MASSACHUSETTS HALL
Harvard's oldest building, built 1718, and occupied by continental troops during the Revolution. It now serves as one of the freshman dormitories.

WORLD'S POPULAR ENCYCLOPEDIA

A modern compilation of essen-
tial facts gathered from all
branches of the world's knowledge
Illustrated throughout

•

VOLUME VI

GLO-IRB

THE WORLD SYNDICATE PUBLISHING CO.
CLEVELAND, O.   NEW YORK, N. Y.

1937

MEN BEHIND THE BOOKS

The value of reference works depends principally upon the authority and knowledge of the men who make them. The following are some of those connected with the original compilation or the revision of the material contained in these books.

FRANCIS J. REYNOLDS
Former Reference Librarian, Library of Congress, Editor-in-Chief of Collier's New Encyclopedia, Reynolds' Atlas and Gazeteer.

ALLEN L. CHURCHILL
Associate Editor of New International Year Book, Contributor to New International Encyclopedia.

HENRY JACKSON WATERS, LL.D.
(Deceased). Ex-President State Agricultural College, Manhattan, Kansas.

GEORGE MAXWELL HOWE, PH.D.
Professor German Department, Harvard University, Cambridge, Mass.

LOOMIS HAVEMEYER, PH.D.
Assistant Professor of Anthropology, Yale University.

ELSIE WRIGHT, A.B.
Western Reserve University, Editor-in-Chief Twentieth-Century Encyclopedia, Research Bureau.

JULIAN DEVRIES, A.B.
Western Reserve University, Associate in Revision of Twentieth-Century Encyclopedia.

DOROTHY CLARKE, A.B.
Lake Erie College, Associate in Revision of Twentieth-Century Encyclopedia.

GLOUCESTER, HUMPHREY, DUKE OF (1391-1447), Eng. soldier; s. of Henry IV. and Mary de Bohun; present at Agincourt, 1415; acted as regent during Henry V.'s absence in France, 1421, 1422; Protector during Henry VI.'s minority.

GLOUCESTER, RICHARD DE CLARE, EARL OF (1222-62), Eng. soldier; the most powerful peer of his day, and leader of the barons in their rising against Henry III.

GLOUCESTER, ROBERT, 1ST EARL OF (d. 1147), Eng. soldier; illegitimate s. of Henry I.; fought for Matilda against Stephen; won battle of Lincoln, 1141.

GLOUCESTER, THOMAS OF WOODSTOCK, 1ST DUKE OF (1355-97), Eng. statesman; s. of Edward III.; practically ruled England, 1386-89; arrested on charge of plotting against Richard II., 1397; soon afterwards died, or was killed, at Calais.

GLOUCESTERSHIRE (51° 45′ N., 2° 30′ W.), W. midland county, England, situated on estuary and lower course of Severn. Bounded N. by Herefordshire, Worcestershire, and Warwickshire, E. by Oxfordshire, S. by Berkshire, Wiltshire, Somerset, W. by estuary of Severn and Monmouthshire. Area, 1,228 sq. miles. Chief towns: Gloucester (capital), Cheltenham, Tewkesbury, and part of Bristol. Surface is varied, with three distinct features: E., Cotswold Hills (highest, Cleeve Hill); center, rich fertile valleys of Severn and other rivers; W., Forest of Dean. Most important rivers include Avon, Lower Avon, Wye, and Thames. Sheep-farming is carried on in hills; in valleys pastureland, orchards, woods, and dairy-farms where celebrated G. cheese is made. W. are coal-fields of Forest of Dean and Bristol. Other minerals include iron, ochre, building-stone, freestone, and quartz. Manufactures—woolens, cottons, silk, gloves, glass, hardware. Extensive canal system. Most noteworthy antiquities are: cath's of G. and Bristol; churches of Tewkesbury and Cirencester; many fine parish churches; remains of Hayles Abbey and castles of Berkeley, Thornbury, and Sudeley.

GLOVE, covering for the hand, usually made of fine dressed skins, silk, wool, or cotton. 'Kid' gloves, made from kid or sheep-skin, are largely made in Paris and other Fr. towns. The most delicate kinds are usually described as suede, in which the inner side of the skin is dressed; and glace, the outer side. As regards the history of g's they appear to have been used from very early times, and are referred to in Homer's *Odyssey*. They probably reached their most decorative stage, in England, in the reign of Elizabeth, when they were often jeweled and otherwise ornamented. In mediæval times the throwing down of a glove was a symbol of defiance.

GLOVER, SIR JOHN HAWLEY (1829-85), Brit. administrator; was administrator of Lagos; served in the Ashanti War (1873); afterwards gov. of Newfoundland, and subsequently of Leeward Islands.

GLOVER, RICHARD (1712-85), Eng. poet; wrote two epics; *Leonidas* and *The Athenaid*; also two tragedies; best remembered by his ballad, *Hosier's Ghost.*

GLOVERSVILLE, a city of New York, in Fulton co. It is on the Fonda, Johnstown and Gloversville railroad, and on the Erie Canal, 50 miles northwest of Albany. Its chief industry is the manufacture of gloves. There are also silk manufactures. A number of great tanneries and a rapidly growing silk center. Here is the Nathan Littauer Hospital, the Carnegie Free Library, and business college.

GLOW-WORMS, see under POLYMORPHA.

GLOXINIA, genus of tropical, gesneriaceous herbs; violet flowers; also greenhouse plant, genus *Sinningia*, especially *S. speciosa.*

GLUCK, ALMA (RIEBA FIERSON) (1886), American soprano; b. in Bucharest, Rumania, in 1886. She came to America in 1889 and was educated at the Normal College, New York and Union College, Schenectady. Studied voice under Signor Buzzi-Peccia, and made her first operatic appearance in *Werther* in 1909. She married Efrem Zimbalist in 1914.

GLUCK, CHRISTOPH WILLIBALD, or RITTER VON GLUCK (1714-87), Ger. composer; b. near Neumarkt; studied at Vienna and Milan, where first opera, *Artaserse*, was presented (1741), followed by *Demofoon*, *Artamene, Poro*, and others belonging to old school of Ital. opera; visited England, 1745; greatly impressed by Händel's works, and later in Paris by Rameau's operas; settled in Vienna, 1756. Between 1762 and 1769 G. produced first great operas of new type: *Orpheus and Euridice*, *Alceste* (with explanatory prefaces), and *Paris and Helena*; visited

Paris, and successfully brought out a music drama, *Iphigenie en Aulide*, 1774, and *Armide*, 1777. His great work, *Iphigenie en Pauride*, 1779, secured him complete and permanent victory over Ital. rival, Piccini; returned to Vienna, 1780.

GLUCOSE. $C_6H_{12}O_6$. Also known as dextrose and grape sugar. The most important member of the group of sugars known as *monoses*. It is found in large quantities in grapes and the hard nodules found in raisins (dried grapes) consist of this sugar deposited from the juice, in which it occurs in solution. It is also found in many other sweet fruits and in the roots, stems and leaves of plants, usually associated with fructose. It may be prepared from cane sugar by boiling with dilute acids, when a mixture of fructose and glucose, known as invert syrup, is produced. To obtain the glucose in a pure condition the process of inversion is carried out in acidified 90% alcohol. After addition of the cane sugar the mixture is kept at a temperature of 50° C for two hours, when it is allowed to cool. The glucose crystallizes out, the more soluble fructose remaining in solution. Anhydrous glucose melts at 146° C, but crystalline glucose, containing one molecule of water, melts at 86°C. It is much less sweet then cane sugar, is soluble in its own weight of water at room temperature, and is a strong reducing agent. It ferments readily with yeast, yielding alcohol and carbon dioxide, and small quantities of fusel-oil, glycerine and other substances. Solutions of the sugar rotate the plane of polarization of polarized light to the right. Hence the name *dextrose* (*q.v.*). With certain metallic hydroxides, notably calcium and barium, glucose forms *glucosates*, compounds soluble in water and readily decomposed by carbonic acid with regeneration of glucose.

GLUCOSIDES are substances yielding sugar, especially *glucose*, on fermentation or *hydrolysis*. For each group there is a special ferment. They are classified by the chemical constitution of the non-glucose part of the molecule into (1) *Ethylene Derivatives* (mustard oils), decomposed by ferment *myrosin*. (2) *Benzene Derivatives* (salicin), decomposed by *ptyalin* and *emulsin*. (3) *Styrolene* and *Anthracene Derivatives*.

GLUE is an impure gelatin with strong adhesive properties.—Bone Glue is made by dissolving grease out of bones by *petroleum*. The *de-greased* bones are then steamed under pressure in cylinders with false bottoms. The glue-liquor collects below the false bottom, is clari-

fied with alum, and concentrated in *vacuo* to 30% dry glue. The liquor, bleached by *sulphur dioxide*, is allowed to cool to a jelly.—Fish Glue has a disagreeable odor. Glue should be free from grit, and of uniform golden color. Cold water should soften and swell it and hot water dissolve it.

GLUKHOV (51° 42′ N., 33° 54′ E.), town, Chernigov, S.W. Russia; kaolin mining.

GLUTEN, adhesive substance derived from kneading wheat flour in water; composed of fibrin and gelatin; highly nutritious; best wheaten flour should contain 11% gluten. Word also used generally of gum.

GLYCERIN, GLYCEROL, GLYCERINUM ($C_3H_5(OH)_3$), colorless, viscid liquid, with a sweetish taste; Sp. G., 1.265; when heated it decomposes, and it dissolves readily in water and alcohol. It is obtained from the action of alkalies or superheated steam on fats and fixed oils, and commercially it is mainly obtained from the spent lyes in soapmaking. It is used as a lubricating agent in the manufacture of nitro-glycerin; in the making of plasters, modeling clay, moist colors; as a preservative and slight antiseptic; as a solvent for coloring fluids and various drugs, (*e.g.*) iodine, tannic acid alkalies, alkaloids, and neutral salts; and medicinally as a purgative.

GLYCOGEN ($C_6H_{10}O_5$), a carbohydrate, white, amorphous powder, found in liver; turns red with iodine.

GLYCONIC VERSE, metres used by Gk. lyric poet Glycon; logacedic tripody or tetrapody, (*i.e.*) a spondee and two dactyls, three trochees and a dactyl, or dactyl and three trochees.

GLYN, ELINOR (MRS. CLAYTON), a British novelist and writer. Publications: *The Visits of Elizabeth*, 1900; *Reflections of Ambrosine*, 1902; *Beyond the Rocks*, 1906; *Three Weeks*, 1907; *Elizabeth Visits America*, 1909; *His Hour*, 1910; *The Reason Why*, 1911; *Letters to Caroline*, 1914; *Three Things*, 1915; *The Career of Katherine Bush*, 1916; *Six Days*, 1922.

GMELIN, the name of a distinguished family of German scientists: *Johann Georg Gmelin* (1709-55), a German scientist and traveler, born in Tübingen. In 1731 he was made professor of natural chemistry and history at St. Petersburg, and in 1733 he undertook a journey to Siberia. In 1749 he was appointed professor of botany and chemistry at Tübingen. He published *Flora Sibirica*, 1747-49, and *Reise durch Sibirien* between 1751-52.

Leopold Gmelin (1788-1853), a German chemist, son of Johann Friedrich, born at Göttingen. He studied medicine at Göttingen and Tübingen, and taught chemistry at Heidelberg for four years, after which he was made professor of medicine and chemistry at Heidelberg, 1817-51. He wrote many scientific works, amongst which is *Handbuch der Chemie*, 1817-19; this was translated into English, 1848.

GLYPTOSAURUS, a fossil land lizard, the remains of which were found in 1871 in Wyoming. It is so called from the fact that the head and parts of the body were covered with bony plates. Several species have been discovered, the largest being about four feet in length.

GMÜND (48° 48' N., 9° 48' E.), town, Württemberg, Germany; gold and silver jewelry.

GNAT, a genus of small dipterous flies of the family of *Culicidae*, very common in a fen or marshy district. There are nine British species, the *Culex pipiens* being the common G. Mosquitoes are included in the family, but are larger in size and bite more effectively.

GNEISENAU, Ger. cruiser 11,420 tons, 23.5 knots, eight 8-2-in. guns, completed 1908), belonged to the Pacific squadron under von Spee at outbreak of the World War; fought in battle of Coronel, Nov. 1, 1914, and was sunk in battle of Falkland Islands, Dec. 8.

GNEISENAU, AUGUST WILHELM ANTON, COUNT NEITHARDT VON (1760-1831), Prussian soldier; served in Amer. War of Independence, on Brit. side; present at Jena; defended Kolberg, 1807; became Blücher's chief of staff; distinguished in Waterloo campaign; gov. of Berlin, 1818; Field-Marshal, 1825.

GNEISS, mineral; name originally used by miners of the Hartz, but now used by geologists to describe certain metamorphic rocks composed generally of layers of quartz and felspar. Some g's are sedimentary, others igneous and differ from granite only by their foliated structure; contain no fossil remains; there are several varieties classed generally according to the distinct minerals they contain; they include muscovite-g., biotite-g., muscovite-biotite-g., mica-g., and syenitic-g. (containing hornblende).

GNESEN (52° 32' N., 17° 33' E.), town, Posen, Germany; old crowning-place of Polish kings.

GNOMES, legendary dwarfs, dwelling in the earth, and supposed to guard its treasures.

GNOMIC POEMS, versified maxims (*Gnomes*), much favored by the ancient Gk. poets.

GNOSTICISM, a name used to embrace a number of sects on the border-land between Christianity and heathen thought. Its root principle was not faith but knowledge (*gnosis*), which was given to the initiated only. In its speculations it mixed up the Platonic theory of ideas (that everything has a spiritual arche-type) with an Oriental dualism which made all matter evil. The supreme God was removed from the world and could only communicate with it by a number of æons, in which various principles and ideas were personified.

G. was antagonistic to Judaism, for it held the God of the O. T. to be the *Demiurge*, a secondary God. The opposition of spirit and matter is a Gr. idea, but into this is united the idea of a conflict in the present world between forces of good and evil, which is Zoroastrian. Gnosticism was essentially mystical and also sacramental; many sacraments analogous to Christian rites were invented. Like other heretics, Gnostics were charged with immorality, and not without cause, as they tended to oscillate between asceticism and licentiousness. Christianity prevailed against the movement, as it also did against the Ebionites, some of whom leaned to Gnosticism.

GNU, OR WILDEBEESTE, name given to two species of antelope (genus *Connochaetes*), differing widely from all others in appearance, having heavy, bull-like head and shoulders, and a tail like that of a horse; horns are present in both sexes. Gnus are gregarious, swift of foot, and dangerous when brought to bay; are frequently seen in zoological collections.

GOA (15° 20' N., 74° E.), Portug. territory on W. coast of India, S. of Bombay; extends 60 miles along Ind. Ocean; area, c. 1,400 sq. miles; immense forests and many rivers; chief exports—salt, spices, fruit, coconuts, copra, manganese, and iron. *Old G.* former flourishing capital, with remaining fine archiepiscopal cathedral and church of Bom Jesus. Numerous palaces and splendid churches in ruins. *Nova G.*, or *Panjim*, present capital, on Mandavi, with viceregal palace, barracks, technical school, harbor, 1882, etc. Taken from Mohammedans by Albuquerque, 1510; Old G. was made capital and rose to great commercial prosperity under Portuguese. Administered by gov.-gen.

GOALPARA (26° 11′ N., 90° 41′ E.), district, Assam, India; fertile, chief crop, rice; exports timber, cotton; subject to earthquakes; unhealthy climate. Area, 3,961 sq. miles. Pop. 462,000. Capital, Goalpara, on Brahmaputra.

GOAT (connected with Lat. *haedus*, a kid). G's. are a genus of ruminant quadrupeds, forming, with sheep, the 'caprine' (Lat. *caper*, goat) section of the Bovidæ family. They are very closely allied to sheep, but distinguished by horns in both sexes (usually more pronounced in the male). These horns are generally long, and directed upward, outward, and backward, while those of sheep are shorter and mostly spirally twisted. Male G's. have beards, and a strong, offensive smell, especially during the rutting season. G's. have shorter tails than sheep, and are marked by the absence of the small pit between the toes of the hind-feet. In habits they are much bolder and more curious than sheep, and do not blindly follow the flock. (The term 'capricious' is derived from G.'s.) Two species exist in N. Africa, and one in S. India, but they are not commonly found below the Himalayas. The domestic G. is very common in the United States, and is greatly valued for its milk, which is especially suited for children and invalids. There are numerous varieties of the wild G. (*Capra hircus*), including the ibex of the Alps, Himalayas, and Arabia; the Bezoar G. or Paseng (pasang), probably the parent of the common domestic G.; The Tur of the Caucasus; the Markhor of the Himalayas; the Spanish G.; and the Thar or Goat-antelope (*Hemiragus*), and the Rocky Mountain G. in the United States. G.'s hides make good leather, and are sometimes used for kid gloves. Of the domesticated breeds the most famous are the Angora and the Kashmir. The former have long, silky hair next to the skin, and an outer covering much resembling wool. The latter have a coat of woolly texture next the skin, and the long, silky hair-covering outside. From this are made the true Kashmir or 'camel's hair' shawls. The two chief varieties of Kashmir G's. (var. *laniger*) are the 'chappoo,' and the more common 'changra.' They abound chiefly in Tibet and Bokhara. The Angora breed has been introduced into Cape Colony (*c.* 1864), Australia, and U. S. A.

GOAT ISLAND, a small island about 70 acres in area, which divides the current of the Niagara Falls. It is connected by a bridge with the American side of the falls.

GOATSBEARD, popular name of cichoriaceous plant, genus *Tragspogon*, order *Compositae*; also fungus of genus *Clavaria*.

GOATSUCKER, OR NIGHTJAR, is a bird of nocturnal habits, feeding on insects which it captures on the wing; beak short and broad, and mouth enormously wide, and fringed with highly modified, bristle-like feathers.

GOBELIN, a famous make of tapestries produced at a factory in Paris. The founder of the firm was Giles G., a XVI.-cent. wool-dyer.

GOBI (*c.* 43° N., 110° E.), Chin. name for extent of desert stretching from Pamirs to Great Kingan Mts. on borders of Manchuria, and from Altai, Sayan, and Yabloni Mts. on N. to most northerly ranges of Kuenlun Mts. on S.; includes large portion of Mongolia; 450 to 600 miles from N. to S., and over 1000 miles from S.W. to N.E.; elevation between 3000 and 5000 ft. and sometimes higher; also called Shamo (sandy desert), and Han-Hai (dry sea). Almost whole surface is sandy or stony desert, without water or vegetation (except for oases) and with little animal life; in some parts are grassy steppes, masses of rocks and crags, and salt lakes. Mountainous tracts, forests, good water, abundant vegetation, and more animal life are to be found in part known as Ordos. Climate has great extremes, with rapid changes. Shifting sands have buried large extents of once cultivated country and habitations, and many discoveries of buried towns and villages have been made; important explorations have been made by Przhevalsky, Sven Hedin, and others. Desert crossed by various caravan routes, some being thousands of years old; among principal routes are those leading from Kalgan (on Chinese frontier) to Urga, from Su-Chow to Hami, and from Hami to Peking. An American expedition headed by Roy E. Andrews, explored the region in 1922-23.

GOBLET (Fr. *gobelet*), large drinking-cup, on stem, but without handles.

GOBLET, RENÉ (1828-1905), leader of Fr. Radical party; prime minister at close of 1886; unequal to facing Boulanger, and resigned, 1887.

GOCH (51° 40′ N., 6° 10′ E.), town on Niers, Rhine province, Prussia; various small manufactures.

GOD (O.E. *god*, Dutch *god*, Ger. *gott*), in heathen times an idol, or object of worship. Since the Teutonic acceptation of Christianity it is the name reserved to the Creator of the Universe. See THEISM.

GOD, CHURCHES OF. See CHURCHES OF GOD.

GODALMING (51° 11′ N., 0° 37′ W.), market town, on Wey, Surrey, England; seat of Charterhouse School.

GODAVARI (16° 30′ N., 82° 15′ E.), river, in Deccan, Brit. India; flows S.E.; discharges by seven mouths into Bay of Bengal; length, c. 900 miles; one of the twelve sacred rivers of India.

GODAVARI (17° N., 81° E.), district, Madras Presidency, Brit. India, in lower valley of Godavari; chief town, Cocanada. Area, 5634 sq. miles.

GODEFROY, DENIS (1549-1622), member of notable Fr. family; prof. of Law at Geneva; was historiographer of France. Jacques G. (1587-1652) pub. new edit. of *Codex Theodosianus*. Théodore G. (1580-1649) wrote *Le Ceremonial de France*.

GODESBERG (50° 41′ N., 7° 9′ E.), town, summer resort, Rhine province, Prussia; mineral springs.

GODFREY, EDWARD SETTLE (1843), an American soldier; b. in Kalida, Ohio. Without finishing his education he enlisted as a private in the Union Army at the beginning of the Civil War, but afterwards entered the West Point Military Academy and graduated in 1867. He served through the Indian wars in the West and in Cuba during the Spanish-American War, retiring in 1907 with the rank of brigadier-general. An article which he wrote in the Century Magazine, *General Custer's Last Battle*, is one of the most valuable personal records of Custer's death.

GODFREY, HOLLIS (1874), an American engineer and writer; b. in Lynn, Mass. He graduated from Tufts College, in 1895, and was engaged in teaching, writing and engineering from 1898 to 1905. He has been consulting engineer to the cities of Philadelphia, and Atlantic City and private corporations. Since 1913 he has been president of the Drexel Institute, in Philadelphia. Many of his articles have appeared in Collier's Weekly, the Review of Reviews, the Atlantic Monthly and numerous technical journals. Among his books are *The Man Who Ended War*, 1908; *The Health of the City*, 1910; *Jack Coller-*

ton's Engine, 1911; and *Dave Morrell's Battery*, 1912.

GODFREY OF BOUILLON (c. 1060-1100), Fr. crusader; led army in first crusade, 1096; took Antioch, 1097, Jerusalem, 1099; became ruler of Jerusalem, with title, 'Defender and Guardian of Holy Sepulchre'; great victory over Moslems at Ascalon, 1099, made him supreme in Palestine.

GODFREY OF STRASBURG (1200), a German poet, who lived in Strasburg. He was the author of many lays but is especially known for his great poem, *Tristan und Isolde*, taken from the legend of the Round Table.

GODFREY OF VITERBO (fl. XII. cent.), author of *Memoria seculorum*, of which part entitled *Gesta Friderici* is important source for career of Emperor Frederick I.

GODIN, JEAN BAPTISTE ANDRÉ (1817-88), Fr. socialist; author of *Solutions Sociales*, 1871; *Mutualite Sociale*, and similar works.

GODIVA (XI. cent.), wife of Leofric, Earl of Mercia, who, at her husband's challenge, rode naked through the streets of Coventry, to secure the relief of the townspeople from the heavy taxation which the earl had imposed; subject to poem by Tennyson. Each year a pageant celebrating the devotion of Godiva is held in Coventry.

GODKIN, EDWIN LAWRENCE (1831-1901), an Irish-American editor; b. in Mayne, Ireland. He was educated at Queens College, Belfast, and during the Crimean War represented the London Daily News at the front. In 1858 he came to the United States as a newspaper correspondent, where he studied law, being admitted to the New York bar, but on the outbreak of the Civil War he went to the front as correspondent for English and American papers. After the war he returned to New York where, in 1865, he founded *The Nation*, and when that paper was merged in a joint ownership with the New York Evening Post, he remained editor of both papers till his death. He wrote *A History of Hungary*, 1856; *The Problems of Modern Democracy* and *Reflections and Comments*.

GODOLPHIN, SIDNEY, EARL OF G. (c. 1645-1712), Eng. politician; page in Charles II.'s household after Restoration; P.C. and Lord of Treasury, 1619; First Lord of Treasury under Charles II., James II., William III., and Anne; promoted Anglo-Scot. Union; dismissed from office, 1710.

GODOWSKY, LEOPOLD (1870), pianist; *b.* in Vilna, Russia. Educated at Berlin Hochschule, 1884 and studied with Saint-Saens, Paris. At age of nine made his first public appearance. Toured Poland, Russia and Germany. 1884-1886 appeared in America. 1895-1900 director of piano at Chicago Conservatory of Music. In 1909 appointed by Austrian Emperor, director Imperial Royal Meisterschule for Piano at Imperial Royal Academy of Music, Vienna, 1912 editor-in-chief of Art Publication Society, St. Louis. Composed pieces for pianos and violins.

GODOY, MANUEL DE (1767-1851), Duke of El Alcudia; Span. courtier and statesman; prime minister, 1792-98; negotiated Treaty of Basel; became Prince of the Peace, 1795.

GODRA, GODHRA (22° 46′ N., 73° 40′ E.), town, Bombay, India; trade in timber.

GODWIN, FRANCIS (1562-1633), Eng. ecclesiastic; bp. of Hereford (1617); author of *Annales of England*, 1630; and a fantastical story, *The Man in the Moon*, first pub. 1638.

GODWIN, MARY WOLLSTONE-CRAFT (1759-97), Eng. writer. Her works include *Vindication of the Rights of Women* and *Original Stories for Children*.

GODWIN, PARKE (1816-1904), an American editor and writer; *b.* in Paterson, N. J. He graduated from Princeton University, in 1834, then took up newspaper work, becoming assistant to his father-in-law, William Cullen Bryant, who was then managing editor of the New York Evening Post. For a time he was editor of Putnam's Magazine. He wrote *A Popular View of the Doctrines of Charles Fourier*, 1844; *Vala, a Mythological Tale*, 1851; *A History of France*, 1861; *Out of the Past*, 1870; *The Biography of William Cullen Bryant*, 1883; and *A New Study of the Sonnets of Shakespeare*, 1900.

GODWIN, WILLIAM (1756-1836), Eng. doctrinaire; *b.* at Wisbech; became Glasite minister, and held charges at Ware, Stowmarket, and Beaconsfield; wrote *Inquiry concerning Political Justice*, a philosophic work showing influence of Rosseau; *History of Commonwealth*, *Caleb Williams*, a novel; and other works.

GODWINE (*d.* 1053), Earl of Wessex; justiciary under Canute; assisted in restoration of Edward the Confessor, 1042; exiled, 1051; *f.* of last Saxon king, Harold.

GODWIT, a spring and autumn migrant, visiting marshy estuarine areas and accompanying sand-flats; long legs and beak, and reddish plumage, with barred tail; nests in Arctic regions.

GOEBEN, AUGUST KARL VON (1816-80), Prussian general; as lieut.-general won great victories over Austria in Seven Weeks War, 1866, commander of VIII. corps against France, 1870; head of First Army, which won St. Quentin, 1871.

GOEBEN and **BRESLAU.** At the outbreak of the World War these Ger. war vessels—*Goeben*, battle-cruiser, 22,-640 tons, ten 11-in. guns, 28 knots, and *Breslau*, light cruiser, 4,281 tons, twelve 4-in. guns, 25 knots—were in the Mediterranean; on Aug. 4, 1914, they bombarded Philippeville and Bona on the Fr. African coast; arrived at Messina (Aug. 5); escaping the Allied fleet, entered the Dardanelles (Aug. 10), and were nominally sold to Turkey (Aug. 13). Rechristened respectively *Sultan Selim* and *Midilli*, they took part in several naval actions in the Black Sea. The former was ultimately disabled by striking a mine near the Bosporus, but was repaired by a lining of cement. On Jan. 20, 1918, they sallied out from the Dardanelles and sank the Brit. monitor *Raglan*. *Breslau* was driven into a minefield and sunk; *Goeben* was damaged and beached at Nagara Point and was bombed by Brit. aircraft, but on June 27 was refloated and taken to Constantinople, being surrendered to the Allies after the Turk. armistice (Oct. 1918).

GOES, DAMIÃO DE (1502-74), Portuguese historian; keeper of archives and royal chronicler, 1548; wrote history of reign of King Manuel, but owing to its truth work condemned and compulsorily revised; G. tried and imprisoned by Inquisition on slight charges; an able and honest historian.

GOETHALS, GEORGE WASHINGTON (1858); American army officer and engineer; *b.* Brooklyn, N. Y. He studied at the College of the City of New York and in 1880 graduated from the United States Military Academy, entering the service in the same year as second lieutenant of engineers. In May 1898 he had risen to the rank of chief engineer of the volunteer forces. He left the volunteer service in the latter part of that year; became major of the engineer corps in 1900; studied at the Army War College, from which he graduated in 1905, and was made major-general in 1915. During his army service, from which he retired in 1916, he was identified with many important engineering works, but his enduring fame was gained as chief engineer in the construction of the Panama Canal (1907-14). In the latter year he was made first civil governor of the Canal Zone. In the World War he served as general manager of the Emergency Fleet Corporation and also as quartermaster-general and member of the General Staff. In 1923 he was appointed Fuel Administrator for New York State during the coal shortage crisis. *d.* 1928.

GOETHE, JOHANN WOLFGANG VON (1749-1832), Ger. poet, dramatist, philosopher, and scientist; *b.* Frankfort-on-Main; at Leipzig G. studied law, 1765-68, and, inspired by Kätchen Schönkopf, wrote *Annette* (charming MS volume of lyrics, pub. 1896), and play, *Die Laune des Verliebten.* Returning to Frankfort, 1768, an invalid, he wrote *Die Mitschuldigen* (comedy). G. graduated as Doctor of Law at Strassburg, 1771; also studied bot., anat., alchemy, etc. At Strassburg he was greatly influenced by his intimate friend, Herder. *Sesenheimer Lieder* (lyrics), inspired by Frederike Brion, were written, 1770. At Wetzler (1772) he became friends with Kestner, whose fiancée, Charlotte Buff, is immortalized in *Die Lieden des jungen Werthers,* 1774, which made him world famous. In 1773 *Clavigo* and the hist. drama *Gotz von Berlichingen* (first really great work) appeared; also some dramatic satires (*Gotter, Helden and Wieland, Pater Brey, Hanswursts Hochzeit,* etc.). At this time G. became engaged for a short while to Lili Schönemann.

In 1775 he wrote the *Faust* of the 'Sturm und Drang' period (pub. as a Fragment, 1790). From 1775 onwards G. lived in Weimar, holding several responsible government posts; formed intimate friendship with Frau von Stein; ennobled, 1782. To the Weimar period belong dramas. *Egmont* (pub. 1778), *Die Geschwister* (1776), *Iphigenie* (prose version, 1778), *Harzreise im Winter,* and *Briefs aus der Schweiz* (1779), etc. The spell of an Ital. visit (1786-88) is seen in *Die Italienische Reise* (pub 1816-17). The dramas, *Iphigenie* (poetical version, 1787) and *Torquato Tasso* (1790), are by many reckoned his masterpieces.

G. accompanied the Duke of Weimar in Fr. campaign, 1792-93; formed deep and lasting friendship with Schiller, 1794; app. director of Weimar Court Theater, 1791-1817; *Metamorphosen der Pflanzen,* 1790; *Beitrage zur Optik,* 1791-1792; *Hermann und Dorothea* (narrative poem), and some of G.'s finest ballads appeared, 1789. In 1806 G. married his mistress, Christiane Vulpius. To his

later years belong *Die naturliche Tochter* (drama, 1804), first part ('Erster Teil') of *Faust,* 1808; the drama which established G.'s reputation as the greatest poet of his time. *Die Wahlverwandtschaften* (novel, 1809), autobiographical *Dichtung und Wahrheit,* 1811; *Uber Kunst und Alterthum,* 1816-32; *Zur Morphologie,* 1817-24; *Wilhelm Meister's Wanderjahre* (romance, 1821), and *Faust,* second part ('Zweiter Teil'), 1833.

GOFF, NATHAN (1843-1920), an American jurist; *b.* in Clarksburg, W. Va. He studied at Georgetown University and the University of the City of New York, took up law and began to practice in 1866. In the following year he was elected to the West Virginia House of Representatives. During 1868-81 he was U.S. district attorney in the district of West Virginia. In 1881 he was appointed Secretary of the Navy by President Hayes. From 1883 to 1889 he was a member of Congress; during 1892-11 he was justice of the Fourth Federal Circuit Court; justice of the U.S. Circuit Court of Appeals, 1912-13, and in 1913 he was elected to the U.S. Senate.

GOFFE, WILLIAM (1605-79), Eng. politician; one of judges of Charles I.; signed death warrant excluded from Act of Indemnity; fled to America.

GOG AND MAGOG.—It is thought that Biblical characters bearing these names are symbolical for nations dwelling N. of Caucasus, and hostile to Jews.

GOGO, GOGHA (21° 39' N., 72° 15' E.), seaport, Bombay, Brit. India, on Gulf of Cambay.

GOGOL, NIKOLAI VASILIEVICH (1809-52), Russ. novelist, poet, and dramatist; famed for his Cossack tales and realistic novels exposing the abuses of officialdom. Amongst his principal works are the *Revizor,* a satirical comedy, and a powerful novel, *Mertvuiya Dushi* (Dead Souls).

GOGRA (25° 45' N., 84° 30' E.), sacred river, India, rises in Himalayas; flows S.E., joins Ganges at Chapra; length, 600 miles.

GOITRE, an endemic disease occurring in various districts, characterized by enlargement of the thyroid gland in the neck, and believed to be caused by the drinking-water (containing lime and magnesium salts) of these districts. Distressful symptoms are due to pressure of the enlarged gland on the windpipe, certain nerves, and other structures in its neighborhood. The treatment is a change of air, rest, and tonics; iron, iodine, or thyroid extract are administered, and if improvement does not take place an operation for removal of part of the gland is carried out. In *Exophthalmic G.*, palpitation of the heart, protrusion of the eyeballs and anæmia accompany the enlargement of the gland; it is believed to be due either to nervous derangement or to excessive absorption of the secretion of the gland.

GOKAK (16° 10′ N., 74° 52′ E.), town, Bombay, India.

GOKCHA, Armenian Sevanga (40° 30′ N., 45° 10′ E.), lake, Transcaucasian S. S. R.; outlet by Zanga into river Aras.

GOLCONDA (17° 22′ N., 78° 26′ E.), fortress and ruined city, Hyderabad, India; capital of a kingdom in XVI. and XVII. cent's; formerly center of diamond cutting and polishing.

GOLD, a precious metal known to the human race from the earliest times and found in all parts of the globe. It is frequently met in association with other metals such as silver, copper, tellurium, platinum, lead and iron. It is heavy, malleable and ductile, and also one of the softest of metals. It is mainly used for coinage, alloyed with silver and copper, and for jewelry and other ornamental purposes. It has always been highly valued because of its unalterability as a material usable for a multitude of trinkets and articles that endure from age to age. The Egyptians and the Greeks seized upon the metal for bedecking their persons, a custom which antedated its use for money. The adoption of gold as the world's standard of value, its universal appeal as the embodiment of riches, its unquestioned acceptance as a safe medium of trade without restriction of amount and its strength as a commodity never sufficiently available to glut the market, has made gold alike the bulwark of the world's business and of corporate and individual wealth.

The modern development of the gold industry dates from 1848, when the metal was discovered in California, producing the famous gold rush there the following year. Soon that state yielded $36,000,000 worth of gold, and the year after $56,000,000, or much more than the annual average world production for the preceding decade. Australia and New England were next revealed as a gold producer, then Russia. Nevada presently became famous by the discovery of the Comstock Lode, which from its first working in 1861 yielded more than $470,000,000. In 1884 came the greatest gold discovery of the time, surpassing Comstock and all previous finds. This was in the Witwatersrand, Transvaal, South Africa, where gold production, up to 1922, had a value approximately, $2,000,000,000. Other sensational discoveries of gold were those in the Klondike, Alaska, in 1894, and in Nome, Alaska, ten years later.

Gold Standard.—There is a need of a standard unit of value in the worlds complex economic system, and for use in general trading relations. The simplest and surest stand of value is the most satisfactory, and gold has been accepted as the best. The hides, tobacco and shells that have been used have proved too unwieldy in a modern world. Gold, on the other hand, is valuable in small quantities; it fluctuates the least in value; it is durable; it will not erode; and it can be stored without damage by fire. Therefore certain countries have adopted by law gold as the sole standard of payment. They are then said to be on the gold standard. In the United States all media of payment were tied up with the value of gold. Every paper dollar had its equivalent in gold stored away in the United States vaults.

In 1931 England abandoned the gold standard, followed by many of the smaller nations.

On April 19, 1933, President Roosevelt announced that the United States would not support the dollar abroad by gold shipments. This meant that the United States had virtually gone off the gold standard, putting into effect a species of inflation. The immediate effect of the proclamation was the fall of the dollar's value abroad to about 92 cents.

On April 20, 1933, the President sent to the Senate his currency inflation bill, further to cheapen money and thus raise prices. The bill, a rider to the Farm Relief bill, contained the following provisions:

1. Authorization for the President to issue $3,000,000,000 of United States notes.
2. Authorization for change in the gold value of the dollar within the range of 50%.
3. Authorization for the acceptance of silver up to the value of $100,000,000 in payment of World War debts.

With over $4,000,000,000 in gold stored away in Washington, the United States had the largest supply of gold of any nation in the world, and, under President Roosevelt's continuous efforts to raise the market value of the metal (which he has done, the price ranging from $20.67 per ounce in Sept., 1933, to $34.06 per ounce in January of the following year) the value of the gold stock of the country materially increased while the dollar proportionately decreased, being valued at 60 cents as of Jan., 1934, raising prices toward a more normal level than the former low scale.

On Dec. 28, 1933, the U. S. Treasury called in all hoarded gold, removing the $100 exemption granted in August after the blanket order in March to return all gold coin to the treasury. In Aug., 1933, about $40,000,000 in gold was returned to the treasury, but according to U. S. Treasury figures, about $311,044,895 in gold coin and $217,-486,829 in gold certificates were still in private hands on Dec., 1933.

On Jan. 15, 1934, President Roosevelt, in a special message to Congress, asked that the U. S. Treasury be given full title to all gold in the Federal Reserve Banks ($3,600,000,000); that the dollar be re-valued at 50 to 60 per cent of its legal gold value, and that a $2,000,000,000 stabilization fund, to be administered by the Secretary of the Treasury, be established. It was estimated that passage of such a bill would permit credit inflation of about $17,500,000,000. After stormy sessions in both the House and Senate, the bill passed and the dollar was re-valued at 60 cents.

Gold production for 1933 was, for the U. S. and territories, valued at $50,337,800 for 2,435,091 ounces on the basis of $20.67 per ounce, the mint prices. The Reconstruction Finance Corporation, which had been buying newly mined gold, succeeded in raising the price of the metal to $34.01 per ounce in October, 1933, at which level it remained until December, 1933, when it rose to $34.06 per ounce. On Jan. 15, 1934, the treasury set a new price for newly mined gold and President Roosevelt authorized mints and assay offices to receive gold on consignment, appointing the Federal Reserve Bank of New York as purchaser, leaving the Reconstruction Finance Corporation, which had been purchasing the gold since October, free to carry on its many other duties. The new price as fixed by the treasury was $34.45 per ounce, less ¼ of 1 per cent for handling charges.

On Feb. 1, 1934, President Roosevelt further devalued the dollar from 60 cents to 59.06 per cent of its old value and at the same time reducing the number of gold grains in the dollar from 25.8 to 15.43. This automatically fixed the price of a fine troy ounce of gold at $35.00. Simultaneously with this action, the country went on a modified gold standard, permitting the export of gold bullion to settle international trade balances. Purchases of gold at the above price were made by the Federal Reserve Bank of New York as fiscal agents for the U. S. Treasury. The profits accruing from the above devaluation amount to approximately $2,700,000,000, of which $2,000,-000 became a stabilization fund. Gold for professional, industrial and artistic use is available only from the treasury at the above price plus a small handling charge. The hoarding of gold became illegal and persons with such supplies found it necessary to smuggle their gold out of the country, bringing it back for sale to the treasury at $35.00 per ounce. The circulation of gold coins was discouraged.

Gold Mining.—In the mining of gold the operation embraces its extraction from alluvial deposits lying loose in river beds and beaches and mixed with sand, gravel or clay and known as placers, and (2) from rock formations, known as lode or quartz mining. Placer mining is the easier to operate, since the ore is largely obtainable on the surface, pure or slightly alloyed with silver, the particles varying from minute grains to substantial nuggets. Placer deposits, which merely required washing of the 'pay dirt' by individual prospectors or small groups without the need of much equipment attracted gold seekers to California. The largest nugget found there weighed 280 ounces. Australia produced a nugget weighing 2,520

—*Photograph by Merl LaVoy*

A PLACER GOLD MINE ON MOOSE CREEK, ALASKA

ounces, valued at about $42,000. Russia yielded one of 96 ounces and the Klondike one of 85 ounces. The discovery of shallow placer deposits account for all the gold rushes, and they are soon exhausted. Deeper deposits, overlain by lava or other strata, are less accessible and require considerable capital and equipment, such as hydraulic and dredging devices, to reach them.

In lode or quartz mining, or the pursuit of gold veins in rock, the ore is reached by shafts in the earth and drifts driven on the vein from the shafts. Sometimes tunnels are driven through the ore body or cross cuts are made through barren rock to the ore. Once found, the vein is opened up, the ore blasted and loaded into cars, whence it goes to the shaft and the surface for metallurgical treatment. Rock deposits may be veins containing gold with metallic sulphides, chiefly iron pyrites; quartz reefs containing gold, chiefly free, but also in sulphides disseminated in the quartz; silicious deposits containing gold, as found in Queenland; or quartz pebbles cemented by silica and iron oxide, the gold being chiefly in the cement, as in the celebrated and (Transvaal) Reef.

In gold-mining equipment for shallow placer work the sluice is invaluable. It is a long box of rough boards for washing the pay dirt by flushing it with water as the gravel is shoveled or dumped in, and is either portable or stationary. For deep placers, if the deposits are near a water supply and otherwise conveniently located, the hydraulic method of obtaining the ore is used. Instead of using pick and shovel and dumping the gravel into gold-saving sluices, water is conveyed to the gravel by pipes from a higher level, the gravel banks being first prepared for the washing by being loosened with explosives. Dredging by means of the endless bucket method is used for deposits in river beds or in ground not profitable or practicable of operation by the sluice system.

Lode or quartz mining calls for hoisting and winding engines, driven by steam, electricity, gas or water; pumps, steam, rod-driven, hydraulic, compressed-air or electric; locomotives for underground transit; air drills and explosives.

After the ore is taken from the mine it undergoes an intricate treatment before it appears as bullion. It is broken by crushers, then ground to fine powder and watered in a device called a stamp mill. There the pulp created by the stamping of pestles and mortar passes over quick-silvered copper plates, which attracts the gold and the amalgam thus formed catches more gold. This opera-

tion leaves a large residuum of the ore containing the gold which has not been attracted by the quick-silver on the copper plates, and which remains to be extracted. The process is called concentration, or the separation of the residual ore and the removal of the less valuable constituents preparatory to smelting. Sometimes concentration is omitted and the ore treated directly by cyanide, which dissolves precious metals from their ores when finely crushed. Another process is flotation of the crushed ore in residuum oil, where sulphides and metallic particles float on top and are skimmed and treated as concentrates, while the earthy and stone materials remain at the bottom and are discharged as tailings. Ordinary concentration is effected by devices that subject the ore to more washing mingled with slow and constant shaking. There are also hydraulic classifiers, which separate the coarser material from the gold. Finally the gold is smelted and poured into bullion molds, and even then it retains some silver, copper, and other metals, which are separated at mints or private refineries. See COINAGE AND MINT.

GOLD BEATER'S SKIN, the thin tough, outer coat of the cæcum, part of the large intestine of the ox. This coat is cleansed and stretched, coated first with fish-glue and then with albumen. Often used as a plaster to stop bleeding of slight flesh wounds.

GOLD, BICHLORIDE OF. See BICHLORIDE OF GOLD.

GOLDEN BULL, an edict issued by Emperor Charles IV. in 1356, to regulate the proceedings at an imperial election; it provided that the election of Holy Rom. Emperor should take place at Frankfort, and the coronation at Aix-la-Chapelle; and that there should be seven electors, the result being decided by majority of votes; these regulations remained in force till close of Holy Rom. Empire in 1806. Name is applicable to any document with golden seal, but is usually confined to important political charters.

GOLDEN CALF. See AARON.

GOLD COAST (5° N., 2° W.), Brit. crown colony and protectorate, including Ashanti and N. territories, on Gulf of Guinea, W. Africa; between Fr. Ivory Coast and Fr. Upper Senegal, Niger on W. and N., and Fr.-Brit. Togoland on E.; length of coast-line, 350 miles; area, c. 80,000 sq. miles. Climate is hot, damp, and unhealthy; country mostly flat and covered with immense forests and swamps; partly navigable rivers are Ankobra and Volta; principal towns are Accra (capital), Addah, Cape Coast Castle, Quittah, Saltpond, Winneba, Axim, Akuse; chief products and exports are palm, kernels, gold, cocoa, manganese ore and diamonds; also ground-nuts, coffee, copra, ivory, etc.; output of gold, which gives its name to the colony, was valued at £1,069,951 in 1933; silver, copper, and iron also found; government railway from Sekondi on coast to Kumasi, 168 miles; lines between Accra and Mangoase (40 miles), and a line from Accra to Kumasi; cables to London and Cape Town; regular steamers from London, Southampton, Plymouth. Once known as notorious resort for fugitives from justice.

G. C. was discovered by Portug., Santander (1470); Diego d'Asambuja built the fort St. Gorge la Mina (present Elmina), 1481; Dutch obtained part of G. C., 1717; Royal African Co. established Dixcove, Winneba, and Accra, 1672; Britain obtained Christianbourg, Augustenbourg, and Fredensbourg from Danes, 1851; and bought Dutch part, 1871-72. Ashanti with chief town Kumasi, was placed under Brit. protection, 1896, and after a dangerous rising (1900) was definitely annexed (1901) with N. territories (which lie N. of 8° N.). See MAP OF AFRICA.

GOLDEN FLEECE (classical myth.), the fleece of the winged ram on which Phryxus and his sister, Helle, the children of King Athamas of Thebes, escaped from the wrath of their stepmother, Ino. The recovery of the fleece was the object of the voyage of the Argonauts under Jason.

GOLDEN GATE, a strait of California. It is about 1 m. in width, and connects the San Francisco Bay with the Pacific Ocean.

GOLDEN HORDE, name given to the Kipchaks, a Tartar race, which, about 1240, rose to power in E. Europe. Their leader was Bātū Khan, whose 'golden' pavilion was erected on the Volga bank.

GOLDEN HORN. See CONSTANTINOPLE.

GOLDEN LEGEND, collection of lives of saints (c. 1250) by Dominican Jacobus de Voragine; Caxton printed Eng. translation (1483).

GOLDEN ROD, the common name for herbaceous plants of the genus *Solidago*, natural order Compositæ. The inflorescence is usually a raceme consisting of small flower-heads; native of N. America, with one common Brit. species.

GOLDEN ROSE, ornament solemnly blessed by Pope on fourth Sunday in Lent, and sent annually to some prince or community he wishes specially to honor on account of services to Church.

GOLDEN RULE, name given to the precept of Christ in *Matthew* 8:12, Luke 6:31, 'Whatsoever ye would that men should do to you, do ye even so to them.'

GOLDFINCH (*Carduelis elegans*), cage bird.

GOLD-FISH, OR GOLDEN CARP (*Carassius auratus*), a common freshwater fish native to China and Japan. In its natural state it is brown in color, but when domesticated it develops the familiar red-gold tint, and occasionally becomes a complete albino, when it is known as the silver fish. It breeds freely in aquaria or ponds, provided the water is kept up to a temperature of 80° F.

GOLD LEAF, a tissue of that metal, beaten out to $\frac{1}{28200}$ in. in thickness. It is beaten to such a fineness for the purpose of gilding various surfaces. The art of gold-beating was known to the ancient Egyptians and was practiced by the potters and decorators of both Greece and Rome. A German monk of the 12th century outlines a process of gold-beating almost identical with that of today, and in the days of their prosperity the skilful Florentines were famous for the art. The gold is sometimes alloyed with silver or copper, and is then cast into ingots. Powerful steel rollers flatten the ingots out to a ribbon $1\frac{1}{2}$ in. wide. After annealing, the ribbon is divided into pieces, each weighing about $6\frac{1}{2}$ grains. These pieces are interleaved in a 'cutch,' the interleaving being effected with small sheets of vellum or tough paper, about 4 in. sq. This 'cutch' or pile is set on a firm marble block and beaten with a seventeen-pound hammer, until the gold has spread to the size of the paper screens. Each gold sheet is cut into four, and again interleaved, this time in a 'shoder,' whose leaves are made of 'gold-beater's skin' (*q.v.*). This 'shoder' or packet is beaten for two hours with a ten-pound hammer. Finally each G. L. is again divided into four and set between layers of very fine gold-beater's skin, in what is technically called a mould. Here the gold is beaten for the last time, usually for four hours. A seven-pound hammer is used. Twenty-five leaves, which are about $3\frac{1}{4}$ in. square, are sold together in a book; and the fineness of the metal is such that a grain of G. L. will gild 56 sq. in. of surface.

GOLDMAN, EMMA (1869), a Russian-Jewish anarchist agitator; *b.* in Kovuo, Russia. After having acquired an advanced education in various universities of Europe, she came to the United States, in 1886, and soon after acquired notoriety in connection with the Haymarket riots in Chicago. In 1906 she established the anarchist publication Mother Earth. In 1917 she was tried for conspiracy under the Draft Law, for which she was eventually sentenced to two years in the penitentiary and fined $10,000. In the fall of 1919 she was deported to Russia, but in spite of her supposed sympathies for the Bolshevist rulers of Russia, was compelled to leave that country for Berlin, Germany. Granted 90 day permit, January 1934, to revisit U.S. She has written *Anarchism and Other Essays*, 1910, and *The Social Significance of the Modern Drama*, 1914.

GOLDMARK, KARL (1832-1915), Hungarian composer; wrote operas *Queen of Sheba*, *Merlin*; *Country Wedding* Symphony, etc.

GOLDONI, CARLO (1707-93), Ital. dramatist; founder of the modern school of Ital. comedy, which replaced earlier pantomimic buffoonery; wrote *Memoires*.

GOLDSBORO, a city of North Carolina, in Wayne co., of which it is the county seat. It is on the Southern, the Atlantic Coast Line, and the Norfolk Southern railroad, and on the Neuse river. It is the center of an important cotton growing district and has also extensive industries, including the manufacture of cotton, cottonseed oil, lumber, rice, furniture, agricultural implements, woolen goods, etc. It has an Odd Fellows' Orphan Home, the Eastern Insane Asylum, a hospital, sanitarium, and a park.

GOLDSMITH, OLIVER (1728-74), Brit. poet, dramatist, and man-of-letters; *s.* of an Irish clergyman; *b.* Pallas, Longford, Ireland; ed. at Trinity Coll., Dublin, and afterwards studied med. at Edinburgh and Leyden. Then he wandered on foot over Europe, and at length, having failed in everything he undertook, turned bookseller's hack in London. After severe struggles G. began to be known in literary society, and made the acquaintance of Johnson, Burke, Reynolds, Garrick, and others. He was plain looking, and marked with smallpox; generous to a fault; extremely foolish in most of his actions; lacking in the ability to make money systematically, or to take care of it when made; but he was beloved by everybody. His *Vicar of Wakefield*, 1766, is one of the masterpieces of Eng. fiction, and his brilliant comedy, *She Stoops to Conquer*, 1773, still maintains its popularity. His play, *The Good-Natured Man*, though little read now, was much esteemed during his lifetime. His poem, *The Deserted Village*, will not readily be forgotten. G. wrote many other works—histories, biographies, essays, and poems. Johnson said of him that he 'left scarcely any style of writing untouched, and touched nothing that he did not adorn.'

GOLDSTÜCKER, THEODOR (1821-79), Ger. scholar; prof. of Sanskrit in Univ. Coll., London; author of *Sanskrit Dictionary* and other works.

GOLETTA (36° 48′ N., 10° 18′ E.), port, Tunisia, N. Africa; connected with Tunis (11 miles S.) by ship canal traversing shallow salt lake.

GOLF, 'The Royal and Ancient Game' of golf is generally regarded as originally a Scot. pastime, but there is good reason for believing that it was first played in Holland. When it was introduced into Scotland is not known, but it was certainly largely played there in the 15th cent. Clubs began to be established early in the 18th cent.; that at St. Andrews—the 'Mecca' of golfers—was founded in 1754. James I. instituted a club at Blackheath, 1608; Charles I. was fond of the game, and is known to have played it on the Links of Leith. It is certain that Scotland kept alive the traditions and practice of the game, which did not find favor in England generally until the second half of the 19th cent. During the last thirty years it has come rapidly into favor in all English-speaking countries, and, indeed, in almost all parts of the world, while in America its popularity has increased enormously. Its practice, interrupted during the World War, has been resumed with even greater vigor. Formerly solely a man's game, it is now equally popular with both sexes.

Golf is played under ideal conditions on ground by the sea, with short, springy turf, diversified with sandy depressions called 'bunkers.' 'Inland' greens are hilly ground or flat meadows in which artificial 'bunkers' and other 'hazards' have to be provided. A full-length course has eighteen 'holes,' placed at 150 to about 500 yds. apart. Holes, about 4 in. in diameter, are placed in smooth 'putting' greens. The game is usually played by two persons, each provided with a small hard ball (of gutta and rubber), or by four persons, two players on each side, who strike the same ball alternately; the match is then called a 'foursome'. The object of each player is to get his ball from the 'teeing-ground' (the starting point for each hole) into the hole with the least number of strokes. The one who plays the holes in the fewest strokes wins the match. For the purpose of driving the ball from good or bad positions a variety of clubs is used. Some of these have wooden heads, others iron, the principal clubs being the driver, brassy (wood); the cleek, iron, mashie, niblick (iron); and the putter (iron, aluminum, or wood). Among the best known players (1933) were: J. Goodman, G. Dunlap, Jr.; Virginia Van Wie, Bobby Jones and MacDonald Smith.

GOLGOTHA, the scene of the crucifixion of Christ, being a small hill just outside Jerusalem. It has been identified with a knoll on the N. side of the city, close to the Damascus Gate, and was probably the place of public execution according to the Mosaic law. The Hebrew word G. means 'a skull', but it is uncertain whether this refers to the shape of the hill or to the skulls of criminals which might be found there.

GOLIARDS, riotous European students of the Middle Ages, whose songs were directed against the asceticism of the Church.

GOLIATH, famous giant of Gath, slain in single combat with David, who was armed only with a sling and stone (1 *Samuel* 17).

GOLTZ, BARON KOLMAR VON DER (1843-1916), Ger. soldier, commonly known as Goltz Pasha; *b.* Bielkenfeld, E. Prussia; fought and was wounded in the Austrian campaign, 1866; became lecturer on military history at Berlin, and wrote his classic works, *Rossbach and Jena* and *A Nation in Arms,* 1883. From 1883 to 1895 he was engaged in reorganizing the Turk. army, and was identified with the Young Turk movement, 1908. The ignominious defeat of Turkey in the Balkan War, 1912, adversely affected his reputation. In 1913 he retired from the Prussian army with the rank of field-marshal. In the World War he was governor of Brussels, Sept.-Oct., 1914, and supervised the defenses of the Dardanelles and the Turk. campaign generally. He died, or was assassinated, on the day after the fall of Trebizond, April 14, 1916.

GOLTZIUS, HENDRIK (1558-1617), Dutch engraver; famed for portraits, and imitations of Michaelangelo.

GOMAL, GUMAL (32° 10′ N., 69° 30′ E.), river and important pass, on borders of India and Afghanistan.

GOMERA (28° 8′ N., 17° 22′ W.); one of Canary Islands; chief town, San Sebastian. Area, 144 sq. miles.

GOMEZ, DE AVELLANEDA, GERTRUDIS (1814-73), Span. dramatist and poet; her literary dramas include *Saul, Baltasar,* and *Alfonso Munio.*

GOMEZ, DIOGO (DIEGO) (fl. 1460), Portug. sailor, explorer, and author; judge at Cintra, 1466; wrote chronicle in Latin on life of Prince Henry the Navigator.

GOMEZ, MAXIMO (1826-1905), Cuban soldier, took part in rebellion of 1868, and was appointed commander-in-chief at rising of 1895, defeating Castillanos at Puerto Principe, 1896, and successfully resisting Span. forces, 1896-8; resented Amer. intervention, 1898, but, on cession of Cuba to U. S., accepted terms offered by the latter.

GOMPERS, SAMUEL (1850-1924), Amer. labor leader; *b.* London, Eng. He came to America at the age of 13 and worked at cigar making. In 1881 he helped to found the American Federation of Labor, with which he was ever since identified. Since 1882, with the intermission of one year, he was president of that organization, and under his direction it has become one of the most powerful labor bodies in the world. Mr. Gompers worked indefatigably to advance its interests and strengthen its influence. He wrote many articles on labor questions and edited the official magazine of the Federation, besides making a vast number of speeches in defense of the rights of labor. In the main his influence was steadying and conservative, and he successfully combated the efforts of radicals and communists to gain control of the organization. In international labor conferences also he stood for law, order and moderation. During the World War, he placed all the resources of the Federation at the disposal of the American Government. He was a prominent figure in procuring enactment of eight-hour legislation, employers' liability laws, and similar measures. He also secured the inclusion in the Clayton Anti-Trust act of a provision that removes associations of wage earners from the provisions of trust legislation. His publications include: *Labor in Europe and America, American Labor and the War, Labor and Common Welfare, Labor and the Employer, Out of Their Own Mouths.* In 1921 he was a member of the Disarmament Advisory Commission. In the Fall of 1924 while in Mexico City he was taken seriously ill. When his condition did not improve he was placed aboard a train and died enroute to the states at San Antonio, Texas, in December 1924.

GONAÏVES, a seaport of Haiti, situated on the W. coast, at the head of the Gulf of Gonaïves, nearly 70 m. N.N.W. of the town of Port au Prince. Played an important part in the declaration of Haitian independence, Jan. 1, 1804.

GONCOURT, EDMOND LOUIS ANTOINE HUOT DE (1822-96 and **JULES ALFRED HUOT DE** (1830-70), Fr. authors of early naturalist school; collaborated in writing histories and novels, including *Portraits intimes du XVIIIe siecle*, *L'Art du XVIIIe siecle*, *Saeur Philomene*, etc.

GONDA (27° 7′ N., 82° E.), town and district, Fyzabad division, United Provinces, India. District: area, 2,813 sq. miles.

GONDAL (21° 55′ N., 70° 52′ E.), native state, in Kathiawar, Bombay, India.

GONDAR (12° 37′ N., 37° 29′ E.), town, Abyssinia, Africa; formerly capital; much decayed; numerous ruined castles, palaces, and churches; cotton, gold, silver, and fine leather manufactures; partly burned by Dervishes, 1889.

GONDIVES, town, W. Haiti; harbor; birthplace of Haitian independence, Jan., 1804.

GONDOKORO (4° 54′ N., 31° 40′ E.), village on Upper Nile, at frontier of Egyptian Sudan; trading center.

GONDOLA, kind of boat; long, narrow, and flat-bottomed, high prow and bow, propelled by single oar; used on Venice canals.

GONDOMAR, DIEGO SARMIENTO DE ACUÑA, COUNT OF (1567-1626), Span. diplomat; ambassador to Eng court, 1613-18 and 1619-22; prevented James I. from joining anti-Span. alliance.

GONFALON, state banner of the Middle Ages, particularly that borne in procession by the magistrates (*fonfaloniers*) of the Ital. republics.

GONIOMETER in its simplest form, Contact g., is a graduated semicircle of metal at the center of which two rules are pivoted together. Between these the angles of large crystals with dull faces are measured. The Reflecting g., used for small bright crystals which reflect sharply defined images, measures the angle between the normals to two faces,

(*i.e.,*) the angle of rotation necessary to superpose the image reflected from the second face on that reflected from the first, while the crystal is rotated about an axis parallel to the edge between two faces.

GONORRHŒA, inflammatory condition of the mucous membrane of the urethra and other genito-urinary passages, caused by a specific organism, the *gonococcus*, and usually resulting from impure sexual intercourse.

GONSALVO DI CORDOVA, see CORDOVA, GONZALO, FERNANDEZ DE.

GONTAUT, MARIE JOSEPHINE LOUISE, DUCHESSE DE (1773-1857), celebrated Frenchwoman, associated with court of Charles X.; her *Memoirs* give an interesting account of period (Eng. trans., 1894).

GONVILLE, EDMUND (*d.* 1351), Eng. ecclesiastic; part-founder of Gonville and Caius Coll., Cambridge.

GONZAGA, Ital. family, rulers of Mantua from 1328 to 1708; often at war with the Viscontis of Milan. Giovanni Francesco II. obtained marquisate for military services to Emperor Sigismund, 1432; and Federigo II. was cr. duke by Emperor Charles V. in 1530. Line became extinct, 1708.

GONZAGA, THOMAZ ANTONIO (1744-1809), Portug. poet; wrote a collection of love poems, entitled *Marilia*, which achieved great popularity.

GOOD, JOHN MASON (1764-1827); Eng. author; chiefly known for his *History of Medicine*, 1795, and his trans. of Lucretius.

GOOD FRIDAY, name given to the Friday before Easter, on which the Savior was crucified. It is kept as a very solemn fast in the R. C. Church, increasingly so in the Anglican, not so much among Nonconformists.

GOODALL, FREDERICK (1822-1904), Eng. artist; at fourteen was awarded the 'Isis' medal of the Soc. of Arts, two years later gaining the silver medal from the same body; at seventeen he exhibited at the Royal Academy; elected A.R.A. 1852 and R.A. 1863; first confined himself to subjects of Eng. life, later to historical subjects. His visit to Egypt, 1857-9, strongly influenced his work, and his Eastern and Scriptural pictures proved very popular with the public. He also met with some success in portraiture. His style was conventional but attractive.

GOODE, GEORGE BROWN (1851-96), an American scientist, *b.* in New

Albany, Ind. After studying at the Harvard Museum of Comparative Anatomy, he became connected in 1874 with the fish commission of the United States Natural Museum. In 1887 he became assistant secretary of the Smithsonian Institution. He was one of the leading authorities on fishes.

GOODELL, CHARLES ELMER (1867), a college president; s. of Harrison and Mary Taylor Goodell. Graduated from Franklin College in 1888 and took postgraduate work at Cornell and at Chicago University. Became professor of history at Franklin College in 1894. Taught at Denison University from 1903 to 1917, in which year he was called to presidency of Franklin College. Member of a number of scientific societies and has contributed to various scientific journals.

GOOD HOPE, CAPE OF. See CAPE OF GOOD HOPE.

GOODING, FRANK R. He was b. in England and came to the United States with family in 1867. Received education in public schools of Paw Paw, Mich. Was for several years a mining contractor, and later took up farming and sheep raising. Was one of the largest sheep owners in Idaho. Served in Idaho State Senate for four years. Became Governor of State of Idaho in 1905. Appointed to fill unexpired term in United States Senate in 1921. Elected to United States Senate for full term 1921-1927. d. 1928.

GOODMAN, JULES ECKERT (1876), American dramatist, s. of Newman and Jeanette Rothschild Goodman. Graduated from Harvard in 1899. Became managing editor of Current Literature, later going to the Mirror. Has written extensively for all leading magazines. His principal plays include *The Test*, *The Man Who Stood Still*, *Mother*, *The Silent Voice*, *The Man Who Came Back*, *Business Before Pleasure*, *Why Worry*, *His Honor*, *Abe Potash*, and *Pietro*.

GOODNOW, FRANK JOHNSON 1859), an American university president; b. in Brooklyn, N. Y. He graduated from Amherst College, in 1879, continuing his studies in Paris and Berlin. He was Eaton professor of administrative law at Columbia University, after 1903, and dean of political science there during 1906-7. During 1913-14 he was legal advisor to the Chinese Government. Since 1914 he has been president of Johns Hopkins University. He is the author of many books, among these being *Comparative Administrative Law*, 1893; *Municipal*

Government, 1910; *Social Reform and the Constitution*, 1911, and *Principles of Constitutional Government*, 1916.

GOODRICH, CASPAR FREDERICK (1847), an American admiral; b. in Philadelphia, Pa. He graduated from the naval academy at Annapolis in 1864, and was promoted through the various grades, becoming rear-admiral in 1904. During 1905-6 he had command of the Pacific Squadron. He retired in 1909. d. 1925.

GOODRICH, SAMUEL GRISWOLD (1793-1860), an American writer; b. in Ridgefield, Conn. He was at first a publisher in Hartford, Conn., then in Boston, Mass., later being editor of The Token, and as such publishing some of the stories of Nathaniel Hawthorne. Then he began to write and publish a series of juvenile books, known as 'the Peter Farley series,' being stories of adventure, history, achievement, etc., written in a vein that proved very popular among children. From beginning to end these books numbered 116 and were read all over the country and in England. He also wrote more serious works, among these being *The Outcast, and Other Poems*, 1837; *Recollections of a Lifetime*, 1857; and his best known work, *An Illustrated Natural History of the Animal Kingdom*, 1859.

GOODRICH, THOMAS (d. 1554) bp. of Ely and Lord Chancellor of England, 1551-52; assisted in compilation of the *Institution of a Christian Man*, and Cranmer's *Bible*, and *Book of Common Prayer*.

GOODWIN, MAUDE WILDER (1856), an American historical novelist; b. in Ballston, Spa, N. Y. Her works, which at one time enjoyed a limited popularity, include *The Head of a Hundred*, *White Aprons*, *Dolly Madison* (a biography), *Historic New York*, 1898; *Four Roads to Paradise*, 1904, and *Veronica Playfair*.

GOODWIN SANDS (51° 19' N.; 1° 35' E.), dangerous shoals, E. of Kent, England; separated from mainland by the Downs; shifting sands; scene of many wrecks; said to be submerged estate of Earl Godwin.

GOODWIN, THOMAS (1600-80), Eng. Puritan preacher; friend of Cromwell's; member of Westminster Assembly, 1643; pres. of Magdalen Coll., Oxford, 1650-60.

GOODWIN, WILLIAM WATSON (1831-1912), an American university professor; b. in Concord, Mass. He graduated from Harvard University.

in 1851. In 1860 he became professor of Greek at Harvard, and remained there in that position for over forty years. He was noted as one of the highest American authorities on the Greek classics. He was the author of *The Syntax of the Moods and Tenses of the Greek Verb*, *A Greek Grammar*, and a revised translation of *Plutarch's Morals*, 1871.

GOODYEAR, CHARLES (1800-1860), an American inventor; *b.* in New Haven, Conn. After leaving school he went into his *f's* hardware business, and during this period he invented a steel pitchfork which had a wide sale. In 1830 the *f's* business went into bankruptcy, and young Goodyear went into the rubber business. Shortly after he invented what was generally called the 'nitric acid gas process,' by which native India rubber was dipped in a preparation of nitric acid, which enabled manufacturers of rubber goods to expose rubber surfaces, hitherto too adhesive to do that. It proved especially valuable in the manufacture of shoes. This invention was superseded by Goodyear's invention of the process of vulcanizing rubber in 1844. He registered over 60 patents, but while others grew wealthy by infringing on his patents, he died in poverty.

GOOLE (53° 42′ N., 0° 52′ W.), market town and port, West Riding, Yorkshire, England; extensive docks, iron foundries; manufactures sugar, agricultural implements.

GOOSE, a collective term for members of the *Anserinae*. The group is largely Arctic in character. The plumage is similar in both sexes; beak tapering and characterized by horny, knobbed tip. Geese are more terrestrial in character than either ducks or swans, and when on the wing travel in typical 'V'-shaped formation, termed by sportsmen a *skein*. The Grey Lag g. is believed to be the progenitor of the domestic species. In Holland and Germany enormous quantities of geese are reared for the market. Strassburg *pate de foie gras* is obtained from geese confined in an apartment kept at a high temperature to produce morbid enlargement of liver.

GOOSEBERRY is the fruit of *Ribes grossularia*, natural order *Ribesaceae*. The shrub has *spines* (modified leaf-bases) and alternate *crenated* three- or five-lobed leaves with dilated *petiole*. The flower has a *monosepalous* bell-shaped *calyx* with five divisions and a *corolla* of five free petals alternating with the divisions of the *calyx*. The five *perigynous* stamens are opposite the petals, and the inferior unilocular *ovary* has two short *styles*. The *ovules* are borne on two *placentas*. The fruit is a berry with a persistent *calyx* at the top, and contains sugar and malic acid. The best growth conditions are cool climate, rich loam, much manure.

GOOSSENS, EUGENE (1893-   ), English composer and conductor, *b.* Bordeaux; ed. at Bruges Conservatoire, Liverpool School of Music and Royal College of Music; conductor of the London Symphony orchestra, Rochester Orchestra, The Russian Ballet, and Carl Rosa Opera company; has written 'Five Impressions of a Holiday', string quartet; a quintet and sextet for strings, and various works for orchestra.

GOPPINGEN (48° 42′ N., 9° 40′ E.), town, on Fils, Württemberg, Germany; cotton and woolen goods.

GORAKHPUR (26° 44′ N., 83° 23′ E.), district and division, United Provinces, India; district, flat, abounds in lakes and marshes; dense forests; chief rivers, Rapti, Gogra, Great and Little Gandak; products—timber and rice; area, 4,535 sq. miles. Chief town, Gorakhpur, on Rapti; river trade, timber, grain.

GORBODUC, legendary Brit. king, subject of the earliest Eng. tragedy, *Gorboduc, or Ferrex and Porrex*, by Sackville and Norton, played before Queen Elizabeth, 1561.

GORCHAKOV, ALEXANDER MIKHAILOVICH, GORTSCHAKOFF (1798-1883), most distinguished member of Russ. princely family; ambassador to Württemburg and Austria; Foreign Minister, 1856; Chancellor, 1863; for some time most powerful minister in Europe. To same family belong Alexander Ivanovich (*d.* 1825), and Andreas Ivanovich (1768-1855), who fought against Napoleon; Mikhail Dmitrievich (1795-1861), Russ. commander-in-chief at Crimea, who conducted defense of Sevastopol; and Peter Dmitrievich (1790-1868), who commanded division at *Alma* and *Inkermann*.

GORDIAN KNOT, inextricable knot fastened to wagon of Gordius; man who loosed it to rule world; Alexander the Great cut it with sword.

GORDIANUS, MARCUS ANTONIUS, Rom. emperor; devoted to study of letters and philosophy; emperor, 238, in 80th year, for a month, jointly with *s.*, Gordianus (killed in battle, 238). His grandson, Gordianus, emperor, 238, inflicted great defeat on Persians; assassinated, 244.

GORDIUM (*c.* 40° N., 31° 35′ E.), ancient capital, Phrygia, on Sangarius; here Alexander the Great cut the Gordian knot.

GORDON, Scot. family; lived in Berwickshire, XII. cent.; descended from

Sir Adam G., lord of Huntly, Aberdeenshire, 1318; became Earls and Marquesses of Huntly and Dukes of G.; dukedom extinct, 1836; granted to Duke of Richmond, descendant in female line, 1876.

GORDON, ADAM LINDSAY (1833-70), Brit. poet; ed. Cheltenham and Oxford; afterwards went to Australia and pub. *Bush Ballads* and other vol.'s of lyrics; committed suicide.

GORDON, CHARLES GEORGE (1833-85), Brit. general and administrator; *b.* Woolwich; served in Crimea, 1855-56; joined military expedition to China, 1860; present at capture of Peking. During Taiping rebellion he took command of some Chin. troops, trained by European and Amer. officers; relieved Chansu, 1863; fought over thirty actions and seized several towns, including Suchow and Chanchufu; final suppression of rebellion largely due to his leadership; refused all pecuniary rewards from Chin. emperor. On returning home G. became Commanding Royal Engineer at Gravesend. Entering service of Khedive of Egypt in 1873, for nearly seven years (the last three as gov. of entire Sudan) he labored indefatigably to establish law and order in Upper Nile district; resigned on failing to arrange peace between Egypt and Abyssinia, 1880; returned to Sudan at request of Brit. Government, 1884, to quell Mahdi's rebellion; shut up in Khartum by rebels; bravely defended city for a year, but was treacherously killed two days before the arrival of relief force under Wolseley.

GORDON, CHARLES WILLIAM (RALPH CONNOR) (1860), a Canadian novelist; *b.* in Ontario, Canada. He graduated from Toronto 'University, in 1883, studied theology and was ordained a Presbyterian minister. During 1890-3 he was a missionary in the lumber regions of the Northwest, becoming pastor of St. Stephen's Church, in Winnipeg, in 1894. He has written many novels, among these being *Beyond the Marshes*, *Black Rock*, *The Sky Pilot*, *The Man from Glengarry*, and *The Major*.

GORDON, GEORGE ANGIER (1853), an American clergyman and theological writer; *b.* in Scotland. He came to this country as a youth and graduated from the Bangor Theological Seminary, in 1877, being ordained a Congregational minister soon after. For a time he was pastor of the Old South Church, in Boston; he was university preacher at Harvard University, during 1886-90 and 1906-9 and was Lyman Beecher lecturer at Yale University during 1901. Among his works are *The Witness to Immortality*, 1893; *The New Epoch of Faith*, 1901; *Through Man to God*, 1906, and *Humanism in New England Theology*, 1920. *d.* 1929.

GORDON, LORD GEORGE (1751-93), *s.* of Duke of G., fanatical leader of Gordon Riots, 1780—a violent protest against removal of R. C. disabilities.

GORDON, JOHN BROWN (1832-1904), a Confederate soldier; *b.* in Upson County, Ga. After graduating from the University of Georgia, in 1852, he studied law and engineering. When the Civil War broke out he was engaged in an engineering project in the Racoon Mts., and immediately organized a company of miners, which was called the 'Racoon Roughs,' with which company he entered the war as captain. At the Battle of Seven Pines he was a colonel, but on account of his general being wounded, he assumed command of his brigade leading it in the fighting so skillfully that he was made a brigadier-general. At the Battle of Gettysburg he gained the Confederates the initial victory by striking the Federal right wing and driving it through the village in disorder. As major-general he had command of nearly half of Lee's army at Appomattox, at which battle he showed his usual high qualities as a soldier. After the war he was twice Governor of Georgia, and served two terms in the U. S. Senate. He wrote *Reminiscences*, 1905.

GORDON-CUMMING, ROUALEYN GEORGE (1820-66), Scot. traveler and hunter; wrote *The Lion Hunter of South Africa*.

GORDON-BENNETT, MOUNT, a peak 15,000 feet above sea level, in Central Africa, in the Ruwenzori Range, near Albert Nyanza. It was discovered by the explorer, Henry Stanley, in 1875 and by him named in honor of his patron, Gordon Bennett, who was financing his expedition in search of Livingston.

GORDY, WILBUR FISK (1854), American educator, *s.* of Elijah Nielson and Martha Gordy. Graduated from Wesleyan University in 1880. Became superintendent of schools, Ansonia, Conn., in 1881. Held same position in Springfield, Mass., until 1911. Lectured extensively on educational subjects throughout New England. Author of the following works, many of which are standard text books: *A School History of the United States*, 1897; *American Leaders and Heroes*, 1901; *Colonial Days*, 1907; *American Beginnings in Europe*, 1911; *Abraham Lin-*

coln, 1917; *Causes and Meanings of the Great War*, 1919.

GORE, CHARLES (1853), Eng. theologian; Fellow of Trinity Coll., canon of Westminster, then bp. of Worcester, 1902-4, of Birmingham, 1905-11; since 1911, of Oxford.

GORE, THOMAS PRYOR (1870), a U. S. Senator; *b*. in Webster County, Miss. Considerable interest has been attached to his personality on account of his being totally blind; at the age of eight he lost one eye by being struck with a stick by a playmate, and at the age of 11 he lost his other eye by an arrow from a cross bow. In 1892 he graduated from Cumberland University, in Tennessee and began to practice law. He removed to Texas, in 1895, where, in 1898, he was a candidate for Congress on the Populist ticket, but was defeated. In 1901 he removed to Oklahoma, where he was elected to the U. S. Senate for the terms of 1909-15 and 1915-21, as a Democrat. Re-elected, 1930.

GORÉE (14° 39′ N., 17° 15′ W.), small island, Fr. Senegal, W. Africa, E. of Dakar; chief town, Gorée; large harbor; formerly important commercial entrepôt.

GORGAS, WILLIAM CRAWFORD (1854-1920), American army surgeon; *b*. Mobile, Ala. He graduated at the University of the South in 1875 and from the Bellevue Hospital Medical College, New York University, in 1879. He was appointed surgeon in the U. S. Army in 1880 and became major surgeon in 1898. In the latter year he was appointed chief officer in charge of sanitary work at Havana, Cuba, and so successfully applied methods of combating yellow fever that he eliminated that disease, which had been the curse of Cuba. His brilliant work in that office caused him to be made surgeon general by a special act of Congress in 1903. In 1904 he was appointed chief sanitary officer of the Panama Canal Zone, and his work there in exterminating tropical diseases paralleled his achievements in Havana. He retired from active service in 1918 and became the director of yellow fever research in the Rockefeller Foundation. Several South American countries availed themselves of his ability in fighting fevers with remarkable results. He was awarded medals and honors by many of the world's greatest scientific societies. Italy decorated him in 1918 and France in 1919.

GORGES, SIR FERDINANDO (*c*. 1566-1647), Eng. soldier and colonist;

was prisoner in Spain; fought for Henry IV. of France; sometime gov. of Plymouth; later became founder and chartered proprietor of Maine, New England, 1639.

GORGET, broad collar-piece, worn with suit-armor in England, XV.-XVII. cent's.

GORGIAS OF LEONTINI, famous Sicilian rhetorician and sophist, *b*. about 480 B.C. In 427 B.C. he was sent to Athens to petition aid against Syracuse. The remainder of his life was spent in Athens as a teacher of rhetoric, and at Larissa. His style was highly ornate, rich, and elaborate, and considerably influenced the oratory of Demosthenes, though its effects on rhetoricians of inferior calibre was vicious. Plato's treatise on rhetoric is called the *Gorgias*, and in it G. is made to express his views on the art of oratory.

GORGONS, THE (classical myth.), Medusa, Stheno, and Euryale, female monsters, dwelling beyond the Western ocean, who turned to stone any mortal who looked upon them. Medusa alone was mortal, and was slain by Perseus.

GORGONZOLA (45° 32′ N., 9° 23′ E.), town, Milan, Italy; famous cheese.

GORILLA, a large man-like ape, which is a native of W. Africa. It can be distinguished from the chimpanzee by the small ears, elongated head, the presence of a deep groove alongside the nostrils, the small size of the thumb, and the great length of the arm, which reaches half-way down the shin-bone in the erect posture. It also differs from the chimpanzee in its greater size; the height of a male G. being from 5½ to 6 ft. In color it is blackish, but the hair on the head and shoulders often has a reddish tinge. It is chiefly a vegetable feeder, but, like most apes, it also preys upon small mammals, birds, and their eggs. The G. spends most of its time on the ground, although it is a skillful climber, and is not so very ferocious, for when attacked it generally avoids an encounter, but when driven into a corner is a dangerous enemy on account of its enormous strength. G's. have not yet been tamed, and fully adult ones have never been seen alive in captivity. Various attempts have been made to add one to the Zoological Gardens, but the animals have all died young.

GORINCHEM, GORKUM (51° 49′ N. 4° 59′ E.), fortified town, on Merwede, S. Holland, Netherlands; salmon fisheries; trade in grain, cattle.

GORKY, MAXIM, pseudonym of Alexei Maximovitch Peshkoff (1868), Russian author. Left an orphan at 9, he led a roaming life, engaging in almost every variety of occupation, and for a time wandered over Southern Russia as a tramp. The sordidness of his experiences prompted an attempt at suicide when he was 19. Later on, these experiences stood him in stead as a realistic writer of stories portraying the lowest depths of human life and experience. His first story, *Makar Chudra,* appeared in 1892, and its striking quality gave notice that a new force had arisen in Russian literature. Many other stories followed, all of them enhancing his reputation. In 1906 he visited several European countries where he received a marked welcome, but a later trip to the United States was marred by criticism from the fact that he was accompanied by a woman, not his wife. His principles were radical, and he frequently came into conflict with the Czar's Government, being twice arrested and banished. At the outbreak of the war he joined the Russian Army and in 1917 took part in the movement that led to the deposition of the Czar. Although he has disagreed with the Bolshevist authorities on some points, he has been to a certain extent the spokesman of the Soviet. During the famine of 1922, his appeals for help to the foreign governments of the world were poignant and powerful. His work, while exceedingly brilliant in characterization, is imbued with the pessimism and sense of futility that mark Russian fiction in general. His publications include: *Twenty-six and One,* 1902; *Heartache, and the Old Woman Izerofel,* 1905, *The Individualists,* 1906; *The Spy,* 1908; *A Confession,* 1910; *My Childhood,* 1915; *In the World,* 1917; *Reminiscences of L. N. Tolstoy,* 1920. *Bystander,* 1930. His plays are: *The Smug Citizen,* and a *Night's Lodging,* the latter portraying the most appalling depths of human degradation.

GORLITZ (51° 9′ N., 15° E.), town, Silesia, Prussia; important commercial center; principal edifice, XV.-cent. Gothic church of St. Peter and St. Paul; cloth, machinery, and glass manufactures.

GÖRRES, JOHANNES JOSEPH VON (1776-1848), Ger. author and publicist; prof. of physics in Coblenz Univ., 1800-14; began to pub. his *Die deutschen Volksbucher,* 1807, and became a leader of the Ultramontane party. His chief work was *Christliche Mystik,* 1842.

GORST, SIR ELDON (1861-1911), Eng. and Colonial politician; b. New Zealand; controller of direct taxes to the Egyptian Government, 1890; under-secretary of state for finance, 1892; financial adviser to Egyptian Government, 1898-1904; assistant under-secretary for foreign affairs, 1904-7; Brit. agent and consul-general in Egypt, 1907-11.

GORTYNA (35° 10′ N., 25° E.), ancient city, Crete, on river Lathæus.

GÖRZ AND GRADISCA, prov. Italy, formerly county and crownland of Austria (45° 57′ N., 13° 38′ E.), between Carniola on E. and Venetia on W.; cap. Görz; surface very mountainous; principal river, Isonzo; extensive vineyards; exports wine and fruit; silk culture an important industry; pop. mainly Slavic and Catholic; prov. belonged to Austria from 1500 till it was given to Italy by Peace Treaty after World War. Area, 1,127 sq. m.

GOSCHEN, GEORGE JOACHIM, VISCOUNT (1831-1907), Brit. statesman and financier; grandson of celebrated Leipzig bookseller, 1752-1828, of same name; First Lord of Admiralty, 1871; ambassador to Constantinople, 1880 opposed Home Rule and joined Unionists; Chancellor of Exchequer 1887-92; converted National Debt, 1888; again First Lord of Admiralty, 1895-1900.

GOSHAWK, a member of the **HAWK** FAMILY.

GOSHEN (30° 18′ N., 32° E.); region, Lower Egypt; settled by Israelites before the Exodus.

GOSHEN, a city of Indiana, in Elkhart co., of which it is the county seat. It is on the New York Central, the Big Four and other railroads, and on the Elkhart river. It is an important industrial community and has manufactures of wool, underwear, rubber goods, furniture, iron, flour, farming implements, and condensed milk. The public buildings include a court-house, 2 high schools, a library and a hospital. The city is the seat of Goshen College.

GOSHEN, a village of New York, in Orange co., of which it is the county seat. It is on the Erie, the Lehigh and New England railroads, about 60 miles northwest of New York City. It is an important agricultural and dairying community and is principally distinguished as a place where trotting and pacing horses are bred, trained and raced. There is a court-house, churches and banks.

GOSHUN, MATSUMURA (1752-

1811), Jap. artist; founder of the Shijo school; work something akin to that of Okyo, but broader in general effect; used color more sparingly, and built up his forms more simply. He was highly successful as a teacher, and his pupil, Keibun, 1779-1843, carried the school to the height of its glory.

GOSLAR (51° 55′ N., 10° 25′ E.), town, Hanover, Prussia, on Gose; has numerous fine old churches and quaint buildings; imperial palace, recently restored, formerly favorite residence of Ger. emperors; silver, copper, lead, sulphur mines; passed from Hanover to Prussia, 1866.

GOSNOLD, BARTHOLOMEW (d. 1607), an English navigator, who sailed from Falmouth, 1602, in the 'Concord,' and discovered Cape Cod and some neighboring islands. He was the leader of an expedition which discovered the Virginian Capes, and founded Jamestown in 1606, where he died.

GOSPEL (literal meaning—good news) was originally applied to the proclamation by Christ of the kingdom of heaven. Canonical g's are first four books of New Testament, with which are associated names of Matthew, Mark, Luke, and John; these were probably written in second half of I. cent. A. D., when the spread of Christianity made written accounts of its origin necessary. First three are called the *Synoptic* g's because of their similarity of matter, method, and style; while St. John's account differs in all three respects. It is now generally believed that St. Mark's G. was written first, and was derived from, and practically identical with, an earlier document; and that Matthew and Luke wrote their accounts by combining this early document with another known as the *Logia*, a compilation of Christ's sayings.

GOSPORT (50° 48′ N., 1° 8′ W.), seaport, Hampshire, England, opposite Portsmouth, with which it is connected by floating bridge; contains Clarence victualling yard; yacht-building.

GOSSAMER, fine threads, or webs, formed by spiders, generally attached to trees or plants; hence anything of a light, flimsy nature.

GOSSARD, GEORGE DANIEL (1868), American college president. Graduated from Otterbein University, Ohio, in 1892. Later a postgraduate student at Johns Hopkins. Ordained in United Brethren Church in 1897. Elected president of Lebanon Valley College, Pa., in 1912.

GOSSE, EDMUND (1849-1928), Eng. critic and miscellaneous writer; was appointed assistant librarian in the Brit. Museum, 1867; removed to the Board of Trade as translator, 1875; librarian at the House of Lords, 1904-14. His most recent works include *Inter Arma*, 1916; *The Life of Algernon Charles Swinburne*, 1917; *Three French Moralists*, 1918; *Diversions of a Man of Letters*, 1919.

GOSSE, PHILIP HENRY (1810-88), Eng. naturalist; a careful observer of *marine fauna*; his *Actinologia Britannica* is a standard work on sea-anemones.

GOSSIP (Anglo-Saxon, *God* and *sib*), word meaning (1) sponsor or godparent, (2) friend, (3) idle tattler, (4) idle talk.

GOTA (58° N., 12° 2′ E.), river, Sweden, flowing from Lake Vener into the Cattegat; length, 50 miles; navigable throughout. Gota Canal, connects Baltic and Cattegat by way of Lakes Vetter and Vener.

GOTAMA, see BUDDHA.

GOTHA (50° 57′ N., 10° 4′ E.), town, Thuringia, Germany; principal building —Friedenstein castle, 1643, with library, cabinet of coins, museum of antiquities, and picture-gallery; contains famous geographical publishing house of Justus Perthes (who pub. well-known *Almanach de Gotha*); important industrial center; manufactures sausages.

GOTHAM, WISE MEN OF, old name given to inhabitants of Gotham, a Nottinghamshire village, who were notorious for their stupidity. Washington Irving applied this name to New York City.

GOTHARD, ST., pass, Alps (46° 30′ N., 8° 40′ E.); 6,936 ft.; from Ticino to Upper Reuss valley; railway tunnel, over 9 m. long, opened in 1882.

GOTHENBURG (57° 39′ N., 11° 59′ E.), seaport, Sweden, on Göta-Elf; large commercial and industrial center; traversed by numerous canals; consists of old and new town, with fine harbor (seldom blocked by ice); chief industries, shipbuilding, machinery, textiles, woodpulp, sugar-refining, brewing; founded by Gustavus Adolphus, 1618; rose to commercial importance during continental blockade, 1806; gives name to famous licensing system.

GOTHIC ARCHITECTURE, see ARCHITECTURE.

GOTHS, Teutonic race whose earliest-known home was the S. shores and islands of Baltic, where they are found in I. cent. A. D. They gradually migrated southwards through central Europe, and early in III. cent. settled in districts to N. of Danube and Black Sea. In this cent. they first came into contact with the Romans, whom they routed at *Abrita* in 251; thereafter for 20 years they ravaged Asia Minor and Balkan regions, and in 270 they obtained the concession of Dacia from Emperor Aurelian. By middle of IV. cent. they had become dominant race of non-Roman Europe, their kingdom stretching in broad band from Black Sea to Baltic. Principal subdivisions of nation are Ostrogoths, or East Goths, and Visigoths, or West Goths. The Visigoths were driven across the Danube by invading Huns, *c.* 375, and settled under Rom. rule; under Alaric they rose in rebellion, overran Greece and Italy, and captured Rome in 410; after Alaric's death they left Italy for Gaul, but were subsequently driven by Franks across Pyrenees, and established a kingdom in Spain which lasted until VIII. cent., when the country was subdued by Muslims. The Ostrogoths were conquered by Huns, *c.* 376, when Ermanaric, the most celebrated Gothic king, committed suicide; they remained in subjection until 451, when they regained independence; and under Theodoric they acquired most of Italy after the break up of Western Empire in 476. After wars with Romans they were eventually defeated by Justinian's general, Narses and left Italy, *c.* 552.

GOTLAND, OR GOTTLAND (57° 30' N., 18° 30' E.), island, Baltic Sea, belonging to Sweden; forms *lan* of G., together with several smaller islands. Chief town, Visby. Coast is steep; interior mostly level, with large extent of forest; cultivates barley, rye, wheat, oats, and beet-sugar; main industries are sheep and cattle-raising, fishing, cement-making, and lime-burning; contains large number of ruined churches.

GOTO, GOTO RETTO, GOTTO (33° N., 129° E.), group of islands lying W. of Kiushiu, Japan.

GOTTFRIED VON STRASSBURG (XIII. cent.), Ger. epic poet; wrote *Tristan and Isolde*, which served as the foundation of Wagner's opera.

GÖTTINGEN (51° 35' N., 9° 56' E.), town, Hanover, Prussia; seat of famous univ. (Georgia Augusta), founded by George II., 1734, with library of over 500,000 vols.; has also Royal academy of sciences, founded 1751; book trade; manufactures scientific and mathe-

matical instruments.

GOUDA (52° 1' N., 4° 42' E.), town on Yssel, S. Holland; Groote Kerch, 1552, has fine stained glass; noted for cheese.

GOUGH, SIR HUBERT DE LA POER (1870), Brit. soldier; educated at Eton and Sandhurst; joined the 16th Lancers, 1889, served in Tirah expedition, 1897-98, S. African War, 1899-1902, and, during World War, in France and Flanders, 1914-18; figured in the Curragh incident (see CURRAGH). He commanded 5th Army on Somme, 1916, before Arras, April, 1917, Flanders, Sept., 1917, and St. Quentin, March, 1918. See WORLD WAR.

GOUGH, HUGH, VISCOUNT GOUGH (1779-1869), Brit. general; brought first Chinese War to successful conclusion, 1842; defeated Mahrattas, 1843; Sikhs, 1844, 1849. By final defeat of Sikhs at *Gujerat* added Punjab to Brit. Empire.

GOUGH, JOHN BARTHOLOMEW (1817-1886), American temperance orator; *b.* in Sandgate, Kent, England; *d.* at Frankford, Pa. He came to America in 1829 and took up book binding, and falling into drunken ways sang for a living in grog shops. In 1842 he signed the pledge at a temperance meeting, and though he once broke his pledge, he became a noted orator and temperance advocate, touring America and England in 1853-1855 and 1857-1860. Publications, *Autobiography*, 1846, enlarged 1870; *Orations*, 1854; *Sunlight and Shadow*, 1880.

GOUJON, JEAN (1515-66), Fr. sculptor and architect; founded Fr. neo-Greek school; designed *Fountain of the Innocents* and other Louvre decorations; though following antique models, his works are modern in sentiment.

GOULBURN (34° 36' S., 149° 43' E.), city, New S. Wales, Australia; seat of Catholic and Anglican bp's; tanneries, boots and shoes.

GOULD, SIR FRANCIS CARRUTHERS (1844-1925), Eng. caricaturist, caricatured for *Truth*, *Pall Mall Gazette*, and *Westminster Gazette*; author and illustrator of *Picture Politics*, *The Modern Froissart*, *Who killed Cock Robin?*, etc.

GOULD, GEORGE JAY (1864-1923), an American capitalist, *s.* of Jay Gould; *b.* in New York City. He entered business in the banking house of W. E. Conner & Company, New York, and succeeded his father as partner in 1885. In 1888 he was appointed president

of the Little Rock and Fort Smith
Railway, and from that time took an
active interest in railway development.
He was president and director in many
important railroad companies, and was
also identified with the railway systems
of New York City. His residence,
Georgiancourt, Lakewood, N. J., was
one of the show places of the country.

GOULD, JAY (1836-1892), American
financier; *b.* Roxbury, N. Y. His father
was a farmer in straitened circumstances.
The son worked on the farm and studied
for a time at Hobart College, where he
learned surveying. He made surveys
of several New York counties and published a history of Delaware County in
1856. In the same year he engaged in
the lumbering and tanning business in
western New York. He gained experience
in banking, and, following the panic
of 1857, made speculative investments
in railroads. He purchased the bonds
of the Rutland and Washington railroad
of which he became president, treasurer
and superintendent, and, shortly after
effecting a consolidation of this road
with the Rensselaer and Saratoga road,
he removed to New York, opened a
broker's office and began his campaign
to gain control of the Erie Railroad. His
manipulation of that stock in conjunction with James Fisk, Jr., was daring
and unscrupulous and virtually wrecked
the road to his own great financial profit.
Still in accord with Fisk, he and his
partner netted $11,000,000 by their
scheme to corner the gold market of
New York, which resulted in the financial crisis and panic known as 'Black
Friday', (Sept. 24, 1869). He invested
heavily in Pacific roads and by branch
constructions and many consolidations
established what is known as the Gould
System. He was the principal figure
in the formation of the Western Union
Telegraph system in 1881 and in the
same year gained control of the New
York Elevated railroad.

GOUNOD, CHARLES FRANÇOIS
(1819-93), Fr. composer; *b.* Paris; won
Grand prix de Rome, 1839; studied sacred
music in Rome, especially Palestrina
and Bach; first opera, *Sappho*, 1851;
Faust, 1859, most popular work and
long the standard type of Fr. opera;
Philemon et Baucis, 1860; *La Reine de
Saba*, 1862; *Mireille*, 1864; *Romeo and
Juliet*, 1867. G. wrote sacred music
during the latter part of his life, two
oratorios, *The Redemption* and *Mors et
Vita*, being among his best works; a
master of orchestration; romantic in
style, with great dramatic passion.

**GOURAUD, HENRI JOSEPH
ETIENNE** (1867), Fr. sold. His brilliant

defense of the Argonne led to his being
called 'the Lion of the Argonne.' He
succeeded General d'Amade as commander-in-chief of Fr. Expeditionary
Force at Dardanelles (May 1915), where
he was severely wounded and lost an
arm. In offensive in Champagne (July-
Aug. 1918) defeated enemy E. of Reims;
drove Germans out of Champagne and
retook Mezières. He was given the rank
of Marshal of France. In Dec. 1919
was appointed high commissioner of
Syria and Cilicia, and the commander-
in-chief of army of Levant. He took
part as commander of a portion of the
French forces in the occupation of the
Ruhr in 1923.

GOURD, *monaecious* annual herbs,
genus *Cucurbitae*, natural order *Cucur-
bitacea*, which trail by tendrils; showy
yellow flower and large juicy fruits.
The *Melon*, *Cucumber*, and *Vegetable
Marrow* are cultivated for table use,
while the *Colocynth* yields a purgative.
The seeds of all have a destructive
action on intestinal parasites. The shell
of g. fruits are used as bottles, dippers,
etc.

GOURGAUD, GASPARD, BARON
(1783-1852), Fr. general; distinguished
for personal devotion to Napoleon in
wars, and voluntarily shared exile at
St. Helena till jealousy of fellow-attend-
ants caused departure; wrote *Campagne
de 1815, Journal inedit de Ste. Helene*,
etc.

GOURKO, BASIL, Russian soldier;
was commander of 1st Cavalry Division
at beginning of World War and fought
on E. Prussian frontier. In Sept.,
1916, became chief of imperial general
staff. After revolution, March, 1917,
was commander-in-chief of western
armies. In June, 1917, he ceased to
occupy his high position; later he was
arrested by Provisional government,
and finally banished from the country
as a counter-revolutionary. He went
to England, and pub. *Memories and Impressions of War and Revolution in
Russia, 1914-1917*, 1918.

GOUT, constitutional disease characterized by inflammation of joints with
deposition of biurate of soda and derangement of various internal organs, particularly the kidneys. The condition is
due to excess of uric acid within the body,
either through excessive consumption
of nitrogenous matter or through
deficient oxidation by the tissues and
organs, accompanied by an obscure
nervous disturbance. G. is hereditary
and is influenced by over-indulgence in
alcoholic beverages, particularly sweet
wines and heavy malt liquors, or in rich
foods, by sedentary occupations and

overwork, by certain poisons, such as lead, or by a combination of insufficient nourishment and bad hygiene.

GOVAN (55° 52′ N., 4° 19′ W.), town, Lanarkshire, Scotland, on Clyde; large shipbuilding yards; engineering works; locomotive manufactures; incorporated with Glasgow, 1912.

GOVERNMENT, ruling authority in state; may also mean the person or persons to whom administration is entrusted and whose duty it is to deal with public affairs at home and to control foreign policy of state. Governments have been classified since the days of Aristotle as monarchical, aristocratic and democratic, but in view of modern developments a truer delineation would be *autocratic, constitutional,* and *popular.* The first of these, under which the monarch directs the lives of his subjects by the fiat of his word, finds no place in modern politics. *Constitutional* government arises where a community, which has formerly been ruled by a bureaucracy, has succeeded, without destroying the bureaucracy, in placing legal limitations upon the executive authority. Governments of this type are those of Japan and Italy, and that of Germany and the various Ger. states under the old regime. Under this system it invariably happens that the federal executive acts contrarily to the wishes of the government as a whole. The executive authority is bound by legal limitations, and by legal limitations only. Under the third type, the *popular* form of government, of which Great Britain, Belgium, and the Brit. Dominions are good examples, the executive exercises its undoubted legal functions according to the wishes of a body which may fairly be said to represent popular or public opinion. These countries are ruled by a nominal head under the title of king. The republic which is both theoretically and actually governed by the people has the United States for its chief example. All republics, including those established after the World War, are modeled after the principles upon which the United States was founded, and which are established in the Constitution. The machinery by which this harmony is achieved is usually that of a cabinet of ministers amenable to a popular chamber, which is itself amenable to a popular electorate. Into one of these three types of government all civilized systems will, it is believed, be found to fall. Government may also be classified according to the solidification or dispersion of ruling power, as centralized, dual, federal, and confederate; in a centralized government entire power is in the hands of the central administrative body, but in the other forms a considerable amount of authority is exercised by local governing bodies.

GOVERNOR, title of chief official of colony, generally also commander-in-chief; the g. represents Crown, and in colonies not possessing self-government has sole executive and sometimes sole legislative power. Canada, Australia, and South Africa have a governor-general; Australian states have gov's and lieut.-gov's; Canadian provinces have lieut.-gov's; S. African provinces have 'administrators.' In the United States the g. is the chief magistrate of a State, and is elected.

GOVERNORS ISLAND. A fortified island in New York Bay at the entrance to the East River. It takes its name from having been the residence of the colonial governors, the first being Wouter Van Twiller, 1637. In 1708 it was a quarantine station. Rumors of a war with France in 1794 impelled the state to give $500,000 for a fort and earthworks and Fort Jay, now Fort Columbus was built. Castle Williams dates from 1811, and in 1861-1865 was used as a prison for Confederates. The island is the headquarters of the Department of the East.

GOWER, JOHN (*d.* 1408), Eng. poet; was a person of means and influence; called by his friend, Chaucer, 'the moral Gower.' His Eng. poem, *Confessio Amantis,* consists of love stories and meditations. He also wrote in Latin, *Vox Clamantis,* dealing with the Peasants' revolt; and in Fr. *Speculum Meditantis,* a poem on married life.

GOWN (O. Fr. *goun*), outer garment without division for legs; now, except for clerical and academic g., appropriated to use of women, and known as dress or frock.

GOWRIE, JOHN RUTHVEN, 3RD EARL OF (1577-1600), Scot. noble; central figure of so-called Gowrie Conspiracy, a plot to seize and dethrone and assassinate James VI., who was lured to G.'s house in Perth on Aug. 5, 1600. G. and his younger *bro.,* Alexander Ruthven, were seized by the king's followers and slain on the spot.

GOWRIE, WILLIAM, 4TH LORD RUTHVEN, EARL OF (*c.* 1545-84), Scot. noble; joined his *f.* in murder of Rizzio, 1566; cr. Earl of G., 1581; led party in 'Raid of Ruthven,' whereby king was seized, 1582; executed.

GOYA (29° 12′ S., 59° 14′ W.), town, on Parana, Corrientes, Argentine Republic, S. America; pastoral district; commercial center.

GOYA Y LUCIENTES, FRANCISCO (1746-1828), Span. artist; famed for portraits, including several Span. kings; also distinguished for genre pictures and etchings.

GOYANA, GOYANNA (7° 25' S., 34° 48' W.), city, Pernambuco, Brazil, S. America; active trade in sugar, coffee, cotton.

GOYAZ (13° S., 48° W.), town and state, Brazil, S. America; between Minas Geraes and Matto Grasso; mountainous; traversed N. to S. by river Tocantius, the Araguay forming W., and Parana-hyba S., boundary; extensive forests; chief occupation, agriculture and stock-raising; some tobacco cultivated and gold mined. Area, 266,000 sq. miles.

GOZO (36° 3' N., 14° 14' E.), island, in Mediterranean, belonging to Britain; 4 m. N. W. of Malta; ancient *Gaulos*. Area, 20 sq. miles.

GOZZOLI, BENOZZO (c. 1420-98), Ital. artist of vast industry; pupil of Fra Angelico; principal work consists of series of frescoes illustrating Old Testament history, in the Campo Santo (Pisa), which occupied him for sixteen years.

GRAAFF-REINET (32° 16' S., 24° 53' E.), town, Cape of Good Hope province, S. Africa; founded by Cape Dutch, 1786; vineyards and orchards.

GRACCHUS, plebeian Rom. family of *gens* Sempronia, of which most noted members were Tiberius Sempronius G. and Gaius Sempronius G., generally known as the *Gracchi*, sons of Tiberius Sempronius Gracchus, consul in 177 B.C., and his wife Cornelia (*q.v.*). Tiberius Sempronius (163-133 B.C.) fought under Scipio against Carthaginians; became tribune, 133, when he passed agrarian law, allotting public lands to the poor; killed with number of followers, by patricians headed by Scipio Nasica. Gaius (158-121 B.C.) became tribune, 123; introduced many reforms, passed corn law, and re-established agrarian law; while at Carthage, his reputation was undermined by enemies at home; on return, rejected for tribunate; escaped from ensuing riots, but was found dead next day; like his *bro.*, a lofty character, an ardent reformer, and a fine orator.

GRACE.—(1) The unmerited favor shown by God to man; (2) as means of salvation has become chief Christian symbol as opposed to works; (3) any favor or the disposition to favor; (4) permission; (5) a legal pardon; (6) attractiveness, virtue, charm; (7) musical: subsidiary embellishment, (*e.g.*) trills.

GRACE, DAYS OF, a certain number of days following the date specified on the face of a bill or note on which it becomes due. Until this period is expired, payment is not necessary. In the United States and Great Britain the usual time allowed is three days. Days of grace have been rescinded in some of the States.

GRACES, THE (classical myth.), were Aglaia, Thalia, and Euphrosyne, *dau's* of Zeus. They personified grace, beauty, and mirth; represented as three beautiful maidens with hands and arms intertwined.

GRACIÁN Y MORALES, BALTASAR, Span. author; the style of his prose allegory, *El Criticon*, has been much admired; Eng. trans. of his *The Art of Wordly Wisdom*, by Jacobs (1892).

GRACKLE (*Eulabes*), a genus of starling-like birds, differing from true starlings in their arboreal habits, their spotted eggs, and rictal bristles; inhabitants of South-Eastern Asia.

GRADISCA. See Görz AND GRADISCA.

GRADO (43° 23' N., 6° 8' W.), town, Oviedo, Spain.

GRADUATE, one who has passed the examinations of a recognized university for the degree of doctor, bachelor or master. Originally graduation was a license to practice a profession. Term 'Graduation' at times applied to prize-giving day in schools and colleges.

GRADUS AD PARNASSUM ('Steps to Parnassus'), dictionary of Latin prosody; an aid to Lat. verse-making.

GRADY, HENRY WOODFEN (1850-1889), American journalist and orator; *b.* in Athens, Georgia, *d.* in Atlanta. Graduated from the University of Georgia in 1868; two years at University of Virginia. He wrote for the Atlanta Constitution, edited the *Courier*, Rome, Georgia, and after failing to establish other papers, bought a quarter interest in the *Atlanta Constitution* in 1881, and was a part owner at his death. He made a great reputation as a correspondent and orator, and helped the north to understand the south. He aided in establishing the Confederate Veterans Home, and to organize the Atlanta Expositions in 1887-1889.

GRAETZ, HEINRICH (1817-91), Jewish historian; wrote *Geschichte der*

Juden (1853-75), best history of Jewish race; pioneer of higher criticism among Jews, but faithful to religion.

GRAEVIUS, JOHANN GEORG (1632-1703), Ger. scholar; Historiographer-Royal to William III. (of England); author of numerous works dealing with classical subjects.

GRAFFITI, name given by archæologists to chalk writings and rough drawings made on ancient buildings at Pompeii and elsewhere.

GRAFLY, CHARLES (1862-1929), American sculptor, *b.* at Philadelphia, Pa.; ed. under Henri Chapu, and Jean Dampt, and at the Ecole des Beaux Arts at Paris. He has received many gold medals, including those at the Paris Exposition (1900), Atlanta (1895), and the gold medal of honor of the Philadelphia Academy of Fine Arts (1899); his works include '*From Generation to Generation,*' '*Vultures of War,*' '*Symbol of Hope,*' and '*Pioneer Mother.*'

GRAFRATH (51° 13' N., 7° 4' E.), town, Rhineland, Prussia; steel and iron works.

GRAFTING, inserting buds or cuts (scions) from one plant (stock) within bark of another so that they unite; used to propagate plants not easily reproducible by seed. Also practiced in animals, mainly for scientific purposes or for the restoration of weakened or lost parts.

GRAFTON.—(1) (29° 39' S., 152° 55' E.), city, New South Wales, on Clarence; agricultural district; sugar-mills.

GRAFTON, a town of Massachusetts, in Worcester co. It is on the New York and Boston & Albany, New Haven and Hartford Railroad, 6 miles southeast of Worcester. The town contains several villages. There is a high school and a public library. Its manufactures include woolen, worsted, and cotton goods, shoes, etc.

GRAFTON, a city of West Virginia, in Taylor co., of which it is the county seat. It is on the Baltimore and Ohio railroad, and on the Tygart's Valley river. The city is an important railroad center and is the terminus of four divisions of the Baltimore and Ohio railroad. It has extensive industries including railroad shops, and plants for the making of flour, machinery, cigars, etc. It is the distributing point for the wholesale grocery trade for the surrounding country. Within the border of the city is a national cemetery.

GRAHAM, SIR GERALD (1831-99), Brit. general; distinguished himself in Crimean and China Wars (1860); commanded in Egyptian War at *Tel-el-Kebir*; wrote *Last Words with Gordon*, and other works.

GRAHAM, HENRY TUCKER (1865-), college president. Ordained Presbyterian minister in 1891. Spent five years as missionary in Japan. President of Hampden-Sidney College (1908-17). Author of *John Randolph of Roanoke*; *An Old Manse*; *Stonewall Jackson*; *The Christian*. Has written extensively for theological papers and magazines.

GRAHAM, SIR JAMES ROBERT GEORGE, Bart. (1792-1861), Brit. statesman; an advanced Liberal, and supporter of the Reform Bill; Home Sec. under Sir Robert Peel (1841-46); First Lord of Admiralty under Aberdeen and Palmertson.

GRAHAM, SYLVESTER (1794-1851), Amer. food reformer; advocate of temperance reform and vegetarianism; introduced 'Graham bread,' made from unbolted flour, and drew up a dietarian and physiological regimen which had many supporters.

GRAHAM, THOMAS (1805-69), Brit-physicist and chemist; appointed Master of the Mint, 1855. His chief researches concerned molecular physics, the absorption of gases by liquids, and the diffusion of gases. He divided substances into crystalloids and colloids, and investigated their behavior towards membranes. He discovered polybasic acids, and obtained three acids from phosphorous anhydride.

GRAHAME, KENNETH (1859-1932), Brit. author; *b.* at Edinburgh, Scotland, in 1859. His best known publications are *Pagan Papers*, 1893; *The Golden Age*, 1895; *Dream Days*, 1898, and *The Wind Among the Willows*, 1908.

GRAHAME-WHITE, CLAUDE (1879-), Brit. aviator and aeronautical engineer, originally a pioneer of petrol-driven car, was first Englishman to obtain aviator's certificate; afterwards established a flying school at Pau, 1909. After outbreak of World War he was appointed flight-commander on special service in R.N.A.S., but resigned, with approval of Admiralty, to carry out government contracts for aircraft. He has written many books on aviation, including *Aircraft in the Great War*, *Air Power*, etc., and also several boys' stories.

GRAHAM'S LAND, Antarctic district (56° to 57° W., 65° to 67° S.), discovered 1832.

GRAHAMSTOWN (33° 13′ S., 26° 32′ E.), city, Cape Province, S. Africa; educational center; seat of Anglican and R.C. bps; agricultural and pastoral district; wool industry.

GRAIL, THE HOLY, a miraculous vessel, which formed subject of many mediæval romances; in most versions of the legend it was a cup sent from heaven, and used by Christ at Last Supper, afterwards coming to possession of Joseph of Arimathea, who collected the Lord's blood in it; on death of Joseph, the grail was taken back to heaven, to be kept there until a hero worthy of it should appear on earth. It enters into the legend of King Arthur and the knights of the Round Table, many of whom, including Galahad, Perceval, and Gawain, set out in quest of it.

GRAIN includes wheat, barley, oats, and various other cereal foodstuffs. Of these wheat is the most important, and its cultivation dates back to remote times. Oats, an important article of food for animals, are largely used in the form of oatmeal for human consumption; and barley, also a cattle-food, is extensively employed in manufactured products. Wheat is grown both in cold and hot climates.

GRAIN ELEVATORS, warehouses for the storage of grain. These buildings are especially adapted for the storage of the various grains, especially wheat, in bulk, resembling large tanks, from which the grain is drawn as though liquid through large pipes into the cars when being loaded for shipping. The grain elevator may be called a peculiarly American institution, being first employed in this country in the Middle West shortly after the wide prairies were first planted with grain, and following this development westward.

They are tall, windowless structures constructed of steel or reinforced concrete and rectangular or cylindrical in design.

In unloading freight cars, the train is placed so that each car is opposite a hopper near the elevator. The grain is discharged, either by power shovels or suction power from the cars into the hoppers into which leg-like tubes extend. These carry the grain to the top of the elevator, where it goes through a cleaning and weighing process before it is carried by conveyor belts to the storage bins throughout the building.

Grain is loaded from elevators into cars by gravity, being carried on conveyor belts from the storage bins to the tubes which extend from the elevator to the freight car.

Marine elevators for loading cars from vessels or *vice versa*, have their elevator legs or tubes mounted on wheels outside the structure, allowing movement along the sides so that the tubes may be set opposite the boat's hatches. These elevators are gigantic in size.

GRAIN PRODUCTION, the growing of those seeds which are utilized as food products, including wheat, corn, rye, barley, oats, and even buckwheat, though botanically the latter is not properly a grain. The production of grain has, naturally, been most extensively developed in the countries with broad, open plains, such as Russia, Canada, Argentina and the United States, rendering other countries economically dependent upon them to a certain extent. After the World War, Russia was, at least temporarily, eliminated from this class. In consequence the European countries were proportionately more dependent on Canada, Argentina and especially the United States, for their supply of cereals. In this country the grain crops are by far the most important in all agricultural production, the value of our cereal crops in 1932 being almost $1,067,611,000, as compared to $3,500,617,000, the total value of all crops, being very little short of half. Of all our grain crops, corn stands forth as the most important, over 107,000,000 acres being devoted to corn as compared to 55,177,000 acres devoted to wheat in 1932 and a little over 75,000,000 acres in 1919, which was the year of largest wheat production in the history of the country. The value of the corn crop in 1932 was $566,930,000, as compared to $254,525,000, the value of the wheat crop in the same year. In quantity the comparison was 726,831,000 bushels of wheat to 2,908,045,000 bushels of corn, being nearly three times as much corn as wheat. Oats rank third in importance; in 1932 41,224,000 acres were devoted to oats, the crop being valued at $175,207,000, and the amount being 1,242,437,000 bu. Thus, in quantity oats were ahead of wheat, but in value considerably less. Barley is the fourth most important crop. In 1932 the crop amounted to 299,950,000 bushels, valued at $59,255,000. In the same year the rye crop amounted to 39,855,000 bushels, valued at $8,981,000. To what extent these gigantic crops of grain constitute a surplus above domestic needs may be judged from the fact that in 1922 the exports of these commodities were as follows: wheat, 54,879,484 bushels; corn, 7,885,855 bushels; oats, 3,486,000 bushels; rye, 1,095,704 bushels; and barley, 7,043,000 bushels. It will be noted that though our corn crop is so much larger than the wheat crop, the surplus is less, corn being very much less used as a human food product in Europe than in the United States. One of the most important factors tending to control grain production in the United States was the organization, in 1929, of the Farmer's National Grain Corporation, an association of the growers of grain for the purpose of marketing their product co-

HARVESTING GRAIN

operatively. In 1933 the control of grain production and prices passed into the hands of the Agricultural Adjustment Administration. (See AGRICULTURE.) To reduce the surplus of wheat and corn and raise prices, the AAA paid bonuses to the farmers for all land taken out of production. Drought and dust storms further reduced crops.

GRAINGER, PERCY (ALDRIDGE), (1882-), mus. composer. Studied at home and under Professor Kwast in Frankfort-on-the-Main. Made debut as pianist at 10 years of age, touring Europe, Australia and South Africa. Come to the United States in 1914 and since then has toured the country from coast to coast. Was a specialist in folk-music and has made more than 500 phonographic reords. Composer of over 70 works for piano, orchestra, chamber music, etc. His best known compositions i n c l u d e *The Sussex Mummers Christmas Carol; Country Gardens; Children's March; The Sprig of Thyme; British Waterloo; The Pretty Maid Milking Her Cow*, etc.

GRAMMAR consists of a code of laws to which the usage of the best writers of an age and language conforms. G. is not a static thing. Speech varies in different areas and in different periods, and the only pattern or standard available is the usage of the best writers and speakers. One language may have very many dialects. Each *dialect* will have an independent g., but in such cases one dialect is usually preferred because it is employed at the court or in the chief univ., or is represented by the finest body of lit. There is, however, a possibility and a probability that the usages of the other dialects may become standard, because it is from the so-called dialect sources that the approved speech is for the most part replenished and renewed. Such growth, therefore, implies various transition stages when alternative forms exist side by side, and time only (and not the grammarian) can choose between them.

Only by patient study of the evolution and development of forms can the seeming irregularities and anomalies of g. be understood. G. falls into two broad divisions—(1) Morphology, which deals with the form, structure, and inflections of words; (2) Syntax, which deals with the arrangement of proper word-forms in groups and sentences. Morphology is concerned with the classification of stems and the classification of inflections. Inflections designate relations to other words in the group (*e.g.*) case, or qualify and limit the meaning of the word (*e.g.*) gender. Languages vary greatly in the number and kind of inflections. Inflections themselves belong to a more or less advanced stage in a language development. *Comparative* g. is necessary for the proper appreciation of the individual systems.

GRAMME, see WEIGHTS AND MEASURES.

GRAMMICHELE (37° 12' N., 14° 39' E.), town, Catania, Sicily.

GRAMONT, ANTOINE AGENOR ALFRED, DUC DE (1818-80), Fr. statesman and diplomat; ambassador to Italy, 1857; Austria, 1861; Foreign Minister, 1870; had considerable share in causing outbreak of Franco-German War; wrote *La France et la Prusse avant la Guerre.*

GRAMONT, PHILIBERT, COMTE DE (1621-1707), Fr. courtier; famed for his handsome person, wit, and gallantries; served under Conde and Turenne; favorite of Louis XVI; later exiled, he appeared at the court of Charles II. of England. His *Memoires*, is a Fr. classic.

GRAMOPHONE, a machine capable of recording sounds such as human speech, music, etc., in such a manner that they can again be reproduced at will, by the same machine which made the record. It was invented by Emile Berliner, at Philadelphia, Pa., in 1888, and consisted of a cylinder with its axis horizontal, rotating at a constant speed, over which was placed a hollow cylinder of wax or similar substance; this was the blank or 'record.' A sharp steel stylus, fastened to a thin diaphragm rested against the cylinder and was moved forward at a constant rate so as to scribe a helix on the wax cylinder. A horn terminated in a small chamber in which the diaphragm was placed. Any sound produced in front of the bell of the horn was concentrated in the diaphragm chamber and caused the diaphragm to vibrate in accordance with the sound waves. This vibration was transferred to the stylus, thus resulting in the production of a groove of varying depth on the record. If after finishing the record, the stylus was again run through the same groove, its varying depth caused the stylus and its connected diaphragm to vibrate, and the original sounds were faithfully reproduced. This device has been highly perfected by various companies. Phonographs are now sold under many names. Superficially these products do not resemble the original gramophone, but the principle of operation is the same. The same principle is used in the Dictograph. See DICTO-GRAPH. The most radical improvement made has been in the records; many of those now in use are discs, although some cylinders are still used (as in the dictograph). The records are of hard, wear-resisting material and are made by a highly developed and accurate system. See TALKING MACHINES.

GRAMPIANS, THE (56° 50′ N., 4° W.), mountain range, Central Scotland, stretching N.E. to S.W. from counties of Banff and Aberdeen to Argyll and Dumbarton; highest summit, Ben Nevis, 4406 ft.

GRAMPUS (*Orca gladiator*), often called the 'killer whale,' is a large member of Dolphin family, sometimes attaining 30 ft. in length; color is black, with white underparts, and a white streak above and behind eye, and dorsal fin is very high; is the fiercest and most voracious member of Dolphin family, and is found chiefly in northern waters.

GRAN CHACO, EL (25° S., 60° W.), Great, low lying alluvial plain in the interior of South America. Bounded on the East by Paraná and Paraguay rivers and on the South and West by Argentina and Bolivia comprising an area of approximately 200,000 square miles. Politically under domination of Paraguay, Bolivia and Argentina. Dispute over boundary between Bolivia and Para-

guay running through El Gran Chaco led to fighting in 1928 followed by arbitration. Fighting, however, was again resumed in 1934.

GRANADA (12° N., 85° 56′ W.), city, Nicaragua, Cent. America, on Nicaragua Lake; manufactures gold-wire chains; exports indigo, hides, cocoa, coffee.

GRANADA (37° 13′ N., 3° 41′ W.), town, Andalusia, Spain; capital of province G.; splendidly situated at base of Sierra Nevada on Darro and Genil. Outstanding features are the Alhambra Alcazabar (citadel), on strongly fortified eminence; Generalife (summer residence of Moorish kings); fine Gothic cathedral (1528), Segrario, with royal mausoleum; monastery of St. Jerome (1492), univ. (1531), and many old interesting houses. G. was founded VIII. cent.; capital of Moorish kingdom, and great trading and artistic center in XIII. cent.; last Moorish stronghold in Spain; taken by Spaniards, 1492.

GRANADA (37° 30′ N., 3° W.), maritime province, S. Spain, formed from part of ancient Moorish kingdom of Granada; generally mountainous, traversed by Sierra Nevada; fine fertile valleys and plains; rich in minerals; produces wheat, barley, wine, sugar, fruit; area, 4928 sq. miles. Pop. 1920, 545,217. Capital, Granada, has a univ.

GRANADA, LUIS DE (1504-88), Span. theologian; provincial of Dominicans in Portugal; a mystical thinker, he was suspected by the Inquisition and his works put on the Index.

GRANBY, JOHN MANNERS, MARQUESS OF (1721-70), Eng. soldier; commanded Brit. troops in Germany, 1760-63; commander-in-chief, 1766.

GRAND ARMY OF THE REPUBLIC. A patriotic association made up of surviving soldiers and sailors of the Civil War and of the militia on active duty in that period and subject to the national call. The association was organized in Chicago in the winter of 1865-1866 by Dr. B. F. Stephenson, the surgeon, and Rev. R. W. J. Rudolph, the chaplain, of the 14th Illinois Infantry. The first post was organized at Decatur, Illinois, April 6, 1866 and the first National Encampment was held at Indianapolis, November 20, 1866. The main purpose of the association is to help the families of dead comrades, caring for their orphans, establishing soldiers homes, and to secure adequate pensions. In 1869 the association ruled against partisanship in political nominations, etc., but this has not always been observed. The G.A.R. is gradually diminishing in membership and only a small number of veterans met on Decoration Day, 1931. In 1932 the membership was 50,000. Headquarters are at Ft. Morgan. Commander-in-chief Capt. Wm. P. Wright, Chicago, Ill. Quartermaster General, Samuel P. Town, Philadelphia, Pa. and Adjutant General, Calvin Brainerd, Chicago, Ill.

GRAND CANYON, term applied to that portion of the Canyon of the Colorado River that lies in northern Arizona. It is far remote from civilization and can be reached only by means of a branch road of the Atchison, Topeka and Santa Fe Railroad. It is one of the most striking natural wonders on the American continent. It has a depth of nearly a mile and a width ranging from 8 to 10 miles. The scenery it affords is rugged and majestic beyond description. The cliffs are of limestone and sandstone with some intervening shales of softer material. The rocks have almost all the colors of the spectrum, and under the influence of sun and shadow form pictures of entrancing beauty beyond the imagination of a dreamer or the brush of an artist. The Colorado River as it rushes through the Grand Canyon is about 300 feet wide, and in time of freshet forms a mighty torrent. Rain and wind have sculptured the cliffs into bewildering and fantastic forms, which, added to by their brilliancy of coloring, make them a stupendous natural spectacle.

The Canyon was first seen by white men in 1541, when Hopi Indians guided Cardenas and his companions to the rim. In 1869 the river through the Canyon was traversed for its entire length by Major Powell, to whom the Government erected a memorial in honor of the exploit. The Grand Canyon is now included in a forest reserve under the supervision of the U.S. Department of Agriculture.

GRAND-DUKE, title dating from the XVI. cent., at present borne by several deposed European rulers. It was also given to the nearest relatives and the children of the Czar of Russia.

GRANDEE, title borne by Span. nobles of the highest rank. Formerly the title carried special privileges.

GRAND FORKS, a city of North Dakota, the county seat of Grand Forks county. It is on Great Northern and Northern Pacific railways, Theodore Roosevelt and Meridian Highways, and is a leading center of North Dakota and northwestern Minnesota with flour mills, packing plant, creameries, produce houses, potato warehouses and sugar beet factory. It is the seat of the University of North Dakota, Wesley College, Lutheran Bible College, St. James Academy, excellent grade and high school.

GRAND GULF, a locality in Mississippi, on the Missouri River, south of Vicksburg. Here, on March 31, 1863 the Confederate batteries were attacked by the Union fleet under Admiral Farragut, and after a severe bombardment which lasted until May 3, the forts surrendered to the naval forces and to the land forces under Generals Grant and Porter.

GRAND HAVEN, a city of Michigan, in Ottawa co., of which it is the county seat. It is on the Grand Trunk, G. R. G. H. & M. Electric, and the Pere Marquette railroads, and at the mouth of the Grand River. The city is a port of entry and has an excellent harbor. It is connected by steamship lines with the chief lake ports. The surrounding country is an important fruit and celery growing region and is the center of an important trade in these products. It has also large fishing industries. Its industries include the manufacture of engines, printing presses, baskets, barrels, pianos, brass novelties, marine boilers, shirts, gloves, etc. There is a public library, a United States customhouse, and a county court-house. The city is the seat of Akeley College for girls. In the neighborhood are Highland Park and Spring Lake.

GRAND INTERNATIONAL BROTHERHOOD OF LOCOMOTIVE ENGINEERS. See BROTHERHOODS, RAILROAD.

GRAND ISLAND, a city of Nebraska, in Hall co., of which it is the county seat. It is on the Union Pacific, the Burlington Route, and the St. Joseph and Grand Island railroads. It is important industrially and has a beet sugar factory, a cement block factory, candy factory, wire factories, broom factories, etc. It has also the railroad shops of the Union Pacific railroad. There is a public library and a hospital. The city is the seat of the Nebraska Soldiers' and Sailors' Home, and Grand Island College.

GRAND JUNCTION, a city of Colorado, in Mesa co., of which it is the county seat. It is on the Denver and Rio Grande, the Colorado Midland, and other railroads, and at the junction of the Grand and Gunnison rivers. The surrounding country is an agricultural and fruit growing region and in the neighborhood are important coal mines.

The industries include machine shops, lumber yards, railroad shops, brick works, and a beet-sugar factory. There is a public library among its public buildings.

GRANDMONTINES, order of hermits (living much like the Camaldolese, *q.v.*) founded by St. Stephen of Thiers (XI. cent.); named from Grandmont, near Muret, where large monastery was founded; order ceased XVIII. cent.

GRAND PRÉ, or **LOWER HORTON.** (1) A post vil. in Nova Scotia, situated in King's co., 15 m. from Windsor. Stands in the midst of very fertile country. Has been made famous as the scene of Longfellow's poem *Evangeline*. Pop. 900. (2) A French tn. in the Ardennes. Notable for severe fighting during the World War.

GRAND RAPIDS, a city of Michigan, in Kane co., of which it is the county seat. It is on the Pere Marquette, the Michigan Central, the Pennsylvania, the New York Central and other railroads, and on both sides of the Grand River, 60 miles northwest of Lansing. The city has direct steamboat communication with Chicago, Milwaukee and other cities. It is the second city of the State in population and commercial importance. The Grand River, which at this point has a fall of 18 feet, supplies excellent water power for the important industries, which include the manufacture of furniture, bicycles, brass goods, flour, brushes, carpet sweepers, refrigerators, etc. Grand Rapids is the largest furniture market in the world. Gypsum quarries in the neighborhood have the largest output in the world. The city is well laid out and has an excellent system of streets. The notable buildings include Blodgett Hospital, Municipal Tuberculosis Hospital, Federal Building, Y. M. C. A. and Y. W. C. A. buildings, and many churches. There are also many handsome business blocks and private residences. There is an excellent school system with 3 senior and 2 junior high schools. Among the public institutions are the Michigan State Soldiers' Home, Union Benevolent Home, Masonic Home and Catholic Home. There is a splendid system of pleasure grounds and public parks. Grand Rapids was founded in 1833 on the site of an Indian village, and was incorporated as a city in 1850.

GRAND RAPIDS, now Wisconsin Rapids, a city of Wisconsin, in Wood co., of which it is the county seat. It is on the Chicago, Milwaukee and St. Paul, the Soo Line, Green Bay and Western, and the Chicago and Northwestern railroads, and on the Wisconsin river, which affords ample electric power. The industries of the city include foundries and machine shops, and plants for the making of paper and pulp, bus bodies, camp stoves. The public buildings include a hospital, library, municipal swimming pool, Elks Club House, and several parks.

GRANDSON, GRANSON (46° 49′ N., 6° 38′ E.), town, Swiss canton Vaud, on Lake Neuchâtel; scene of defeat of Charles the Bold by Swiss, 1476.

GRANGEMOUTH (56° 2′ N., 3° 45′ W.), seaport town, Stirlingshire, Scotland, on Firth of Forth; large docks, shipbuilding yards; exports coal, iron.

GRANGER, JAMES (1723-76), Eng. biographer; vicar of Shiplake (Oxon); wrote *Biographical History of England*, in which portraits were first introduced; hence 'to Grangerise' is to insert illustrations from other books.

GRANGERS or **GRANGES,** nickname of an agricultural association founded in America, 1867, for farmers' education and co-operation. See Husbandry Patrons of.

GRANITE, unstratified rocks, composed of quartz, felspar, and mica, occurring in masses. G's are the most abundant of igneous rocks, and have been subjected to great pressure; they belong to various periods, ranging from the pre-Cambrian to Tertiary. They vary in hardness and color according to their composition.

GRANITE CITY, a city of Illinois, in Madison co. It is on the Chicago and Alton, the Chicago, Peoria and St. Louis, the Cleveland, Cincinnati, Chicago and St. Louis, and other railroads. The city is opposite St. Louis, Mo. It has great industrial importance and has manufactures of iron, steel castings, pig iron, corn products, coke, lead articles, babbit metal, sheet steel. There is a public hospital.

GRANT, ETHEL WATTS - MUMFORD, an American author. Studied art at Julien Academy, Paris. Took up writing in connection with illustration and travel sketches. Her writings include *Whitewash*, 1903; *The Cynic's Calendar*; *A Joke - Book*. 1904; *The Hundred Love Songs of Kamal*, 1905; *Out of the Ashes*, 1913; *The Grim 13*, 1917; Her plays are *Good Night Nurse*; *The Scenario*; *Sick-a-Bed*; *Easy Money*'

It Pays to Smile, from story by Nina Wilcox Putnam; *The Wedding Song*, and others.

GRANT, FREDERICK DENT (1850-1912), an American soldier, *s.* of Ulysses S. Grant; *b.* St. Louis, Mo. He served in the Civil War, rising to the rank of colonel, and at its close entered West Point, graduating in 1871. He resigned from the army in 1881. He served as minister to Austria and was police commissioner of New York from 1894 to 1898. At the outbreak of the Spanish-American War he was made brigadier-general of volunteers. He continued service in the regular army and commanded in the Philippines and several departments in the United States. He was made a major-general in 1906.

GRANT, GEORGE MUNRO (1835-1902), Canadian educationist; principal of Kingston Univ. (Ontario); author of *Ocean to Ocean, Our National Objects and Aims*.

GRANT, JAMES (1822-87), a British novelist, *b.* at Edinburgh. He was taken to Newfoundland when a boy, but returned at the age of seventeen and entered the army. After four years' service he resigned and took up literature instead. In 1846 he published the *Romance of War*, which gained some reputation for him. In 1875 he was received into the communion of the Roman Church. Amongst his works are *Adventures of an Aide-de-Camp*; *Frank Hilton*; *Bothwell*; and *Old and New Edinburgh*.

GRANT, PERCY STICKNEY (1860-1927), Amer. clergyman. Graduated at Harvard in 1883 and from the Episcopal Theological School in 1886. Ordained in 1887. Held various charges in Fall River and Swansea, Mass. Since 1893 rector of Church of the Ascension, New York City. He was noted for his independence on theological subjects. Conducted an open forum for public discussion of questions of the day. He resigned his pulpit in 1924. Author: *Ad Matrem*, 1905; *Socialism and Christianity*, 1910; *The Return of Odysseus*, 1912; and *Fair Play for the Worker*, 1918.

GRANT, ROBERT (1852), American jurist and novelist. *b.* in Boston. Graduated from Harvard 1873 and the Law School 1879; appointed judge of probate and insolvents for Suffolk county in 1893. A member of the American Academy of Arts and Letters. Publications *Little Tin Gods on Wheels*; *Confessions of a Frivolous Girl*; *Unleavened Bread*, 1900; *The Law Breakers*,

1906; *The Chippendales*, 1909; *The High Priestess*, 1915; *Law and the Family*, 1919.

GRANT, ULYSSES SIMPSON (1822-1885), American soldier and 18th President of the United States. *b.* at Point Pleasant, Ohio, *d.* at Mount MacGregor near Saratoga Springs. Of Scotch ancestry his grandfather Noah Grant was a soldier in the Revolution. He was the oldest of six children born to Jesse Root Grant and Hannah Simpson, and named Hiram Ulysses but having been designated as Ulysses Simpson in his appointment to the U.S. Military Academy he retained that name. Having obtained a good common school education he entered the U.S. Military Academy in 1839 and graduated in 1843, and was assigned to the Jefferson barracks in Missouri. In 1844 he accompanied the 4th Infantry to Louisiana and appointed 2nd lieutenant. Joined General Zachary Taylor's army in occupation the next year. In the Mexican War he fought in the battle of Palo Alto and was present when Monterey fell. The 4th Infantry having joined Gen. Scott, the young lieutenant went through the successful campaigns that terminated with the capture of the City of Mexico. He was made 1st lieutenant and captain for bravery at Molino del Rey and Chapultepec. Returning to the United States in 1848 Grant married Miss Julia B. Dent of St. Louis. Three sons and a daughter were born to them, the eldest being Frederick Dent Grant (*q.v.*). In 1854 Grant resigned from the army and tried various occupations as farmer, real estate agent, and lastly as a clerk in his father's leather store in Galena, Ill. At the beginning of the Civil War he offered his services to the Government by letter and received no reply. Having raised and drilled a company at Galena he was made a mustering officer and then Colonel of the 21st Illinois Infantry Volunteers (June 17, 1861). Assigned to a military district under Fremont in Missouri his command included western Kentucky and southern Illinois. His first act was to seize Paducah, Ky., and with 3000 men on transports from Cairo he made a demonstration against Belmont, Mo., to hold the Confederates at Columbus, Ky., from reinforcing General Price in Missouri. In February 1862 with gunboats under Commodore Foote attacks were made on Forts Henry and Donelson. Foote captured Fort Henry and February 16, Grant took Fort Donelson, for which he was promoted Major-General. With Halleck's army he fought at Shiloh and helped to drive the Confederates out of Corinth. Halleck having been appointed commander-in-chief of all the Federal armies, Grant succeeded him in the field. In October 1862 he commanded the Dept. of Tennessee and the army of Mississippi which captured Vicksburg July 4. In the battle of Chattanooga, November 23-25, Grant defeated General Bragg and received the thanks of Congress and a gold medal. The rank of Lt.-General was revived for him in March, 1864. He had control now of all armies of the United States. Sherman commanded all troops west of the Alleghenies and north of Natchez. Grant's army between Washington and Richmond had for its objective Lee's Northern Army of Virginia. The Battles of the Wilderness and Spottsylvania Court House were Federal victories but June 3, Grant's troops were repulsed with great slaughter at Cold Harbor. The capture of Petersburg was followed by the siege and fall of Richmond and April 9, 1865, Lee surrendered to Grant at Appomattox Court House. By a special Act of Congress Grant was appointed General July 25, 1866. He was nominated for President by the Republicans in 1868 on the first ballot. In the election Grant had 214 electoral votes to 80 for Seymour. He was renominated and re-elected in 1872 defeating Horace Greeley. Grant's administrations were notable for reduction of public debt; treaty with England in 1871; settlement of the Canadian boundary and fisheries question, the 15th Amendment to the Constitution; commercial treaty with Mexico, etc. General Grant made a trip around the world in 1877-1879. At the Republican Convention in 1880 he led for 36 ballots, when Garfield was named. In the same year Grant became a partner in a brokerage firm in New York and was victimized by his partner who was sent to prison. Congress restored him to the army in 1885 with rank of General and retired. His last years were spent on his *Memoirs* for which the public paid $500,000. Cancer of the throat from which he had long suffered led to his death in July 1, 1885. A stately tomb on the Hudson, at New York marks his resting place.

GRANTH, sacred writings of Sikhs; name derived from Sanskrit word *grantha*, 'a fastening together'; originator of Sikh religious sect was Baba Nanak, a Hindu, whose writings are contained in the *Adi Granth Sahib*, a compilation made by Guru Arjan, and written in various dialects.

GRANTHAM (52° 55′ N., 0° 39′ W.), market town, Lincolnshire, England, on Witham; fine XIII.-cent. church;

in grammar school Newton was ed. in vicinity, on May 13, 1643. Cromwell won his first victory over Royalists; iron manufactures.

GRANULATION, the act of forming into grains. The process by which a metal is reduced into grains is brought about by melting the metal and then pouring it in a thin stream into cold water. The metal divides itself into grains which are each practically perfect spheres. Metals which are easily melted are often poured in a molten state into a wooden box and violently shaken. This results in the metal granulating into much finer portions.

GRANULITE (Lat. *granulum*, a little grain), name of two classes of rocks of granite class and of same family as gneiss. Muscovite and biotite freely occur in g., but as a rule it is composed mostly of quartz feldspar. G. often contains small garnets.

GRANVILLE. (1) (48° 51′ N., 1° 37′ W.), fortified seaport, seaside resort, Manche, France; deep-sea fisheries; shipbuilding; active trade; unsuccessfully besieged by the Vendeans in 1793; by British in 1803.

GRANVILLE, GEORGE LEVESON-GOWER, 2ND EARL (1815-91), Brit. politician; M.P. for Morpeth, 1836; Foreign Under-Sec., 1840; held office in all Liberal governments till 1886; promoted exhibition, 1851; Colonial Sec., 1868; Foreign Sec., 1870-74, 1880-85. Liberal leader in Upper House for many years.

GRANVILLE, JOHN CARTERET, EARL (1690-1763), Eng. politician; supported George I. against Jacobites; ambassador to Sweden, 1719; Sec. of State, 1721; Lord-Lieut. of Ireland, 1724-30; secured recall of patent for 'Wood's halfpence.' Sec. of State, 1742-44; formed ministry with Lord Bath which lasted two days, 1746; Pres. of Council, 1751-63.

GRANVILLE, WILLIAM ANTHONY (1863), college president. Graduate of Sheffield Scientific School, Yale, 1893. Served as instructor of mathematics at Yale from 1895 to 1909. Elected President of Pennsylvania College, Gettysburg, Pa., in 1900. Author of the following text books: *Differential and Integral Calculus*, 1905; *Plane Trigonometry*, 1909; *Special Trigonometry*, 1909; *Elementary Analysis*, 1909.

GRAO (39° 30′ N., 0° 19′ W.), town. Valencia, Spain.

GRAPE. See VINE.

GRAPE FRUIT. See SHADDOCK.

GRAPE SUGAR. See GLUCOSE.

GRAPHITE, also called plumbago (Lat. *plumbum*, lead) and blacklead, a form of carbon and one of softest of minerals, occurring in older crystalline rocks such as gneiss and schist, and found in great purity in Burrowdale, Cumberland, also in Canada and Bohemia. Color is iron grey. G. is used for pencils, giving a smooth surface to casting moulds and lubrication.

GRAPHOPHONE. See GRAMOPHONE.

GRAPHS, diagrams, generally drawn for convenience on squared paper, which are intended to illustrate or prove a calculation or an array of facts. For instance, if a table showing the average height of a number of men was required, the simplest form would be a g. with the number of men of similar height arranged in ascending order on the side line with a scale in inches marked along the base. G's of this kind take the form of a tall curve narrowing as it ascends and generally symmetrical; the normal variability curve is of this type. G's are also employed in marking contour lines, barometric conditions, and for temperature charts, while their service is widely employed in math's, especially in Algebra.

GRAPTOLITES, an order of extinct *Hydromedusae*, occurring in the Lower Palæozoic rocks; believed to be related to existing *Calyptoblasts*, though differing in important details. The harder parts alone remain to us, and these, when preserved in the original condition are found to consist of *chitin.*

GRASLITZ (50° 21′ N., 12° 27′ E.), town, Czecho-Slovakia; manufactures cottons and laces, upholstery.

GRASMERE (54° 27′ N., 3° 1′ W.), lake, Westmoreland, England; 1 mile long; also village on lake, associated with Wordsworth, De Quincey, and Coleridge.

GRASS. The presence of grassland depends not so much on soil as on rainfall. Grasses have shallow roots and require frequent showers during their growing season. The earth is naturally divided into *woodland, desert,* and *grassland,* but an increase of pasture at the expense of woodland may spoil the pastures of a locality. Nearly all pastures are sown with mixed grasses. Of these *Phleum pratense* (timothy grass) is cheap, and used for crops of more than one year's duration. *Lolium perenne* (perennial rye-grass) is cheap, and very popular. *Alopecurus pratensis* (meadow fox-tail) is expensive, and therefore

often adulterated.

Grasses are herbaceous *monocotyledonous* plants with jointed stems, hollow except at the bases of the leaves. They belong to the natural order *Tramineae,* which includes *cereals, grasses,* and *bamboos.* The *embryo* has one *Cotyledon,* which remains behind in the seed-coat to absorb the *endosperm.* The primary root is soon replaced by other roots from the base of the stem. The long, narrow leaves are parallel-veined and have long membraneous sheaths, which enclose the stem, being split on the side opposite the leaf-blade. The leaves are arranged in two opposite series. In the buds the leaves may be rolled or folded. The flowers are arranged in *spikelets* (*i.e.* are borne on the axis without stalks). These may be grouped together in various ways. If the *spikelets* are borne on branches of the main axis the *inflorescence* is a *panicle,* which is loose as in the *oat,* or close and cylindrical as in the *fox-tail* grass. In the *wheat* the *spikelets* form a compound *spike.* The number and character of the flowers in a *spikelet* vary, and the sepals and petals are absent or scaly. The *spik..et* bears a number of scales in two rows; the two basal scales have no flowers, and are called *glumes.* The other scales represent *bracts* and carry flowers in their axils. They constitute the lower or outer *palae* or *flowering glumes.* A long process, the *awn,* is sometimes carried by the lower *palae.* Above the lower *palae* is the flower, above which there is a scaly *bracteole* called the *upper* or *inner palae.* The flower has three or two *stamens* inserted below the *pistil* and borne on long, slender filaments. The *anthers* are versatile. The *pistil* consists of one *carpel* bearing two feathery *stigmas,* and the *ovary* contains one *ovule.* The fruit is a *caryopsis* (*i.e.*) has the seed-coats and fruit-wall fused together, while the seed is *albuminous.* Two little scales, *lodicules,* are found at the base of the ovary. The *stigma* ripens first and the wild grasses are cross-fertilized, but the cultivated *cereals* are self-pollinated. All are *wind-pollinated.* Perennial grass grows either by *rhizomes, runners,* or *suckers,* or by branching at the base form tufts.

GRASSE (43° 39′ N., 6° 54′ E.), town, Alpes Maritimes, France; celebrated for manufacture of essences and perfumes.

GRASSE, FRANÇOIS JOSEPH PAUL, COMTE DE (1722-88), Fr. naval leader; commanded the French fleet which aided Americans in the Revolution; defeated and captured by Rodney, 1782.

GRASSHOPPERS (*Locustidae*) form a family of Orthoptera, differing from true locusts in possessing long, tapering antennæ and four-jointed terminal leg-segments. Many are green in color, and all are herbivorous, and in the main nocturnal, when their chirping music is commonly heard. There are moderately few small species in temperate regions, but in the tropics there is great diversity in size, shape, and color.

GRASS-TREE, popular name for Australian liliaceous plants of genus *Xanthorrhea*; yield resin.

GRATIANUS (375-80), Rom. emperor whose weakness led to revolts; rebellion of Maximus in Britain and Gaul ended in assassination of G.; ardent Christian.

GRATIANUS, FRANCISCUS (XI. cent.), Ital. monk; compiler of the *Decretum Gratiani*, first treatise on canon law (*q.v.*).

GRATIOLA, a genus of scrophulariaceous plants, is world-wide in distribution. The best-known species is *G. officinalis*, the common hedgehyssop, which was formerly used in medicine.

GRATTAN, HENRY (1746-1820), Irish orator and statesman; *b.* Dublin; after studying law in London was called to Irish Bar; entered Irish Parliament, 1775; as leader of national party, advocated removal of authority exercised by Brit. Parliament over Irish Parliament, his attitude leading to enrollment of 80,000 Irish volunteers, ostensibly for defense of Ireland; Britain was compelled to yield to Irish demands, and Ireland obtained Home Rule. In 1800 he opposed bill for Union of Great Britain and Ireland, to which parliamentary corruption and Irish rebellion of 1798 had led; but he afterwards sat in the United Parliament, and until his death worked incessantly for Catholic emancipation.

GRATTIUS, FALISCUS, Rom. poet; author of *Cynegetica*, verse treatise on hunting, etc.

GRAUDENZ (53° 29′ N., 18° 43′ E.), fortified town, on Vistula, W. Prussia, Germany; has iron foundries and breweries; successfully defended against Fr. in 1807.

GRAVEL, fragments of rock, worn round by the action of water. Shore g. is composed of small stones washed up by waves; river gravel, stones washed down by rivers to 'pockets'; includes stones varying in size from that of a pea to a hen's egg. Anything smaller than former is called 'sand'; larger, 'shingle.'

GRAVELINES (51° N., 2° 6′ E.), fortified seaport, Nord, France, on Aa; fisheries; scene of victory of Spaniards over Fr., 1558.

GRAVELOTTE (49° 6′ N., 6° E.), village, Alsace-Lorraine, Germany; scene of Ger. victory over Fr., 1870.

GRAVES, ANSON ROGERS (1842), graduated from Hobart College in 1866, and from the General Theological Seminary in 1870. Ordained in 1871. Held various charges in Nebraska, Minnesota, New Hampshire and Vermont. Consecrated bishop of the Platte in 1890, resigned in 1910. Author, *The Farmer Boy who Became a Bishop* (autobiography); *Sermons for Lay Readers*. Also many tracts for various religious occasions.

GRAVES, FREDERICK ROGERS (1858), American bishop. Educated at Hobart College and General Theological School from which he graduated in 1881. Ordained priest in Protestant Episcopal Church in 1882. Missionary in China until 1883. Professor of Theology, Theological School Shanghai until 1893. Consecrated bishop in 1893. Has written many works on theological subjects in Chinese.

GRAVES, HENRY SOLON (1871), educated at Yale and took special studies in forestry at Harvard; M.A. Harvard, 1911. Became professor of forestry and director, Forest School, Yale University, 1900-10. Chief of U.S. Forestry Service, 1910-20. Author, *Forest Mensuration*, 1906; *Principles of Handling Woodlands*, 1911. Also many bulletins issued by Department of Agriculture. Lieutenant Colonel Corps of Engineers, U.S. Army in France, 1917.

GRAVES, JOHN TEMPLE (1856), American journalist. Educated at University of Georgia. Became editor of Daily Florida Union, Jacksonville, Fla., in 1881, and thereafter edited various papers in Atlanta and Rome, Ga. Editor-in-chief, New York American, 1907-15. Editorial writer on Hearst newspapers since 1915. Orator on many notable occasions. Author, *History of Florida of To-day*; *History of Colleton, S.C.*; *Speeches and Selections for Schools*. Has contributed to various leading magazines as advocate for universal peace by arbitration and on national preparedness. Pres. of U.S. Press Club in 1913. *d.* 1925.

GRAVESEND (51° 27′ N., 22° E.), market town and river port, Kent, England, on Thames; chief pilot station for river; favorite resort of Londoners; boatbuilding yards; iron foundries; extensive market gardens in vicinity.

GRAVINA (40° 49′ N., 16° 24′ E.),

town, on Gravina, Italy; bp.'s see; cathedral.

GRAVITATION is the attraction which bodies have for one another due to their *mass.* Newton formulated the *Law of G,* thus: 'the force of the attraction which bodies have for one another is directly proportionate to their masses, and inversely proportionate to the square of their distances apart.' This is the most general property of matter, and no exceptions to Newton's Law are known. If a body is thrown up into the air, it falls to the earth after a longer or shorter period of time, depending upon the greatness of the force opposed to that of gravity. Such a body has a certain attraction for the earth, but since the mass of the earth must necessarily be larger than that of any body on it, the force with which the body attracts the earth must be negligible compared to that with which the earth attracts the body. When the force impelling the body to move upwards is expended, the pull of the earth on the body becomes evident. The value of gravity is 32·2 ft. per sec., and it is unaffected by the nature of the matter. The value of gravity is less at the equator than at the poles, but this does not affect ordinary calculations. By very exact experiment the force of attraction which a body exerts on the earth can be determined. Through the force of g. the sun and various other planets affect the earth, while the earth affects the moon, acting through a distance of 240,000 miles.

The mutual attraction between a body and the earth is represented by its *weight.* The presence of large masses, such as mountains, does not alter the weight of any substance for practical purposes. Weight always acts downwards through the *center of gravity,* (*i.e.*) the point through which the *resultant* of all the forces due to gravity must pass. When a body is lifted a certain resistance is felt. This resistance is the force with which the body is attracted to the earth. Water flowing from a horizontal hose gradually curves towards the earth as the force by which it is expelled horizontally becomes exhausted, and gravity becomes noticeable. A drop of water as it falls towards the ground soon loses its spherical shape and becomes pointed, due to the attraction of the earth on the surface nearest it. See RELATIVITY, THEORY OF.

GRAY, ASA (1810-88), botanist; *b.* Paris, N.Y. He studied medicine and became assistant professor of botany at the College of Physicians and Surgeons New York City, afterwards occupying the chair of natural history and botany at Harvard, 1842-73. He made an exhaustive study of North American flora and acquired note as an authority on taxonomy and morphology. His writings embraced popular textbooks for the young, especially on the growth of plants, and philosophical expositions on the theory of natural selection.

GRAY, DAVID (1838-61), Scot. poet; author of *The Luggie* and some sonnets.

GRAY, DAVID (1870), American author. Graduated from Harvard in 1892; Columbia, Ph.D. in 1904. Instructor in English, University of Texas, 1902-5. Instructor, associate professor and professor since 1905, Leland Stanford University, California. Has written, *Emerson,* 1917; *The Original Version of Love Labor Lost with a Conjecture of Love Labor Won,* 1918. Also the following plays: *Hannibal,* 1893; *A Superficial Girl,* 1899; *The Call of Bohemia,* 1909. Has contributed to periodicals largely on Shakespearian criticism. Served in World War.

GRAY, ELISHA (1835-1901), inventor; *b.* Barnesville, O.; *d.* Newtonville, Mass. He was a competitor of Alexander Graham Bell in inventing devices for the telephone. While studying at Oberlin College he supported himself by carpentry, and later designed a number of electrical appliances, including the self-adjusting telegraph relay, the telegraphic switch and annunciator for hotels, the telegraph repeater, the private telegraph line printer, and the telautograph, by which written messages could be sent over the telephone or telegraph. He challenged the claim of Bell as the inventor of the telephone, claiming priority on the specifications for a speaking telephone filed by him in 1876, but the Supreme Court awarded the patent to Bell. He manufactured electrical apparatus at Chicago and Cleveland and founded the Gray Electric Company at Highland Park.

GRAY, GEORGE (1840-1925), Amer. jurist. Graduated from Princeton in 1879 and from Harvard Law School. Practiced law in New Castle and Wilmington, Del. Attorney-General of Delaware, 1879 to 1885. Appointed United States Circuit judge in 1899 serving until 1914. Member of Peace Commission after Spanish - American War in 1898. Member of International Permanent Court of Arbitration at the Hague. Member of American-Mexican Commission in 1916. Trustee of Carnegie Endowment for International Peace.

GRAY, HORACE (1828-1902), jurist *b.* Boston, Mass.; *d.* Nahant, Mass. He was admitted to the bar in 1848 after graduating at Harvard and studying law there, and established a practice in Boston. In 1864 he was appointed a judge of the Massachusetts Supreme Court, becoming its chief justice nine years later. President Arthur in 1881 made him an associate justice of the U.S. Supreme Court, of which he remained a member till his death.

GRAY, THOMAS (1716-71), Eng. poet; *b.* London; ed. Eton and Peter house, Cambridge; spent two years abroad, in company with Horace Walpole; and afterwards returned to Cambridge, where he spent the rest of his life. He declined the laureateship, on the death of Cibber; but in 1768 was app. prof. of Modern History at Cambridge. His poems include *Ode on a Distant Prospect of Eton College*, 1747, which was followed by *Pindaric Odes*, *The Fatal Sisters*, *The Descent of Odin*, and in 1750 he completed, and sent to Walpole, the MS. of the *Elegy in a Country Churchyard*. Probably no Eng. poem has found wider acceptance than the *Elegy*, or has provided more quotable passages.

GRAYLING, general name for various trout-like Salmonidæ fish; genus *Thymallus*.

GRAYSON, CARY TRAVERS (1878), rear admiral and navy surgeon; *b.* Culpeper County, Va. He was educated at William and Mary College and the University of the South. He received the degree of M.D. in 1902 and two years later graduated from the U.S. Naval Medical School while acting assistant surgeon in the Navy. He passed from that rank through the regular grades of promotion, becoming medical director and rear-admiral in 1916. He cruised round the world in 1905-6 and was naval surgeon of the President's yacht during the Roosevelt and Taft administrations. He became physician to the President in 1912 and served in that capacity during Woodrow Wilson's occupancy of the White House. In 1934 President Roosevelt appointed Dr. Grayson National Chairman of the Red Cross.

GRAZ, GRATZ (47° 4′ N., 15° 26′ E.), cap. Styria, Austria, on Mur; has interesting XV.-cent. cathedral; seat of univ. founded 1586; other features of interest are the Landhaus, Stradt-Park ancient fortress of Schlossberg (destroyed by the Fr. in 1809), the Joanneum Museum, and the picture-gallery; bishop's see; active industrial center; manufactures machinery, iron-ware, leather-ware, wine.

GREAT AMERICAN DESERT, term applied to a large arid area in the western part of the United States and the northern part of Mexico. Much of the territory formerly included in that designation has, however, since been reclaimed by irrigation and is now suitable for grazing and agriculture. Its boundaries are roughly the Rocky Mountains and their continuing ranges in New Mexico and Texas on the east, and the Cascade ranges and the Sierra Nevadas on the west. The region is about 700 miles across in its greatest width, and extends from the Canadian border to Mexico and a considerable distance into that country. The really arid wastes comprise perhaps 550,000 square miles in the United States and somewhat less than that in Mexico. The highest desert stretches are in central Nevada at an altitude of from 5,000 to 6,000 feet; the lowest are in Death Valley, Cal., 427 feet below sea level, and Salton Desert in that State, which is also below sea level. There are few permanent streams, though torrents sometimes descend from the mountain to be quickly swallowed up by the thirsty sands. Sometimes no rain falls for a year, and the average annual precipitation ranges from 5 to 10 inches. Cactus, sagebrush and rough grasses are almost the only plant growths. The temperature for days at a time exceeds 100 degrees and often reaches 130 degrees.

GREAT AWAKENING, religious revival which began in New England in 1740 under leadership of George Whitefield and subsequently spread over America.

GREAT BARRIER REEF, coral reefs off E. coast Queensland, Australia; length, 1300 miles; distance from coast, 15 to 155 miles; supposed form of old Australian coast-line; area, about 100,-000 sq. miles; broken by several natural navigation channels.

GREAT BARRINGTON, a town in Massachusetts, in Berkshire co. It is on the New York, New Haven and Hartford railroad, and on the Housatonic river and main automobile routes. Within its limits are included the villages of Housatonic and Van Deusen. The town is in the Berkshires and is noted for its picturesque scenery. It is a popular summer resort and residence place for people of wealth. There is a public library and several private schools. The industries include the manufacture of cotton goods, vacuum bottles and paper.

GREAT BASIN (*c.* 32° to 45° N., 112° to 122° W.), area in W. Cordilleran region of U.S.; *c.* 200,000 sq. miles in extent; surface is varied, and includes mountain chain known as Basin Range, which has smooth valleys with shallow salt lakes; the largest is Great Salt Lake.

GREAT BEAR LAKE (66° N., 120° W.), lake, N.W. Canada; discharges through Great Bear River into the Mackenzie River.

GREAT BRITAIN (49° 57'-58° 40' N., 1° 46' E.-6° 13' W.), large islands off W. coast of Europe, consisting of England, Scotland, and Wales. The island has an extreme length of *c.* 605 m.; breadth, *c.* 320 m.; total area, *c.* 88,500 sq. m. The most northerly point is Dunnet Head, in Caithness; most easterly, Lowestoft Ness, Suffolk; most southerly, Lizard Point, Cornwall; most westerly, Ardnamurchan Point, Argyll. See also BRITISH EMPIRE.

GREAT CIRCLE, any circle of longitude, or the meridian circle at the equator.

GREAT EASTERN, a British merchant vessel of 18,915 tons, built in 1854-57. She became of note as the largest craft in the world up to that period. She was constructed of iron and had paddle and screw means of propulsion. Her length extended 680 feet, and her breadth 82½ feet, or with her paddle boxes, 118 feet. She had six masts, five of which were of iron, and 7,000 yards of sail. Eight engines worked her screws and paddles, capable of 11,000 horse power. She was costly, unprofitable and unfortunate from the start. After a number of runs to New York, she became a troop ship, then a cable-laying ship, and finally declined to a sightseeing object. In 1888 she was broken up.

GREAT FALLS, a city of Montana, in Cascade co., of which it is the county seat. On the Great Northern and Chicago, Milwaukee and St. Paul railroads. It is the south gateway to the large Kevin-Sunburst oil fields, and the famous Glacier National Park. It has the only copper wire mill west of the Mississippi River, largest electrolytic zinc plant and ferro-manganese plant in the world, as well as the largest fresh water springs in the world, with a daily flow of 350,000,000 gallons, second largest hydro-electric power plant in the west. Is an industrial, jobbing, railroad and commercial center. Within the city are several parks. The neighboring country is of great scenic beauty. The Great Northern, and the Chicago, Milwaukee and St. Paul railways have ten lines of railway radiating in every direction from Great Falls. Great Falls is termed

"Niagara of the West" and has excellent fishing streams in the vicinity.

GREAT HARWOOD (53° 46' N., 2° 24' W.), town, Lancashire, England; collieries; cotton mills.

GREAT LAKES OF NORTH AMERICA, the collective name for six freshwater lakes—Superior, Michigan, Huron, St. Clair, Erie, and Ontario—situated between Canada on N. and U.S. on S. (41°-49° N., 76°-92° W.), and forming upper waters of St. Lawrence R. Superior, largest lake, is connected with Huron by St. Mary R.; Michigan (lying wholly in U.S.) joins Huron at Straits of Mackinac; Huron empties itself into Erie by St. Clair R., and lake, and Detroit R.; between Erie and Ontario are Niagara R. and Falls. Lakes opened up to navigation, and differences of levels overcome by system of canals with numerous locks. The lakes are frozen for four or five months in winter. Some of the largest and most important towns in N. America situated on shores of lakes. Chicago, on Michigan, and Buffalo, on Erie, share greater part of lake traffic. Around lakes are extensive coal-fields, iron mines, fruit and grain-growing regions. Area exceeds 90,000 sq. m.

GREAT REBELLION, wars in Great Britain, 1642-52, between Royalists and Parliament. See ENGLAND.

GREAT SALT LAKE, a great sheet of water lying in Northwest Utah along the western base of the Wahsatch Mountains, 4,200 feet above sea level. It has a length of about 80 miles and is from 20 to 32 miles wide, but has no great depth, being generally quite shallow. The lake is the chief drainage center of the Great Basin and has a number of inlets, or tributaries, one of which, the Jordan, brings the fresh waters of Lake Utah. It contains several islands, the largest of which, Antelope, is about 18 miles long. It has no fish, but several species of insects people its waters, and its shores are frequented by numerous water fowl. The area is variable, due to the lake's lack of outlet except evaporation. Its clear water consequently holds much saline matter always in solution. Sometimes the water flowing in exceeds the evaporation, resulting in an increase of the lake's area, which has varied between 1,700, 2,280, and 2,360 sq. miles. For the past fifty years the lake has been receding, due to irrigation and a reduced flow from the inlets.

GREAT SLAVE LAKE (62° N., 115° W.), lake, N.W. Canada discharges by Mackenzie River into Arctic Ocean; *c.* 300 miles long; average breadth, 50 miles.

GREAT SLAVE RIVER, a river in Canada which flows from the Province of Alberta to the Northwestern Territories, into Great Slave Lake. Its total length is about 300 miles and it is navigable for practically its entire length during the open season. The valley through which it passes is of great fertility but is largely unsettled.

GREAT SOUTHERN OCEAN, narrow expanse of water encircling the globe almost completely, between parallels of 40° and 66½°.

GREATER PUNXSUTAWNEY, a borough in Pennsylvania, in Jefferson co., 45 miles N.W. of Altoona. It is in the midst of an extensive coal and iron region and its chief industry is connected with coal mining.

GREBES (*Podicipedidae*), a cosmopolitan family of swimming birds, with short, close plumage, brown on upper and white and very glossy on under surface.

GRECO, EL, DOMINICO THEOTOCOPULI (*d.* 1614), Cretan artist; pupil of Titian; spent many years in Spain, under the patronage of Philip II.; was an artist of striking and original genius.

GRECO-TURKISH WAR, 1897, see GREECE: *History.*

GREECE, republic, S. E. Europe (35° 42′ N., 19° 30′ E.), consisting of southern part of Balkan Peninsula and numerous islands—Euboea, N. Sporades, Cyclades, etc., on E., Crete, Cerigo, etc., on S., Ionian Islands on W.; bounded by Albania, Jugo-Slavia, and Bulgaria on N., Black Sea, Sea of Marmora, Dardanelles, and Ægean Sea on E., Mediterranean Sea on S., Ionian Sea on W.; mainland is almost bisected by Gulfs of Patras, Corinth, and Ægina, and severance is completed by canal across narrow isthmus of Corinth (3½ m.), which leads to southern Morea or Peloponnesus. The coasts are high, rocky and indented. Cape Matapan is most southerly point on mainland of Europe. The northern part consisted, until 1923, of Macedonia and Thrace, secured by the Balkan and World Wars. Farther S. is Thessaly, ceded by Turkey, 1881. The country is traversed on the W. by the limestone Dinaric Alpine fold, Mt. Taygetos, (7,890 ft.), part of which forms the Pindus Mts.; between the roughly parallel ridges are deep valleys (Arachthus, Achelous) and mountain basins

(Arta, Agrinion); the Ionian Islands are a partially submerged ridge. Along the E. coast a ridge runs through Olympus, 9,750 ft., Pelion, Euboea, to island of Mykonos, enclosing lacustrine plains (Thessaly) and landlocked gulfs (Volo). Earthquakes are frequent, especially in S.W. The lower courses of the Maritza, Struma, and Vardar in the N. are in Gr. territory; entirely Greek are the Vistritza, Salamvria, Hellada on E., Arta, Aspro, and Ruphia on W. Climate is Mediterranean; snow lies above 4,000 ft.; rainfall heaviest on W.; deforestation has reduced rainfall and reserves of soil; marshlands are malarial. Below 1,500 ft. the cypress, myrtle, olive, and other evergreens prevail; vine, fig, orange, tobacco, and (locally) cotton and date flourish; above 1,500 ft., where moisture is sufficient, are oak and chestnut forests; from 3,500 to 5,500 ft. beech and pine thrive; higher still flora is Alpine. Fauna is Mediterranean, including wolves, jackals, deer, bears, lynx, badgers, vultures, and snakes (two varieties poisonous). Agriculture, which is backward, is predominant occupation. Chief products are grapes for currants (mostly from Ionian Islands and S. side of Gulf of Corinth and Patras); olives, tobacco, figs and fruit, cereals are wheat, barley, rye, and corn. Principal minerals are iron ore, lead, zinc, salt, chromite, iron pyrites and lignite. Chief manufactures are smelting, textiles, and some shipbuilding. Exports include currants, figs, olive oil, wines, tobacco, hides, ores, marble, and sponges; imports, manufactured goods, corn, timber, cattle, sugar, salt fish, coal. Railway mileage, 1931, 1,727; the ship canal across Isthmus of Corinth is rarely used by foreign vessels; the mercantile marine has a tonnage of *c.* 1,417,071. Athens is cap.; chief ports, Piraeus, Syra, Patras, Salonica, Volo, Corfu, Kalamata, Laurium, Canea (Crete); Dede-Agach, with free access, secured by Treaty of Peace, for Bulgars.

Area and Population.—The increase of terr. and pop. as a result of the World War gives Greece in Europe an area of *c.* 50,257 sq.m. with *c.* 6,480,000 inhabitants. Pop. includes three main stocks; (1) aboriginal Mediterranean brunettes, purest in Crete; (2) dark, sallow, brachycephalic alpine highlanders, typically represented in Albania; (3) scanty remains of tall, fair, or ruddy northerners whose successive invasions (Thraco-Phrygian, *c.* 1500 B.C.; Dorian, 1000 B.C.; Galatian, 275 B.C., etc.) mark the main turning-points of Aegean history. It is Albanian blood which mainly differentiates modern from anc. Greeks. Most of the inhabitants belong to the Gr. Orthodox Church; but complete toleration exists. Elementary education is free and nominally compulsory between ages of five and twelve. In Athens are a univ., a polytechnic, an industrial academy, and two schools of agriculture.

History. Greece is a republic. The former king was George, son of Constantine, who was forced to abdicate in 1917. A year after Constantine's death in 1922, George was forced to quit the country and two years later the republic was founded. The army is conscript, between ages of 21 and 57. The total strength, 1933, was 583,450 officers and men.

Admiral Koundouriotis became head of the new republic, serving through the political vicissitudes rife in the country from 1925 to 1929 when he was forced to resign because of ill health. He was succeeded by Alexander Zaimis. Panayoti Tsaldaris was made premier on March 10, 1933.

Thrace, Imbros and Tenedos, commanding the Dardanelles, were added to Greek territory in 1919-20 but, by the Lausanne Treaty, were ceded back to Turkey in 1923. In the same year, Greece by treaty with Yugo-Slavia ceded to that country for fifty years a free zone in the harbor of Salonica, giving the Serbs an outlet to the Aegean sea. This was confirmed by three treaties signed in 1926, enlarging the zone and giving Greece all rights to Serbian railroads from the boundary in exchange for 20,000,000 French francs. Arbitral powers were vested in a resident official of the League of Nations and the Free Zone went into effect in March, 1929. In 1924 Bulgaria was allowed a commercial outlet to the Aegean in the port of Kavala which was joined to her frontier by a narrow corridor under the supervision of the League. Possession, however, has not yet been effected (1933). The invasion by Greek troops of Bulgarian territory in 1925 was settled in December of that year by the League of Nations which imposed indemnity against Greece of about $219,000 which was paid in Dec.

1929. A treaty of friendship between Greece and Turkey was signed at Istanbul June 10, 1930 which settled all outstanding questions following the exchange of population brought about by the Lausanne Treaty, Greece agreeing to pay an indemnity of $2,125,000. An amity treaty with a ten year peace pact was signed at Ankara on Sept. 16, 1933.

In 1927 Greece funded her war debt to both Great Britain and the U. S., each payable in 62 years. The American debt was funded at $19,-659,836. In the same year the U. S. agreed to advance a loan to Greece of $12,167,000 at par, bearing 4 per cent interest and to be repaid in 40 years. The bill was authorized by Congress in 1929 and the money paid to Greece a few months later. Under approval of the League of Nations a $15,000,000, 6%, 40 year loan was floated by Greece which, in addition to the American loan, enabled her to stabilize the drachma.

History: Prehistoric Times. The term *Aegean Civilization* is used to denote the culture of Greece and the Ægean islands, with outposts both E. and W., before the coming of the historic Greeks. It is a civilization whose discovery has only been made within the last generation by the unearthing of various archæological remains. It has no literary records except inscriptions, which are still undeciphered. It seems certain now that in primitive times these lands were inhabited by a long-skulled, dark-skinned people to which the name of Mediterranean race has been given. The Stone Age came to an end about 3000 B. C., and from that time civilization greatly improved and a state of culture was reached unsurpassed till classical times. The center of this was Crete, especially the cap., Cnossus; recent excavations show the various stages of culture, sometimes called Minoan (from King Minos); and Dr. A. J. Evans divides it into Minoan I., II., and III., each in three subdivisions, coming to an end about 1000 B. C. The art is quite distinct from that of neighboring races, though it shows affinities with Egypt and

Phœnicia. The occurrence of Ægean objects in the tombs of Egyptian kings has enabled us approximately to date the civilization to which they belong. Minoan civilization reached a high pitch about 2000 B. C., then after a temporary decline its highest point about 1600, when the city was burnt. It revived somewhat, but was finally destroyed about 1000, when this civilization in Crete came to an end, though it may have lingered a little in Cyprus and elsewhere. The destroyers were probably still uncivilized Greeks from the north. On the mainland the chief centers were Mycenæ (where it is sometimes called *Mycenaean*) and Tiryns. Anc. Ægean costume, curiously, resembled modern dress more than classical. Its religion was a form of nature worship. A goddess, who appears possibly in the Gr. Artemis and Aphrodite, and her divine son and partner were the chief deities. Whether an Indo-European tongue was spoken or not is uncertain.

Ancient History. The Greek people are a branch of the great Aryan or Indo-European family. They came down from the mountain district that stretches from the Alps to the Himalayas, and dispossessed a people of advanced civilization that held the lands round the Ægean Sea.

The Greeks were divided into three great families—Ionians, Æolians, and Dorians; the Dorians came last and established themselves in the south. Argo, Sparta, Corinth, Messenia, and Ægina formed their chief settlements. Their invasion drove many Ionians and Æolians to Asia Minor, where some of their kinsmen must already have been settled. Athens and Eubœa were chief Ionian districts in Greece proper, Bœotia chief Æolian.

The Ionians of Asia Minor, no doubt inspired by contact with the more civilized East, first developed Gr. science, literature, and art: Miletus, Smyrna, Chios, Samos, and later Ephesus, are their chief settlements; Lesbos was the chief Æolian. In the S., Dorians spread across the Ægean, to Crete, Rhodes, and Cnidus.

By 700 B. C. Gr. trade was flourishing, and many colonies were founded along the coasts of the Black Sea, Thrace, S. Italy, Sicily, and other lands. Miletus, Megara, and Chalcis in Eubœa, were the chief colonizing cities, and trade ranged from the Caucasus and Egypt in the E. to S. Gaul and Spain in the W. The Phœnicians were their principal rivals, and Carthage, with Etruria, always opposed them.

In Greece proper, Argos established her position as head of the Peloponnese, but Sparta soon challenged her. Finding a need for expansion, the Spartans, organized as a race of warriors under the constitution of Lycurgus, conquered all Laconia and Messenia, and by 500 B. C. had established themselves at the head of a league which embraced nearly all the Peloponnese; a great victory over Argos, 495, left Sparta undisputed head of Greece at time of Pers. wars.

Tyrants (unconstitutional monarchs) established themselves in some cities between 700 and 500 B. C. Periander of Corinth, Cleisthenes of Sicyon, Thrasybulus of Miletus are the chief; their influence was largely for good, but no tyranny could long stifle Gr. love of freedom.

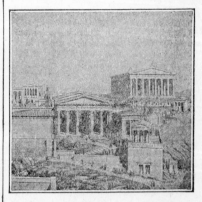

THE ACROPOLIS (c. B.C. 450)

Athens comes into prominence in the 6th cent.; her great lawgiver, Solon, set a high ideal, which the tyranny of Pisistratus did little to destroy. After the expulsion of the tyrants, 510, the constitution was organized by Cleisthenes on a more democratic basis.

Persian Wars.—The Gr. cities of Asia Minor had first been attacked by Lydia, and all subdued except Miletus; in 546 Cyrus of Persia overthrew Crœsus of Lydia; all Ionia was reduced thereafter, except Miletus, which made a separate treaty. Darius, 521-485, determined to extend his empire into Europe, but first had to deal with the Ionic revolt, led by Miletus and Chios. The Athenians helped to burn Sardis, but the revolt failed for lack of unity, and their defeat at Lade, 494, destroyed the Ionians.

Thereafter Darius' general, Mardonius, secured Thrace and Macedonia, 493, but failed to reach Greece. A second expedition, under Datis and Artaphernes, sailed across the Ægean, took Eretria, and landed at Marathon, 490, but was defeated by the Athenians under Miltiades. The third expedition, 480, was led by Darius' successor, Xerxes. Themistocles had organized the Athenian fleet in the interval, and Athens, Corinth, and Ægina were the protagonists in the decisive victory of Salamis, after Leonidas and the 300 Spartans had nobly died in defense of Thermopylæ. Xerxes fled, leaving Mardonius in Bœotia. A simultaneous attack on Sicily by Carthage was defeated by Gelo, tyrant of Syracuse. Next year the Greeks under the Spartan Pausanias defeated Mardonius at Platæa; a victory by sea and land at Mycale finished the war, which determined the fate of Europe. The subject cities were gradually freed by the Confederacy of Delos, a mar. league led by Athens.

This confederacy developed into an Athenian empire, and its members gradually became subjects. Cimon and Pericles successively developed Athenian strength—the former winning great victories at the Eurymedon, 467, and in Cyprus (against Persia) in the E.; while Pericles, the organizer of Athenian democracy, aimed at land empire. Athens crushed Ægina, defeated Corinth, and established a short-lived supremacy in central Greece, ended by a defeat at Coronea, 447, by Thebes.

Sparta had had trouble in the Peloponnese after the Pers. wars, but had recovered, and caused a rising of the Helots (serfs); gradually the antipathy between the Empire and the League rose, fostered by Corinth, Athens' great trade rival, until it culminated in the Peloponnesian War, 431,404: Athenian *v.* Spartan, Ionian *v.* Dorian, democracy *v.* oligarchy. Athens met with success at Sphacteria, 425, but was defeated by Thebes at Delium, 424, and Brasidas the Spartan made havoc of their Thracian possessions. From 421 to 413 the Peace of Nicias closed open hostilities. Sparta defeated her old rival Argos at Mantinea, 418, while Athens ambitiously tried to gain Sicily and attacked Syracuse, 415; but the great Sicilian expedition met with a memorable disaster. This led Sparta to renew the war; her capable admiral, Lysander, aided by Pers. money, eventually defeated Athens at Ægospotami, 405, and starved the city into surrender. During this time Athens' one capable man, Alcibiades, proved untrustworthy, and internal dissensions aided her fall; the conquerors granted easy terms.

Sparta now took over the Athenian Empire, but mismanaged it; her allies turned against her, and she began to fail, partly for lack of men, as shown by an attempt by Agesilaus to attack Persia. Athens revived somewhat; Thebes developed strength under Epaminondas, who defeated the Spartans at Leuctra, 371, and organized Arcadia and Messenia against them; a further victory at Mantinea, 362, ended Spartan power, but Epaminondas was killed—his work had been entirely destructive.

Macedonian Empire.—Worn out by struggles, the Greeks of central and southern Greece fell a prey to the semi-alien power of Macedon under Philip; the resistance of Thebes and Athens, led by the orator Demosthenes, ended at the battle of Chæronea, 368. His son Alexander had larger schemes: in the name of Greece he attacked Persia; in the three great battles of the Granicus, 334, Issus, 333, and Arbela, 331, he defeated the Persians by the famous Macedonian phalanx, and extended his sway to the Hindu-Kush and the Indus. He tried to hellenize the East, but his premature death, 323, left his work half done. His generals divided his empire: the western part of Asia Minor remained Gr. for centuries, but beyond the Euphrates the Oriental element eventually triumphed.

In Greece-proper Macedon resumed the position of a semi-alien but dominant state, and the chief feature is the rise of federations, of which the chief were the Ætolian and Achæan leagues. In 198 Rome began to look eastwards, first to protect the Greeks from Macedon, then, in their own interests, to govern them; eventually it became necessary to subdue them, and the destruction of Corinth, 146, marked the end of Gr. independence.

The Greeks in Sicily, after the Athenian expedition, found a strong enemy in Carthage, who took in succession Himera, Selinus, and Acragas, and threatened Syracuse, which was saved by the tyrant Dionysius. The struggle continued intermittently with varying fortunes till Rome intervened to help the Greeks, and the first Punic War, 264-241 gave Sicily to Rome.

Greece came under Roman control in 146 B.C., when Mummius, the Roman general sent to support Sparta, captured and ruined Corinth and defeated the Achæan League. Macedonia then became a province of Rome, and with Achæa was governed by a prætor. Many Gr. institutions were left unaltered, but the cities were deprived of all political importance. The country enjoyed considerable prosperity, which was interrupted by national rising led by Mithridates in 1st cent. B.C.; this was suppressed by Rome with great severity by 84 B.C., after which the country was in evil case for some time. It revived under the empire, and was recognized as supreme in the field of culture. Christianity was introduced in the 3rd cent., and from this time old paganism gradually declined.

Mediaeval and Modern History.— Greece suffered from invasions of Western Goths in 3rd cent., Vandals and Eastern Goths in 5th cent., Slavs from the 6th cent. onwards. After break-up of Roman Empire, Greece formed part of Byzantine dominions till 1204, when it was seized by Latins. During 13th cent. it was sub-divided into fiefs; greater part of country conquered by Turks by 1460; Venetians for some time retained several of the islands, and warred against Turks from time to time, but by 1718, whole country was under domination of Porte. Greeks, who remained in subjection till 1821, were allowed by their Turk. masters to acquire considerable wealth, and the increase of education and culture which followed resulted, early in 19th cent., in a revival of national feeling. In 1821 open rebellion broke out, and the war of Gr. independence began with a rising in Moldavia. The Turks vainly tried to suppress revolt by terrible cruelties and massacres, but within the year they were expelled, Greece regained her freedom, and a national constitution was framed. Turkey, however, obtained reinforcements, under Ibrahim Pasha, from Egypt, and reconquered country in 1825. The Gr. cause was then taken up by Britain, Russia, and France, whose combined forces destroyed the Turk. and Egyptian fleets at Navarino, 1827; further Russian victories on land completed Turk. discomfiture, and in 1830 the independence

of Greece was declared by the London protocol. In 1832 a monarchy under Otho of Bavaria was established; but his despotic rule proved so unpopular that a revolution occurred, and he had to leave the country in 1862. Prince George of Denmark became king in 1863, with consent of Britain, France, and Russia. Under him the country enjoyed a fair degree of prosperity until the outbreak of war with Turkey, the king's unwillingness to engage in which made him somewhat unpopular. Dissatisfaction in Greece concerning the Greco-Turk. boundary and possession of Crete resulted in Greco-Turkish War in spring, 1897. In Thessaly Greeks suffered series of defeats—Larissa, Pharsala, and Velestino being taken by Turks, who were also victorious in Epirus at Homopulos and at mouth of river Luro. Tsar intervened; armistice arranged which resulted in agreement whereby Greece paid an indemnity of $18,000,000, but lost little territory. Outbreak of a military revolutionary movement in 1909-10; rivalry with Rumania on the Macedonian question, which in 1905, 1906, and 1910 resulted in the breaking off of diplomatic relations between the countries; constant difficulties with European Powers on account of Crete; declaration of war against Turkey by Greece, Oct. 18, 1912 (see BALKAN WARS); assassination of king March 18, 1913; succeeded by his son Constantine, who renewed war with Bulgaria, June-Aug. 1913, and as result enlarged boundaries of the kingdom along N. Ægean coast.

Greece and the World War.—At the outbreak of the World War the Gr. premier was Eleutherios Venizelos, who five years previously, by his solution of the Cretan difficulty, had saved both Greece and the dynasty. It was he who had formed the Balkan League, and naturally he was eager to fulfil the treaty obligations of 1913 should Serbia be attacked by Bulgaria. From the first he believed that the future of Greece was bound up with the victory of the Allies, and he was strongly in favor of armed intervention on their behalf. Constantine, the king, was a pro-German, brother-in-law and warm admirer of the Kaiser. He was only prevented from openly siding with the Central Powers because of the vulnerability of his country to naval attack. Consequently, his best service to his friends was to maintain a neutral attitude. About May 1915 Baron Schenck appeared in Greece, and at once began a pro-German propaganda, which had considerable success. The Russians were then retreating; the British were making no headway in Gallipoli, and many

Greeks had lost faith in the Allies. Thwarted by the king, Venizelos resigned, and was succeeded by Gounaris, but at the general election in June he won a sweeping victory. The king's illness was made the excuse for delaying the meeting of Parliament. On Aug. 21, Venizelos again assumed the reins of power as prime minister.

Between the election and his return to power the Allies proposed that Greece should give up Eastern Macedonia to Bulgaria in order to keep her out of the war, and to this Venizelos agreed. At once the royalists denounced him as a traitor, and there were many defections from his side. Early in September, with the quasi-concurrence of the government, Venizelos invited the Allies to send 150,000 troops to Salonica, promising that Greece would mobilize. The king signed the mobilization order, but when on Oct. 6, while the Allied troops were arriving, he repudiated the declaration of Venizelos that no resistance would be offered to their passage, that statesman had no option but to resign. A stop-gap government was installed. On Oct. 14, 1915, Bulgaria declared war on Serbia, and shortly afterwards the Allies offered Cyprus to Greece if she would actively intervene on their behalf. The offer was refused. Later on in the month Venizelos and his friends carried a vote of want of confidence in the government, which resigned. Another premier was set up; but as he was at the mercy of the Venizelists, Parliament was dissolved and a general election was announced for the following December. The election was a perfect farce: the crown used every endeavor to prevent its opponents from holding meetings and going to the polls. A royalist Parliament was elected, and Constantine again made professions of strict neutrality.

In Aug. 1916 the Bulgars invaded Gr. territory. The Gr. frontier fortress of Rupel, in the valley of the Struma, had already been surrendered to them on May 26, and the Gr. port of Kavala was yielded to them on Sept. 12. These ignominious surrenders alienated many Greeks who had formerly supported Constantine. Venizelos held mass meetings, and begged the king to place himself at the head of the nation and defend its honor. Meanwhile the first step in active revolution had been taken. An officer of Cretan gendarmerie had induced three regiments of the 11th Division to join a movement for defending Gr. soil from Bulgarian aggression. The Allies also protested, and in a note denounced the December elections as illegal, and demanded an honest election. A few days later they applied pressure by refusing to allow Gr. ships to enter or leave harbor. The king replied by stirring up the army reservists against the Allies, who responded by demanding the disbandment of the army, the holding of fresh elections, and the dismissal of pro-German officials. The presence of Brit. warships forced Constantine to agree to these demands. The government resigned, and another premier was appointed.

Rumania had declared war on behalf of the Allies on Aug. 27, and again the question of treaty obligations arose. Venizelos now announced that if Greece did not join the Allies it would be his duty to head a revolution. For a moment Constantine was alarmed, but fortified by reassurances from the Kaiser, held out against Venizelos, who now began to take action. On Sept. 24 Crete disowned the Athens government, and joined the national movement under her old prime minister. With headquarters at Salonica, he set up a government of national defense, his leading coadjutors being Admiral Condouriotis and General Danglis. Men flocked to his banner, and were armed and munitioned by the Allies. Constantine now perpetrated another piece of treachery by ordering the 4th Army Corps at Kavala to surrender. The troops were disarmed and sent to Germany to prevent the possibility of their being utilized by the Allies. In the meantime a succession of notes had been passing between the Athens government and the Allies, and further acts of naval pressure had forced Constantine to deport Schenck and his fellows. Nevertheless, he was still engaged in trying to thwart and trick the Allies.

Early in October Admiral Dartige du Fournet demanded and received the surrender of the Gr. fleet under the threat of blockade. Constantine, who had massed his troops in Thessaly on the flank of the Allies, now made his last effort to join hands with the Bulgars. The situation was extremely dangerous. Allied blue-jackets were landed to occupy certain of the forts round Athens, and thus to control the railways. Rioting took place, and on Nov. 16 the Allies demanded the surrender of the mountain batteries before Dec. 1. This had not been done by the time fixed, and the Allies prepared to land some 2,000 troops. Meanwhile Constantine had posted his men in positions from which they could command the buildings in which the Allied troops were to be housed. Firing began almost immediately the Allied troops landed, and 131 French and British were killed and 250 wounded. In the evening the Allied warships proceeded to bombard the city. Constantine again temporized, and a reign of terror began. Venizelists were imprisoned and murdered, and the Allies proceeded to blockade the coasts. On Dec. 15 the Gr. Government was ordered to stop the movement of all troops and material to the N., and Constantine was forced to yield, and after an ultimatum he also had to agree to apologize for the attack on the Allied troops, and to salute their flags publicly. This was done on Jan. 20, 1917. In May of that year, however, the king was as defiant as ever; bands of his irregulars threatened the Salonica lines of communication; and there were fears that when the crops of Thessaly were reaped they would be handed over to the enemy. The Allies thereupon bought the crops, and landed a Franco-Brit. column to protect the reapers. By this time nine-tenths of the people had joined the national cause. Constantine was still a stumbling-block, and on June 10 his abdication and that of the crown prince were demanded within forty-eight hours. On June 14 he left Greece, and his second son, Alexander, succeeded to the throne. Venizelos formed a new cabinet, and thereafter Gr. troops participated in the Salonica campaign. At the peace settlement Greece received most of the territories of Turkey in Europe, various Ægean islands, Cyprus, and the Smyrna dist. of Asia Minor. In 1919 Alexander morganatically married Mlle. Manos. He died on Oct. 25, 1920, from the bite of a pet monkey. Condourtiotis was appointed regent, and the question of the dynastic succession was referred to the people in the ensuing elections. The elections resulted in a strong expression on the part of the people for the return of Constantine and his establishment as king, and in January 1921, he returned to Greece and was welcomed with acclamation. Under his direction aggressive measures were taken to carry on warfare with Turkey in Asia Minor, and a large army was raised for that purpose. The campaign continued throughout 1921 and the greater part of 1922 without decisive results to either Greece or Turkey. In the autumn of 1922, however, the Turks under Mustapha Kemal, in a series of aggressive attacks, disastrously defeated the Greek army and put an end to the war. Smyrna was taken and burned. The whole area of Asia Minor came into the hands of the Turks. See TURKEY. The Greek cabinet at once resigned and so great was the popular displeasure with the king that Constantine abdicated in favor of his son, George. He retired to the island of Palermo where he died January 11, 1923. The government was now controlled by a revolutionary committee with George as the nominal head.

The generals and statesmen who were held responsible for the disasters in Asia Minor were tried for treason and several were executed. Among those tried was Prince Andrew, the king's brother. He was, however, acquitted. As a result of these disasters Greece lost most of the territory acquired through the Treaty of Sévres. The Turkish government, under the direction of Mustapha Kemal demanded return of all territory, including Thrace, and the deportation from that territory of all the Greeks. These demands were practically all granted at the Lausanne conference (q.v.) in 1923. See LAUSANNE CONFERENCE OF. There was much suffering among the Greek refugees from Asia Minor and from Thrace. From the latter country the greater part of the population fled. As the result of the murder of Italian officials in Janina, Italy seized Corfu, and compelled the payment of a large indemnity in Sept., 1923.

The *Greek Religion* was an important aspect of Gr. civilization. Recent research into anthropology, comparative religion, and mythology has made it possible to view it in relation to other systems of belief. Though Gr. religion possessed no doctrinal system, there are certain definite characteristics which marked it off from that of neighboring peoples. It has been defined as 'anthropomophic polytheism.' Some elements of it were brought in by the Greeks; others were taken over from the older non-Aryan peoples of the Mediterranean, of whose importance we have only lately come to know. One authority distinguishes two types—the Olympic, the joyous worship of the gods; and the Chthonic, the propitiation of malevolent deities. Certainly the Greeks conceived the gods to be like 'big men' with human passions, while to the Romans they were more shadowy. Greek religion was profoundly influenced by the introduction of the cult of Dionysus, and by Orphism. These superimposed a mystery religion upon older cuits. In the cent's immediately preceding the Christian era Greece was more than ever influenced by Oriental worship and modes of thought, and thus prepared the way for Christianity. See GREEK CHURCH.

Language.—The Gr. language belongs to the Indo-European group. Little is known of the pre-Hellenic population of Greece, and surviving elements of the language, chiefly in place-names, show no kinship with the Gr. tongue. But this evidence is not conclusive, and the eventual deciphering of Cretan records may prove an unexpected and uncontestable argument in favor of a close relationship. As it is, Prof. Ridgeway holds that the Achæans adopted the language of the Pelasgians they conquered.

The physical features of Greece and the adjacent islands fostered a diversity of dialects. The country is broken and irregular, and mountain barriers separate state from state. Gr. dialects are usually classified into Æolic, Doric, Ionic, and Attic. It was not till the unification of Greece under Macedonian rule that the dialects broke down and a common dialect was established (*koine dialektos*). Of this one of the best-known examples is the Greek of the N.T.

The Gr. alphabet differs from the Roman. The language is synthetic and inflectional. In Greek we find reduplication verbs. In nouns only five cases survive out of the original eight— nominative, vocative, accusative, genitive, and dative. Greek, like Sanskrit, has three numbers—singular, dual, and plural. The conjugation of the verb is extraordinarily fine and subtle, and is unparalleled in its power of expressing delicate shades of meaning. A fully conjugated verb has three voices and 507 forms.

The vowel-music of the Gr. language is extremely rich. Especially beautiful are the diphthongs Gr. words terminate either in a vowel or in the consonants n, r, s, and x (the preposition *ek* alone excepted). This gives the language great flexibility, beauty, and grace. The vocabulary is very copious, and yet it retained perfect purity.

The Attic dialect, through the supremacy of Athens, became the dialect of refinement and culture, but the others were adopted as literary dialects in various branches of poetic composition.

Literature.—Greek literature falls into six divisions—(1) Early literature, up to *c.* 475 B.C., including epic and lyric (2) Attic, up to *c.* 300 B.C., including the drama and the development of prose; (3) Alexandrian period of the decadence, up to *c.* A.D. 146; (4) the Græco-Roman period, up to *c.* 529; (5) the Byzantine period, up to 1453, the date of the capture of Constantinople by the Turks; (6) Modern Greek, up to the present day.

Ancient.—Gr. literature, as it was a spontaneous growth and uninfluenced by previous and extraneous models, affords a peculiarly instructive study of a natural evolution. The progress of Gr. letters is traced from impersonal epic to personal lyric, and from individualistic lyric to democratic drama. Prose developed later than poetry, and side by side with the drama. Anc. Gr. poetry commences with the *Iliad* and the *Odyssey*—the supposed work of Homer. Sprung as these epics certainly were from a ballad epoch, in the shadowy times of unwritten literature, their construction is so artistic and their unity (despite a few inconsistencies) so complete that they must have taken their final form from the genius of a great artist. The groundwork of the poems is a body of Achæan ballads transmuted by the Æolian bards of Asia Minor and finally shaped by Ionic genius. Their dialect is Ionic, with an admixture of Æolic, and the metre is hexameter.

The epic tradition was continued by the so-called cyclic poems, which completed the tale of Troy divine. In the 8th cent. B.C. arose the great poet Hesiod. The keynote of the Homeric poems is joyousness unalloyed by stern reflection; the Hesiodic poems are essentially didactic; the gospel of the *Works and Days* is a gospel of toil unceasing. The didactic tradition was continued by the early cosmologists—(*e.g.*), Xenophanes and Parmenides. Attributed to Homer is a collection of hymns (the *Homeric Hymns*) addressed to various deities. These hymns really belong to the 6th cent. B.C., when a recitation of the poems of Homer was one of the competitions of the Panathenæa. The reciter was called a rhapsodist, and the hymns were the preludes which were sung to the presiding gods.

The epic period was succeeded by the lyric age. Lyric verse, like epic, had its origin among the Ionians, and is the outcome of the intellectual awakening that followed the great migratory enterprise. There are two broad divisions of lyric—elegiac and iambic. Elegiac metre consists of the smooth, flowing hexameter, followed by the broken flow of the pentameter, a metre peculiarly well adapted for meditation and reflection. Elegiac verse suits manifold subjects: Tyrtæus employed it for martial themes, Mimnermus for erotic, Solon for gnomic, and Simonides for commemorative. Subsequently elegiac and iambic verse lost their instrumental associations, and Gr. melic poetry was confined to the Dorian and Æolian species. The Æolian was personal and monodic: the Dorian was civic and choral. Æolian verse had its most glorious representative in Sappho. The fragments of her poetry show deep passion and supreme beauty of form. Pindar gave to the Dorian choral lyric the breadth of Panhellenic spirit.

Out of the dithyramb (triumphal song to Dionysus) was developed drama. In the history of the early development of the dithyramb stand Arion and Stesichorus, but the real history of the drama commences with Thespis of Icaria, who introduced one actor, and so made dialogue possible with the leader of the chorus. To this stage belonged **Phry-**

nichus, the author of the historical drama, *The Capture of Miletus*. Æschylus introduced the second actor, and reduced the importance of the chorus—an epoch-making advance. Thus dialogue became dominant, and three parts became possible, as an actor could take two roles. Among the dramas of Æschylus that remain is the great trilogy on the house of Agamemnon. The *Agamemnon* tells of the murder of the king by Clytemnestra, the *Choephori* deals with the Nemesis that tracked the avenger Orestes, and the *Eumenides* shows the final reconciliation between the Furies and the avenger. The dramas of Æschylus are essentially idealistic. The laws of heaven fulfil their purpose, and that purpose is good, though attained at the cost of individual sacrifice. This is the dominant thought—the fathers sin, and their sins are visited upon the children unto the third and fourth generations.

Sophocles is less universal in his themes. With him the psychological problem is supreme. Tragedy arises where there are duties in conflict, where the will is other than the deed. Thus Antigone has to choose between duty to the written law, or duty to the greater unwritten law. Œdipus had to front the awful consequences of a rash action.

With Euripides we pass from idealistic to realistic drama. The hero, though he be demigod of story, becomes a man, and the conflict he has to face is some subtle, sophistical problem of contemporary Athenian life. Too frequent use is made of the *Deus ex machina*, and the chorus is made a mere embellishment with no vital connection with the story.

Gr. comedy, like tragedy, had its origin in the cult of Dionysus. It springs from the harvest festivals. Old comedy is represented by Eupolis and Aristophanes, with its fearless ridicule of contemporary events and personalities. The middle comedy criticizes movements and not individuals. The new comedy, represented by Menander, deals with the humorous aspects of domestic life. See also under DRAMA.

The earliest traces of Gr. prose belong to the 6th cent. B.C., and these are mainly genealogies and cosmologies. Herodotus was the father of literary Gr. prose. His sentences follow the 'loose' construction. His history is intended to corroborate his theory of the conflict of the East and West. Thucydides is a much more critical historian. His sentences are periodic in structure, and his chief virtue is the revelation of character. His style is restrained and sterling. He is the most characteristically Gr. prose writer. The work of Xenophon is less profound in character, less perfect in finish.

Gr. oratory vacillates between the plain and the ornate, the simple and the florid, till it culminates in the perfect balance of style attained by Demosthenes.

The writings of Plato cannot be overlooked. As a stylist he is almost as great as he is as a philosopher.

The poetry of Alexandria was not truly Greek in character. It was artificial and scholarly; its appeal was very limited. Theocritus was the most natural poet of the Alexandrian school. Less spontaneous were Apollonius Rhodius, Bion, and Moschus.

Byzantine literature, though it affords much invaluable information, has no permanent value or purely literary qualities.

Modern Gr. literature has produced nothing that is really great. Some of the ballads, folk-songs, and pastorals are beautiful in sentiment and sweet in expression, but the glory of Gr. literature is of the ancients.

Art.—Gr. art may be conveniently classed under three heads—architecture, sculpture, and painting. From what survives of the architecture and sculpture, one can conjecture with some degree of certainty to what heights of perfection Gr. art developed in these two branches; but the remains of Gr. painting give us no adequate idea of what was the degree of development in that art.

Architecture.—Out of primitive or Mycenæan arch., which showed genius of a bold and virile type, the Doric, Ionic, and Corinthian orders were developed. The column is the distinguishing feature of these three types, as it is perhaps the distinguishing feature of Gr. arch. in general. The column had its origin in the tree trunk used as a prop in primitive dwellings. In Greek the columns were fluted and slightly tapered. The Doric column is simplest and most impressive, being capped by a simple square abacus. Its development culminated in the exquisite proportions of the Parthenon. The distinguishing feature of the Ionic column is the volute and torus. The Corinthian pillar is more ornate, and belongs to a later age in the history of Gr. architecture. Tradition states that its head, with the graceful leaf designs, was suggested to its inventor, Callimachus, by the twining of the leaves of the acanthus plant. The Corinthian pillar was susceptible to embellishment, and with the decay of the pure Gr. genius it degenerated into designs tawdry and trivial.

Gr. arch. at its best is marked by a noble and simple symmetry. That definiteness which is so characteristic of the Gr. genius is reflected in the exquisite precision of the temples and their chaste beauty. Greece in the structure of her temples was true to her motto, that there ought to be 'Nothing in excess.' See ARCHITECTURE.

Sculpture.—To pass from Gr. arch. to Gr. sculpture is a natural step, because the metopes of the temples were adorned with the finest masterpieces of sculpture, and within the temples stood the statues of the gods. Gr. sculpture, like the other Gr. arts, is in spirit ethical and ideal. It is an exquisite mingling of the human and the divine. Inspiration was sought from the gods, on whom the Gr. mind loved to dwell, but the sculptor's material was found in the palæstra. It was the perfection of the human physique, produced by the system of Gr. physical culture, which produced the magnificent statuary which will ever be the glory of Greece and a wonder of the world. The temple statue developed out of the rude image of a deity rough-hewn out of a tree trunk. Up to class. times, such rude images survived in the anc. temples; and the Hermes busts that stood, in the time of the highest civilization of Greece, at the cross-roads mark the transition from tree trunk to marble statue. Moreover, just as the most perfect of Gr. columns, the Doric, was marked by a solemn simplicity of line, so the finest examples of Gr. statuary were marked by a sublime freedom from all traces of sentimentality. The pose, too, of the statue at first showed the obvious influence of the tree-trunk type. The members were arranged in rigid symmetry, the legs and arms being stiff and straight.

At the period of the perfection of Gr. sculpture—the period of Pheidias and his school—the statue had lost its rigidity, but still retained a suggestion of calm and dignified composure. Gr. art was really on the decline when the sculptor sought to portray complex distortions of the frame, though the beauty of such a group as the *Laocoon* of the Rhodian school cannot be denied. Such distortions are conspicuous by their absence in the sculptures of the Parthenon, which, if they are not the actual work of the great Pheidias, belong to his school. The calm dignity of these works has fixed them for all time as the perfect types of classic beauty. Just as in literature the noble grandeur of Æschylus and Sophocles was followed by the more human and sentimental dramas of Euripides, and just as in arch. the solemn severity of the Doric column was superseded by the ornate and more complex designs of the Corinthian order, so the sentimentality of the decline invaded Gr. sculpture. Thus,

if Pheidias is the Æschylus of Gr. sculpture, Praxiteles is the Euripides. As Euripides made his gods human, so Praxiteles made his statues human. His statue of Venus, colored (as Gr. statues usually were), seemed the very incarnation of sensuous beauty; and if the exquisite tenderness of the famous statue of Hermes with the infant Dionysus (the best-preserved and most authentic masterpiece of Gr. sculpture) is a sign of the decay of the sublime in Gr. art, it is not a sign of the decay of its beauty.

Painting.—As no paintings of the class. age in Greece survive, criticism on this art is reduced to conjecture. One can make deductions from Roman wall-paintings excavated at Pompeii. Very probably Gr. painting was weak in regard to perspective. More valuable material is derived from Gr. vase-painting. The specimens which have survived of Mycenæan vase-painting reveal beauty of the bold and virile type, and stand comparison in some respects with the art of the best period. The Dorian conquest, as it temporarily threw back the progress of Gr. civilization, seems to have had a similar influence on art. The art of vase-painting evolved from crude geometric designs and rigid figures arranged with labored balance. The potter of the early ages set black figures on a light background. The result always tended to be ludicrous. Later, red figures on a dark background were introduced. Lines of expression and anatomy were applied in black glaze. Normally the vase was black and red. White and brown embellishments belong to a later age. The decline in Gr. vase-painting is traced by the growth of elaborate detail and ornament.

Greek art borrowed from the art of the East, but what it borrowed it made its own, by infusing into it its characteristic spirit of beauty and idealism. While the art of the East distorts the human frame and degenerates into the quaint and grotesque, Gr. art ennobles what is real and rises into beauty and sublimity. Moreover, there is a chastity in Gr. art which is unique in the history of the world. The Gr. artist knew that what is imperfect cannot be made perfect by elaboration and embellishment. The key to Gr. art is found in the method of the sculptor, who studied the perfect human physique of the wrestling-ground and, working by an inductive method, conceived hence his ideal of the divine nature. This conception gave birth to the beauty which is truth, for it was always faithful to what is. Gr. art, therefore, idealizes the real rather than realizes the ideal. See MAP, TURKEY.

GREEK ACADEMY. See ACADEMY

GREEK CHURCH. The correct name is the Holy Oriental Orthodox Catholic Apostolic Church, the term Greek simply indicating its early history. It comprises that group of Christian churches in the East, which, while not owing allegiance to Rome, has preserved an ecclesiastical and sacerdotal system much resembling hers, and has continued with but little change from primitive times. The Gr. Church consists of four ancient patriarchates—Jerusalem, Alexandria, Antioch, and Constantinople, and several national churches in communion with these, but independent in government. Most important of these are the Hellenic Church, the Russian Church, the Orthodox Church of the late Austrian Empire, the National Churches of Serbia, Rumania, Bulgaria, and the Churches of Cyprus and Mount Sinai.

In doctrine, the Eastern Church agrees on the whole with the Roman. The only point on which there is essential difference is the manner of the procession of the Holy Ghost. The Oriental Church maintains that He proceeds from the Father alone, and its dislike to the Latin addition of the phrase *Filioque* to the Nicene Creed has been the chief obstacle to reunion, although the questions of primacy and infallibility of the Pope also present difficulties.

GREEK FIRE, liquid inflammable and explosive mixture, used in mediæval warfare.

GREEK LANGUAGE AND LITERATURE. See GREECE.

GREELEY, a city of Colorado, in Weld co., of which it is the county seat. It is on the Union Pacific, the Denver, Laramie and Northwestern, and the Colorado and Southern railroads, and on the Cache la Poudre river. The city is the center of an important agricultural and cattle-raising region and it has a large trade in potatoes, flour, wheat and other agricultural products. Its industries include lumber yards, flour mills, a beet-sugar factory. Here is the State Teachers' College, and there is also a public library and two parks. The city was the site of the so-called 'Greeley Colony' named after Horace Greeley, which was the first agricultural community in the State.

GREELEY, HORACE (1811-72), journalist; *b.* Amherst, N.H.; *d.* Pleasantville, N.Y. He was the son of a poor farmer and at fourteen was apprenticed to a printer in Vermont after a meagre education. He became a journeyman compositor, finding employment in New York State and Pennsylvania printing plants, and in 1831 came to New York City where, with a partner, he later set up a small printing shop and issued the *New Yorker*, a literary weekly. This venture proved that the journeyman printer possessed editorial gifts which eventually made him famous. It led to his successful editorship of the *Jeffersonian*, a Whig campaign paper, and of the *Log Cabin*, a popular weekly. Meantime he acquired a high repute as a political writer. In 1841 he established the *New York Tribune* as an independent Whig daily and edited it with a remarkable brilliance and force for thirty years, making it a national organ of great influence. He was in Congress for a brief period, 1848-9. In 1861 he was nominated as Republican candidate for U.S. Senator from New York, but was defeated, and he met with other failures to obtain public office. Opposing the renomination of President Grant in 1872, he consented to become presidential candidate of the Liberal Republicans with the endorsement of the Democrats. Grant defeated him by over 700,000 votes, the only states he carried being Georgia, Kentucky, Maryland, Missouri, Tennessee and Texas. His death occurred before the votes were counted.

GREELY, ADOLPHUS WASHINGTON (1844), Arctic explorer and army general; *b.* Newburyport, Mass. He served throughout the Civil War as a private in a Massachusetts infantry regiment of volunteers. Later, as second lieutenant in the regular army, he was assigned to the signal corps, of which he became chief officer in 1887, ranking as brigadier-general. In 1906 he was promoted to major-general. His explorations in the Arctic began in 1881, when he commanded an expedition to establish circumpolar stations for meteorological and other purposes in that region. There were twelve in the party and they attained the highest point north then reached (83° 24′), which was in Grinnell Land. Their non-return caused a relief expedition to be sent the next year, and another in 1883, both of which failed to reach them. A third rescue party under Commander Winfield S. Schley found them in June, 1884, at Cape Sabine. Greely's men were reduced to seven, five having died through cold and famine in the 1883 winter, and the survivors were on the point of starvation. The Royal Geographical Society of London and the Societè de Geographie of Paris awarded him medals for his services to geographical science. He supervised the development and extension of military telegraph communication, including cable and wireless, with Porto Rico, Cuba, the Philippines and Alaska, and conducted the relief measures for the San Francisco earthquake sufferers in 1906. In 1908 he retired. His writings record his various activities in the government service and include works on American weather, auroras, the California earthquake, Alaska, and polar discoveries.

GREEN, ANNA KATHERINE (1846-1935), American author, b. in Brooklyn, New York. She was educated at Ripley Female College at Poultney, Vt., and in 1884 married Charles Rohlfs, actor and furniture designer. In 1878 Miss Green published *The Leavenworth Case*, and established herself as a successful writer of mystery stories. From that year until 1922 she turned out a succession of popular books. These include: *That Affair Next Door*; *The Millionaire Baby*; *The House of the Whispering Pines*; and *The Step on the Stair*. Many of her stories were dramatized and were successful on the stage and the screen.

GREEN, HETTY HOWLAND ROBINSON (1835-1916), an American business woman. She accumulated a large fortune in New York City, largely through shrewd investments in real estate. Property valued at $100,000,000 was bequeathed at her death to her son, Colonel E. H. R. Green, and her daughters.

GREEN, THOMAS HILL (1836-82), Eng. philosopher; ed. Rugby and Balliol Coll., Oxford; elected fellow, 1860; prof. of Moral Philosophy, 1878. His *Prolegomena to Ethics* and lectures on the *Principles of Political Obligation* were pub. after his death.

GREEN, WILLIAM HENRY (1825-1900), Amer. Hebrew scholar; wrote a *Grammar of the Hebrew Language*, and numerous works of Biblical criticism.

GREEN, WILLIAM MERCER (1876), American bishop. Graduated from University of the South, 1896. Ordained in 1900 in Protestant Episcopal Church. Rector of churches in Knoxville, Tenn.; Meridian, Miss.; Vicksburg and Jackson, Miss. Consecrated bishop coadjutor of Mississippi in 1919. Has written extensively on theological subjects for church magazines and journals.

GREEN BAY, a city of Wisconsin, in Brown co., of which it is the county seat. It is on the Chicago and Northwestern, the Chicago, Milwaukee and St. Paul, and other railroads, and on Green Bay and Fox rivers. The city is at the head of the lake and foot of river navigation. It has an excellent harbor and there is a large trade in lumber, coal, grain, flour, and machinery. There are several Roman Catholic and Lutheran parochial schools. A ship canal connects the Mississippi River with Lake Michigan, using the Wisconsin and Fox rivers. The cost of this was over $10,000,000.

GREEN EARTH, popular name for various soft minerals, specially *glauconite* (*q.v.*), celadonite, and chlorite.

GREEN MOUNTAINS. See APPALACHIAN MOUNTAINS.

GREEN MOUNTAIN BOYS, a band of Vermont men who took an active part in the Revolutionary War under the leadership of Ethan Allen, and defended the frontier against attacks from Canada. The corps was raised by Allen before the revolution to resist encroachments on Vermont territory made by the authorities of New York State, who claimed rights to it. At the outbreak of the war the Green Mountain Boys seized and held the British fortresses on the New York border.

GREEN RIVER, in Kentucky, rises near the State's center in Lincoln County and flows irregularly west, south and northwest through the western coal field of Kentucky to the Ohio river, of which it is a tributary, a few miles above Evansville, Ind. It is about 300 miles long and for some 200 miles from the Ohio is navigable for small steamers.

GREEN RIVER, in Wyoming, Utah and Colorado, rises in the Wild River Mountains of West Wyoming and flows south and east into Colorado, then generally south into Utah. There it joins the Grand river, one of the main forks of the Colorado. Its course forms a number of remarkable canyons in the Uinta Mountains. It is 720 miles long and drains an area of 47,220 sq. miles.

GREENAWAY, KATE (1846-1901), an English artist and illustrator of books in London. Her father was John G., an engraver and draughtsman. She studied at South Kensington and at the Slade Schools. In 1868 she first exhibited water-color drawings at the Dudley Gallery, London. In 1873 she began to illustrate for *Little Folks*, and commenced her series of Christmas cards for Marcus Ward; they were full of quaint beauty and charm, and became extremely popular. In 1877 she began to draw for the *Illustrated London News*. The charming freshness of her illustrations in her books, one of which, *Under the Window*, sold to the extent of 150,000 copies, made her famous. Her drawings of children dressed in the style of the early 19th century, are full of artistic grace and delicate quaintness. Among her best known illustrated books are: *A Birthday Book for Children*, *The Pied Piper of Hamlin*, *Mother Goose*, and *Little Ann*.

GREENBACK PARTY, a political party of the United States which favored greenbacks, or paper currency, to exchange for interest-bearing bonds. They called themselves the Independent Party. The rise in gold value of greenbacks, or paper currency after the Civil War caused much distress in the West where business was regulated to the high scale of prices prevalent in the war. The purpose of the Act of 1866 was to slowly retire greenbacks, and created much opposition. The further proposition in 1868, to make bonds, when no medium of payment was specified, paid in coin, developed the 'Ohio Idea.' This was that all bonds be paid in greenbacks at the government's option. The idea spread and controlled the Democratic Convention. Agitation over the greenback question was revived in 1874, and on November 25, a Greenback Convention met at Indianapolis to protest against the Resumption Act, and passed three resolutions: (1) All banks and corporations currency should be withdrawn, (2) That no currency be allowed except government paper and exchangeable on demand for 3.65 per cent bonds, (3) That coin should be paid only for interest on the national debt and for that part of the principal which promised it. In 1876 with hard-money, Samuel J. Tilden a prospective presidential candidate, the Greenback Party was formed and convened May 17, at Indianapolis. Peter Cooper of New York was nominated for president and Newton Booth of California for vice, but the latter declined, and was succeeded by Samuel F. Cary. Besides the three points mentioned the repeal of the Resumption Act of 1875 was demanded. In the election the Greenback vote was 81,737. In the States election the next year the vote was 187,095. The party then merged with the Greenback-Labor party.

GREENE, FRANCES NIMMO, educated at Tuscaloosa Female College. Taught for a number of years in public schools of Alabama. Has contributed largely to newspapers and magazines, short stories and other forms of fiction. Author, *King Arthur and His Court*, 1901; *Into the Night*, 1909; *The Right of the Strongest*, 1913; *The Devil to Pay*, 1917; *America First*, 1917; and *American Ideals*, 1921.

GREENE, FRANCIS VINTON (1850), army officer; *b*. Providence, R.I. Graduating from West Point in 1870, he entered the artillery as second lieutenant and was transferred to the engineers. He became major-general of volunteers in 1898. From 1877 to 1879 he served as U.S. military attaché at St. Petersburg, and was with the Russian army in the Russo-Turkish war, witnessing the decisive battle of Plevna among other engagements. He was police commissioner of New York City from 1903 to 1904. His contributions to military literature included works on Russia and her army, the Revolutionary War, Mississippi campaigns of the Civil War, and a life of Gen. Nath. Greene. *d*. 1921.

GREENE, JEROME DAVIS (1874), American banker. Graduated at Harvard in 1896; Harvard Law School, 1897-99. Secretary to president of Harvard 1901-05. Secretary to Harvard corporation 1905-10; General manager Rockefeller Institute of Medical Research, 1910-12. Associated with John D. Rockefeller in management of his business and philanthropic interests, 1912-14. Secretary Rockefeller Foundation 1913-17. Member of firm of Lee Higginson & Co. since 1918. Overseer of Harvard University, 1911-13, 1917-23.

GREENE, JOHN PRIEST (1849), American college president. Graduated from La Grange College, Mo., in 1872 and from Southern Baptist Theological Seminary in 1879. Ordained in Baptist ministry in 1872. President of William Jewell College, 1892 to 1920. Author of *Commentary in Pastoral Epistles*; *The Happy Man*, and *The Ideal Man*.

GREENE, NATHANIEL (1742-86), American soldier; *b* Patawomut, R.I. He worked as a child at the forge and on the farm, and educated himself in his spare moments. In 1770 he was chosen a member of the General Assembly for Coventry and thereafter engaged actively in public affairs. He was ardent in the cause of the Colonies against the British crown, and in 1775 was appointed as brigadier-general to command a Rhode Island contingent in the army at Boston. From that time he was not absent a day from military service until the end of the Revolutionary War. He was perhaps the ablest general of the Continental Army, next to Washington. He served with distinction at the battles of Harlem Heights, Trenton, Princeton, and Germantown. At Brandywine, his brilliant work alone preserved the army from utter destruction. From March 1778 until August 1780 he held the office of quartermaster-general, and in the latter year, resuming active service, won a brilliant victory at Springfield. In October of that year he took command of the Southern army, which was at the time utterly disorganized, and in less than a year, regained from the enemy nearly all the territory that they had conquered in Georgia and the Carolinas. In that remarkable campaign were included the battles of the Cowpens, Guilford Court House, Hobkirk's Hill and the drawn battle of Eutaw Springs. For his services in that zone of operations Congress gave him a medal, and the states of North and South Carolina and Georgia made him valuable grants of property. He died from sunstroke in 1786.

GREENE, ROBERT (1558-92), an English author of brilliant parts whose works were conspicuous in Elizabethan literature. He belongs to the early molders of the English novel, drama and lyric. His life was disreputable, but his profligacy was little reflected in his writings, which were marked by delicacy of spirit. He was educated at Cambridge, married a woman of good family, deserted her and lived with thieves and cutthroats. Like Shakespeare, he wrote plays for the Queen's actors; also prose romances, satires, finely wrought poems and pamphlets on crime based on his own wild life. His chief dramatic works are *Friar Bacon*, *Friar Bungay* and *James IV. of Scotland.*

GREENE, SARAH PRATT (1856), American author. Educated at Mt. Holyoke, Mass. Author: *Cape Cod Folks*, 1881; *Some Other Folks*, 1882; *Towhead*, 1883; *Last Chance Junction*, 1889; *Vesty of the Basins*, 1892; *The Moral Imbeciles*, 1898; *Winslow Plain*, 1902; and *Power Lot*, 1906.

GREENFIELD, the county seat of Franklin co., Mass. It is the trading center of a highly developed industrial and agricultural section of Western New England and is noted for its production of small tools. Principal industrial products, tools, silver ware, rakes, snow shovels, pocket books, hats, etc. There are five banks with combined resources amounting to twenty-one million dollars.

GREENGAGE, the name given to a certain kind of small round plum, grown especially for dessert. It is less hardy than some kinds, and requires shelter and a good deal of care in cultivation, which follows the same lines as those of the plum.

GREENLEAF, SIMON (1783-1853), Amer. lawyer; author of a *Treatise on the Law of Evidence*, 1842-53.

GREENLAND, Danish *Gronland* (70° N., 40° W.), large island belonging to Denmark; between Baffin Bay and Atlantic Ocean, N.E. of America; larger part in Arctic circle; stretches from 59° 45' N., beyond 82° - 83°; extreme length, about 1650 miles; greatest breadth, about 800 miles; area, 827,300 sq. miles; interior a lofty plateau, 9,000 to 10,000 ft. high covered by an ice cap, 1,000 ft. thick. Entire island likened to gigantic ice filled mountain rimmed bowl; highest peak, Petermann's Spitze, 9000 ft., near Franz Joseph Fjord; coast-line broken by numerous bays and fjords of great depth— Scoresby (180 miles long), South Strom, Petermann Fjords, Kane Basin, Inglefield Gulf, etc.; Disco, on west coast, is the largest of many islands; no large rivers; drainage mainly done by enormous glaciers, which move with surprising rapidity, and small streams of melted snow and ice; largest glaciers are Humboldt, Petowik, Jakobshaven, and Great Karajak; part of northeast and northwest coasts still unexplored. Fauna includes lemming, musk-ox, white wolf, polar bear, reindeer, fox, and hare; numerous birds; copse-woods on coast; climate colder on east coast owing to north polar current; west coast washed by Atlantic water. Principal settlements are Julianehaab (most southerly station), Frederikshaab, Godthaab, Sukkertoppen, Godhaven, Egedesminde, Kristianshaab, Jakobshaven, Umanak, and Upernivik (most northern settlement).

G. was first discovered by Norse settlers from Iceland, X. cent.; the Norwegian, Erik the Red, established two colonies, c. 986; under Norwegian rule, 1261; western settlements destroyed by Eskimos, XIV. cent.; rediscovered by John Davis, 1585-87, followed by Hudson, 1610, Baffin, 1616; Egede established several Dan. missionary stations on W. coast, 1721; Julianehaab founded, 1775; E. coast explored by Scoresby, 1822, Graah, 1829-30, 2nd Ger. North Pole Expedition, 1689-70, Nathorst, 1899, Amdrup, 1900. G. first crossed by Nansen (E. to W.), 1888; northern limits traced by Peary, 1892; exploration of inland ice by Nordenskiold, 1883, Von Drygalski, 1892, Garde, 1893; Mylius Erichsen, 1906-8, followed by Mikkelsen, 1909-12, explored extreme N.E. Principal exports: fish, fur, graphite and cryolite; copper, lead, iron, zinc are found. In 1931 deposits of excellent coal were found. Large cod and haddock fisheries on W. coast; trade a monopoly of Dan. Government. On the coast it is populated by Eskimos and some Danes. See MAP N. AMERICA.

GREENOCK (55° 56′ N., 4° 45′ W.), burgh, prosperous seaport and manufacturing town, on Clyde estuary, Renfrewshire, Scotland; picturesquely situated; birthplace of James Watt; head of large fishery district; shipbuilding is largely carried on, also iron-working, especially construction of boilers and engines; sailcloth and woolen factories; sugar-refining; rope-works, tanneries, etc.

GREENOUGH, HORATIO (1805-52), sculptor; b. Boston, Mass.; d. Somerville, Mass. He modeled in clay and worked at sculpture as a boy. After his graduation from Harvard he went to Rome to study, and thereafter spent most of his life in Italy. He executed, 1843, the great statue of Washington which fronts the Capitol at Washington, D. C., and also busts of John Quincy Adams, Chief Justice Marshall, Webster, Lafayette and Clay. His work includes a number of grouped figures, notably *The Rescue*, symbolizing the triumph of civilization which was also placed in Washington.

GREENSBORO, city of N. Carolina in Guilford co., of which it is the county seat. There are extensive manufactures of cotton and tobacco. The surrounding country produces large quantities of tobacco. It is the seat of the State College for Women, the Greensboro College for Women, Oak Ridge Military Institute and Guilford College. There are also three negro colleges. It is the home office of 12 insurance companies.

GREENSBURG, a city of Indiana, in Decatur co., of which it is the county seat. It is on the Cleveland, Cincinnati, Chicago and St. Louis railroad. The city is the center of an important agricultural and natural gas region, and in the neighborhood are important limestone quarries. The industries include flour mills, and a wire factory. Here is the State Odd Fellows' Home. There is a park and a public library.

GREENSBURG, a town of Pennsylvania, in Westmoreland co., of which it is the county seat. It is on the Pennsylvania Railroad. The surrounding country is rich in coal and natural gas. The city is an important industrial community and has a plant for the making of steam heating apparatus, steel works, glass works, nut and bolt works, etc.

GREENSLET, FERRIS (1875), grad. from Wesleyan University in 1897. Associate editor Atlantic Monthly, 1902-7. Literary adviser and director of Houghton, Mifflin and Co. since 1910. Author: *Joseph Glanville*, 1900; *The Quest of the Holy Grail*, 1902; *Walter*

Pater, 1903; *Life of Lowell*, 1905, and *Life of Thomas Bailey Aldrich*, 1908.

GREENVILLE, a city of Mississippi, in Washington co., of which it is the county seat. It is on the Yazoo and Mississippi Valley, and the Columbus and Greenville Ry. and on the Mississippi river. It is connected by steamboat with various parts of the river. There is a large trade in cotton, and the industries include cottonseed oil mills, cotton compresses, and lumber mills. The public institutions include parks and playgrounds and a public library.

GREENVILLE, a city of North Carolina, in Pitt co., of which it is the county seat. It is on the Norfolk Southern, and the Atlantic Coast railroads, and on the Tar river. The city is the center of an important tobacco, cotton, and corn growing district, and its industries include tobacco factories, cotton mills, and cottonseed oil mills. It is the seat of the East Carolina Teachers' Training School.

GREENVILLE, a city of Ohio, in Darke co. It is on the Cincinnati Northern, Dayton and Union, and the Pittsburgh, Cincinnati, Chicago and St. Louis railroads, and on Greenville creek. It has grain elevators and several industrial establishments. It is famous as being the scene of the signing of a treaty between the Indians and General Anthony Wayne

GREENVILLE, a borough of Pennsylvania, in Mercer co. It is on the Pennsylvania, the Erie, and the Bessemer and Lake Erie railroads, and on the Shenango river. It has important industries, including plants for the making of steel railroad cars, tanks, steel fabricating, flour, foundry and machine shop products. There are also extensive railroad shops. The borough is the seat of Thiel College.

GREENVILLE, a city of South Carolina, the seat of Greenville county, on Southern, Charleston & Western Carolina, Piedmont & Northern and Greenville and Northern railroads. It is the center of the textile manufacturing industry in South Carolina. Its industries also include manufacturing of fabricated steel, textile machinery; fabricated houses; automobile parts; underwear, medicine and food stuffs. Seat of Furman University, Greenville Woman's College; two business colleges. It has morning and evening newspapers, monthly publications, and so forth.

GREENVILLE, a city of Texas, in Hunt co., of which it is the county seat. It is on the Missouri, Kansas and Texas, the Texas Midland, and the St. Louis Southwestern railroads. The surrounding region is an extensive agricultural area. The industries include cottonseed oil mills and cotton compresses. It is the seat of Burleson College, Wesley College, and Holiness University.

GREENWICH (51° 28′ N., 0°), parliamentary borough, county of London, England, on S. bank of Thames; has celebrated Royal Observatory in G. park. G. Hospital (handsome building on site of royal palace) was made hospital for seamen by William and Mary; now Royal Naval Coll.

GREENWICH, a borough of Connecticut, in Fairfield co. It is a residential community and has many beautiful private residences. The borough is in a town of the same name.

GREENWOOD, a city of Mississippi, in Le Flore co., of which it is the county seat. It is on the Southern, and the Illinois Central railroads. The city is the center of an extensive cotton growing region and its industries include the manufacture of oil, cotton compresses, wagons, lumber, ice, etc. There is a Carnegie library, an Elks home and a court-house.

GREENWOOD, a city of South Carolina, in Greenwood co., of which it is the county seat. It is on the Seaboard Air Line, the Piedmont and Northern, and other railroads. Its industries include the manufacture of lumber, cottonseed oil, cotton, spools, etc. Here is Brewer Normal School for Negroes, the Lander Female College, and Bailey Military Institute.

GREER, DAVID HUMMELL (1844-1919), Episcopal bishop; b. Wheeling, W. Va.; d. New York City. He studied theology at Gambier Episcopal Seminary, Ohio, after graduating from Washington College, Pa., in 1862, and was ordained in 1868. His first ministries were in the South. Following them came a long tenure, 1871-85, of the rectorship of Grace Church, Providence, R.I., which he resigned to become rector of a leading church in New York City, St. Bartholomew's. In 1904 he was elected bishop-coadjutor of New York after declining three other bishoprics. He became head of that diocese in 1908, succeeding Bishop Potter, and held the office to his death.

GRÉGOIRE, HENRI (1750-1831),

Fr. politician and ecclesiastic; sided with Third Estate, 1789; bp. of Blois, 1790; advocated destruction of royal authority, but tried to prevent king's execution; wrote *Memoires, Historie des Sectes Religieuses,* and other works.

GREGORAS, NICEPHORUS (fl. 1300 - 60), Byzantine historian; his *Roman History* covers the period, 1204 to his death.

GREGORIAN CALENDAR. See CALENDAR.

GREGORIAN CHANT. See MUSIC.

GREGOROVIUS, FERDINAND (1821-91), Ger. historian; principal work, *History of the City of Rome in the Middle Ages,* 1859-72

GREGORY, name borne by sixteen popes and one antipope. The most important were the following:—

Gregory I., Saint, surnamed the Great (c. 540-604), was b. at Rome; inherited great wealth, which he devoted chiefly to service of Church; became a monk in one of monasteries founded by himself. Elected pope in 590. His *Liber Pastoralis* was one of the works trans. into Anglo-Saxon by order of Alfred the Great. His name is traditionally associated with *Gregorian chants.* G. was last Latin Father of Church.

Gregory II., Saint (d. 731); b. Rome; when deacon accompanied Pope Constantine to Constantinople as canonist; became pope, 715; sent St. Boniface as missionary to Germany; opposed the Gk. emperor's (Leo III.'s) taxation and proscription of image-worship.

Gregory VI. (d. 1047); archpriest of San Giovanni by the Latin Gate, and godfather of the profligate Benedict IX., from whom in innocence bought Papacy, 1045; deposed, 1046, for simony, and exiled to Germany; man of great learning and uprightness.

Gregory VII., Hildebrand (c. 1020-85), was the pope who did most to establish ecclesiastical supremacy of the Papacy, and laid foundations of its temporal power. Before his election as pope in 1073, he had directed the policy of the four preceding popes, had managed to place their election entirely in hands of cardinals, and was in reality the most prominent and influential man in the Church. With Henry IV., Holy Rom. emperor, who took oath of obedience in 1074, and subsequently repudiated it, he took a high-handed course; he deposed the simoniacal prelates appointed by the emperor and cited him to appear at Rome. When Henry retorted by getting his supporters to pronounce Hildebrand deposed, the latter excommunicated Henry; and the emperor found it necessary, in order to avoid deposition, to do penance at Canossa in Italy in 1077.

Gregory VIII. (*d.* 1121), antipope, 1118; banished from Rome in 1121.

Gregory VIII. (*d.* 1187), was pope for short time in 1187; concluded treaty of peace with Emperor Henry VI., and began to make arrangements for a crusade, but died before these were completed.

Gregory IX. (*d.* 1241), was elected pope, 1227. His pontificate is marked by long struggle against Emperor Frederick II., whom he excommunicated 1227. Dispute was afterwards renewed, and emperor again excommunicated in 1239. Frederick then prepared to besiege Rome, and was marching towards the city, when G. died.

Gregory X. (1208-76) was member of Visconti family; went on crusade; elected pope 1271; reunited Eastern and Western Churches.

Gregory XI. (1330-78) was elected to Papacy in 1370; retransferred papal see to Rome in 1397; tried to suppress heresy and to reform religious orders.

Gregory XIII. (1502-85), was elected pope, 1572; founded Jesuit College at Rome; reformed calendar (*q.v.*), 1582; strongly opposed heresy; built Gregorian Chapel at St. Peter's.

Gregory XVI. (1765-1846), was elected pope, 1831; an autocrat, he discouraged democracy on principle, but encouraged learning and research in all directions.

GREGORY, AUGUSTA, LADY (1853) an Irish author and playwright, born in Roxborough county Galway. She was one of the founders and chief supporter of the Irish National Theatre movement, and was the author of many plays, some of which were produced. She also published several books of poems and translations. *d.* 1932.

GREGORY, EDWARD JOHN (1850-1909), Eng. artist; Pres., R.W.S., 1898; excellent technique.

GREGORY, ST. (*c.* 213-70), bp. of Neocæsarea from 240; an energetic prelate and theologian; much increased the Church's strength during his episcopate.

GREGORY, ST., OF NAZIANZUS (329-89), called (like St. John) 'the Theologian'; wrote five orations, delivered against Macedonians and Eunomians in 379. G. was scarcely an original thinker, but a graceful and powerful expounder; also wrote poems and letters to Basil, bp. of Cæsarea. These two, with Gregory of Nyssa, are known as *Cappadocian fathers*.

GREGORY, ST., OF NYSSA (*c.* 331-86), bp. of Nyssa; one of 'Cappadocian fathers'; wrote many works, perhaps best is his *Catechetical Oration*.

GREGORY, ST., OF TOURS (530-94), theologian and historian; ordained 563; chosen bp. of Tours by people, 573; took part in various political quarrels of Merovingian kings; wrote several theological works, but greatest work is *History of the Franks*.

GREGORY, THE ILLUMINATOR (*fl.* 290), saint and abp. of Cæsarea; his history is partly legendary; said to have been brought up in Christian faith at Cæsarea.

GREGORY, THOMAS WATT (1861), lawyer; *b.* Crawfordsville, Miss. He was educated at the universities of Virginia and Texas and admitted in 1885 to the bar of the latter State, where he established a law practice in Austin. The State engaged him as counsel in prosecuting cases against its anti-trust laws, and in 1913 he had charge of the investigation and prosecution of the New Haven railroad as a special Assistant Attorney General of the federal government. From 1914 to 1919 he was Attorney General in President Wilson's cabinet, thereafter resuming law practice in New York City. *d.* 1933.

GREIZ (50° 39' N., 12° 13' E.), town, Germany, capital of Reuss (the Elder), on White Elster; woolen manufactures.

GRENADA (12° 5' N., 61° 40' W.), one of Brit. W. India Islands, most southerly of Windward (*q.v.*) group; mountainous; several crater lakes and mineral springs; very fertile, good climate; chief products—cocoa, fruit, spices, wool; capital, St. George; colonized by Fr., 1650; taken by British, 1762; held by French, 1779-83, then ceded to Britain. Area, 133 sq. miles.

GRENADE, earliest form of modern explosive shell. It was a ball of metal, or strong glass, filled with explosives, and exploded by a fuse; thrown by hand. SEE BOMBS.

GRENADIER, originally the name applied to the soldiers of a company attached to each regiment, who led the assault on trenches and ortresses, and hurled hand *grenades*.

GRENADINES (12° 45' N., 61° 15' W.), group of small islands, Brit. West Indies, between islands of Grenada and St. Vincent, and forming dependency of these islands; exports corn and cattle.

GRENFELL, (SIR) WILFRED THOMASON (1865), English missionary and explorer; *b.* Parkgate, near Chester, England. He was educated at Marlborough College of the University of London and Oxford University. He practiced medicine for some years in London, and in 1892 went to Labrador as superintendent of the Labrador Medical Mission, to which he has ever since devoted his life and labors. His daring and self sacrifice have earned him an international reputation. He has written voluminously concerning the work in which he was engaged. His publications include: *Off the Rocks*, 1906; *A Man's Faith*, 1908; *Labrador*, 1909; *Down to the Sea*, 1910; *What the Church Means to Me*, 1911; *On Immortality*, 1912; *The Attractive Way*, 1913; *The Prince of Life*, 1914; *Labrador Days*, 1919. He has contributed largely to religious and secular magazines and has written an autobiography under the title of *A Labrador Doctor*.

GRENOBLE (45° 12′ N., 5° 42′ E.), town, France, on river Isère; capital of Isère department; ancient *Gratianopolis*; old capital of Dauphiné; ceded to France, 1349; a Prot. stronghold; beautiful situation among mountains, near famous Chartreuse Monastery (*q.v.*); first-class fortress; has univ. and cathedral; manufactures kid gloves, liquor, cement, straw hats, etc.

GRENVILLE, GEORGE (1712-70), Brit. prime minister, 1763; attacked liberty of press in Wilkes' case, 1764; carried out imposition of Stamp Tax in colonies, 1765, the immediate cause of America's secession.

GRENVILLE, SIR RICHARD (*c.* 1541-91), Eng. mariner; commander of *Revenge* in expedition against Azores, 1591; had celebrated fight for fifteen hours against fifteen Span. ships; *d.* shortly after action.

GRESHAM, SIR THOMAS (1519-79), Eng. merchant; helped to consolidate and improve Eng. trade by building Royal Exchange, 1566-71; devoted much of his wealth to educational and charitable purposes.

GRESHAM, WALTER QUINTON (1832-95), statesman and jurist; *b.* Harrison County, Ind.; *d.* Washington, D.C. He studied at the Indiana State University, read law in Corydon, Ind., and was admitted to the bar in 1853. He served with distinction in the Civil War as lieutenant colonel of an Indiana regiment, being promoted by Grant and placed in charge of a brigade at Vicksburg. He also commanded a division in Sherman's march to the sea, and in 1864 retired as major-general of volunteers after being seriously wounded and disabled from service. In 1869 he was appointed a judge of the federal circuit court and in 1882 became postmaster-general. Two years later he was Secretary of the Treasury for a brief period, and again became a circuit judge. In 1893 President Cleveland made him his Secretary of State.

GRESSET, JEAN BAPTISTE LOUIS (1709-77), Fr. poet and dramatist; famed chiefly for his humorous poem, *Vert Vert*, 1734; *Oeuvres Completes*, 1811.

GRETNA, a city of Louisiana, in Jefferson parish, of which it is the parish seat. It is on the Missouri and Pacific, the Texas and Pacific, and other railroads. It has important industries including the manufacture of cottonseed oil, lard, soap, barrels, fertilizers, etc. Here is a Catholic college. The public buildings include a court-house.

GRETNA GREEN (55° N., 3° 3′ W.), village, Dumfriesshire, Scotland, near the Border; long famous for 'runaway' marriages—Eng. couples taking advantage of the greater ease with which the marriage ceremony could be performed in Scotland.

GREUZE, JEAN BAPTISTE (1725-1805), Fr. artist; famed for his genre pictures and female studies. His works, as a rule, have a moral tendency; among best known are *The Broken Pitcher* (Louvre), *Girl with Doves* (Wallace Collection), and *Girl with Dead Canary* (Scot. National Gallery).

GREVILLE, CHARLES CAVENDISH FULKE (1794-1865), Clerk of the Council in Ordinary, 1821-65; is famed for his *Memoirs*, pub. 1875-87, valuable for sidelights on social and official life in the first half of XIX. cent.

GRÉVY, FRANÇOIS PAUL JULES (1807-91), President of the French republic, *b.* at Moot-sous-Vaudrey Jura, and studied law in Paris, becoming an advocate in 1837. In 1848 he was elected by the republicans of his department to the constituent assembly, of which he became vice-president. He vigorously opposed the second empire under Louis Napoleon, and confined his attention to the bar till 1868, when he was returned as deputy for the Jura, and was elected president of the national assembly in 1871, being re-elected in 1876, 1877, and 1879. On the resignation of Marshal MacMahon in 1879, he was elected president of the republic. In 1885 he was re-elected for a further period of seven years, but, on the discovery of his son-in-law Daniel Wilson's dishonest traffic in the decorations of the Legion of Honor, he was obliged to resign office.

GREW, JOSEPH CLARK (1880), American diplomat. Graduated from Harvard in 1902. Deputy consul-general, Cairo, Egypt, 1904-06. 3rd Secretary of Embassy, Mexico City, 1906-7; St. Petersburg, 1907-8; Secretary, Embassy Berlin, 1912-16. Counsellor of Embassy at time of break of diplomatic relations with Austria-Hungary, Vienna, 1917. Secretary General of American Commission to negotiate peace, 1918. Appointed envoy and minister to Denmark in 1920 and to Switzerland in 1921. Appointed Ambassador to Turkey, 1927.

GREY, CHARLES, 2ND EARL GREY (1764-1845), Brit. politician; b. at Falloden, Northumberland; First Lord of Admiralty, 1806; after Fox's death became Foreign Sec. in 'All the Talents' ministry; succ. to earldom, 1807; carried act abolishing African slave trade. G. became Prime Minister in 1830; the Reform Bill was introduced by Lord John Russell, 1831, and carried, 1832, by G.'s obtaining royal permission to create sufficient peers to ensure its passing; retired, 1834.

GREY OF FALLODON, EDWARD, 1ST VISCOUNT (1862), Brit. statesman. Appointed under-secretary for foreign affairs, 1892-5, with Rosebery as his chief; secretary of state for foreign affairs, 1905-16. In 1907 concluded Anglo-Russian agreement, which settled outstanding Asiatic rivalries. Added to his reputation during Morocco crisis, 1909, and by inducing the belligerents in the Balkan War to sign the Peace of London, May 30, 1913. His earnest efforts to preserve peace after the Austrian ultimatum to Serbia are set forth in the White Paper issued in Aug. 1914. On Aug. 1 defined Britain's attitude in a masterly speech. Impaired vision necessitated a brief retirement from active duties in June 1915; cr. viscount, July 1916. On Asquith's resignation, Dec. 1916, Viscount Grey retired from Foreign Office. Lord Rector of Edinburgh Univ. 1920. d. 1933.

GREY FRIARS. See FRANCISCANS.

GREY, SIR GEORGE (1812-98), Brit. Colonial administrator, politician, and bibliophile; led exploring expeditions in N.W. and Western Australia, 1837-38; gov. of S. Australia, 1841, of New Zealand, 1846, conciliating the Maoris; gov. of Cape Colony, 1854-61; tried to federate South African States; crushed Kaffir revolt; gov., New Zealand, 1861;

ended Maori War, 1870; premier of New Zealand, 1877-84.

GREY, HENRY, 3RD EARL GREY (1802-94), Brit. politician; M.P., 1826; Colonial Under-Sec., 1832; War Sec., 1835; Colonial Sec., 1846-52; advocated emancipation of slaves; established free trade between colonies and mother country; opposed Crimean War.

GREY, LADY JANE (1537-54), Eng. 'Nine days' Queen'; granddau. of Henry VIII.'s sister Mary; early acquired wide knowledge of classical and modern languages; m. Lord Guildford Dudley, whose f., Duke of Northumberland, proclaimed her Queen in 1553; but on Mary's accession she was sent to Tower; beheaded, 1554.

GREY, ZANE (1872), author; b. Zanesville, Ohio, where he received a high school education, studying later at the University of Pennsylvania. He came to New York City and in 1904 embarked on a literary career with the publication of Betty Zane, a novel of Western life and the forerunner of a number of like stories of the plains, desert, lonely trails and forests, which earned him considerable popularity. In 1921 appeared The Call of the Canyon; in 1922, The Vanishing American, and in 1923, Wanderer of the Wasteland.

GREYHOUND, dog of Eastern origin, thoroughbred racer; run in many coursing meetings in this country; Scotch, Italian, Irish, and English breeds.

GREYTOWN (1) called also San Juan del Norte, a tn. and port of Nicaragua on the Caribbean Sea, at the mouth of the San Juan R. It is a port of call for mail packets, and monopolizes the import and export trade of the country. Pop. 2,500. (2) A tn. of Natal in the Umvoti Valley, 65 m. S.W. of Pietermaritzburg.

GRIDLEY, CHARLES VERNON (1845-98), naval officer; b. Logansport, Ind.; d. Kobe, Japan. He graduated from the U.S. Naval Academy in 1863, when he joined the sloop-of-war Oneida and shared in the operations of the West Gulf Squadron in the Civil War. He was an instructor at the Naval Academy from 1875 to 1879 and subsequently filled various naval posts until 1897, when he became captain and was assigned to command the Olympia, flagship of the Asiatic squadron. Admiral Dewey, who commanded the squadron, made him one of his chief advisers. The Olympia took part in the battle of Manila Bay in the Spanish-American War of 1898, and Gridley was seriously injured while conducting her fight from the conning tower. He died a few weeks after.

GRIEG, EDVARD HAGERUP (1843-1907), Nor. composer and pianist; of Scot. descent; *b.* Bergen; studied at Leipzig under Richter and Reinecke; Copenhagen, under Gade; excelled in shorter pianoforte pieces and songs; most popular work, *Peer Gynt* music.

GRIERSON, SIR JAMES MON-CRIEFF (1859-1914), Brit. general; distinguished himself in S. African War at capture of Johannesburg and Pretoria, 1900; on Count Waldersee's staff in China, 1900-1; sent to France to command a corps in the World War, 1914, but died before taking up duties; wrote *The Armed Strength of Russia, Germany, and Japan*; *Staff Duties in the Field*, 1891; *Records of the Scottish Volunteers*, 1909.

GRIFFIN, a city of Georgia, in Spalding co., of which it is the county seat. It is on the Central of Georgia and Southern railroads. Its industries include canning, and the manufacture of cotton. Here is a State Agricultural Experiment Station.

GRIFFIN, GERALD (1803-40), Irish novelist; author of *The Collegians*, 1829, upon which Boucicault founded *The Colleen Bawn*; also other novels, plays, and lyrics.

GRIFFIN, GRYPHON, mythical monster which was said to guard the earth's treasures. It is usually represented as having the body and hind legs of a lion and the wings and beak of an eagle; a figure in heraldry.

GRIFFIS, WILLIAM ELLIOT (1843), Congregational minister and Oriental authority; *b.* Philadelphia, Pa. He saw service in the Civil War, after which he studied at Rutgers College and in 1870 went to Japan to apply American methods to schools there. From 1872 to 1874 he was professor of physical sciences at the Imperial University, and introduced technical education into Japan. Returning to the United States, he studied for the ministry, graduating from the Union Theological Seminary in 1877, and filled pastorates until 1903, when he turned to literature to promote a better understanding of Oriental civilization. His publications chiefly embrace works on Japan, China and Corea. *d.* 1928

GRIFFITH, ARTHUR (1872-1922), President of the Irish Parliament and founder of Sinn Fein; *b.* Dublin; *d.* there. He was the son of a Roman Catholic compositor who belonged to an old Irish family, despite his supposedly Welsh name, and began life setting type and reading proofs on a Dublin news-paper. While at this work he acquired an acquaintance with foreign languages, metaphysics, mathematics, science and history. He revised school books, and had an ambition to become a philologist and compile a polyglot dictionary. He managed to get abroad, studying at a continental university, and wandered as far as South Africa, where he worked in a diamond mine. After a study of European conditions, especially the Magyar problem in Austria-Hungary, he returned to his native land about 1890 swayed by the belief that Ireland must solve her troubles by taking her cue from the Magyars. He established his famous weekly, the *United Irishman*, which was frequently suppressed, and in 1905 founded the Sinn Fein (*Ourselves*) organization and launched its principle as a national doctrine.

The new patriotic organization did not make much headway until 1916, when the undercurrents of its strength came to the surface and produced the Easter rebellion of that year. The Sinn Fein party swept the Irish elections in 1918, and elected him member of Parliament for Cavan. He was an outstanding figure in the subsequent negotiations with the British Government for securing Irish independence to end the revolutionary struggle and bloodshed that rent Ireland after Sinn Fein's triumph at the polls. With the establishment of an Irish Parliament, he was elected President of the Dail Eireann in January, 1922, after the republican leader, De Valera (*q.v.*) and his followers had deserted the House. He died the following August.

GRIFFITH, DAVID (LEWELYN) WARK (1880), a moving picture director, *b.* in La Grange, Ky. He was educated in the public schools and for several years was on the stage as an actor. He first took part in moving pictures in 1908 as an actor and then became a director. He was among the first of the moving picture directors to show appreciation of the possibilities of the screen and his productions were of unusual excellence. They include, *Birth of a Nation, Broken Blossoms,* and *Orphans of the Storm*. During the World War he was chairman of the War Cooperative Commission.

GRIFFITH, SIR RICHARD JOHN (1784-1878), Irish geologist; carried out boundary survey of Ireland, completed, 1844.

GRIGGS, EDWARD HOWARD (1868), educator and lecturer; *b.* Owatonna, Minn. He graduated from Indiana University, where he also taught Eng. literature, 1889-91. Afterwards he became professor of that department, serving for two years, meantime giving instruction in ethics at Leland Stanford. He was professor of ethics at the latter university from 1893 to 1897, later heading the department of education as well. In 1899 he became known as a university lecturer, giving extension courses throughout the United States and Canada, and also as a writer. He lectured on Dante, great autobiographies, Italian cities, human progress, Maeterlinck, moral leaders, Plato's philosophy and Browning, his lectures on these and other subjects being afterwards published in a series of handbooks. He also edited and contributed to B. W. Huebsch's *Art of Life* series. His more lengthy works include *Moral Education, The New Humanism, Philosophy of Art,* and *The Soul of Democracy.*

GRIGGS, JOHN WILLIAM (1849), lawyer; *b.* Newton, N.J. He began practicing law in Paterson, N.J. after his graduation from Lafayette College in 1868 and his admission to the bar in 1871. He was a member of the New Jersey legislature from 1876 to 1888, serving both in the general assembly and senate, and in 1896 became governor of the State, resigning in January, 1898, when President McKinley appointed him to his cabinet as Attorney General. He relinquished that office in 1901 to join the Permanent Court of Arbitration at The Hague and officiated as a member of that tribunal till 1908. Later he resumed the practice of law in New York City and became identified with large business interests. *d.* 1927.

GRILLE (Fr.), metal screen or grating; usually fitted into a door for purpose of observation.

GRILLPARZER, FRANZ (1791-1872), Austrian dramatist and poet; regarded as perhaps the greatest dramatic poet of his country; his plays include *Sappho,* 1819; and *Das Goldene Vlies,* 1821; *Konig Ottokar's Gluck und Ende,* 1825; *Des Meeres und der Liebe Wellen,* 1840, and others.

GRIMALDI, GIOVANNI FRANCESCO (1606-80), Ital. artist and architect; hist. subjects, portraits, and landscapes; architect to the popes.

GRIMM, FRIEDRICH MELCHIOR, BARON VON (1723-1807), Ger. author; famed for his *Correspondance Litteraire,* an invaluable commentary on contemporary events; lived mostly in Paris.

GRIMM, JACOB LUDWIG KARL (1785-1863), Ger. philologist; *b.* at Hanau; first important appointment was that of librarian to King Jérôme at Wilhelmshöhe in 1806. In 1816 he joined his bro., Wilhelm Karl, 1786-1859, at the Cassel library as sub-librarian. The lives of the bro's were devoted to a scientific study of the Ger. languages and folk-lores, and their researches were epoch-making. They collaborated in the famous collection of fairy-tales. Jacob wrote a *Deutsche Grammatik, Geschichte der Deutschen Sprache,* and a *Deutsche Mythologie.*—Grimm's Law, term loosely applied to rules regulating 'consonantshift' in various Indo-European languages. The elder G. applied it to the change into Teutonic dialect, then into High German, (*e.g.*) Lat. *pater,* English (from Teuton dialect) *father,* German *vater;* Latin *tu,* English *thou,* German *du.*

GRIMM'S LAW. See GRIMM, JACOB L. K.

GRIMSBY, GREAT GRIMSBY (53° 34' N., 0° 4' W.), seaport, on Humber, Lincolnshire, England; important commerce; chief fishing port in country; has docks covering area of about 150 acres. Industries include shipbuilding, brewing, tanning, flax-dressing.

GRIMSEL PASS, situated in the Bernese Alps, Switzerland. It is over 7,000 ft. high, and leads to the valley of the Aar, being crossed by a carriage road. At the foot of the pass is the Grimsel Hospice. It was here that the French were victorious over the Austrians in 1799.

GRINDAL, EDMUND (*c.* 1519-83), Eng. abp.; engaged in religious disputation, 1549; was one of clerics who examined the Forty-two Articles, 1552; cr. bp. of London, 1559; abp. of York, 1570; of Canterbury, 1575.

GRINDING. See ABRASIVES.

GRINGOIRE, PIERRE (*c.* 1480-1539), Fr. poet and dramatist; author of satirical comedies directed against Pope Julius II., the enemies of Louis XII., and the vices of society; subject of play by T. de Banville.

GRINNELL, a city of Iowa, in Poweshiek co. It is on the Chicago, Rock Island and Pacific, and the Minneapolis and St. Louis railroads. Its industries include the manufacture of gloves, washing machines, cab bodies, etc. There is a public library. The city is the seat of Grinnell College.

GRINNELL, GEORGE BIRD (1849); ethnologist and author; *b.* Brooklyn, N.Y. He graduated from Yale in 1870 and from 1874 to 1880 was assistant in osteology at the Peabody Museum,

New Haven, Conn. He edited *Forest and Stream* from 1876 to 1911, and for most of that period was also its president. In 1886 he founded the Audubon Society. His publications embrace about twenty volumes, chiefly on ethnological subjects relating to the Indians and the early West.

GRINNELL LAND, an Arctic region above Baffin Bay and adjacent to the northwest part of Greenland, from which it is divided by Kennedy Channel. A large portion of this tract is known in Europe as Ellesmere Land; the remainder, to the north, is called Grant Land. The name of Grinnell Land has also been attached to a tongue of land stretching to the northwest of North Devon, an island to the south of Ellesmere Land. The regions were so named in honor of Henry Grinnell, who equipped two American expeditions in search of Sir John Franklin in 1850 and 1853. With Greenland the larger Grinnell Land is the most northerly region of the earth. It has a snow-free area in summer of 1,000 sq. miles, covered with luxuriant vegetation. The fox, wolf, musk-ox, reindeer, ermine and hare are among its fauna. Peary visited it in 1898-9. In 1881-4 Lieut. Greely, U.S.A., afterwards rescued by Commander Schley, went up Kennedy Channel and explored Grinnell Land westward.

GRIQUALAND EAST and GRIQUALAND WEST, divisions of the Cape Province, Union of South Africa.

GRISELDA, GRISELDIS, female character, immortalized by her patience and virtue, in Boccaccio's *Decameron*; derived thence by Chaucer (*Clerkes Tale*); subject of a ballad, *Patient Grissel*, 1565.

GRISI, GIULIA (1811-69), Ital. prima donna; sang in Paris, London, and New York.

GRISONS (46° 40' N., 9° 30' E.), most easterly canton of Switzerland; largest, but most thinly populated; chief town, Coire or Chur. Juf and St. Moritz are among highest villages in Alps. Principal industry, cattle breeding; maize and chestnuts grown; wine produced; mineral springs found; climate severe. Canton is visited yearly by great numbers of tourists, especially at Davos, Arosa, and Engadine; has few railways, but many fine roads. Ger., Ital., and Romansch dialects spoken.

GRISWOLD, ALEXANDER VIETS (1766-1843), Episcopal bishop; *b.* Sunsbury, Conn.; *d.* Boston, Mass. He was ordained in 1795. For twenty-six years, 1804-30, he was rector of St. Michael's Church, Bristol, R.I. and the following five years of St. Peter's, Salem, Mass. In 1811 he became the first bishop of the eastern diocese of the Episcopal Church as then organized, officiating as such in conjunction with the rectorships he held.

GRISWOLD, RUFUS WILMOT (1815-57), Amer. editor; pub. *Poets and Poetry of America*, 1842, and other anthologies; also biographical and critical editions of Poe and other writers.

GRISWOLD, SHELDON MUNSON (1861), American bishop. Graduated from Union College in 1882 and from the General Theological Seminary in 1885. Ordained in 1885. Rector of churches in Ilion, N.Y., Little Falls, N.Y., and Hudson, N.Y. Elected missionary bishop of Salina in 1902. Suffragen bishop of Chicago, in 1917.

GRIZZLY BEAR. See BEAR.

GROAT, mediæval, thick, silver coin, worth four-pence, first issued in England in XIV. cent., and in circulation until latter half of XVII. cent.

GROCYN, WILLIAM (c. 1446-1519), Eng. scholar and ecclesiastic; Gk. lecturer at Oxford; prebendary of Lincoln, 1485.

GRODNO. (1) Prov., Poland, was annexed by Russia after Polish 'partition', 1795; surface flat, covered with forests, chiefly pine, and swamps; chief rivers, Niemen, W. Bug, Narev, and Bobr; center of woolen industry. Area c. 14,900 sq. m.; pop. 2,000,000. (2) Fort. tn. (53° 40' N., 23° 50' E.), on Niemen, 533 m. by rail from Petrograd; important railway and road junction; anc. palace of Polish kings and more modern palace built by August III.; manufactures tobacco and has considerable trade in timber. Pop. 34,916. In Feb. 1915 the Germans reached the Niemen, N. of Grodno, and on Sept. 2 the fortress fell after a brief defense by the Russian rearguard.

GROIN, in human anatomy the fold between the lower part of the abdomen and the thigh; in arch. the curve formed by the intersection of two arches.

GROLL, ALBERT LOREY (1866) American painter. Educated at Royal Academy, Munich. Was a landscape artist and has been awarded many prizes and medals including St. Louis Exposition, 1904; Buenos Aires and Santiago Expositions, 1910; Inness Gold Medal, 1911; San Francisco Exposition, 1915. His works are to be seen in the Corcoran Art Gallery, Washington; Minneapolis Museum; National Gallery, Washington;

New York Water Color Club and various other galleries of the country.

GRONINGEN (53° 13' N., 6° 35' E.), province, N.E. Holland; low and flat; rich pastures; climate damp; chief occupation dairy-farming and grazing; some fishing and boat-building. Area, 909 sq. miles.

GRONINGEN (53° 13' N., 6° 34' E.), town, Holland; capital of G. province, at junction of Drentsche Aa and Hunse; Martini-kerk, 1477, Brœder-kerk, town hall, antiquity museum, univ. 1614, fine art academy and many XVI.- and XVII.-cent. houses.

GRONNA, ASLE J. (1858-1922), U.S. Senator and farmer; b. Elkader, Iowa. He became identified with agriculture and banking pursuits in the Dakotas for many years and was politically affiliated with North Dakota, to whose territorial legislature he was elected in 1889. After serving in the U.S. House of Representatives from 1905 to 1911 as a member from that State, he was selected as Senator to fill the vacancy caused by this death of Martin N. Johnson. He was re-elected for the term 1915-21, and at its expiration retired through failing health.

GROS, ANTOINE JEAN, BARON (1771-1835), a French painter, b. in Paris, was the son of a miniature painter. He studied first at David's studio, and afterwards traveled in Italy where he became acquainted with Napoleon Bonaparte, having been introduced by Josephine. He was given an official position by Bonaparte and became a military painter. In 1824 he was made a baron by Charles X. for his paintings in the Pantheon. He committed suicide by throwing himself in the Seine. His best pictures are: *Bonaparte at the Bridge of Arcole*; *Napoleon visiting the Plague-stricken at Jaffa*; *The Battle of Eylau*; *The Meeting of Charles V. and Francis I.*, and among his classic style, *Hercules and Diomedes*.

GROSBEAK, the name applied to some of the species of the family Fringillidæ, belonging to the order Passeriformes, and including the various kinds of finches. In these birds the beak is stout and very much developed. Among the species may be mentioned the Pine G. (*Pyrrhula enucleator*), found in the regions of the N., and the Hawfinch (*Coccothraustus vulgaris*), occasionally found in Britain.

GROSS, SAMUEL D. (1805-84), an American surgeon, b. at Easton, Pa. He was for many years professor of surgery at the Jefferson Medical College, Philadelphia, and was the author of many books on surgery. In 1861 he was president of the American Medical Association.

GROSSMITH, GEORGE (1847-1912), Eng. comedian; associated with the operas of Gilbert and Sullivan.

GROSSTESTE, ROBERT (c. 1175-1253), an English scholar. He studied at Oxford and Paris and became a master of Hebrew and Greek languages. He was lecturer at Oxford for many years and his reputation for learning spread throughout Europe. In 1235 he was elected Bishop of Lincoln, but quarreled with Pope Innocent IV. on the question of bestowing English benefices on foreigners. He wrote much and some of his writings have been published.

GROSSWARDEIN (Hungarian *Nagyvarad*), an old tn. of Hungary, cap. of Bihar, on the Rapid Körös, about 150 m. S.E. of Budapest. It contains an old fortress and many public buildings, among them two bishops' palaces, as it is the seat of both Roman Catholic and Greek Catholic bishops. Near to this town are hot mineral springs.

GROSVENOR, EDWIN AUGUSTUS (1845), historian and college professor; b. Newburyport, Mass. He was a graduate of Amherst College and from 1873 to 1890 occupied the chair of history at Robert College, Constantinople. He returned to Amherst in 1892 as professor of European history, and later of modern government. He also taught history at Smith College. His publications include translations from the French on historical subjects, works on Constantinople, and a survey of contemporary history.

GROSVENOR, GILBERT HOVEY (1875), geographer and editor; b. Constantinople, Turkey. In 1890 he graduated from Robert College, Constantinople, and later studied at Amherst. In 1903 he was appointed editor of the National Geographic Magazine after serving as assistant and managing editor, meantime also becoming a director of the National Geographic Society. He wrote on modern explorations and on Peary's polar expeditions and edited *Scenes from Every Land.*

GROTE, GEORGE (1794-1871), Eng. historian; b. at Clay Hill, Kent; M.P., 1832-41; began systematic study of Gk. history in 1822; pub. famous *History of Greece*, in 12 vol's, 1846-56; also wrote *Plato and other Companions of Socrates*, *Aristotle*, and some minor works. G. was prominent supporter of Univ. Coll.,

London, and of Univ. of London, becoming vice-chancellor in 1862; buried in Westminster Abbey. His democratic views well fitted him to interpret Athenian history and culture.

GROTEFEND, GEORG FRIEDRICH (1775-1853), Ger. scholar; famed for his successful deciphering of the Babylonian cuneiform writing.

GROTESQUE, extravagant style of ornament containing unnatural forms of animals, the human figure, etc.

GROTIUS, HUGO, HUIG VAN GROOT (1583-1645), Dutch politician and jurist; b. Delft; entered profession of law; wrote Latin plays and verses; app. historiographer to United Provinces, 1603; sent to England to make arrangements concerning Greenland whale fisheries, 1613. In the disputes in Holland between rigid Calvinists and the followers of Arminius, G. tried to restrain the Calvinist clergy by maintaining supremacy of State in Church affairs, and composed edict counselling toleration, the publication of which aroused popular resentment. G. was arrested and sentenced to lifelong confinement; but his wife, who shared his imprisonment, soon afterwards contrived his escape; going to Paris, G. later held the post of Swed. ambassador. His most celebrated works are *De Jure Belli et Pacis*, a treatise on jurisprudence, and *Annales et Historiae de Rebus Belgicis*, an historical work.

GROTON, a town of Connecticut, in New London co. It is on the Thames River and on Long Island Sound, and is opposite New London. Here was Fort Griswold which is famous for the massacre of an American garrison by the British, in 1781.

GROUCHY, EMMANUEL, MARQUIS DE (1766—1847), Fr. soldier; supported Revolution and rose rapidly in republican army; distinguished at *Hohenlinden*, *Wagram*, and in Russia in 1812; marshal, 1814; defeated Blücher at *Ligny*; exiled from France after *Waterloo*, returning in 1821.

GROUND-NUT, a term often applied to the edible parts of the roots of various plants. Amongst the best known may be mentioned the earth nut (*Bunium esculentum*) and the roots of the *Apios tuberosa*.

GROUND-RENT, in Eng. law, is the rent paid to the owner of the freehold in the ground.

GROUP INSURANCE. See INSURANCE.

GROUPS, THEORY OF, a branch of mathematics dealing with the sets of operations which may be performed on a given set of objects; has wide applications in higher mathematics, notably in the theory of invariants, of algebraic and especially of differential equations, of geometrical transformations, etc.

GROUSE include black g. (*Tetrao tetrix*) and red g. (*Lagopus scoticus*), so named from color of male plumage. They inhabit moorland areas; birds of strong but heavy flight; cock is polygamous, fighting for mates; nest on ground, open, containing from six to ten eggs; males of the two species further distinguished by lyrate curvature of tailfeathers in black g.

GROVE, SIR GEORGE (1820-1900); Brit. publicist; chiefly wrote about Palestine exploration and music; secretary, Crystal Palace, 1852; director, Royal College of Music. *Dictionary of Music* and other works.

GROVE CITY COLLEGE, a co-educational, non-sectarian institution situated at Grove City, Pa. It was founded in 1876. Campus of 600 acres, has 9 college buildings. Annual enrollment is approx. 680 students. Music, Commerce, Science.

GROW, GALUSHA AARON (1823-1907), member of Congress; b. Windham County, Conn.; d. Glenwood, Pa. He practiced law in Susquehanna County, Pa. after graduating from Amherst College in 1844, and six years later was elected to the House of Representatives, serving till 1863, first as a Free-Soil Democrat, then as a Republican. He was Speaker from 1861 to 1863 and effected the passage of the Homestead Law after a ten-years' fight. He was Congressman-at-large from Pennsylvania from 1894 to 1903, when he retired.

GRUB, the larvæ of insects, or more particularly the underground larvæ of Crane Flies or Daddy-long-legs, known as 'the grub'—destructive to corn crops.

GRUB STREET, former name of Milton Street, near Moorfields, London, where in Dr. Johnson's time lived colony of needy hack-writers, penny-a-liners, 'whence any mean product is called G.S.'

GRUMENTUM (40° 20′ N., 16° 30′ E.), ancient town, Lucania, S. Italy, on Aciris.

GRUNDY, MRS., character in Morton's play, *Speed the Plough*, 1800, who does not appear, but whose opinion is much feared by a neighboring farmer's wife; hence the Eng. archetype of puritanical prudery and straight-laced conventionality.

GRUYERE (46° 35′ N., 7° 5′ E.), town, Fribourg, Switzerland; famous cheese.

GRYPHIUS, ANDREAS (1616-64), Ger. poet and dramatist; wrote lyric poetry of considerable merit; the former including *Peter Squenz*, *Horribilicribrifax*, etc.; the latter, *Carolus Stuardus*, *Katharina von Georgien*, and others.

GUACHARO, or OIL BIRD (*Steatornis*), a Picarian bird confined to Trinidad and the coastal region of the N.W. of South America; so called on account of the fat contained in the nestlings, which is used for lighting and as a butter-substitute by the natives; a twilight feeder, which nests in caves.

GUADALAJARA (40° 50′ N., 3° W.), province, Spain; generally level; fertile; traversed by Tagus; produce chiefly agricultural; area, 4676 sq. miles. Pop. 210,000. Capital, Guadalajara; has fine old ruined palace; cotton and woolen industries.

GUADALAJARA (21° 9′ N., 103° 2′ W.), town, Mexico; capital of Jalisco State; contains cathedral, univ., art academy, mint; many interesting churches; various charitable institutions; important trade, cotton, woolen, iron, and steel manufactures, leather, pottery.

GUADALQUIVIR (36° 47′ N., 6° 22′ W.), river, Spain; rises in Sierra de Cazorla; flows S.W. for 360 miles, into Atlantic; navigable to Seville; ancient *Baetis*.

GUADELOUPE (16° 12′ N., 61° 40′ W.), island in Lesser Antilles (W. Indies), forming important Fr. colony with five island dependencies; capital, Basse Terre; climate hot, but healthy; soil fertile and well cultivated. Sugar, coffee, and rum are exported. G. was discovered by Columbus; acquired by France, 1634; taken by British, 1794, 1810; restored to France, 1814. Area, 687 sq. miles.

GUADIANA (37° 10′ N., 7° 20′ W.), river, Spain and Portugal; rises in Span. province, Albaceté; flows through Ciudad Real, Badajoz, and Portug. province Alemtejo; separates Huelva from Portug. province Algarve; falls into Atlantic; length, 500 miles; navigable 40 miles above mouth; ancient *Anas*.

GUADIX (37° 19′ N., 3° 8′ W.), town, Granada, Spain.

GUADUAS (c. 5° S., 74° 50′ W.), town, Colombia, S. America, near Magdalena River, 50 miles N.W. of Bogotá.

GUAIACUM, genus of trees, natural order *Zygophylleae*; dark greenish, dense, hard wood heavier than water. The heart wood and resin of *G. officinale* and of *G. jankum* from the W. Indies have an acrid and aromatic taste and a balsamic odor.

GUALEGUAYCHÚ (33° 2′ S., 58° 34′ W.), town, river port, Argentina, S. America, on Rio Gualeguaychú; meat products, hides.

GUAM, the largest of the Ladrone Islands, also known as the Mariana Archipelago, and was occupied by the United States in 1898. Located lat. 13° 26′; long. 44° 43′ E. It is 32 miles long and 4 to 10 miles wide, and the area is about 210 sq. miles. The southern part is hilly; the northern part a coral formed plateau. About 30,000 acres are cultivated. The forests are rich in fine woods and also furnish coconuts, pineapples, bread fruit, and custard apples. The fields produce rice, hemp, tobacco, cacao, coffee, melons, etc. The only native mammals are rats, bats, and flying foxes. Goats were introduced and have largely multiplied, and there are some deer. The island has no snakes and the scorpions and centipedes are harmless. Cows and pigs flourish from the abundant food. There is much rain, but the climate is temperate except in midsummer. Heavy storms are frequent and a typhoon July 6, 1918 ruined crops and deprived most of the inhabitants of their homes. The people call themselves Chamorros, speaking a Malay dialect. The majority are in villages. The chief harbors are Apra and Tarofofo. In 1930 the population was 18,509. 1,118 Americans are residents. Agana is the capital. The island is under the U.S. Navy Dept. as a navy station, the governor being a naval officer appointed by the president. See Map, Asia.

GUAN (*Penelope*), a native of tropical America, is a handsome relative of common poultry bird; of blackish-bronze color, with naked throat furnished with large pendant scarlet wattle.

GUANABACOA (23° 7′ N., 82° 19′ W.), town, sea bathing resort, Cuba, West Indies; residential suburb, 5 miles E. of Havana.

GUANACO, HUANACO, animal included in *Camelidae*; native throughout southern half of S. America; smaller and thicker set than camel, and without, hump.

GUANAJUATO (21° N., 100° 48′ W.), inland state, Mexico; mountainous in N., the southern portion forming part of a fertile plain; chief river, Rio Grande de Lerma; very rich in minerals, gold, silver, lead, tin, iron; some cattle reared; cotton and woolen manufactures, tanneries. Area, 11,374 sq. miles.

GUANAJUATO, SANTA F ÉDE GUANAJUATO (21° N., 100° 48′ W.), city, capital of G. State, Mexico; center of large mining district; manufactures cotton, pottery; founded by Spaniards, 1554.

GUANCHES, GUANCHOS, original inhabitants of the Canary Islands; supposed to have been of Berber stock, of fine physique, and a highly intelligent race; now practically extinct.

GUANO, valuable fertilizing manure, consisting chiefly of the excrement of sea-birds that feed on fish. Deposits to a depth of 60 ft. have been found off the coast of Peru, Bolivia, and Chile. A good substitute has been found in fish g., obtained by grinding to powder the heads and bones of cod and herring. The chief constituents of g. are phosphoric acid and nitrogen (ammonia).

GUANTA (10° 6′ N., 64° 47′ W.), seaport town, Bermudez State, Venezuela, S. America; exports coffee, sugar.

GUANTANAMO, a town in the chief coffee-growing district of Cuba, 13 m. N. of Caimanera, its port, and 49 m. E. of Santiago de Cuba. One of the four naval stations ceded to the United States by Cuba in 1901. Exports sugar and lumber.

GUAPORE, a river of South America, rising in the Brazilian province of Matto Grosso. After a course of about 500 miles it unites with the Mamore and forms the Madeira river.

GUARANIS, S. American Indians inhabiting Paraguay and Uruguay.

GUARANTEE, a promise by one person to be answerable for the debt, default, or miscarriage of another. Originally at common law it need not be in writing, but the Statute of Frauds provided that 'no action shall be brought whereby to charge the defendant upon any special promise to answer for the debt, default, or miscarriages of another person, unless the agreement upon which such action shall be brought or such memorandum or note thereof shall be in writing and signed by the party to be charged therewith, or some other person thereunto lawfully authorized.'

GUARATINGUETA (22° 45′ S., 45° 15′ W.), city, São Paulo, Brazil, S. America, on Parahiba; agricultural center.

GUARD, COAST. See COAST GUARD.

GUARD, NATIONAL. See ARMY, UNITED STATES.

GUARDAFUI, CAPE (10° 50′ N., 51° 20′ E.), cape, N.E. of Abyssinia, Africa.

GUARDI, FRANCESCO (1712-93), Venetian artist; prolific painter, whose works are similar to those of his master, Canaletto; fine examples in Louvre and Manfrini Palace, Venice.

GUARDIAN, a custodian in law of persons incapable of caring for themselves, and especially persons under 21 years of age. A guardian is entitled to the care and custody of the person in his ward and must give a careful accounting of disbursements and receipts. Trust companies are largely employed in the business of guardianship.

GUÁRICO (8° 30′ N., 67° 30′ W.), state, Venezuela, S. America; Capital, Calabozo. Area, 25,631 sq. miles.

GUARINI, GIOVANNI BATTISTA (1537-1612), Ital. poet; friend of Tasso, whom he succ. as court poet at Ferrara. His masterpiece is *Pastor Fido,* 1590, a pastoral drama, the scene of which is laid in Arcadia. The literary style is highly finished, and the work is invaluable as a picture of contemporary manners and vices.

GUARINO DA VERONA, GUARINUS (1374-1460), Ital. scholar; an important figure in connection with the revival of Gk. learning in Italy; translated and wrote commentaries on Gk. authors.

GUARNIERI, JOSEPH DEL GESU, GUARNERI (1687-1745), principal member of a Cremona family of famous violin-makers.

GUATEMALA. (1) Republic of Central America, bounded by Mexico, Brit. Honduras, Gulf and Republic of Honduras, Salvador, and Pacific Ocean; cap. Guatemala la Nueva. Surface consists of low-lying marshy plains along Pacific coast. N. and W. of these lies the Sierra Madre, the watershed between the Pacific and the Atlantic, with many volcanoes, including Tajamulco, 13,800 ft., Acatenango, 13,615 ft., Fuego, 12,570 ft. Farther N. and E. extend mountainous country and great plain of Peten, mostly Ind. pasture-land. Principal river is Montagua, 250 m.; lakes include Lake of Peten, Gulfo Dulce, Atlitan. There are vast forest lands; copious rainfall on Atlantic slope.

Guatemala was taken by Spaniards, 1524; independence declared, 1821, and Guatemala joined Confederation of Central America; present republic established, 1847; San Salvador defeated, 1863; Carrera dictator, 1845-65; constant strife with neighboring states led to Central America; present republic established, 1847; San Salvador defeated, 1863; Carrera dictator, 1845-65; constant strife with neighboring states led to Central American Arbitration Treaty, 1907. In World War Guatemala was the first Central American republic to sever diplomatic relations with Germany, 1917.

In 1930 delegates from Guatemala and Honduras signed a treaty in Washington submitting to arbitration the 90 year old boundary dispute between them. A committee of five of which Chief Justice Charles E. Hughes was chairman handed down its award on Jan. 1933, dividing the area under dispute on the basis of actual occupation. In Jan. 1928 universal suffrage became effective. Area, 48,290 square miles. See Map Central America.

GUATEMALA LA NUEVA, cap. of above, Central America, (14° 36′ N., 90° 30′ W.); on plain c. 5,000 ft. above sea-level, and 70 m. from its port, San José, on Pacific. Among chief buildings are cathedral, government house, mint; numerous educational institutions, churches, hospitals; wool and cotton.

GUATEMALA ANTIGUA, or *Old Guatemala* (14° 27′ N., 90° 37′ W.), the original city, founded 1527, was destroyed by flood, 1541, and by earthquake, 1773; the third capital was then removed to present site, about 15 m. N.E.

GUAVA, tropical American shrub (*Psidium Guayaba*) and its fruit, much used for jelly and preserves; family *Myrtaceae*.

GUAYAMA (18° N., 66° 5′ W.), town, Porto Rico, W. Indies; exports sugar, rum, coffee.

GUAYAQUIL (2° 10′ S., 79° 56′ W.), city, chief port, Ecuador, S. America; built mainly of wood. Among principal structures are government buildings, town hall, cathedral, bp.'s palace, univ. G. exports cacao, coffee, rubber; has shipyards and various manufactures. The city was formerly regarded as the most unhealthy in the world, on account of the prevalence of yellow fever. Gen. W. C. Gorgas, acting for the Rockefeller Foundation, cleared the city of this plague in 1919.

GUAYAS (2° 30′ S., 80° W.), maritime province, Ecuador; S. America; most important, industrially and commercially, of the republic; climate hot, humid, unhealthy; soil fertile; agriculture is chief pursuit; principal products—cacao,

coffee, tobacco, sugar-cane; capital, Guayaquil. Area, 8300 sq. miles.

GUAYMAS (28° 10′ N., 110° 50′ W.), seaport, Mexico, on Gulf of California; good harbor; exports metals, hides.

GUBBIO (43° 22′ N., 12° 34′ E.), city (ancient *Iguvium*, or *Eugubium*), Perugia, Italy, at foot of Monte Calvo; has a cathedral (XIII. cent.) and ducal palace (XIV. cent.); the famous Eugubine Tablets, discovered in the neighborhood in 1446, are preserved in the museum; manufactures, majolica.

GUBEN (51° 58′ N., 14° 42′ E.), town, Brandenburg, Prussia, on Neisse; woolen cloth, yarn

GUDGEON, small freshwater fish, genus *Gobio*, of carp family.

GUDRUN, legendary *dau.* of King Hettel, betrothed to King Herwig of Heligoland, but carried off by Hartmuth, king of Norway; famed for heroic fortitude and resignation.

GUELPH (43° 30′ N., 80° 21′ W.); city, river port, Ontario, Canada; seat of Ontario Agric. Coll.; flour mills, woolen mills.

GUELPHS AND GHIBELLINES, names of great conflicting parties into which Germany and Italy were divided in later Middle Ages, XII.-XV. cent.; names Italianized from German *Welf* and *Waiblingen*, warcries of Saxony and Empire respectively; Ghibellines were aristocratic party, supporting the emperor; Guelphs (or Guelfs) were democratic party, favoring the pope. House of Brunswick and Hanover are Guelphs by descent, whence British throne has been held by a Guelph since George I. In 1914 the name of 'Windsor' was substituted for 'Guelph' as the family name of the royal house of England.

GUERBER, HELENE ADELINE, an author. She was educated abroad. In addition to writing many books she was also the editor of French and German textbooks. Among her works are: *Myths of Greece and Rome*; *Myths of Northern Lands*; *Legends of the Virgin and Christ*; *Stories of the Wagner Operas*; *Story of the Chosen People*; *Story of the Greeks*; *Story of the Romans*; *Story of the English*; *Story of the Thirteen Colonies*; *Story of the Great Republic*; *Stories of Shakespeare's Comedies*; *Stories of Shakespeare's Tragedies*; *Stories of Shakespeare's English History Plays*; *The Book of Epic*; *Joan of Arc*, *French Composition*.

GUÉRIN, JEAN BATISTE PAULIN (1783-1855), Fr. artist; famed for portraits; works include *The Dead Christ, Cain and Abel, Anchises and Venus.*

GUERIN, JULES (1866), an American artist, *b.* at St. Louis, *s.* of Richmond L. and Louise Davis Guerin. He studied art under Benjamin Constant and Jean Paul Laurens. He was the director of color and decoration at the Panama P.I. Exposition and painted the decorations for the Lincoln Memorial Building, Washington and also for the Pennsylvania Station, New York City. In addition to the Yerkes Medal, he was awarded a silver medal, at the St. Louis Exposition in 1904 and a gold medal at the Panama P.I. Exposition in 1915.

GUÉRIN, MAURICE DE (1810-39), Fr. author; distinguished both as poet and prose writer; prose is marked by masterly style; shows remarkable sympathy with nature. His sister, Eugénie, 1805-48, whose *Journal* and *Letters* are highly valued, was intimately associated with his work.

GUERNSEY (49° 27′ N., 2° 35′ W.), second largest of the Channel Islands, 30 miles W. of Normandy; surface undulating, sloping gradually N. to S.; climate mild; popular health resort; produces large quantities of fruit, flowers, and vegetables; famous breed of cattle; some granite quarried, and fishing carried on. Capital, St. Peter Port; good harbor; residence of lieut.-gov. Area, 25 sq. miles.

GUERNSEY LILY, or *Nerine Sarniensis*, a Cape plant belonging to the order Amaryllidaceæ. The flowers are of a delicate pink color.

GUERRERO (17° 40′ N., 101° W.), Pacific state, Mexico; mountainous; rich in minerals; fertile; produces coffee, cereals, tobacco; capital, Chilpancingo; chief port, Acapulco. Area, 25,000 sq. miles.

GUERRILLAS, name given to bands of armed men who carry on an irregular warfare on their own account. They belong peculiarly to Spain, and in 1808-14 they fought against the French. Some joined Wellington and rendered him service, but when peace was concluded formed themselves into robber bands. The term Guerrilla Warfare is used to denote war carried on by bands in an unorganized manner. In the Basque provinces at the time of the civil wars of Spain, G. W. was frequent. The subject was dealt with at the Hague Conference in 1899, and the rules made were reaffirmed in 1907.

GUEUX, LES ('the Beggars'), name

given to the Netherlanders who, in the XVI. cent., revolted against the oppression of Philip II. The 'Beggars of the Sea' harassed the Span. navy.

GUGLIELMI, PIETRO (1727-1804), an Italian musical composer, *b.* at Massa Carrara. He studied under Durante, and produced his first operatic work at Turin in 1755. In 1762 he went to Dresden to conduct the opera there, and some years afterwards appeared in London. In 1793 he became musical director at the Vatican. He was a writer of operas, both comic and serious, as well as of oratorios and orchestral pieces. His best operas are *La Didone; Enea e Lavinia; I due Gemelli; La Pastorella Nobile; La Bella Pescatrice.*

GUIANA, part of S. America (1°-8° 30′ N., 51° 30′-61° 30′ W.), between Orinoco and Amazon rivers, embracing Venezuelan, Brit., Dutch, Fr., and Brazilian Guianas. Physical geography is much the same in all three colonies. Along the coast are flat, swampy tracts, with rich, fertile soil; beyond this, the land rises to undulating savannas, behind which are mountainous regions covered with almost impenetrable forest. Guiana contains innumerable rivers, which form chief means of communication; almost all larger streams are connected by creeks and channels, and are navigable up to rapids and falls. Vegetation is remarkably rich and luxuriant; sugar, coffee, rice, cocoa, fruits cultivated; forests yield fine timbers, balata, rubber, oil, balsams, gums, tonka beans, nuts, etc. Birds are particularly brilliant in plumage, and include humming-birds, parrots, macaws, and orioles; tiger-cats, jaguars, tapirs, peccaries, manatees, capybaras, alligators, and great variety of insects to be found. Gold and diamonds are produced. Inhabitants are chiefly Europeans, Indians, and negroes. Climate not unhealthy though tropical; earthquakes and hurricanes practically unknown.

British Guiana, largest of three colonies, is bounded on W. by Venezuela, S. by Brazil, and E. by Dutch Guiana. Chief towns are Georgetown, cap., on mouth of Demerara R., and New Amsterdam, on Berbice R.; in W. are Pacaraima Mts., culminating in Roraima, on Venezuelan boundary; principal rivers are Essequibo, Corentyn, Berbice, Demerara, Mazuruni, and Cuyuni; railways connect Georgetown with New Amsterdam, Demerara with Essequibo, and a line runs from Demerara a few miles along W. coast. Among principal exports are sugar, rum, rice, molasses, coffee, balata, timber, shingles, and gold. New goldfield discovered on S. frontier in 1914; promising diamond fields; iron ore and manganese. Administration is under governor, assisted by elected legislative council. Area, 89,480 sq. m.

Dutch Guiana, or *Surinam*, bounded on W. by Brit. Guiana, S. by Brazil, and E. by Fr. Guiana; cap., Paramaribo, near mouth of Surinam R.; contains great extent of dense forest and unexplored country; well watered. Exports embrace sugar, rum, balata, timber, and gold. Area, 54,291 sq. mi.; pop. 155,888, exclusive of negroes of forests.

French Guiana, or *Cayenne*, bounded on W. by Dutch Guiana, S. by Tumac Humac Mts., and E. by Brazil. Cayenne, cap. and chief center of population. Fr. Guiana is penal settlement and the least prosperous of three colonies: little agricultural industry; gold-mining principal occupation. Area, 34,740 sq. m.

Guiana was sighted by Columbus in 1498; later visited by adventurers in search of El Dorado; in 1595 and 1617 explored by Raleigh; first settlements made by Dutch in Demerara and Essequibo (c. 1613); English settled in Surinam and French in Cayenne; in 1616 English seized Dutch and Fr. Guiana, but restored them (1617), and handed over Surinam to Netherlands in exchange for New York. By 1674 Dutch claimed all territory now known as Dutch and Brit. Guiana; after prolonged struggle British captured Berbice, Demerara, and Essequibo, and in 1831 formed colony of Brit. Guiana. Venezuelan and Brit. Guiana boundaries fixed in 1899. Fr. and Brazilian boundary dispute settled in 1900. Brit. and Brazilian frontier question settled by award of King of Italy in 1904. See Map, South America.

GUIART, GUILLAUME (fl. 1300), Fr. poet-chronicler; his *Branche des royaulx lignages*, dealing with the history of the Fr. kings, is valuable for the later period.

GUIBERT OF NOGENT (1053-1124), Fr. historian; wrote *Gesta Dei per Francos*, an account of the First Crusade.

GUICCIARDINI, FRANCESCO (1483 1540), Ital. politician and historian; *b.* Florence; ambassador to Span. court, 1512; became papal ruler of Reggio and Modena, 1515; of Parma, 1521; of Romagna, 1523; of Bologna, 1531; supported the Medici at Florence, and successfully defended Duke Alexander from charges leveled against him at imperial court in 1535. Alexander's successor, Cosimo, dismissed G., who withdrew from public life. He wrote *Storia d'Italia* and other hist. and political works; *Storia d'Italia* is a masterly analysis of Ital. history between 1494 and 1532.

GUICHARD, KARL GOTTLIEB (1724-75), military historian and Prussian officer; of Fr. descent; fought for Prussia in Seven Years War, 1757-62;

GUIDO OF AREZZO, GUIDO ARETINUS (*c.* 995-1050), Fr. Benedictine monk and musician; birthplace uncertain; invented 'Harmonic' or 'Guidonian Hand' and was first to use stave with lines and spaces.

GUIDO RENI (1575-1642), Ital. artist principal master of the Bolognese school; *b.* Bologna; studied first under Calvaert, and later under Caracci. Removing to Rome, he obtained the patronage of Pope Paul V. His best work in Rome is considered to be *Aurora and the Hours* (on the ceiling of the Rospigliosi Palace).

GUIENNE, GUYENNE (45° N., 1° E.), ancient province, S.W. France; now divided into departments of Gironde, Dordogne, Lot, Aveyron, Lot-et-Garonne, and Tarn-et-Garonne. G. belonged to England (1154) after marriage of Eleanor of Aquitaine to Henry II.; long disputed by English and French; annexed by French, 1453.

GUILDFORD (51° 14′ N., 0° 34′ W.), market town, Surrey, England, on Wey; remains of ancient Norman castle; noted grain and live-stock markets; flour-mills.

GUILDHALL, hall of London municipality; erected, 1411; destroyed, 1666; re-erected, 1669; restored, 1789; important library and art gallery.

GUILDS, GILDS, mediæval associations formed for the protection and development either of commerce or some particular trade. The earliest were of a semi-religious character, providing, amongst other things, for the payment for masses for souls of the departed, and some of them so remained until their suppression by Henry VIII. in 1547. The industrial g., however, was classed under two distinct heads— the 'gild merchant' (merchant g's), an organization which came into existence in England soon after the Norman Conquest, and the 'trade' or 'craft' g., which first began to flourish during the XIV. cent. On the Continent the g. was of earlier origin. Members of the merchant g. enjoyed the privilege of regulating the trade of a borough. Their influence was very great, especially in freeing industrial cities and ports from the power of feudal lords. The trade g. was an association of craftsmen in the different branches of industry, to protect the common interests of the members. A subsequent development of the trade g's were the various *livery companies*, each of which followed its particular craft or 'mystery.' The word 'guild' is now generally used in connection with social or religious improvements societies, such as temperance g's, communicant's g's, etc.

GUILLAUME, CHARLES EDOUARD (1860-   ), French physicist, b. Switzerland; ed.atNeuchatel; best known for his invention of invar, an alloy with a very small coefficient of expansion, used in making instruments of precision; awarded the Nobel Prize for Physics (1920), became director of the International Bureau of Weights and Measures.

GUILLEMOT AND AUK FAMILY (*Alcidae*), a family of marine swimming birds confined to the colder regions of the northern hemisphere, characterized by short wings, heavy body, and fully webbed anterior toes, the first toe being absent. The most interesting and largest member of the family was the flightless Great Auk or Garefowl (*Alca impennis*), distinguished by its large, deep beak, equalling the head in length, black plumage on the upper surface and white on the under, as well as on a patch above the eyes. Confined to the North Atlantic, its chief breeding-places were rocky islands off Iceland and Newfoundland, where incessant slaughter for more than two centuries brought about its extinction in 1844. Its remains have been found in Orkney.

GUILLOTINE, machine used in France for decapitating criminals. Its chief feature, a heavy blade, with sharp oblique lower edge, can be made to fall by its own weight between two grooved upright posts, on to the neck of the victim fastened below; derives its present name from its reputed inventor, Dr. Guillotin (1792), but similar instruments had been in use before the Fr. Revolution.

GUIMARAES (41° 28′ N., 8° 11′ W.), fortified town, Portugal; cutlery, paper, leather; noted sulphur springs in vicinity.

GUINEA, dist. of W. Africa, stretching along the shores of Gulf of Guinea, between Senegal and Cape Negro, (7° N., 2° W.), divided into Upper Guinea (E. and W.) and Lower Guinea (N. and S.). Guinea includes coast regions of Sierra Leone, Gold Coast, Lagos, Nigeria (Brit.); Fr. Guinea, Ivory Coast, Dahomey, Fr. Equatorial Africa; Togo, Kamerun, Port. Guinea and Angola (Port.); Span. Guinea; Belgian Congo; Liberian Republic; also Guinea Islands—Fernando Po, Annabon

(Span.), Principe, Sao Thome (Port.). See Map, Africa.

GUINEA. See Coins.

GUINEA-FOWL (*Numida*), genus of Pheasants; Common G., or Pintado (*N. meleagris*) of W. Africa, is domesticated in Britain; head is naked, plumage is speckled with white. G's in wild state are gregarious.

GUINEA-PIG or CAVY (CAVIA), a genus of small rodents native to S. America, but now domesticated in most countries. Sometimes considered as a separate species (*Cavia cobaya*), the familiar common cavy is probably a domesticated form of the *Cavia aperea* of Guinea and Brazil, introduced by the Dutch into Europe in the 16th century. The domesticated kinds are mostly white, or marked with yellow and black, or tawny-colored. They have short limbs, the fore-feet having four toes, the hind feet only three. Their ears are short and rounded, and they have no tails. Gs. are very prolific, producing young five or six times a year. They are much used in bacteriological laboratories for the study of germ-diseases.

GUINEA-WORM (*Filaria medinensis*), a parasite of man common in tropical districts, particularly on the Guinea Coast, its habitat being the subcutaneous tissues of the back and legs, where it forms swellings which develop into abscesses.

GUINES (22° 50′ N., 82° W.), town, Cuba, W. Indies; sugar-cane, tobacco.

GUINEY, LOUISE IMOGEN (1863-1923), poet; b. Boston, Mass. She graduated from Elmhurst Academy, Providence, and also studied under private tutors. Besides poetry she wrote considerable prose, and edited the works of Mangan and Matthew Arnold. Her writings date from 1884 and were largely produced in England, where she became permanently domiciled.

GUINOBATAN (12° 50′ N., 123° 43′ E.), town, Luzon, Philippine Islands; hemp.

GUIPUZCOA (43° 6′ N., 2° 10′ W.), maritime province, N. Spain; surface mountainous; fruit, timber, cattle; rich in minerals (iron, lignite, copper); flourishing industries; good fisheries; climate mild, healthy; many mineral springs; capital, San Sebastian. Area, 728 sq. miles.

GUISCARD, ROBERT (1015-85), Norman conqueror of Sicily; Count of Apulia, 1057; reduced Sicily, 1061-72; conquered Bari, 1071; drove Henry IV. from Rome and restored pope, 1083-84.

GUISE, DUKEDOM OF, held by younger branch of family of Lorraine, founded by Claude of Lorraine, 1st

Duke of G., who served with distinction in Italy under Francis I., and later in Luxembourg, 1542; his *dau.* Mary m. James V. **of** Scotland, and his two eldest *sons* attained great importance. Francis, 2nd duke, elder *s.* of Claude, acquired great military reputation by his defense of Metz against Charles V., 1552, and his conquest of Calais, 1558; he subsequently captured Guînes and Arlon, and in 1562 defeated the Huguenots at *Dreux*; was for many years the most powerful personage in France; assassinated in 1563. His *bro.* Charles entered the Church, and became cardinal of Lorraine; he was prominent minister of Henry II., and introduced Inquisition in France. Henry, 3rd duke (1550-88), is chiefly noted for his opposition to Huguenots, whom he defeated at *Jarnac* and *Moncontour*, 1568, and against whom he formed Catholic League, 1584; he also had considerable share in instigating the massacre of St. Bartholomew's Eve in 1572, and opposed Henry of Navarre; he was assassinated in 1588. Henry, 5th duke, failed to secure crown of Naples, 1647, 1654. Title became extinct with death of Mary, Duchess of G., in 1688.

GUITAR, a stringed instrument of Oriental origin somewhat similar to the lute; popular in Spain and Italy. G. has a flat back with curved sides, large sound-hole, and six strings—the three highest of gut, the three lowest of silk, spun over with silver wire; sound is produced by plucking the strings with the fingers of right hand, while the left hand is used for altering the pitch by pressing a fretted finger-board; music is written in treble clef, but sounds an octave lower than written.

GUITEAU, CHARLES JULIUS (1840-1882), slayer of President Garfield. He was a Chicago lawyer who had vainly applied to the President for the post of American consul at Marseilles, and was also believed to have become hostile to Garfield through being influenced by the latter's stalwart opponents, led by Roscoe Conkling. He shot Garfield on July 2, 1881, in the waiting room of the B. & O. railway station in Washington, D. C. The President succumbed to his wound on Sept. 19. Guiteau was tried and convicted for murder, the defense pleading insanity, and was hung in the District of Columbia jail on June 30, 1882.

GUITERMAN, ARTHUR (1871), an American author; *b.* at Vienna, Austria, *s.* of Alexander and Louise Wolf Guiterman, Americans. He graduated from the College of the City of New York in 1891 and from then until 1906

was engaged in editorial work on the Woman's Home Companion, the Literary Digest and other magazines. He was a lecturer on magazine and newspaper verse at the New York University School of Journalism from 1912-15, contributed *Rhymed Reviews* to Life, and ballad and lyric verse to various other magazines and was the author of *The Mirthful Lyre*, 1918; *Ballads of Old New York*, also *Chips of Jade*, 1920 and *A Ballad Makers Pack*, 1921 and others.

GUITRY, LUCIEN (1860), Fr. actor, made début as Armand in *La Dame aux Camelias* (1878), and has appeared successfully in many roles, including creation of part of *Chantecler* in Rostand's play (1910). *d.* 1925.

GUITRY, SACHA (1885), Fr. dramatist and actor, *s.* of Lucien Guitry; a dramatist of great versatility, displaying genius for light comedy in such plays as *La Pelerine Ecossaise*, and for serious and moving scenes-(*e.g.*), *Pasteur*. His *Le Mari, la Femme, et l'Amant* was one of the successes of Fr. stage in 1919. In May and June 1920 there was a Guitry season at Aldwych Theater, London, when *Nono, La Prise de Berg-op-Zoom, Pasteur, Jean de la Fontaine, L'Illusioniste,* and *Mon Pere avait Raison* were well staged, the chief parts being taken by the author, his wife (Mlle. Yvonne Printemps), and his father. Other works include *Le Kurtz, Les Nuees d'Aristophane, Petite Hollande*. Several of his plays were produced in the United States in 1922 and 1923.

GUIZOT, FRANÇOIS PIERRE GUILLAUME (1787-1874), Fr. politician and author; *b.* at Nîmes, of Huguenot stock; ed. at Geneva and Paris; early turned his attention to literature; appointed prof. of Modern History at Sorbonne, 1812, in which year he m. Pauline de Meulan, writer on educational subjects. In 1814 he was app. Sec. Gen. of Interior under Louis XVIII., but retired from office after Napoleon's escape from Elba in 1815. After final defeat of Napoleon, G. obtained office under Ministry of Justice; was conspicuous member of *Doctrinaire* party; dismissed from office, 1821, he devoted himself to historical research; entered Lower House in 1830; as Minister of Education, 1832-36, he had principal share in development of modern system of education in France. Ambassador to Britain, 1840, but was presently recalled to France to form cabinet; became Foreign Minister, and in 1847 succ. Soult as Premier. His attempts to foster friendly relations with Great Britain were at first crowned with success; but in 1846 the *entente* was broken by the discovery of the Span. marriage intrigues, which discredited both G. and the king. G. remained in office till Revolution of 1848, when with difficulty he escaped to England. G. wrote *Histoire de la Revolution d'Angleterre depuis Charles I. a Charles II.*, an important hist. work; also author of *Histoire de la Civilisation en France*, *Histoire de la Civilisation en Europe*, a biography of Washington, and other works.

GUJARAT, GUZERAT (22° N., 72° E.), region, Bombay Presidency, India; includes the N. districts of the presidency, the Gaekwar's territories, and numerous native states.

GUJRANWALA (32°10′N.,74°14′ E.), district, Lahore, Punjab, India; chief river, Chenab; manufactures brassware; area, 3,198 square miles. Capital, Gujranwala.

GUJRAT (32° 47′ N., 74° 9′ E.), chief town, Gujrat district, Punjab, India; cotton goods; brassware; scene of defeat of Sikhs by Brit. under Gough, 1849. District area, 2,051 square miles.

GULBARGA (17° 19′ N., 76° 54′ E.), town. Hyderabad State, India.

GULFPORT, a city of Mississippi, in Harrison co., of which it is the county seat. It is on the Louisville and Nashville, and on the Illinois Central railroads, and on Mississippi Sound. There is an excellent harbor and the city is an important port of entry. It has a large trade in lumber, naval stores, cotton, etc. Its industries include fertilizer works, canning factories, and sawmills. There is a United States custom house and a post-office building.

GULF STREAM, a warm, slow-moving oceanic current, from 40 to 100 miles wide, and over 300 fathoms deep, issuing from Gulf of Mexico; flows N.E. along E. coast of N. America to near Newfoundland, where, turning E., it merges into a drift current; causes mildness of Brit. and Norwegian climate.

GULL FAMILY (*Laridae*), a family of about 115 species of strong-flying and swimming birds with completely or partially webbed feet. They are mostly marine, and live upon fishes and crustacea, but some have taken to an inland life, breeding in marshy places and feeding on worms and insect grubs. They are found on all the oceans. Amongst them are the Terns or Sea Swallows (*Sterna*), so called because of their forked tails—active

graceful birds which lay their eggs in depressions on sandy shores; with them are reckoned the tropical Noddies (*Anous*). The Skimmers or Scissor-Bills (*Rhynchops*), with long, scissor-like beak, the lower mandible of which protrudes far beyond the upper, occur in Africa, S.E. Asia, and America. Lastly, the Gulls and Kittiwakes may be distinguished by possessing completely webbed feet, a beak shorter than the head, with the upper mandible shorter than the lower, and forming a slight hook at its tip.

GULLY, WILLIAM COURT, 1ST VISCOUNT SELBY (1835-1909), Brit. politician; Conserv. M.P., Carlisle, 1886; Speaker, House of Commons (1895-1905); peerage and pension (1905); member, Hague Arbitration Court(1907)

GUM ($C_6H_{10}O_5$) is an amorphous *carbohydrate*, the watery solution of which is a jelly with adhesive properties. Gums are exudatious from the stems of plants. *Tragacanth*, from *Astragalus gummifer*, yields two gums, *Tragacanthin* and *Arabin*. The oak and beech give *Xylan*, which on hydrolysis yields the sugar *Xylose*. The gum from *Acacia Senegal* is *Arabin*, used to suspend insoluble oils, powders, etc.

GUM, BRITISH. See DEXTRIN.

GUMBINNEN (54° 35′ N., 22° 9′ E.), town, on Pissa, E. Prussia, Germany; textiles, iron foundries.

GUMBO, or **OKRA**, an annual African herb, natural order *Malvaceae*, with edible fruit.

GUMTI (25° 33′ N., 83° 20′ E.); river, India; joins Ganges, 17 miles N.E. of Benares, after S.E. course of 500 miles.

GUN-COTTON, explosive substance, is approximately $C_{12}H_{14}(NO_3)_6O_4$, *cellulose hexa-nitrate*, the washed and dried product obtained by soaking cotton-wool in a mixture of three parts of concentrated *sulphuric acid* and one part of *nitric acid* (Sp. Gr., 1.5) for twenty-four hours. It is insoluble in a mixture of alcohol and ether. When lighted, it burns quietly and quickly without smoke. When fused with a detonator it explodes with violence. Gun-cotton forms two non-explosive compounds, *colloidon* and *celluloid*. See EXPLOSIVES.

GUNNERY, or **BALLISTICS**, is that portion of artillery science which deals with the flight of projectiles, and the means whereby accurate shooting from a firearm can be attained. 'Interior ballistics' is the study of the pressure in the bore of a gun caused by the gases of the explosive which give initial velocity to the projectile. 'Exterior ballistics' is the theory of the flight of a missile traveling at high velocity, and acted on by the force of gravity and the resistance of the air. For comparatively slow motions, the retardation caused by the air varies with the square of the velocity; but with the ogival rotating projectile of a modern gun, so many other considerations come into play that the conditions of flight are mainly determined by experiment. A missile is now fired through equidistant electric screens, and the time of flight between their severed wires noted by a chronograph. By formulæ used in conjunction with experimental ballistic tables, the trajectory or path of any shot at a given velocity can be demonstrated. When once the ranges (corrected for wind, temp., muzzle velocity, etc.) are found, the sights of the gun or the rifle are adjusted for each distance, and their manipulation becomes a matter of mere drill.

GUNNISON, a riv. of Colorado. Its source is in the N. of Saguache co., and its course is W. and N.W., until it enters the Grand R. at Grand Junction, about 25 m. E. of the western borders of Colorado. There are numerous cañons.

GUNPOWDER, an *explosive* obtained by mixing *saltpetre, charcoal,* and *sulphur* together. Its discovery is attributed by some to Schwartz, a Ger. monk, and by others to Roger Bacon. It was known as an explosive, and used as a scientific amusement long before its propelling powers were known. It was probably first employed as a *propellan* by Edward III., since he possessed cannon. The chief combustible is charcoal, which is made from *dogwood, willow,* or *alder.* The charcoal must be free from grit and burn easily, leaving little ash. When made, the charcoal is ground, sifted, and carefully stored. The sulphur, after purification by distillation and melting, is cast in moulds and then ground and sifted. *Potassium nitrate* forms a very suitable source of oxygen as it does not become deliquescent. Each constituent is weighed carefully and passed through a sieve of known mesh. After moistening, the materials are *incorporated* or moved, twisted, and turned in every direction by iron rollers working on a circular bed. The whole apparatus can be douched with water if friction causes ignition. The product is '*mill-cake.*' The *mill-cake* is pressed and becomes *press-cake.* The higher the density the slower is the initial rate of burning. Excess of moisture reduces the explosiveness. The *press-cake* is broken up and granulated, the grains being afterwards separated and sorted by sieving. Final processes give different shapes (number of faces) to the grains to suit various requirements. The products of combustion should be *nitrogen* and *carbon dioxide* as gases, and *potassium sulphate* and *carbonate* as solids.

GUNPOWDER PLOT, conspiracy of Eng. Rom. Catholics (on account of James I.'s refusal to redress their grievances) to blow up with gunpowder the Houses of Parliament when the king and his ministers were there on Nov. 5, 1605. Originator of plot was Robert Catesby, the other conspirators including Thomas Percy, Sir Everard Digby, Francis Tresham, and Guy Fawkes. Barrels of gunpowder were secretly lodged in coal cellar underneath House of Lords, and it was arranged that Fawkes should fire it at the appointed time. On Oct. 26 an anonymous letter, generally attributed to Tresham, was received by Lord Mounteagle; this aroused suspicion and led to discovery of plot; cellars were searched on Nov. 4, and Fawkes was arrested; other conspirators took to flight, but were presently overtaken when some, including Catesby, were killed and others taken prisoner. Fawkes and others were executed, and Tresham died in captivity.

GUNTER, ARCHIBALD CLAVERING (1847-1907), novelist and playwright; *b.* Liverpool, Eng.; *d.* New York. His parents emigrated to California when he was quite young, and there he became a mining engineer and afterwards a stockbroker in San Francisco. Literature attracted him and he ventured to New York City to live by his pen. *Mr. Barnes of New York,* his most successful novel, by which his name is best known, was published in 1887 after being rejected by almost every American publisher. *Mr. Potter of Texas* followed and met with a like success. Succeeding novels resembled them in their fertility of situated and rapid movement. His most popular works were dramatized.

GUNTER, EDMUND (1581-1626), Eng. mathematician; ed. Oxford; became prof. of Astronomy, Gresham Coll., London, 1619; invented the *chain* for land measurement, also *Gunter's scale,* for working navigation problems.

GUNTRAM (561-592), king of Burgundy; *s.* of Clotaire I., and inheritor, with his bro's, of the Frankish dominions; possessed some administrative ability, but few social virtues.

GUNTUR (16° 18' N., 80° 29' E.), town, Madras, India; trade in cotton and grain.

GUPTA, Ind. dynasty, c. 320-480 A.D., founded by Chandragupta Maurya under Samudragupta, dominions comprised nearly whole of India; succumbed to Bengal.

GURDASPUR (32° 3' N., 75° 27' E.), district, Lahore, Punjab, India; area, 1,889 sq. miles. Chief town, Gurdaspur.

GURGAON (28° 37' N., 77° 4' E.), district, Delhi, Punjab, India; chief town, Gurgaon; trade in grain. Area, 1984 sq. miles.

GURKHAS, or GOORKHAS, the principal race in Nepal (India). They are a sturdily built people, excellent soldiers; rendered valuable service in suppression of the Indian Mutiny.

GURNEY, EDMUND (1847-88), Eng. philosopher and scientist; ed. at Cambridge, studying classics and medicine but best known for his pioneer work on pyschical research; with Myers and Podmore edit. *Phantasms of the Living*; an acute, scientific thinker.

GURNEY, JOHN (1750-1809), Eng. banker; of a Norwich Quaker family; *f.* of Elizabeth Fry; his *s.* Samuel G., (1786-1856), largely extended the banking business, and was a noted philanthropist.

GUSTAVUS I., VASA (1496-1560), king of Sweden; *b.* at Lindholm, Upland; fought against Danes, 1517-18. His *f.* and other leaders of Swed. party were executed by Christian II. of Denmark, 1520; G. raised an army, and after various battles expelled Danes from Sweden; crowned king of Sweden, 1523. G. established Lutheran religion; excluded bp's from Senate; formed alliance with Denmark; put down peasant insurrection; Diet declared crown hereditary in his house, 1560.

GUSTAVUS II., ADOLPHUS (1594-1632), king of Sweden, hero of Thirty Years War; succeeded, 1611; warred against Denmark, 1611-13, Russia, 1614-17, and Poland, 1617-29; from Russia he acquired Karelia and Ingria, from Poland, Livonia, Courland, Esthonia. He landed in Germany with 13,000 troops in 1630; captured Stettin; failed to relieve Magdeburg, but inflicted severe defeat on Tilly at Breitenfeld, 1631; he attacked and defeated Wallenstein at Lützen, 1632, but was himself slain during the action.

GUSTAVUS III. (1746-92), king of Sweden; succ. in 1771. G. warred against Catharine II. of Russia, 1788-90; and at the naval engagement of Svensksund inflicted a crushing defeat upon the Russians; concluded peace by Treaty of Värälä in 1790; assassinated, 1792.

GUSTAVUS IV. (1778-1837), king of Sweden; succ. 1792; deposed as insane, 1809.

GUSTAVUS V. (1858), King of Sweden; succeeded father, Oscar II. (1907); fifth sovereign of the house of Ponte Corvo and the great-grandson of Marshal Bernadotte.

GÜSTROW (53° 48' N., 12° 11' E.), town, on Nebel, Mecklenburg-Schwerin, Germany; has cathedral and ancient ducal castle; ironworks; active trade.

GUTENBERG, JOHANNES (c. 1398-1468), Ger. printer; *b.* Mainz; followed various mechanical employments until 1450, when he entered into partnership with Johannes Fust (or Faust), a goldsmith, who furnished the capital to start a printing business. G. is credited with the invention of printing by movable blocks. The partnership was subsequently dissolved, Fust taking an action at law for the recovery of money advanced. G. afterwards started a rival press.

GUTHRIE, a city of Oklahoma, county seat of Logan co. It is on the main line of the Atchison, Topeka and Santa Fe Railroad, as well as the Ft. Smith and Western and El Reno and Western. Has both senior and junior high schools, and the largest Masonic Temple in the world. It is the industrial center of North Central Oklahoma.

GUTHRIE, THOMAS (1803-73), Scot preacher and philanthropist; wrote three *Pleas for Ragged Schools*; promoted establishment of Industrial Schools for destitute children.

GUTTA-PERCHA is the evaporated milky *latex* of the trees *Dichopsis gutta* and *Dichopsis oblongifolia*, Natural Order *Sapotaceae*. The trees, which are native to the Malay Peninsula, are felled, cut by a special method and the latex collected. Mature trees are the best. When felled during the wet season about 30 oz. per tree are obtained. After evaporation g.-p. is sent to the market as blocks of a dirty greyish appearance often with a reddish tinge. Chemically it consists of a *hydrocarbon* and two *oxygenated resins.*

GUTTENBERG, a town of New Jersey, in Hudson co. It is on the Hudson River. Its chief industry is the quarrying of stone. It has several industrial establishments.

GUY OF WARWICK, hero of a XIII.-cent. Eng. metrical romance, who traversed the world performing knightly deeds of valor to win the hand of Felice. *dau.* of the Earl of Warwick.

GUY, THOMAS (1644-1724), Eng. philanthropist; founded Guy's Hospital (1721), and subscribed to other charities.

GUYNEMER, GEORGES (1894-1917), French aviator; *b.* Paris; *d* Poelcapelle, Belgium, in action. He was the *s.* of a French officer and historian and was educated at Stanislas College and the École Polytechnique in Paris. He had an aptitude for science, mechanics and mathematics; was drawn to aviation by the achievements of Santos Dumont, Bleriot, Paulhan and others. When the World War began in 1914 he enlisted in the aviation corps as a student mechanic and became one of the most remarkable airman of his time. His first flights were at the Pau School, and after an apprenticeship there he joined the celebrated French 'Storks' as a corporal. He soon acquired fame for his aerial battles with German airmen from the Aisne to Verdun and over the Somme and Belgium. His active air service lasted from June 8, 1915, to September 11, 1917, ending with his life at 23, in which period he brought down 53 enemy machines without taking account of those that fell too far from the official observers, those only disabled, or those that reached safety with a pilot or passenger dead. His last flight was with a German biplane over Poelcapelle, Belgium, in the Ypres Sector, where he was found dead in his wrecked machine, shot through the head. His body and machine disappeared in the heavy shelling which subsequently ploughed the district and were never found.

GUYON, JEANNE MARIE BOUVIER DE LA MOTHE (1648-1717), Fr. mystic; disciple of the doctrine of quietism or spiritual perfection; persecuted and imprisoned for her opinions, which were regarded as heretical; wrote *Autobiography* and numerous works..

GUYOT, YVES (1843), Fr. journalist and publicist; first to cast suspicion upon the verdict in the notorious Dreyfus trial, in the *Siecle*; pub. several works on Socialism; member of Chamber of Deputies (1885-92); minister of public works (1889-92). *d.* 1928.

GWALIOR (24° 30′ N.; 77° 50′ E.), native state in Central India, consisting of several detached districts; situated partly in basin of river Jumma and partly in that of the Nerbudda; drains into Bay of Bengal and Arabian Sea; area, 29,047 sq. miles. Capital, Gwalior, in the N. At capital stands famous old citadel, on precipitous rock. Other towns are Dhar and Indore in the S.

GWYN, NELL, ELEANOR (1650-87); Eng. actress; originally an orange-seller; famed for her performances in comedy; mistress of Charles II.; had two sons, one of whom became Duke of St. Albans.

GYGES (687-54 B.C.), king of Lydia. Plato tells that he was a herdsman who discovered a magic ring which rendered the wearer invisible. With its aid he assassinated the king of Lydia and seized the throne.

GYLIPPUS (fl. V. cent. B.C.), Spartan general who rescued Syracuse from Athenians, 414 B.C.; Athenian captives were then slain, possibly by G.'s advice.

GYMNASIUM, a place used for the performance of athletic exercises; in ancient Greece it was an elaborate combination of halls and courts for exercises, wrestling, and running, with baths and porticos, frequented by philosophers, who instructed the youths who took part in the exercises (*e.g.*), the Academy, where Plato taught; in modern Germany the g. is an advanced school, preparing for the univ's, corresponding to the public schools and high schools of Britain and America.

GYMNASTICS, athletic exercises practiced for improving the condition and development of the body, as opposed to athletic sports and games (*e.g.*), running, jumping, football, golf, into which the competitive element enters. G. were practiced by the Greeks as training for open-air sports and games, and recognized as of benefit to health, and a valuable adjunct to the moral and literary training carried on in the same buildings as the physical training. In mediæval times horsemanship, field sports, and exercises with arms took the place of the older and more systematic training of the body, and it was not until the second half of the XIX. cent. that the therapeutic value of g., as known to Hippocrates and Galen, was again recognized. Physical exercises are regularly taught in Britain in the elementary schools, while the higher schools and univ's have gymnasia fitted up with apparatus, which is less elaborate now than it was a few years ago.

Clubs for gymnastic exercises are common everywhere, and g. play an important part in the training of the army. G. are practiced with benefit for such conditions as digestive derangements and (under medical supervision) diseases of the lungs and heart. The dumb-bell, which has been employed since Elizabethan times, is the most generally popular gymnastic apparatus, its weight being easily proportioned to the person using it, and bar-bells, or two-handed dumb-bells, and Indian clubs are also much used. The vaulting-horse, parallel bars, trapeze, swinging rings, horizontal bar, and bridge ladder are more elaborate gymnastic apparatus on a larger scale, but, although these and similar apparatus have been very popular for many years, there is a tendency to-day to discard them in favor of free gymnastic exercises without any apparatus. In the United States, France, Germany, Sweden, Denmark, Switzerland, Italy, among other countries, g. are much practiced and much esteemed for hygienic purposes, and many competitions of gymnastic teams are held, the Olympic Games even including such competitions among its events.

GYMNOSPERMS, naked - seeded plants in which the seed lies on the surface of the *carpel*, and is not enclosed in an *ovary*. They form the smaller, less developed and more ancient of the two divisions of the *Phanerogams* or *Spermaphyta* (seed-bearing plants). G's are divided into four classes, all trees or shrubs—(1) *Conifers*; (2) *Cycads*; (3) *Gnetales*; (4) *Ginkgoales*. These classes, although differing widely in appearance, have in common with each other and their fossil ancestors—(*a*) exposed *ovule* at which the pollen can get directly; (*b*) simplicity of wood structure; (*c*) formation of *endosperm* before fertilization.

GYMPIE (26° 15′ S., 152° 38′ E.), town, Queensland, Australia; gold-mining center.

GYNECOLOGY, GYNÆCOLOGY, the branch of medicine which deals with the diseases peculiar to women, a subject which has received much attention since ancient times, Egyptian and afterwards Gk. and Rom. physicians making a special study of it, while Galen gave it a place of some importance in his works. The rise and development of modern scientific g. began about the first half of the XIX. cent., when Récamier (1774-1852) began to advocate the use of the speculum and sound, and Simpson, Hughes Bennett, and others did much to advance its progress.

GYP, psuedonym of Gabrielle Riqu-

etti de Mirabeau, Comtesse de Martel de Janville (1850), Fr. novelist; her works deal freely with social conventions, and include *Chiffon's Marriage, Petit Bob, Mlle. Eve, Elles et Lui.*

GYPSIES, name given to a nomadic race found all over Europe, great part of Asia, in N. and S. America, Africa, and Australia. They have also been known in England as 'Egyptians (of which Gypsy is a diminutive), 'Greeks,' 'Heathens,' 'Bohemians,' etc. The g. calls himself *Romany* or 'Rómano'; and his language, which is practically the same in all countries, is *Romani chiv.* Where the g. first came from is unknown. They are generally described by themselves as of *Little Egypt,* which some students have identified with Epirus. They probably first appeared in Europe in the early part of the XIV. cent., and seem to have reached England at about its close. It is recorded that certain g's danced before James V. of Scots at Holyrood; and, in 1540, the same king granted permission to 'oure louit Johnne Faw, lord and erle of Litill Egipt,' to punish any offenders against the Romany laws. At first they seem to have been well received in Europe, and were known for skilled metal-workers, but subsequently charges of kidnapping and other crimes were brought against then, and in England and other places they were mercilessly hunted down and imprisoned or put to death. In past times these nomads used to be famed for their skill in music and dancing, besides metal-working. Now the chief male occupation is horse-dealing; the female, fortune-telling and basket-making. Amongst common surnames are Smith, Boswell, Stanley, Lee, and Lovell. The Eng. g's conform to no religion; and their moral code is far from strict. Amongst physical characteristics may be noted lithe figures, olive skin, dark, lustrous eyes, exceedingly fine teeth, and black or dark hair.

GYPSUM, $CaSO_4+2H_2O$, mineral composed of hydrated sulphate of lime; occurs abundantly in the more recent sedimentary rocks, although it may occur in any geological age. Varieties: *alabaster,* which is white and resembles marble; *selenite,* transparent and crystalline; *satin spar,* has pearl-like lustre. G. contains a large amount of water, and when this is evaporated off in kilns plaster of Paris is left. This, when mixed with water again, quickly sets, and is used for moulds, casts, etc. G. is also used in a powdered form as agricultural manure, and in the manufacture of porcelain.

GYPSY MOTH. An insect belonging to the genus Porthetria. First described by Linnaeus in 1758, and called by him Bombyx dispar. The male moth is brown and flies freely, while the female is white and does not fly. It is very abundant in France, Germany and Russia, where it is considered a pest owing to the great damage done by the caterpillars to trees, shrubs and plants. Even conifers are sometimes attacked and killed. The caterpillars hatch in the spring and become full-grown about the middle of July. They pupate in loose cocoons and the moth emerges in about two weeks. The female lays her eggs in August, depositing them on tree trunks, fences, and even rocks. The eggs occur as yellow, horny masses. The moths were introduced into this country by an unfortunate accident. In 1869, Leopold Trouvelot was experimenting with various breeds of silkworms, at Medford, Mass., with the purpose of developing a hybrid resistant to the pebrine silkworm disease. Some of his specimens accidentally escaped, among them being the Gypsy Moth. Trouvelot, realizing the possibility of serious consequences, promptly informed the authorities, but little was done to combat the moth until 1889, when the ravages caused by the caterpillars in the state of Massachusetts began to cause alarm among farmers and landowners. In the following year, the state legislature appointed a commission for the extermination of the insect, and later the work was carried on by the State Board of Agriculture. For ten years the fight was carried on, at a cost of about a million dollars. By 1900 the ravages of the insect had been so greatly reduced that public opinion would no longer permit further expenditures. In recent years, the insect has again increased in numbers, and there seems every probability that the fight against it will have to be renewed with increased persistence. Whether it can ever be exterminated seems doubtful and only by constant watchfulness can its numbers be kept within reasonably safe limits.

GYROSCOPES and **GYROSTATS** are instruments by means of which the dynamics of a rotating body such as the earth or a spinning-top have been investigated. In the *Gyroscope*, invented towards the end of the 18th cent., the principal axis of rotation always passes through a fixed point, and accordingly the rotating wheel or disk is mounted in *gimbals*. The *Gyrostat* was invented by Kelvin to illustrate the movement of a rotating body left free to wander about on a horizontal plane. It illustrates the action of a top spun on a table. When the gyroscope is rotated at a very high speed it resists any forces coming from without and tending to change its axis of rotation. Hence it can be used to give stability to a moving body through its inertia. The *moment of inertia* can be calculated, and is equal to the product of the mass of each particle of the body into the square of its distance from the axis of rotation. It will, therefore, to some extent depend on the geometrical shape of the body.

The *radius of gyration* of a rotating body is the distance from the axis of rotation at which, if the whole mass of the body were concentrated there, the energy of rotation of the body would be the same as it really is. The first practical application of the gyroscope was Sersen's apparatus for providing a false horizon at sea when the real one was obscured by fog. It consisted of a top with a highly polished upper plane surface. *Centrifugal machines, cream separators*, are really tops held in a frame and obliged to rotate about a vertical axis—(*i.e.,*) they are an application of the gyrostatic principle in which one degree of freedom is suppressed. Other modifications of this principle are used on the platforms of quick-firing guns and for searchlights on board ships. A gyroscopic fly-wheel travels in its original direction only when it is perfectly free in all directions in space. In the form of a small heavy wheel fixed in gimbals rotating at at least 2,000 revolutions per minute it is used to control the course of a torpedo or submarine. The fly-wheel acts on a valve to which rudders are attached. The rolling of a ship can be neutralized by the presence of a gyrostat the movement of which is restrained in one direction, and the same principle can be used to give stability to a mono-rail car. In 1911 the gyroscopic compass was invented, and the gyroscope was used for steadying cinematograph cameras. Bicycle wheels furnish an instance of gyrostatic movement. Any deviations from the original direction of the movement can be corrected by forces of the required direction acting through the handle-bars. Many complicated composite movements can be explained by the fact that, given forces acting in the proper direction, it is possible to overcome the inertia due to gyrostatic movement. The earth can be considered as a large top with a slow backward motion of the equinoctial points due to the attractive force by the sun, moon, and planets. The axis of the earth describes in space a conical motion in about 26,000 years. Various applications of the gyroscope have been used to demonstrate the inclination of the earth's axis. Large gyroscopes installed in ocean vessels are found to stabilize the motion and to prevent seasickness.

GYTHIUM (36° 46′ N., 23° 34′ E.), seaport town of ancient Greece, on Gulf of Laconia; was Spartan naval station; now mostly submerged.

HAARLEM AMSTERDAMSCHE POORT

H

H, eighth letter of the Eng. alphabet; derived from the Phoenician, and originally consisted of two upright and three transverse bars. It is an aspirate, or simple breath sound, neither consonant nor vowel; sounded in words of native origin, but in a few words derived from the Latin, such as 'hour' and 'honour,' mute.

HAAKON, OR HACO, name of several kings of Norway. (1) H. I. *the Good* 915-61, passed his youth in England, and on return to Norway dethroned his brother Eric; defeated Danes, and was converted to Christianity; was murdered by sons of Eric. H. IV. 1204-63 won over-lordship of Iceland and Greenland; was defeated by Alexander III. at Largs, Scotland 1263, dying in Orkneys on way home. H. VII. 1872, *s*. of King Frederick VIII. of Denmark, became King of Norway on its separation from Sweden 1905; married Princess Maud Charlotte 1869, *d*. of Edward VII. Heir, Crown Prince Olaf.

HAAN, WILLIAM GEORGE (1863), American army officer. *B*. at Crown Point, Indiana, Oct. 4, 1863. Graduated from U. S. Military Academy 1889; Captain U. S. artillery corps 1901; major 1907, colonel 1916, brigadier-general 1917 and major-general 1921. Active service Cuba and Philippines 1898-1901; General Staff 1903-1905; Chief of Staff Eastern Dept. 1912-1914; Commander 57th Artillery Brigade corps Camp MacArthur, Texas, 1917, of 32nd Division N. G. 1918; brigadier general U. S. A. 1918, commander 3rd Division offensives Marne and Argonne, France; of 7th army corps, Germany, Nov. 1918 to April 1919; Assistant chief of Staff U. S. A. June, 1919. Decorations D.S.M. (U.S.) and Legion of Honor and Cross, France. *d*. 1924.

HAARLEM (52° 22′ N., 4° 40′ E.), town, capital of N. Holland, Netherlands, on Spaarne; the Cathedral of St. Bavo (Groote Kerk) dates from XV. cent.; has collections in art and science, an academy of science, and several royal schools; trade in flower bulbs; surrendered to the Spaniards, 1573.

HAARLEM LAKE (52° 20′ N., 4° 40′ E.), Dutch Harlemmer Meer, a former shallow lake of the Netherlands, about 20 miles in length, 2 miles S.E. of Haarlem; drained in 1853.

HAAS, JOHN A. W. (1862), College President. *B*. in Philadelphia. In 1884 Backelor of Arts, University of Pennsylvania, 1887, Master of Arts and Bachelor of Divinity. Was a student of Lutheran Theological Seminary. Ordained Lutheran Minister. From 1888-1896, pastor of Grace Church, 1896-1904 St. Pauls Church, New York. Since 1904, professor of philosophy, and president of Muhlenburg College. University preacher at Harvard College. Member of Association of College Presidents of Pennsylvania. Was president of Lutheran Ministerium of Pennsylvania. Author of Commentary on the Gospel of Mark in Lutheran Commentary, 1895, Bible Literature, 1903, Trends of Thought and Christian Truth, 1915. Contributor and co-editor of Lutheran Cyclopaedia, 1899. Biblical Criticism, 1903.

HAASE, FRIEDRICH (1827-1911), Ger. actor; retired, 1898; one of the leading players of the modern Ger. stage.

HAASE, HUGO (1863-1919) German Socialist; *b*. at Allenstein, E. Prussia, of Jewish extraction; studied law at Königsberg Univ.; entered Reichstag in 1897; succeeded Bebel as president of Social Democratic party; during Great War seceded from main body of Socialist party on the question of voting war credits in the Reichstag 1915; one of the authors of the revolution which brought about the abdication of the Kaiser; co-operated with Majority Socialists in formation of a People's Government; shot on steps of Reichstag by a Viennese named Voss Oct. 8, 1919; *d*. from blood-poisoning Nov. 7.

HABAKKUK, eighth minor prophet of Old Testament, of whom personally nothing is known, but probably a Levite. Book is dramatic in form, consisting of colloquy between prophet and Jehovah; former begins by lamenting surrounding violence and is told that

God has raised up Chaldaeans as instrument of judgment; prophet then complains of greater wickedness of Chaldaeans, and is told that they shall perish after accomplishment of their task. Then follows a series of woes pronounced against Chaldaeans; and in conclusion the prophet breaks into a sublime lyrical poem, describing a divine theophany. H. is quoted in *Acts*, *Romans*, *Galatians*, *Hebrews*.

HABBERTON, JOHN (1842-1922), Amer. novelist and journalist; chief work, *Helen's Babies*, 1876.

HABEAS CORPUS, in law, writ protecting personal liberty of the citizen. Where a person is detained on criminal charge without being brought to trial, or where he is unlawfully detained by private individuals, any one may on his behalf apply for writ of H.C. commanding warden of prison, or person detaining the individual on whose behalf the request is made, to bring him before the court in order that the reasons for his detention may be investigated; if there by no sufficient reason, the court will then order him to be set at liberty, or, if he is a child, will order him to be given up to his lawful guardians. Writ must be issued by judge on good reason being shown.

The act was passed in 1679. The right of habeas corpus is secured by the Constitution of the United States, and has been incorporated into the jurisprudence and Constitution of every State.

HABERDASHER, retail dealer in mens' furnishings; the name is used by Chaucer.

HABIBULLAH KHAN (1872-1919), Amir of Afghanistan; succeeded to throne on death of father, Abdur-Rahman 1901; was not at first inclined to be friendly with Ind. Government, but attitude was changed as result of visit to India 1907. During World War he kept country neutral, though section of nobility headed by his *b.* wished to intervene in Turkey's favour; was assassinated Feb. 20, 1919.

HABSBURG, OR HAPSBURG, Ger. noble family, deriving name from castle of Habsburg on Aar, built about 1020. Rudolph of Habsburg, who became Holy Roman emperor in 1273, acquired Austria in 13th cent.; his descendants held empire at various times, and from 1438 the imperial title remained practically hereditary in house of Habsburg. Family was remarkable for its continuous acquisition of territories in the E.; it annexed Styria, Carinthia, Tyrol; and Bohemia and Hungary were both subject to it for some time. Practice of subdivision frequently weakened family, but all their dominions were reunited under Frederick III. and his *s.* Maximilian. Latter married Mary of Burgundy 1477, and established his family as great European power. In reign of Charles V. Spain was united to empire; when he abdicted 1556 it was transferred to his *s.* Philip, while the empire passed to his *b.* Ferdinand. Family thus divided into Spanish (elder) and Austrian (younger) branches. Span. line became extinct with the death of Charles II. of Spain in 1700; Austrian Habsburgs claimed throne, but war with France resulted in its passing to Bourbons. Austrian Habsburgs were founded by Ferdinand I.; lands were divided among his sons at his death, but were reunited under Ferdinand II. 1619. Male line became extinct with the death of Charles VI. in 1740; he had previously issued document known as the Pragmatic Sanction, securing succession of his *d.* Maria Theresa. She married Francis of Lorraine, who became emperor in 1745. Henceforth Habsburg-Lorraine family were Holy Roman emperors till 1806, and from that date till conclusion of World War 1918 emperors of Austria.

HACHETTE, JEANNE, famous Frenchwoman who, when the Burgundians, in 1472, had practically reduced Beauvais, tore down their flag and re-inspired the garrison to resistance.

HACKENSACK, a city of New Jersey, in Bergen co., of which it is the county seat. It is on the New York, Susquehanna and Western, and the New Jersey and New York railroads, and on the Hackensack River, 14 miles northwest of New York City. It is chiefly a residential city but has important industries including the manufacture of brick and silk. The public buildings include a court house, public library, and a high school. The city is connected with neighboring towns and cities by electric railroads. A settlement was made here by the Dutch in the latter part of the 17th century, and during the Revolution Hackensack was occupied in turn by the British and American armies.

HACKNEY, metropolitan borough of London, England, 3 miles N.E. of St. Paul's.

HACKNEY, horse for riding or driving as distinguished from finer breeds, such as hunters or racehorses; carriage for hire; 'to hackney' is to make common, by frequent use.

HACKETT, FRANCIS (1883), Literary Critic. *B.* in Ireland. Educated at

Clongowes Wood College, Kildare, Ireland. In 1900 came to America. From 1906-1909 editorial writer, Chicago Evening Post. Editor, 1909-1911, Friday Literary Review of same paper. Since 1914 associate editor of New Republic. Author of, Ireland, A Study of Nationalism, 1918. Horizons, 1918, The Invisible Censor, 1920.

HACKETT, JAMES HENRY (1800-1871), American actor. B. in New York, March 15, 1800; d. in Jamaica, Long Island, Dec. 28, 1871. He made his first stage appearance in 1826 and soon became noted for playing Yankees and Westerners. In 1832 he first acted Falstaff, a part in which he was considered above all rivals in his day. He played in England also with marked success. During his management of various theatres he made a considerable fortune. Publications: 'Notes and Comments on Shakespeare', 1863. See IRELAND, 'ACTORS AND ACTRESSES OF GREAT BRITAIN AND THE UNITED STATES' NEW YORK, 1886.

HACKETT, JAMES KETELTAS (1869-1926),Actor-Manager. Bachelor of Arts of College of the City of New York, 1891. Student at New York Law School. In Philadelphia, 1892 made debut on stage. Became a leading man at twenty-four. His most successful play, 'The Prisoner of Zenda'. Has been interested in many theatres including Grand Opera House, Chicago: Tremont Theatre, Boston; Savoy Theatre, New York. Producer of many plays as manager or actor among which are 'The Walls of Jericho', 'Rupert of Hentzau', 'The First Gentleman of Europe', 'The Grain of Dust', and 'Craig Kennedy'. Manager of many stars. In 1919 awarded the Red Cross Badge for exceptional service.

HADAD, name found in Bible ,as Ben H. (s. of H.); kings of Damascus called Ben H. possibly assumed title from Syrian god H.

HADDINGTON (55° 57' N., 2° 47' W.), county town on Tyne, Haddingtonshire, Scotland; ancient royal burgh; among chief buildings are the XV. cent. abbey church ('Lamp of Lothian'), Corn Exchange, and Knox Memorial Institute; important grain market; cornmills. Alexander II., John Knox, Samuel Smiles, and Jane Welsh Carlyle were natives.

HADDINGTONSHIRE, OR EAST LOTHIAN (55° 55' N., 2° 45' W.), maritime county in S. E. of Scotland, bounded by Firth of Forth, Ger. Ocean, Berwickshire, and Edinburghshire; total area, 280 sq. miles; county town, Haddington. Of great historical interest,

with numerous antiquities. Royal burghs are Haddington, Dunbar, and North Berwick

HADDOCK (*Gadus oeglefinus*), fish found plentifully in N. hemisphere; belongs to Cod family; length of male, c. 2 ft., of female (which lays about one million pelagic eggs), c. 15 inches.

HADEN, SIR FRANCIS SEYMOUR (1818-1910), Eng. surgeon and artist; pres. and part founder of the Royal Society of Painter-Etchers; stands in the foremost rank of etchers, and author of numerous works on etching.

HADERSLEBEN, DAN. HADERSLEV (55° 15' N., 9° 10' E.(, seaport town, Schleswig-Holstein, Prussia, on inlet of Little Belt; iron foundries.

HADES, see HELL.

HADING, JANE (1859), Fr. actress; has played with Coquelin; achieved great success in *Le Maitre de Forges, La Chatelaine, Le Demi-monde*, etc.; toured in U. S.; acted in London in *Sapho* and *Retour de Jerusalem*, etc.; one of the most famous *comediennes* of her day.

HADJ, HAJJ, Arabic name for the pilgrimage to Mecca, the person performing it being afterwards known as Hadji. Pilgrimages to Jerusalem are also so called.

HADLEY, ARTHUR TWINING (1856), American university president. B. in New Haven, Connecticut, April 23, 1856. He graduated with highest honors from Yale in 1876 and studied at the University of Berlin 1878-1879. (LL, D. Yale, Harvard, Columbia, Brown, and others). Lectured on railroad administration 1883-1886; professor of political science 1886-1891; politicial economy 1891-1899; president, Yale University 1899-1921; President Emeritus, 1921; Roosevelt professor in Berlin 1907-1908; lectured at Oxford University, England, 1914; president of the American Economic Association 1899-1900. Publications 'Freedom and Responsibility', 1903; 'The Standard of Public Morality', 1907; 'Undercurrents in American Politics', 'The Moral Basis of Democracy', 1919. *d.* 1930.

HADLEY, HENRY K. (1871), American composer; b. at Somerville, Mass., in 1871. He studied music in Boston under S. A. Emery, and G. W. Chadwick and also in Vienna. In 1895 he was appointed instructor of music at the St. Paul School, Garden City, L. I. 'The Four Seasons' a symphony received the Paderewski and New England Conservatory of Music prizes; 'The Culprit Fay' rhapsody for orchestras the prize from the Federation of Musical Clubs. He is the composer of over 150 songs, and of many overtures and a cantata, and two serious operas 'Safie' produced at Mayence and 'Izora, Montezuma's Daughter', also four comic operas. In 1907-1909 he was choir-master at the Mayence Opera House and also played his pieces in European cities. Conductor Seattle Symphony orchestra, 1909 and of the San Francisco Symphony 1911-1915.

HADLEY, HERBERT SPENCER (1872-1927), Governor. *B.* in Kansas. In 1891 Bachelor of Arts of University of Kansas. At Northwestern University, Bachelor of Laws with first honors, 1894. From 1894-1898 practised at Kansas City. First assistant city counselor, 1898-1901. From 1901-1903 at Jackson County, Missouri, prosecuting attorney. From 1905-1909 was attorney-general of Missouri. Prosecutor in cases against the Harvestor Trust, Standard Oil Company, Insurance and Lumber Trusts and race track gamblers of St. Louis. From 1909-1913 governor of Missouri. From 1913-1915 was special counsel for railways W. of Chicago in federal valuations of railways. Since 1917, professor of law at University of Colorado. From 1919-1921 counsel for State Railroad Commission.

HADRAMUT (18° N., 40° E.), district along S. coast of Arabia from Yemen on W. to Oman on E.; narrow belt of land, chiefly mountainous; many wadis, or valleys, without running water, except after rains; country irrigated by wells. Main productions are wheat, millet, indigo, dates, and tobacco. Chief towns—Shibam, Tarim, Keshin, and Makalla. Shrines of Kabr Salih and Kabr Hud visited by pilgrims.

HADRIAN, PUBLIUS ÆLIUS HADRIANUS (76-138 A.D.), emperor of Rome. After distinguishing himself in wars in Dacia and holding various important offices of state, he succeeded Trajan as emperor in 117; soon afterwards he gave up his claim to Armenia, and made peace with Parthians, to whom he retransferred Assyria and Mesopotamia. He spent several years of his reign in visiting all the provinces of his empire, and in course of his first journey, which he began *c.* 119, he visited Britain, where he caused a wall, Hadrian's Wall, to be built beteeen Bowness-on-Solway and Wallsend-on-Tyne, to secure Rom. provinces to the S. from incursions of Caledonians. The wall was repaired by Severus and considerable portions remain. He lived for some time at Athens, where he built magnificent temple; founded Ælia Capitolina on site of Jerusalem; put down Jewish insurrection, 134.

HADRUMETUM (*c.* 35° 50′ N., 10° 30′ E.), ancient city, N. Africa; on E. coast Tunisia; originally a Phoenician and later a Rom. colony; site now partly occupied by modern Susa.

HAECKEL, ERNEST HEINRICH (1834-1919), Ger. biologist; prof. of zool. at Jena. His biological achievements lay in two main directions; minute systematic classification and general biological philosophy. In the first, he pub. masterly monographs on several divisions of protozoa, sponges, and coelenterates; in the second, propounded his 'gastraea' theory, based upon his 'fundamental biogenetic law'—that the ontogeny or development of the individual is a recapitulation of the phylogeny or development of the race. This theory has won wide acceptance among naturalists, and though it has undergone some modifications, still lies at the base of all modern zoological classifications. Of Haeckel's more popular works, his *History of Creation* (4th Eng. ed. 1892) has been widely read. *The Last Link,* 1899 contains his final conclusions on the origin and descent of man, as based upon the latest available palaeontological discoveries.

HÆDUI, ÆDUI, Gallic people dwelling between Saône and Loire; gave allegiance to Julius Caesar.

HÆMATITE, OR HEMATITE (Ger. *Hamin,* blood), a distinct iron ore of fibrous structure, consisting chiefly of peroxide iron, and found in Cumberland, Lancashire, in Spain, Scandinavia, and near Lake Superior. Thefe are two varieties, red and brown, the former being variety of red oxide, and giving the name on account of its blood-like colour.

HÆMATOCELE, collection of blood in the tunica vaginalis of the testis or in the spermatic cord, due to injury or, rarely, to maligant disease; treatment is rest, cold wet dressings or ice-bag to promote absorption, or, in chronic cases, a slight operation to remove the clot may be necessary.

HÆMOGLOBIN. See BLOOD.

HÆMORRHOIDS. OR HEMORRHOIDS. SEE PILES

HAESELER, GOTTLIEB, F. A. A., COUNT VON (1836-1919), Prussian field-marshal, fought against Denmark, 1864, and Austria, 1866; commanded an army corps in Franco-Ger. War, and was oberquartiermeister of the army of occupation, 1871; afterwards was given command of 11th Regiment of Uhlans, and was also engaged on compilation of official history of the war. At the outbreak of World War was attached to the crown prince as adviser, particularly in the Argonne and at Verdun, but retired owing to opposition to continuance of the operations at the latter place. Later, while he was engaged at War Office in Berlin, he was responsible for death warrant of Nurse Edith Cavell.

HÃFIZ (d. 1389), the greatest of Persian lyric poets. His real name was Muhammad Shams ed-Din; b. and d. at Shiraz, but little is known of his life. His book, or *Divan*, consists of *ghazals* (short odes), which, though sensuous in tone, are claimed to be mystical in meaning, and impregnated with Sufi philosophy. They are known by heart in Persia. Eng. trans. by McCarthy, Payne, and others.

HAFNIUM. An element isolated in 1913 by Dr. Alexander Scott of the British Museum from a black sand obtained from New Zealand. It was not definitely identified by him as a new element until 1922, when the Danish chemists, Coster and Hevesy, discovered the same element in xirconium minerals. The claim is also made that the element was discovered several years previously by Prof. G. Orbain, a well known French chemist, but there appears to be some doubt as to whether this element, named 'celtium' by the professor, is identical with the hafnium of Coster and Hevesy. The element is stated to be very similar to the metal zirconium and has an atomic weight of approximately 180. Its oxide, as prepared by Dr. Scott, is a cinnamon colored powder. If the new element is found to have a commercial value, it can probably be produced in large quantities, as the deposit of sand in New Zealand, from which it was isolated, is reported to be seven miles in length and of considerable depth, and it is also believed to exist in appreciable quantities in some Norwegian zirconium minerals.

HAGEDORN, HERMANN (1882), American Author. *B.* in New York. Educated at Harvard and Columbia Colleges and University of Berlin. From 1909-1911 at Harvard, instructor of English. Writer of one act plays produced by Harvard Dramatic Club. At Harvard in 1917 delivered the Phi Beta Kappa poem An Ode of Dedication. Author of 'The Silver Blade' 1907: 'The Woman of Corinth', 1909; 'A Troop of the Guard', and Other Poems, 1909; Barbara Picks a Husband', 1918; 'The

Boys Life of Theodore Roosevelt', 1918; 'Life of Roosevelt', 1919; 'That Human Being', (Leonard Wood), 1920; 'Roosevelt in the Bad Lands', 1921.

HAGEN (51° 22′ N., 7° 28′ E.), town, Westphalia, Prussia; ironworks; textile industries.

HAGENAU (48° 35′ N., 7° 48′ E.); town, on Moder, Alsace-Lorraine, Germany; cotton and woollen industries.

HAGENBECK, KARL GOTTFRIED WILHELM HEINRICH (1844-1913), dealer in wild animals; organized expeditions in quest of big game; inaugurated 1875, ethnographical exhibitions; acquired large tract of land at Stellingen, near Hamburg 1902, for animal park in which animals were allowed to roam freely over restricted areas; system now widely adopted in zoological gardens.

HAGERSTOWN, a city of Maryland, in Washington co., of which it is the county seat. It is on the Baltimore and Ohio, the Cumberland Valley, the Norfolk and Western, the Western Maryland railroads, and on Antietam Creek. It has important industries, including the manufacture of knit goods, leather goods, pipe organs, machinery, steam engines, etc. Hagerstown is the trade center for the western part of Maryland. It has a courthouse, two high schools and a $500,000 Y. M. C. A.

HAGGADA, part of Talmud, which gives ethical and hist. commentary on and amplification of Bible; to it is joined the *halkaha*, or legal exposition of the Scriptures; it is of great literary value.

HAGGAI, first Hebrew prophet after the return from Exile; contemporary of Zerubbabel and Joshua, whom he was inspired to support in rebuilding of Temple, the reconstruction having been suspended for fourteen years. His prophecy dates from 520 B.C., and consists of four parts: the first reproves apathy of the people in not carrying out the work; the second gives an assurance that the new temple shall equal the glory of the former one; the third promises blessing; and fourth contains message of encouragement for Zerubbabel. H. is quoted in *Hebrews* 12₂₆.

HAGGARD, SIR HENRY RIDER (1856-1925), Eng. novelist; secretary to governor of Natal 1875; member of special commission to the Transvaal 1877; with General Brooke hoisted Brit. flag over S. African Republic at Pretoria 1877; master, High Court of the Transvaal 1878; returned to England and studied law; became barrister 1884; investigated agricultural conditions in

England 1901-2; Brit. Government special commissioner to report on Salvation Army settlements, U.S., etc. 1905; travelled round world as member of Dominions Royal Commission 1912-17. The most famous of his numerous publications are *King Solomon's Mines* 1886, *She* 1887, *Allan Quatermain* 1888, *Queen Sheba's Ring* 1910. He has also written on land questions.

HAGGIS, Scots pudding, consisting of sheep's lung, heart, and liver, chopped fine, and mixed with oatmeal, suet, and spices; boiled for three or more hours in a sheep's stomach.

HAGIOLOGY, as the critical study of lives of saints, has only existed for two cent's, but collections of lives were made from time of Eusebius; called *menologies* in Eastern and *legendaries* in Western Church; among important collections are *Sanctorum priscorum patrium vitoe* (pub. by Lippomano, 1560) and *Vitoe patrium* (by Rosweyde, 1615).

HAGONOY (14° 25' N., 120° 45' E.), town, Philippine Islands; fertile region; produces rice, Ind. corn, and sugar; woven fabrics.

HAGOOD, JOHNSON (1873), Army Officer. *B.* in South Carolina. Educated at University of South Carolina, and a graduate of United States Military Academy. Second lieutenant of second artillery in 1896 and was promoted through the grades to Brigadier-General in 1921. From 1896-1901 did garrison duty in Rhode Island, Connecticut and South Carolina. From 1901-1904 was instructor in department of philosophy, United States Naval Acadmy. From 1912-1913 was commander of Fort Flagler, Washington. Was in France during World War. In battles on British, French and American Fronts. Decorated in 1919 with Distinguished Service Medal. Inventor of Hagood tripod mounting mortar deflection and other apparatus for sea-coast defense.

HAGUE, THE (Dutch's *Gravenhage*), cap. of Netherlands (52° 3' N., 4° 18' E.), 2 m. from North Sea; traversed by numerous canals; royal palace, castle of Counts of Holland (Dutch Parliament House), famous picture-gallery, museums, fine Bosch Park, etc.; originally a hunting lodge of Counts of Holland, 12th cent.; numerous treaties arranged here; Triple Alliance between England, Sweden, and Netherlands 1668; peace between Austria, Spain, and Savoy 1717; identified with peace movement; famous Peace Conferences 1899, 1907; Carnegie Palace of Peace completed in 1913; but for the World War a Peace Conference would have been held in 1917. Chief industries, copper and lead smelting, iron foundries, printing works, carriages, gold and silver. Forty five nations, including the U.S. were members of The Hague Court in 1931.

HAGUE, ARNOLD (1840-1917); American geologist. *B.* in Boston, Oct. 3, 1840; *d.* 1917. Graduating from the Sheffield Scientific School, Yale, after three years study in Germany, he was appointed assistant-geologist of the United States explorations of the 40th parallel. Author of 'Volcanic Rocks of the Great Basin', 1884. 'The Volcanic Rock of Salvador,' 1886; 'Geology of the Yellowstone Park', 1895; 'Atlas of the Yellowstone Park', 1904, etc.

HAGUE TRIBUNAL. See ARBITRATION, INTERNATIONAL; PEACE MOVEMENT.

HAHN-HAHN, IDA, COUNTESS VON (1805-80), Ger. novelist; her stories are sentimental and deal chiefly with aristocratic life. The best are *Ulrich*, *Grafin Faustine*, and *Eudoxia* (Eng. trans. of two last).

HAHNEMANN, SAMUEL CHRISTIAN FRIEDRICH (1755-1843), a German physician and founder of homoeopathy, *b.* at Meissen, in Saxony. He studied medicine at Leipzig and Vienna, and took his degree in 1779 at Erlangen. He practised first at Dresden, then, in 1789, settled at Leipzig. He was not satisfied with the state of the science of medicine and in 1796 advanced a new principle, 'the law of similars,' *i.e.* that diseases should be treated by those drugs which produce symptoms similar to them, in the healthy. Four years later he published his doctrine on a system of smaller doses of drugs. In 1810 his chief work was printed, *Organon der rationellen*, *Heilkunde*, explaining this system, which he named homoeopathy. The hostility of the apothecaries forced him to leave Leipzig and find protection with the Grand-duke of Anhalt-Köthen. Fourteen years afterwards he went to Paris and practised homoeopathy with great success.

HAIDINGER, WILHELM KARL, RITTER VON (1795-1871), Austrian mineralogist and geologist; *b.* Vienna; came to live at Edinburgh, 1822; app. Counsellor of Nimes, 1840, and lectured on mineralogy, 1843; discovered optical appearances known as 'H's brushes.'

HAIDUK.—(1) Hungarian infantry soldier; term applied in XVI. cent. to mercenary soldiers who protected frontiers against Turks, and received various privileges as reward. (2) Retainer.

HAIFA (32° 48' N., 35° 1' E.), seaport

town, ancient *Sycaminum*, Syria, on Bay of Acre, at foot of Mt. Carmel.

HAIG OF BEMERSYDE (DOUGLAS HAIG), 1ST EARL (1861), *s.* of John Haig of Cameron Bridge, Fife; educated Clifton and Brasenose, Oxford (hon. fellow, 1915); joined 7th Hussars 1885; served in Sudan and S. African War; inspector-general cavalry, India 1903-6; general 1904 for distinguished service; director of military training 1906-7; director of staff duties at army headquarters 1907-9; chief of staff, India 1909-12; general officer commanding, Aldershot 1912-14. At the outbreak of the World War was placed in command of the 1st Army, which held the right of the Brit. line from the eastern suburbs of Mons to the little town of Binche, and contained six battalions of the Guards. At the battle of the Marne his army, after a hard struggle, dislodged the enemy at La Trétoire, and made large captures of guns and prisoners. During first battle of Ypres he rendered distinguished services, and on Dec. 15, 1915, succeeded Viscount French as commander-in-chief of the Brit. forces in France. Much of the success of the Allies was due to his uniformly friendly relations with the French, and to his ready acceptance of an Allied command with Foch as generalissimo. Made field-marshal on Jan. 1, 1917, and Knight of the Thistle in July. After brilliant advance of Aug. 1918, was awarded the military medal from France. Appointed March 1919, field-marshal commanding-in-chief the forces in Great Britain. Received Order of Merit June 1919, and in Aug. of the same year an earldom, the sum of $500,000 and the thanks of Parliament. *d.* 1928.

HAILE SILASSIE I, (Ras Taffari), Emperor of Abyssinia. *b.* 1891; Crowned king, 1928; proclaimed Emperor, 1930. Granted his subjects a constitution, 1931, establishing a Parliament and ceasing to be absolute monarch.

HAILSTONES. When water-drops, suspended in the air, are carried upward by air-currents there is a consequent fall in their temperature, and this may be so great as to cause them to freeze. While h's so formed are small they may still be carried upward, and more water will condense upon them until they are so large that they fall to the earth.

HAINAN, KIUNG-CHOW-FU (19° N., 109° 45' E.), island in province of Kwang-tung, extreme S. of China, lying between China Sea and Gulf of Tong-king; extending *c.* 150 by *c.* 100 miles; capital, Kiung-chow (with port Hoihow). Island is almost entirely agricultural; centre and S. are mountainous,

and earthquakes and typhoons occur; there are good harbours; exports include timber, rice, and sugar.

HAINAUT, HAINAULT (50° 30' N., 4° E.), province, Belgium; surface generally level; traversed by the Sambre, Scheldt, Dender, and Haine; rich coal-fields; fertile soil; agriculture and mining chief pursuit of inhabitants; capital, Mons. Area, 1437 sq. miles.

HAINES, THOMAS HARVEY (1871), Psychologist. *B.* in New Jersey. Educated at Haverford and Harvard Colleges. From 1912-1913 at London, Munich and Zurich studied neurology and psychiatry. At Ohio State University from 1901-1915 assistant professor of philosophy and professor of philosophy. From 1913-1914 first assistant physician of Boston Psycopathic Hospital. At Ohio Bureau Juvenile Research, 1914-1917 clinical director. 1915-1920 at Ohio State University professor of medicine. From 1917-1918 at Camp Stewart and Camp Dix was psychological examiner Surgeon General of United States of America. Director in 1921 of Arizona Mental Hygiene Survey.

HAINICHEN (50° 58' N., 13° 6' E.), town, Saxony, Germany; centre of Ger. flannel manufacture.

HAI-PHONG (20° 51' N., 106° 39' E.), seaport, Tong-king, Fr. Indo-China, on branch of Red River delta; rice.

HAIR, a characteristic of all mammals, even if in some it is reduced to a few bristles on the lips, as in whales. It is a product of the superficial skin or epidermis, is nourished by blood-vessels, and consists of a spongy centre and a harder outer layer. In mammals the temp. of the body must be kept at a constant high pitch; hair conserves the heat gained at the expense of energy and checks excessive dissipation of heat by radiation. It sometimes undergoes profound modifications. Thus in the hedgehog and porcupine, belonging to different orders, it develops into long, hard, and sharp spines, which are clearly specialized defensive structures. Only one kind of hair may be present, as in the cat, but often the long, coarse, apparent over-hair is supplemented by a fine, soft, thick under-fur, as in seals. The double coat is developed in animals exposed to cold temperatures—*e.g.*, martens of N. American and Europe, Arctic and Antarctic foxes, the ermine from Asia and Europe, etc. Hair, like feathers, is seasonably moulted, and the winter coat, which is thickest and warmest, often changes in northern animals to a colour matching or approaching that of the snow amongst which they move. Histologically, hairs are outgrowths of epidermis; develop in little pits (follicles) epidermis (root-sheath) forms inner layer of follicle; corium rises up at base of follicle as a vascular papilla; hair itself may be divided into body or shaft, and root; shaft has externally a cuticle of overlapping scales; beneath is pigmented fibrous layer, while sometimes in centre is dark-coloured medulla composed of angular cells. Root of similar structure, but enlarged, and consists chiefly of young growing cells. Each hair follicle has attached to it little bundle of muscular fibres by which it can be erected; when they contract under influence of emotion (e.g., fear) produces 'goose skin.' Colouring of hair depends on nature and amount of pigment.

Human hair and beards are possibly sexual ornaments. Racial varieties are: curly or smooth, generally fair hair of N. Europeans; crisp and short, woolly, very black hair of most negroes; black coarse straight hair of Mongols, Chinese, Amer. Indians; crinkly black hair of Australian Blacks.

Chairs are stuffed with short horse-hair; cloth is woven from long horse-hair and hair of goats, especially the Angora variety. Felt, for roofing and packing for pipes, is manufactured from cowhair. Artists' brushes are made from hair of camel and sable, clothes brushes from hog bristles

HAITI, OR HAYTI, the second largest island in W. Indies (17° 37′-20° N., 68° 20′-74° 28′ W.), separated from Cuba (the largest) by the Windward Passage, and from Porto Rico by Mona Passage. Cap. Port-au-Prince. Haiti isl. is divided into two republics—Haiti in W., and Santo Domingo in E. Republic of Haiti, originally a Fr. colony, was formed in 1804. Language of whites is French; religion is R.C. In 1910 education was made compulsory. It possesses a small fleet and army. Surface is mountainous, ranges running to both coasts. Highest peak, Loma Tina (10,300 ft). These mountains are covered with pine, oak, and other forests—much valuable timber being produced. Rivers are not navigable. There are many large lakes. Earthquakes are frequent and hurricanes common; climate is hot in low-lying parts, but healthful elsewhere. Cotton, rice, maize, sugar, coffee are cultivated. Haiti is rich in minerals, gold, silver, iron, copper, etc. Revolutions and bloodshed characterized the political history of Haiti, and in 1915 the republic signed a treaty with the United States whereby the United

States agreed to aid her in establishing a responsible government and in improving conditions on the island. Under the direction of the American marines, a native constabulary, the Garde, was established; swamps were drained; agriculture improved; and native Haitians trained to carry on the work begun by the Americans. In August, 1933, the two countries signed a new treaty stipulating that the country once more be turned over to native control, and on August 15, 1934, the marines evacuated Haiti. Stenio Vincent was elected president for the term 1931-1936.

HAJIPUR (25° 41′ N., 85° 14′ E.), town, Muzaffarpur, Bihar and Orissa, India, on Gandak; has large river trade.

HAKE (*Merluccius vulgaris*), fish common in Atlantic and Mediterranean; predatory habits; mem. of Cog (*q.v.*) family.

HAKE, THOMAS GORDON (1809-95), Eng. poet; sometime engaged in medical profession; associated with the Rossetti circle; his volumes include *New Day Sonnets, Madeline.*

HAKLUYT, RICHARD (*c.* 1553-1616), Eng. geographer and ecclesiastic; having taken orders, he held several livings and became archdeacon of Westminister 1602. He was early devoted to the study of navigation. He was the intimate friend of Drake, Raleigh, Gilbert, and others. His *Divers Voyages* appeared in 1582; and his monumental work, *The Principal Navigations*, was pub. 1589-1600. He also wrote and trans. several minor works, and his unpublished MSS. were afterwards used by Samuel Purchas in his *Pilgrims.*

HAKODATE (41° 47′ N., 140° 51′ E.), seaport, island Yezo, Japan, on Bay of Hakodate; exports sulphur, dried fish, rice.

HAKON. See Haakon.

HAL (50° 43′ N., 4° 13′ E.), town, on Sienne, Brabant, Belgium; place of pilgrimage.

HALAESA (*c.* 38° N., 14° 15′ E.), ancient town, N. coast of Sicily.

HALBERSTADT (51° 54′ N., 11° 3′ E.), town, Saxony, Germany; XIV. cent. cathedral; sugar, cigars, machinery. It has large railway shops.

HALCYON, a poetical name for the kingfisher. According to fable, it laid its eggs in nests that floated on the sea, about the time of the winter solstice, and was said to have the power of charming the winds and waves during the period of incubation. Thus the term 'halcyon days'.

HALBERT, HALBERD, military weapon, consisting of an axe-like head, and spike, fixed on a long pole being a combination of the bill and pike; first used in England in reign of Edward IV.; was commonly employed during reign of Henry VII.; did not fall into disuse until reign of George III.

HALDANE, ROBERT (1764-1842), Scot. theologian; served in navy during Fr. war, then devoted himself to religion; helped to form 'Soc. for the Propagation of the Gospel.'

HALDANE OF CLOAN, 1ST VISCOUNT (RT. HON. RICHARD BURDON HALDANE), (1856-1928), Brit. statesman; educated at Edinburgh and Göttingen; Grey scholar and Ferguson scholar in philosophy of the four Scottish universities 1876; called to Eng. bar 1879; Gifford lecturer in St. Andrews Univ. 1902-4; M.P. for Haddingtonshire 1885-1911; Q.C. 1890; P.C. 1902; counsel for United Free Church before House of Lords 1904; took office for first time as secretary of state for war 1905, and held it until appointed lord chancellor 1912-15. Has written *Essays on Philosophical Criticism* (with Prof. Seth), *Life of Adam Smith, Education and Empire,* 1902; *The Pathway to Reality,* 1905; is translator (with Kemp) of *Schopenhauer's World as Will and Idea* (3 vols.). As secretary for war he established the Territorial System, and practically created the British Expeditionary Force that went to France in 1914.

He resigned in the cabinet crisis of May, 1916, but continued to act as a member of the judicial committee of the Privy Council, and in a variety of ways assisted in the prosecution of the war.

HALDIMAND, SIR FREDERICK (1718-91), Brit. gen. of Swiss birth; entered Brit. Military service and served with distinction in America; Gov.-Gen. of Canada 1778-85.

HALE, EDWARD EVERETT (1822-1909), Unitarian clergyman and author. *B.* in Boston, April 3, 1822; *d.* June 10, 1909. He was pastor of the Church of the Unity 1845-1856; then of the South Congregational Society, a Unitarian Church, and pastor emeritus from 1901 until his death. He helped to organize the Kings Daughters, Look Up Legion, etc., and edited Old and New, and Lend a Hand, periodicals. He is best remembered as the author of 'The Man Without a Country' which appeared in 1863, and published about 70 books. Among the best known are *Philip Nolan's*

Friends, New England Boyhood, Historic Boston, 1898; *Lowell and His Friends,* 1899; *Memories of 100 Years,* 1900, and with his sister Susan Hale a series of travel books *Family Flights Through France, etc.*

HALE, EDWARD EVERETT, JR. (1863-   ), Univ. Professor, *b.* in Massachusetts. Bachelor of Arts of Harvard, 1883 and Doctor of Philosophy, Halle 1892. 1886-1890 at Cornell was instructor and professor of English. At University of Iowa, 1892-1895 professor of English. Since 1895 at Union College. Author of *Constructive Rhetoric,* 1896. *Lowell,* 1899; *Dramatists of Today,* 1905; *Seward,* 1910; *Life and Letters of Edward Everett Hale,* 1917.

HALE, EUGENE (1836-1918), American politician. *B.* in Turner, Maine, June 9, 1836; *d.* in Washington, D. C., Oct. 27, 1918. Admitted to the bar in 1857 he was a member of the Maine Legislature 1867-1868, and 1880; Congress 1868-1870 (in the last term chairman of the Republican Congressional Committee), delegate to the Republican National Conventions 1868, 1876, 1880. He declined the appointment of Postmaster-General in 1847 and of Secretary of the Navy in 1877. He succeeded Hannibal Hamlin in the U. S. Senate in 1881 and was re-elected 1887, 1893, 1899, 1905 and 1909. Retired in 1911.

HALE, FREDERICK (1874-   ), United States Senator. *B.* in Detroit, Mich., Oct. 7, 1874. Graduating from Harvard University in 1896, A.B., he was admitted to the bar and has since practiced law in Portland, Maine. In 1904 he was elected to the House of Representatives, Maine; member of the Republican National Committee, 1912-1918 and was elected to the U. S. Senate 1917-1923.

HALE, GEORGE ELLERY (1868-   ), American astronomer, *b.* Chicago, Ill.; ed. at the Mass. Institute of Technology; one of the foremost observers of his day; inventor of the Spectro-heliograph for photographing the sun; now perfecting the spectro-helioscope for the visual observation of the solar atmosphere.

HALE, HENRY CLAY (1861-   ), American army officer. *b.* in Knoxville, Ill., July 10, 1861. Graduated from the U. S. Military Academy, 1883; Colonel 20th Infantry, 1915; major-general, 1917; aid-de-camp to General Wesley Merritt at St. Paul, Chicago and Governor's Island 1893-1899; member General Staff 1903-1906; Philippines 1906-1909; adjutant-general Dept. of the Lakes 1909-1910; Dept. of Missouri, 1910-1911;

commander of Camp Zachary Taylor, Louisville, 1917; commander 84th Division A.E.F. France, 1918; of Combat Division, Germany, Dec., 1920 to Feb., 1922; major general 1921, commanding 1st Division U.S.A., Camp Dix, N.J.

HALE, JOHN PARKER (1806-73), Amer. statesman, Democrat, and pioneer Abolitionist; Free Soil candidate for presidency, 1852; faithfully supported Union and Lincoln.

HALE, LOUISE CLOSSER (1873-1933), American actress and author. Born in Chicago. Educated at the public schools of Indianapolis. She married Walter Hale the artist in 1899. First stage appearance was in Bernard Shaw's 'Candida' in 1895. She has been identified with important productions in the United States and London. Author of 'The Actress', 1909; 'Her Soul and Her Body', 1911; 'We Discover New England', 1915; 'We Discover the Old Dominion', 1916, and 'An American's London'. 1920.

HALE, LUCRETIA PEABODY (1820-1900), American author. Sister to E. E. Hale (q.v.). B. in Boston, Sept. 2, 1820; d. there Jan. 12, 1900. She is best remembered as the author of stories for young people, and as the creator of the amusing Peterkin Family as described in 'The Peterkin Papers', 1882, and 'Last of the Peterkin's', 1886. Among other books are 'The Lord's Supper and its Observances', 1866, and a movel 'The Wolf at the Door', 1877.

HALE, SIR MATTHEW (1609-76), famous Eng. judge and chief justice; took no part in Civil War; justice of Common Pleas, 1653; chief baron of Exchequer, 1660; Chief Justice of England, 1671; wrote numerous works on law and history; many of his collected MSS. at Lincoln's Inn library.

HALE, NATHAN (1755-1776), American revolutionary soldier. B. in Coventry, Conn., June 6, 1755; d. in New York, Sept. 22, 1776. After graduating from Yale College in 1773, he taught school and intended to enter the ministry, but moved by patriotism he enlisted in 1775 and became a captain in 1776. After the retreat from Long Island he volunteered to penetrate the enemy's lines for information. Disguised as a Dutch schoolmaster he succeeded in his mission, but was caught by Howe who ordered his execution the next morning. His last words were 'I only regret that I have but one life to lose for my country-See PARTRIDGE 'NATHAN HALE, THE IDEAL PATRIOT', 1902.

HALE, PHILIP (1854-1934), Music and dramatic critic, b. in Vermont.

Educated at Yale College. Admitted to the Bar in Albany, New York in 1879. From 1882-1884 at Berlin studied music under Haupt and Bargiel. Studied in Paris under Guilmant, 1885-1887. Organist in Troy and Albany ,New York. From 1889-1905 at Dr. de Normandie's Church, Boston. 1890-1891 was musical critic of Boston Post. 1891-1903 on Boston Journal. Since 1903 Boston Herald. Editor from 1897-1901 Musical Record, Boston. Boston Symphony Program Books.

HALE, WILLIAM GARDNER (1849); Amer. scholar; author of *The Anticipatory Subjunctive in Greek and Latin, The Sequence of Tenses in Latin*, etc. d. 1928.

HALEBID (13° 13' N.; 76° 2' E.); village, state of Mysore, S. India; on site of Dorasamudra, ancient Hoysala capital.

HALES, JOHN (1584-1656), Eng. author; his political writings include *Declaration of the Succession of the Crowne Imperiall of Inglande, Discourse of the Common Weal*, etc.

HALES, STEPHEN (1677-1761), Eng. physiologist and inventor; curate of Teddington in Middlesex; made investigations in plant and animal physiology and on gases; on treatment of stone in bladder and kidneys; devised a ventilating machine, and a process for distilling sea-water.

HALESOWEN (52° 28' N., 2° 3' W.); market town, Worcestershire, England; large iron•and steel works.

HALEVI, JUDAH BEN SAMUEL (d. 1140), Span.-Hebrew poet; famed for religious poems.

HALEVY, JACQUES FRANÇOIS FROMENTAL ÉLIE (1799-1862), Fr. composer; real name, Levi; chief operas: *La Juive, Les Mousquetaires de la Reine*. Musical author.

HALÉVY, LUDOVIC (1834-1908), Fr. dramatist and novelist; chiefly associated with Henri Meilhac. They wrote the libretti for operas by Offenbach and Bizet (*La Belle Helene, La Grande Duchesse de Gerolstein, Carmen*, etc.), *Froufrou*, and other plays. His successful novels include *L'Abbe Constantin* and *La Famille Cardinal*.

HALF-TONE. See ENGRAVING.

HALIBURTON, THOMAS CHANDLER (1796-1865), an author, was b. in Nova Scotia. Called to the bar there, he eventually rose to be chief justice, to which high office he was appointed in 1828. He retired in 1856, when he came to England, where he resided until his death. He was the author of many books, including histories of his native province; but it is for his writings under the pseudonym of 'Sam Slick' that he became best known. The three series of *The Clockmaker, or Sayings and Doings of Sam Slick of Slickville*, 1837-40, were reprinted in England and attracted much attention. His wit was racy, and the rigour of his outspokenness was only gilded by the humorous coating under which he disguised it. There is a memoir by F. Blake Crofton 1889.

HALIBUT, HIPPOGLOSSUS VULGARIS, large flat fish of predatory habits, found in N. hemisphere; distinguished by large mouth, right-sided eyes, and narrowness of body; length, 2-5½ ft.; female lays up to five million pelagic eggs.

HALICARNASSUS, modern Budrun (37° N., 27° 20′ E.), ancient Gk. city, Caria, Asia Minor, on Ceramic Gulf; site of the world-famous mausoleum, built 352 B.C.

HALIFAX, a city and cap. of Nova Scotia, Canada, situated on the E. coast on a fortified eminence on Chebucto Bay. The harbour is 6 m. long and 1 m. wide, and is open all through the year, having splendid anchorage. It has two entrances which are formed by McNab's Island, situated in the mouth, and in the N. it is connected by a narrow channel with Bedford Basin, which is deep enough for the largest vessels. Until 1905 this was the sole point in Canada with a garrison of British regular troops. It is the Atlantic terminus of the Inter-colonial, Canadian Pacific, and other railways. The harbor is one of finest in the world; is well fortified; seat of Dalhousie Univ.; large sea trade, especially in fish, apples, lumber, and agricultural produce; large quantities of munitions exported during Great War. In Dec. 1917 a large area of the city was destroyed, and over 5,000 people killed and injured, as result of explosion following collision in Halifax harbor of Fr. steamship loaded with munitions and Norweg. relief ship; part of suburb Dartmouth, on opposite side of harbour, was laid in ruins.

HALIFAX, GEORGE MONTAGUE DUNK, 2ND EARL OF (1716-71), Brit. administrator; president, Board of Trade 1748; lord-lieutenant of Ireland 1761; secretary of state in Bute's cabinet 1762, and in Grenville's 1763-5; secretary of state in Lord North's government at time of his death.

HALIFAX, GEORGE SAVILE, 1ST MARQUESS OF (1633-95), Eng. politician and author; opposed bill excluding James, Duke of York, from succession 1680; lord privy seal 1682. Under James II. became president of Council 1685, but shortly afterwards was dismissed from office; was one of the commissioners sent by James II. to arrange terms with William of Orange; held office as lord privy seal in early part of William's reign, but retired in 1690.

HALL, ARTHUR CRAWSHAY ALLISTON (1847), Bishop. *B.* in England. Educated at Christ Church, Oxford and Universities of Vermont and Columbia. Minister of Church of England; licensed preacher in Diocese of Oxford as member of Society of St. John the Evangelist. Assistant minister in 1874 of church of the Advent, Boston. From 1882-1891 minister at Mission Church of St. John the Evangelist. Was consecrated bishop in 1894. Author of *The Virgin Mother, Christ's Temptation and Ours, Charges on Liberty and Loyalty, A Companion to the Prayer Book, The Christian Doctrine of Prayer, Meditations on the Lord's Prayer. d.* 1930.

HALL, ASAPH (1829-1907), an American astronomer, *b.* in Goshen, Conn. He graduated from the University of Michigan and after serving as instructor in several colleges was made professor of mathematics in the United States Navy. He made several important astronomical discoveries including that of the two moons of Mars, which were named by him Dimos and Phobos.

HALL, BASIL (1788-1844), a British naval officer, *b.* at Edinburgh. He entered the navy in 1801, and was present at the battle of Corunna in 1809, on board the *Endymion.* In 1816 he went to China with Lord Amherst's embassy, and described the incidents of the commission and the explorations in the Eastern seas, etc., in his *Account of a Voyage of Discovery to the West Coast of Corea and the Great Loo-Choo Islands,* 1818. He also published *Philosophical Transactions; Extracts from a Journal written on the Coasts of Chili, Peru, and Mexico;* and *Fragments of Voyages and Travels,* which contains, besides the subject-matter of the title, some interesting accounts of the navy in the early part of the 19th Century. In 1842 H.'s mind gave way, and he ended his days in Haslar Hospital.

HALL, CHARLES CUTHBERT (1852-1908), American Presbyterian clergyman. *B.* in New York, Sept. 3, 1852; *d.* there March 25, 1908. Graduating from Williams College in 1872 and the Union Theological Seminary in 1873, he completed his studies in London and Edinburgh. Was pastor of the Presbyterian Church at Newburgh, N. Y., 1875-1877; First Presbyterian Church, Brooklyn, N. Y., 1877-1897; elected president of the Union Theological Seminary, 1897. Among his publications are 'Does God Send Trouble', 1894; 'Gospel of the Divine Sacrifice', 1896; 'Christ and the Human Race', 1905, and 'Christ and the Soul', 1909.

HALL, CHARLES FRANCIS (1821-1871), Arctic explorer. *B.* in Rochester, New Hampshire, in 1821; *d.* in Thank God Harbor, Greenland, Nov. 8, 1871. He led two expeditions to trace the unfortunate Franklin expedition, 1860-1862 and 1864-1869 and from the natives of King Williams Land learned of the fate of 79 of the 105 members of Franklin's party. In 1871 he commanded the government ship Polaris in a north Pole expedition and reached 82° 11′ N. the highest northern latitude then attained. Publications 'Arctic Researches and Life Among the Exquimaux', 1864; 'Narrative of the 2nd Arctic Expedition', 1879. See DAVIS 'THE POLARIS NORTH POLE EXPEDITION'.

HALL, FLORENCE MARION HOWE (1845), Author. *B.* in Boston. Educated at private schools. Studied music with Otto Dresel, Boston. Was first chairman of correspondance of New Jersey of General Federation of Women's Clubs. Vice-president of department of education of New Jersey State Federation of Women's Clubs from 1911-1913. Regent continental Chapter of Daughters of American Revolution. Author of 'Social Customs', 1887; 'The Correct Thing', 1888, 1902, 'Flossy's Play-days', 1906; 'Social Usages at Washington,' 1906; 'Handbook of Hospitality in Town and Country', 1910; 'The A B C of Correct Speech', 1916. In 1913 edited the Julia Ward Howe and the Woman Suffrage Movement. *d.* 1922.

HALL, FREDERIC ALDIN (1854), University Chancellor. *B.* in Maine. Educated at Drury and Tufts Colleges and Universities of Washington and Missouri. 1878-1891 principal of Drury Academy. 1898-1901 dean of Drury College. At Springfield, Missouri, 1899-1901 director of Summer School. Chancellor of Washington University since 1917. Trustee of Drury College. From 1900-1910 director and superintendent St. Louis City Missionary Society. Member of Archaeological Institute of America, Phi Beta Kappa. Decorated in 1918, Order of the Redeemer. Author of 'Homeric Studies for young Readers'; 'Outline of the Odyssey'; 'Outline of the Orestrian Trilogy'; 'Iphigenia in Literature'. *d.* 1925.

HALL, GRANVILLE STANLEY (1846-1924), Univ. president. *B.* in Ashfield, Mass., Feb. 1, 1846. He graduated from Williams in 1867 (A.B. A.M.) Union Theological Seminary 1867-1868 and studied in Germany, 1871-1872. Was professor of psychology Antioch College, 1872-1876; instructor in English, Harvard, 1876-1877; professor of psychology Johns Hopkins, 1881-1888; president and professor of psychology Clark University 1888-1920. He founded and edited the American Journal of Psychology 1887-1921. Fellow of the American Academy of Arts and Sciences, etc. Publications include 'Adolescence', 1904; 'Educational Problems', 1911; 'The Foundations of Modern Psychology', 1912; 'Supreme Standard of Life and Conduct', 1920; 'Recreations of a Psychologist', 1920.

HALL, JAMES NORMAN (1887), Author. *B.* in Colfax, Iowa. Bachelor of Philosophy of Grinnell College. Author of 'Kitchener's Mob', 1916; 'High Adventure', 1918; 'Faery Lands of the South Seas', (with C. Nordhoff), 1921.

HALL, JOHN LESSLIE (1856), College Dean. *B.* in Richmond, Va. Educated in Randolph-Macon College. Doctor of Philosophy of Johns Hopkins University, 1892. In 1921 Doctor of Laws of William and Mary College. 1888-1907 professor of English and History, English literature and languages since 1907 and dean of faculty of William and Mary College. Author of 'Translation of Beowulf', 1892; 'Old English Idyls', 1899; Judith, Phoenix and Other Anglo-Saxon Poems', 1902; 'English Usage', 1917; Joint editor of Baskerville, Harrison and Hall's Anglo-Saxon Reader, 1900; 'Half-Hours in Southern History'.

HALL, LYMAN (1725-1790), A signer of the Declaration of Independence. *B.* in Connecticut in 1725. Graduating from Yale College in 1747 he later moved to St. John's parish, Georgia. Many people from New England had settled there who were active in persuading Georgia to cast in her lot with the Colonies. In 1775 Hall was sent as delegate to the Congress and was allowed to debate, but not to vote, as he was Georgia's only representative. Later he was one of the five delegates to Congress elected by the State. He was re-elected 1776 and 1780, and was governor of Georgia 1783-1785.

HALL, PERCIVAL (1872), College President. *B.* in Georgetown, District of Columbia. Bachelor of Arts, Harvard College, 1892; Master of Arts, Gallaudet

College, 1893; Doctor of Literature, Washington University, 1914. From 1893-1895 instructor at School for the Deaf, Washington Heights, New York; instructor and professor of mathematics, 1895-1910 and since 1910 president of Gallaudet College; president board of directors Columbia Institute for the Deaf; president of Convention of American Instructors of the Deaf.

HALL, THOMAS CUMING (1858), Theologian. *B.* in Ireland. Bachelor of Arts, Princeton College in 1879 and in 1882 graduated from Union Theological Seminary. Doctor of Divinity of Marburg, 1921. In 1883 ordained Presbyterian Minister; 1883-1886 pastor in Omaha. At 41st Street Church from 1886-1893. At the Fourth Church 1893-1897 in Chicago. At Union Theological Seminary, 1898-1917 professor of Christian Ethics. 1921-1923 professor of philosophy, faculty of University of Göttingen. Author of 'The Power of an Endless Life', 1893; 'The Social Significance of the Evangelical Revival in England', 1899; 'The Synoptic Gospels', 1900; 'Social Solutions in the Light of Christian Ethics', 1910.

HALLAM, ARTHUR HENRY (1811-33), Eng. poet, elder *s.* of Henry Hallam, the historian; his sudden death at Vienna inspired Tennyson's poem *In Memoriam*; literary *Remains*, ed. by his *f.* pub. in 1834.

HALLAM, HENRY (1777-1859), Eng. historian; careful investigator; produced work incisive, judicious, and accurate; chief works include *View of the State of Europe during the Middle Ages*, 1818; *Constitutional History of England from Accession of Henry VII. to Death of George II.* 1827; *Introduction to the Literature of Europe in the Fifteenth, Sixteenth, and Seventeenth Centuries*, 1838-39, etc.

HALLE-AN-DER-SAALE (52° 5′ N., 8° 22′ E.), town, Prussian Saxony, Germany; cathedral and famous university, founded 1694, 2500 students; salt-works.

HALLECK, FITZ-GREENE (1790-1867), American poet and writer. *B.* in Guildford, Conn., July 8, 1790; *d.* there Nov. 19, 1867. At the age of 18 he was employed by a bank and continued there for 20 years. John Jacob Astor engaged him as confidential agent and also appointed him one of the first trustees of the Astor Library. In 1849 Mr. Halleck retired to his native town. From early youth he had written prose and verse. With Joseph Rodman Drake he wrote 'The Croaker Papers' for the N. Y. Post in 1819; 'Fancy' a satire, is

his longest poem. He is best remembered to-day by the stirring martial poem 'Marco Bozzaris'. His 'Complete Poems', in one volume were published. See WELLS' 'LIFE AND LETTER OF FITZ-GREENE-HALLECK'.

HALLECK, HENRY WAGER (1815-1872), American soldier. *B.* in Westernville, N. Y., Jan. 16, 1815; *d.* Louisville, Ky., Jan. 9, 1872. Graduating from the U. S. Military Academy in 1839, he engaged in engineering work in Washington and New York. Secretary of State, California, 1847-1849; Inspector of lighthouses 1852-1854 and then resigned for law practice in San Francisco. Was president of the Pacific and Atlantic R. R., 1850-1861. In 1861 during the Civil War he was in command of the Department of Missouri; directed the western campaign of 1862, and captured Corinth, and in July of that year was made general-in-chief of U. S. armies until superseded by Grant in March, 1864, Chief-of-Staff to 1865; commanded the military division of the James, 1865, of the Pacific, 1865-1869, and of the South until death. Author of 'Elements of Military Art and Science', 1864; 'Bitumen' and 'International Law', 1861.

HALLELUJAH, ALLELUIA (Heb. 'Praise the Lord'), exclamation of religious praise or exaltation; *Psalms* 113-118, called H., in R.C. Church, as song of gladness, not used throughout Lent.

HALLER, ALBRECHT VON (1708-77), Swiss anatomist, phsyiologist, pathologist, botanist, and poet; after wide course of study he practised as physician at Bern, and became prof. of Medicine, Anatomy, Bot., and Surgery at Göttingen 1736; establishing a botanic garden, anatomical museum, school of obstetrics, etc.; retured to Bern as a magistrate; his most valuable researches are in physiology and bot., and he took a prominent part in the literary movement of the time, writing three political romances and descriptive lyrical and other poems.

HALLETT, RICHARD MATTHEWS (1887), Author. *B.* at Bath, Maine. At Harvard College, 1907; Bachelor of Arts 1910; Bachelor of Laws. Author of 'The Lady Aft', 1915; 'Trial by Fire', 1916; (Serials) 'The House of Craigenude', 'Ticklish Waters' and in 1921 'The Canyon of the Fools'. Writes for the Saturday Evening Post.

HALLEY, EDMUND (1656-1742); Eng. astronomer; ed. Queen's Coll., Oxford; stayed at St. Helena, 1676-78; made catalogue of stars of S. hemisphere and arranged them in constellations; discovered 1682 comet which bears his name, and correctly predicted its return in 1759; made astronomer-royal, 1719.

HALLEY, JOSEPH ROSWELL (1826-1905), an American statesman, *b.* in Stewartsville, N. C. He studied law and entering politics became prominent as an orator and speaker. He served throughout the Civil War receiving the rank of major general. He was governor of Connecticut in 1866 and was president of the Republican National Convention of 1868. He served in Congress from 1872 to 1876 and was president of the United States Centennial Commission, from 1873 to 1876. He was elected to the Senate in 1881, serving until 1905.

HALLEY'S COMET. See COMET.

HALLIWELL-PHILLIPS, JAMES ORCHARD (1820–89), Eng. scholar; his works include an edit. of Shakespeare, 1853–65; *Life of S.* 1848; *Dictonary of Old English Plays*, 1860, etc.

HALL-MARKS, the marks placed on gold or silver articles to indicate the quality of the gold or silver; *e.g.*, in the case of gold, a crown and the number 22 indicate that the article is of 22 carat gold (*i.e.*, contains 22 parts of gold out of 24). On silver ware the marks indicate respectively that the articles are of 11 oz. 10 dwt. and 11 oz. 2 dwt. fineness, showing the proportion of pure silver in 1 lb. (= 12 oz.) of the metals thus marked. Hall-marks on silver plate were introduced in the 13th cent. by the Eng. Guild of Goldsmiths and Silversmiths; these were the king's mark, the maker's mark, and the year's mark. Some provincial towns have their own assay marks. The lion *passant* was introduced in 1554; from 1784 to 1890 the sovereign's portrait was used.

HALL OF FAME, a building on University Heights, New York City, on the grounds of the New York University. It was erected from a gift of $100,000, afterwards increased to $250,000 for a building to be called 'The Hall of Fame for Great Americans'. On the ground floor of the buildings is a museum, 200 feet long by 40 feet wide, consisting of a corridor and six halls to contain mementos of the names inscribed above. The collonade is 600 feet, with provision for 150 panels, each to bear the name of a famous American. Only those persons who shall have been dead 25 years or more are eligible to be chosen. The names are selected by a committee composed of prominent persons. The Hall was dedicated on May 30, 1901, when 25 national associations each unveiled one of the brass tablets in the collonade. On May 30, 1907 eleven new tablets were unveiled. Up to 1933 the names of 62 men and 7 women had been inscribed on the tablets. In May, 1923 the busts of Edgar Allen Poe, George Washington, General Grant, Miss Maria Mitchell and Mark Hopkins were unveiled.

HALLOWE'EN (Oct. 31), the Eve of All Saints' Day; usually devoted to merry-making and divination.

HALLUCINATION, term applied to a false appreciation of sense impressions, the individual believing that a sense-organ has received an impression from some object which has in reality no physical existence. The hallucination may involve any of the senses, but most commonly it is auditory or visual, due to the more striking character of such impressions and to the more constant use of the ears and eyes; it may, in rare cases, involve two senses. Hallucinations may be experienced by certain individuals under conditions of quite normal health and sanity, to which no precise cause can be assigned; they may be experienced under conditions differing but slightly from the normal, as when one or other of the senses has been subjected to a strain, or when the body has been in want of food for a considerable period, or when an individual is under the influence of certain drugs (opium or Indian hemp) or in the transitional state between sleep and waking, or in a state of hypnosis, or under conditions of intense emotional excitement; they may be experienced when the body or mind is in a diseased condition, as in diseases of the heart, lungs, or abdominal organs, or in delirium tremens, hysteria, or epilepsy, as well as in conditions of more advanced mental disease, melancholia, mania, monomania, and other forms of insanity. The condition precedent of all forms of hallucination is partial or total dissociation of consciousness.

The physiological explanation of hallucination is that in the cerebral cortex certain centres normally work in association with others, all being capable of stimulation by sensory stimuli. If some of the association-paths between centres are blocked, as in fatigue, disease, etc., the excitements in one centre will radiate into unusual paths, and so excite centres not usually excited from these paths. The perception thus aroused, however, will naturally be referred to the ordinary sensory stimulus, and the result is a hallucination. There is a disturbance of the normal relation between the central and the peripheral nervous elements.

HALLUIN (50° 47′ N., 3° 8′ W.); fortified town, Nord, France; textiles.

HALMAHERA (1° N., 128° E.), island of the Dutch East Indies, E. of Celebes; area, *c.* 6800 sq. miles; consists of four peninsulas, each traversed by a mountain chain from 3000 to 4000 ft. high, with several active volcanoes. Chief town, Gilolo.

HALMSTAD (56° 39′ N., 12° 49′ E.), seaport, Sweden, on Cattegat; breweries, cloth manufactures; exports granite. It is an important railroad and steamship center. Pop., 1930, 18,400.

HALO, a luminous circle around sun or moon, caused by refraction of light passing through ice-crystals suspended in the atmosphere; true h's are large circles of definite diameters, 45° and 92°, which are seldom both seen together; usually whitish, but occasionally exhibit prismatic colours, red being on inside; smaller coloured circles sometimes seen round the moon are due to diffraction of light by cloud or mist.

HALO, originally a circular metal plate to preserve heads of statues; adopted by Christian artists as symbol of holiness; may be cruciform, square, or stellate; but generally takes form of circle or ring; found also in early Oriental paganism.

HALOGENS are Fluorine, Chlorine, Bromine, and Iodine. Each forms monobasic gaseous acid.

HALPINE, CHARLES GRAHAM (**MILES O'REILLY**) (1829-1868), American journalist and poet. *B.* in Oldcastle, County Meath, Ireland, Nov. 20, 1829; *d.* in New York, Aug. 3, 1868. After studying at Trinity College, Dublin, he came to Boston in 1851 and was assistant-editor of the Boston Post. With B. P. Shillaber (Mrs. Partington), he started a comic weekly 'The Carpet Bag' which failed. As Washington correspondent of the N. Y. Times his letters attracted attention, and he joined the staff of the N. Y. Herald. In the Civil War he enlisted in the 69th N. Y. Volunteers, became assistant adjutant-general under Hunter and a Colonel with Halleck, resigning in 1864, brevetted brigadier-general. Was noted for his humorous verse. Publications 'Life and Adventures, Songs, Services, and Speeches', 1864; 'Poetic Works', 1865.

HALS, FRANS (*c.* 1580-1666), Dutch artist; famed for portraits and genre subjects, in the latter of which he is one of the greatest of Dutch masters. He was particularly successful in dealing with scenes of carousal, depicting laughter, etc. (e.g. *The Laughing Cavalier*). Fine examples of his work are in the galleries of Amsterdam and Haarlem. He was notorious for his drunken and disorderly life. His *b.*, Dirk H., and his *s.*, Frans H., the Younger, were also artists of distinction.

HALSBURY, HARDINGE STANLEY GIFFARD, 1ST EARL OF (1825-1921). Brit. Conservative statesman; Lord Chancellor, 1895-1905; M.P. for Launceston, 1877-85; Solicitor-Gen. 1875-80; cr. Baron H., 1885; Earl, 1898; formerly held large criminal practice; was engaged in Tichborne trial; gave judgment in House of Lords 1904 in the appeal of Scot. Free Church against the Scot. .U F. Church; led extreme 'Die-Hard' party in Lords against Parliament Bill.

HALSEY, FRANCIS WHITING (1851-1919), Author and editor. *B.* in Unadilla, N. Y., Oct. 15, 1851; *d.* in New York, Nov. 20, 1919. Graduating from Cornell in 1873 he engaged in journalism, first with N. Y. Tribune, 1875-1880, then the N. Y. Times, 1880-1902, editing the Times Saturday Review from its first number in 1896 to 1902. He was literary adviser for D. Appleton, 1902-1905, and for Funk and Wagnalls, 1905-1919. Author of 'The Old Northern Frontier', 1901; 'Our Literary Deluge', 1902. Editor 'American Authors and Their Homes', 'Authors of Our Day in Their Homes', 1902; 'Women Authors of Our Day in Their Homes'; 'The World's Famous Orations' (with W. J. Bryan), 1906; 'Great Epochs in American History', 1912; 'Seeing Europe with Famous American Authors', 1914, etc.

HALSTEAD, MURAT (1829-1908). American journalist. *B.* in Ross, Butler co., Ohio, Sept. 29, 1829; *d.* in Cincinnati, July 2, 1908. He studied at Farmers College near Cincinnati and began to write for newspapers at 18. In 1854 he bought an interest in the Commercial, of Cincinnati, which was afterwards combined with its rival The Gazette as The Commercial-Gazette and became the organ of the Republican Party in Ohio. In 1890 Mr. Halstead moved to Brooklyn, New York and edited The Standard-Union. During the Spanish War he was special correspondent in the Philippines. Author of 'The Story of Cuba', 'Life of William McKinley', 'Story of the Philippines', 'The History of American Expansion', 'The Boer and British War', 'War between Russia and Japan', etc.

HAM, one of the sons of Noah (*Genesis*), founder of the Hamitic race, including the Ethiopians, Egyptians, and others.

HAM. See MEAT PRODUCTS.

HAMADAN (34° 55′ N., 48° 20′ E.); town, Persia, near foot of Mt. Elvend; important entrepôt of trade; extensive manufactures of leather; contains tomb of Avicenna, and another, said to be that of Mordecai and Esther; occupies site of ancient *Ecbatana*.

HAMAH, OR HAMATH, famous Hittite city, referred to in Bible, situated on the Orontes, about 100 miles from Damascus; conquered by the Assyrians, VIII. cent. B.C.

HAMBURG, free city and state, Germany (53° 33′ N., 10° E.), on N. branch of Elbe; second largest city in Germany; greatest seaport and commercial town on Continent. The old town is intersected by canals (Fleete), and is surrounded by fine shaded promenades. To N. lie two wide sheets of water, the Binnen- and Aussen-Alster separated by Lombard's Brücke; fashionable quarter surrounds Binnen-Alster. Docks on both sides of river cover huge area; part of harbor in a free port. Hamburg trades chiefly with Britain and America, also with Scandinavian, Russian, S. Amer., Eastern, and other ports; chief imports are sugar, tea, coffee, chocolate, lard, rice, wine, herrings, skins, leather, wax, hemp, tobacco, jute, indigo, oils, rubber, coal; chief industries are food-stuffs, breweries, shipbuilding, machinery, chemicals, furniture, musical and scientific instruments, and factories where above imports are treated. Little of mediaeval Hamburg survives owing to great fire 1842. Among the chief buildings are St. Peter's, St. Nicholas's, and St. Michael's churches, Rathaus, Kunst-halle, museums, etc. Hamburg has important schools of navigation and commerce, and before Great War had a world-famous zoological garden. Hamburg was founded by Charlemagne 808; in mid-13th cent. formed Hanseatic League with Lübeck and Bremen; made free imperial city 1510; joined Deutscher Bund 1815; Nord-Deutscher Bund 1866; Ger. Empire 1871; and Zollverein 1888; great cholera plague 1892. During World War Hamburg suffered greatly, its shipping trade, on which it depended largely for prosperity, being destroyed. In early days of revolution of 1918 the city was the scene of a good deal of rioting, and two warships in harbor were blown up. Hamburg state (area, 160 sq. m.) is a republic governed by senate and house of burgesses, and after revolution of 1918 constitution was made more democratic. Pop., 1930, 1,133,000.

HAMBOURG, MARK (1879), Russian pianist and composer; *b.* Bogutchar, South Russia. He studied music under Leschetitzky at Vienna, where he obtained the Liszt scholarship in 1894. His concert debut was made at Moscow in 1888 and was followed by a successful tour of the leading European capitals.

He also toured America, 1899-1900, 1902-03, 1907; South Africa, 1905-1907 and made his first Canadian tour in 1910. He has become a naturalized British subject. His publications include *Variations On a Theme by Paganini, Volkslied, Impromptu Minuet* and *How To Become a Pianist*, 1922.

HAMBY, WILLIAM HENRY (1875); Writer. *B.* at Wright County, Missouri. Educated at Drury College and University of Missouri. From 1895-1905 was owner at, Boulder, Colorado; Meadville, Missouri; Marceline, Missouri of newspapers. Writes special articles and fiction for various magazines including McClure's, Century and Saturday Evening Post. Author of 'Tom Henry of Wahoo County', 1911; 'Getting and Holding', 1910; 'The Sound of the Hammer', 1914; 'If a Man Fails Seven Times', 1917; 'The Way of Success', 1918; 'The Desert Fiddler', 1919; 'Crooked Water', 1921; 'Vagabond's End', 1921. *d.* 1928.

HAMELIN, FRANÇOIS ALPHONSE (1796-1864), Fr. admiral and naval administrator; was engaged in bombardment of Sebastopol 1854; as Minister of Marine was responsible for construction of the first ironclad, *Gloire,* launched 1859.

HAMELN (52° 7′ N., 9° 21′ E.); town, Hanover, Prussia; formerly fortified; many quaint buildings associated with legend of the Pied Piper; iron- and paper-works.

HAMERTON, PHILIP GILBERT (1834-94), Eng. artist and author; wrote *Etching and Etchers, The Intellectual Life,* and numerous other works of art criticism.

HAMILCAR BARCA (*d.* 228 B.C.); Carthaginian general; maintained Carthaginian rule against Romans in Sicily; 247-241; opposed Romans in Spain, *c.* 236-228; great military genius; *f.* of Hannibal.

HAMILTON, a city of Ontario, Canada, in Wentworth co., of which it is the capital. It is on the Grand Trunk, the Canadian Pacific, and the Toronto, Hamilton and Buffalo railroads, and on Burlington Bay. It has an excellent harbor and the city is an important commercial center and has steamship connection with lake ports. It is the center of an important fruit growing region of western Ontario. Excellent water power is furnished by the Decew Falls, 35 miles southeast of the city. Natural gas is supplied from the Welland field. Hamilton has over 500 manufacturing establishments which include a great variety of industries.

HAMILTON, a city of Ohio, in Butler co., of which it is the county seat. It is on the Baltimore and Ohio, the Pennsylvania System, Erie and Cincinnati, and Cincinnatti and Dayton railroads, and on both sides of the Great Miami River and on the Miami and Erie Canal. Abundant water power is supplied by the river for the extensive industries which include the manufacture of paper, stoves and furnaces, safes and bank vaults, machine tools, blankets and underwear, and the refining of sugar. The public institutions include Notre Dame Academy, the Hamilton Children's Home, and the Mercy Hospital.

HAMILTON (55° 47′ N.; 4° 3′ W.), town, on Clyde, Lanarkshire, Scotland; near it is Hamilton Palace, a seat of the Duke of Hamilton; in neighbourhood are remains of ancient castle of Cadzow; chief industry, coal and iron mining. Pop. 1921, 39,420. (37° 45′ S., 142° 1′ E.), town, Victoria, Australia; has fine racecourse; is centre of agricultural and pastoral district

HAMILTON, chief town, on Hamilton I., Bermudas, W. Indies (32° 16′ N., 64° 55′ W.), safe harbor; Brit. garrison.

HAMILTON COLLEGE, educational institution located at Clinton, N. Y. It was founded by a Congregational missionary, Samuel Kirkland, in 1793, but owing to lack of funds the building itself was not opened until 1798. Designed at first as an academy for both white and Indian children, the institution gradually expanded its curriculum and facilities until in 1812 it was chartered by the State as Hamilton College, in honor of Alexander Hamilton, who had contributed to its funds and assisted in its growth. It offers two courses of study: the Classical and the Latin-Scientific. It has fine laboratories, thorough equipment and a library of over 70,000 volumes. In 1933 it had an enrollment of 450 students and there were 48 members in the Faculty.

HAMILTON (53° N., 60° W.), river, Labrador, Canada; flows into the Atlantic through Hamilton inlet.

HAMILTON, Scot. family, descended from Walter Fitz-Gilbert, a supporter of Bruce who was granted barony of Cadzow in return for his services; his *s.* David was captured at Neville's Cross, 1346, and was founder of chantry in Glasgow Cathedral, 1361. In 1445 Sir James H. of Cadzow became Lord H., and in 1503 his *s.* James was cr. Earl of Arran. The second Earl of Arran was tutor to Mary, Queen of Scots, for whom his eldest *s.* James was proposed as husband. James afterwards lost his reason, and his *b.* John, as head of family, became 1st Marquess of H. in 1599; he was accused of share in murder of Regents Lennox and Murray.

James, 1st Duke of Hamilton 1606-49, 3rd marquess, obtained dukedom in 1643; served under Gustavus Adolphus, 1631; took part in disputes between Charles I. and Covenanters, and went to Scotland with the king in 1641; for a short time he deserted the Royalist cause and threw in his lot with Argyll, but was subsequently restored to favour. In 1648 he commanded Scots army in England in support of king, but was defeated and captured at Preston, and executed in the following year. William, 2nd Duke 1616-51, Royalist in Civil War, was mortally wounded at Worcester. James, 4th Duke 1658-1712, opposed Union of Parliaments. James, 6th Duke, m. Elizabeth Gunning. Present Duke 13th succ. 1895. Dukes of Abercorn are cadet branch of H. family, and Earls of Haddington also came from Walter FitzGilbert.

HAMILTON, ALEXANDER (1757-1804), American statesman. *B.* in Charles Town, Nevis Island, West Indies, Jan. 11, 1757; *d.* in New York, July 12, 1804. He was a natural *s.* of James Hamilton and Rachel Levine, a woman of French extraction separated from her husband. After his mother's death her relatives cared for him and sent him to the United States to be educated. Graduating from King's College now Columbia in 1773, he became noted for his brilliant advocacy of the cause of the Colonists. Captain of the first Continental Artillery Company he fought in the battles of Long Island White Plains, Trenton, and Princeton and in 1777 was Lt. Colonel and aid-de-camp on Washington's staff. In 1780 he married Elizabeth Schuyler, *d.* of General Schuyler of New York. At the siege of Yorktown he headed a storming party that captured an important British redoubt. After the war he practiced law; was a member of the Continental Congress 1782-1783, the Annapolis Convention of 1776 and Constitutional Convention of 1787. A member of Congress 1787-1788 he was the first U. S. Secretary of the Treasury 1789-1795. After parties were formed he led the Federalists being opposed by Jefferson, the Republican leader. When a French war was threatened in 1899-1800, John Adams through deference to Washington made Hamilton the actual head of the army. The Federals were defeated in 1800 through the publication of an anti-Adams pamphlet written by Hamllton. When Burr and Jefferson were nominated, Hamilton forgot his differences with the latter and worked for his success. Burr never forgot this, and found a pretext to call Hamilton out. They fought a duel at Weehawken, July 11, 1804 when Hamilton was mortally wounded and d. July 12, 1804. He was brilliant in framing constructive measures of government and his services to the young nation cannot be overestimated.

HAMILTON, CLAYTON (MEEKER) (1881), Author, lecturer, editor. *B.* in Brooklyn, N. Y. Bachelor of Arts of Polytechnic Institute of Brooklyn, 1900. 1901-1904 at Barnard and Columbia College tutor in English. Since 1903 extension lecturer at Columbia. At Classical School for Girls, 1900-1920 lecturer. 1903-1906 at New York Department of Education. At Brooklyn Institute Arts and Sciences 1913-1919; dramatic critic and associate editor from 1907-1909 of the Forum, The Bookman, 1910-1918 Vogue, 1912-1920. Author of 'The Stranger at the Inn', 1913; play and other Books, 'Materials and Methods of Fiction', 1908; 'Studies in Stagecraft', 1914; 'Seen on the Stage', 1920. From 1920-1922 associate editor at Goldwyn Studios.

HAMILTON, EMMA, LADY (*c.* 1765-1815), was the humbly born and beautiful wife of Sir William H., ambassador at Naples; principally remembered as mistress of Nelson; subject of many pictures by Romney; *d.* in poverty at Calais.

HAMILTON, GAIL pseudonym of Mary Abigail Dodge *c.* 1830-96, Amer. author; wrote *Woman's Wrongs* 1868, etc.

HAMILTON, SIR IAN STANDISH MONTEITH (1853), Brit. general; entered army 1873; fought under Roberts in Afghanistan 1878-80; with Low in Chitral relief expedition 1895; commanded 3rd Brigade in Tirah War 1897-8. On outbreak of S. African War appointed chief of staff of the Natal relief force under Sir G. White; commanded at Elandslaagte (Oct. 21, 1899); through siege of Ladysmith; subsequently commanded mounted infantry division; chief of staff to Kitchener 1901, and again commanded mobile columns in W. Transvaal. Quartermaster-general of army 1903-4. At outbreak of World War appointed to commnad 4th Army, which he was organizing when sent to take charge of land forces at the Dardanelles. He was relieved of his command in Oct., 1915. He pub. *A Jaunt in a Junk*, 1884; *Fighting of the Future,* 1885; *Icarus*, 1886; *A Ballad of Hadji*, 1887; and in 1920 issued his *Gallipoli Diary* (2 vols.),

HAMILTON, LORD GEORGE FRANCIS (1845), Brit. statesman; M.P. 1868-1906; under-secretary of state for India 1874-8; vice-president of Council 1878-80; first lord of the Admiralty 1885-92; chairman of London School Board 1894-95; secretary of state for India 1895-1903; chairman of commission of Poor Law and Unemployment 1905-9; chairman Mesopotamia Commission 1916-17.

HAMILTON, SIR WILLIAM (1730-1803), Brit. diplomatist and antiquarian; envoy at Naples; his wife became the mistress of Lord Nelson.

HAMILTON, SIR WILLIAM, BART. (1788-1856), Scot. philosopher; ed. Balliol Coll., Oxford; app. prof. of Civil History at Edinburgh, 1821, and of Logic and Metaphysics, 1836; pub. *Philosophy of the Unconditioned*, 1829; edit. Reid's works, 1846, and *Discussions in Philosophy, Lit., and Education*, 1852-53.

HAMIRPUR (25° 58' N., 80° 11' E.), town, capital of H. district, Allahabad, Brit. India; at junction of Betwa and Jumna; cotton and grain.

HAMITIC LANGUAGES AND PEOPLES.—Hamitic Languages are agglutinative or inflectional, and are generally grouped as the Ancient Egyptian, N. African, and Ethiopian or Cushite languages; of these the first are still represented by liturgy of Coptic Church, second by modern Berber dialects, and third by tongues spoken in Abyssinia and elsewhere.—Hamitic Peoples are generally classed as belonging to Caucasian family; include Berbers of N. Africa, Ethiopians, Egyptians, and other races. They are generally dark in complexion and of fine physique.

HAMLET, the hero of one of Shakespear's greatest tragedies which is founded upon a legend in the *Historia Danica* of Saxo Grammaticus (13th century). Shakespeare, however, owed little but the outline of his plot to Saxo, whose hero, Amleth, only feigned his madness and plotted a deliberate vengeance a year before carrying it out.

HAMLIN, ALFRED DWIGHT FOSTER (1855), American architect; *b.* Constantinople, Turkey. He was the *s.* of Cyrus Hamlin (*q.v.*). He graduated at Amherst College in 1875, and later pursued architectural studies at the Massachusetts Institute of Technology and at the Ecole des Beauxs-Arts, Paris. He joined the teaching staff of Columbia

University in 1883 as special instructor and later became professor of history and architecture in that institution. He has written extensively for periodicals. His publications include a *History of Architecture*, 1896; *European and Japanese Gardens, in collaboration*, 1902; *Cyrus Hamlin, Missionary*, 1903; and *History Of Ornament, Ancient and Mediaeval*, 1916. *d*. 1926.

HAMLIN, CHARLES SUMMER (1861), Member of Federal Reserve Board. *B.* in Boston; educated at Harvard and Washington and Lee Universities. Practised at Boston as lawyer from 1886-1893 and 1898-1913. 1893-1897 assistant secretary of the United States Treasury and again from 1913-1914. 1914-1916 member of Federal Reserve Board of Washington. For term of 1916-1926 reappointed. In 1887-1888 defeated for Massachusetts senate. Ran for secretary of State in 1892, but defeated. Defeated for Democratic nomination for governor in 1902-1910. In 1897 Special Commissioner to Japan from United States. At Harvard College, 1902, 1903 lectured on United States Government. Author of 'Index Digest of Interstate Commerce Laws', 1907; 'Index Digest of Federal Reserve Act', 'Index Digest of the Federal Reserve Bulletin', 1921.

HAMLIN, CYRUS (1811-1900), American missionary and educator; *b.* Waterford, Maine. He graduated at Bowdoin College in 1834 and at the Bangor Theological Seminary three years later. He chose the foreign field, and from 1837 to 1859 was a missionary to Turkey. In 1860 he became president of Robert College in Constantinople, one of the most notable educational institutions in the Near East. In 1877 he returned to this country and became a professor in Bangor Theological Seminary. Later he was president of Middlebury College, Vermont 1880-85. He was an expert in the Turkish and cognate tongues, and some of his writings were in the Armenian language. His publications in English include *Among the Turks*, 1887; and *My Life and Times*, 1893.

HAMLIN, HANNIBAL (1809-1891), an American statesman, *b.* near Paris Hill, Me. Studying law, he began to practice in Hampden, Me., in 1833, was several times elected to the state legislature, then, in 1842, was elected to Congress on a Democratic ticket. He entered the U. S. Senate in 1848 and served continuously till 1856, when he resigned to become governor of Maine, but a month later resigned as Governor to return to the U. S. Senate. On account of his Unionist sympathies he turned Republican at the outbreak of the Civil War and was elected Vice-President of the United States on the same ticket with Lincoln. During 1881-83 he was U. S. Minister to Spain.

HAMLINE UNIVERSITY, coeducational institution located at Hamline, Minn. It was originally established at Redwing, Minn., but was closed in 1869, an interval of eleven years elapsing before teaching was resumed at its present location. It has a course of study leading to the usual college degrees, a library of 15,000 volumes and an endowment fund of $1,100,000. In 1933 it had 503 students and 34 teachers.

HAMM (51° 40′ N., 7° 50′ E.), town, Westphalia, Prussia, on Lippe; iron foundries, wire-works; thermal baths; ancient capital of Mark.

HAMMER, tool consisting of a steel head, fixed generally on a wooden shaft, and used for striking purposes. The powerful 'steam-hammer,' now largely used in engineering works, was invented by James Nasmyth, about 1840.

HAMMERFEST, seaport town, Norway (70° 40′ N. 23° 45′ E.) on island of Klavö; the most northerly town in Europe; mean ann. temp. 36° F.; exports fish. fish oil, hides, and down.

HAMMERSMITH (51° 29′ N., 0° 14′ W.), borough, Middlesex, England; on N. side of Thames, forming part of W. London.

HAMMERSTEIN, OSCAR (1847-1919), an American theatrical and political manager, *b.* in Berlin, in 1847. In 1863 he came to the United States, where he engaged in the business of making cigars, and through several labor-saving devices accumulated a large fortune. He then engaged in many theatrical and operatic enterprises. After managing several theatres in New York, he built the Harlem Opera House, and afterwards the Manhattan Opera House, a large edifice to compete with the Metropolitan Opera House. He also built opera houses in Philadelphia and in Boston. He conducted several brilliant seasons of opera in New York, but on account of financial difficulties was obliged to make an agreement with the Metropolitan Opera Company to produce no more opera for ten years. Under his auspices appeared several of the most famous operatic stars, including Mary Garden. His ventures in Philadelphia and London were financial failures. He wrote several short comedies and operettas.

HAMMOND, a city of Indiana, in Lake co. It is on the Baltimore and

Ohio, the Chesapeake and Ohio, the Pere Marquette and other railroads, and on the Grand Calumet River. It is an important industrial community and has railroad supply shops, foundries, chemical works, packing houses, and steel works. Its public buildings include two high schools.

HAMMOND, JOHN HAYS (1855), mining engineer. *B.* in San Francisco, March 31, 1855. Educated at public and private schools;the Sheffield Scientific School 1876, and the Royal School of Mine Freiburg, Saxony. Geologist with the U. S. Geological Survey of the California gold fields in 1880. Consulting engineer of Union Iron Works, San Francisco, and of the Central and Southern Pacific railways. His mining experiences have been world-wide. In 1893 he was chief mining engineer for the Barnato Brothers and then for Cecil Rhodes; consulting engineer of Consolidated Gold Fields Co., South Africa, the British S. A. Co., and the Rand, Fontein Gold Mining Co. He was one of the four reform leaders in the Transvaal in 1895-1896. Though not in sympathy with the Jameson Raid he was arrested and condemned to death, the sentence being commuted to fifteen years imprisonment. He was finally released on paying a fine of $125,000. Returning to America in 1900 he was associated with great mining enterprises in the United States and Mexico. President Taft appointed him special ambassador to represent the United States at the coronation of George V. President of the Panama-Pacific Exposition Commission to Europe in 1912. Chairman of the Worlds Court Congress, 1914-1915; President of the National League of Republican Clubs; Chairman of the Federal Coal Commission, 1923.

HAMMOND, JOHN HAYS, JR. (1888), Inventor. *B.* in San Francisco, Cal. In 1910 at Sheffield Scientific School (Yale) Bachelor of Science; inventor of type of torpedo for coast defense, controlled by wireless energy from coast fortifications. This invention was recommended to congress by Board of Ordnance and Fortifications for purchase by United States. Invented incendiary projectiles used by allied armies in World War. Inventor of system of automobile torpedo firing type in latest battleships of United States. Approved by the United States Navy and Signal Corps, United States, a system of selective radio telegraphy. On Bartlett Expedition for Polar exploration his system of aerial coast surveying was used. Member of advisory Committee of Langley Aerodynamic Laboratory of Smithsonian Institute; fellow of American Geographic Society; was director of American Society of Aeronautic Engineers; honorary member of National Institute of Inventors.

HAMMOND, WILLIAM ALEXANDER (1828-1900), American surgeon; *b.* Annapolis, Md. He graduated at the University of the City of New York in 1848. In the following year he entered the army as assistant surgeon, rising through various grades until he was made surgeon-general in 1862. After the war he practised his profession in New York City, later devoting much of his time to literature. His publications include *Sleep and Its Nervous Derangements,* 1869; *Disease of the Nervous System,* 1871; besides novels, of which may be cited *Robert Severne, A Strong-Minded Woman, Mr. Oldmixon and Dr. Grattan,* 1884.

HAMMONTON, a city of New Jersey; in Atlantic co. It is on the Pennsylvania, Reading, and on the Seashore railroads. Surrounding it is an extensive fruit growing and poultry raising region of which it is the center. It has important manufactures of shoes, cut glass, underwear, optical instruments, etc.

HAMMURAPI, sometimes c a l l e d Hammurabi or Khammurabi, King of Babylon (2124-2081 B.C.). He was the *s.* of Sinmuballit and the sixth ruler of the first Babylonian Dynasty. A reference in the 14th chapter of *Genesis* would indicate that he participated with Chedorlaomer in a raid on Syria. During the first half of his reign he was occupied with the conquest of Mesopotamia. It is probable that Assur and Nineveh were included in his kingdom, although they may have acknowledged a shadowy suzerainty of Assyria. He was one of the greatest and noblest of Babylonian kings, and his celebrity is based not so much on his conquests as on his wisdom and organizing ability. Many important undertakings for the benefit of his kingdom such as the building of canals, construction of granaries as a safeguard against famine and the development of the financial resources of his realm are recorded in ancient inscriptions. He took pride in the title 'King of Righteousness'. He reorganized the judiciary, freed himself to some extent from the domination of the priesthood and devoted himself to the administration of justice. The code of Hammurapi (*q.v.*) is one of the most enlightened and interesting law compilations of ancient times.

HAMMURAPI OR HAMMURABI, CODE OF, a system of laws codified by the Babylonian king of that name (*q.v.*) engraved on a block of diorite discovered by De Morgan on the Acropolis of Susa 1901-02. There are 282 paragraphs in the code, comprising laws that deal respectively with property and persons and having many subdivisions. There is no religious legislation in the code, which is civil throughout. The legal principles on which the code are based are in the main wise and humane, and compare favorably with those of the Mosaic code. The latter in fact may have been influenced to some extent by the former. The weak, the poor, the widow and the orphan are protected against injustice from the powerful and rich. A woman had the right to own and dispose of property and she could also divorce her husband on certain grounds. Even the slave had certain legal rights. An advanced economic condition is shown by laws concerning land owners, deposits, loans, debts and other features of trade, property and commerce. It is impossible to tell how much of the code is due to Hammurabi's own conceptions of justice and equity and how much had already been embodied in collections of law compiled by earlier monarchs, but the principles laid down are far in advance of those contained in the legislation of other nations of that period.

HAMPDEN, JOHN (c. 1595-1643), Eng. politician; entered Parliament, 1621; chiefly famous for his refusal to pay ship-money (q. v.) in 1637; his trial before Court of Exchequer resulted in judgment against him, 1638. He was a determined opponent of Charles I., and a member of Short and Long Parliaments; had share in prosecution of Strafford; was one of five members impeached by Charles in 1642. On outbreak of Civil War he raised troops for Parliament; mortally wounded at Chalgrove Field, 1643.

HAMPDEN, WALTER, (WALTER HAMPDEN DOUGHERTY), (1879), Actor. B. in Brooklyn, N. Y.; student at Harvard and Bachelor of Arts, 1900 of Polytechnic Institute of Brooklyn. In 1901 with E. R. Benson's Company, made first appearance on stage in England. For three seasons at the Adelphi Theatre in London, was leading man. In 1905 succeeded the younger Irving as Hamlet. Returned to United States in 1907 and supported Alla Nazimova at Bijou Theatre, New York. Appeared in 'The Servant in the House', 'The Master Builder', 'The Yellow Jacket' and others. Has toured in Shakespearean repertoire.

HAMPDEN-SIDNEY COLLEGE, institution located at Hampden-Sidney, in Prince Edward co., Va. It was founded under Presbyterian auspices in 1776 and seven years later was incorporated under the laws of Virginia. Some of the most famous names of Revolutionary history, such as Patrick Henry, James Madison and others, were among the incorporators of the institution. The college owns a property of 250 acres. It has classical and scientific courses leading to the usual degrees. The library has more than 25,000 volumes. In 1933 there were 319 students in attendance and a teaching staff of 16 professors.

HAMPSHIRE, SOUTHAMPTON, Hants (51° N., 1°30' W.), county, S. England; bounded N. by Berkshire, W. by Dorset and Wiltshire, S. by Eng. Channel, E. by Surrey and Sussex. Isle of Wight, separated from mainland by Solent and Spithead, is included in county. On coast are Portsmouth Harbour, Southampton Water, Christchurch and Poole Bays; inland are fertile valleys, hills, and woods.

Chief towns: Southampton (one of chief ports in kingdom), Portsmouth, Winchester, Christchurch, Lymington, and Romsey, seaside resorts at Bournemouth, Milford, Southsea; and in Isle of Wight, Cowes, Ryde, Ventnor, and Newport; Aldershot, military training centre. Sheep, cattle, and horse-rearing, fishing, shipbuilding, brewing, tanning are carried on.

HAMPSTEAD (51° 33' N., 0° 11' W.); a N.W. district and residential suburb of London; associated with the names of Pope, Keats, Shelley, and many other men-of-letters; H. Heath is a popular pleasure-ground.

HAMPTON, a town of Virginia, in Elizabeth co., of which it is the county seat. It is on the Chesapeake and Ohio Railroad and is connected by steamship lines with various ports. Hampton is a favorite summer resort. It has excellent bathing ground at Buckroe Beach, on Chesapeake Bay. It is within two miles of Fortress Monroe. Its chief industry is oyster and crab fishing. It has, however, manufactures of brick and fish oil. Hampton is the seat of the Hampton Normal and Agricultural Institute for Negroes, and it has also a national soldiers' home and a national cemetery.

HAMPTON, village, Middlesex, England (51° 25' N., 0° 22' W.), on Thames. Pop. 10,500. *Hampton Court*, a former royal residence; fine gallery of paintings.

Hampton Court Conference was summoned by James I. 1604, as a result of Millenary Petition, presented by the Puritan clergy 1603, proposing changes in the Prayer-book. Conference, which consisted of Archbishop of Canterbury, bishops, church dignitaries, and four moderate Puritans, was a farce from point of view of Puritans, and no reasonable concessions were made.

HAMPTON, WADE (1818-1902), American Confederate commander; *b.* Columbia, S. C. He graduated from the University of South Carolina, studied law but never entered on its practice, devoting his time to the management of his extensive plantations. He served in both houses of the South Carolina legislature. He was a Union Democrat, but went with his State when it seceded, raised and equipped at his own expense a large body of troops called 'Hampton's Legion' and served on the Confederate side with great distinction throughout the war. He fought at Bull Run, Seven Pines, Gettysburg and in the Shenandoah. By 1864 he had reached the rank of lieutenant general and had command of Lee's entire cavalry force. Later, with Johnston, he fought bravely but unsuccessfully to stem Sherman's march to the sea. He assisted vigorously in the reconstruction of the South following the conflict. Served as governor of his State 1876-78 and in the latter year was chosen to the United States Senate, serving until 1891. He was U. S. commissioner of railroads from 1893 to 1897.

HAMPTON NORMAL AND AGRICULTURAL INSTITUTE. Founded in 1868 for the education of negroes and Indians at Hampton, Va. under the auspices of the American Mission Association; chartered in 1870. The inception of the institution was largely due to General Samuel Chapman Armstrong, director 1868-1893. The institute has an endowment fund of about $1,500,000, yearly income about $500,000; the property covering 188 acres near Hampton Roads contains 60 buildings. There are four educational divisions, academic, agricultural, trade, and graduates. Students may work for wages six days in the week all the year, and attend night school for eight months. Their wages are held as a bond that they will carry out the promise to finish their education. The Graduates course comprises agriculture, business, domestic arts and sciences, library methods, and school teaching. Booker T. Washington was a graduate. Total number of students, 1933-34, 2,387. Value of plant and equipment, est. almost $2,000,000. Pres. Geo. T. Phenix.

HAMPTON ROADS, an arm of the Chesapeake Bay, (at the mouth of the James River. It is between Hampton and Norfolk, Va., with Newport, Old Point Comfort, Fortress Monroe and Fort Wool in the neighborhood. It is a favorite summer and winter resort and has a bathing beach, bathing places and many historical sites in the neighborhood. It is notable as being the scene of the famous battle between the Monitor and the Merrimac during the Civil War.

HAMSUN, KNUT (1860), Norweg; author; his novel *Sult*, trans, *Hunger* 1899, is perhaps most grimly powerful description of slow starvation in literature; awarded Nobel Prize for literature 1920. Other works include *Mysterier* 1893; *Norn*, 1894; *Siesta*, 1897; *Kratskow*, 1904. *d.* 1920.

HANAU (50° 9′ N., 8° 55′ E.), town Hesse-Nassau, Prussia, on Main; gold and silver work; diamond-cutting; scene of defeat of Bavarians by French, 1813.

HANCOCK, a city of Michigan, in Houghton co. It is on the Copper Range, the Mineral Range and other railroads, and on the Duluth to Liverpool Waterway. Within the limits of the town are several important copper mines. It has also smelting works, foundries, machine shops, and other industries, also dairying and creameries. It is the seat of a Finnish college.

HANCOCK JOHN (1737-1793); American statesman. *B.* Jan. 23,1737; *d.* in Quincy, Mass., Oct. 8, 1793; graduating from Harvard College in 1754 he joined his uncle in business and inherited £80,000 on the latter's death in 1764. He was several times elected a member of the Massachusetts General Court. The seizure of his sloop 'Liberty' in 1768 caused the riot in which the royal customs commissioners were nearly killed. After the 'Boston Massacre' of 1770 he was one of a committee who requested the governor to remove the troops. His oration at the funeral of the victims gave such offence to the governor that orders were given to arrest him and Samuel Adams. They were both members of the Provincial Congress over which Hancock presided. After the Concord fight Gage offered pardon to all rebels but Hancock and Adams. He was chosen president of the Continental Congress in 1775 and signed the Declaration of Independence the next year. Resigning the presidency in 1777, he remained a member until 1780, and was again elected 1785-1786. Appointed a major-general to command Massachusetts forces in the Rhode Island Expedition of 1780, he was member of the Massachusetts Constitutional Convention and governor in 1780 and annually re-elected except 1783-1785 until his death. President of the convention of 1788 that adopted a Federal constitution.

HANCOCK, WINFIELD SCOTT (1824-1886), American soldier. *B.* in Montgomery Square, Pa., February 14, 1824; *d.* at Governor's Island, New York Harbor, Feb. 9, 1886. Graduating from the U. S. Military Academy in 1844 after service in the west he made a good record in the Mexican War and in 1855 was quarter-master at Fort Myers, Florida, during the Seminole trouble. In 1857-1858 he was on the Kansas border and quarter-master Southern Dist. of California 1859-1861; as brigadier-general of volunteers in the Civil War he commanded a brigade in the Army of the Potomac and fought at Williamsburgh and Antietam; Major-general U. S. Volunteers in Nov. 1862, he led a division at Fredericksburg which lost in that fight 2,015 out of 5,000 men. At Chancellorsville ,May 5-4 1863 he saved the Federals at a critical time and was soon called to command the Second Corps. At Gettysburg, July 2, he commanded the Federal left wing and July 3 the left centre. In a great Confederate attack Hancock lost 4,000 out of 6,000 men, and was shot from his horse. He was appointed major-general 1866 and commanded military depts. Missouri, Texas, Louisiana, 1866-1868, and Dakota 1869-1872. He ran for president in 1880 and was defeated by Garfield, the vote being 4,454,416 to 4,444,952.

HAND, see SKELETON.

HAND BALL. See ATHLETICS.

HANDCUFFS, pair of articulated steel bracelets, self-locking, fastened to each other by a chain. Used to secure prisoner; not applicable to prisoner on suspicion unless he behaves violently or attempts escape.

HANDEL, GEORGE FREDERICK (1685-1759), Anglo-Ger. composer; *b.* Halle; showed musical precocity from earliest childhood; first teacher—Zachau, organist; app. organist at Schloss and Domkirche, and studied law at Univ. of Halle, 1695; joined opera orchestra, Hamburg, 1703; visited Italy, 1709, where he became friend of Scarlattis and Corelli; app. *capellmeister*, Hanover, 1710. H. twice visited England, 1711-15; offended Elector of Hanover, but on latter's accession as George I. became reconciled by writing *Water Music* in king's honor; director of music to Duke of Chandos, 1718; directed Ital. Opera for Royal Academy of Music, London, 1720, which eventually failed; settled in England, becoming naturalised, 1726; lost eyesight towards end of life. Among

best works are: Operas—*Almira, Nero,* 1705; *Daphne, Florinda,* 1708; Latin Psalms—*Dixit Dominus* and *Laudate Pueri;* oratorios—*Concerto in F,* 1715; *Passion* Oratorio, 1716. To Eng. period belong over forty operas no longer performed, and his greatest oratorios— *Chandos Anthems,* 1718-20; *Saul, Israel in Egypt,* 1738; *Samson, Messiah,* 1741; *Joseph,* 1743; *Judas Maccaboeus,* 1746; *Joshua,* 1747; *Jephtha,* 1751.

HAND GRENADES. See GRENADES; BOMBS, AMMUNITION.

HANDICAPPING, the putting of competitors in a game or contest upon an equality, by imposing penalties upon the more powerful or skilful. Time allowances, based upon tonnage and sail area, are granted in a yacht race, and in a motor-car speed trial upon weight and horse-power.

HANDWRITING, see PALAEOGRAPHY.

HANFORD, a city of California, in Kings co., of which it is the county seat. It is on the Southern Pacific and the Gulf, Colorado and Sante Fe railroads. Surrounding it is an extensive agricultural and oil producing region of which it is the center. Its industries include also fruit canning factories. It is a favorite summer resort and has two sanitariums. Among the public buildings is a public library.

HANG-CHOW-FU (30° 20′ N., 120° 10′ E.), city, port, Che-Kiang, China, on Tsien-Tang River; centre of silk manufacture; opened to foreign commerce in 1896.

HANGING, the method of execution employed as punishment for capital offences. As the penalty for homicide it has been employed in America and England from very early times. Thieves and pirates were hanged in chains, *i.e.* gibbeted in England—down to a comparatively recent period. The bodies were left hanging until they gradually decayed away. Hanging in chains was discontinued after 1832, and the last public execution took place in 1868. Executions are now carried out within prison walls, in the presence of the sheriff and other officials.

HANGING GARDENS. See BABYLON.

HANGO (59° 47′ N., 22° 59′ E.), seaport, Finland, on Gulf of Finland; exports wood and fish.

HANKOW, city, river port, Hupeh, China (30° 36′ N., 114° 16′ E.), on Han, at junction with Yang-tse-Kiang; harbour accessible to Ocean steamers; wireless station; large transit trade; centre of commerce and finance; chief exports, tea, eggs.

HANNA, MARCUS ALONZO (1837-1904), senator of U. S. A.; important financier; chief supporter of Republican party under McKinley; one of founders of National Civic Federation, 1901.

HANNAY, JAMES (1827-73), Scot. author; wrote *Satire and Satirists*, 1854; two nautical novels, and other works.

HANNIBAL, a city of Missouri, in Marion county. It is on the Burlington, the Wabash, and the St. Louis and Hannibal railroads, and on the Mississippi River, 110 miles northwest of St. Louis. There is steamboat communication with all the river ports. The city has important industries including the manufacture of lime, cement, shoes, flour, planing mill products, foundry products, etc. There is a public library, public high school. Hannibal was the birthplace of Samuel L. Clemens (Mark Twain).

HANNIBAL (247-183 B.C.), a celebrated Carthaginian general, the *s.* of Hamilcar Barca. He was educated in his father's camp and trained in all the arts of military warfare. He was taken to Spain when only nine years old, and there made an oath to his father upon an alter of eternal hostility to Rome. On his father's death (229 B.C.), Hasdrubal, the son-in-law and successor of Hamilcar, placed him in command of the troops in Spain, and in 221, on the assassination of Hasdrubal, he was unanimously proclaimed by the soldiers the ruler of Carthaginian Spain, his election being later ratified by Carthage. H. crossed the Tagus and subdued the Celtiberian tribes, and before 219 he had reduced all the country S. of the Iberus, with the exception of Saguntum. In the spring of that year he laid siege to Saguntum, which surrendered after a resistance of eight months. The Romans, having made an alliance with that city, regarded H.'s action as an intended provocation to war, and demanded his surrender, which, being refused, war was formally declared between the two nations. H. prepared his army in the winter of 219, and left Spain in the following spring with some 90,000 foot, 12,000 horse, and 50 elephants (Polybius, iii. 34, 18). In the early summer he performed his brilliant march across the Alps, and on reaching Northern Italy, defeated Publius Scipio at Ticinus and at Trebia. After spending some months in winter quarters, he marched into Etruria early in 217 to the banks of the Arno. The Carthaginian army endured

great suffering from the unwholesome swamps, and H. himself lost the sight of one eye. The Roman army under Flaminius was encamped at Arretium, which H. passed by on his way S. Flaminius hurried in pursuit and fell into an ambush near Lake Trasimene, the Romans being practically wiped out and the consul slain. Rome now elected dictator Q. Fabius Maximus, who, on account of his caution, won the name of 'Cunctator'. He continually harassed the Punic forces, without risking a hand-to-hand engagement. H. marched S. to Capua and into Apulia. In 216 he encountered Æmilius Paulus and Terentius Varro, and inflicted a most crushing defeat upon the Romans on the r. b. of the Aufidus, below Cannae. He wintered in Capua, nad several other southern towns revolted from Rome to his side. It has been said that the luxury prevailing in Capua enervated his troops; whether this be true or not, 216-215 mark the turning-point of his career. H. obtained some successes in the S., taking Tarentum in 212; but he did not feel himself strong enough to attack the stronghold of Rome until his army was reinforced. His *b.*, Hasdrubal, approached with his troops from Spain, but at the R. Metaurus met the Roman army under Livius and Claudius, and with most of his men was slain. H. maintained his ground in the wild, mountainous region of Bruttium from 207-203, in which year he was recalled to Africa on the success of the younger Scipio. In 202 he met Scipio at Zama, where he was defeated for the first time. He urged his countrymen to make peace with Rome and himself signed the treaty which forbade Carthage to wage war outside her own dominions without permission from Rome 201. The Romans continually urged the banishment of H., and it was felt in Carthage that the family of Barca was too great for the state. In 195, compelled by the jealousy of factions at home as well as by the enmity of Rome, he sought refuge with Antiochus III., King of Syria, who was allied with Egypt against Rome. Antiochus was defeated at Thermopylae 191, and at Myonnesus, 190, and H., fearing to be given up as a hostage of war, fled to the court of King Prusias of Bithynia. In 183 Rome sent Quintus Flamininus to demand the surrender of the fugitive, and, accordingly, to escape being placed in the hands of his enemy, H. took poison in 183. The Second Punic War may more fitly be called the Hannibalic War, for he is the one prominent figure throughout it. For military strategy and statesmanship he can only be compared with another great hero of history, Napoleon Bonaparte.

HANNINGTON, lake, Brit. East Africa; named after Bp. James Hannington.

HANNINGTON, JAMES (1847-85), Eng. missionary; first bp. of Equatorial East Africa.

HANNO (V. cent. B.C.), Carthaginian navigator; author of *Periplus*, an account of his travels.

HANNO 'THE GREAT' (III. cent. B.C.), Carthagnian general, leader of the aristocrats, and opposed to Hamilcar.

HANOI, capital, Tonkin, Fr. colony 1873; native industries.

HANOTAUX, GABRIEL (1853), Fr. statesman and author; was minister for foreign affairs 1894-8; elected to Academy 1897; author of *Historie du Cardinal de Richelieu*, which gained him the Gobert Prize, *La France en* 1614, *Jeanne d' Arc, LaFrance Contemporaine, Histoire de la Guerre de* 1914 (9 vols.), etc. Del. League of Nations, 1921.

HANOVER (1) Prov., Prussia (52° 30' N., 9° E.), surrounded by North Sea, Holstein, Mecklenburg-Schwerin, Saxony, Brunswick, Hesse-Nassau, Westphalia, Lippe, Pyrmont, and Netherlands; traversed by Harz Mountains in S.E.; remainder forms part of great N. Ger. plain, covered with moor and immense stretches of heath, such as Lüneburger Heide; chief rivers, Elbe, Weser, Ems, Leine; traversed by numerous canals; principal towns, Hanover (cap.), Hildesheim, Osnabrück, Göttingen (with univ.), Borkum and Norderney (famous watering-places); rich agriculture; also coal, salt, silver, copper, iron ore, lead, pottery, asphalt, flax, tobacco, etc.; famous poultry rearing (especially geese).

Ernst August of Brunswick became Elector of Hanover 1692, and was succeeded by his *s.*, George Ludwig, who became George I. of England 1714; the union of Britain and Hanover under the Guelphs lasted until Queen Victoria's accession 1834, when Hanover passed to Ernst August (Duke of Cumberland), *b.* of William IV. Hanover sided with Austria during Austrian War of Succession 1727, with Prussia during Seven Years' War, and against Fr. Republic 1793. Hanover was made a kingdom by Congress of Vienna 1814; joined Zollverein 1854; sided with Austria against Prussia 1866; Hanoverians forced to capitulate at Langensalza, and Hanover annexed to Prussia 1866; Area, 14,862 sq. m.

HANOVER, N. H. See DARTMOUTH COLLEGE.

HANOVER, town, Prussia (52° 22'

N., 9° 44' E.), cap. of Hanover prov., on Leine; fine parks and suburbs, picture galleries, museums, stately town hall, public and royal libraries, large theatre, state palace with magnificent internal decorations and valuable art collection; manufactures—hardware, chemicals, machinery, linen, cloth, pianos, tobacco.

HANOVER, a borough of Pennsylvania, in York co. It is on the Pennsylvania, and the Western Maryland railroads, and is surrounded by an important agricultural and iron ore region. Its industries include the manufacture of cigars, silks, water wheels, flour, furniture, wire, clothing, etc. There is a public library and a handsome high school and two parks.

HANOVER COLLEGE, educational institution under the auspices of the Presbyterian Church, founded in 1827 at Hanover, Indiana as an academy and chartered as a college in 1833. Since 1880 it has been co-educational. It has departments of arts, letters, science, law, philosophy, and education. Tuition is free. It has an endowment fund of about $300,000 and a library of 25,000 volumes. In 1933 its enrollment of students numbered 355, and there were 21 members in the faculty.

HANSEATIC LEAGUE, confederation of N. German towns, formed in XIII. cent. for mutual protection and for promotion of commercial privileges; exercised great influence in Europe for more than two cent's. and at one time included ninety free cities, of which most important were Lübeck. Hamburg, and Bremen, these three being still known as Hanse towns. The first confederation was formed early in XIII. cent. at Wisby, which for some years remained centre of Baltic trade, but was eventually superseded by Lübeck. Lübeck and Hamburg were united for trading and protective purposes from 1241 onwards; in 1252 they received certain privileges from Flanders, and in 1266-67 were allowed to establish their own associations in London. Early in XIV. cent. the confederation obtained important concessions from Bruges, and at later date from Bergen; in this cent. also it came into conflict with Waldemar of Denmark, who was defeated; war ended with treaty of Stralsund, 1370, by which League gained increase of power. Its importance began to decline in the XV cent.; waged war against Holland without success in first half of this cent., hostilities ending with treaty of Copenhagen in 1441. In following cent. it waged unsuccessful war against Norway and Sweden, and by 1670 had ceased to exist.

HANTHAWADDY (17° N., 96° E.), district, Lower Burma, India; constituted a seaprate district in 1880; capital, Rangoon. Area, 3023 sq. miles.

HANUMAN (Hindu myth.), monkey god who bridged the distance between India and Ceylon to aid Rama when searching for his wife, Sitâ; hero of *Ramayana.*

HANUS, PAUL HENRY (1855), University Professor. *B.* in Silesia Prussia. In 1859 came to United States. Bachelor of Science, 1878 of University of Michigan. 1906 at University of Colorado, Doctor of Laws. Teacher, except for one year since 1878. 1891-1901 assistant professor of history and art of teaching, professor 1901-1921, professor emeritus since 1921. Member 1909-1919 of Massachusetts State Board of Education. 1909-1917 chairman of executive board, Boston Vocation Bureau. Author of 'Elements of Determinants', 1886' 'Geometry in the Grammar, School', 1894; 'A Modern School', 1905; 'School Efficiency', 1913; 'School Administration and School Reports', 1920. Writes for educational journals.

HAPARANDA (65° 52′ N., 24° 3′ E.), town, Norbotten, Sweden, at head of Gulf of Bothnia.

HAPGOOD, ISABEL FLORENCE (1850), American author and translator; *b.* Boston, Mass. She had remarkable linguistic ability and employed it in felicitous translations from Russian, French, Italian and Spanish authors. For many years she wrote special articles and book reviews for the New York Evening Post and the New York Sun. Besides her numerous translations, she has written *The Epic Songs of Russia,* 1886; *Russian Rambles,* 1895; *A Survey of Russian Literature,* 1902. *d.* 1928.

HAPGOOD, NORMAN (1868), American journalist and diplomat; *b.* Chicago, Ill. He graduated from Harvard in 1890 and from the Harvard Law School three years later. He engaged in newspaper work as dramatic critic and writer of special articles for the New York Commercial Advertiser and the Bookman 1897-1902. He was editor of Collier's Weekly 1903-1912 and of Harper's Weekly 1913-16. In 1919 he was appointed United States Minister to Denmark, but resigned the position within a year. In 1922 he became editor of Hearst's International Magazine. His publications include *Literary Statesmen and Others,* 1897; *Daniel Webster,*

1899; *The Stage in America,* 1901 and *Industry and Progess,* 1911.

HAPSBURG. See HABSBURG.

HARA-KIRI, method of suicide, obligatory or voluntary, by disembowelment, practised by the Samurai class in Japan; later adopted by all classes as ideal form of self-destruction. It was done by a self-inflicted cut across the abdomen with a dagger, followed by a sword stroke by another hand, which severed the head from the body. As an obligatory act, abolished in 1868. On the day of the Jap. emperor's burial 1912, General Nogi and his wife committed hara-kiri.

HARA, TAKASHI (1754-1921), a Japanese statesman. He served for a time as an official in the foreign office at home and abroad, and obtained the rank of Vice-Minister in 1895. He was one of the organizers of the Liberal party, and visited the United States as Minister of Communications in 1908. He was appointed Premier in 1918. His strong and assertive rule won him many enemies among the Conservatives, and he was assassinated on November, 4 1921.

HARALD, I., HAARFAGER (850-933), king of Norway; won battle of Hafrsfjord, 872, and conquered whole of Norway.

HARALD III., HAARDRAADA (1015-66), king of Norway; fought against Saracens; after succeeding to Norwegian throne he tried to conquer Denmark, but without success; invaded England 1066; killed at Stamford Bridge.

HARBINGER, one who goes before; originally one whose business was to provide accommodation.

HARBIN, KHARBIN (45° 46′ N., 126° 35′ E.), town, on Sungari, Manchuria; railway workshops; breweries, flourmills. Important commercial center.

HARBOR, a port or haven, which by its natural conformation or artificial construction affords safe refuge and anchorage to ships. A h. should be easily accessible in any weather, and should have a sufficient depth of water at all tides; the majority of h's, however, are tidal, and are provided with enclosed docks into which vessels enter at high tide. The dock gates are closed before the ebb, and a uniform level is thus maintained. Every effort is made to secure the utmost possible depth of water, as it has been calculated that the value of a h. increases as the cube of the depth. The entrance to the h. must be proportiomed to the area, as upon this depends the tranquillity of the harbor.

HARBOR GRACE, Newfoundland, port located on Conception Bay, 27 miles N.W. of St. John's in a direct line. Its harbor is large and capacious, and in case of storm an inner harbor, well protected, offers secure anchorage. It is second in commercial importance only to St. John's. It is the headquarters of a Roman Catholic diocese and the Catholic cathedral is the chief architectural feature of the town.

HARBORD, JAMES GUTHERIE (1866), an American soldier, *b.* in Bloomington, Ill. He graduated from the Kansas State Agricultural College, in 1886, and three years later enlisted in the army as a private, passing through the non-commissioned grades within two years, after which he was commissioned second lieutenant of cavalry. From 1903 to 1914 he served as assistant chief of the Philippines constabulary, with the rank of colonel. From May, 1917, until May, 1918, he was chief of staff of the American Expeditionary Force in France. During June and July of 1918 he had command of the Marine Brigade which fought at Chateau Thierry. He commanded the Second Division which participated in the Soissons offensive during July 18-20, 1918. Shortly after he was given command of the Service of Supply, becoming again Chief of Staff in May, 1919, being promoted to the rank of major-general in the regular army in September. In 1921 he was appointed department chief of staff of the U. S. Army, but resigned to enter business in 1922. Chairman of the Board, Radio Corp. of America. Director, Nat'l Broadcasting Co.

HARBURG (53° 28′ N., 9° 59′ E.), seaport, Hanover, Prussia, on Elbe; manufactures palm-oil, rubber goods, chemicals; active trade.

HARCOURT, SIMON, 1ST VISCOUNT HARCOURT (c. 1661-1727), Eng. lord chancellor; called to Bar, 1683; solicitor-gen., 1702; helped to promote Union with Scotland; attorney-gen., 1707, 1710; defended Sacheverell, 1710; Lord Keeper of Great Seal, 1710; Lord Chancellor, 1713; P. C., 1721.

HARCOURT, SIR WILLIAM, GEORGE GRANVILLE VENABLES VERNON (1827-1904), Brit. statesman; P.C., 1866; knight and solicitor-gen., 1873; Sec. of State under Liberal government, 1880; Chancellor of Exchequer, 1886, 1892-95; reformed incidence of death duties, 1894. His Local Veto Bill was one of the causes of Liberal defeat, 1895; leader of Opposition, 1895-98, and continued to be prominent parliamentary figure; constant political writer.

HARCOURT, WILLIAM VERNON (1789-1871), Eng. ecclesiastic canon of York, etc.; deeply interested in scientific subjects; founder and pres. of Brit. Association.

HARDANGER, FJORD (60° 20′ N., 6° 10′ E.), inlet, on W. coast, Norway; magnificent scenery; tourist resort.

HARDEE, WILLIAM JOSEPH (1815-73), American Confederate military commander; *b.* Savannah, Ga. He graduated at the United States Military Academy in 1838; served in the Mexican War and when the Civil War broke out entered the Confederate service as colonel. He fought with distinction at Shiloh, where he headed an army corps, and commanded the left wing at the battle of Perryville. He was entrusted with the command of Savannah against Sherman in the last months of the war. From 1862 his rank was that of lieutenant general.

HARDEN, MAXIMILIAN (1861), Ger. journalist and publicist; began life as an actor, then became dramatic critic; founded famous weekly review, *Die Zukunft*; caused great sensation by exposure of court scandals 1907; stood trial, but drove his accusers from public life; his paper suppressed on several occasions during World War; did not scruple to expose blunders of the Pan-Germans; popular lecturer. *d.* 1927.

HARDERWIJK (52° 22′ N., 5° 37′ W.), seaport, Netherlands, on Zuider Zee; chief exports, grain, fish.

HARDICANUTE, OR HARDACNUT (c. 1019-42), king of England; *s.* of Canute; succ. his half-bro., Harold, 1040.

HARDIE, JAMES KEIR (1856-1915), British Labor leader and politician; worked in coal mines between ages of 7 and 24; in Parliament 1892-5; again from 1900 till his death; proprietor and ed. *Labor Leader*; visited India and Australia in 1907; leader of Labor party in House of Commons 1906-15.

HARDONG, SAINT STEPHEN (c. 1050-1134), third abbot of Citezux; received St. Bernard into abbey and helped Cistercian reform.

HARDING, HENRY, VISCOUNT H. (1785-1856), Brit. gen. and Ind. gov.; distinguished in Napoleonic wars; Gov.-Gen. of India, 1844-47; fought in second Sikh War, 1845-46; commander-in-chief of Brit. army, 1852-56; field-marshal, 1856.

HARDING, WARREN GAMALIEL (1865-1923), twenty-ninth President of the United States; *b.* near Blooming Grove, Ohio. His *f.* was a physician in moderate circumstances, and the future

WARREN GAMALIEL HARDING (1865-1923)
29th President of the U. S. A.

President, in the intervals between sessions of the district school that he atsended, worked at various occupations on farms, in the village and at one time with the construction force of a railroad. In 1879 he entered Ohio Central College at Iberia and studied there for three years. For a time he was the editor of the college paper and this gave him a bent toward newspaper work which persisted after he left the institution. He learned the printer's trade and became an expert at typesetting, both by hand and machine. Then he entered the service of the Marion (Ohio) Daily Star, first as reporter, later as editorial writer, and in 1884 purchased the paper. Soon his energetic and fearless editorials began to attract attention outside the confines of the town, and he became a leader and moulder of public opinion in the State. When the paper had become very profitable and influential, he organized the Harding Publishing Co., and made it possible for such of his employes as so desired to become stockholders in the business. His broad and generous policy has kept him immune from strikes and labor troubles.

Engaging actively in Republican politics, he was chosen a member of the Ohio State senate 1900-04. The qualities he showed as a debater and legislator in this body led to his election as lieutenant governor 1904-06. In 1910 he was the Republican candidate for governor, but was defeated. He supported Taft in the presidential campaign in 1912, and in 1914 was elected to the United States Senate by a plurality of more than 100,-000 votes. In that body he served on a number of important committees, including those on Commerce and Foreign Relations, and won the respect and esteem of his colleagues by his moderation, tact and sagacity. He was eloquent in debate, the impressiveness of his views being added to by an unusually rich and resonant voice. For some time before the meeting of the Republican National Convention, it had become evident that he would be one of the leading candidates for the Presidential nomination, and when that convention met he was chosen to head the ticket on the tenth ballot, receiving 692½ votes to 156 for Major General Leonard Wood, his nearest competitor. His speeches during the campaign materially furthered his cause, and on Nov. 2, 1920 (his 55th birthday), he was chosen President by the largest plurailty ever given to a candidate. The electoral vote stood: Harding 404; Cox 127. The popular vote was: Harding 16,138,914; Cox, 9,142,438.

Mr. Harding was inaugurated President, March 4, 1921. His choice of a Cabinet met with general approval, especially the selection of Charles E. Hughes as Secretary of State. In the administration of his office, President Harding was cautious, deliberate and independent. He did not ask to dominate Congress, nor on the other hand did he yield to its domination. On several occasions he addressed in person a joint Congressional session on subjects that he had much at heart. He vetoed the soldiers'bonus bill that both Houses had passed. He saw with regret the failure of the Ship Subsidy bill, which he had vigorously advocated. He was unceasing in his efforts to bring Government expenditures within Government income. Notable features of his administration were the signing of the separate treaty with Germany, the adjustment with Japan of the controversy over the Island of Yap and the Conference on the Limitation of Armaments, which was called by him and which resulted in the signing of six important treaties designed to assure the peace of the world. In Feb. 1923, he sent a message to the Senate urging participation by the United States in the World Court, consideration of which however, was deferred by that body intil the next session in December.

In July, 1923, Mr. Harding undertook an extensive tour through the western part of the United States and Alaska. During its progress he made many speeches explaining and expounding the great policies of his administration. He was received in Alaska with great enthusaism as he was the first President to visit that Territory. He died suddenly in San Francisco, Aug. 2, 1923. During the latter days of his administration he advocated the Permanent Court of International Justice and also opened the investigation of the Teapot Dome (*q.v.*) (Wyo.) oil leases, which had been illegally given to a private corporation.

In 1891 Mr. Harding married Miss Florence Kling of Marion, Ohio. They had no children.

HARDING, WILLIAM P. GOULD (1864), Banker. *B.* in Alabama. Graduate of University of Alabama. At Berney National Bank, 1886-1896 bookkeeper to cashier. Vice-president, 1896 and from 1902-1914 president of First National Bank of Birmingham, Member of Federal Reserve Board of Washington and governor Federal Reserve Board 1916-1923. 1918-1919 mining director of War Finance Corporation. President of Alabama State Bankers Association and Birmingham Chamber of Commerce, *d.* 1930.

HARDINGE OF PENSHURST,

CHARLES, 1ST BARON (1858), Brit. diplomat; entered diplomatic service 1880; secretary of legation to Teheran 1896; secretary of embassy at Petrograd 1898-1903; ambassador to Russia 1904-6; permanent under-secretary for foreign affairs 1906-10; viceroy of India 1910-16; under-secretary for foreign affairs 1916-18; appointed ambassador to France in succession to Lord Derby Sept. 1920-22.

HARDT MOUNTAINS (49° 18' N., 7° 40' E.), N. extension of Vosges mountains, in Bavarian Palatinate, Germany; average elevation, 1300 ft.

HARDWAR (29° 58' N., 78° 13' E.), town, on Ganges, United Provinces, Brit. India; place of pilgrimage; every twelfth year a sacred festival is held.

HARDY, ARTHUR SHERBURNE (1847), American educator, author and diplomat; *b*. Andover, Mass. He graduated from the United States Military Academy in 1869, served nearly a year in the army and then spent some years abroad studying civil engineering. From 1878 to 1893 he was professor of mathematics in Dartmouth College. He edited the Cosmopolitan Magazine 1893-95; entered the diplomatic service and was U. S. Minister to Persia 1897-99 to Greece, Rumania and Serbia 1899-01 to Switzerland 1901-03 and to Spain 1903-05. His publications include *Elements of Calculus*, 1890; *His Daughter First*, 1903; *Aurelie*, 1912; *Diane and Her Friends*, 1914; *Helen*, 1916 and *No. 13, Rue du Bon Diable*, 1917. *d*. 1930.

HARDY, THOMAS (1840-1928), Eng. novelist and poet; famed for his 'Wessex' novels, including *Far from the Madding Crowd* 1874; *Tess of the D' Urbervilles*, 1891. Of late years he has devoted himself entirely to poetry, and has pub. *Wessex Poems*, written 1865 onwards 1898; *The Dynasts*, a Napoleonic drama 1904-8, and several vols. of lyrical poems; his two latest vols. are *Selected Poems* 1916, and *Moments of Vision* 1917; *Collected Poems*, 1919.

HARDY, SIR THOMAS MASTERMAN, BART. (1769-1839), Brit. vice-admiral; captain of the *Victory* at *Trafalgar*, and greatly esteemed by Nelson, who *d*. in his arms.

HARE, LEPUS EUROPŒUS, rodent closely allied to rabbit, but larger and speedier owing to superior development of hind limbs; differs also from rabbit in solitary life, in not forming burrows, and in young being born fully furred and with open eyes.

HARE, AUGUSTUS JOHN CUTHBERT (1834-1903), Eng. author; wrote *Memorials of a Quiet Life*, and numerous travel books.

HARE, SIR JOHN (1844), Eng. actor; first appearance on stage, Liverpool 1864. His most notable appearances were in *Caste*, *A Pair of Spectacles*, *A Quiet Rubber*. *d*. 1921.

HAREBELL, Campanulaceous plant (*C. rotundifolia*) with blue flowers; popularly termed bluebell; name also applied to wild wood-hyacinth.

HARELIP, congenital vertical cleft in upper lip; may be *single* or *double*; often associated with cleft palate.

HAREM OR SERAGLIO, name given in Muhammadan countries to the apartment in a palace or house set apart for the use of the wives and concubines of the owner. The name is also applied collectively to the women themselves. The law of the Koran only permits of a man having four wives, but he is not limited in the number of his concubines. Each wife has a separate establishment within the h., and is waited upon by a separate staff of servants. A woman must always appear veiled except before her husband or immediate male relatives. The h. is guarded by eunuchs.

HARFLEUR (49° 29' N., 0° 17' E.), seaport town, Seine-Inférieure, France; potteries, distilleries; iron foundries.

HARGRAVES, EDMUND HAMMOND (1816-91), discoverer of Australian goldfields; went to Australia 1824, then tried gold-digging in California 1849; returned to Australia and found gold 1851 at Lewis Pond Creek (Blue Mts.).

HARGREAVES, JAMES, a Lancashire weaver, inventor of spinning-jenny, through which he suffered much persecution from fellow-workmen; *d*. 1778.

HARI-RUD, HERI-RUD (34° 40' N., 61° E.), river, Afghanistan; rises in the chain of Koh-i-Baba, flows N. and W., and loses itself in the Tejend oasis.

HARKNESS, ALBERT (1822-1907), Amer. classical scholar; author of numerous extensively used textbooks, including *Complete Latin Grammar* 1898.

HARLAN, JOHN MARSHALL (1833-1911), American jurist; *b*. Boyle co., Kentucky. He graduated from Center College of that State, and after a course in law at Transylvania University began the practice of law at Frankfort. He served on the Union side in the Civil War as colonel. He was attorney general of his State 1863-66 and was a candidate for the nomination of vice-president in the Republican National Convention in 1872. In 1877 he was made associate justice of the United States Supreme court, in which position his opinions were notable for their breadth of view and knowledge of underlying legal principles. In 1893 he served as a member of the Bering Sea Arbitration Tribunal.

HARLAN, OTIS, Actor. *B.* in Zanesville, Ohio. Made his professional debut in New York at 14th Street Theatre. Played part of Romantic Young Man in 'A Hole in the Ground', 1887. Toured in 'Little Puck' with Frank Daniels. Played Major Yell in 'A Texas Steer'. In 1896 scored success in 'A Black Sheep' as Hot Stuff. 1907 toured in 'The Parisian Model' with Anna Held; 'Little Boy Blue', in 1911. Scored many successes in films.

HARLAND, HENRY (1861-1905)' pseudonym 'Sidney Luska', Anglo-American author; *b.* St. Petersburg, Russia.' He received his education at Harv. University, was for a time in the surrogate's office, New York 1883-86 and later edited 'The Yellow Book' in London, Eng. His publications, which have had a wide circulation in English-speaking countries, include *The Land of Love*, 1887; *My Uncle Florimond*, 1888; *The Cardinal's Snuff-box*, 1900 and *My Friend Prospero*, 1904.

HARLAND, MARION. See TERHUNE, MARY VIRGINIA.

HARLAW, battlefield near Inverurie, Aberdeenshire, where Earl of Mar defeated Donald, Lord of the Isles, 1411.

HARLEM RIVER, a tidal river which separates the island of Manhattan from the mainland. It joins the Hudson River on the W. by way of Spuyten Duyvil Creek, and joins the East River at Hell Gate. The total length of the river is about 7 miles. It is spanned by several bridges and is pierced by tunnel carrying city subway lines. The Harlem Canal, which connects with the East River was opened on June 17, 1895. The Harlem River is one of the important commercial arteries of New York City.

HARLEQUIN, familiar figure in the modern pantomime; supposed to be an invisible mischievous sprite; derived originally from early Ital. comedy.

HARLINGEN (53° 10' N., 5° 24' E.), seaport, Friesland, Netherlands, on Zuider Zee; various manufactures; exports dairy and farm produce.

HARMODIUS, a young Athenian, who with his friend, Aristogeiton, was concerned in the assassination of the tyrant, Hipparchus. Both were slain, but after death were revered as heroes 514 B.C.

HARMON, JUDSON (1846), an ex-governor of Ohio, *b.* in Newton, Ohio. He graduated from Denison University, in 1866, studied in the Cincinnati Law School, then began to practice. He was mayor of Wyoming, Ohio, during 1875-6; judge of the State Court of Common Pleas, 1876-7; of the State Superior Court, 1878-87; Attorney-General in the cabinet of President Cleveland, 1895-7; and since 1896 he has been professor of law at the University of Cincinnati. He was Governor of Ohio during 1909-11 and again during 1911-13. *d.* 1927.

HARMONIA (classical myth.), *d.* of Ares and Aphrodite, and wife of Cadmus; was possessor of a necklace which brought woe to those who wore it.

HARMONIC ANALYSIS is a general mathematical method of investigating certain physical problems such as wave motion, pendulum motion, vibrations of strings and springs, etc. A particle is said to move with Simple Harmonic Motion if, starting from rest, it moves in a straight line with an acceleration always directed towards a fixed point.

HARMONICA, term applied to musical instruments consisting of glasses tuned with more or less water, and producing sound by friction, or bell instruments of percussion; in vogue during XVIII. cent. now a toy instrument.

HARMONIUM, a keyed instrument, somewhat resembling piano and organ, which produces sounds by means of 'free vibrating reeds', used in churches, halls, etc., in place of the costlier organ. Although the guiding principle was then far from new, h's were first constructed in France by Grenié at the beginning of XIX. cent. and called *Orgue Expressif*. Various improvements were made in France and elsewhere (notably by Debain, Alexandre, and Mustel of Paris); but h.-construction was revolutionised by invention of *American Organ*.

HARMONY is the combination of several sounds. These combinations are termed *Chords*, which in their formation and progression are determined by fixed laws. The union of any bass-note with its 3rd and 5th (for instance, C, E, G) is called a chord or *Triad*; it may be either 'Concord' or 'Discord,' and may be formed on any note of the major or minor scale. *Concords* or *Common Chords* are those which seem complete in themselves. *Discords* are incomplete in themselves, and must be resolved to a concord before the ear is satisfied. By the addition of the 7th to any triad the *Chord of the 7th* is formed, the principal one being the *Chord of the Dominant 7th*, which usually resolves to the tonic chord.

HARMSWORTH, SIR ALFRED CHARLES. See NORTHCLIFFE, LORD.

HARNACK, ADOLPH VON (1851), Ger. Church historian; prof. at Leipzig, Giessen, Marburg, and Berlin; was appointed general director of Royal Library, Berlin 1905; his historical insight has gained him world-wide reputation; his publications include *Lehrbuch der Dogmengeschichte* 1886-90; *Grundriss der Dogmengeschichte* (trans 1893); *The Sayings of Jesus*, 1908. *d.* 1930.

HARNESS. See SADDLERY.

HARO, Norman cry to a ruler for redress of wrong.

HAROLD I., HAREFOOT (*d.* 1040), king of England; succ. Canute as his elder *s.*, though opposed by *b.* Harthacnut in Wessex.

HAROLD II. (*c.* 1022-66), Eng. king; Earl of Wessex, 1053; elected king, 1066; routed and killed his *b.* Tostig and Hardrada, king of Norway, at Stamford Bridge, 1066; was defeated and slain at Hastings by William the Conqueror.

HAROUN AL-RASCHID. See HARUN ER RASCHID.

HARP, largest and one of the oldest instruments; played by plucking or striking strings with fingers or plectrum; has survived from earliest times in almost original form—triangular and remarkably graceful in line. H. was in common use in ancient Egypt, and held in highest honour by Celts, Franks, and Northmen. Old Brit. and continental bards accompanied their lays on h. The national symbol of Ireland is still the h. (*Clairseach*).

HARPER, GEORGE M'LEAN (1863) an American University Professor; *b.* in Shippensburg, Pa. He graduated from Princeton University, in 1884, was on the staff of the New York Tribune for a year, then spent two years abroad. On his return he was employed for two years on the staff of Scribners' Magazine. Since 1900 he has been professor of English literature at Princeton University. He is the author of 'The Legend of the Holy Grain', 1896; 'Masters of French Literature', 1901; 'W i l l i a m Wordsworth; his Life, Work and Influence', 1916; 'John Morley and Other Essays', 1920; and 'Wordsworth's French Daughter', 1921.

HARPER, IDA HUSTED. Writer, lecturer. *B.* in Indiana. Graduate of Muncie, Indiana High School. For two years studied at University of Indiana. Leland Stanford, Jr. University for two years. Conducted 'A Woman's Opinions' department in Terre Haute Saturday Evening Mail. For five years, department editor for New York Sunday Sun. Four years on Harper's Bazaar. Speaker at International Woman Suffrage Alliance in London, Paris, Amsterdam and Berlin. Author 'Life and Work of Susan B. Anthony', 1898, 1908; 'History of Woman Suffrage to Close of 19th Century, (with Susan B. Anthony).

HARPER, WILLIAM RAINEY (1856-1906),an American university president, *b.* in New Concord, Ohio. He graduated from Muskingum College, in 1870. During 1879-86 he was professor of Hebrew at the Baptist Union Theological Seminary, in Chicago; and professor of Semitic languages and biblical literature at Yale University, during 1886-91. In the latter year he became president of the newly established University of Chicago. For some years he was director of the Chatauqua system. He wrote *Elements of Hebrew*, 1890; *The Trend in Higher Education*, 1905 and *The Priestly Element in the Old Testament*, 1905.

HARPER'S FERRY, a town in West Virginia, in Jefferson co. It is on the Baltimore and Ohio Railroad, and on the Shenandoah and Potomac rivers. It has great historical importance from its association with John Brown. It was the site of a United States Government foundry, arsenal and armory which, in 1859, was seized by John Brown and a band of associates. Brown was quickly captured and was executed. The government buildings were burned in 1864 to prevent their falling into the hands of the Confederates. The Union army, in 1862, surrendered here to 'Stonewall' Jackson. Harper's Ferry is the seat of Storer College.

HARPIES, THE (classical myth.); monsters who served the gods; bird-like and horrible; best known from connection with the blind Phineus, whose food they kept defiling or carrying off; they were driven off by Argonauts (*q.v.*).

HARPIGNIES, HENRI (1819-1916), Fr landscape painter, of great delicacy and finish.

HARPOON, powerful dart used in whale-fishing; formerly thrown by hand, but now chiefly fired from a harpoon-gun.

HARPSICHORD, prototype of the modern grand piano, which still retains external appearance of earlier instrument. Instead of hammer action of piano, harpsichord had its tones produced by action of points of quill or of hardened leather called "jacks," which plucked or twitched strings when keys were depressed; was superseded by piano in latter part of 18th cent.

HARPY EAGLE. See EAGLE.

HARRADEN, BEATRICE (1864), Eng. novelist; best-known books: *Ships that Pass in the Night,* 1893; *Interplay,* 1908; *Where your Treasure is,* 1918; *Spring shall Plant,* 1920.

HARRAN, CHARRAN (33° 30' N., 36° 35' E.), town of Palestine; supposed dwelling-place of Laban in the Old Testament.

HARRAR, HARAR (9° 19' N., 42° 6' E.), town, Abyssinia, N. E. Africa; encircled by walls; trading center; coffee, durra, tobacco.

HARRIER, breed of hounds, for hunting hares, like small foxhound.

HARRIMAN, EDWARD HENRY (1848-1909), an American financier, *b.* in Hempstead, L. I., N. Y. He was the *s.* of a clergyman and received his early education in Trinity School, in New York City. At the age of fourteen he entered the office of a stock broker as a clerk. So adept did he become in the business of finance that before the age of 22 he was a member of the New York Stock Exchange. In 1872 he founded the firm of Harriman & Co., and speculated so successfully that in a few years he controlled a large fortune. In 1883 he and Stuyvesant Fish began certain financial operations involving control of the Illinois Central, the Union Pacific, the Central Pacific and the Southern Pacific railroad companies, and the Oregon Railroad and Navigation Co. The outcome was that Mr. Harriman secured control of the traffic, between Chicago and the Pacific Coast. In 1901 he entered into the notorious struggle with James J. Hill for control of the Northern Pacific Railroad, in which, however, he was beaten, and again by Thomas F. Ryan, by the latter in a fight for control of the Equitable Life Insurance Co. The result was a financial crisis, leading to an investigation of the Harriman lines by the Interstate Commerce Commission, in 1906, which showed Harriman to hold a virtual monopoly of trans-continental transportation. He *d.* leaving an estate of over $100,000,000.

HARRIMAN, Mrs. EDWARD HENRY (1851-1932) Wife of Edward Henry Harriman. American philanthropic and social leader. Named as sole beneficiary and executrix of husband's will, she received an estate valued at more than $100,-000,000 which included vast railroad holdings in which she took an active interest. She was donor of the E. H. Harriman Memorial Medals given each year to railroads showing the greatest results in accident prevention and safe transportation. She endowed the Chair of Forestry at Yale University and gave 10,000 acres of ground and $1,000,000 to the State of New York for erection of a playground now known as Harriman Park. She also founded and supported the American Orchestral Society Inc. for the training of young musicians.

HARRIS, ABRAM WINEGARDNER (1858-   ), Univ. President. *B.* in Philadelphia. Has degrees from various colleges. From 1880-1881 at Williamsport, Pa. teacher of mathematics in Dickinson Seminary; 1881-1884 tutor of mathematics and registrar, 1885-1888 at Wesleyan University instructor of history; 1888-1891 assistant director and 1891-1893 director. From 1893-1901 at Unviersity of Maine, president; at Port Deposit, Maryland, director of the Jacob Tome Institute; 1906-1916 president of Northwestern University. Since 1916, secretary of Board of Education of Methodist Episcopal

Church. 1915-1917 president of Amercian Social Hygiene Association. Trustee of Drew Theological Seminary and Wesleyan University.

HARRIS, CORRA MAY (WHITE), (MRS. L. H. HARRIS) (1869-1935), an American author, *b.* at Farm Hill, Ga. She received a private education and began to write in 1899, her first articles appearing in The Independent. Her series of "Brasstown Valley Stories" appeared in the American Magazine during 1905-9. Among her books are: *A Circuit Rider's Wife, Eve's Second Husband, The Recording Angel, Happily Married, Daughter of Adam, My Son, My Book and My Heart,* and *Happy Pilgrimage.*

HARRIS, FRANK (1854-1931), Irish-American editor and writer, *b.* in Galway, Ireland. He came to the United States at the age of sixteen and later studied at the universities of Kansas, Paris, Heidelberg, Strassburg, Gottingen, Berlin, Vienna and Athens. In 1875 he was admitted to the Kansas bar, but later returned to Europe, becoming editor of The Evening News and The Fortnightly Review, in London. He later returned to the United States, becoming owner and editor of Pearson's Magazine, in New York. He is the author of "The Bomb—a Story of the Chicago Anarchists of 1886", 1909; "The Man Shakespeare", 1909; "Unpathed Waters", 1913; "Contemporary Portraits", 1914; "Great Days", a novel, 1914; "The Life and Confessions of Oscar Wilde", 1916; and two further series of his "Contemporary Portraits", 1919 and 1921, and *My Life and Loves.* He died in 1931. *The Life of George Bernard Shaw* was published posthumously in October, 1931.

The death of Frank Harris, author, editor, critic, meant the loss of a turbulent, vigorous figure in the literary world. Frank Harris was never a neutral bystander. He was always a combatant.

In England, where he became the editor of *The Saturday Review,* he gathered about him such clever young men as Max Beerbohm, H. G. Wells, and George Bernard Shaw, making this magazine one of the best critical periodicals in England.

HARRIS, ISHAM GREEN (1818-1897), an American statesman, *b.* in Tullahoma, Tenn. From 1849 to 1853 he was a member of Congress and was Governor of Tennessee from 1857 to 1863. He served as an officer in the Confederate army during the latter part of the Civil War. After the end of the war he engaged in the practice of law in Memphis, and in 1887 was elected United States Senator. He was successively re-elected until his death. In

FRANK HARRIS

1893 he was chosen president pro tempore of the Senate.

HARRIS, JOEL CHANDLER (1848-1908), an American writer, b. in Eatonton, Ga. As a youth he served a term as a printers' apprentice, then took up newspaper work, becoming a member of the staff of the Savannah Daily News in 1871. Five years later he became connected with the Atlanta Constitution, on whose staff he remained for over 25 years. It was in that paper that his famous 'Uncle Remus' sketches first appeared. His negro dialect stories have facinated the children of two generations, and are now as widely read as ever. Among his many books are *Folk Lore of the Old Plantations*, 1880; *Daddy Jake, the Runaway*, 1889; *Balaam and His Master*, 1890; *Mr. Rabbit at Home*, 1895 and *Uncle Remus and Br'er Rabbit'*, 1907.

HARRIS, JOHN HOWARD (1847), University President. *B.* in Indiana, Pa.; served eighteen months with the Union Army; Bachelor of Arts, 1869 of Bucknall University, Doctor of Philosophy, 1884; Lafayette College, Doctor of Laws of Colgate and Dickinson Colleges in 1891. Founded the Keystone Academy in 1869 and principal from 1869-1880. 1889-1919 was president of Bucknall University. Professor of Psychology same since 1889.

HARRIS, THOMAS LAKE (1823-1906), Amer. poet and founder of a new religion accepted by many prominent people; of great gifts, but practised black magic and probably fraud.

HARRIS, WILLIAM TORREY (1835-1909), Amer. educational reformer and philosophical writer.

HARRISBURG, a city of Illinois, in Saline co., of which it is the county seat. It is on the Cleveland, Cincinnati, Chicago and St. Louis, and the Southern Illinois Railway and Power Company railroads. The surrounding country is an extensive agricultural and coal mining region. The industries include flour mills, electric power plant, brick plant. Among the public buildings is a library and a post office.

HARRISBURG, a city of Pennsylvania, the capital of the State, and the county seat of Dauphin co. It is on the Pennsylvania, and the Philadelphia and Reading railroads, and on the Susquehanna River, 106 miles W. of Philadelphia. It is an important railroad center, is at the cross roads of national highways, and has direct connection with the coal and iron resources of the State. Harrisburg is a handsome city, and is surrounded by picturesque country. The State Capitol, which is one of the finest State executive buildings in the country, is located in the midst of a beautiful park of 10 acres. Fort Washington, just across the Susquehanna River, marks the most northern point of the Confederate advance during Lee's invasion of Pennsylvania. Gettysburg is 46 miles to the south. The river is crossed by the Rockville four-track railroad bridge, 5 miles to the north. There are two railroad bridges in the heart of the city and two vehicular bridges. Hershey Park, the model town of the Hershey Chocolate Co., is 12 miles to the east. Harrisburg has an excellent school system with 28 elementary and two high schools, and many private schools. The total enrollment is about 15,000. It is the seat of Roman Catholic and Episcopal bishops and has many hotels, a large hospital, a home for the friendless, and a children's industrial home. The city is of great importance industrially and manufacturers boilers, bricks, castings, brooms, leather, cotton goods, iron, steel, clothing, shoes, silk, flour, etc. There is also a large trade in dairy and farm products. There are 18 national banks and trust companies. The city was founded in 1785 by John Harris and was incorporated as a borough in 1791. It became the capital of the State in 1812 and in 1860 received its charter.

HARRISON, a city of New Jersey, in Hudson co. It is on the Pennsylvania, the Lackawanna and the Erie railroads, and on the Passaic river. It is an important industrial community and has manufactures of cotton, thread, electric supplies, trunks, leather goods, iron and steel products, furniture, etc. It has a public library and a high school. The city was settled in 1688 and was incorporated in 1873.

HARRISMITH (28° 24' S.; 28° 36' E.), town Orange Free State, S. Africa; exports wool and hides.

HARRISON, BENJAMIN (1833-1901), twenty-third President of the United States. *B.* in North Bend, Ohio, Aug. 20, 1833; *d.* in Indianapolis, Ind., March 13, 1901. He was a great-grandson of Benjamin Harrison who signed the Declaration of Independence and grandson of William Henry Harrison, ninth President of the United States. Graduating from Miami University, Ohio, in 1852 and admitted to the bar in 1853 he practiced law in Indianapolis and in 1861 was elected reporter of the state Supreme Court. In the Civil War he helped recruit, and was colonel of the 70th Indiana Volunteers which formed part of the 20th army corps under Hooker in the campaign from Charleston to Atlanta. He served with distinction at Peach Tree Creek commanding a brigade, and at Nashville, and brevetted brigadier-general, was mustered out in June, 1865. He was defeated running for governor of Indiana in 1876; member of the Mississippi Commission, 1879; chairman of the Indiana Delegation to the Republican National Convention, 1880; senator, 1881-1887; delegate to Republican National Convention, 1884, and in 1888 was nominated for president, receiving in the election 233 electoral votes to 168 for Cleveland. During his administration the McKinley tariff law was passed, the new navy extended, civil service reform advanced, the Pan-American Congress convened, and the Behring Sea fisheries question arbitrated with Great Britain. At the Republican National Convention of 1892 Harrison was renominated, but in the election received only 145 votes to Cleveland's 276. In 1899 he was counsel of Venezuela in the Anglo-Venezuelan Arbitration Commission; member for the United States at the Hague Peace Conference, 1899; and of the Board of Arbitration. Author; 'This Country of Ours', 1897 and 'Views of an Ex-President', 1901.

HARRISON, MRS. BURTON (CONSTANCE CARY) (1843-1920), an American author, b. in Vancluse, Va. In 1867 she married Burton N. Harrison, who had been the secretary of the Confederate President, Jefferson Davis, and was captured with him. She was well on into middle age before she began to write, but the many novels she wrote after that acquired a wide popularity. Among them are *Bar Harbor Days*, 1887; *Sweet Bells Out of Tune*, 1893; *A Bachelor Maid*, 1894; *A Princess of the Hills*, 1901; *Recollections, Grave and Gay*, 1911. She also wrote several plays, one of them, *The Unwelcome Mrs. Hatvh*, first produced in 1901, being played by road companies for many years after.

HARRISON, FRANCIS BURTON (1873), an American governor-general of the Philippines, b. in New York. He graduated from Yale University, in 1895, and from the New York School of Law, in 1897, was admitted to the bar, in 1898, then enlisted as a private in the army for the Spanish-American War, becoming a captain and adjutant-general of Volunteers. He was elected to Congress from New York for the terms 1903-5, 1907-13, was re-elected for 1913-15, but resigned on being appointed Governor-General of the Philippines, in 1913, which position he held till 1921.

HARRISON, FREDERIC (1831-

1923), Eng. jurist, Positivist, and critic; b. London; educated Oxford, called to bar 1858; prof. of jurisprudence, Inns of Court 1877-89; helped to codify Eng. law; follower of Comte; studied Labour problems; distinguished literary critic and historian, whose writings have a high value among students. Chief works are *Oliver Cromwell* 1888, *Ruskin*, 1902; *Chatham*, 1905; *The Creed of a Layman*, 1907; *Autobiographic Memoirs*, 1911; *Among My Books*, 1912; *The Positive Evolution of Religion*, 1912; *On Society*, 1918; *Obiter Scripta*, 1919. His s., Austin 1873, edited the *English Review* from 1910, and has wrote on Anglo-Ger. questions; he opposed Mr. Lloyd George in Carnarvon Boroughs (Dec. 1918).

HARRISON, (LOVELL)BIRGE (1854-1929); b. in Philadelphia, Pa.; pupil in Paris of Cabanel; 1889-1893 painted in the South Seas, Australia and Western United States. In 1887 awarded silver medal at Paris Salon. Buffalo Exposition 1901 a medal. Medal at Chicago Exposition in 1893. Gold medal, Philadelphia, 1907. His paintings in oil are in museums in Marseilles, Paris, France. St. Louis, Chicago, St. Paul, Nashville, Oakland, California, Toledo, Washington, Memphis, Omaha, Atlanta. Director of landscape school of Art Students League, 1910. Member of New York Water Color Club. Society American Artists. Fellow Pennsylvania Academy of Design. Author of 'Landscape Painting', 1909. Writes for Art Magazines.

HARRISON, MARY ST. LEGER (1852), an English novelist who wrote under the pen name of Lucas Malet. She was the youngest d. of Charles Kingsley and was b. in Eversley. She married William Harrison, who died in 1897. Her novels, which were of unusual literary merit and strength, include *The Counsel of Perfection, The Wages of Sin, Sir Richard Calmady, The Far Horizon*, and *Adrian Savage*.

HARRISON, THOMAS (1606-60); Eng. Roundhead; present at Marston Moor, Naseby, and siege of Oxford; signed king's death warrant; held military command during Cromwell's absence; instrumental in expelling Long Parliament; opposed Cromwell's protectorate; suspected of plots, he was twice imprisoned; executed at Restoration.

HARRISON, WILLIAM HENRY (1773-1841), 9th President of the United States, b. in Berkeley, Va. He was about to graduate in medicine when the death of his father caused him to return to his own choice and enter the Army. He saw a great deal of active service against the Indians, then resigned in 1798 to settle at North Bend, near Cincinnati. He was sent to Congress as the first delegate from the Northwest Territory. Part of this region was marked off as the Territory of Indiana, of which he was appointed first governor, as well as Superintendent of Indian Affairs. After protracted negotiations with the Indians under Tecumseh, he set out, in 1811, with 900 men, to punish them, and severely defeated them in the famous battle of Tippecanoe. During the War of 1812 he was given the rank of major-general and made commander-in-chief of the Northwest. After serving a term in Congress he retired, in 1829. Im 1839 he was nominated candidate for the Presidency by the Whigs and was elected over his adversary, Van Buren, by 294 electoral votes to 60. He only survived his inauguration as President a month.

HARROGATE (54° N., 1° 33′ W.), town, Yorkshire, England; health resort, noted for saline, chalybeate, and sulphur springs.

HARROW, agricultural implement for breaking the soil into fine pieces after it has been ploughed, and for covering the seed sown; chief varieties are the straight-tooth and the spring-tooth.

HARROW-ON-THE-HILL (51° 34′ N., 0° 20′ W.), town, Middlesex, Eng.; famous for school founded by John Lyon, 1571.

HARRY, blind minstrel of Scot. court in latter part of XV. cent.; wrote long epic poem called *William Wallace.*

HARSHA, HARSHAVARDHANA, last native ruler of the whole of N. India 606-648 A.D.

HART, ALBERT BUSHNELL (1854), an American university professor and historical writer, *b.* in Clarksville, Pa. He graduated from Harvard University, in 1880, continued his studies in Germany, then began teaching, specializing in history, being professor of history at Harvard University, since 1897 and professor of government as well since 1910. He has written many magazine articles and books, among the latter being *Introduction to the Study of Federal Government,* 1890; *Foundations of American Foreign Policy,* 1901; *Manual of American History, Diplomacy and Government,* 1908; *The War in Europe,* 1914; *America at War,* 1917; and *Causes of the War,* 1920.

HART, CHARLES (fl. 1660). Eng. actor who played leading parts in Restoration tragedies; grandson of Shakespeare's *s.* Joan; *d.* 1683.

HART, SIR ROBERT (1835-1911); Anglo-Chinese official; entered Consular service, China, 1854; inspector-gen. of Chin. Customs department, 1863; greatly increased revenues; his house, containing valuable official documents, burnt down in Boxer rising, 1900; retired in 1907.

HARTE, FRANCIS BRET (1839-1902), *b.* in Albany, N. Y., in 1839; *d.* in Aldershot, Eng., May 6, 1902. In 1854 he was attracted to California then in the height of the gold excitement. After teaching school for a time and making a failure of gold-mining he became a compositor on the Golden Era, in which his early sketches appeared. Later he joined the Californian wherein his 'Condensed Novels' and parodies were published. Secretary of the U. S. Branch mint in 1864, he became editor of the Overland Monthly in 1868. in whose pages appeared *The Luck of Roaring Camp.* He went to New York in 1871 and wrote stories for the Atlantic Monthly until appointed U. S. consul at Crefeld, Germany in 1878, and at Glasgow in 1880. After 1885 he made his home in London. Notable among his shorter fictions are *Miggles, The Outcasts of Poker Flat* and *M'llis,* 1871; *An Heiress of Red Dog,* 1879; *Flip,* 1882; *A Phyllis of the Sierras,* 1888. Stories: *The Bell Ringer of Angeles,* 1894; *A Problem of Jack Hamlin's,* 1894. Long stories and novels: *Snowbound at Eagles, Cabriel Conroy, Criesy,* 1889; *A Waif of the Plains,* 1890; *A Ward of the Golden Gate,* 1890; *Clarence,* 1895; *In the Hollow of the Hills,* 1895; *Three Partners,* 1897. Poems: *East and West Poems,* 1871; *Echoes of the Foothills,* 1874; *Some Later Verses,* 1898. Bret Harte was at his best in short pieces, he was unequal to long flights. His continued residence in Europe had a weakening effect on later work.

HARTFORD, a city of Connecticut; the capital of the State and the county seat of Hartford co. It is on the New York, New Haven and Hartford railroad, and on the Connecticut River, 36 miles northeast of New Haven. It is an important commercial city and is a port of entry. Hartford is one of the most attractive cities in New England, and is the seat of many important institutions, including Trinity College, Hartford Congregational Theological Seminary, American Asylum for the Deaf, Insane retreat, old people's home, young people's Christian association building. There is a Roman Catholic cathedral and many other handsome churches. The capital is of unusual architectual merit and the city hall is also an attractive building. The latter was used as a

State house for nearly 100 years, and was the meeting place of the famous Hartford Convention. Other historical buildings are Center Church, erected in 1807, the Wadsworth Athenaeum, and the Hartford Public Library and Morgan Memorial. Near the center of the city is a tablet which marks the site of the Charter Oak, a famous tree, in the hollow of which was hidden the Connecticut charter to save it from Sir Edmund Andros, who wished to seize it. The State House is an impressive building erected at a cost of over $3,000,000. The city has great industrial importance. It manufactures machinery, tools, firearms, carriages, sewing machines, typewriters, engines, brushes, electrical appliances, brass goods, etc. It is the greatest insurance center in the United States and is the home office of many of the largest fire, accident and life insurance companies. Hartford was first settled by the Dutch in 1623. This, however, was abandoned and the first permanent settlement was made by the English in 1636. This was called Newton. In 1637 the name was changed to Hartford. The city was incorporated in 1784 and became the State capital in 1873.

HARTFORD CITY, a city of Indiana, in Blackford co., of which it is the county seat. It is on the Pennsylvania, N. Y., Chicago and St. Louis, and the Nickel Plate and other railroads. The surrounding country is an extensive natural gas and oil region. There are manufactures of paper, tile, bricks, glass, overhead doors, etc.

HARTFORD CONVENTION, a gathering held in 1814 to discuss measures for securing New England interests against the S. and W., especially with regard to the war of 1812. The Federalists opposed the war on several grounds, their chief objection being that it was destroying all American commerce in order to punish Great Britain for crippling a part of it. Thus, all through the war they harassed the government, but by 1814 the destruction of New England industries had become intolerable, and a convention was called. This met at Hartford, and George Cabot, of Massachusetts, was chosen president. Various proposals were made, but before anything definite could be arranged, a satisfactory peace was made, and all disasters were forgotten in the blaze of the battle of Orleans.

HARTINGTON, LORD SPENCER CAMPTON CAVENDISH, MARQUIS. See DEVONSHIRE, DUKE OF.

HARTLEPOOL (54° 42′ N., 1° 11′ W.), seaport, Durhamshire, England; including municipal borough of H. and county borough of West H. H. is an old market town; West H. is modern, with municipal buildings, Athenaeum, exchange, etc.; considered as one port which has large trade; engineering works, shipbuilding, iron and brass foundries, flour and paper mills.

HARTLEY, DAVID (1705-57), Eng. philosopher, physician, and psychologist; wrote *Observations on Man*; called founder of *Association* school of psychologists.

HARTMANN, KARL ROBERT EDUARD VON (1842-1906), Ger. philosopher; wrote *Philosophy of the Unconscious* 1869 and many other works; a pessimist, but believed that by social progress some happiness might be attained.

HARTMANNSWEILERKOPF, height (3,000 ft.) of S. Vosges, Haute-Alsace, France (47° 53′ N., 7° 8′ E.); was centre of prolonged struggle during World War. Fr. troops reached its W. slopes (Dec. 1914), and a company of Alpine troops captured and established themselves on its summit early in 1915, but were cut off by Ger. force and two-thirds of their number killed. During offensive in Alsace (Jan. 1915) the French again secured summit, and again the detachment was killed or captured. French again returned to charge (March 24) and after severe fighting reached summit (March 27). On April 26 the hill was again the scene of severe fighting. Thereafter neither side held the crest.

HARTFORD THEOLOGICAL SEMINARY, a training school for ministers of the Congregationalist Church, founded in 1834 as the Theological Institute of Connecticut, in East Windsor. In 1865 it was removed to Hartford and its name changed to its present one. It is governed by a Board of Trustees, elected by the Pastoral Union, an association of about two hundred ministers. Newton Case Memorial Library, greatest theological library in U. S. housed there.

HARTRANFT, JOHN FREDERICK (1830-1889), an American soldier, b. in New Hanover, Pa. After studying law he entered the army and served throughout the Civil War, reaching the rank of major general. He was selected to execute the sentences passed upon the assassins of President Lincoln. From 1872 to 1878 he was governor of Pennsylvania.

HARTSHORN, the horn of the common stag, which in composition differs from that of the ox, etc., being nearly identical with that of bone. The substances derived from the horns were the volatile liquor, salt, and oil, and the ash which remains when the horns are calcined in air. The fluid parts are got by distillation, and the salt formed is carbonate of ammonia. From this pure ammonia is obtained, which, when condensed in water, constitutes the spirit of H. The volatile alkali, or spirit of H., is now seldom obtained from that source; the ammonia sold in shops being obtained from gas-liquor, etc.

HARTSHORN, SPIRIT OF, the name for a solution of ammonia which used to be obtained from the horns of the stag, and which has now been replaced by carbonate of ammonia or sal-volatile.

HARTT, ROLLIN LYNDE (1869), Writer. *B.* in Ithaca, New York. In 1892 Bachelor of Arts of Williams College and of Andover Theological Seminary, 1896. Was ordained Congregational Minister, 1896. Pastor of churches in Helena, Mont. and Leverett, Mass. 1899-1900 traveled in America gathering material for magazines. On staff of *Literary Digest*, Boston Transcript and Chicago Tribune. In 1920 did publicity work for Methodist Centenary. Author *The Clerk of the Day, The People at Play, Ruth of the Dolphin, Confessions of a Clergyman* (which he wrote anonymously) author of *As I Was Saying* which ran daily in the New York Tribune. Contributes articles to magazines.

HARUN-EL-RASHID (763-809), V. Abbasid Caliph of Bagdad; famed for the greatness of his empire, the splendour of his court, and his patronage of learning and letters; one the greatest princes of his day;known to Eng. readers from his association with the *Arabian Nights.*

HARUSPICES, ARUSPICES (singular, *Haruspex*), Rom. prophets whose duty it was to explain omens, particularly to inspect entrails of offerings; probably Etruscan practice adopted by Rome.

HARVARD, JOHN (1607-1638), the founder of Harvard University, *b.* in England. After graduating from Cambridge University, in 1635, he emigrated to Massachusetts, of which colony he was made a freeman in 1837. Little is known of his private life, and in the records of the colony a few scraps here and there only indicate public activity, such as the statement that he was one of a commission 'to consider of some things tending toward a body of laws.' At his death his property was valued at £1,600, one half of which he gave to the 'schoale or colledge' which had been

established in 1836 but which hitherto had languished on account of lack of funds, and was henceforward called Harvard College, and later Harvard University. He also bequeathed a library of 300 volumes to the institution. A monument was erected to his memory in Charlestown cemetery by the alumni of Harvard College, in 1828, Edward Everett making the official address at the unveiling.

HARVARD OBSERVATORY, an institution for astronomical observation and research, established in 1843, by public subscription, as an annex to Harvard University. A branch station is established on a mountain 8,000 feet in altitude, near Arequipa, Peru. Among its most important instruments are one 15 inch and one 6 inch equatorial telescopes, one 8 inch transit circle, a 11 inch Draper photographic telescope, an 8 inch photographic telescope and a meridian photometer. The annals and records of the institution fill sixty volumes. A special grant was recently made by the Carnegie Institute for a study of the collection of photographs at the main observatory at Harvard. The amount of material, including photographs and photographic charts of the sky that have been collected require a special building for their accommodation. The Sears Tier of the Observatory was added in 1846 and two years later Edward Bromfield Phillips bequeathed the University $100,000 especially for the observatory. It has now an endowment fund of $900,000. Its staff consists of a director, four professors and 40 associates.

HARVARD UNIVERSITY. The oldest educational institution in the United States, founded in Cambridge, Mass. in 1636. In that year the General Court of the colony of Massachusetts Bay voted £400. to found a college to educate 'English and Indian youth'. The first building was erected at New Town, later Cambridge, in 1637. In 1688 a young non-conformist clergyman John Harvard, *d.* at Charleston, and left £750., and his library of 300 books to the college which was named after him. The first president was the Rev. Henry Dunster, and the first graduating class 1642, had nine members. In that year the General Court established a board of overseers consisting of the governor, deputy governor, and magistrates of the colony, and teaching elders of five towns. In 1650 the Court granted a charter; the internal administration including the president, five fellows, and the treasurer. A change came in 1780 when the governor, lieut. governor and council and senate of the Commonwealth of Massachusetts took the place of the colonial officials on the board of overseers. In 1865 the graduates were given the right to elect overseers. Non-residents became eligible as overseers in 1880. The progress of the college was long hampered by religious differences, lack of funds, the burning of Harvard Hall in 1664, and adhesion to the cause of the colonists in the Revolution. In 1782 a medical department with three professors was established and a medical school in 1816; a Law School in 1817, and Divinity School in 1819, the Lawrence Scientific School in 1847, and a Dental School in 1867. The college became a university after Charles W. Eliot (*q.v.*) became president 1869. In 1890 the Graduates School of Arts and Sciences became independent, and in 1906 the Graduates School of Applied Science. University Extension work was started in 1910, Graduates School of Medicine, 1912 and Graduates School of Business Administration 1913. Schools and Departments. Harvard College and the Graduates School, established in 1872. Law, Divinity, and Dental Schools previously mentioned. The Bussey School of Agriculture and Horticulture 1870; The Arnold Arboretum, forestry and arboriculture 1872; Astronomy, 1843; with a branch station on a mountain at Arequipa, Peru; University library of 1,181,635 volumes; the Gray Herbarium, 1864; the University Museum and Botanic Gardens, 1809 and the University Summer School. Twenty-four acres are devoted to athletics and the Stadium seats 30,000. There is also the Harvard Club House, 1901 and Widener Memorial Library, 1915. The invested funds, etc., of the University are about $108,000,000. Annual income of the University 1930, $14,000,000. Students registered in 1933, 8,227. Faculty 1,770. President J. B. Conant.

HARVEST (O. E. *hoerfest*, autumn), the period of gathering in crops or fruit; also the crops or fruit so gathered. Religious festivals to celebrate the h. date back to remote times.

HARVEST MOON. See MOON.

HARVESTING MACHINES are mechanical devices for cutting and gathering wheat or similar grains, and binding them into bundles. Some types are equipt to thresh and sack the grain in addition to cutting and gathering it. Probably the first mention of harvesting machines was made by Pliny in 23 A.D. when he described the Gallic 'header'. It was not until 1806 however, when Gladstone proposed a harvesting machine that the attention of inventors was directed to this field of endeavor.

Salmon of Woburn in 1807 devised a machine somewhat similar to Gladstone's. Neither of these machines was considered practical and little advance was made before 1822, when Henry Ogle, also an Englishman developed a side draft machine. Progress thereafter was rapid, several models being presented in the following decade. In 1833 Obed Hussey of Md. and C. H. McCormick of Va. presented machines which embodied the side draft feature and vibrating or reciprocating cutters and which may be considered the basis of modern machines. In these however the grain had to be raked off and bound by hand, binding machines not having been developed at this stage. Nelson Platt in 1848 and many others, followed with self raking machines, the grain being left in gavels by the side of the machine. The advent of the binding machine (see BINDING MACHINES) in 1850, in which the sheaves were bound by cord or twine marked the beginning of the development of the modern machine now so widely used in the extensive grain raising areas of the United States and in other countries. These machines, head, thresh, clean and sack the grain in one operation. They are usually drawn by a tractor, which does the work of the 30-40 horses otherwise necessary to draw the machine. Such a machine will harvest 60 to 125 acres of grain per day, doing in 10 minutes what it would take three hours to do manually.

HARVEY, a city of Illinois, in Cook co. It is on the Illinois Central, the Grand Trunk, the Baltimore and Ohio, and other railroads, and on the Calumet River. The city is chiefly a residential suburb of Chicago, It has, however, important industries including the manufacture of mining machinery, gas stoves, automobiles, cement, railroad supplies, etc. There is a public library.

HARVEY, GABRIEL (c. 1545-1630); Eng. poet; wrote sonnets, satires, and controversial pamphlets; was the intimate friend of Spenser; and claimed to have introduced hexameter verse into Eng. lit.

HARVEY, GEORGE BRINTON MAC-CLELLAN (1864-1928), Amer. editor and diplomat; *b.* Peacham, Vt. He was educated at the Peacham Academy and entered newspaper work as reporter for the Springfield Republican, Chicago News and New York World 1882-86. He was insurance commissioner of New Jersey 1890-91 and from 1891 to 1893 was managing editor of the New York World. He engaged in business as constructor and promotor of electric railroads 1894-98. In 1899 he purchased the North American Review, of which he has since been editor. From 1900 to 1915 he was president of Harper and Bros. Publishing Company. In politics he has been in the main an independent Democrat. He was a warm supporter of Woodrow Wilson for the presidency, but later became antagonistic to him and vigorously attacked his policies. In 1921 he was appointed by President Harding as U. S. Ambassador to Great Britain. He wields a trenchant pen and is a powerful platform speaker. He has never hesitated to express his views, sometimes with a freedom that has provoked surprise and criticism. One such occasion was at the Pilgrims' dinner in London in 1921 when with a vigor and directness unusual for a diplomat he declared that the United States had no intention of becoming a member of the League of Nations. Another utterance of his that attracted wide attention was his statement in 1923 that Lord Balfour had erred in declaring that the United States required Great Britain to guarantee its loans to other Allied Governments. He resigned as Ambassador in Oct., 1923.

HARVEY, WILLIAM (1578-1657), Eng. physician, discoverer of the circulation of the blood; *b.* at Folkestone, *s.* of a yeoman in good circumstances; ed. at the grammar school, Canterbury; at Caius College, Cambridge (B.A., 1597); and at Padua Univ. (M.D., 1602). Returning to England, he commenced to practise medicine in London, becoming a fellow of the Coll. of Physicians 1609, physician to St. Bartholonew's Hospital 1609, and Lumleian lecturer at the Coll. of Physicians 1615. He began to expound his theory of the movements of the heart and the circulation of the blood in his first course of lectures as Lumleian lecturer, but it was not until 1628, when he pub. his treatise, *Exercitatio Anatomica de Motu Cordis et Sanguinis*, that he made his great discovery. See BLOOD, CIRCULATION OF. H. was appointed physician to James I. and to Charles I., having charge of the young royal princes at the battle of Edgehill; he lived at Oxford for some years, being elected warden of Merton College, but on the surrender of the city to the Parliamentarians he returned to London to live in retirement. He was elected pres. of the Coll. of Physicians 1654, but declined the position, and *d.* after being long affected by gout, in London.

HARWICH (51° 51' N., 1° 17' E.), port, Essex, England; packet station for Holland; fine harbour and docks; large export and import trade; strongly fortified.

HARVEYIZED STEEL. See IRON AND STEEL.

HARZ MOUNTAINS (51° 41' N.; 10° 37' E.), a mountain range of N.W. Germany, extending through part of Prussia, Brunswick, and Anhalt, between Leine and Saale; divided into Ober, Unter, and Vorharz; highest peak, Brocken (*q.v.*), 3,745 ft.; length, 57 miles; breadth, 20, and area, 784 sq. miles; rich in iron, copper, lead, silver, sulphur, zinc, granite, marble; large fir and pine forests; numerous mineral springs; figures prominently in Ger. legend and lit.

HASA EL. See EL HASA.

HASDRUBAL (slain 221 B.C.), succ. his f.-in-law, Hamilcar Barca, as leader of the Carthaginians. Hasdrubal, Hamilcar's younger *s.*, aided his *b.* Hannibal in the Punic Wars against Rome.

HASHISH, OR HASHEESH, the Arabic name, meaning literally 'dried herb', for the various preparations obtained from the flowering tops of the Indian hemp plant (*Cannabis indica*). It is used as an intoxicant in several Eastern countries (called 'bhang' in India), and is either smoked, chewed, or drunk. It is valuable as a narcotic and is sometimes employed in medicine as an anodyne. The English word 'assassin' is probably derived from the Arabic 'hashishin,' *i.e.* hemp-eaters, who committed great excesses when under the influence of hashish.

HASLINGDEN (53° 43' N., 2° 20' W.), town, Lancashire, England.

HASPE (51° 20' N., 7° 20' E.), town, Westphalia, Prussia; industries—ironfounding, iron, steel, and hardware.

HASSAM, CHILDE (1859), an American artist, *b.* in Boston, Mass. After a common school education he studied art, first in Boston, then in Paris. His work, both in painting and etching, is represented in many foreign galleries, and in the permanent collections of the Pennsylvania Academy of Fine Arts, the Carnegie Institute, in Pittsburgh, Pa., the Boston Arts Club, the Corcoran Gallery, in Washington, D. C. and the Metropolitan Museum of Art.

HASSAN (13° N., 76° 7' E.), town, Mysore, India. Pop. *c.* 9000. District has area of 2,546 sq. miles; produces coffee, cereals.

HASSE, JOHANN ADOLPH (1699-1783), Ger. composer; very popular in XVIII. cent.; composed innumerable operas, besides symphonies, masses, etc. with genuine pleasing melodies.

HASSELT (51° 56' N., 5° 20' E.), town, Limburg, Belgium.

HASSENPFLUG, HANS DANIEL LUDWIG FRIEDRICH (1795-1862), Ger. politician; held state offices in Hesse-Cassel, 1832-37; in Hohenzollern Sigmaringen, 1838; Luxembourg, 1839; Prussia, 1841-50; head of Hesse government, 1850.

HASTINAPUR, capital of the Pandavas in the Hindu epic, *Mahabharata*; traces c. 20 miles N.E. of Meerut, United Provinces, India.

HASTINGS—(1) (50° 52' N., 0° 36' E.), municipal, parliamentary, and county borough, Sussex, England; fashionable watering-place and one of Cinque Ports. Small shipbuilding and fishing industry. Site of battle of H. 1066 is 6 miles inland.

HASTINGS, a city of Michigan, in Barry co., of which it is the county seat. It is on the Michigan Central and the Chicago, Kalamazoo and Saginaw railroads, and on the Thornapple river. It is an important industrial city and has manufactures of cigars, flour, pumps, carriages, wagons, etc. There is a public library and a city hall.

HASTINGS, a city of Nebraska, in Adams co. It is on the Burlington, Missouri Pacific, Chicago & Northwestern, Union Pacific and other railroads. It is the center of an important farming and stock raising district. Has numerous factories and wholesale houses. It is the seat of Hastings College and other educational institutions. Here is Ingleside Insane Hospital. It is the home of the Westinghouse Radio Station KFKX, the pioneer rebroadcasting station of the world.

HASTINGS-UPON-HUDSON, a village of New York, in Westchester co. Although it is chiefly a residential suburb of New York City it has important industries including the manufacture of copper wire cable, copper, brass, dyestuffs, chemicals, etc.

HASTINGS, Eng. family; descended from Sir Henry de H. d. 1268, supporter of Montfort. Family held H. barony from c. 1290; earldom of Pembroke, 1339-89; extinct in XVI. cent. Barony is now held by Astley family. Another branch of family became barons, 1461; Earls of Huntingdon, 1529.

HASTINGS, FRANCIS RAWDON, 1ST MARQUESS OF HASTINGS (1754-1826), Brit. soldier and adminis-

trator; served in Amer. War, 1775-82; gained victory at Hobkirk's Hill; led force to assist Duke of York in Flanders, 1794; master general of ordnance, 1806; Gov.-Gen. of Bengal and commander-in-chief in India, 1812; defeated Gurkhas; extended Brit. territories, 1816; crushed Pindaris and Mahrattas, 1817-18.

HASTINGS, THOMAS (1860), Architect. *B.* in New York. In 1884 graduated from Ecole des Beaux Arts, Paris. Partner of John M. Carrere in firm of Carrere and Hastings since 1884. Firm were architects of many famous buildings including New York Public Library, Ponce de Leon and Alcazar Hotels at St. Augustine, Florida and the National Academy of Design. In 1907, member of Commission of Fine Arts. Member of American Academy of Arts and Letters. Was president of Society Beaux Arts Architectes. Chevalier of Legion of Honor, France. *d.* 1929.

HASTINGS, WARREN (1732-1818), Brit. administrator; *b.* at Churchill, Oxfordshire; entered East India Companys' service, 1750; resident at court of Murshidabad, 1758; member of council, 1761; second in council at Madras, 1768; pres. of council and Gov. of Bengal, 1772. H. effected reforms in system of government; transferred centre of administration from Murshidabad to Calcutta; reformed military and police organisation.

The consolidation of Ind. Empire was largely due to his administrative genius. He became Gov-.Gen. of India, 1773. Members of council were inimical to him, and condemned all his measures. He was accused by Brahmin Nuncomar of receiving bribes; shortly afterwards Nuncomar was accused of forgery, found guilty, and hanged, a circumstance tending to alienate public sympathy from H. During these events H. sent in his resignation, but subsequently remained in office. Between 1777 and 1785 he conducted war against Mahrattas and against Hyder Ali; suppressed insurrection of Chait Sing, Rajah of Benares, and deposed him; caused begums of Oude to give up land and treasure, 1780, some of which he afterwards restored. He returned to England in 1785, and was impeached by Burke in a famous speech, 1786, for oppression, maladministration, and corruption. Trial lasted seven years, after which he was acquitted, 1795. Costs of trial swallowed up his entire fortune, but he subsequently obtained pension from East India Co.

HAT, name given to head-covering, with brim, the principal materials used being silk, fur, wool, merino, straw. The frame of a silk h. is composed of calico and other materials, stiffened in shellac, and is shaped on a block. The crown and brim are then sewn on, the silk covering and trimmings added, and the finished article is then polished for wear. Opera hats are covered with silk or merino, and a collapsible steel frame provides means of adjustment. Felt hats are made from fur, fur and wool, or wool alone, according to quality. See COSTUME.

HATCH, to incubate from eggs; to develop a hidden scheme; term used by surveyors for shading, and by engravers for similar lines; lower part of divided door.

HATCHMENT, diamond-shaped panel, enclosing arms of a deceased person, suspended on wall of his dwelling for short period after death.

HATHAWAY, ANNE. See SHAKE-SPEARE, WILLIAM.

HATHOR. See EGYPT (Ancient Religion).

HATHRAS (27° 36′ N., 78° 11′ E.), town. United Provinces, Brit. India.

HATTERAS, CAPE, a low extent of land, in North Carolina, forming part of a sandbank. Here the coast line turns from north east to due north. Severe storms are frequent here and navigation is dangerous at times. At the point of the Cape is a lighthouse, 190 feet above the sea.

HATTIESBURG, a city of Mississippi, in Forrest co., of which it is the county seat. It is on the Southern, Gulf and Ship Island, Mississippi Central and Gulf, Mobile and Northern Railroads, and on the Leaf River. It is the center of an extensive lumbering region and its industries include railroad shops, woodworking shops, machine shops, fertilizer factories, etc. It is the seat of the Baptist Women's College and State Teachers College.

HATTO I. (c. 850-913), bp. of Mainz; alleged to have been eaten at Bingen (where the Mouse Tower is still shown) by rats as a punishment for his cruelty.

HATTON, SIR CHRISTOPHER (1540-91), Eng. lord chancellor; held various positions under Elizabeth; denounced Mary, Queen of Scots, in Parliament, 1587; Lord Chancellor, 1587; was favorite of Elizabeth; encouraged literature.

HAUFF, WILHELM (1802-27); Ger. poet and novelist; b. Stuttgart; best works: Lichtenstein (novel), Phantasien im Bremer Rathskeller; Reiter's Morgengesang (poems).

HAUGWITZ, CHRISTIAN AUGUST HEINRICH KURT (1752-1831), Pruss. politician; ambassador to Vienna, 1792; entered Berlin cabinet, 1792; began negotiations resulting in treaty between Britain and Prussia, 1794; influenced treaty with France, 1795; as Foreign Minister signed treaty of Schönbrunn, 1805.

HAUNTING by spirits of the dead has been observed or credited in all ages. Until recently belief in ghosts was generally discredited, but owing to 'Psychical Research' and elaborate investigation of various phenomena many people believe there is some foundation for ghost stories in fact; possibly mysterious experiences are due only to telepathic suggestion.

HAUPT, LOUIS MUHLENBERG (1844), an American civil engineer, b. in Gettysburg, Pa. He graduated from the United States Military Academy in 1867. After several years of service in the army he resigned to become engineer of Fairmount Park, Phila. He was professor of civil engineering at the University of Pennsylvania, from 1872 to 1892, when he resigned to engage in private practice. He was a member of the Nicaragua Canal Commission and of the Isthmian Canal Commission, and was chief and consulting engineer for many important projects including several ship canals. He was the author of many books on engineering and kindred subjects and invented several devices for reclaiming land.

HAUPT, PAUL (1858); an American Orientalist, b. at Gorlitz, Germany. He was educated at the University of Leipzig and Berlin. For several years he was professor of Assyriology at the University of Göttingen. In 1883 he was chosen professor of Semitic languages and director of Oriental Semitic at Johns Hopkins University. He wrote much on Oriental subjects and was editor of the Polychrome Bible, and other editions of the Hebrew texts. d. 1926.

HAUPTMANN, GERHART (1862); Ger. poet and dramatist; his works include historical and realistic dramas and comedies; Einsame Menschen was his first real success, 1891; Die Weber 1892 is a study of conditions of life among hand-weavers of Silesian mountains; Und Pippa tanzt is a masterly fairy tale. Most successful when he turns to field of legend and simple childlife. He received Nobel Prize for literature, 1912.

HAUSAS, HOUSSAS, African race inhabiting W. Africa between Lake Tchad and the river Niger; busy traders; language spoken by over 15,000,000 people.

HAUSEN, MAX VON (1846), Ger. soldier, of royal Saxon birth, entered a Saxon Jager battalion and served in wars of 1866 and 1870-1. At outbreak of World War he was placed in command of 3rd Ger. Army. Pub. *Errinnerungen an der Marnefeldzug*, 1914, 1920. *d.* 1922.

HAUSER, KASPAR (1812-33), mysterious youth appeared in Nuremberg, 1828, who could give no account of himself, and possessed no memory of his previous life. A letter in his possession stated that he was born in 1812. Earl Stanhope, and others, took charge of him, and he *d.* from a wound in his breast. Nothing was discovered as to his origin. Subject of a novel by Wasserman.

HAUTBOY. See OBOE.

HAUSSMANN, GEORGES EUGÉNE BARON (1809-91), Fr. administrator; as Préfet de la Seine 1853-69 greatly embellished Paris, by planning and opening new streets and boulevards.

HAUTE-GARONNE (43° 20′ N., 1° E.), S. W. department, France; area, 2,457 sq. miles; crossed by Garonne produces timber, cereals, wine, fruit; chief town, Toulouse.

HAUTE-LOIRE (45° 10′ N., 3° 50′ E.), department, central France; area, 1,930 sq. miles; surface mountainous; crossed by Loire; coal, timber, cereals, lace; chief town, Le Puy.

HAUTE-MARNE (48° 10′ N., 5° 10′ E.), N. E. department, France; area, *c.* 2,420 sq. miles; surface slopes upwards from N. to S., where is plateau of Langres; crossed by Marne; cereals, vegetables, wine, iron; chief town, Chaumont.

HAUTES-ALPES (44° 40′ N., 6° 20′ E.), S.E. department, France; area, 2,178 sq. miles; drained by Durance; sheep raised; chief town, Gap.

HAUTE-SAÔNE (47° 40′ N., 6° 10′ E.), E. department, France; area, 2,074 sq. miles; crossed by Saône; nearly half surface under cultivation; produces cereals, cherries; iron, steel, and copper works, cotton manufacture; chief town, Vesoul.

HAUTE-SAVOIE (46° N., 6° 25′ E.), E. department, France; area, 1,774 sq. miles, mountainous; beautiful scenery; produces wine; chief town, Annecy.

HAUTES-PYRÉNÉES (43° N., 0° 10′ E.), department, S.W. France; bounded S. by Spain, W. by Basses-Pyrénées, E. by Gers, E. by Haute-Garonne. Chief towns, Tarbes, Lourdes, and Bagnères-de-Bigorre; principal rivers, Gave de Paw, Adour, and Neste. In N. are plains and hills, and in S. Fr. Pyrenees. Cattle- and sheep-rearing, horse-breeding, fruit-growing, and wine-making carried on.

HAUTE-VIENNE (45° 50′ N., 1° 15′ E.), central department, France; area, 2,119 sq. miles; crossed by Vienne, Isle; produces fruits, cereals, porcelain; chief town, Limoges.

HAÜY, RENÉ JUST (1742-1822), a French physicist and mineralogist, *b.* at St. Just, educated at the colleges of Navarre and Lemoine, and became a teacher at the latter. In 1781 he discovered the geometrical law of crystallisation associated with his name, which he afterwards expounded in his *Traite de Mineralogie*, 1801. For this he was elected to the Academy of Sciences in 1783. In 1794 he became curator in the School of Mines, and in 1802 professor of mineralogy at the Museum of Natural History. He suffered considerably during the Revolution. He also made valuable observations in pyro-electricity. His other works include *Traite elementaire de Physique*, 1803, and *Traite de Cristallographie*, 1822.

HAVANA, OR HABANA, cap. and seapt. of Cuba (23° 6′ N., 82° 25′ W.), situated on N. side of island; chief commercial city of W. Indies. Havana consists of old or inner town, with narrow, dirty streets, and well-laid-out new part, with beautiful promenades and gardens. Notable features are the old Spanish cathedral 1724, governor's and bishop's palaces, admiralty, State univ., library, museum, theatres, arsenal, bull-ring, and splendid harbour with strong fortifications (Punto and Morro castles, Cabanas fort, etc.); chief industries; famous Havana cigars, sugar, chocolate, coffee, rum, molasses woollen fabrics and straw hats.

Founded by Diego Velasquez on S. coast 1515, and removed to present position, 1519; captured by French, 1563, by English 1762, and restored 1763. In 17th cent. chief naval station of Span. W. Indies fleet; blockaded by Amer. fleet 1898, and made independent 1902. Scene of Cuban Revolt, 1933.

HAVEL (52° 43′ N., 12° 11′ E.), river, Prussia, Germany; unites with Elbe above Wittenberge.

HAVELOCK, SIR HENRY (1795-1857). Brit. soldier; served in Burma,

1825-26; Afghan wars, 1839; distinguished in Mahratta and Sikh campaigns, 1843, 1845; commanded division in Persia, 1857; sent to India during Mutiny; defeated rebels at Fatehpur, Cawnpore, and other places; relieved Lucknow, 1857.

HAVELOK, THE DANE, hero of Anglo-Scandinavian romance, *s.* of Birkbagen, king of Denmark, who, by treachery, was set adrift on raft, which bore him to the Lincolnshire coast. He was befriended by a fisherman, Grim; subsequently m. a distressed Eng. princess, and became king of Denmark and part of England; Eng. versions of Middle Eng. poem by Skeat and others.

HAVERFORD COLLEGE, an educational institution founded by the Society of Friends in Haverford, Pa., in 1833, and being the first establishment of the kind to come under their auspices. Its buildings, numbering 17, and the grounds, cover 226 acres, and are valued at about $3,000,000. In 1933 the faculty numbered 38 and the students 300. Wm. H. Comfort, Pres.

HAVERGAL, FRANCES RIDLEY (1836-79), an English poetess, *b.* at Astley, Worcestershire, *d.* of the Rev. William Henry H. She was a talented child, and began to write verses at the age of seven. Her best work is religious, and is characterized by graceful expression, sympathetic feeling, and introspective insight. Many of her hymns are well established favorites, and are included in numerous collections for use in churches. Her works, originally published as *Ministry of Song*, 1870; *Under the Surface*, 1874; *Loyal Responses*, 1878; were collected in 1884 by her sister, who, in 1880, had published *Memorials of Frances Ridley Havergal.*

HAVERHILL, a city of Massachusetts, in Essex co. It is on the Boston and Maine Railroad, and on the Merrimak River, 33 miles N. of Boston. It is an important manufacturing city and among its industries are plants for the making of boots and shoes, hats and woolen goods, leather, lumber and brick. It is also the center of an extensive farming and dairying district. There are many notable public buildings, four national banks, an excellent system of streets and sewers, and electric railways. The city was originally an Indian village called Pentucket, and was settled in 1640. It was incorporated in 1645 and was chartered as a city in 1869. Haverhill was the birthplace of John Greenlief Whittier and was his home for many years.

HAVERSACK, canvas bag to strap on shoulders; originally receptacle for oats (*haver*), which were the usual fare of soldiers on the march.

HAVERSTRAW, a city of New York, in Rockland co., formerly known as Warren. It is on the West Shore and also on the New York and New Jersey railroads, and on the Hudson River. It is notable for being the largest brick manufacturing city in the world. Other industries include cotton goods, bleaching and printing, silk weaving, etc., dynamite and baskets. In the vicinity are many points of historic interest. The city has parks, street railways, daily and weekly newspapers, and a national and state bank.

HAVRE, OR LE HAVRE DE GRÂCE, second greatest seaport of France (49° 29′ N., 0° 6′ E.), in Seine-Inférieure, on estuary of Seine; first-class fortress, with church of Notre-Dame, town hall, museum, marine arsenal, etc., large shipbuilding yards, cannon foundries; machinery, glassware, lace, cotton goods, etc. During World War vast numbers of troops for various fronts disembarked here.

HAWAII, OR THE HAWAIIAN IS-LANDS are situated in the North Pacific. They were formerly known as the Sandwich islands, and have been American territory since 1898. Their latitude is from 19° 54′ to 22° 15′ N., and their longitude 154° 50′ to 160° 30′ W. They thus extend N.W. to S.E. for about 390 miles on the northern edge of the tropics. The islands serve as the crossroads of the Pacific, as they are more than 2,000 miles from the nearest mainland. They are 2,089 miles from San Francisco, 4,680 miles from Panama, 3,800 from Manila, and 4,950 miles from Hong Kong. The area of the territory is 6,449 square miles and comprises twenty islands, of which nine are inhabited, the latter being the main island, Hawaii, 4,016 square miles, Maui, 728; Oahu, 598; Kauai, 547; Mokokai, 261; Lanai, 140; Niihau, 73; Kahoolawe, 44; and Molokini, 2.7 square miles. The island of Hawaii, by which the group is commonly designated, constitutes nearly two-thirds of the entire territory, but Oahu, on which the Hawaiian capital, Honolulu, is situated, is the more important island.

These two islands and Maui contain large areas of fertile plains and valleys between the mountains and the coasts. All the islands are mountainous and of volcanic origin. Like other Pacific islands, they form the summits of towering volcanic masses projected up from the sea bed, with steep and rocky coasts and precipices extending several miles. Hawaii island has the loftiest peaks.

Mauna Kea and Mauna Loa, 13,085 and 13,650 feet high respectively. Mauna Loa is an active volcano at times and contains on its eastern slope the famous Kilauea crater, about nine miles in diameter, which is in frequent eruption and the largest active volcano in the world. A much larger but extinct crater, measuring from 20 to 30 miles in circumference, is Haleakala (House of the Sun), rising more than 10,000 feet above sea level on the island of Maui. Where the land does not rise up sheer, there are occasional sandy beaches, and, more frequently, coral reefs. The islands have no waterways that can be called rivers. The mountains pour down torrential streams, but the watercourses formed are short and quite unnavigable, though useful for irrigation.

The islands came into the possession of the United States as the outcome of a growth of American interests there extending from the beginning of the ninteenth century. They were discovered by Captain Cook in 1778. After the American revolution the Sandwich Islands, as they were then known, were frequently visited by Yankee trading craft and became their chief center in the Pacific. The work of American missionaries and the appointment by President Monroe of an American agent of commerce and shipping increased the connection between the two countries, and American settlers came. The United States had a military force on the islands to protect American commerce, and to check desertions and mutinies by seamen on whalers and other ships, and in 1825 a small naval force was sent. Later there were occasional negotiations between the United States and the Hawaiian monarchy for the improvement of the relations between the two countries in view of growing commercial interests and the need of protecting American rights. The U. S. government also sought to oppose interference with the island's independence by foreign powers. This policy was induced in 1843 by the action of a British naval commander, who occupied the islands and demanded that Hawaii declare her allegiance to Great Britain. The British government repudiated his action and later Great Britain and France undertook not to seek control of the islands even under a protectorate.

Steps towards American annexation began as early as 1851, when the Hawaiian government provisionally ceded the islands to the United States to checkmate feared French designs. The United States refused to take them, but its navy kept a fleet handy for Pacific service. Three years later a treaty was drafted admitting the islands as a state of the American Union, but was not proceeded with. A reciprocity treaty signed in 1867 promised an expansion of American influence, but was rejected by the Senate. From that year onward annexation of the islands intermittently occupied succeeding American Secretaries of State with periodic soundings of the Hawaiian government on the subject. In 1875 the United States by another treaty obtained certain exclusive trade privileges in the islands; in 1884 it obtained the right to enter Pearl Harbor and establish a coaling station. Finally, in 1893 an annexation treaty was signed with a provisional government which was established following the deposition of Queen Liliuo Kalani. This step was the outcome of a revolution headed by an American, Sanford Ballard Dole (q. v.) a judge of the Hawaiian Supreme Court. President Harrison sent the treaty to the Senate, but President Cleveland withdrew it in order to examine the whole situation. Any lingering doubts as to the expediency of annexing the islands were dispelled by the action of Germany and other powers in annexing other Pacific islands. The republic formed by Dole and his followers wanted union. The Spanish-American war of 1898, which brought the Philippines and other islands within American territory led both houses of Congress, on July 7 of that year to a joint resolution by large majorities annexing the islands, which in 1900 were organized as a Territory and admitted into the Union.

Sugar, pineapples, rice and coffee form the island's leading products. The largest industry is the production of sugar, which in 1933 extended over plantations—mostly irrigated land-aggregating 138,000 acres, producing 1,008,000 tons. The growing and canning of pineapples produced in 1931 nearly 12, 726,-291 cases. In 1932, 388,068,857 lbs. valued at $20,591,503 were shipped to the U.S. The United States gets most of the island's products and sends in return manufactured goods, food products and general merchandise and commodities in large volume. The total exports to the United States in 1932 had a value of $82,688,205 and the imports $58,504,391, both a considerable falling off from the value of trade done the fiscal years immediately previous. Rice yielded a large crop in 1933, and coffee too was an important export.

The farms in 1930 covered 2,815,026 acres, of which 440,579 were improved and 747,636 woodland, and had a value of $111,780,432. There were 5,955 farmers, of whom 633 were white, 510 Hawaiian, 4,191 Japanese and 335 Chinese. Most of the farms were owned by the occu-

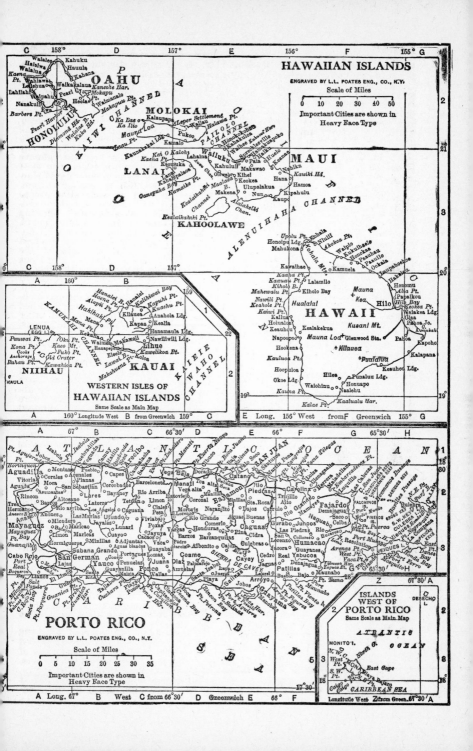

pants. There is almost no manufacturing done in the Hawaiian islands.

The U. S. government maintains a considerable army on the islands. As to their revenue, it is chiefly derived, as in the States, from taxing real and personal property. The federal government's share in the island's productiveness is shown in the custom receipts, income and other taxes, which yielded, 1932, $8,707,471 for Washington. At Pearl Harbor, on Oahu, the U. S. navy has a large base as well as an aviation field and powerful radio station. The governor of the islands was Lawrence M. Judd, appointed (1929-33) to succeed Wallace R. Farrington.

The population in 1930 was 368,336, of which 139,631 were Japanese, and only 50,860 were Hawaiian or part Hawaiian. The rest were Portuguese, Americans and other Caucasian races, 44,895, Filipinos 63,052, and Porto Ricans, Spaniards, Koreans and negroes. The chief city is Honolulu, the capital, with a population, 1930 of 173,582.

On Feb. 2, 1934, Joseph B. Poindexter, former attorney general of Montana, was appointed by President Roosevelt to the governorship of Hawaii, succeeding Lawrence M. Judd.

HAWARDEN (53° 11′ N., 3° 1′ W.), town, Flint, N. Wales. Hawarden Castle was Gladstone's seat.

HAWES, STEPHEN (*d. c.* 1523), Eng. poet; Groom of the Chamber to Henry VIII.; his works include *Pastyme of Pleasure*, 1509; *Convercyon of Swerers*, 1509; *The Exemple of Vertu*, 1512, etc. His works contributed to the formation of the Eng. literary language.

HAWICK (55° 26′ N., 2° 48′ W.), burgh, Roxburghshire, Scotland, on both sides of Teviot; chief manufacturing town in S. Scotland. district rich in historic houses.

HAWK FAMILY (FALCONIDÆ), a large family of diurnal birds of prey (*Accipitrines*), comprising nearly 500 species found all the world over. They are distinguished from other birds of prey by the presence of a voice-box at base of windpipe, of a circlet of feathers surrounding the oil gland, of an aftershaft on the feathers, and by their feathered heads. The following are a few of the many types belonging to the Hawk family: the New World Caracaras (*Polyborinoe*) feed on living prey or on carrion, run rapidly, and nest on the ground. They differ from all other Hawks in having three toes instead of two, connected by a web. Long-legged Hawks, with the lower leg-joint or metatarsus at least equal to that

above it, the tibia, form the group *Accipitrinoe*, found in all lands.

HAWKE, EDWARD, BARON HAWKE (1705-81), Brit. admiral; *b.* London; entered navy at an early age and became commander when twenty-eight; served against Spain in W. Indies; rendered good service at Toulon, 1744; in 1747, off Belleisle, and in 1759, in Quiberon Bay, he inflicted ruinous defeats on Fr. fleets; also led an unsuccessful expedition against Rochefort in 1757; Admiral of the Fleet, 1768; First Lord of Admiralty, 1766-71; cr. peer, 1776.

HAWKER (*Hawker*, XVI. cens.); itenerant vendor.

HAWKER, HARRY GEORGE (1881); Australian airman of Cornish origin; took pilot's certificate at Brooklands, 1911; won Michelin prize, 1912; took part in *Daily Mail* 'Round Britain' competition, 1913. During the World War was engaged in testing machines for Sopwith Co. Made new world's record for height at Brooklands, 1916. In June, 1919, with Commander Mackenzie Grieve, attempted to fly across Atlantic, but engine trouble compelled their descent in mid-ocean. *d.* 1921.

HAWKESWORTH, JOHN (*d.* 1773); Eng. writer; edit. Captain Cook's *Journals*, 1773; edit. Swift, and pub. much miscellaneous work.

HAWKINS, ANTHONY HOPE pseudonym Anthony Hope (1863), Eng. novelist; has achieved distinction in the romantic style with *The Prisoner of Zenda*, 1894; and in light modern comedy with *The Dolly Dialogues* and similar works; his later books have been comedies of a more serious character, and include such novels as *The God in the Car*, *Quisante*, *Tristram of Blent*, etc.; his most recent works are *Captain Dieppe*, 1918 and *Beaumaroy home from the Wars*, 1919; author of several plays: *The Prisoner of Zenda* has been successfully dramatized. *d.* 1933.

HAWKINS, SIR JOHN (1532-95), Eng. admiral; engaged in slave trade; defeated by Spanish, 1567; treasurer of navy, 1572; rear-admiral, 1588; fought against Armada; *d.* on voyage to West Indies.

HAWKINS, SIR RICHARD (1562-1622), Eng. admiral; *s.* of Sir John H.; commanded *Duck* galliot in Drake's raid on Span. Main, 1585; captain of *Swallow* in attack on Great Armada, 1588; sailed in the *Dainty* for the Pacific, 1593; plundered Valparaiso, and, in San Mateo Bay, kept up a three days' fight with two Span. galleons; finally capitulated, and was for ten years prisoner; subsequently ransomed; knighted by James I., and made vice-admiral of Devon.

HAWKWOOD, SIR JOHN L'ACUTO (*d.* 1394), Eng. soldier-of-fortune; served under Black Prince in France; afterwards fought as mercenary in Italy, assisting Pisa against Florence, Milan against pope, pope against Milan, and finally entered Florentine service, **1378**; see RUSKIN'S FORS CLAVIGERA.

HAWTHORN (37° 49′ S., 145° E.), town, Victoria, Australia.

HAWTHORN, a tree, *Cratoegus oxyacantha*, natural order *Rosaceoe*, suborder *Pomeoe*, with *polypetalous* white or red flowers and numerous *stamens* in whorls; the *stigma* ripens first, but *self-pollimation* is possible. The fruit is a *pome*, the *carpels* of which are stony. H's are commonly used for hedges and for ornamental purposes.

HAWTHORNE, HILDEGARDE, an American author, *b.* in New York. She received a private education, at home and abroad, after which she began her literary work, contributing articles, poems and short stories to the magazines. For many years she has been a book reviewer on the New York Times. Among her books are *A Country Interlude*, 1904; *The Lure of the Garden*, 1911; *Old Seaport Towns of New England*, 1916; *Rambles Through College Towns*, 1917 and *Girls in Bookland*, 1917.

HAWTHORNE, JULIAN (1846); an American writer and the *s.* of Nathaniel Hawthorne, *b.* in Boston, Mass. He graduated from Harvard University, in 1867, then studied engineering in Germany. For a while he held a position in the Department of Docks in New York City, but after 1872 began writing. Among his books are *Bressant*, 1872; *Garth*, 1875; *American Literature*, 1891; *Hawthorne and His Circle*, 1903, and *The Subterranean Brotherhood*, the latter written after his imprisonment, in 1914, and based on his experiences in the penitentiary.

HAWTHORNE, NATHANIEL (1804-1864), American novelist. *B.* in Salem, Mass., July 4, 1804; *d.* in Plymouth, New Hamp., May 18, 1864. He came of stern Puritan ancestry circumstance that colored his literary work. Graduating from Bowdoin College in 1829, *Fanshowe* was published anonymously in 1828. He first signed his name to *Four Tales* which appeared in The Token. The first volume of *Twice Told Tales* came out in 1873. So little was he read, that he took the position of weigher at the Port of Boston 1839-1841, being dismissed when a new party came in power. *Grandfathers Chair*, sketches from New England history for children was published in 1841, and for about two years he was a member of the Brook Farm Community. Having married Miss Peabody of Salem, he settled in Concord where he wrote two series of *Twice Told Tales* and *Mosses From an Old Manse*, 1843. Literary work was still so unprofitable that he obtained the position of Surveyor of Customs at Salem, 1846-1849. His masterpiece *The Scarlet Letter* appeared in 1850 and was hailed at home and abroad as a work of genius. From 1852 to 1856 he was American consul at Liverpool, Eng., and wrote *The English Note Book* and *Our Old Home*. *French and Italian Note Books* appeared in 1857-1858. Among his other works not previously mentioned are *The Wonder Book*, 1851; *The Blithedale Romance*, 1852; *Tanglewood Tales*, 1853; *The Marble Faun*, 1860; *Dr. Grimshaw's Secret* unfinished, was published in 1882 and *Septimust Fulton* also unfinished in 1871.

HAWTREY, CHARLES HENRY (1858), Eng. actor-manager and playwright; his adaptation of *The Private Secretary* 1884 achieved remarkable success, as also did *A Message from Mars*, 1899. *d.* 1923.

HAXO, FRANÇOIS NICOLAS BENOIT BARON (1774-1838), Fr. general and most famous of Napoleon's engineers.

HAY. By the word hay we mean the dried stems and leaves of herbaceous plants, the grasses (Gramineae), clover and allied plants (Leguminosae), which are used as fodder for domestic animals, during periods when green food is not available. The methods of preparing hay vary considerably in details in different localities, but in principle they are the same. The herbage is first mown and then spread out, turned, and shaken in the fields to dry under the action of wind and sun. The more quickly this drying process is finished the finer is the aroma of the hay, and the more palatable is it to animals. It is next gathered into windrows and finally stored in hayricks. The time of drying varies from two to ten days, but under unfavorable weather conditions the hay is frequently damaged or spoiled. Insufficient drying may cause subsequent mouldiness (due to fungoid growth) or heating (due to bacterial action) in the rick, but this is sometimes held to improve the product. In England it is usual to cut permanent meadows for hay; while in Scotland a special hay crop is more generally grown. The chief hay plants are clover and the grasses—the most important being rye-grass, timothy, foxtail, cocksfoot, sweet vernal, the oat grasses, and several species of fescue. See GRASS.

HAY, IAN (John Hay Beith) (1876-), British novelist, *b.* at Rusholme; ed. at Edinburgh and Cambridge; received the M.C. in the war; best known for *The First Hundred Thousand* (1915); *Carrying On* (1917); and *The Last Million* (1918); also wrote *A Safety Match* (1911); and *Paid With Thanks* (1925).

HAY, JAMES, JR. (1881-), writer *b.* at Harrisburg, Va. Author of *The Winning Clue*, 1919; *The Melwood Mystery*, 1920; *No Clue*, 1920; *The Unlighted House*, 1921. Managed publicity for Geo. Washington Bicentennial Commemoration, 1931-32.

HAY, JOHN (MILTON) (1838-1905), American statesman; *b.* in Salem, Ind. Graduating from Brown University in 1858, he studied law with his uncle Milton Hays and was admitted to the bar in 1861. Having worked for Lincoln in his first election, Hay was made one of the president's secretaries. After Lincoln's death he was appointed secretary of legation in Paris, and in 1867 charge d'Affaires in Vienna, resigning the next year. First secretary of legation, Madrid, 1868-1870 he returned to this country to become an editorial writer on the N. Y. Tribune. After marrying the *d.* of Amasa Stone of Cleveland, Ohio, he moved to that city and was engaged in literary work until 1879, when appointed by President Hayes, Assistant Secretary of State. In 1881 he took charge of the N.Y. Tribune, and began with Nicolay the great work on Lincoln, 1881-1887. In 1897 he was appointed minister to Great Britain, and Secretary of State from 1898 until his death. He obtained justice for China after the Boxer revolt, securing her integrity and an 'Open door' policy from European nations. He negotiated the Hay-Pauncefote Treaty and supported the Hague Conference, inducing the Powers that claimed an indemnity from Venezuela to submit the question to The Hague tribunal. He signed the treaty with Colombia that granted right of way for the Panama Canal, and persuaded Great Britain to submit the Alaska boundary question to arbitration. Roosevelt on his succession urged Hay to remain as Secretary of State and he retained the office when Roosevelt was re-elected. Publications *Pike County Ballads, Castilian Days, The Bread Winners*, a novel, 1885; *Complete Poetical Works*, 1916: *The Addresses of John Hay* were published after his death. He edited *Complete Works of Abraham Lincoln*, 1894.

HAYASHI, BARON GONSUKE (1861-), Jap. diplomatist; secretary of legation, 1896; was subsequently ambassador in Rome and in Peking. Prior to becoming ambassador in London, 1920 was governor of Kwantung Leased Territory. Amb. to Ct. of St. James, 1920-25.

HAYDEN, FERDINAND VENDEVER (1829-1887), American geologist, *b.* in Westfield, Mass.; served in the Civil War, rising to rank of lieutenant colonel; spent many years in exploring the Rocky Mountain region and edited a number of geographical and geological reports for the United States government. He also wrote several books on the exploration of the West.

HAYDN, FRANZ JOSEPH (1732-1809), Austrian composer; *b.* Rohrau, near Vienna; a wheelwright's *s.*; joined St. Stephen's Cathedral choir, Vienna, 1740; app. conductor of Count Morzin's band, 1759; patronized by Esterhazy family; exceedingly popular in Vienna, then greatest European music centre. Among his pupils was Beethoven. H. greatly influenced his young friend, Mozart. H. was a slow but prolific composer; the first great writer of quartet and the 'Father of Symphony', paving the way for Beethoven. Compositions: 118 symphonies, including *Farewell*, 1772; *Toy*, and 12 written for Eng. visits, 1791-1794; 83 quartets, trios, operas, and oratorios—greatest, *The Creation*, 1799 and *The Seasons*, 1800.

HAYDON, BENJAMIN ROBERT (1786-1846), Eng. his. painter; *b.* at Plymouth; studied at Royal Academy. Quarrels with the Academy and debt troubles made his life a burden, and he committed suicide. His best pictures are *The Judgment of Solomon* (1814), *Christ's Entry into Jerusalem*, and *The Resurrection of Lazarus*.

HAYES, PATRICK JOSEPH (1867-), an American Roman Catholic prelate, *b.* in New York City. He graduated from Manhattan College, in New York, in 1888, and was ordained a priest in 1892. During 1903-14 he was president of Cathedral College, at the end of which period he was consecrated auxiliary bishop of New York. In 1919 he was appointed Archbishop of New York. Cardinal, 1924.

HAYES, RUTHERFORD BIRCHARD (1822-1893), Nineteenth president of the United States, *b.* in Delaware, Ohio, Oct. 4, 1822; *d.* in Fremont, Ohio, Jan. 17, 1893. Graduating from Kenyon College, Gambier, Ohio, in 1842, and the Harvard Law School, 1845, he was admitted to the bar and after some country practice established an office in Cincinnati. When the Civil War broke out he joined the Federals as a major of volunteers. Promoted brigadier-general he was brevetted major-general for distinguished services in the West Virginia campaign of 1864, especially in the battles of Fishers' Hill and Cedar Creek, Va. The Republican Party elected him to Congress 1868-1872-1875. In 1876 he was nominated for President by the Republicans while the Democrats chose Samuel J. Tilden. The contest over the election that followed was unique in American political history. The election returns in South Carolina, Louisiana, and Florida gave rise to charges of fraud from both sides. A commission was appointed to investigate the returns and decided that Hayes had received 185 Electoral votes to 184 for Tilden. President Hayes during his administration worked for Civil Service reform against his party's opposition. He brought the South relief by removing troops without whose backing the 'carpet-bag' governments could not have held power. Specie payments suspended since the Civil War, were resumed. After leaving office Mr. Hayes did notable service in the interests of education and prison reform in the South.

HAY-FEVER, HAY ASTHMA, OR SUMMER CATARRH, disease, often hereditary, occurring in the summer, which has been shown to be due to extreme sensibility to the pollen of grasses at that time floating in the atmosphere; characterised by headache, swelling with watery discharge of the nasal mucous membrane, paroxysms of sneezing, and cough. Treatment is change of air, with avoidance of vegetation; cocaine or suprarenal extract applied to the mucous membrane, or destruction of the sensitive part of it by the cautery; and tonics, e.g. arsenic or quinine preparations, for the general system. A serum has been prepared, which sometimes gives relief.

HAYLEY, WILLIAM (1745-1820), Eng. poet and biographer; his poetical works include *Triumphs of Temper*, *Essays and Epistles*, which were very popular; declined laureateship; also wrote *Lives* of Cowper 1803-4, Milton, and Romney.

HAYMARKET SQUARE RIOT, a riot in Haymarket Square, Chicago, 1886, in which seven policemen were killed and sixty wounded by a bomb when dispersing an anarchist meeting. A number of anarchists were hanged.

HAYNAU, JULIUS JACOB (1786-1853), Austrian field-marshal; execrated in Liberal countries for his severity towards revolutionaries.

HAYNE, ROBERT YOUNG (1791-1839), Amer. politician; senator, 1823; advocated free trade; Gov. of S. Carolina, 1832; opposed Jackson.

HAYNES, ELWOOD (1857), Inventor; b. at Portland, Ind. Bachelor of Science of Worcester Polytechnic Institute in 1881. At Johns Hopkins from 1884-1885. Teacher of sciences from 1885-1886 at Eastern Indiana Normal School. 1886-1880 was manager of Portland Natural Gas and Oil Company. President since 1898 of Haynes Automobile Company. In 1881 discovered tungsten chrome steel, 1897 alloy of chomium and nickel, 1900, alloy of cobalt and chromium. On exhibition at the Smithsonian Institution is the oldest automobile in existence and which he constructed and designed in 1893-1894. First person to use aluminum in automobile engine, 1895. In 1903 invented and built rotary valve gas engine. In 1911 discovered 'stainless Steel' which was patented in 1919. Trustee of Western College. Member of Society of Automobile Engineers, Iron and Steel Institute, London, American Chemical Society. d. 1925.

HAY-PAUNCEFOTE TREATY, a treaty negotiated by John Hay (*q.v.*) on the part of the U.S.A., and Lord Pauncefote on behalf of Great Britain, abrogating the Clayton-Bulwer Treaty (*q.v.*), and providing for the construction of a Panama Canal (*q.v.*) under U.S. control and for its neutralisation on the same basis as Suez Canal. When submitted to the senate in 1900 it was ratified, but with such amendments, especially regarding its neutralisation, that Great Britain refused to ratify them. A further treaty was negotiated in 1901 and passed by the senate. It demanded no guarantee of neutrality. although the general principle of neutrality of the Clayton-Bulwer Treaty was retained, and in time of war the U.S. were given certain rights of control not definitely specified.

HAYS, WILL H. (1879), American, lawyer and cabinet officer; b. Sullivan, Ind. He graduated from Wabash College in 1900 and was admitted to the Indiana bar in the same year. He was city attorney for Sullivan 1910-13 and took an active part in political management both in local and State affairs. His adroitness as a manager of political campaigns soon gained him a national reputation, and in 1918 he was elected Chairman of the Republican National Committee. He managed the Presidential campaign of Mr. Harding, and on the election of the latter was offered the position of Postmaster General in the cabinet. He held this office for a year and then resigned to become the head of the organization of motion picture producers of the United States, 1922.

HAYTI. See HAITI.

HAYTON (fl. 1250), king of Cilicia, 1224-69; allied himself with Mongols; travelled in W. Africa, Mongolia, and elsewhere, an account of his travels being written by Kirakos Gandsaketsi; abdicated, 1269, and entered monastery.

HAYWARD, ABRAHAM (1801-84), Eng. author; by profession a barrister, but became an extensive contributor to the *Quarterly Review* and other critical journals; pub. *Biographical and Critical Essays, Eminent Statesmen and Writers*, etc.; possessed a prodigious memory and exercised much influence on public opinion.

HAYWARD, SIR JOHN (c. 1560-1627), Eng. historian; pub. *The First Part of the Life and Raigne of King Henrie IV.*, 1599; *Lives of the Three Norman Kings of England*, 1613; *The Life and Raigne of King Edward VI.*, 1630.

HAYWARD, WILLIAM (1877), lawyer; b. in Nebraska; graduate of Nebraska City High School. Bachelor of Laws of University of Nebraska, 1897. In 1897 he began practise at Nebraska City; Captain in Spanish American War and later Colonel; 1901-1902 county judge of Otoe County, Nebraska; chairman 1907-1909 of Republican State Central Committee; from 1910-1911 traveled around world. Member of law firm of Wing and Russell, 1911-1912; from 1913-1914 assistant district attorney of New York; manager of Charles S. Whitman's campaign for governor; counsel to New York legislative committee to investigate public service commissions; public service commissioner 1st District, New York, 1915-1920; resigned 1918. Recruited, organized and trained the 15th Infantry, N.G.N.Y. One of first regiments to go to France in 1917. Under fire 191 days, longest of any American regiment. Decorated by France and United States. United States attorney, Southern District of New York, 1923-25.

HAYWOOD, ELIZA (c. 1693-1756), Eng. novelist; wrote *Secret History of the Court of Caramania*, 1727 and other novels.

HAZARA (34° N., 73° 5′ E.), district, Peshawar, India; surface is valley between mountain ranges; drained by affluents of Indus.

HAZARD, game of dice, fashionable in the XVIII. cent.

HAZARD, CAROLINE (1856), ex-College President. *B.* in Rhode Island. Educated privately and studied abroad. Honorary Master of Arts, 1899, University of Michigan; Doctor of Literature, 1899; Brown College, Doctor of Laws, 1905; Tufts College. From 1899-1910, president of Wellesley College; member of American Academy of Political and Social Science, American History Association. Author : *Life of J. L. Diman*, 1886; *Thomas Hazard, Son of Robert*, 1893; *Narragansett Friends Meeting*, 1894; *The College Year*, 1910; *The Yosemite and other Verse*, 1917. Was chairman of First Liberty Loan, 1916; War Savings Campaign, 1917; United War Work Campaign, 1918.

HAZARIBAGH (23° 59′ N., 85° 20′ E.), town, Bihar and Orissa, India. Pop. 15,799. District has area of 7020 sq. miles.

HAZEBROUCK (50° 44′ N., 2° 31′ E.), town, Nord, France.

HAZEL, a shrub (*Corylus avellana*), natural order *Cupuliferoe*. It is *monoecious*, but the *stamens* and *carpels* do not occur in the same flowers. The *staminate* flowers hang in *pendulous inflorescences* named *catkins*. The small bud-like *carpellary inflorescences* are distinguished by the protruding tufts of red *stigmas*. These are borne on special *dwarf* shoots. The fruit is a one-seeded edible nut (cob or filbert), around which the *bracts* form a green cup.

HAZELTON, a city of Pennsylvania, in Luzerne co. It is on the Pennsylvania, the Lehigh Valley, and the Wilkesbarre and Hazelton railroads. Surrounding it is an extensive anthracite coal mining region, of which it is the center. In addition the city's industries include railroad shops, iron works, and plants for the making of flax, brooms, macaroni, chewing gum, etc., it has a Miners' State Hospital and is the seat of Hazelton Seminary.

HAZLITT, WILLIAM (1778-1830); Eng. essayist and critic; b. Maidstone; s. of Unitarian minister; studied theol., and later, art, but subsequently took up journalistic work; formed friendships with Leigh Hunt and the Lake poets. He published *The Round Table*, 1817, a vol. of literary sketches; *Characters of Shakespeare's Plays*, 1817; *View of the English Stage*, 1818; *Lectures on the English Poets*, 1818; *English Comic Writers*, 1819 *Dramatic Literature of the Age of Elizabeth*, 1821; *Table Talk*, 1821-22; *The Spirit of the Age*, 1825;

Life of Napoleon Buonaparte, 1828-30, etc.

HEAD. The human body is obviously separable into head, trunk, and limbs, of which the first is naturally divided into skull and face. Vertebrates possessing a head are termed *Craniata*, the higher types of which have the hard bony case of the skull containing the brain, which is continuous with the spinal cord, while the cavity of the face is almost entirely occupied by the mouth and pharynx, into the latter of which the upper end of the alimentary canal opens. It will be seen that the fundamental structure of the human body is that of a double tube, the dorsal and ventral, and in a comparison of the head with the trunk it will be found that in the former the dorsal tube is large relatively to the ventral. This condition is reversed in the trunk. The head is also remarkable on account of the large number of organs of special senses which it contains, such as those of smell (nose), taste (tongue), sound (ear), sight (eye), (See under these headings), hence there is no necessity to enlarge here on the vital character of this part of the human body.

Development.—In the embryo the distinction between the head and trunk by the formation of a cervical constriction is a change of comparatively late occurence, though long before this constriction appears, the characteristic features of the parts have become apparent. At first the head may be said to consist wholly of the cranial part; the face being developed later from a series of outgrowths or bars of the cranium.

HEADACHE, is present at the commencement of all fevers and many other diseases. When persistent, it may be due to tumour, or other changes in the brain. The term H. is often used to include neuralgia, or pain due to the nerves or nervous structure, as the eye, when it may be relieved by appropriate glasses to correct the otherwise fairly normal vision. The H. may also be caused by the fact that the glasses used are inappropriate, when measures should be taken to have them changed as soon as possible. H. may also be due to the general circulation, as in diseases of the kidney and heart. Ordinary headaches are usually symptomatic of some form of strain, worry, indigestion or other minor ailments and invariably disappear with the cause. Hermicrania or headache of one side of the head, when persistent, is sometimes traceable to defective teeth, tonsils and other infections or some form of nervous disorder or brain injury. Migraine, the name given to the severe, blinding type of headache is the most stubborn to treat. Little or nothing is known concerning it or its origin. It occurs in apparently normal, healthy people as well as in epileptics and those similarly afflicted. They are usually preceded by some sort of aura or warning such as a feeling of unusual well being, drowsiness, deep refreshing sleep or some slight bodily pain. The attack lasts from a few hours to several days during which time the sufferer is totally incapacitated. There is no treatment or cure. Persistent or frequently occurring and recurring headaches, no matter how slight are symptoms of some bodily derangement and should have competent medical attention. The popular notion that eyestrain is always the cause of headaches has no scientific basis nor is the belief that certain kinds of food or overeating will cause them. Headaches of this type are indicative of gastric or optical derangement and are not to be classed with migraine.

HEAD-HUNTING, OR HEAD-SNAPPING, a custom once prevalent among all Malay races, but now rapidly dying out, of obtaining and treasuring the heads of their enemies. Even to-day it survives among the Dyaks of Borneo and other Eastern tribes. It is believed to have had its origin in religious motives, the worship of skulls among the Malays being universal, and is said to have existed in the Philippine

Islands in 1577. The chief examples of head-hunters are the Was, a hill-tribe on the northeastern frontier of India, and the Nagas and Kuhus of Assam. Severe repressive measures, however, have led to the decrease of the custom.

HEALTH, the condition of the body in which the various functions are performed normally. A district is said to be healthful if the prevailing conditions are accompanied by a scarcity of diseased individuals.

HEAD HUNTERS OF EAST AFRICA

HEADLEY, JOEL TYLER (1814-1897), an American historian, *b*. in New York. He graduated from Union College in 1839. He took an active part in politics and in 1855 was elected Secretary of State of New York. He wrote many popular books on historical subjects. These include, *Napoleon and his Marshals*; *Oliver Cromwell*; *Life of Washington* and *The Great Rebellion*.

HEALING, MENTAL. See AUTO-SUGGESTION.

In order that H. may be maintained in an individual or in a community, attention must be directed to the following among other considerations: (1) The duty of individuals in keeping their bodies clean and free from disease by attention to food, clothing, habits, and hereditary or occupational tendencies; (2) the duty of the community in relation to the drainage of houses and towns, the building of healthful houses, removal of waste matter, legislation against hurtful employments, and the prevention and stamping out of disease. The science of hygiene has done a great deal in both of these directions. By means of exhibitions, lectures, handbooks, and instruction in schools, the individual has been taught to look after and preserve his H. by attention to simple sanitary rules. To keep the body in H. the proper preparation of good food is essential, and girls and women are being encouraged and instructed in this art by means of lectures and classes in the city, and often by house visitation by the district visitor of H. in the country. The body must be kept clean by baths, and steps are being taken by town councils to ensure that the individual may be enabled to take a bath in comfort and at no great expense. Special organisations and physicians of specialised experience probably have more to do with such cures than the actual chemical constitution of the waters.

HEALTH ASSOCIATION, T H E AMERICAN PUBLIC. A conference was held in New York, April 18, 1872, when the representatives of five states and five cities appointed a committee to organize a national association for the advancement of sanitary science. In September the committee made a report, a constitution was adopted and officers were elected. The purposes of the association are served by annual meetings when papers are read and addresses made, which are published in The American Journal of Public Health. The association exerts a wide influence in spreading the knowledge of sanitary science. Membership, 1932, 4,000.

HEALTH INSURANCE, a form of insurance whose main object is to protect the wage earner or salaried man from unemployment during sickness. It had its beginnings in the British 'friendly societies', organized over a century ago, these being voluntary, co-operative groups of men and women who paid a few pennies a week as dues and during sickness enjoyed a financial benefit from the treasury of the organization, enough to cover the minimum of living expenses. In the United States these societies took on special development in the form of the numerous secret fraternal orders, such as the Independent Order of Odd Fellows, the Elks, etc., the glamor of pagantry being added to the pecuniary benefits. Another form of life insurance companies is the great 'mutuals', also co-operative in form, though practically the membership has little control. Here, in theory at least, the policy holders are supposed to receive in benefits the sum total of the company's receipts, except what is laid aside in a reserve fund. A

third form is the purely commercial enterprise, carried on as a profit-making business by a corporation. The form of health insurance which promises in the future to become predominant is compulsory state insurance, such as was instituted in Germany, in 1884. In 1916 the American Association for Labor Legislation attempted to have bills for compulsory insurance in the industries passed in the legislatures of Massachusetts, New York and New Jersey. While these attempts failed, enough interest was aroused in Massachussets to have a special commission appointed to study the subject. This idea is supported by the U. S. Commission on Industrial Relations, the U. S. Federal Health Service and the U. S. Department of Labor.

HEALY, GEORGE PETER ALEXANDER (1808-94), Amer. artist; excelled in portraits; painted several Amer. Presidents and other public men.

HEALY, TIMOTHY MICHAEL (1855), Irish politician and lawyer; called to Irish bar, 1884; Q.C., 1899; bencher, Gray's Inn, 1910; M.P., 1880-1917; together with William O'Brien founded the Independent Nationalist party; alert, dexterous, resourceful, Eloquent, and ironically witty debater; was one of bitterest opponents of Parnell's continued leadership; secured insertion of 'Healy clause' (that in future no rent should be chargeable on tenants' improvements) in Land Bill of 1881; author of *A Word for Ireland*, 1886, etc. In 1922 he was appointed Governor-General of the Irish Free State. *d.* 1931. See IRELAND.

HEANOR (53° 1′ N., 1° 22′ W.), town, Derbyshire, England; coal, iron, hosiery.

HEARING. See EAR.

HEARN, LAFCADIO (1850-1905), a writer on Japan; *b.* Ionian Islands, of Irish and Gr. parentage; some years a journalist in America; became subsequently naturalized in Japan, where he married Jap. wife and turned Buddhist; author of *Glimpses of Unfamiliar Japan*, 1894; *Shadowings*, 1900, etc., which vividly protray Jap. character and social conditions.

HEARNE, SAMUEL (1745-92), Eng. Arctic discoverer; found copper by Coppermine River, whose mouth he discovered.

HEARNE, THOMAS (1678-1735), Eng. antiquary; edit. Camden's *Annals*, Fordun's *Scotichronicon*, Leland's *Itinerary* and *Collectanea*, and numerous other antiquarian works.

HEARSE (Fr. *herse*, from Lat. *hirpex*, harrow), vehicle used to convey body to grave; usually black framework wit glass sides. The framework resembles that of barrow-like candle-stands used in Rom. Catholic funeral ceremonies; formerly a funeral monument.

HEARST, PHEBE (APPERSON), (1842-1919), an American philanthropist. In 1861 she married George F. Hearst, United States Senator from California. At his death he left her an immense fortune from which she donated about four million dollars to the University of California for new buildings. She also gave $200,000 to the American University of Washington and made many other large gifts to educational and other institutions. She was the *m.* of William R. Hearst.

HEARST, WILLIAM RANDOLPH (1863), American newspaper publisher; *b.* San Francisco. He studied at Harvard 1882-85, and then assumed publication of the San Francisco Examiner, formerly the property of his father. He bought the New York Journal in 1895, changing the name of the morning edition later to the American. He founded the Chicago American in 1900, and since that time has become owner of a large number of newspapers and magazines, including the Boston American, Los Angeles Examiner, Chicago Examiner, Atlanta Georgian, New York Deutsches Journal, Cosmopolitan Magazine, Hearst Magazine, Good Housekeeping, Harper's Bazaar, Motor Magazine, Motor Boating Magazine and others. He served in the 58th and 59th Congresses as representative from a New York district. He was a candidate for the office of Mayor for New York in 1905 and 1909, being both times defeated. He was Democratic nominee for Governor of New York State in 1906 but was defeated by his Republican opponent, Charles E. Hughes. He controls the syndicate known as the International News Service. The policies of his papers have been radical, and he has been unsparing in his attacks on men and institutions that aroused his antagonism.

HEART, a cone-shaped, hollow, four-chambered, muscular organ, about the size of the closed fist, which acts as the central pump of the circulatory system, and is situated in the central part of the chest, resting upon the diaphragm, between the two lungs. It is held in place by the great vessels which leave or enter the organ, and by a serous membrane, the *pericardium*, in the form of a double bag, which ensheaths it completely, holding the h. in position by its attachment to the upper surface of the diaphragm.

The two upper and posterior chambers of the h., or the *auricles*, are the receiving chambers for the blood; the right auricle receives the impure or venous blood conveyed to the h. by the superior and inferior *Vena cava*, carrying the blood from the upper and lower parts of the body, and the *coronary vein*, carrying the venous blood from the substance of the h. itself; the left auricle receives the purified blood from the lungs, conveyed to it by the pulmonary veins.

From the auricles the blood passes to the two lower and anterior chambers, or *ventricles*, which are larger than the auricles and have strong muscular walls; the right ventricle propels the impure blood to the lungs, where it is purified, while the left ventricle, which is the strongest and most muscular chamber, propels the purified blood throughout the body. The right auricle communicates with the right ventricle by an opening which is guarded by a valve, the *tricuspid*, opening towards the ventricle and composed of three triangular flaps which are attached by fibrous cords to muscular projections on the walls of the right ventricle. The opening by which the left auricle communicates with the left ventricle is guarded in the same way by a valve, the *mitral*, composed of two flaps. At the point where the pulmonary artery leaves the right ventricle, and similarly where the aorta leaves the left ventricle, there is a valve to prevent the flow of blood back to the respective chambers, composed in each case of three pocket-like cusps.

The action of the h. consists, first, of the simultaneous contraction of the auricles, which drives the blood into the flaccid ventricles, the quantity and weight of the blood in the large veins preventing any flow backwards into them; this is followed by the contraction of the ventricles, which drives the blood into the main arteries, the reflux of blood into the auricles being prevented by the closure of the tricuspid and mitral valves; after the contraction of the ventricles there is a pause, when the h. is at rest, then the contraction of the auricles recommences, and so on. The heart's mechanism is subject to the absolute control of two sets of nerves. These are the cardiac branches of the two nervous systems, the cerebro-spinal and sympathetic. The action of each system is antagonistic to the other, that is, the sympathetic system causes acceleration of the heart beats while the cerebro-spinal has the opposite effect. Under normal conditions there is an equilibrium in the activity of the two systems which results in a steady, rythmic action of the heart.

HEAT is that particular form of energy which consists in the kinetic and potential energy of the molecules of matter (see ENERGY). The ultimate particles of any mass are, at all temperatures above the lowest, in the state of agitation; each atom may be moving as a whole, and it may have internal motions; the molecules (consisting of an assemblage of two or more atoms chemically alike or different) may have similar motions, and with them there may be associated potential energy due to the separation of their constituent atoms. All energy dependent on such motion or position is classed as heat, using the term in its strictest sense. The popular acceptation of the term is different, and is associated with the relative hotness or coldness of a body as perceived by the senses—*i.e.*, it is related to the *temperature* of the body, not to the heat-energy contained in the body.

The term *latent heat* is applied to heat which when supplied to a body produces no change in temp. so as to be appreciated by a thermomenter—*e.g.*, when a solid becomes liquid, the heat required for the change is called the latent heat of fusion of the solid; from liquid to vapour we have the latent heat of vaporization. Correctly speaking, the heat has been transformed into potential energy due to the separation of the molecules of the ice during the passage of the substance into the liquid form. *Radiant heat* is not heat in the sense used above, but is energy of wave motion in the ether, and only differs from light in the length of its waves.

In ordinary circumstances—*i.e.*, when no change of physical state takes place—any change in the heat-energy contained in a body produces a change in the state of hotness or coldness of the body, and to this state the name *temperature* is given. In order to give numerical expression to temp. a scale is chosen. The common attribute of all temp. scales is that they have two definite points, fixed by reference to two definite conditions of a standard substance as regards its hotness or coldness, and this interval of temp. is divided into a certain number of degrees. Any instrument which will indicate by means of such a scale the temp. of a body is termed a *thermometer*.

Being one form of the objective reality which we term energy, heat must be capable of measurement. The unit of heat generally employed in scientific work is the *calorie*, which is the amount of heat required to raise the temp. of 1 gram of water from 15° to 16° C. For engineering purposes the *Brit. thermal unit* is employed. It is the amount of heat required to raise the temp. of 1 lb. of water by 1° F., and is equal to 252

calories. Another unit in practical use is the amount of heat required to evaporate 1 lb. of water at the boiling-point under standard atmospheric pressure, and is equal to 243,583 calories. The determination of a given quantity of heat in terms of these units is dealt with below. Heat must also have quantitative relations with other forms of energy, and it is found that 1 calorie is equivalent to 42 million *ergs*, and that the British thermal unit is equivalent to 776 foot-pounds.

Heat may be transferred from one body to another or from one part to another of the same body in three ways—viz., conduction, convection, radiation. In most cases all three modes of heat transference operate together. In *conduction*, heat is passed from one particle to an adjoining particle at a lower temperature (or on a larger scale from one body to another in contact with it) until the temperatures are uniform. In some substances (good conductors—*e.g.* silver, copper, and metals generally) the transference takes place rapidly. In others (bad conductors—*e.g.*, woollen cloth, wood, etc.), it takes place slowly.

Heat has also very important effects when supplied to or withdrawn from a body. Indeed, there are few physical properties of matter which, otherwise constant, are not thus affected. The first effect is, in general, a change in temp. The relation between the amount of heat added to a body and the consequent rise in temp. is expressed by the *specific* heat of the substance, and this is defined as the number of units of heat required to raise the temp. of unit mass of the substance by 1° C. The method of determining specific heats is detailed below.

The next important effect of adding heat to a body is to change the volume, and in general all bodies increase in volume when heated. The increase is expressed numerically by the *co-efficient of linear expansion*, which is the increase in length of unit length of a substance when heated by 1° C. The co-efficient of cubicle (or volume) expansion is correspondingly defined, and it is approximately thrice the linear coefficient. In gases, the coefficient of volume expansion is approximately ·00366. The expansion of bodies when heated and their contraction on cooling finds many useful applications in industry and in the arts. Obviously, there is need for a substance that will not be so affected, and this has been found in an alloy of steel and nickel, containing 36 per cent. of nickel, known as *Invar*, which has the remarkably low coefficient of expansion of ·00000087, about thirteen times smaller than the coefficient of either of its constituents. It is now used for pendulum rods in clocks, and in various measuring instruments.

The third important effect of heat on matter is change of physical state. In general, the continuous addition of heat to a body causes it to pass from the solid to the liquid, and then to the gaseous (or vaporous) state. It is probable that if the means were available, all bodies could be made to assume any of these three states, provided that such assumption involves no chemical change. Changes of temp. also cause changes in the viscosity of fluids, electric resistance magnetic properties of matter, etc. Lastly, there must be noted the important fact that 'the velocity with which a chemical system strives to reach its state of equilibrium increases enormously with the temp.' (Nernst). Usually, the rate at which a chemical reaction takes place is doubled or trebled by a rise in temp. amounting to 10° C.

Calorimetry is concerned with the measurement of quantities of heat. The apparatus used is termed a *calorimeter*. In the metric system the unit quantity of heat is the *calorie*, and *great calorie* = 1,000 calories. Substances other than water, except liquid hydrogen, do not require so much heat for 1° rise—*e.g.*, ice, mercury, copper, air, steam. Mercury absorbs about .003, copper about .091 calories. These numbers are the specific heats (S.H.), and increase with increase of temp. of measurement. Carbon, boron, and silicon show this increase remarkably, so that at high temperatures they tend to conform to *Dulong and Petit's law*, specific heat—atomic weight = 6·4 nearly. A simple calorimeter may be made from a small sheet-copper vessel supported on corks and isolated from air-currents by being placed inside a larger vessel. Such a vessel has a definite *water-equivalent*, which may be found by placing a given mass of heated water (A) at temp. *t* inside it and stirring it, when a rapid fall takes place due to heat taken by the calorimeter and the stirrer. If *tc* is the original temp. of the calorimeter and *tf* the final temp. of the water and calorimeter, the water equivalent (W.E.) is WE = A $(t-tf\ tf-tc)$.

Once this is found, the specific heat of a body may be found where it is practicable to place such a body at a given temp. in a given mass of liquid in the calorimeter. If M be the mass of the substance heated to temp. *ts m* the mass of the water (any liquid of known specific heat would do), *to* the original temp. of the water, *we* the water equivalent of the calorimeter, and *tf* the final temp. of the mixture, then the specific heat (S.H.) of the substance i· given by SH.M $(ts-tf) = (m+we)\ (tf-\ )$, or if some other liquid of specific heat *sh* be used, SH.M $(ts-tf) = (sh.m+we)\ (tf-to)$.

For any body the specific heat — mass gives the water equivalent or *thermal capacity*. A substance with a low specific heat like mercury comes rapidly to the temp. of its environment and is suited for thermometers. Water, again, stores much heat, is heated and cooled slowly, and is adapted for heating purposes. This property of water also causes certain meteorological effects. For gases and vapours there exist a specific heat when the volume is kept constant, and a specific heat when the pressure is constant. The latter is greater than the former, owing to the work done in expansion against the pressure. The specific heats of steam in steam-engine theory and of air in gas- and oil-engine theory are of high importance.

Again, the latent heat of fusion of a solid, *e.g.* ice, is determined by finding the number of calories of heat required to convert 1 gram of ice at 0° C. into water at the same temp. Similarly the latent heat of steam (more correctly of vaporization of water) is determined.

HEAT, ANIMAL. See Animal Heat.

HEAT, CONDUCTION OF. See Conduction of Heat.

HEAT ENGINE. See Thermo-Dynamics.

HEAT MEASUREMENTS. See Calories.

HEAT REGULATORS. Devices, usually automatic or semi-automatic, for the control and regulation of the amount of heat generated by any of the usual means, such as coal or coke fire, oil or gas flame, electric resistance or arc, etc. The correct name for this class of apparatus is temperature regulators, since they control primarily the temperature of a certain place and only secondarily the heat manifested. Such contrivances are widely used to control the temperature of rooms, bake ovens, metallurgical furnaces, drying rooms and kilns, refrigerators, and for similar purposes. For more complete description, see Automatic Heat Regulators.

HEATH, HEATHER, LING, comprises a group of woody, low-growing shrubs, natural order *Ericaceoe. Erica tetralix* (cross-leaved heath) and *E. cinerea* (bell-heather) are insect-pollinated and *gamopetalous. Calluna vulgaris, Erica vulgaris, Ling* or *Heather,* has sepals resembling petals, very small petals, and is wind-pollinated. All are moor-plants, mostly evergreen, with narrow rolled leaves to prevent excessive evaporation.

HEATH, BENJAMIN (1704-66), Eng. writer on classical and religious subjects; *f.* of Benjamin H. 1771-85; headmaster of Harrow, who formed the noted *Bibliotheca Heathiana.*

HEATH, WILLIAM (1737-1814), Amer. general; failed in attack on Fort Independence, 1777; member of Board of War, 1779; Senator, 1791.

HEATHEN, Teutonic word of doubtful derivation, applied after acceptance of Christianity to those who clung to the Teutonic deities.

HEATHER. See HEATH.

HEATHFIELD, GEORGE AUGUSTUS ELLIOTT, BARON (1717-90), Brit. general who as gov. of Gibraltar defended it against French and Spaniards, 1779-82.

HEATING AND VENTILATION. These two subjects, while apparently distinct, are really so closely connected that it is customary to consider them together. They cover the proper conditioning of the air for health and comfort, as regards both temperature and purity. Deficient heating of dwellings or public buildings, or even conveyances, is comparatively rare in this country, but owing to the fact that the discomfort produced by foul air is not felt acutely in its early stages, improper ventilation is much more common. The various devices used for heating enclosed spaces have come to be considered such fundamental necessities, that it is difficult to realise how recent is their origin. The open fire was the only device known over the greater part of the world until less than two hundred years ago, and even chimneys were not used until the twelfth century. The first stove, invented by Benjamin Franklin, was constructed in 1744, and although steam was used for heating in England as far back as 1750, it was a hundred years later before it was applied for the same purpose in the United States. The Romans are believed to have made some use of a hot water heating system, and in 1816 a plant on modern principles was constructed in England, but it was not until 1870 that the system was introduced into the United States. Even the hot air furnace, which is often looked upon as of ancient origin, dates only from 1835, when the first furnace was constructed at Worcester, Massachusetts.

The temperature to which dwellings and other buildings are heated varies considerably in different countries. In the United States and Canada, 68-70° F. is considered necessary for comfort, but in England a temperature of 62° F. is preferred. Apparently, the lower outside temperature creates a demand for higher temperatures within. The heating of a building is brought about either by radiation, by connection or by a combination of the two. An open fire radiates heat and so heats the walls, the furniture and the body. The steam or hot water radiator heats the air by convection, and also warms surrounding objects by radiation. The hot air furnace relies entirely upon convection, the house being warmed by currents of hot air.

Modern Methods of Heating. The open fireplace still remains, the principal method of heating dwellings in Europe. In the United States and Canada, however, it is considered utterly inadequate, and has come to be looked upon merely as a pleasant and desirable adjunct to the central heating equipment. The *stove* is still widely used in country districts. It is much more efficient than the open fireplace, but is dusty, clumsy and is apt to produce foul air. The *hot air furnace* is very common in small houses. It is cheap to install, and owing to the fact that it continually draws fresh air into the house, it is healthy. In the older type of furnace, hot air from a central chamber travels to different parts of the house through large pipes; in the more modern *pipeless furnace,* the air of the entire house is warmed through a central register located on the ground floor. With the ordinary hot air furnace, trouble is frequently experienced in obtaining uniform heating. During a high wind the sheltered side of the house becomes overheated, while the side to windward receives no heat at all. In the pipeless type, this trouble is not experienced, heating being uniform throughout the house. The *steam furnace* consists of a boiler, located in the cellar, which generates steam under pressure and distributes it to radiators in different parts of the house. In large buildings the radiators are sometimes placed in the basement and air is warmed by being drawn over them and then conveyed to the rooms to be heated. The *vapor vacuum system* is a modification of steam heating. Instead of being under pressure, the steam in this system is under a slight vacuum. In this way the knocking and hissing of radiators is avoided. *Hot-water* systems are similar to steam systems, but instead of steam being generated in the boiler, a volume of hot water is heated and circulates, by convection, to all parts of the house. It begins to supply warmth, therefore, long before the boiling point is reached, which gives it an advantage over the steam system. More radiating surface is required, however, to give the same heating effects. The *gas-steam* radiator is a miniature boiler and radiator combined. At the base of the radiator is a reservoir of water, heated by gas nets. When steam is formed, the pressure automatically lowers the gas flame, so that the temperature is kept practically constant. The *boiler-radiator* is similar in principle, but coal is used in place of gas, and, if required, connecting pipes will carry the hot water to radiators in adjoining rooms. The system is of value for small houses or bungalows which have no cellars. *Electric heating* is too expensive for general use, but is employed for heating street cars, and electric trains, and also finds application in small domestic heaters for occasional use

Ventilation. The value of a sufficient supply of fresh air is becoming recognized to an increasing degree. The owners and designers of factories, offices and workshops are realizing that expenditure on ventilating systems is true economy, resulting in better work and less loss of time through sickness. The well-known effects of bad ventilation, including headache, lassitude and decreased resistance to disease, are due to the poisoning of the air by the carbon-dioxide exhaled from the lungs. It is estimated that an adult person requires 3,000 cubic feet of air per hour. In actual practice, it is found that 250-300 cubic feet of air space is sufficient. This is due to the constant supply of fresh air which must occur even in a room with closed doors and windows and no special ventilating device. The room, of the ordinary dwelling is, of course, far from being hermetically sealed. The leakage around doors, windows and by the chimney is enormous. There is, therefore a danger of over enthusiasm in the matter of ventilation, and it should be taken as a fundamental rule that when the current of fresh air is sufficient to be perceptible and to produce unequal cooling of the air, either the system is at fault or the ventilation is excessive. The opening of windows, top and bottom, is the simplest form of ventilation. More elaborate systems involve the use of fans or air pumps, and sometimes, in large public buildings, the air is carefully filtered and cleaned by passing through canvas or cotton, and then either cooled or heated according to conditions, and pumped through pipes to different parts of the building.

HEAVEN, the firmament, or empyrean; the atmospheric region, and the space in which the sun, stars, and planets are seen; the abode of God; the dwelling-place of the blest; a state of supreme happiness, etc.

HEBBURN (54° 58' N.; 1° 45' W.).

town, Durham, England; shipbuilding yards.

HEBE (classical myth.), d. of Zeus and Hera; cup-bearer to the gods; subsequently became wife of Hercules; gave place to Ganymede. She is usually represented as a beautiful maiden, bearing wine-cup and pitcher.

HEBER, REGINALD (1783-1826), Eng. hymnologist; bp. of Calcutta 1822; a man of great learning and piety; now chiefly remembered by his hymns, *From Greenland's Icy Mountains,* etc.

HÉBERT, JACQUES RENÉ (1757-94), Fr. revolutionary; led sect of *Hebertistes* against the *Girondins;* edit. *Le Pere Duchesne;* instigated September Massacres; guillotined.

HEBREW LANGUAGE (*see* Literature and Religion in other parts of this article). Hebrew langauge is hardly excelled by any in euphony, power and brevity. It is a Semitic language to whose composition elements from several Semitic languages contributed. Hebrew, in its full purity appears in the earlier books of the Bible, in the mediæval poetry of Judah Hallevi, Eben Ezra, etc., and in the modern poems of Byalik and others. Most ancient Hebrew is believed to have resembled the Phoenician, and to be best represented by the Maccabean coins. The alphabet consists of twenty-two letters, or consonants, written from right to left, and called *aleph, beth, gimmel, dalled,* etc. The vowels are expressed by marks above or below the letters, a system called the *Massoretic* punctuation. These accents and marks of punctuation are very numerous. There are no capital letters. The prose writings posterior to the Babylonish captivity are generally tinged with Aramaisms, especially the Mishnah, while the mixed idiom of the Talmud may be termed Chaldaic. Now there are three kinds of Hebrew alphabets in use: the most common in print being the square, or Assyrian (properly Babylonion), supposed to have been introduced by Ezra; the cursive, for writing; and the rabbinical or mediæval, chiefly used in commentaries and notes, (Rashi).

HEBREW LITERATURE, denotes works written in the Hebrew language. The earliest beginnings of Hebrew literature were probably poetical, stimulated by great national occurences and deeds of ancient heroes, suffused with religious feeling. These poems are in most cases considered older than the narratives in which they are incorporated. The early literature is almost entirely based on the Old Testament, which comprises the highest literary productions of the race for a period of about 800 yrs. There are exhibited in the course of it, not only the normal changes, which such a lapse of time always makes in a language, but deeper cutting differences, *e.g.* in Daniel, Chronicles, Nehemiah, and Ecclesiastes, there is a very large proportion of Persian words. Yet there is a distinctly unifying tendency noticeable over the whole, and this is especially true of the Psalms, which do not probably belong to any particular period, but are a collection of slow and gradual growth. The traditional view that Moses was the author of the Pentateuch in its present form, would make this the earliest part of Hebrew Literature (*c.* 800 B.C.), but modern inquiry has arrived at other conclusions. The Hebrew traditions respecting Israel's origins and early history were probably first cast into written form in the 10th or 9th cent. B.C., by the Judean prophets, who give the story of the Patriarchs, of Moses and the Exodus, of the journey through the wilderness and the conquest of Canaan. The later form of the language, with its admixture of Aramaic and Persian elements, became the common language of the people, and the older portions were in great part translated into this vernacular for use in the synagogues. This formed the *Targum*. Another process came into being, of amplification, not only of the Mosaic Law, and that given in the Pentateuch, but also of the Oral or traditional Law, which had been handed down among the elders; this compilation formed the *Halakhah*, and was collected in written form by Judah-ha-Nasi in the *Mishnah*. Side by side with this there grew up a mass of expository writings which received the name of *Midrash*, and the compiling of which went on till the 5th cent. A.D. As time wore on, these explanatory works themselves became the subject of critical commentary out of which grew the *Talmud* (first printed edition, Venice, 1520). With the *Talmud*, the period of old Hebrew literature, which had been mostly a collection of anonymous commentaries, may be considered to end. Thenceforward important works were produced by particular teachers, (the *Geonim*), who, no doubt, often represent opinions of a school. The greatest of all Jewish commentators, Rashi (Solomon Izhaki), who died at Troyes in 1105, seems to have confined himself wholly to Jewish learning. For the study of the Bible and Talmud he is indispensable. The greatest of all mediæval Jewish scholars was *Maimonides*, (Moses ben Maimōn) (*q.v.*). With the 13th cent. Hebrew literature may be said to have reached the height of its development. Later writers used over again, to a large extent, the material of their predecessors, and from the XV. cent., onwards, Hebrew literature ac-

quired a more personal and less religious character. The introduction of printing (first dated Hebrew printed book, Rashi, Reggio, 1475), gave occasion for a number of scholarly proof-readers, and compositors, some of whom were also authors, such as Elias Levita, a grammarian and lexicographer; Dei Rossi, who endeavoured to investigate Jewish history in a scientific spirit; and Joseph ben Joshua, a historian living in Italy; and in the 17th cent., Leon di Modena and David Conforte. In addition to these works which were mainly of an historical and scientific nature and possess no striking literary merit, the liturgical literature grew steadily in volume.

MODERN HEBREW LITERATURE. Henceforth, Hebrew thinkers and scholars contributed powerfully to modern culture, through the medium of various European languages, and its modernized vernacular, which is termed 'Yiddish.' Modern Hebrew literature became universal in scope. It took its rise in Italy (M. H. Luzzatto, 1707-47), whence it shifted to Germany. Here, at first, it showed a rationalistic and cosmopolitan tendency through the influence of Moses Mendelssohn (1729-86), who attempted to tear Hebrew literature out of its groove and infused it with a new and more practical spirit. In Russia and Lithuania, Hebrew literature assumed a humanitarian spirit, which found expression through Kalman Schulman (1819-99), and J. L. Gordon (1831-92). Since the day of P. Smolenskin (1842-85), Hebrew literature has been largely dominated by the idea of a national revival, which idea has found complete expression in the essays of Asher Ginzberg (Ahad Ha'am).

Poetry has made rapid strides. Perhaps the leading Jewish national poet, who writes in Hebrew is, Chaim Nachman Byalik (*q.v.*). Dr. Saul Tschernichowski (1875-); Dr. Jacob Cahan (1880-), an idealist; and Zalman Schneor (1886-), are other modern poets. Among the most notable story writers of modern times are, Isaiah Domoshevitzky (known as J. Bershadsky), (1870-1908), one of a group who wrote in a melancholy and morbid spirit; and S. J. Agnon, a master of Hebrew style; while the adaptation of the Hebrew language to the needs of modern life owes much to Eliezer Ben-Yehuda (1858-1923); I. D. Berkowitz; M. Smilianski; and R. Brainin. Probably the greatest Hebrew journalist is the well known Zionist leader, Nahum Sokolow, who writes also in many other languages. Before the World War, eastern Europe was the chief center of Hebrew literature; during the war it came to a complete standstill and then the center of activity shifted to Palestine, although there was a revival in Europe and a development in America.

HEBREW RELIGION. From the Semites sprang Judaism, . Christianity and Mohammedanism (or Islam). The Hebrews were Western Semites. The age to which Biblical writers evidently ascribe Abraham and the beginning of Hebrew religion is approximately that of the Middle Egyptian empire. A firm foundation is afforded by the Amarna age, which is approximately that of Moses, and by which time religion had reached an advanced stage. Materials for earlier Hebrew religion are not adequate, being uncertain and of late date. The evidence of the Tell-el-Amarna tablets shows that from 2000-1400 B.C., the Hebrew Religion was much under Babylonian influence, and until about 600 B.C., they were merely one of a congeries of Semitic tribes closely akin not only in blood and language, but also in religion. There were probably tribal deities, much as in Arabia before Muhammad. Before Moses, there was some progress in the direction of monotheism, though only monolatry was attained.

The cult of Yahweh, Israel's god, was, however, purer than that of other Semitic deities, though when the Hebrews entered Canaan they took over some religious ideas and practices from the peoples whose land they conquered. The conflict between Israel and the neighbouring peoples developed a new order—the prophets. At first they were only *seers*, those possessed of 'second sight'; then they became the witnesses and declarers of God's will to men. Prophecy was one of the most remarkable developments of Hebrew religious genius, and one which marked it off from other peoples, whose religion started similarly, but failed to rise to any great height. The impure rites against which the prophets inveighed were not a native Hebrew growth. Probably the greatest influences in the monotheistic belief in the one and only god *Yahweh*, were Samuel, King David, and Solomon, who built the first Temple (10th cent.) at Jerusalem, the house of worship and sacrifice to Yahweh. In the VIII. cent. B.C., Amos and Isaiah denounced a religion merely of rites and sacrifices, and preached gospel of righteousness— the religion as something largely ethical was only just beginning to emerge. But higher spiritual results could not be attained before the national kingdoms of Israel and Judah had been overthrown and the people had endured the weary discipline of the Exile.

The religious teaching of Jeremiah and his career present, it has been said,

as close a parallel to that of Christ as any in the Old Testament. Religion, too, became more individual, and the feeling of personal responsibility to God was realised; 'The Soul that sinneth it shall die.' The conception of the 'suffering servant,' *i.e.*, the Hebrew nation, was evolved. Meanwhile the turning-point in religious history was the reformation under King Josiah, 621 B.C., when the 'Law of the One Sanctuary' was established. Henceforward people had to come up to Jerusalem to sacrifice, and about this time the Book of *Deuteronomy* was produced. Though these tended in some ways to a too *legal* religion, it was probably only thus that monotheism could be safely secured. After the return from the first Exile the reconstruction of religion in the restored nation was largely due to Ezekiel, who with the functions of a prophet also combined those of a priest. The elaborate sacrificial system which was to last till the destruction of the Temple was organized, and during the 5th cent. B.C., the so-called Priestly Code, the latest embodiment of Hebrew ritual, was evolved.

From this period until the time of Christ, several important developments took place. Hebrew religion became intensely legal, and its idea of God, transcendant. The nation passed through the fiery trial of the conflict with debased Hellenism under the Seleucid kings, and was brought through by the energy and devotion of the Maccabees, (many portions of the Book of *Isaiah*, often thought to be earlier, are assigned to this date.) The Exile left its mark on Hebrew theology, particularly in angelology; eschatology became prominent, and various conceptions of a coming Messiah floated in men's minds. Each of these was destined to have enormous effect on early Christian theology; the genesis of the ideas is in some cases uncertain, but the ideas of angels and of a resurrection were due to Soroastrian influence, and the various woes through which Israel has passed gave rise to the longing for a better age. In the Book of *Enoch* the Messiah is pre-existent—an important development. Hebrew thought also came into contact with Gk. philosophy, so the 'Wisdom' literature was written, and the curious tendency to personification or semi-personification of divine attributes and spiritual forces, 'half persons and half powers,' resulted from this or other causes. Thus, Hebrew religion, at the time of Christ, while retaining its ancient sacrifices and traditions, was a complex thing, in which various elements were mingled.

HEBREWS. See JEWS.

HEBREWS, EPISTLE TO THE, one of the most important N. T. writings.

The epistle is anonymous, and although many conjectures have been made, the authorship has not been established. It is certain that the author was a Jew who had a knowledge of Jewish and Gr. literature and of contemporary philosophy. According to an old theory, the author was Luke; Apollos, suggested by Luther, may be nearer the truth; Tertullian refers to epistle and says it is the work of Barnabas; Harnack's view that it was written by Aquila and Priscilla is the most likely. There is no direct evidence to whom it was sent; the conjecture is that it was written to a Jewish Christian community, most probably in Rome, for the purpose of defending Christian belief and hope. There was an urgent danger that those to whom the author was writing were falling away from Christianity; he exhorts them to hold fast and cultivate patient endurance and faith, imitating the heroes of the faith and looking unto Jesus. Christianity is the perfect and therefore final religion, because it brings free access to God.

The date of the epistle is about A. D. 70.

HEBRIDES, NEW. See NEW HEBRIDES.

HEBRIDES, THE, OR WESTERN ISLES (57° 45′ N., 6° 50′ W.), a large group of islands extending over 200 miles along the western coast of Scotland. They are divided roughly into the Inner and Outer Hebrides, being divided by the Minch and Little Minch. The principal islands of the Outer Hebrides are Lewis-with-Harris, North Uist, Benbecula, South Uist, Barra, the Shiants, St. Kilda, and the Flannan Isles, or Seven Hunters, about 20 miles northwest of Gallon Head in Lewis. The Inner Hebrides include Skye; Small Isles, which are Canna, Sandy, Rum, Eigg, and Muck; Coll; Tyree; Lismore; Mull; Ulva; Staffa; Iona; Kerrera; the Slate Islands, which include Seil, Easdale, Luing, Shuna, and Torsay; Colonsay; Oronsay; Scarba; Jura; Islay; and Gigha. The Hebridean Islands are more than 500 in number, but only about one-fifth of these are inhabited. The population of the whole is estimated at about 70,000, while the most populous of the islands are Lewis-with-Harris, Skye, and Islay. The general surface is moorland and mountainous, with many lakes, and only a very small portion can be cultivated. The scenery is nearly treeless, stark and wild, having a grandeur that comes from the very bleakness of the wind-swept isles.

Potatoes and turnips are the only crops that succeed, being the only crops hardy enough to survive, although in some of the islands barley and oats can be grown. The most general occupations are sheep-raising and cattle-raising, which added to fishing, and tourist trade, sustain the inhabitants. Industries include distilling, slate-quarrying, and manufacture of tweeds, tartans and woolens. The larger islands are in communication with the mainland by means of steamers from Glasgow, Oban and Mallaig. Most of the people belong to the United Free Church, and the islands unite with the counties to which they belong in sending members to parliament. In 1846 a potato failure caused nearly universal destitution, which was relieved by paying the passage of about 5,000 inhabitants to Australia. Immigration to Canada is now prevalent.

HEBRON (31° 31′ N., 35° 8′ E.) town, Palestine; has enclosure built over rock cave, which is traditional tomb of Abraham and other patriarchs.

HECATÆUS OF ABDERA (IV. cent. B.C.), Gk. philosopher; a source of Diodorus Siculus.

HECATÆUS OF MILETUS (c. 550–470 B.C.), Gk. historian and geographer; wrote *Travels about the Earth* and a hist. work in which he endeavored to separate mythology from fact; latter contained in Müller's *Fragmenta Historicorum Graecorum*.

HECATE (classical myth.); d. of Perses and Astraea, sometimes identified with Persephone; was the goddess of witchcraft and enchantments, also of fertility, her power extending over heaven, earth, and hell. She was sometimes represented as triple-bodied, at other times as a tall woman, with sword and torch. Dogs and black lambs were sacrificed to her.

HECHT, BEN. (1893-   ); author; b. in New York City. Educated at Racine, Wisconsin High School. Started in 1910 with Chicago Journal, since 1914 with Daily News. From 1918-1919, correspondent in charge of Berlin Office, Daily News. Writes short stories and is author of *Erick Dorn*, 1921, and *A Jew in Love*, 1930, co-author of successful play *Front Page*.

HECKER, FRIEDRICH FRANZ KARL (1811-81), Ger. revolutionary; member of Baden Chamber of Deputies, 1842; with object of founding Ger. republic, raised military force against government, but was defeated, 1848, withdrew to Switzerland; subsequently served on Federal side in Amer. Civil War.

HECKER, ISAAC THOMAS (1819-88), Amer. R. C. evangelist; of Ger. parentage; became R. C., 1844.

HECKSCHER, AUGUST (1848-)
An Amer. capitalist. Born in Hamburg,
Germany. Educated at Weinheim, Germany and Neuchatel, Switzerland. Came
to the U.S. in 1868. Founded the Hechscher Foundation for Children in 1921,
one of the best and most extensive organizations of its kind, to promote the
welfare of children throughout the U.S.

HECTOR (classical myth.), Trojan
hero; *s.* of Priam and Hecuba, husband
of Andromache, *f.* of Astyanax; killed
Ajax in single combat, and slew Patroclus; was himself afterwards slain by
Achilles.

HECUBA (classical myth.), wife of
Priam, king of Troy; at the fall of the
city became the spoil of Odysseus; subject of a tragedy by Euripides.

HEDGE, feature of agriculture now
largely giving place to the fence. Hedging and ditching at the king's command
were among the duties of the Anglo-Saxon thegn.

HEDGEHOG OR URCHIN (*Erinaceus*), a short-snouted Insectivore characterised by spiny covering and short
tail; nocturnal; feeds on worms, lizards,
snakes, eggs, and even rats and mice;
hibernates in winter.

HEDIN, SIR SVEN ANDERS (1865),
Swed. Asiatic explorer; travelled extensively in the East, but first gained his
reputation by crossing the Pamirs in the
depth of winter, 1893; crossed the desert
of Takla-Makan, nearly losing his life,
1895; floated down the Tarim, 1899 and
solved the problem of Lobnor; he dug
out of the sand evidences of Chin.
civilization of the 3rd cent.; subsequently
explored in Persia and Tibet; discovered
a great range in the N. of the Himalayas
1907-8, which was named after him the
Hedin Mts. During early months of
World War acted as correspondent for
Swed. press with the Ger. armies.

HEDJAZ. See HEJAZ.

HEDONISM, ethical theory which
may be of two kinds—(1) that every
man makes pleasure his goal; (2) that
pleasure is the only ultimate good. The
ancient Cyrenaics and (differently)
Epicureans were hedonists.

HEEL, back division of foot; possibly
regarded as hinge in walking, hence to
h. over, to turn; anything that covers
the h.

HEEM, JAN DAVIDSZ VAN (fl.
XVII. cent.), Dutch painter; chief
painter of flowers, insects, glass, and
similar still-life studies, of his school.
His *s.* Cornelius fl. XVII. cent., was a
lesser master in the same kind.

HEEMSKERK, MARTIN JACOBSZ
(1498-1574), Dutch religious painter of
Ital. school; many of his principal works
were burned at Haarlem in 1572; those
left are remarkable for sculpturesque
figures.

HEFLIN, JAMES THOMAS (1869),
United States Senator. *B.* in Alabama
Educated at Southern University and A.
and M. College. In 1893 was admitted
to bar. Mayor of Lafayette for two
terms. From 1894-1896 register in
chancery. Was member from 1986-1900
of Alabama House of Representatives.
1896-1902 member of Democratic State
Executive Committee. Secretary of
State, 1902-1904. Elected to Congress
in 1904 for unexpired term. Re-elected
for term 1915-1921. Resigned Nov. 1,
1920 and elected next day as United
States Senator. Re-elected 1925-31.

**HEGEL, GEORG WILHELM
FRIEDRICH** (1770-1831), Ger. philosopher, founder of Absolute Idealism; *b*
Stuttgart; ed. Tübingen Univ.; went to
Jena, 1801, and app. prof., 1805. In
1808, app. rector at Nuremberg gymnasium; prof. at Heidelberg, 1816, and at
Berlin, 1818. Henceforth the leading
philosophic thinker in Germany. Chief
works, *Phenomenology of Spirit*, 1807;
Science of Logic, *Encyc. of Philos.
Sciences*, *Philosophy of Rights*, 1821; and
the posthumous lectures of *Aesthetics,
Phil. of Religion*, and of *History*.

HEGESIAS OF MAGNESIA (fl. III.
cent. B.C.), Gk. orator; much condemned in the Augustan Age; author of
life of Alexander the Great.

HEGESIPPUS (fl. IV. cent. B.C.),
Athenian statesman.

HEGEMON OF THASOS (V. cent.
B.C.), Gk. comic writer; praised in
Aristotle's *Poetics*.

HEGEMONY (Gk. *hegemonia*, leadership), primacy of one state in a federation, *e.g.* pre-eminence of Athens in the
Delian Confederacy.

HEGESIPPUS (fl. II. cent.), patristic
writer.

HEGESIPPUS, putative author of
De Bello Judaico, IV.-cent. rendering of
Josephus.

HEIDELBERG. City, Baden, Germany (49° 24' N., 8° 42' E.), beautifully
situated on Neckar, near Rhine, surrounded by hills covered with forests and
vineyards. St. Peter's Kirche (15th
cent.), Gothic Heilige-Geist-Kirche, Jesuiten-Kirche; town hall; fine castle on
hill, 330 ft. high, with great vat capable
of holding 50,000 gallons of wine; cele-

brated univ. 1385; beer, wine, and book industry; scientific instruments; residence of counts palatine (c. 1155-1721); great centre of Ger. Calvinism; sacked by French 1688. 1693; annexed to Baden, 1903.

HEIDELBERG (26° 30′ S., 28° 20′ E.), town, Transvaal, Brit. S. Africa.

HEIDELBERG CATECHISM, THE, Prot. catechism compiled by order of Elector Frederick III. in 1563, by Zacharias Ursinus and Caspar Olevianus; accepted by Heidelberg synod, but attacked by extreme Lutherans; on somewhat different lines from most catechisms, it possesses great spiritual beauty, and has been often translated.

HEIDELBERG COLLEGE, Ohio, a seat of learning for both sexes situated at Tiffin. It dates from 1890, when the college from which it sprang, founded in 1850 by the Reformed Church, was reorganized. The liberal arts are taught, as well as theology, commerce, art and music, and it has preparatory and summer schools. In 1932 there were 435 students and 37 teachers headed by C. E. Miller.

HEILBRONN (49° 8′ N., 9° 13′ E.), town, Württemberg, Germany; has XI.-cent. Ghotic church and other interesting buildings; industrial centre. Pop. 45,000.

HEILPRIN, ANGELO (1853-1907), an American scientist, born in Hungary, but came to U. S. in 1865. Educated in Europe. Professor of paleontology and geology at Academy of Natural Science, Philadelphia, 1880. Went on Peary Relief Expedition, 1892, and travelled extensively in America and Africa for scientific research. Was present (1902) in Martinique at the time of the eruption.

HEINE, HEINRICH (1797-1856), Ger. poet; b. Düsseldorf, of Jewish parents; studied law at Bonn, Göttingen, Berlin; adopted Christianity, 1825; pub. *Reisebilder*, 1826; *Buch der Lieder*, 1827, which made him the most popular poet of Germany; visited England, 1837; *Engliche Fragmente* appeared, 1831. H. settled in Paris, 1831; after unhappy love affairs with his cousins; to this period belong *Franzosische Zustande*, 1833; *Der Salon*, 1834; *Ludwig Borne*, 1840; *Die Romantische Schule*, 1836 (prose works); *Atta Troll*, 1847; *Romancero*, 1851 and *Letzte Gedichte und Gedanken*, 1835, 1855, rank among his finest poetical works; bedridden, 1848-56; d. Paris. H. ranks as perhaps the most cosmopolitan Ger. poet; belongs partly to Romantic movement, partly to 'Young Germany' revolt; great lyric and *spiritual* writer.

HEINTZELMAN, STUART (1876), Army Officer. B. in New York City. Graduated from United States Military Academy, 1899 and 1905, honor graduate of Infantry and Calvary School. In 1899 second lieutenant of cavalry, 1st lietenant, 1901, Captain, 1905, Major, 1917, Lieutenant Colonel, 1917; Colonel Regular Army, 1920. In Philippines 1900-1902. From 1907-1909 with China Relief Expedition, 1909-1912, 1914-1916 instructor in Army Service Schools. In France, 1917-20, appointed asst. chief of staff, director military intelligence. Awarded Distinguished Service Medal and decorated by France and Italy. Command't. Ft. Leavenworth school, 1929.

HEIR, originally inheritor in fee (*h. at law*),afterwards inheritor, next of kin, or devisee. *H. apparent* is person who will inherit if he lives; *h. general* is h. at law; h. *presumptive*, person who will inherit if conditions remain the same; *right h.* is next of kin.

HEJAZ, kingdom of Arabia, on the shores of Red Sea (25° N., 38° E.), bounded N. by Syria, E. by Nefud desert and Nejd, S. by Tehama. Contains Tehama range of mts., and is almost all stony desert; N. portion desolate and thinly populated; in S.more cultivation, dates, wheat, and barley being chief products. Chiefly interesting on account of sacred cities of Mecca and Medina, which it contains along with seaports Jiddah and Yambu; railway connecting cities of Hejaz with Damascus. Name changed to Arabian Saudian Kingdom, 1932. After the participation of Turkey in the Great War, 1915, this region was the scene of severe and prolonged fighting. For recent history, see ARABIA, and HUSSEIN IBN ALI. Area, 96,500 sq. m.

HEKLA. See VOLCANOES.

HEL, HELA, the goddess of death in Scandinavian mythology; *d.* of Loki and Angurboda; to her went all who died by disease; dwelt in Niflheim, place of eternal snow and darkness.

HELDENBUCH, DAS, Ger. poetic cycles of XIII. cent.; chief figures are Dietrich of Bern, Wolfdietrich, Hugdietrich, and Ortnit. The first printed edition appeared without date, the second, 1491; many modern edit's.

HELDER, THE (52° 57′ N., 4° 45′ E.), port. Holland; strongly fortified.

HELEN OF TROY (classical myth.), *d.* of Zeus and Leda, wife of Tyndareus, king of Sparta; famed for her beauty; became the wife of Menelaus, but eloped with Paris, *s.* of Priam, king of Troy, which act led to the Trojan War.

HELENA, a city of Arkansas in Phillips co., of which it is the county seat. It is on the Missouri and Northern Arkansas, the Iron Mountain and Southern, and other railroads, and on the Mississippi River, 90 miles S.W. of Memphis, Tenn. It is connected by steamship lines with all the important river ports and is a shipping point for lumber and cottonseed oil. Its industries include the manufacture of cottonseed oil, boxes, cotton goods, machinery, canned goods, and lumber. It has a public library, Jefferson High School, Sacred Heart Academy, and a national bank.

HELENA, a city of Montana, the capital city of the state and county seat of Lewis and Clark counties. It is on the Missouri Pacific and Great Northern railways. It is the financial center of the state, and is the commercial and business center of Montana, Northern Idaho, and Eastern Washington. It has abundant water power from the Missouri River. Branches of the Federal Reserve and of the War Finance Corporation are located here. It is surrounded by splendid scenery and by rich agricultural and stock raising country. It is noted for its famous mines. It has a splendid educational system which includes Protestant and Catholic universities. There are three hydro-electric plants on Missouri River close to Helena. The largest lead and zinc smelter in the world is at East Helena. The city has fine public buildings, and good street railway service.

HELENA, ST. (*c.* 247-328), wife of Rom. emperor Constantius I., and *m.* of Constantine the Great; accepted Christianity and made pilgrimage to Jerusalem, where she is said to have discovered the Cross and built churches of the Holy Sepulchre and Nativity.

HELENA, ST. See St. Helena.

HELENUS, *s.* of Priam; mentioned in the *Iliad,* and prominent character in later Gk. legend.

HEINRICH, KARL (1873); Ger. financier; was a prof. of political economy in Berlin Univ., entered Foreign Office, 1901 as an expert in colonial affairs and economics; he took a prominent part in connection with Anatolian Ry. concession, and became director of Deutsche Bank, 1908. Shortly after outbreak of World War he was made secretary to Imperial Treasury, in which capacity he created vast amounts of paper money, and skilfully contrived to bolster up successive war loans by transferences of 'paper.' His finance was based on expectations of huge indemnities from vanquished, and though his dexterous handling of facts and figures sustained for a time public confidence in Germany in her 'inexhaustible resources,' he could not prevent steady fall of mark on foreign exchanges. In 1916 he became secretary of state for the interior, and deputy imperial chancellor, but resigned towards end of 1917. He was Germany's chosen negotiator of economic terms for her enemies, and, as ambassador to Russia 1918, was real author of supplementary treaties imposed on Bolshevists; pub. a book on origin of the war, 1919.

HELICON (38° 17′ N., 22° 53′ E.), mountain range, Boeotia, Greece; traditional home of Muses.

HELICOPTER. This name is applied to a type of flying machine, heavier than air, capable of raising itself vertically in the air, by means of propellers turning on vertical axes.

The scientists of the eighteenth and nineteenth centuries were much interested in this type of machine, and made many models in an attempt to demonstrate the practicability of their ideas. Such men as Sir George Cayley, J. Degen, Sarti Stringfellow and many others gave much attention to this branch of aeronautics, believing that it was the only solution to the problem of aerial navigation.

The name Hélicoptére was first associated with the model of Penaud, 1872, which depended for its lifting power on 'vertical screws'. Many elaborate models were built after this, utilizing springs, twisted elastic bands, and even steam engines as their source of power. All were unsuccessful. In 1923 during experiments in France a machine was kept in the air for three minutes. A year later a direct lift machine rose 1772 ft. in a direct line. In 1930 D'Ascanio built a successful helicopter in Italy. During the same year experiments were being made in the U. S. with the Curtiss-Bleecker helicopter. These machines are designed on the basis of one or more air screws turning on a vertical axis. See Aeronautics.

HELIGOLAND, OR HELGOLAND isl., Germany, North Sea (54° 11′ N., 7° 52′ E.), 28 m. from mainland; triangular in shape, rising to 200 ft.; consists of Unterland and Oberland, connected by a wooden staircase; Dünen I. (lower isl.), separated from Rock I. by violent storm, 1720, contains land-locked harbor capable of sheltering large ships; also formerly famous seaside resort; once possessed by Schleswig-Holstein; taken by

Danes, 1714; by British, 1807; ceded to Germany, 1890. Area, ¼ sq. mi.; Heligoland was powerfully fortified by Germany at cost of many million dollars. During World War formed a forward base for Ger. fleet; by Peace Treaty (June 28, 1919) fortifications, harbors, and military establishments were destroyed, and defenses prohibited for the future.

HELIGOLAND BIGHT, BATTLE OF (Aug. 28, 1914), earliest naval action of World War, undertaken to assert British command of the North Sea up to the enemy's gates; Germans had wind of operation, and planned counter measures. *Arethusa* and *Fearless*, leaders of 1st and 3rd flotillas respectively, engaged several enemy light cruisers; Brit. 'Cat Squadron', under Admiral Beatty, came to rescue, and destroyed or finished off three German light cruisers, *Mainz*, *Koln*, and *Ariadne*; Germans also lost a destroyer. Brit. loss did not exceed 35 killed and 40 wounded; Germans lost well over 1,000. No Brit. vessel sunk. Battle had great deterrent effect on enemy.

HELIODORUS (fl. *c.* III. cent. A.D.), author of the *Aethiopica*, a Gk. story which had great influence on Renaissance writers.

HELIOGABALUS, ELAGABALUS (*c.* 205-22), Rom. emperor; became priest to sun-god Elagabal; emperor, 218; assassinated during army mutiny, 222.

HELIOGRAPH, signalling instrument that reflects sun's rays by mirrors; range of 190 miles has been reached.

HELIOMETER is an instrument used for measuring the sun's diameter and for micrometrical work on the stars. It is based on the fact that measures can be made by double images. The heliometer consists of an *achromatic* telescope with its object glass divided (by a plane passing through the optic axis of the telescope) into two segments, one fixed in the telescope tube, the other mounted so that it can be moved in a plane perpendicular to the telescope's optic axis. The movement is obtained by the revolution of a screw connected with an apparatus for counting the revolutions. In very recent heliometers this reading is checked independently by a *micrometer* which measures directly the separation of the segments. From two measurements the actual diameter can be calculated. Recent modifications of the apparatus aim at increasing facility of movement and avoiding the effects of temp. changes.

HELIOPOLIS (the On of the Bible), city of Lower Egypt, near Cairo, slightly N. of the Nile Delta; was one of the principal centers of sun-worship and of Egyptian learning. H. was also the name of Baalbek.

HELIOSCOPE, a kind of telescope, particularly adapted by means of blackened or smoked glasses which only partially reflect the light, for viewing the sun.

HELIOSTAT, instrument for reflecting a beam of sunlight in a fixed direction. A mirror is mounted on a spindle driven by clockwork whose rate can be adjusted. The clockwork case is so arranged as to allow the initial adjustment to be made.

HELIOTHERAPY, treatment by sunlight, developed early in 20th cent. by Bernard and Rollier; exposure to rays should be gradual, a small portion of the skin being exposed at a time until the treatment can be tolerated on the whole body for as long as three to four hours daily. Since cold air has a stimulating effect, heliotherapy is more beneficial in a temperate than tropical climate. The rays of greatest therapeutic value are the ultra-violet (*q.v.*) or actinic rays, the shortest in the solar spectrum. These may be applied artificially as well as naturally. The sun treatments are stimulating to the mind as well as to the body, a factor which often is important in the disease that is treated. In addition, the rays increase the power of the blood to destroy bacteria, supply thermal energy, destroy harmful toxins, and raise the calcium, phosphorus and iron content of the blood. Heliotherapy is used for treatment of surgical tuberculosis, rickets, nervous asthma, psoriasis, and other skin diseases, in convalescence from weakening fevers, and in stimulation of the endocrine glands.

HELIOTROPE, a plant with a sweet scent, belonging to a genus of 200 species of the natural order *Boraginaceoe*. They are small hairy shrubs. Heliotrope (*Cherry-Pie*) has terminal *spikes* of lilac flowers.

HELIOTROPISM, turning of a plant towards light; stems curve towards sun (*positive h.*), roots and stems of certain climbers turn away from sun (*negative h.*).

HELIUM. A gaseous element with an atomic weight of 3.99, being the lightest of the known elements with the exception of Hydrogen, which has the atomic weight 1.00. It was discovered in the sun, by means of the spectroscope, long before its existence on the earth was demonstrated. The discovery was made by Jannsen and Lockyer in 1868 and it was later found, by Ramsay, in the gases evolved from the mineral cleveite. It also occurs in the air to the extent of about one part, by volume, to 250,000 parts of air. It is believed to be the final product in the disintegration of radium, the so-called alpha rays having been identified by Ramsay as particles of helium. Because of its lightness and its non-inflammability and general chemical inertness, the suggestion was made by English chemists during the European war, that it should be used in place of hydrogen for filling airships and balloons. Up to that time, however, it had been prepared only on a laboratory scale, and there was no known source of supply from which it could be obtained in large quantities. The co-operation of the U. S. Bureau of Mines was sought, and under their direction the Jeffries-Norton and Linde processes for the extraction of helium from natural gas were developed. The principal constituents of natural gas are nitrogen, methane and helium, and the separation of the gases is brought about by freezing to extremely low temperatures. At 318° F. below zero, nitrogen and methane become liquified, while helium remains in a gaseous condition. The separation then becomes an easy matter, the helium being drawn off from the liquid gases. The process was developed too late to be of value during the war, although when the Armistice was signed quantities of the gas were awaiting shipment to France. Since the war, however, considerable experimental work has been carried out with the gas, and the results are considered satisfactory. Although helium is denser than hydrogen, its greater safety more than counterbalances the loss in buoyancy.

HELL, the abode of the dead; also the place of punishment of the wicked, numerous times mentioned in the New Testament. Alternative names are the Gk. *Hades;* Heb. *Gehenna;* Scand. *Hela.*

HELLANICUS OF LESBOS (V. cent. B.C.); Gk. historian; wrote history of Attica, 683-404; a chronological work on the Carnean games; also histories of Troy and Persia.

HELLEBORE is a genus of herbs belonging to natural order *Ranunculaceoe.* —Hellebore (*Christmas Rose*) has five or more petaloid spears. The 'petals' are slipper-shaped *nectaries.* The stigma ripens first (*protogynous*) and self-pollination is impossible. The fruit is an aggregation of three *follicles.*

HELLENISM, a type of culture peculiar to the ancient Greeks. The Gk. character as reflected in Hellenic religion, poetry, art, and philosophy makes for clearness, measure, and balance, and eschews the vague, the undefined, the excessive. The Gk. ideal is therefore the antithesis of the Gothic. In architecture the Gothic mind expressed itself in soaring arches and mysterious curves. The Gothic mythology deals with vast, titanic, cloud-like beings, neither human in character nor restricted in power. The Gk. mind is well illustrated by the motto of the ancient Delphic temple, 'Nothing in excess'. In Gk. mythology the outstanding characteristic is the extraordinary definiteness of the gods and goddesses. Each god has his peculiar attributes, his fixed bodily shape, and his allotted functions. Mystery has no place in the Gk. Pantheon. Similarly in philosophy the theory that virtue lies in preserving the 'mean' is characteristically Gk. Thus bravery is regarded as a mean between rashness on the one hand and cowardice on the other.

HELLER, EDMUND (1875-   ), naturalist, *b.* in Illinois; was member of many important expeditions. Wrote papers on fish, reptiles and birds. Director Milwaukee Zoo, 1928.

HELLESPONT, ancient classical name of the Dardanelles, the strait connecting the Sea of Marmora and Sea of Ægean Sea; so called from Hellé, *d.* of Athamas and Nephele, who, fleeing from the cruelty of her stepmother, Ino, fell from the air into the strait and was drowned.

HELMET, headpiece in armor. Early h's were simply caps made of leather or metal, with attachments for protection of face and neck. In mediaeval times some h's had a fixed nasal, while others had movable covers for protecting both upper and lower face, the whole head being covered during action. In XIV. cent. barred visors came into use. The *armet* first appears about 1443, and was a closed h., used only by horsemen. The XVI.-cent. *morion* had a projecting brim. Modern h's worn by policemen and firemen are made of metal, felt, leather, or cork. The use of helmets in the shape of steel hat was revived in the armies of all the principal countries in the World War.

HELMHOLTZ, HERMANN LUDWIG FERDINAND VON (1821-94); Ger. philosopher and physicist; prof. of Physiology in Heidelberg, and later of Physics in Berlin. He discovered nerve-cells in *ganglia,* invented the opthalmoscope, and measured the velocity of nervous impulse. It was by his inspiration Hertz commenced his work, which resulted in discovery of 'Hertzian' waves of wireless telegraphy. H. also perfected notion of electron.

HELMSTEDT, HELMSTADT (52° 13' N., 11° E.), town, Brunswick;

Germany; ruined Benedictine abbey, fine churches; seat of univ. till 1809.

HELMUND (31° N., 61° 50' .E), river, Afghanistan; has its source in Hindu Kush Mountains and flows to Lake of Hamun or Seistan.

HÉLOISE. See ABELARD.

HELOTS, the ancient serf population of Greece and the property of the Spartan State. They are supposed by some authorities to have been the original inhabitants of Laconia. They were employed in agricultural pursuits by the Spartans, and in war were required to perform military service. A revolt of the h's, in 464 B.C., was with difficulty suppressed.

HELPER, HINTON ROWAN (1829-1909), an American writer, b. in North Carolina. For a time he lived in California. He was brought into great prominence by his *The Impending Crisis of the South*, published in 1857, an antislavery work. He published other works which had less success. From 1861 to 1867 he was United Stages consul at Buenos Aires.

HELPS, SIR ARTHUR (1813-75), Eng. essayist and historian; Clerk to Privy Council 1860-75; author of *Friends in Council, Companions of my Solitude, Conquerors of the New World*, etc.

HELSINGBORG (56° 2' N., 12° 42' E.), port, Sweden; fine harbor, docks; manufacturing centre.

HELSINGFORS, cap. of Finland, on Gulf of Finland (60° 14' N., 24° 57' E.); splendid harbor, strongly guarded by fortress of Sveaborg; exports timber, corn, and butter; manufacturers sugar, beer, linen, tobacco, etc.; has a univ. and cathedral, and is seat of government of republic of Finland. During spring of 1918 a good deal of street fighting took place in town between Red and White Guards, the latter triumphing through Ger. aid. See FINLAND.

HELVETIC CONFESSIONS, ecclesiastical constitutions of Reformed Churches; drawn up in Switzerland; that of 1536 was prepared under influence of Bullinger and Bucer but was largely superseded by the second H.C., written by Bullinger in 1562.

HELVETIC REPUBLIC was established in Switzerland, 1798, after conquest by French.

HELVETII, inhabitants of S. Gaul (modern Switzerland). Caesar praises their bravery. Their invasions of Italy were suppressed by Caesar's victory at *Bibracte* and the establishment of Rom. colonies. They were separated from Gaul by Tiberius. The H. gave name Helvetia to Switzerland.

HELVETIUS, CLAUDE ADRIEN (1715-71), Fr. philosopher; became farmer-general of taxes, 1738, gaining great wealth; retiring to country estate, wrote *De l'esprit*, which evoked storm of abuse. Many have denied its originality. Bentham was influenced by him. H.'s view of morals was utilitarian.

HELY-HUTCHINSON, JOHN (1724-94), Irish lawyer and politician; entered Irish Parliament, 1759; provost of Trinity Coll., Dublin, 1774; Sec. of State, 1777; advocated removal of Catholic disabilities, and free trade.

HELYOT, PIERRE (1660-1716), Fr. Franciscan historian; devoted many years to writing standard celebrated *Histoire des Ordes monastiques, religieux, et militaires.*

HEMANS, FELICIA DOROTHEA (1793-1835), Eng. poet; b. Liverpool; m. Captain H. 1812; but separated 1818. Her poetry is marked by excess of sentiment.

HEMEROBAPTISTS, Jewish sect (possibly Essene), whose members observed daily ablution.

HEMICYCLE, semicircular plan characteristic of Rom. architecture and re-adopted at the Renaissance.

HEMIPTERA, OR BUGS, are *Insecta* invariably characterised by modification of mouth organs to form a suctorial, jointed proboscis, generally flexed so as to occupy a position on under side of body. The wings are four in number as a rule, and are external growths developed in successive moults from the hinder dorsal portions of the middle and posterior body-segments. They differ considerably in character in the two great sub-orders, *Heteroptera* and *Homoptera*, the pairs varying in texture and folding flat on the back in the former, and in the latter covering the abdomen. The two sub-orders are further distinguished by the extent of the flexure of the head, this being much less in the *Heter.* than in the *Homo.* The young resemble the adult in general features, the transition from the juvenile to the adult being gradual. Amongst the most interesting forms, from an economic standpoint, are the *Aphides* or *Plant Lice*, which often swarm in incredible numbers over the host plant, and the scale insects or *Mealy-bugs*, which form small hard scales on fruit, twigs, etc. The *Anopleura* (Lice) are degenerate wingless members of this order.

HEMISPHERE, a half sphere. It is applied especially to one of the halves in which the earth may be supposed to be divided.

HEMLOCK, a herbaceous plant, *Conium Maculatum*, natural order *Umbelliferoe*, with white *inflorescence* of compound umbels and purple-spotted fluted *glaucous* stem. The leaves and fruit have a disagreeable odor and contain *alkaloid* poisons.

HEMORRHAGE, the escape of blood from a blood vessel; in bleeding from an *artery*, bright red blood spurts in jets, keeping time with the beating of the heart; in bleeding from a *vein*, dark blood flows steadily; and in *capillary* bleeding, the blood oozes from a raw-looking wound surface. Bleeding into the tissues is termed *extravasation*; bleeding from the nose, *epistaxis*; vomiting of blood, *hoematemesis*; coughing up of the blood from the air-passage, *hoemoptysis*; the presence of blood in the urine, *hoematuria*; in the faeces, *meloena*. To arrest bleeding, pressure is applied to the bleeding point, or a tourniquet is tied round the limb between the bleeding point and the heart; the application of cold, especially for an oozing wound, hot water (130° F. and over), perchloride of iron, or suprarenal extract, are also found to be valuable remedies.

HEMORRHOIDS. See PILES or HAEMORRHOIDS.

HEMP is an annual herb, *Cannabis sativa*, natural order *Cannabineoe*. Originally an inhabitant of Persia it is now grown in all parts of Europe, because its bast fibres are used in the rope industry. The plant is *dioecious* with opposite lower leaves and deeply *partite* strongly *dentate*, rough alternate upper leaves, with two lateral *stipules*. The male *inflorescence* is a *raceme* and the female flowers occur in the axils of the leaves. Petals are absent. The fruit is one-seeded. Intoxicating preparations for drinking and smoking, *e.g.* Arab. *Hashish*, Indian *Bhang*, are made from the female flowers, resin, and leaves.

HEMPEL, FRIEDA (1885), Operatic Soprano. *B.* in Germany, educated at Sterns Conservatory, Berlin, under Mme. Nicklass Kempner. In 1905 at Royal Opera House, Berlin, made professional debut in 'Merry Wives of Windsor'. From 1905-1907 appeared in Schwerin Opera House. Toured Europe and was the principal guest soprano at Covent Garden, London, Warsaw, Brussels, San Sebastian, Grand Opera, Paris, and principal opera houses throughout Europe. decorated by King of Belgium, Emperor of Germany; one

of five Imperial German Court Singers. From 1907-1912 at Royal Opera, Berlin, was principal coloratura soprano. With Metropolitan Opera Co. since 1912. Married Wm. B. Kahn, 1918, div. 1926.

HEMPSTEAD, a village of Nassau co., New York, on the southern coast of Long Island, 20 miles E. of New York City. It forms a part of the town of Hempstead, which includes the villages of East Rockaway, Freeport, Hempstead, Lawrence, Rockville Center, and a part of Floral Park. All these are residential places. Pop. 1930, 12,650.'

HENBANE, a flowering beinnial plant, *Hyoscyamus niger*, natural order *Solanaceoe*. It contains in its leaves and flowers two *alkaloid* poisons, *Hyoscyamine* and *Hyoscine*, and a poisonous oil.

HENDERSON, a city of Kentucky, in Anderson co., of which it is the county seat. It is on the Louisville and Nashville, Illinois Central and other railroads, and on the Ohio River. It is the center of an extensive timber, coal and salt region. It is connected by steamship lines with Louisville, Memphis and other points on the river and from it are shipped large quantities of tobacco and grain. Its industries include tobacco factories, car works, lumber mills, and carriage and wagon factories. It has also plants for the making of flour products, wool products, and churns. Pop. 1930, 11,668.

HENDERSON, ALEXANDER (1583-1646), Scot. Presbyterian divine; prof. at St. Andrews; one of commissioners to interview Charles I., who liked him; tried to mediate between Charles and Parliament, 1642; Moderator of General Assembly; has been called 'the second founder of the Reformed Church in Scotland.'

HENDERSON, RT. HON. ARTHUR (1863), Brit. Labor leader; served apprenticeship as moulder in Newcastle; held various positions in Trade Union movement; took part in munice. affairs; mayor of Darlington, 1903; M.P. for Barnard Castle, 1903-18); secretary of Labor party, 1908-10 and 1914-17; chief whip of Labor party, 1914; and became chairman at outbreak of war; joined first Coalition government] as president of Board of Education, 1915-16; paymaster-general and Labor adviser to government, 1916; joined second Coalition as member of war cabinet without portfolio; went on government mission to Russia (May, 1917), as outcome of which resigned Aug. of same year; defeated at general election, 1918; but elected for Widnes (Sept., 1919). In the election of 1922 he was elected by the Labor party, and was one of the prominent party leaders in Parliament in 1923; Home Secretary, 1924; Secretary of State, Foreign Affairs, 1929. In 1934 he was awarded the Nobel Peace Prize for his service as President of the Disarmament Conference, which opened in 1932.

HENDERSON, JOHN (1747-85), Famous Shakespearean actor; rival of Garrick.

HENDERSON, WILLIAM JAMES (1855-   ), American music critic and author, b. at Newark, N.J.; ed. at Princeton; associate editor, *Standard Dictionary*; became music critic on the New York *Sun* in 1902; wrote *Richard Wagner*; *The Art of Singing.*

HENDIADYS (Lat. from Gk. *hen dia duoin*, one by two), term in rhetoric for connecting two equivalent nouns by 'and'; common Virgilian usage, *e.g.* '*Vinclis et carcere frenat*,' or *Italiam Lavinaque litora.*'

HENDON (51° 36' N., 0° 14' W.), town, Middlesex, England; chief English flying ground.

HENDRICK, BURTON JESSE, (1871-   ), Writer. *B.* in New Haven, Conn. At Yale, 1895, Bachelor of Arts and 1897 Master of Arts. 1896-1898, editor of the New Haven Morning News; 1899-1905, on staff of New York Evening Post; 1905-1913 staff writer for McClure's Magazine; associate editor of World's Work since 1913. Author of *The Age of Big Business*, (in Yale Chronicles of America); *Life and Letters of Walter Hines Page.* A book *The Victory at Sea* of which he was co-author with Admiral William S. Sims won the Pulitzer prize of $2,000.00 for the best book published on United States History in 1920 and in 1928 he won the Pulitzer Prize in biography for *The Training of an American.*

HENDRICKS, THOMAS ANDREWS (1819-1885), former Vice-President; *b.* near Zanesville, O.; *d.* Indianapolis. He studied law and was admitted to the Indiana bar in 1843 after graduating at South Hanover College, Indiana. He became a member of the state legislature, served in the U. S. House of Representatives, 1852-3, and from 1863 was in the Senate. He was twice defeated as a Democratic candidate for governor of Indiana, but his third candidature, 1872 was successful. As running mate with Tilden on the Democratic ticket in the presidential election of 1876, he was elected Vice-President by popular vote, but the Electoral Commission (*q.v.*) awarded the election to the Republicans. In 1884 he was again nominated as Vice-President, this time on the successful Cleveland ticket, and served as such for a brief period till his death.

HENEY, FRANCIS JOSEPH (1859-   ), lawyer; *b.* in New York. In 1883 admitted to the bar; was one of the lawyers in litigation over Mexican land grants in Arizona. 1893-1894 attorney general of Arizona; discoverer of conspiracy to protect guilty politicians. Judge, since 1931, Superior Court of Calif.

HENGELO, HENGELOO (52° 16' N., 6° 47' E.), town, Holland.

HENGIST and **HORSA,** two bro. Jutes, the first of the Teutonic invaders, called in to aid the Brit. king, Vortigern *c.* 450, against the Picts. Horsa was subsequently killed in battle, but Hengist made himself king of Kent, 458.

HENGSTENBERG, ERNST WILHELM (1802-69), Lutheran ecclesiastic; studied at Bonn, specially devoting himself to Old Testament and Oriental languages; prof. at Berlin, 1826; vigorously defended conservative positions in Biblical criticism.

HENLEY, JOHN (1692-1758), Anglican clergyman, from 1729, at Lincoln's Inn Fields; called 'Orator Henley'; attracted attention by absurd innovations as preacher.

HENLEY, WILLIAM ERNEST (1849-1903), Eng. poet; *b.* Gloucester; edit. successively *The Magazine of Art*, *National Observer*, and *New Review*; collaborated with R. L. Stevenson in several plays; part author of a Slang dictionary and a *Life* and edition of Burns; a trenchant and fearless critic; wrote some exquisite lyrics.

HENLEY-ON-THAMES, market tn. and munic. bor., Oxfordshire, Eng. (51° 32' N., 0° 54' W.); favorite summer resort, noted for its beautiful surroundings; is famous among amateur oarsmen for annual regatta, begun in 1839.

HENNA, the powdered leaves of *Lawsonia inermis.* These contain a red stain used, in Persia and India, to dye the finger nails, etc.

HENNEPIN CANAL. See CANAL.

HENNEPIN, LOUIS (1640-1710), a French missionary and explorer. He was born in Belgium. In 1873 he visited Canada and five years later joined La Salle on his famous expedition down the Mississippi. He explored the Illinois to its mouth and the upper Mississippi. In

1680 he was captured by Sioux Indians and was adopted into their tribe. During his captivity he visited the Falls of St. Anthony and having escaped returned to Fort Frontenac in 1681. He returned to France in 1683 and published his famous book *Description of Louisiana.* The second book, *New Discoveries in Three Great Countries,* published in 1697, claimed to have shown that he descended the Mississippi to its mouth. This claim has never been proved false. The third book, *A New Voyage,* was published in 1698.

HENNEQUIN, PHILIPPE AUGUSTE (1763-1833), Fr. hist. painter and engraver patronised by Napoleon. His grandson, Alfred Néocles 1842-87, was a prominent comic playwright.

HENRI, ROBERT (1865-1929), artist; *b.* in Cincinnati; educated in Schools in New York and elsewhere; student in Julien Academy, Ecole des Beaux Arts, Paris and Pennsylvania Academy of Fine Arts; studied in Spain and other countries without instruction. His picture 'La Neige' purchased in 1899 by the French Government for the Luxembourg Gallery, represented in collections of Art Institute, Chicago, New Orleans Art Association, Dallas Art Association and many others. Awarded gold medal at Philadelphia Art Club in 1909. Portrait prize at Wilmington Society of Fine Arts in 1920. Member of National Institute Arts and Letters and others.

HENRIETTA MARIA (1690-66), consort of Charles I. of Great Britain; *d.* of Henry IV. of France; raised money for king during Civil War; encouraged impeachment of five members; fled to France, 1644; twice visited England after Restoration.

HENRY I., BEAUCLERC (1068-1135), king of England; youngest *s.* of William the Conqueror; succ., 1100. Elder bro., Robert, claimed crown, but was defeated and imprisoned, his duchy of Normandy being added to H.'s dominions. Various conspiracies formed in Normandy in favour of Robert's *s.*, William, were supported by Fr. king, whom H. defeated at *Bremule,* 1119. H.'s *s.* William was drowned in *White Ship,* 1120. Exchequer was instituted in this reign.

HENRY II. (1133-89), king of England; *s.* of Matilda and Geoffrey Plantagenet; grandson of Henty I.; succ. 1154; revoked Stephen's grants of crown lands, and revived King's Court and Exchequer; at first supported by his minister, Becket, whom he cr. abp.; quarrelled with Church, issued Constitutions of Clarendon, 1164, which Becket opposed; after latter's murder, 1170, H. had to

make various concessions to Church; conquered Ireland, 1172; crushed barons' rebellion, 1173, and reduced their power by legal reforms; sons intrigued against H. towards end of reign.

HENRY III. (1207-72), king of England; succ. his *f.*, King John, 1216; during minority French were expelled from England; assumed government, 1227; unsuccessfully invaded Poitou, 1230; defeated at *Taillebourg,* 1242; aimed at arbitrary power; left many important offices vacant; aroused hostility of barons, who compelled him to assent to Provisions of Oxford, 1258, subsequent annulment of which resulted in outbreak of Barons' War; H. defeated at *Lewes,* 1264; henceforth a cipher.

HENRY IV. (1367-1413), king of England; *s.* of John of Gaunt; fought in East, 1392-96; helped to suppress Gloucester's rebellion, 1397; banished, 1398. On Richard II.'s seizing his estates, H. invaded England, defeated Richard, and became king, 1399; defeated Scots, 1402; defeated Percies, who had joined Glendower's revolt, at *Shrewsbury,* 1403; crushed Scrope's rebellion, 1405; subdued Percies, 1408, and ended Welsh rebellion; opposed Lollards.

HENRY V. (1387-1422), king of England; *s.* of Henry IV.; succ. 1413; repressed Lollards; invaded France and won battle of *Agincourt,* 1415; successfully besieged Rouen, 1417-19; formed alliance with Philip of Burgundy, 1419; m. Princess Catherine of France; attained regency of France and succession to Fr. crown by Treaty of Troyes, 1320; spent remaining years in suppressing Fr. risings against Eng. rule; took Meaux, 1422.

HENRY VI. (1421-71), king of England; *s.* of Henry V.; succ., 1422; minor till 1442; Cade's rebellion suppressed, 1450; Fr. possessions lost, 1453; insane in 1453, subsequently recovered. Wars of Roses began, 1455; ended in 1461 with H.'s defeat, when Edward IV. became king. H. was murdered in Tower, 1471. He founded Eton School, and King's Coll., Cambridge.

HENRY VII. (1457-1509), king of England; founder of Tudor line; half-bro. of Henry VI.; m. Edward IV.'s *d.* Elizabeth; defeated Richard III. at *Bosworth Field* 1485; and became king; instituted Court of Star Chamber, 1487; suppressed Lambert Simnel's rebellion by victory at *Stoke,* 1487; supported Brittany against France; formed alliance with Span. and Ger. Kings, and invaded France, 1492; concluded commercial treaty with Flanders, 1496; overthrew Perkin Warbeck's insurrection;

defeating his supporters at Blackheath, 1497; amassed large fortune; strengthened crown at expense of nobles.

HENRY VIII. (1492-1547), king of England and Ireland; second *s.* of Henry VII.; succ. of 1509, and m. Catharine of Aragon, his *b.'s* widow; invaded France, winning *Battle of Spurs*, 1514; held conclave with Francis I. at Field of Cloth of Gold, 1520, but sided with Francis's rival, Charles V.; made peace with France in 1527. Having no male heir, H. desired divorce; Wolsey's failure to obtain the necessary papal decree led to his downfall. H. disavowed papal supremacy in England, and, with Cromwell's aid, broke with Rome and established himself as head of Eng. Church; divorced Catharine, 1533, and m. Anne Boleyn, who was beheaded in 1536; dissolved monasteries, 1536, and put down Pilgrimage of Grace, 1537. After Anne Boleyn's execution, H. m. Jane Seymour, their *s.* afterwards reigning as Edward VI.; subsequent wives were Anne of Cleves, Catharine Howard and Catharine Parr. Later years marked by wars with France and Scotland; led expedition to France; took Boulogne, 1544.

HENRY I., THE FOWLER (*c.* 876-936), Holy Rom. emperor; duke of Saxony, 912; elected king of Romans, 919; acquired Lorraine, 923; defeated Slavs, Danes, Hungarians.

HENRY II., THE SAINT (973-1024), Holy Rom. emperor; succ. Otto III., 1002; king of Italy, 1004; crowned emperor at Rome, 1014; waged intermittent war with Poland, 1002-18; liberated Bohemia from Polish yoke, 1004; concluded peace at Bautzen, 1018; supported Benedict VIII. against Greeks, 1021.

HENRY III., THE BLACK (1107-56), Holy. Rom. emperor; *s.* of Conrad II.; Ger. king, 1028; emperor, 1029; waged was with Bretislaus of Bohemia, whom he finally forced to acknowledge his suzerainty, 1041; defeated Hungarians, 1045, and reinstated Peter of Hungary; emperor by Clement II., whose election to papal chair be had obtained; put down rebellion in Lorraine, 1050; built Worms, Mainz, and Spires cathedrals.

HENRY IV. (1050-1106), Holy Rom. emperor; *s.* of Henry III. elected Ger. king, 1053; emperor, 1056; engaged in struggles with Swabia and Carinthia; deposed and defeated Otto of Bavaria, 1071; waged war against Saxony and Thuringia, 1073-88; came into conflict with Pope Gregory VII. (*q.v.*), who excommunicated him in 1076, and forced him to do penance at Canossa, 1077. H. subsequently repudiated his vow of obedience, deposed pope, and elected antipope, Clement III.; invaded Italy, 1081; took Rome, 1083; was crowned emperor, 1084. Ger. princes elected another king, but H. gradually overcame all opponents. Later years marked by further disputes with popes and Ger. princes; abdicated, 1105.

HENRY V. (1081-1125), Holy Rom. emperor; *s.* of Henry IV.; elected Ger. king, 1098; emperor, 1106; subdued Robert of Flanders, 1106; reign marked by dispute with pope concerning investitures. H. took Paschal II. prisoner, 1111; was excommunicated, 1112; ban removed and dispute settled by Concordat of Worms, 1122; waged intermittent war with Lothair of Saxony; later years marked by war in Holland and invasion of France.

HENRY VI. (1165-97), Holy Rom. emperor; *s.* of Frederick I.; elected Ger. king, 1169; m. Constance, heiress to throne of Sicily, 1186; crowned king of Italy, 1186; emperor, 1191; succession to Sicily opposed by Tancred, after whose death H. became king; coalition formed against him in Germany, 1191, but he put down all opponents both there and in Italy.

HENRY VII. (*c.* 1269-1313), Holy Rom. emperor; *s.* of Henry III., Count of Luxembourg; elected Ger. king, 1308; emperor, 1309; tried to unite Germany and Italy, and was crowned at Milan, 1311; revolts occurred, in dealing with which he met with little success; *d.* while marching to Naples.

HENRY I. (1008-60), king of France; waged war with Odo, Count of Blois, and William, Duke of Normandy.

HENRY II. (1519-59), king of France; persecuted Protestants; recovered Boulogne from England, 1550; took Metz, Toul, Verdun, from Emperor Charles V.; recovered Calais, 1558.

HENRY III. (1551-89), king of France; reign marked by war between Catholics and Huguenots; participated in massacre of St. Bartholomew, 1572; very dissolute; assassinated.

HENRY IV., HENRY OF NAVARRE (1553-1610), king of France; king of Navarre, 1562; leader of Huguenots; m. Margaret of Valois, *s.* of Charles IX., 1572; succ. to Fr. throne, 1589; had to fight Spain and the League; became Catholic, 1593; peace with Spain, 1598; passed Edict of Nantes in favour of Huguenots, 1598; developed agriculture and commerce; introduced silk industry; carried out financial reforms; directed influence against Hapsburgs; assassinated by Ravaillac. See FRANCE: *History.*

HENRY I. (*c.* 1210-74), king of Navarre; *s.* of Theobald I.; *m.* Blanche of Artois; his *d.* Johanna *m.* Philip IV., by which marriage the crowns of Navarre and France were united.

HENRY II. (1503-55), titular king of Navarre; *s.* of Jean d'Albret; his claim to the crown, in right of his wife Catherine of Navarre, was successfully disputed by Ferdinand I. of Spain. He *m.* Margaret, Duchess of Alencon, and had issue, Jeanne d'Albret, *m.* of Henry IV. of France.

HENRY OF PRUSSIA, PRINCE (1862), *b.* of ex-Kaiser William II.; *b.* at Potsdam; followed an army career; was sent to China, 1900, to 'avenge' Boxer outrages; on diplomatic mission to U. S., 1902; subsequently nominally inspector-general and grand-admiral of Ger. navy.

HENRY VII. (1221-42), Ger. king; elected, 1220; led rebellion against *f.*, Emperor Frederick II., 1233, but submitted, 1235; imprisoned.

HENRY RASPE (*c.* 1202-47), Ger. king; aided Emperor Frederick II.; Landgrave of Thuringia, 1242; Ger. king, 1246; defeated Conrad.

HENRY II. (1489-1568), duke of Brunswick-Wolfenbüttel; opposed Reformation; defeated by League of Schmalkalden, 1542; defeated Albert of Bayreuth, 1553.

HENRY I. (1512-80), king of Portugal; succ., 1578, and proved a feeble administrator. He had previously held the archbishoprics of Braga, Lisbon, and Coimbra; was cr. cardinal, 1542.

HENRY, four kings of Castile.—Henry I., reigned 1214-17.—Henry II. 1333-79, became king, 1369, after killing bro., Peter the Cruel; supported France against England.—Henry III., 1379-1406, succ., 1390; called Cortes to Madrid, 1394.—Henry IV., 1425-74, succ., 1453; deposed, 1468.

HENRY (*c.* 1174-1216), emperor of Constantinople; *s.* of Baldwin, Count of Flanders; shared in Fourth Crusade; noted for bravery, toleration, and wise administration.

HENRY STEWART (1725-1807), Cardinal York, was younger *s.* of James, the Old Pretender, *b.* of Charles Edward, the Young Pretender; cr. cardinal, 1747; called himself 'Henry IX.' on death of his *b.*, 1788.

HENRY THE LION (1129-95), duke of Saxony and Bavaria; defeated Abotrites, and extended his dominions; established claim to Bavaria, 1156; acquired Lübeck, 1158; aided Frederick I. of Poland and Italy; waged war against Denmark, which ended, 1171; went as pilgrim to Jerusalem, 1172; banned by emperor, 1180; submitted, 1181; obtained Brunswick and Lüneberg; banished, 1189; subsequently rebelled against Henry VI.

HENRY THE PROUD (*c.* 1108-39), duke of Saxony and Bavaria; put down revolt in Bavaria; supported Lothair against Hohenstaufens.

HENRY, PRINCE OF BATTENBERG (1858-96), *s.* of Prince Alexander of Hesse and Countess von Hauke; *m.* Princess Beatrice of England, 1885; engaged in Ashanti War; *d.* off Sierra Leone.

HENRY FITZ HENRY (1150-38), Eng. prince; 2nd *s.* of Henry II., and subsequently heir to the throne; was frequently at variance with his *f.*; famed for knightly accomplishments; *d.* of fever.

HENRY OF BLOIS (1101-71), bp. of Winchester, 1129; nephew of Henry I. and *b.* of King Stephen; papal legate, 1139-44; ardent ultramontanist; quarrelling with Stephen, proclaimed their cousin Matilda queen, 1141; reverted to Stephen's side; but never regained his favor.

HENRY OF HUNTINGDON (*c.* 1084-1155), Eng. chronicler; was archdeacon of Huntingdon; his *Historia Anglorum* extended to 1154, and was first pub. 1596.

HENRY OF GERMANY (1235-71), *s.* of Richard, Earl of Cornwall, *b.* of Henry III.; murdered as a Royalist by Simon de Montfort's sons.

HENRY OF PORTUGAL, THE NAVIGATOR (1394-1460), Portug. prince; *s.* of John I. and Philippa, John of Gaunt's *d.*; served with great distinction at siege of Ceuta, 1415; subsequently took great interest in navigation and discovery, and for years sent expeditions along W. coast of Africa at his own expense; among his discoveries were the Madeira Islands and Azores, where he established colonies; constructed observatory at Sagres, near Cape St. Vincent; in later years he again distinguished himself in the field in Morocco, and took Alcazar the Little in 1458; encouraged education.

HENRY OF TOULOUSE, OR DE BRUYS (fl. early XII. cent.), Fr. evangelist who influenced development of the Albigensian movement (*q.v.*); preached moral reformation rather than new tenets, but attacked the Church and caused the personal intervention of St. Benedict, who crushed the movement.

HENRY, JOSEPH (1797-1878), an American scientist, *b.* in Albany, New York. Educated at Albany Academy, he afterwards contemplated adopting the medical profession, but in 1835 he was unexpectedly appointed assistant engineer on the survey of a route for a state road from the Hudson R. to Lake Erie and he at once embarked with zeal upon the new enterprise. He appears to have been the first to adopt insulated wire for the magnetic coil. He was the first to magnetise iron at a distance, and he was also the first to apply the telegraph to meteriological research. From 1868 he was chosen annually as president of the National Academy of Sciences, and he was also president of the Philosophical Society of Washington from the date of its organization in 1871.

HENRY, MATTHEW (1662-1714), Welsh Presbyterian preacher; held charges at Chester and Hackney; famed as author of *Exposition of the Old and New Testaments*, a work of sincerity and charm, left unfinished at his death.

HENRY, O. See under PORTER, SYDNEY.

HENRY, PATRICK (1736-1799), Revolutionary leader and orator; *b.* Hanover co., Virginia; *d.* Charlotte co. He was of Scotch and Welsh descent, had little school education, married in penury at eighteen, failed in store-keeping and farming, and finally studied law, like his father, who was judge of the Hanover court. He was admitted to the bar of his native county in 1760, and became immediately successful, due to the revelation his practice made of his powers of oratory. His eloquence was effectively used in 1763 when he exploded with indignation in court in a speech challenging the right of George III. to annul the acts of the colonial legislatures. As a raw rustic he became in 1765 a member of the Virginia House of Burgesses, where he presented resolutions directed against the Stamp Act (*q.v.*) and affirming that the colonial assembly should have the sole and exclusive right to levy taxes. Thereafter he projected as a leader of the revolutionary cause against the exactions of the then misguided colonial policy of Great Britain. At the first colonial Congress that met in Philadelphia in 1774 he sounded the first note of the new nationalism then in the throes of birth, urging that there should be no more designations of New Englanders, New Yorkers, Pennsylvanians or Virginians, but that all were Americans. 'I am not a Virginian', he said, 'but an American'. The next year, before the second Revolutionary Congress, he made the speech in which he originated the famous declaration 'Give me liberty; or give me death', while advocating the arming for immediate war against Great Britain of the Virginia militia, which he later commanded. He became Virginia's first governor in 1776 and framed its first constitution, serving till 1779. He sat in the legislature from 1780 to 1784, and was again governor for the two years following. He was a bitter opponent of the Federal Constitution and vainly exercised his passionate oratory against its ratification. He charged that the power conferred upon the federal authority curtailed State rights, and succeeded in having amendments incorporated that represented a bill of rights for the States. His death cut short a renewed term of service in the Virginia legislature, to which he was re-elected in 1799.

HENSCHEL, SIR GEORGE (1850-1934), baritone singer, composer, and conductor; naturalized Englishman, 1890; sang with great success at Brussels, 1873; Cologne, 1874; and London, 1877; settled in London, 1877. He was the first conductor of the Boston Symphony Orchestra. His compositions include songs, an opera, a comic opera, a *Requiem Mass*, *Stabat Mater*, and *Te Deum*. He retired in 1914.

HENSLOW, JOHN STEVENS (1796-1861), Eng. scientist; prof. of Mineralogy, and later of Bot., at Cambridge. His discoveries established the *phosphate industry* in England.

HENSLOWE, PHILIP (*d.* 1616), Eng. theatre owner; built the 'Rose' and 'Fortune' theatres, and held shares in others, where many famous Elizabethan plays were performed. His *Diary* (MS. in Dulwich Coll.) contains valuable information relative to his period.

HENTY, GEORGE ALFRED (1832-1902), Eng. war correspondent and boys' author; served in purveyor's department in Crimea; acted as newspaper correspondent in Franco-Prussian and Turco-Servian Wars and other campaigns; wrote about eighty popular historical and military stories for boys.

HEPHÆSTION (*d.* 324 B.C.), Macedonian soldier who m. Drypetis, *s.* of wife of Alexander the Great, whose inseparable friend he was.

HEPHÆSTION (II. cent. A.D.), Gk. grammarian; wrote a valuable work on Gk. prosody; Eng. trans. by Barham, 1843.

HEPHÆSTUS (classical myth.), the god of fire and metal-working (Roman Vulcan); *s.* of Zeus and Hera; lame from birth; was flung from Olympus by his *f.*, whose anger he had incurred. He forged the thunderbolts of Zeus, made the armor of Achilles, the crown of Ariadne, etc. The chief seat of his worship was the isle of Lemnos.

HEPPLEWHITE, GEORGE, noted Eng. cabinet-maker, who fl. during latter portion of XVIII. cent.; contemporary of Chippendale, but his work was of a lighter and more elegant character. Painted designs upon satinwood were a feature of many of his productions.

HEPTARCHY, condition or government by seven persons; generally applied to the 'Saxon H.' in Britain, dating from about the VI. cent., when the country was divided into seven kingdoms: Kent, Sussex, Wessex, Essex, Northumbria, East Anglia, and Mercia.

HEPTATEUCH, first 7 books of Old Testament.

HERA (classical myth.), known by the Romans as Juno, *d.* of Cronus and Rhea; wife of Zeus; *m.* of Hephaestus, Ares (Mars), Hebe, and Eileithyia. As queen of heaven she participated in the supreme honors paid to Zeus; famed as the embodiment of wifely chastity; celebrated for her surpassing beauty, of which she was extremely vain. She was devoted to the Greeks and their country, and was principally worshipped at Argos and Samos.

HERACLEA, several ancient Gk. towns.—H. Lucania, where Pyrrhus defeated Romans, 280 B.C.; H. Minoa, Sicily, naval post of Carthaginians. H. Pontica, Bithynia, destroyed by Romans, I. cent. B.C.

HERACLEONAS, Byzantine emperor for a short space in 641 A.D.

HERACLIDÆ, children of Heracles, who sought asylum in Athens from Eurystheus, king of Mycenae. After several unsuccessful attempts they conquered the Peloponnesus and founded the kingdoms of Sparta, Messenia, and Argos.

HERACLIDES OF PONTUS (IV. cent. B.C.), Gk. philosopher.

HERACLITUS (*c.* 53-475 B.C.), Gk. philosopher; of aristocratic birth; called the *Weeping Philosopher*; did much for study of metaphysics; thought 'everything is and is not,' and that in diversity true unity was to be found; fire is the original principle, and out of it the soul was created.

HERACLIUS (*c.* 575-642), Byzantine emperor; beset by Avars from Danube, and by Persians in East; made Treaty with Avars, 620; defeated Persians, 627-28; lost Syria and Egypt to Arabs.

HERALD, originally an officer whose duty it was to convey messages from commander of force to his opponent; function afterwards included making military proclamations of all kinds, and, later, superintendent public ceremonies and processions. About XIV. cent. colleges of h's were founded in most European countries to record armorial bearings of nobility and gentry.

HERALDY, science of blazoning coats of arms. *Armorial bearings*, or devices blazoned on shields, were unknown in England at time of Norman Conquest; by 13th cent. they were in general use throughout Europe, and a regular science of heraldry had been developed; probably largely influenced by the Crusades, as in warfare, where closed helmets rendered recognition impossible. some bold representation on the shield, as mark of identity, became necessary to the leaders. These being of the upper class, armorial bearings came to be the prerogative of that class, and were, and still remain, the outward sign of noble or gentle rank, the granting or creation of which rests with the sovereign.

In mediaeval times the undifferenced arms belonged to a single holder, from whom it descended to his heirs, while cadet branches had to show their cadency by various marks of difference. Marks of difference are still in use, although not compulsory in England; the *label*, a file of three points placed across top of shield, is now properly used only by the eldest son, while the signs of younger sons are the crescent, mullet, martlet, amulet, etc. These marks are quite small, and are generally placed in centre near top of shield. *Marshalling arms* is the disposition of several coats of arms of the same shield, to show descent, marriage, alliance, etc. In modern times, when a man marries an heiress the two coats of arms are generally marshalled by the wife's arms being shown on a small escutcheon superimposed on the husband's coat and their children bear the two coats quarterly—the father's arms in the first and fourth quarters, the mother's in the second and third. When the wife is not an heiress the arms are marshalled by impalement—*i. e.*, the shield is parted and the husband's arms are shown on right side, while the wife's are shown on left.

Technical name for whole device is *achievement*, which consists of arms (shield and device), helmet, mantling, wreath, crest, and motto. Other adjuncts are supporters, compartment, *cri-deguerre*, standard, badge, augmentation, all of which may be possessed by commoners. Knights of any order may have circle and badge of order, and peers may add coronet of rank. *Shield* consists of colored background called the field, and device thereon known as charge; it varies in shape. *Helmet*, placed above shield, may vary in shape, style, and design, but certain rules regulate its position and form. *Mantling* is cloth hanging from point on top of helmet; originally plain cloth to protect armour from weather. *Wreath* is used to attach crest to helmet; originally a fillet of silk twisted round it. *Crests* only came into general use in England in 16th cent., and are now most important adjunct of armorial bearings. *Mottoes* are a late development, and only appeared when standard was represented as a drawing and no longer carried in battle; they became usual in late 17th cent. *Supporters* are granted to Knights of the Garter, Thistle, St. Patrick, and to Knights Grand Cross and Grand Commander of any order who petition and pay for them, and to peers. They are sometimes granted as mark of royal favor. The *compartment* is for the supporters to stand upon; generally a golden scroll. *Cri-deguerre* is very exceptional; it was a family battle-cry, and could be inserted on standard. *Badges*, simple devices used for purpose of speedy recognition, date from even earlier times than armorial bearings. *Standards* originally represented arms, like the shield, but were later charged with badge as more easily recognizable. *Augmentations* are additions to existing arms granted by sovereign for services rendered; they may be supporters, additional crest, innerscocheon, etc. Peers' coronets, another accessory to shield, are gilt metal circlets varying in pattern according to rank.

Turning to details of shield, the *field* is the tincture of the back-ground, which may be a color, metal, or fur. Colors are *gules*, *azure*, *sable*, *vert*, *purpure* (red, blue, black, green purple); metals, *or* and *argent* (gold, silver); principal furs, *ermine* (white, with black spots), *ermines* (black with argent spots), *erminois* (gold, with black spots), *vair*, and *potent* (silver and blue in alternate divisions) The field may be of one or more tinctures, variously disposed. Partition lines are generally plain, but there are twelve varieties of such lines, named *engrailed*, *invected*, *embattled*, *indented*, *dancetty*, *wavy*, *nebuly*, *raguly*, *potente*, *dovetailed*, *flory*, and *rayonne*.

The ordinary charges, called *ordinaries*, are nine in number. The *pale*, *fesse*, and *bend* are bands which respectively cross shield perpendicularly, horizontally, and diagonally. Cross is a common bearing from very early times

and occurs in various forms, as *cross flory*, *cross patee*, *cross botonny*, etc. *Saltire* is a diagonally set cross, in form of St. Andrew's cross. *Chevron*, an early charge, resembles a gable. *Pile* is wedge-shaped device from chief to foot of shield. *Chief* is band at top of shield. *Quarter* is dexter top quarter of shield. Pale, bend, saltire, and chevron all have diminutives, respectively *pallet*, *bendlet*, *gyron*, *chevronel*. Diminutive of quarter, is *canton*; of canton, *chequer*. *Fesse* duplicated becomes a *bar*; diminutive, *barrulet*. Other ordinary charges are the *lozenge*, diamond-shaped figure; *flaunches*, sides of shield cut off by curved lines; *innerscocheon*, small superimposed shield; *tressure*, inner border of shield decorated by fleur-de-lys *mascle*, voided lozenge; *fret*, voided lozenge and saltire interlaced.

Principal animal used as heraldic charge is lion, whose position may be *rampant*, *passant*, *statant*, *sejant*, *sejant-erect*, *couchant*, *dormant*, or *salient*. A lion full-faced is *gardant*; head looking backwards, *regardant*. These terms are supposed to apply with few exceptions to all heraldic animals. Mythical animals represented are dragon (four-legged), wyvern (two-legged), griffin, unicorn, pegasus, and other winged animals. Other animals are given sea characteristics, series including mermaids, sea-wolves, sea-lions, etc. Eagle is most important bird represented in armoury; it is generally found *displayed* (with spread wings), and often double-headed. Other positions of birds are *close*, *volant*, and *rising*. Pelican resembles eagle. Peacock with spread tail is called 'peacock in his pride.' Fish are less frequent; positions are *hauriant* (erect) and *naiant* (swimming). Flowers and trees often occur; fleur-de-lys is generally considered a conventional iris; rose is represented without stalk or leaves, unless mentioned; trefoil, quatrefoil, and cinquefoil are conventional forms of leaves.

HERAT (34° 26′ N., 62° 8′ E.), city, in Afghanistan, situated on Hari-Rud, 2,500 ft. above sea-level; owing to central position, of great hist. and political interest, and formerly of commercial importance. Once a large city with magnificent buildings, now a mass of ruins; strongly fortified by ditch, walls with 5 gates, and a citadel on N. side; built in form of quadrangle, with 4 principal streets (called Chahar-Suk) meeting in centre; other streets filthy and almost desolate. Great Mosque, or Mesjid-i-Juma, remains of mosque of Mosaalla tomb of Abdullah Ansari, ruined palaces of Bagh-i-Shah and Takhd-i-Sefer, marble mausoleums, and other ruins testify to former splendor.

H. was scene of struggles throughout history of Central Asia; date of foundation unknown; flourished under princes of house of Timur, when finest buildings were erected. Pop. including Persians, Tajiks, and Chahar-Aimaks, 20,000.

HERAULT (43° 30′ N., 3° 20′ E.), S. department, France; area; 2,402 sq. miles; surface rises from S. coastal plain to Cévennes in N.W.; drained by Hérault, Orb.; wine, fruits, coal; chief town, Montpellier.

HERBARIUM, OR HORTUS SIC-CUS, a classified collection of plants which have been dried and preserved so that their characteristic features are illustrated as far as possible.

HERBART, JOHANN FREIDRICH (1776-1841), Ger. philosopher; studied at Göttingen, 1805; prof. at Königsberg, 1809; prof. of Philosphy, Göttingen, 1833-41. The importance of H.'s work is largely in psychology, and he arrived at his results by a combination of metaphysics, mathematics, and experience.

HERBERT, GEORGE (1593-1633), Eng. ecclesiastic and poet; after vainly seeking perferment at court, took orders, and was made rector of Bemerton, Wilts 1630. In *The Temple*; *Sacred Poems and Private Ejaculations*, pub. the year after his death, are some of the finest religious poems in the language.

HERBERT, HENRY WILLIAM (1807-58), Eng. novelist and sporting writer; wrote, under the name of 'Frank Forester,' *Field Sports of the United States, Young Sportsman's Complete Manual*; also historical works, including *The Chevaliers of France, The Captains of the Old World*, etc.

HERBERT, VICTOR (1865-1924), conductor; b. in Ireland. At age of seven began musical education under leading masters in Germany. Principal violoncello player in Court Orchestra at Stuttgart; heard in concerts in Europe. In 1886 came to New York as solo violoncellist of Metropolitan Opera Company. Was connected with orchestral organizations as soloist and conductor including Siedl's and Thomas'. Since 1894, bandmaster of 22nd Regiment Band, New York. From 1904 to 1924 conductor of Victor Herbert's New York Orchestra. Composer of 'Prince Ananias', 'The Wizard of the Nile,' 'The Fortune Teller', 'The Idols Eye' and compositions for orchestras.

HERBERT OF CHERBURY, EDWARD, BARON (1583-1648), Eng. soldier, diplomat, and writer; b. at Eyton-on-Severn; fought in Netherlands,

1610, 1614; ambassador to France, 1619-21, 1622-24, having been imprisoned by Parliament in 1642, he took no part in Civil War. Author of *De Veritate*,an important metaphysical work, *De Religione Gentilium*, a comparative history of religion and other philosophical treatises. Hist. works are *Life and Raigne of Hehry VIII.* and *Expeditio Buckinghami ducis.*

HERBS, plants with no woody tissue in stems.

HERCULANEUM, ruined city of Italy, situated at eastern base of Mt. Vesuvius. In 79 A.D. it was annihilated by eruption, when a stream of lava nad shower of ashes covered it so completely that it was lost sight of for cent.'s; since early XVIII. cent., however, excavations have been more or less constantly going on, and now a good part of the city is open to view, including the theatre and two small temples; the discoveries render possible the reconstruction of domestic life of the ancients, and many beautiful wall-paintings and statues have been brought to light, as well as philosophical MSS., coins, mosaics, etc. City was traditionally connected with Hercules; taken by Romans in Samnite Wars, and again in Social War, 88 B.C.; an important town at time of its destruction.

HERCULES, HERACLES (classical myth.), *s.* of Zeus and Alcmene, wife of Amphitryon, king of Thebes. As he grew to manhood be became celebrated for his great stature, strength, and beauty. He performed many feats of valor. Subsequently he was driven mad by the enmity of Hera, and killed his own children. At a later date, Eurystheus, king of Mycene, imposed upon him the punishment of twelve great labors: to slay the Nemean lion; to destroy the Hydra; to capture the Arcadian stag; also the Erymantian boar; to cleanse the Augean stables; to slay the Stymphalian birds; to capture the Cretan bull; to capture the wild mares of Diomedes; to secure the girdle of Hippolyte, the Amazon; to capture the oxen of the giant, Geryon;to obtain the golden apples of the Hesperides; and to bring up Cerberus from the lower world.

HERCULES, PILLARS OF (*Herculis Columnoe*, the name given to the twin rocks which guard the entrance to the Mediterranean at the E. extremity of the Straits of Gibraltar. According to Pliny and Strabo, Hercules tore asunder the rocks which had before entirely divided the Mediterranean Sea from the ocean. Another legend asserts that he forced the two rocks into temporary union to make a bridge for the safe conveyance of the herds of Geryon to Libya, and another that he narrowed the Strait so as to shut out the sea-monsters which had previously made their way in from the ocean and infested the Mediterranean.

HERD, a company of animals, usually cattle, assembled or driven together.

HERDER, JOHANN GOTTFRIED VON (1744-1803), Ger. author; *b.* Mohrungen (East Prussia); studied med. and theology at Konigsberg, 1762-64; greatly influenced by Kant and Hamann; teacher at Riga, 1764-69, where he wrote *Fragmente uber die neue Deutsche Litteratur* and *Kritische Walder* (prose works); visited France, 1769; intimate friends with Goethe at Strassburg, 1770; court preacher at Buckerburg, 1771-75; to this period belong *Uber den Ursprung der Sprachen,* 1772; *Von Deutscher Art und Kunst,* 1773; *Auch eine Philosophie der Geschichte zur Bildung der Menschheit,* 1774, prose works; app. court preacher at Weimar, 1776; *Volkslieder,* (1778-79, songs and ballads), *Vom Geist der Hebraischen Poesie,* 1782; *Ideen zur Philosophie der Geschichte der Menschhiet* (pub. 1785-94), prose works, and his famous translations of the *Span. Romances of the Cid* rank as his best works.

HEREDIA, JOSE MARIA DE (1842-1905), Fr. poet, chief of the "Parnassiens"; pub. *Les Trophees,* 1893; a series of sonnets, a poetical history of humanity, the work of thirty years, perfect of their kind.

HEREDIA Y CAMPUZANO, JOSE MARIA (1803-39), of Cuba, one of greatest Span. poets of the century.

HEREDITAMENT, legal term for hereditable possession; "tenements and h's" is constant phrase of land conveyance.

HEREDITY. Organic relations between generations, especially between parents and offspring. A constancy of likeness or stability of type through successive generations. When ancestral as well as parental characteristics are exhibited, the person in whom they appear is said to be atavistic. Pathological or abnormal conditions of parents, or grandparents often reappear in offspring, provided such a condition is congenital. Hugo DeVries in 1889, following in the steps of Gregor Mendel (1886) who formulated the laws which bear his name, sought to combine the fact of continuity with part of the theory of pangenesis. However, it was not until 1900 that Mendel's laws came to light again when similar results were obtained not only by DeVries in Holland but by Castle, Davenport and Morgan (*q. v.*) in the United States. In December, 1933 Dr. C. B. Davenport of the Carnegie Institution of Washington, in his annual report as head of the Institution's department of genetics, revealed that the actual unit of heredity is the gene, a miroscopic cell within the chromosome, less than eight-millionths of an inch in diameter and is also the actual creator of life. According to the latest findings the gene consists of a compound molecule, that is, a bundle of several smaller molecules that are made up of clusters of atoms. Life is created by their ability to divide into other molecular groups meanwhile retaining qualities of the parent molecule.

Inasmuch as pathological conditions, innate or congenital, tend to be transmitted, the suggestion lends itself that public opinion should be informed and educated concerning the undesirability of abnormal people propagating their defects. Among the long list of inheritable tendencies and weaknesses are insanity and many of the numerous afflictions of the nervous system as a whole. Legislation in some states provides for the sterilization of such types (among which it included the habitual criminal) while in Germany (1934) the practice has been made law.

HEREFORD (52° 3′ N., 2° 43′ W.), city, municipal and parliamentary borough, Herefordshire, England, pleasantly situated on Wye; contains beautiful cathedral, with various styles of architecture from Norman to Perpendicular; chief features are central tower, north porch, bp.'s cloisters, and tower called Lady Arbour; trades chiefly in agricultural produce.

HEREFORD (54° 7′ N., 8° 40′

E.), town, Westphalia, Prussia; formerly site of Benedictine abbey.

HEREFORDSHIRE (52° 10′ N., 2° 45′ W.), county, England, on Welsh border; bounded N. by Shropshire, E. by Worcestershire, S. by Monmouth and Gloucestershire, W. by Radnor and Brecknock; area, 833 sq. miles; chief towns are Hereford (capital), Leominster, Ross, and Ledbury; rich, fertile county, well watered by Wye, celebrated for its beauty, and its tributaries, Lugg, Arrow, Frome, and Monnow; hills separate various valleys; in E. are Malvern Hills and in S. W. Black Mts. Soil produces fine wheat, barley, and hops; orchards occupy large area; celebrated cattle, sheep, and horses reared.

HERERO OVAHERERO, Bantu race;

HEREFORD CATHEDRAL, ENGLAND

The cathedral exemplifies all styles of architecture from the Norman to the Perpendicular. It was built from 1079 to 1535, although the west. front, replacing that which fell in 1786, was completed as recently as 1905. The total length of the cathedral outside is 342 ft., inside 327 ft. 5 in., the nave being 158 ft. 6 in. and the lady chapel 93 ft. 5 in. The principal features are the intricate metal-work screen, the central tower, the north porch and the organ, built originally by Renatus Harris. In the south choir aisle is the Mappus Mundi, or Map of the World, dating from about 1314, the work of a Lincolnshire monk, Richard of Haldingham.

inhabiting Damaraland, South-West Africa.

HERESY (Gk. 'choice'), used classically of a sect. In New Testament used of Pharisees and Sadducees, and by St. Paul of parties within the Church. Gradually h. came to mean theological difference, and has generally denoted any departure from the recognized belief of the Church. It is often said that the growth of h. within the Church forced her to define dogmas, that is the contradiction of opposition to that which had always been accepted, but never defined. The first five cent's of Christianity saw a series of religious doctrines and movements developed, which were rejected by the Church as a whole, of which Gnosticism and Arianism were the chief. The Fathers denounce h. in unmeasured terms, few even admitting the honesty of the heretics. The Early Church had defended the rights of each man to choose his own religion, but when Christianity had become the religion of the Empire the Church sought the help of the state to suppress h. The Mediaeval Church was ruthless, and sought by every possible means to crush it out, though recent research has shown there was more of it than is sometimes imagined. The Reformation did not involve either dogmatic freedom within the Church nor freedom from persecution by the state. Calvin was as severe as Laud. Many Christian Churches allow a certain latitude of dogmatic interpretation, particularly in modern times. Religious toleration has been gradual, in R.C. countries coming only in the XIX. cent., and it is only partial in Russia to-day. Laws against heretics date from 1400 (Statute *De Heretico Comburendo*). Episcopalian and Puritan harried one another by turns in the XVII. cent.

HEREWARD 'THE WAKE', Eng. patriot who, after the Norman Conquest, long defied the authority of William I., and dwelt secure in the morasses of the Isle of Ely. He was at length subdued, but escaped capture.

HERFORD. OLIVER (1863), author. Educated at Lancaster College, England and Antioch College, Ohio; studied art at Julien's Academy, Paris, and Slade School, England. Author of *Alphabet of Celebrities*, 1899; *A Childs Primer of Natural History*, 1899; *More Animals*, 1900; *Rubaiyat of a Persian Kitten*, 1904; *The Fairy God-Mother-in-Law*, 1905; *The Astonishing Tale of a Pen and Ink Puppet*, 1907; *Hearticulture*, 1908; *Simple Geography*, 1909; *Cupid's Fair Weather Book*, 1909 *Peter Pan Alphabet*, 1909; *The Mythological Zoo*, 1914; *Jingle Jungles*, 1915; *Cynic's Calendar*,

1917; *The Laughing Willow*, 1918; *This Giddy Globe*, 1919; *The Herford AEsop*, 1921.

HERGESHEIMER, JOSEPH (1880); Author. *B.* in Philadelphia, Pa.; student of Quaker School and Pennsylvania Academy of Fine Arts. Author: *The Lay Anthony*, 1914; *Mountain Blood*, 1915; *The Three Black Pennys*, 1917; *Gold and Iron*, 1918; *Java Head*, 1919; *The Happy End*, 1919; *Linda Condon*, 1919; *Steel*, 1920; *San Christobal de la Habana*, 1920; *Cytherea*, 1921. Writes for Century, Forum and Saturday Evening Post. *The Bright Shawl*, 1922; *Java Head* produced as a motion picture, 1922. Writes for magazines, 1933.

HERIOT, GEORGE (1563-1623), Scot. goldsmith; known as 'Jingling Geordie'; acquired considerable wealth in the exercise of his calling, which, after his death, was devoted to the building and endowment of 'Heriot's Hospital', Edinburgh.

HERISAU (47° 23' N., 9° 17' E.); town, Switzerland.

HERKIMER, NICOLAS (1716-1777); an American soldier, *b.* in New York. He was in command in Fort Herkimer, N. Y. when he was attacked by Indians and in 1777 was the leader of a militia force sent to relieve Fort Stanwicks which was besieged by British and Indians. In the battle of Oriskany which followed he was mortally wounded. See ORINSKY, BATTLE OF.

HERKIMER, a village of New York, in Herkimer co., of which it is the county seat. It is on the New York Central, Otsego and Herkimer and N. Y. State railways, and on the New York State Barge Canal. It is surrounded by an extensive dairying country of which it is the center. Its industries include the manufacture of knit goods, office desks, upholstered furniture, paper boxes, etc.

HERKOMER, SIR HUBERT VON (1849-1914), Bavarian (naturalized Eng.) portrait and subject painter; worked for *Fun* and the *Graphic*; exhibited *After the Toil of the Day* at the Royal Academy, 1873; founded school of art at Bushey, 1883; among his best pictures are *The Last Muster, On Strike*, and portraits of Ruskin, Wagner, and Tennyson.

HERMÆ, architectural term for pillars with head, usually that of Hermes, at the top; large numbers found in Gk. towns where they were objects of worship; used as boundaries.

HERMAGORAS (fl. early I. cent.

B.C.), Gk. who founded school of rhetoric at Rome.

HERMANN I. (*d.* 1217), landgrave of Thuringia; one of chief figures in Ger. history of his time.

HERMANN, COUNT OF WIED (1477-1552), elector and adp. of Cologne; deposed for introducing Reformation into his dominions.

HERMANN OF REICHENAU (1013 54), Ger. monk of Reichenau and author of *Chronicon ad annum*, 1054.

HERMANNSTADT (Hung. *Nagy-Szeben*), tn., Rumania (45° 48′ N., 24° 8′ E.), chief town of Szeben co., on the Cibin (Szeben), in the S. of Transylvania, at the N. foot of the Carpathians. The principal features are the numerous churches, and the antique town house containing the 'Saxon' archives and a collection of armor. The town also possesses the collections of the Transylvanian Carpathian Soc., and a law academy. Distilling, pottery, soap and candle making, printing, milling, and other industries are carried on. It was in the possession of the Turks from 1663 to 1692. During the World War was captured by Rumanians during their invasion of Transylvania (Sept., 1916); retaken by Falkenhayn (Oct., 1916), after a battle. At the Peace Conference it passed along with Transylvania to Rumania.

HERMAPHRODITUS, deity of both sexes in Gk. mythology. H. in Ovid's *Metamorphoses* was *s.* of Hermes and Aphrodite, and united at her request to a nymph who had fallen in love with him.

HERMAPHRODITISM. See SEX.

HERMAS 'THE SHEPHERD' OF, was written at Rome in the first half of the II. cent., traditionally by H., *b.* of Pius, bp. of Rome. It enjoyed at first a high reputation, and was nearly included in the canonical Scriptures. H. was a prophet, and he represents the Church under the guise of a female figure. The work is arranged under Visions, Mandates, and Similitudes. H.'s function is to deliver a message of repentance, declared to him by an angel. It was probably written at different times; theologically it has Adoptionist tendencies.

HERMENEUTICS (Gk. *hermeneuein*, to explain, from Hermes, Zeus's messenger), art of interpreting the wisdom of the ancients, or divine law

HERMES (classical myth.), known to the Romans as Mercury, the swift-footed messenger of the gods, who also conducted the dead to Hades. He was notorious for cunning and dissimulation, was the patron of commerce, and the god of Eloquence. His parents were Zeus and Maia. He is generally represented as a beautiful, naked youth, bearing a caduceus.

HERMES TRISMEGISTUS, name by which the Greeks denoted the Egyptian god Thoth, looked on as the originator of learning and culture; considered in the early centuries A.D. to be author of many occult treatises known as the Heremetic Books, an encyclopaedia of Gk. learning.

HERMIPPUS (fl. early V. cent. B.C.); Athenian poet who wrote satirical comedies.

HERMIT, one who lives apart from others, a frequent practice of Early Christian saints; Paul, the initiator of the practice. St. Anthony, and St. Jerome are well known, Founder of the pillar h's was Simeon Stylites.

HERMIT-CRAB. See CRAB; MALACOSTRACA, COMMENSALISM.

HERMON (33° 26′ N., 35° 50′ E.); or Jebel-es-Sheikh, highest peak of Anti-Lebanon range, Syria; height, *c.* 9150 ft.; on slopes are ruined temples.

HERMOSILLO (22° 23′ N., 110° 58′ W.), city, capital of Sonora State, Mexico, distilleries, wine, silver; has a mint.

HERNE (51° 34′ N., 7° 15′ E.); town; Westphalia, Prussia.

HERNE, JAMES A. (1839-1901), an American actor and playwright, *b.* in Troy, N. Y. He was on the stage the greater part of his life, but his chief fame rests on his plays, especially Shore Acres, which was one of the most popular pieces every enacted on the American stage. Other well known plays are *Hearts of Oak*, *Drifting Apart*, and *Margaret Fleming*. His *d.* Crystal Herne, was a well known actress.

HERNE THE HUNTER, ghostly huntsman, said to haunt Windsor Great Park by night. He is referred to in Shakespeare's *Merry Wives of Windsor*.

HERNIA is the term in surgery applied to the protrusion of an organ, or part of an organ, through an opening in the wall of the cavity in which it is normally contained; most commonly denoting such a protrusion of an organ of the abdomen, popularly termed 'rupture.' The most common situations of abdominal h. are the groin (inguinal canal), the upper part of the thigh (crural canal), and the naval or umbilicus, and the cause may be either *congenital*, due to arrested development of certain parts, or to hereditary weakness of the abdominal wall, or *acquired*, from various causes which may weaken the abdominal walls or increase the internal pressure of the abdomen, *e.g.* pregnancy, hard coughing in chronic bronchitis, and similar violent efforts, or injury.

HERNÖSAND (62° 35' N., 17° 49' E.), port, Sweden,

HERO FUND, CARNEGIE. See CARNEGIE HERO FUND.

HERO AND LEANDER (classical myth.), two famous lovers of ancient times. H. was priestess of Aphrodite, at Sestos, and L. a handsome youth of Abydos, who nightly swam the Hellespont to visit his love, guided by a lamp; on a night of storm, the lamp was extinguished, and L. drowned. H., in despair, cast herself into the sea.

HERO OF ALEXANDRIA (I. or II. cent. B.C.), Gk. mathematician and writer on mechanical and physical subjects; invented, as toys, number of machines and automata; wrote *Catoptrica* (on reflecting surfaces). three books on *Mechanics, Pneumatica* (descriptions of his machines), *Automatopoietica*, and numerous treatises on *Geometre*.

HEROD, princes of Judaea. H. the Great, was appointed king of all Judaea in 40 B.C., and in 37 B.C. he took Jerusalem and deposed Antigonus, the last Asmonaean prince; he rebuilt Temple, and laid out a new palace on Zion; had great numbers of his relatives put to death, and ordered massacre of Innocents; *d.* in 4 B.C.—H. Antipas, tetrarch of Galilee and Peraea; beheaded John the Baptist; deposed 40 A.D.—H. Philip, tetrarch of region beyond Jordan; founded Caesarea Philippi; m. Salome, *d.* 33 A.D.—H. Agrippa I. *d.* 44 A.D., king of Judaea; *s.* of Aristobulus; *g.s.* of H. the Great; Caligula showered honors and favors upon him, and he became one of the most powerful kings of the East; imprisoned St. Peter, and put James, *b.* of John the Evangelist, to death; according to *Acts* 12, *d.* 'eaten of worms.' H. Agrippa II. *d. c.* 100 A.D., *s.* of H. Agrippa I., last king of H. the Great's line; appears in *Acts* 26.

HERODAS, HERONDAS (III. cent. B.C.), Gk. poet and writer of mimes; probably native of Cos. A papyrus with seven mimes of H. was discovered in 1890. The scenes are very lively and vivid.

HERODIANS, associated by Christ with the Pharisees for condemnation (*Mark* 8₁₅; cf. 3₆); supposed to have been a Jewish political party in favor of Herod, king of Judaea, 37-4 B.C.

HERODIANUS, Gk. historian; fl. during first half of III. cent. A.D., and wrote a valuable narrative of his period.

HERODIANUS, ÆLIUS (fl. II. cent. A.D.), Alexandrian scholar whose treatises on Gk. prosody and style are valuable.

HERODIAS, the *g.d.* of Herod the Great and Mary Marimne. She first married her uncle, Herod Philip, and afterwards left him and lived with her *b.*, Herod Antipas. Through her scheming Herod was persuaded to put to death John the Baptist, who had denounced the relations between her and Herod.

HERODOTUS (c. 490-420 B.C.), early Gk. historian, generally regarded as the father of history; *b.* at Halicarnassus, Asia Minor; during his youth occurred the great uprising of Greeks against Persians; spent many years in travelling, visiting Egypt, Babylon, Greece, and other countries, and was thus able to give lifelike descriptions of the various peoples mentioned in his history. The latter is an account of the great victory of Greeks over Persians, and is also an epitome of the life and thought of the time; the main theme is preceded by a lengthy introduction which relates the earlier history of both nations, and gives incidentally long accounts of many other great nations with which they came in contact. The part dealing with his own times is of great hist. value, but much of his work on earlier periods is untrustworthy. His style is unstudied and harmonious, and is praised by both ancient and modern writers.

HEROIC, THE (Gk. *heros*, a superior being). Nearly every country has its h. age, in which men performed more than mortal feats. Historians have not yet decided whether the hero should be regarded as an original god or the god as a deified hero, but there is a strong current of opinion in favor of the latter view. Science has done much of late years in sifting the myths and obtaining a historical residuum, Niebuhr's treatment of early Rom. history marking an epoch in this process. The result has been, so far, to establish a line of demarcation, the h. being claimed for history, the mythical remaining among religions. Thus, so far, efforts to humanise Zeus and Woden have failed, but the heroes of Greece and Troy, whose deeds are sung in Homer, receive a place in modern accounts of Ægean civilisation, and the symbolism of the stories of regal Rome has been so plausibly explained as to be generally accepted as historial.

The h. in romance again, is very valuable for history. Charlemagne is mentioned by name in the *Chanson de Roland*, but in many cases pseudonyms are given, sometimes well-known (for instance, Dietrich of Bern, hero of a cycle in the XIII. cent. *Heldenbuch*, is Theodoric).

HEROIC VERSE amongst the Greeks and Romans was the hexameter measure used by Homer, and Virgil; synonymous term amongst the Fr. for Alexandrine verse; in Eng. verse it is the name given to two-rhymed iambic lines, each consisting of ten syllables. It was first popularised by Chaucer; was the favorite measure of Dryden and Pope; but sank into disfavor in the early part of the XIX. cent. See COUPLET.

HERON (ARDEA CINEREA), a large marsh bird with long legs and a stout, powerful beak; plumage slaty grey above, with pale breast and neck, whilst head is characterised by a dark crest. The h. is a voracious feeder, devouring eels, fish, worms, water-voles, field-mice, which it impales on its beak. The breeding haunts are termed heronries, and the nests are large, flat structures, built in groups in high trees. H.-hawking was a favorite sport in falconry.

HERPES, inflammation of the skin, accompanied by the appearance of vesicles on the surface, due to inflammation of the cutaneous nerve supplying the part; *herpes labialis* occurs about the lips in acute fevers, pneumonia, or even in a severe cold, soon passing away; *herpes zoster* usually occurs on the body along the course of an intercostal nerve, neuralgic pain usually preceding the eruption.

HERRERA, FERNANDO DE (*c.* 1534-97), Span. poet who introduced Ital. Renaissance into Spain.

HERRERA, FRANCISCO (1576-1656), the elder, and his *s.*, Francisco H., the younger (1662-85), Span. painters; the former famous for depth in subject and treatment, and founder of a Span. school.

HERRERA Y TORDESILLAS, ANTONIO DE (1549-1625), Span. historiographer-royal; wrote history of early Span. colonies in America.

HERRICK, MYRON T. (1855), U. S. ambassador; *b.* Huntington, Ohio. He graduated from Ohio Wesleyan University and studied law at Cleveland, where he practised from 1878 to 1886. Afterwards he engaged in large banking, rail-

road and manufacturing enterprises and entered politics as a Republican. In 1903 he was elected governor of Ohio, and from 1912 to 1914 served as ambassador to France, where he became an outstanding American figure during the early stages of the World War. He promoted the establishment of the American ambulance hospital in the Élysée Pasteur at Neuilly and organized the American Relief Clearing House. The French government bestowed on him the grand cross of the Legion of Honor and the British government presented him with a piece of old English plate as a tribute to his war services to their nationals. Honorary degrees of LL.D. were also conferred on him by Columbia, Harvard, Yale, Princeton and other seats of learning. *d.* 1929.

HERRICK, ROBERT (1868), university professor and novelist; *b.* Cambridge, Mass. He graduated from Harvard in 1890, then taught at the Massachusetts Institute of Technology and afterwards at the University of Chicago, where in 1905 he was appointed professor of English. He wrote a number of novels, beginning with *The Man Who Wins*, 1895; and including *The Common Lot*, 1904; *Wanderings*, 1925; *Waste,* 1926, and *Little Black Dog*, 1931.

HERRICK, ROBERT (1591-1674), English poet; *b.* London; *d.* Dean Prior, Devonshire. He was the *s.* of a goldsmith and studied at Cambridge, becoming a chaplain. In 1629 he became vicar of Prior Place, Devon, but in 1647 was ejected from his parish by Parliamentary troops owing to his royalist sympathies. Upon the restoration of Charles II. in 1662 he was reinstated to his old living. As a poet his viewpoint was pastoral and idyllic. He also wrote religious poems, but the main body of his work was amatory and descriptive, much of it of an exquisite lyrical quality and of perfect form. A number of his lines survive, as fresh and as melodious as when written, in present-day anthologies, among them *Cherry Ripe*, and *Gather Ye Rosebuds*. His literary mentor was Ben Johnson. His poems were collected and published under the titles of *Hesperides* and *Noble Numbers*.

HERRIN, a city of Illinois, in Williamson co. It is on the Burlington and Quincy, the Illinois Central and the St. Louis, Iron Mountain and Southern railroads. It is the center of an important coal mining region and its industries include machine shops, foundries and a powder plant. In 1922 riots between striking miners and strike breakers resulted in the killing of 50 non-union miners after they had surrendered their arms. The leaders of the mob were indicted and tried in 1923. The result of the trials was acquittal.

HERRING FAMILY (*Clupeidoe*), the most valuable of all groups of fishes, on account of their importance as food fishes. They are marine and surface feeders and are taken in drift nets. Most are small fishes, with large, thin, silvery scales and without a lateral line, but the related Mexican Silver-King, or Tarpon, a favourite game-fish, may reach a length of 6 feet. The Menhaden (*Brevoortia tyrannus*) is one of the most valuable of Amer. fishes. Its young are preserved as 'sardines.' The egg of the herring is one of the few fish eggs that do not float. The smaller Sprat (*c. sprattus*), with serrated belly, the young of which, with those of the herring, are known as 'Whitebait'; the silver and green Pilchard (*C. pikchardus*), the young of which are Sardines; the Shad, which may weight 8 lb., and spawns, like the Salmon, in rivers; and the Anchovy.

HERRING-BONE, term in masonry for arrangement of bricks in h.-b pattern.

HERRINGS, BATTLE OF THE (Feb. 12, 1429), so called because of Eng. force, under Sir J. Fastolf, carrying provisions to Orleans, defended themselves behind barrels of herrings, and repulsed a Fr. attack under Comte de Clermont.

HERSCHEL, CAROLINE LUCRE-TIA (1750-1848), the sister of Sir William H., whom she assisted in his astronomical observations, *b.* in Hanover, She lived with her brother at Bath from 1772, and acted as his assistant when he was appointed astronomer-royal. Between 17-86-97 she discovered eight comets, five undoubtedly unobserved before, and many of the smaller nebulae and star clusters included in her brother's catalogue were her discoveries. In 1798 she published for the Royal Society, *Catalogue of Five Hundred and Sixty-one Stars observed by Flamsteed*. In 1828 the Astronomical Society awarded her their gold medal, and elected her an honorary member in 1835.

HERRNHUT (51° 1′ N., 14° 45′ E.), town, Saxony, Germany; Moravian sect established colony here, 1722.

HERSCHEL, SIR JOHN FREDER-ICK WILLIAM, BART. (1792-1871), Eng. astronomer; only *s.* of Sir William H.; *b.* Slough (Bucks); grad. at Cambridge, 1813, and was Senior Wrangler and Smith's Prizeman; spent some time after his *f.s* death reviewing the nebulae and star clusters his *f.* had discovered;

to these he added several hundreds more, and made observations on over 3,000 double stars; set up at his own expense an observatory near Cape Town, 1834, and there completed his survey of the whole heavens, publishing his results in 1847.

HERSCHEL, SIR WILLIAM (1738-1822), astronomer; *b.* Hanover; came to England, 1757, and held various musical appointments, studying maths. and astron, in spare time; began 1779 systematic survey of individual stars with a 7-ft. reflecting telescope constructed by himself; discovered, 1781, planet *Uranus* (being thereupon granted a pension of £400 a year), and later its satellites. He also discovered two of *Saturn's* satellites, and observed the phenomena of its rings. In 1787 he completed the erection of a 40-ft. reflector at Slough (Bucks), and continued his studies there.

HERSCHELL, FARRER, 1ST BAR-ON HERSCHELL (1847-99), Eng. Lord Chancellor; *b.* at Brampton, Hants; called to Bar, 1860; app. Q.C., 1872; Recorder for Carlisle, 1873-80; M.P., 1874; Solicitor-Gen. under Gladstone, 1880; defeated for Lonsdale in general election of 1886, but in same year was app. Lord Chancellor and raised to the peerage; again sat on the Woolsack, 1892-95; Chancellor of London Univ., 1893; G.C.B., 1893. While in Washington, as pres. of Anglo-Amer. boundary commission, he met with accident which resulted in his death, 1899.

HERSTAL, HERISTAL (50° 41′ N., 5° 38′ E.), town, Belgium; centre of iron and steel manufactures.

HERTFORD (51° 48′ N., 0° 5′ W.), town, Hertfordshire, England; has castle originally built in X. cent.; in neighbourhood is Haileybury Coll.

HERTFORDSHIRE, HERTS (51° 45′ N., 0° 15′ W.), county, England; bounded N. by Cambridge, E. by Essex, S. by Middlesex, S.W. by Buckingham, N.W. by Bedford; area, *c.* 634 sq. miles. Beautiful undulating county of hills, valleys, parks, and woods; in N. is branch of Chiltern Hills, highest being Kensworth Hill. Principal rivers are Lea, Stort, Colne, Maran, and artificial New River; chief towns, Hertford (capital), St. Albans, Hemel Hempstead, Watford, Hitchen, Bishop Stortford, and Ware. Wheat principal grain grown; water-cress, fruits, roses cultivated; stock raised; manufacturing industries small; brewing at Watford; straw-plaiting, paper-making, tanning, and brick-making carried on. Grand

Junction Canal crosses S.W. part of county.

H. contains battlefields of St. Albans and Barnet; Waltham Cross and St. Albans Abbey.

HERTHA, NERTHUS, in Teutonic myth, the personification of the Earth; worshipped by Norsemen, Germans, and A-Sasons.

HERTLING, GEORG, COUNT VON (1843-1919), Ger. writer and politician; became prof. in the univ. of Munich and wrote several historical and philosophical works; entered Reichstag in 1875; employed by Bismarck during the Kulturkampf to secure concessions from Rome, and was leader of the Catholic centre. In 1911 became president of the council and minister of foreign affairs in kingdom of Bavaria, but was gradually drawn towards Prussia and labored for the supremacy of that country; succeeded Dr. Michaelis as Ger. Chancellor (Nov. 1917), and held that office when treaties of Brest-Litovsk and Bukharest were made. He retired in Oct. 1918.

HERTZ, JOSEPH HERMAN (1872), a Jewish theologian rabbi and chief rabbi of the United Hebrew Congregation of the British Empire. He was *b.* at Rebrin, Hungary, and as a child emigrated to New York City, where he received his education. He was rabbi at Syracuse, N. Y. until 1898 and from that year to 1911 at Johannisburg. In 1912 he was rabbi of a church in New York City and in the year following was chosen chief rabbi of the British Empire. His published works include *Ethical System of James Martineau, The Jew in South Africa,* and *Book of Jewish Thoughts.*

HERTZ, HEINDRICH RUDOLF (1857-94), Ger. physicist; was assistant to Helmholtz and later prof. of Physics at Carlsruhe Polytechnic. *Wireless telegraphy* is a practical application of one of his investigations. He demonstrated the similarity between *electromagnetic, light,* and *heat waves,* and worked at *electric discharges* in gases.

HERTZBERG, EWALD FRIEDRICH, COUNT VON (1725-95), Pruss. lawyer and politician; after holding several posts in government service, he became chief minister in 1763; supported foreign policy of Frederick the Great, and for several years guided policy of Frederick William II.; dismissed from office for opposing the king in his dealings with Great Britain, Poland, and Russia, 1791; wrote on Ger. lit.

HERTZEN, ALEXANDER (1812-70), Russ. author; *b.* Moscow; banished as political offender, 1834; left Russia, 1847, and lived in Italy, Geneva, London, Paris, where he died; best works, *Kto Vinovat,* novel; political works. *Baptized Property, Kolokol, Golosa iz Rossii* (Voices from Russia), etc.

HERULI, Teutonic people said to have been driven S. when the Danes settled in Denmark; allied with the Goths against the Rom. Empire.

HERVÈ, GUSTAV (1871), a French Socialist leader, *b.* near Brest. For many years he was professor of history of the University of Sens, but the publication of pacifist articles in 1901 brought about his dismissal. In 1905 he was imprisoned for opposing compulsory military service, and was, in the years following, several times arrested and imprisoned for the same offense. He incurred strikes among the working men and upheld sabotage. He was considered the most radical of French Socialists. When France declared war against Germany, however, he heartily supported the government and took part in military service.

HERVEY ISLANDS. See COOK ISLANDS.

HERVEY, JAMES (1714-58), Anglican clergyman who played part in Methodist revival; author of *Meditations among the Tombs,* 1745.

HERVIEU, PAUL ERNEST (1857-1915), Fr. psychological novelist and dramatist; great originality and charm of style; among his novels are *Diogene-le-Chien,* 1882; *Flirt,* 1890; *L'Armature,* 1895; and his plays include *Les Paroles restent,* 1892; *La Course du Flambeau,* 1901; *Le Reveil,* 1905; and *Connais-toi,* 1909; his works deal chiefly with sex problems.

HERWARTH VON BITTENFELD, KARL EBERHARD (1796-1884), Pruss. field-marshal; commanded right wing at Königgrätz and directed movements of 1870.

HERZEGOVINA. See BOSNIA-HERZEGOVINA.

HERZEN, ALEXANDER (1812-70), a Russian author and publisher, *b.* at Moscow. In 1835 while still a student he was tried and exiled to Viatka for a too free expression of his political views. In 1840 he returned to St. Petersburg and held an official post, but in consequence of too great frankness he was sent to Novgorod in 1842, and left Russia in 1847 to pass the remainder of his life between Paris, London and Geneva. In London he established his *Free Russian Press* from which emanated a large number of works dealing with the cause of reform in Russia and the periodicals *Bell* and *Polar Star*, which were smuggled into Russia and obtained an enormous influence. When the Polish insurrections of 1863 broke out, H. espoused the insurgents' cause, and lost his influence in Russia. He wrote *Memoires de L'Imperatrice Catherine III.*, 1869, and some novels, as well as his political works. His collected Russian works were published at Geneva in 1870.

HERZL, THEODOR (1860-1904), Jewish politician; *b.* at Budapest; founded Zionist movement, and in 1896 wrote *Der Judenstaat*, advocating the establishment of a Jewish autonomy in Palestine; to this end he organised a number of congresses at Basel.

HERZOG, JOHANN JAKOB (1805-82), Ger. ecclesiastical historian; prof. of Theology at Halle, then at Erlangen.

HESEKIEL, JOHANN GEORG LUDWIG (1819-74), Ger. author; famed for his patriotic songs, pub. under title of *Preussenlieder* and *Neue Preussenlieder*; *Lofe of Bismarck*, etc.

HESILRIG, SIR ARTHUR (*d.* 1661), Eng. politician and soldier; Roundhead in Civil War; raised cavalry force for Parliament; conducted defence of Newcastle, 1647-48; imprisoned at Restoration, and *d.* in Tower.

HESIOD (*c.* VIII. cent. B.C.), one of the earliest Gk. poets; *b.* Ascra, in Boeotia. His poems are (1) *The Works and Days*—a didactic work on peasant life; (2) *The Theogony*—an account of the origin of the gods and heroes; (3) *The Shield of Hercules*—a description of the hero's shield, in imitation of Homer's account of the shield of Achilles; exemplar for Vergil.

HESPERIDES, THE (classical myth.), three maidens, Ægle, Arethusa, and Hesperia, *d.*'s of Erebus (darkness) and Nox (night); guardians together with the hundred-headed dragon, Ladon, of the tree bearing golden apples, which was presented by Gaea (Earth) to Hera, on her marriage with Zeus.

HESPERUS, Gk. name for planet Venus when seen as evening star.

HESS, HEINRICH HERMANN JOSEF, BARON VON (1788-1870), Austrian field-marshal; won laurels as chief-of-staff to Radetzky in Italy.

HESS, KARL ERNST CHRISTOPH (1755-1828), Ger. engraver, whose three sons, Peter 1792-1871, Heinrich Maria, 1798-1863, and Karl, 1801-75, were prominent painters.

HESSE, republic of Germany, (50° 30′ N., 9° E.), in S.W. of Prussia, comprising the provinces Oberhessen, Starkenburg, Rheinhessen, and eleven small enclaves; watered by Rhine, Lahn, Main, Fulda; chief towns—Darmstadt (cap.), Giessen, Mainz, Wörms, Offenbach; has famous mineral springs, iron, salt, manganese ore; industries—leather goods, chemicals, furniture, hardware and machinery, tobacco, beer. Hesse ruled by landgraves from 13th cent. till 1567; then divided into Hesse-Kassel, Hesse-Darmstadt; Hesse-Marburg, etc., which by 1866 were annexed by Prussia, with exception of Hesse-Darmstadt, from that date simply known as Hesse. Formerly a grand-duchy, the state was proclaimed a republic in Nov. 1918. Area, 2,966 sq. m.

HESSE-DARMSTADT (50° 15′ N., 9° E.), former grand-duchy of Germany, formed by division of Hesse, 1567; since 1866 known simple as Hesse.

HESSE-HOMBURG, old landgraviate, Germany; incorporated with Prussia, 1866.

HESSE-KASSEL, now part of Prussian province of Hesse-Nassau (51′ N., 9° 20′ E.), formed by the division of Hesse, in 1567, and founded by William IV. (the Wise); ruled by landgraves until 1803; then Landgrave William IX., having fought against French, received title of Elector; Elector Frederic William having sided with Austria, Hesse-Kassel was annexed to Prussia (1866).

HESSE-NASSAU (*c.* 51° N., 9° E.), Pruss. province, Germany; area, 6,062 sq. miles; magnificent forests; wine, fruits; mineral springs.

HESSE-ROTENBURG, former landgraviate, Germany; partly incorporated with Hesse-Cassel, 1834.

HESSIAN-FLY OR CECIDOMYIA DESTRUCTOR, the name of a species of dipterous insects belonging to the family Cecidomyiidae; they are minute fragile flies, having very few wing nervures; the elongated antennae are furnished with rings of hairs. This fly does great injury to crops, and in some parts of the world causes considerable loss when it has once attacked cereals; the larvae is lodged at a point in the stem of the wheat enfolded by a leaf; the stem consequently weakens and bends. When about to pupate, the larvae of *C. destructor* exudes a substance from its skin and this forms a remarkable cocoon, which is called flax-seed.

HESSIANS, the name given to mercenary troops from the German States, and especially from Hesse-Cassel, employed by George III. in 1775 against the American colonies. In many instances their conduct was extremely brutal. Some of them, taken prisoners, settled in the United States after the war.

HESTIA, Gk. goddess of the hearth. The hearth in the city prytaneum was sacred to H., and the fire never allowed to become extinct; brands were taken from it to light the city fire in a new colony.

HESYCHASTS (Gk. *hesychazein*, to be quiet), name given to a Greek sect which arose among monks of Mount Athos in XIV. cent.

HESYCHIUS (fl. IV. or V.cent. A.D.), Gk. philologist of Alexandria.

HESYCHUS OF MILETUS (fl. V. cent. A.D.), Byzantine historian.

HETEROMERA, a sub-order of beetles, with five joints on tarsi of fore and middle legs and four on hind legs. It includes the Tenebrionidae, with the common 'meal-worm,' the larva of *Tenebrio molitor*; the churchyard beetles (*Blaps*), whose funereal appearance, and habits of frequenting dark places and of feeding upon animal refuse, have gained them their name;the blister and oil beetles (Cantharidae), which often contain an irritant capable of blistering the skin.

HETEROPTERA. See HEMIPTERA.

HETMAN (Russian *Ataman*), a Polish word used as military title for the commander-in-chief of their army when the king was not present. It was adopted by Russian as a title for the head of the Cossacks (*q. v.*), and once held by the Cesarevitch. It is also used for the elected elder of the *Stanitsa* in Cossack administration. See COSSACK.

HEUGLIN, THEODOR, BARON VON (1824-1876), a German traveler and explorer. He made many trips in Africa and the Soudan. He also made a journey to Spitzbergen and Nova Zembla. He published several volumnes of African travel and natural history.

HEVELIUS, JOHANN (1611-87), Ger. astronomer; studied sun-spots; discovered four comets, and suggested revolution of such bodies round the sun; founded lunar topography.

HEWITT, ABRAM STEVENS (1822-1903), ironmaster and social reformer; *b.* Haverstraw, N. Y. He was educated at Columbia College, where he later taught mathematics. He also studied law, and was admitted to the bar in 1844, but abandoned the legal profession to engage

in the manufacture of iron and steel in partnership with Edward Cooper, *s.* of Peter Cooper (*q.v.*). The firm (Cooper and Hewitt) was the first to mould iron girders and supports for fireproof buildings and bridges and promoted the introduction of the open-hearth process of making steel into the United States. In 1886 he was elected mayor of New York City, defeating Henry George and Theodore Roosevelt. Previously he had served several terms in Congress. As a democrat he supported Tilden's claim to the presidency in 1875, when he was chairman of the National Democratic Committee. He aided many institutions by bounteous gifts, especially the Cooper Union Institute (*q.v.*), founded by his father-in-law, Peter Cooper.

HEWITT, PETER COOPER (1861-1921), manufacturer and inventor; *b.* New York City; *s.* of Abram Stevens Hewitt and *g.s.* of Peter Cooper. He was educated at Columbia and at Stevens Institute, Hoboken, specializing in electrical engineering. Entering business with his father, he became a director of the Cooper-Hewitt and several other corporations and a trustee of Cooper Union. As an electrical engineer, he invented the mercury vapor lamp and the mercury vapor rectifier that bear his name, and a number of other mechanical appliances. He invented also devices to simplify the processes of manufacturing glue at the Peter Cooper factory; also a hydroplane, improved methods of hatching fish, and developed the use of mercury vapor in the operation of wireless telegraphy.

HEWLETT, MAURICE HENRY (1861-1923), Eng. novelist and poet; keeper of Land Revenue Records and Enrolments 1896-1900; pub. essays, *Earthwork out of Tuscany*, 1894; *The Masque of Dead Florentines*, 1895; then *Songs and Meditations*, 1897; first novel, *The Forest Lovers*, 1898, followed by *Richard Yea-and-Nay, The Queen's Quair, The Stooping Lady, Halfway House, Love and Lucy*, and many others; poems include *Song of Renny, Song of the Plow*, etc.; an interpreter of mediaevalism and of the English countryside.

HEXAMETER, dactylic measure, and the noblest of the Gk. and Roman verse measures, used by Homer and Vergil and other early poets. The form has been used in Ger. poetry and also in Eng. poetry, the best examples of the latter use being Kingsley's *Andromeda*, Clough's *Bothie*, and Longfellow's *Evangeline*.

HEXAPLA (the sixfold), an edit. of the Old Testament by Origen (fl. III. cent.), giving six versions.

HEXATEUCH, the Pentateuch and the Book of *Joshua*, joined to the Pentateuch as also treating of the conquest of Canaan.

HEXHAM (54° 58′ N., 2° 7′ W.), town, Northumberland, England, on Tyne; quaint old market town with narrow streets; most interesting feature is Abbey Church, with remains of ancient monastery; site of battle between Yorkists and Lancastrians, 1464; manufactures gloves and leather; coal and baryte mines near; trade chiefly agricultural.

HEYN, PIETER PIETERZOON (1578-1629), Dutch admiral; seized Span. bullion fleet, 1628; killed in action against Dunkirk pirates.

HEYNE, CHRISTIAN GOTTLOB (1729-1812), a German classical scholar, *b.* at Chemnitz in Upper Saxony. Although very poor, he was a student at Leipzig University, and in 1753 obtained a post in the Bruhl Library, Dresden. His edition of *Tibullus* which appeared in 1755, secured him the support of Ruhnken of Leyden, and although he suffered many vicissitudes during the Seven Years' War, the scholar was instrumental in obtaining for him, in 1763, an appointment as professor at Göttingen. His other works include editions of the *Enchiridion* of Epictetus; Virgil, 1767; Homer, Pindar, and Apollodorus, as well as many reviews of books. See LIFE BY LUDWIG HEEREN, 1813.

HEYSE, PAUL JOHANN LUDWIG (1830-1914), Ger. poet, dramatist, and novelist; renowned for his ovellen (short stories), such as *L'Arabbiata*; has also written fine lyrics, several narrative poems, and about thirty plays; Nobel prize, 1910.

HEYWOOD (53° 35′ N., 2° 14′ W.), town, Lancashire, England.

HEYWOOD, JOHN (*c.* 1497-1580), Eng. dramatist and epigrammatist; a distinguished writer of i n t e r l u d e s, amongst which were *The Play of Love, The Pardoner and the Frere,* and *The Play of the Wether.* He was also author of many noted epigrams.

HEYWOOD, THOMAS (*d.* 1650), Eng. dramatist; very voluminous and popular writer of plays chiefly with a domestic interest; his best include *A Woman killed with Kindness,* 1603; *Rape of Lucrece,* 1608; *Fair Maid of the Exchange, Love's Mistress;* also wrote *An Apology for Actors.*

HEZEKIAH (fl. VIII.. to VII. cent. B.C.), king of Judah; had great difficulty in putting down revolts of subject states; Bible relates how Sennacherib of Assyria invaded Judah and lost 180,000 men in single night by stroke of the 'angel of the Lord,' but episode is doubtful. H. was famous prophet and administrator; builder of aqueducts at Jerusalem.

HIATUS (Lat. gap), term in logic for break in chain of reasoning; generally, temporary pause.

HIAWATHA, a legendary superman immortalized in the mythology of the Iroquois tribe of American Indians, and the subject of a narrative poem of Longfellow's bearing his name. He was supposed to have been of miraculous birth and to have come among the Indians on a civilizing mission. They credited him with having instructed them in the science of medicine and of navigation and to have produced maize (Indian corn) as a food, but with the appearance of a white man on American soil he disappeared in an ascension to the land of the Hereafter, called the kingdom of Ponemah. Schoolcraft's *Algic Researches* perpetuates the legend, but makes Hiawatha an Ojibway Indian. Longfellow based his poem in the story, which resembles the Finnish epic *Kalevala.*

HIBBEN, JOHN GRIER (1861), University president; *b.* Peoria, Ill. Graduating from Princeton in 1882, he studied for the ministry at the Theological Seminary of that university, and also at the University of Berlin. In 1887 he was ordained and occupied the pastorate of the Presbyterian church in Chambersburg, Pa. until 1891, when he returned to Princeton as instructor in logie and psychology, becoming professor of logic in 1903. In 1912 he was elected president of the university in succession to Woodrow Wilson upon the latter's resignation to take office as President of the United States. His writings comprise mainly essays on logic and philosophy and he edited, 1905, *Epochs of Philosophy,* 12 vols. France made him an officer of the Legion of Honor. *d.* 1933.

HIBBERT LECTURES, a series of lectures founded by trustees of Robert Hibbert, 1770-1849, a Jamaica merchant who conveyed to trustees, 1847, 50,000 dollars to found scholarships and fellowships, lectures being included since 1878; the first series was delivered by Max Müller.

HIBBING, a city of Minnesota, in St. Louis co. It is on the Missabe and Northern, and the Great Northern railroads. It is in the great Mesabe iron ore range which is the most productive in the

United States, and is the chief shipping point for iron ore from this range. Within the city limits are ten important mines.

HIBERNATION, the state of quiescence or torpor in which many organisms tide over natural conditions unfavorable to their active life. The state of h. has much resemblance to a deep and prolonged sleep, and indeed sleep is often the starting-point which leads to h.; but there are great differences between the two types of unconsciousness. In h. the functions of the body are so reduced that the animal becomes practically inanimate, nutrition ceases, respiration is almost stopped, and, most strange of all, the body termperature, which may have been anything from 35° to 40° C. in mammals, falls almost to that of the surrounding air, with the fluctuations of which it now fluctuates. Almost the first moment of awaking, however, restores the lowered temperature to its normal pitch.

HIBERNIA (ALSO IERNE), ancient Rom. name for Ireland.

HIBERNIANS, ANCIENT ORDER OF. A Catholic Irish organization. The original purpose of the society was to protect the Catholic faith and priesthood in Ireland, but later it developed into a charitable and benevolent society, while politically working for the independence of Ireland. Some writers say that it originated about 1642 after the revolt in the North, and others in 1661 when Cromwell outlawed the Irish people and forbade Catholic worship. It is well established that Rory O'Moore founded the society as it is today sometime in the 17th century when it was known as The Defenders. The present name was adopted after Catholic Emancipation in 1829. The society spread to England and Scotland, to the United States in 1836, and later to Canada, Mexico and Hawaii. Since 1884 National Conventions of the order have been bi-annual. It supports the Gaelic League, and endowed a Celtic Chair at the Catholic University of America. A Ladies Auxiliary was founded at the National Convention, Omaha, in 1894. The society expends over a $1,000,000 a year in sick and death benefits. National president in 1933, M. W. Delaney, Chicago, Ill. Membership 100,000 (1933).

HIBISCUS, genus of plants of order Malvaceae, usually tropical or sub-tropical; *H. syriacus* grows in the open in America; *H. cannabinus* (Ambare hemp) is an Ind. plant, fibre being often known as Bombay hemp; *H. abelmoschus* is used in India for clarifying sugar.

HICCUP, HICCOUGH OR SINGULTUS, is a sudden spasmodic contraction of diaphragm, accompanied by closure of glottis, caused by abnormal stimulation of any part of phrenic nerve; is a reflex act frequently following irritation of mucous membrane of stomach, and usually easily cured by holding breath, or by a draught of cold water. When persistent it may be symptomatic of a serious condition—*e.g.*, peritonitis—and is also common in last stages of exhausting illness.

HICHENS, ROBERT SMYTHE (1864), Eng. novelist; gave up music for literature; won recognition with *The Green Carnation*, 1894; and since then has pub. *An Imaginative Man, Flames, The Woman with the Fan, The Garden of Allah* (successfully dramatized, 1920), *The Call of the Blood, Barbary Sheep, Bella Donna, Snake Bite*, 1919; *Mrs. Marden*, 1919; *The First Lady Brenden*, 1931, and *Mortimer Brice*, 1932; a play, *The Daughters of Babylon*, and has produced stage versions of his own stories.

HICKORY, an Amer. tree, genus *Carya*, with strong elastic wood, easily decayed by worms and moisture, but greatly valued as fuel; used for golf-clubs, hammer and tool handles.

HICKS, ELIAS (1748-1830), Amer. Quaker and anti-slavery agitator.

HICKS-BEACH, SIR MICHAEL. See St. Aldwyn, Viscount.

HIDALGO (Span. *hijo de algo, s. of* something), Spaniard of gentle birth.

HIDALGO (*c.* 20° 30′ N., 98° 45′ W.)' state, Mexico; gold, silver, cereals' coffee.

HIDALGO Y COSTILLO, MIGUEL (1753-1811), Mexican priest; led revolt against Spaniards; defeated at Calderon Bridge; put to death.

HIDE, the space that might be ploughed with a single plough, and would suffice to maintain a family or the household of a mansion-house. Authorities are not agreed upon the exact area. In Anglo-Saxon times and in Domesday Book the h. is given at 30, 40, 50, and 80 acres.

HIDES. See Skins, Leather.

HIEMPSAL II. (fl. I. cent. B.C.), king of Numidia; deposed, but reinstated by Romans under Pompey.

HIERAPOLIS.—(1) ancient ruined town in N.E. Syria, on high road from Antioch to Mesopotamia; possessed great temple, and was once one of the chief seats of worship of Astarte. (2) ancient city of Great Phrygia, lying between Lycus and Meander and near Laodicea and Colossae; possessed temple to Cybele, and hot springs; early seat of Christianity, Church being founded by St. Paul.

HIERARCHY, government in sacred things; applied to varying ranks of Church officers.

HIERATIC, term given to a more cursive form of Egyptian hieroglyphics.

HIERAX (fl. c. 300), Egyptian Biblical commentator, who exercised strong influence for asceticism in the early Church.

HIERO, name of two tyrants of Syracuse.—H. I. defeated Etruscans, 474 B.C.—H. II. made treaty with Rome, 263 B.C.

HIEROCLES OF ALEXANDRIA (V. cent. B. C.), Gk. philosophical writer.

HIEROGLYPHICS, name given to figures sculptured or written on Egyptian monuments and papyri, and found on monuments of the Aztecs; translation found by the Rosetta Stone 1799. See CUNEIFORM WRITING.

HIERONYMITES, order of hermits whose rule was founded on the Augustinian; established in Italy and Spain, XIV.-XV. cent.

HIERONYMUS OF CARDIA (fl. IV. cent. B.C.), Gk. commander under Alexander the Great and his successors; his history is chief historical source of the period.

HIERRO, FERRO (27° 43′ N., 18° W.), island, Canary Isles (q.v.), Atlantic. Pop. 6,000.

HIGDON, (HIGDEN), RANULF (c. 1300-c. 1363), Eng. chronicler; monk of Chester and author of the excellent *Polychronicon.*

HIGGINSON, ELLA Author, b. at Council Grove, Kans. (1862), Educated in private schools and Oregon City Seminary. Conductor of literary department of Seattle Sunday Times. Writes verse, novels, and short stories. Author: *The Flower that Grew in the Sand,* 1896; *A Forest Orchid,* 1897; *From the Land of the Snow Pearls,* 1897; *When the Birds Go North Again,* (poem), 1898; *Mariella of Out-West,* 1904; *The Voice of April-Land,* 1906; *Alaska, The Great Country,* 1908; *The Takin In of Old Miss Lane,* (This book won the McClure prize of $500.00 for best short story); *The Vanishing Race,* 1912; *The Message of Anne Laura Sweet.* (This book also a prize winner).

HIGGINSON, FRANCIS JOHN (1843), rear-admiral; b. Boston, Mass. He served throughout the Civil War

after graduating from the U. S. Naval Academy, taking part in leading engagements, including the bombardments at Forts Jackson and St. Philips, the capture of New Orleans, and the battle at Fort Sumter. Naval service afterwards took him all over the world in various squadrons. He became commodore in 1898, when he commanded the *Massachusetts* in the Spanish-American war. The following year he was promoted to rear-admiral, and from 1901 to 1903 commanded the North Atlantic fleet. He retired in 1905.

HIGGINSON, HENRY LEE (1834-1919), banker and philanthropist; b. New York City. He was educated at Harvard and showed a strong bent for music, which he later studied in Vienna. The Civil War drew him into the Union army, where he served as a lietuenant-colonel of cavalry. In 1868 he joined the Boston financial house of Lee, Higginson & Co., and became of national note as a banker and philanthropist. He contributed generously to the funds of Harvard University, of whose corporation he was elected a fellow, and also gave large sums for charitable purposes. He was especially notable as a lavish patron of music, and founded and maintained the Boston Symphony Orchestra.

HIGGINSON, THOMAS WENTWORTH (1823-1911) author; b. Cambridge, Mass.; d. there. He studied for the ministry at the Harvard Divinity School and from 1847 to 1850 was pastor of a Unitarian Church in Newburyport. Between 1852 and 1858 he held another pastorate at Worcester, Mass., then abandoned the ministry to take part in the anti-slavery movement, to which he was devoted. In the Civil War he was colonel of the first regiment of freed slaves and was wounded. After the war he applied his gifts to authorship and became an advocate of educational and political reforms, specially women suffrage. His writings, which comprise many volumes and cover the period of 1863 to 1907, including Young Folks' History of the United States, 1875, which was translated into French and German; Larger History of the United States, 1885; and biographies of Margaret Fuller, Longfellow and Whittier.

HIGH CHURCH. See ENGLAND, CHURCH OF.

HIGH COMMISSION COURT, established by Queen Elizabeth, 1559, dealt with ecclesiastical cases; members were Crown nominees; misused by Laud; abolished, 1689. Similar court in Scotland, 1606-38.

HIGHGATE, a suburb, N. of London, in the co. of Middlesex, about 4½ m.

N.W. of St. Paul's. It is noteworthy as having been the place where Bacon and Coleridge died, and also for its cemetery containing the remains of Lyndhurst, Faraday, and George Eliot, among other celebrities. Whitington's stone is at the foot of H.Hill, and is said to indicate the place at which he turned again after hearing Bow Bells.

**HIGHLAND PARK, a city of Michigan, in Wayne co. Its chief industry is the manufacture of automobiles and motors, and the development of this industry has greatly increased its industrial importance within recent years.

HIGHLANDS are to be distinguished in formation alike from table-lands and mountains. Generally speaking H. may be said to exist in the E. of the Old World in the E. of Australia, and in the E. of N. America. They occur in broad, expansive masses, unlike high mountains, which are much more localised. Their structure, moreover, is peculiar. Both valleys and watersheds or divides radiate, and the river systems are like great branching trees; the distribution, as in mountainous countries, of parallel ranges separating valleys is only rarely visible—the Appalachians are an exception; as a rule the valleys branch like fingers in the inner H., thus collecting tributary streams, whilst they broaden and deepen as they pass outward. H. are formed by the denudations or washing out of valleys, as, for example, the H. of Scotland, and by slow crustal movements, and sometimes by volcanic activities.

HIGHLANDS, THE, N. and N. W. district of Scotland. See SCOTLAND.

HIGHNESS, title of honor, used in speaking of or to princess, grand-dukes, and minor royalties. Members of Imperial family addressed as 'Imperial H.'; of Royal family, 'Royal H.'

HIGH PLACE (Hebrew *Bamah*), often means place of worship (originally on hilltops); h. p's were the centre of religious worship among Canaanites; the rites associated with them drew down the fierce denunciations of the prophets; abolished in reformation of Josiah, 621 B.C., but restored later.

**HIGH POINT, a city of North Carolina, in Guilford co. It is on the Southern, and the High Point, Thomasville and Denton railroads. Its industries include the manufacture of hosiery, print cloth and silk. It has also railroad and street car shops.

HIGH PRESSURE ENGINES. See ENGINES.

HIGH PRIEST. See PRIEST.

HIGH RELIEF, relief work whose degree of projection is half natural circumference.

HIGH SCHOOLS. The high school in the United States has developed as a stepping-stone to enable pupils of the pupil or elementary schools to reach college if they want to continue their education on the higher levels. It has grown on lines that make it a distinctive outgrowth of American education. Generally it provides a four-year course of secondary education. In practice this tuition, added to the eight years primary instruction imparted by the lower schools, suffices in the majority of cases for pupils whom the necessity of earning a livelihood prevents from taking up college studies. In the early days of public education, the academies, which ousted the old Latin grammar schools, served the purpose of high schools. The academies prepared elementary pupils for college, but they were private institutions charging fees that were prohibitive except for students who had parents of means.

The growth of public instruction proceeded for some time without poor elementary pupils having any facilities for continuing their education, either to fit them for practical pursuits or to prepare them for college. The high school came to supply the first-named need and slowly displaced the expensive academies. The latter could not compete with new institutions, which provided a similar secondary education without fees. Private academies survive, but for the most part they are select preparatory schools catering to a restricted class.

The high school did not primarily set out to prepare students for college, but their deposition of the academies left a gap in middle education which the growing educational requirements of the people at large duly called upon the high school to fill. To-day the high school has an extensive curriculum, embracing courses in the classics, literature, languages, arts, sciences, commerce, technology and manual training. In large communities several of these departments, such as the commercial, mechanical and manual training, called for separate buildings, and have developed into important institutions. The high schools have attained such a distinguished place in the country's educational system that they rank with, where they do not eclipse, many seats of higher learning, so much so that they have become known as 'people's colleges'. In 1930 there were

24,000 such institutions. See Education.

HIGH SEAS, seas over which no individual sovereignty is recognised by international law.

HIGHWAY, public road, which every one has right to use; generally created by legislation or by dedication, but uninterrupted use of any road for certain time may also establish right-of-way. Obligation to repair highway, rests generally with municipalities through which they pass, but may devolve upon owner of land the road passes through.

HILARION, ST. (291-372), abbot; after hermit's life of Egypt, introduced the monastic system into Palestine.

HILARIUS (fl. XII. cent.), mediaeval goliardic poet, possibly of Eng. birth.

HILARY, ST. (d. 367), bp. of Poitiers who wrote learned theological books and treatises against Arians; his day is Jan. 13, and has given name Hilary to Eng. legal term between Michaelmas and Easter (these terms were abolished, 1873), and to Lent term at the Univ. Oxford.

HILARY, ST. (c. 400-49), bp. of Arles, 429; the dispute as to his episcopal right led to strengthening of papal influence over the Gallican Church; festival, May 5.

HILDA, ST. (614-80), Eng. abbess; took the veil about 647; became abbess of Hartlepool, and subsequently founded 658 Whitby Abbey for monks and nuns; exercised great influence on the religious life of her period.

HILDEBERT O F LAVARDIN, GILDEBERT, ALDEBERT (c. 1050-1133), bp. of Le Mans, 1096; adp. of Tours, 1125; noted preacher and theological writer.

HILDEBRAND. See Gregory VII.

HILDEBRAND, LAY OF, Ger. alliterative poem, (IX. cent.); variant of the Persian story of *Sohrab and Rustum*; a father, long absent from home, returns, and is challenged to single combat by a youth whom he, too late, discovers to be his son.

HILDEGARD, ST. (1098-1179); Ger. religious mystic; became abbess of Disibodenberg (Lorraine), and subsequently founded, 1147, a nunnery near Bingen; famed for prophetic powers.

HILDEN (51° 7′ N., 6° 46′ E.); town; Rhenish Prussia, Germany.

HILDESHEIM (52° 8′ N., 9° 58′ E.); town in Pruss. province of Hanover, at base of Harz Mountains, with fine cathedral (XI. cent.), St. Godehard Church (XII. cent.), St. Michael's; town hall, Carthusian monastery, Knochenhauer-Amtshaus, and many other old houses; chief industries—machinery, vehicles, church bells, bricks, sugar-refining, cigars. A free city of Empire in XIII. cent., H. joined Hanseatic League, 1249; annexed to Prussia, 1866.

HILDRETH, RICHARD (1807-65); Amer. editor and writer of finance, slavery, etc.

HILL, geographical term for height above a bank and below a mountain.

HILL, AARON (1685-1750), Eng. dramatist and poet; wrote numerous pieces for the stage, of which *Zara*, his chief success, was derived from Voltaire.

HILL, AMBROSE POWELL (1825-1865), Confederate army general; b. Culpeper County, Va.; d. Petersburg, Va. After graduating at West Point he fought in the Mexican War and against the Seminole Indians in Florida. The outbreak of the Civil War aligned him with the South as a colonel. He took part in the battle of Bull Run; commanded the Confederate right at Antietam; hea ed a division under Stonewall Jackson at Fredericksburg and Chancellorsville; became lieutenant-general in 1863; when he commanded a corps of the Army of Northern Virginia; led the Confederate center at Gettysburg; and was killed in the attack on Petersburg, Va., while reconnoitering.

HILL, DANIEL HARVEY (1821-1889), Confederate army general and educator; b. York District, S. C.; d. Charlotte, N. C. He graduated from West Point in 1842 and saw service in the Mexican War. He left the army for a scholastic career, and between 1849 and the outbreak of the Civil War was professor of mathematics and military tactics at Washington College, Va., professor of mathematics at Davidson College, N. C., and president of the North Carolina Military Institute, Charlotte. He joined the Confederate army in the Civil War, and as a lieutenant-colonel commanded a corps at the battle of Chickamauga after taking part in the Peninsula Campaign, as well as in the battles of Beaver Dam Creek, Gaines' Mill, South Mountain and Antietam; and commanding the Richmond and Petersburg defenses in the Gettysburg campaign. In 1865 he surrendered to the Union forces in North Carolina with General J. E. Johnston, under whom he served in the closing days of the war. Following the peace he founded and edited 'The Land We Love', and became president successively of the Arkansas University and of the Agricultural College at Milledgeville, Ga.

HILL, DAVID BENNETT (1843-1910), U. S. Senator and lawyer; *b.* Havana, N. Y. He studied law and opened a practice at Elmira, N. Y., where he became a leader of the bar. He was active in Democratic state politics as an assemblyman, president of the Democratic State Conventions, mayor of Elmira, lieutenant-governor, and, 1885-91, governor of the State. From 1891 to 1897 he was U. S. Senator from New York and opposed many of President Cleveland's policies. Throughout his public career he projected as an outstanding figure in New York State politics and in 1892 was a leading candidate for the Democratic presidential nomination.

HILL, DAVID JAYNE (1850), American educator and diplomat; *b.* Plainfield, N. J. He graduated from Bucknell University in 1874, became professor of rhetoric in that institution, 1877-79 and president in 1879. In 1888 he was chosen president of Rochester University, resigning his position in 1896 in order to spend three years abroad in the study of diplomacy and international Law. From 1898 to 1903 he was first assistant Secretary of State. He was Minister to Switzerland, 1903-05 to Holland, 1905-08, and Ambassador to Germany, 1908-11. He has served as delegate on various important international bodies, notably the Second Peace Conference at the Hague. His publications include *Principles and Fallacies of Socialism*, 1885; *Genetic Philosophy*, 1893; *The Conception and Realization of Neutrality*, 1902; *World Organization as Affected by the Nature of the Modern State*, 1911; *The People's Government*, 1915; *The Rebuilding of Europe*, 1917; *Present Problems in Foreign Policy*, 1919; *American World Policies*, 1920. *d.* 1932.

HILL, DAVID SPENCE (1873), University President; *b.* in Nashville, Tenn. Holds degrees from various universities including Randolph-Macon College and State University of Arizona. 1897-1904 instructor at Smith Academy of Washington University, at Ralph Sellew Night Schools, St. Louis, 1901-1904, at Peabody College for Teachers, Nashville, as professor of history and philosophy of education; 1907 and from 1907-1911, professor psychology and education, Professor elect of psychology and education. 1911 at University of Nashville.

1911-1913 at Tulane University of Louisiana professor of psychology and education. At University of Montana, 1913, professor of Summer School. Since August, 1919, president of State University of Wisconsin. Author of *Individual Differences in Children of the Public Schools*, 1913; *An Experimental Study of Delinquent Boys*, 1913; Joint author of *Educational Research in Public Schools*, 1915; *Introduction to Vocational Eeducation*, 1920. Wrote for psychological and educational journals.

HILL, FREDERIC TREVOR (1866), lawyer and author; *b.* Brooklyn, N. Y. He was educated at Yale and Columbia, obtaining the LL. B. degree from the latter university in 1899. He joined the army in the World War, served on General Pershing's staff and was promoted to colonel. France made him a chevalier of the Legion of Honor. His publications include a number of novels, among them *The Thirteenth Juror*, 1913, collections of short stories, and several works on legal subjects. He wrote also on the lives of Washington, Lincoln, Grant and Lee, and, 1920, a book on aeroplane construction.

HILL, GEORGE BIRKBECK NORMAN (1835-1903), Eng. writer, especially noted for editions of Dr. Johnson's works.

HILL, GEORGE WILLIAM (1838-1914), astronomer; *b.* New York City. Graduating from Rutgers College in 1859, he joined later the staff of the American Ephemeris and Nautical Almanac, of which he became editor. He made notable researches into celestial mechanics, wrote largely on that subject and on mathematics, and threw light on the lunar theory, for which he received the gold medal of the Royal Astronomical Society of London, in 1887. He received also the Damoiscan Prize of the Academy of Sciences of Paris, 1898 and the Copley Medal, 1909. His most distinctive work is *A New Theory of Jupiter and Saturn*, 1890.

HILL, JAMES (JEROME), (1838-1916), American railroad developer and financier; *b.* near Guelph, Ontario, Canada. His early educational opportunities were limited, and he entered business life at the age of 15, settling in St. Paul, Minn., and working as clerk and agent in the Mississippi River steamboat business from 1856 to 1868. In 1870 he established the Red River Transportation Company, doing business between St. Paul and Winnipeg. The purchase in 1878, in company with others, of the defaulted bonds of the St. Paul and Pacific Railroad Company, marked his entrance into the railroad business, in which he became one of the most powerful and remarkable figures on the American continent. He concentrated all his tremendous energy on the development and perfecting of the great system that, by a series of consolidations, became the Great Northern Company, which not only included a railroad to the Pacific Coast, but also embraced a line of steamers running to China and Japan. He was also a great factor in the building of the Canadian Pacific. The country owes him a debt of gratitude for his contribution to the development and prosperity of the Northwest. He resigned from the presidency of the system in 1907 to become chairman of the board of directors, which office he relinquished in 1912. Apart from his business interests, he took a keen and active interest in art, literature and civic betterment.

HILL, LOUIS WARREN (1872), Railway Chairman; *b.* in Minnesota. Bachelor of Philosophy of Yale College in 1893. Held positions on railroads of which his father was president. President of Great Northern Railway, 1907-12. Director since 1929.

HILL, ROWLAND (1744-1833), famous Eng. preacher.

HILL, ROWLAND, VISCOUNT (1772-1842), a British general, nephew of the preacher Rowland Hill, was *b.* at Prees Hall, near Hawkstone. He commanded the 90th regiment in Abercromby's Egyptian Expedition, 1801, and served throughout the Peninsular War as Sir Arthur Wellesley's ablest coadjutor. He captured the forts of Almarez, for which he was created Baron, 1814. He distinguished himself by his brigade charge at Waterloo, and succeeded Wellington in 1828 as commander-in-chief.

HILL TIPPERA, TRIPURA (23° 30′ N., 91° 40′ E.), native state, adjoining Bengal, India; area, 4,086 sq. miles; rice, cotton.

HILLARD, GEORGE STILLMAN (1808-1879), lawyer and author; *b.* Machias, Maine; *d.* Boston. He graduated from Harvard Law School in 1832 and established an extensive practice at Boston, at the same time taking part in politics as a state assemblyman, in editing the Christian Register, and the Jurist, and in the editorial conduct of the Boston Courier, in which he acquired an interest. From 1866 to 1870 he was United States district attorney for Massachusetts. He edited the works of Edmund Spenser and his voluminous writings include a biography of General George B. McClellan.

HILLEL, called *Hazaken* ('the elder') and *Hababli* ('the Babylonian') (*c.* 75 B.C.-10 A.D.), a Jewish rabbi, was a native of Babylon. When he was already verging towards old age, he began to study law under Shemaieh and Abtalion in Jerusalem, and soon grew famous for his profound lore, whereby, according to the Talmud, he comprehended all tongues, even those of trees and beasts. Being well-nigh penniless, his learning was only acquired by exceptional zeal and self-denial. It is unlikely that he was ever president of the Sanhedrin, yet his humility and loving-kindness, and what has been described as the 'sweetness and light' of his personality, ensured the popularity of his teaching, which, like that of Jesus, was ever averse from 'sacerdotal traditionalism' and blind adherence to legal ordinance.

HILLER, FERDINAND (1811-85), a musical composer, played a concerto of Mozart at the age of ten, and in 1827 was present at the deathbed of Beethoven. *B.* at Frankfort-on-Main, he visited Weimar, Vienna (with Hummel, his master), Paris (where he lived from 1828-35), Italy, St. Petersburg, and England, etc. From 1850 till his death, he was municipal capellmeister at Cologne. His numerous compositions include chamber, orchestral, and vocal music; these display conspicuous inequalities, but since its first publication, his oratorio entitled *Die Zerstorung Jerusalems*, 1839, has been recognised as a masterpiece.

HILLES, CHARLES DEWEY (1867); Republican organizer and insurance manager; *b.* Belmont County, Ohio. After a high school and academy education he engaged in institutional work between 1890 and 1909 as superintendent of the Boys' Industrial School of Ohio and of the New York Juvenile Asylum at Dobbs' Ferry. In 1909 he entered the government service as assistant secretary of the Treasury and in 1911 became secretary to President Taft for the remainder of the latter's term of office. While occupying that post he was chosen chairman of the Republican National Committee and as such took a prominent part in the Taft presidential campaign 1912. The following year he entered business as a member of the firm of Dwight and Hilles, New York City, resident managers of the Employers Liability Insurance Corporation. He retained a close association with the Republican organization and in 1922 was chosen chairman of the National Republican Club. Entered business, 1933.

HILLIARD, NICHOLAS (*c.* 1537-1619), Eng. craftsman and miniature painter, whose works are the treasures of collectors. His *s.* Lawrence (*d.* 1640) excelled him in the same field.

HILLIARD, ROBERT COCHRAN (1857-1927), Actor, *b.* in N. Y.; started professional career in his own theatre, The Criterion, Brooklyn in *False Shame*, 1886. Has taken leading parts in *Mr. Barnes of New York; Richard Gray* in *Adrift* which he wrote. He also played part of John Earl of Woodstock in *Sporting Life.* He was also half owner of this play. Starred in *The Sleepwalker, The Mummy.* In 1905 created role of Dick Johnson in *The Girl of the Golden West.* Played in *The Pride of Race, The Argyle Case,* and *The Littlest Girl* (written by himself). Starred with Paul Arthur in *The Nominee.*

HILLIS, NEWELL DWIGHT (1858), Congregational minister and author; *b.* Magnolia, Iowa. He graduated from McCormick Theological Seminary, in 1877, when he entered the Presbyterian ministry, filling pulpits of that denomination at Peoria and Evansville, Ill. until 1894. The following year he became pastor of an independent congregation forming the Central Church, Chicago, and in 1899 of Plymouth Congregational Church, Brooklyn, N. Y. He acquired considerable note as a preacher, lecturer and author. His publications have a stimulating and constructive note and bear upon the problems of modern life. He edited the lectures and sermons of Henry Ward Beecher, with whom and Phillips Brooks, he became ranked as a preacher. *d.* 1929.

HILLQUIT, MORRIS (*b.* Riga, Latvia, 1869, *d.* N. Y. 1933) Amer. Socialist and lawyer came to U. S. with parents in 1886. Grad. N. Y. U. Law School, 1893.

Joined Socialist party 1888. Gained prominence as speaker and as delegate to various nat'l. conventions he played an important part in shaping the party's policies. Served as Nat'l. Committeeman from N. Y. (1902-6) and as a member of the Natl. Exec. Com. of the party after 1907. Was delegate to several international. Soc. congresses and in 1904 appointed a rep. on Int'nat'l. Soc. Bur.

at Brussels. His writings on Socialism considered authoritative. Among them are: *History of Socialism in U. S.* (1903), *Socialism in Theory* and *Marx to Lenin* (1921).

HILLSBORO, a city of Texas, in Hill co., of which it is the county seat. It is on the Missouri, Kansas and Texas, the St. Louis Southwestern and the Trinity and Brazos Valley railroads. It is the center of an extensive agricultural region. Its industries include flour mills, planing mills, and hay press work.

HILLSDALE, a city of Michigan, in Hillsdale co., of which it is the county seat. It is situated on the New York Central Railroad. It is the manufacturing and commercial center of the county. Its industries include flour, gas engines, clothing, furniture, screens, etc. It is the seat of Hillsdale College. It has parks and several handsome public buildings.

HILPRECHT, HERMAN VOLRATH (1859), German-American Assyriologist; *b.* Hohenerxleben, Germany. He came to the United States in 1886 after studying at Bernburg and Leipzig, and edited the Oriental department of the *Sunday-School Times*, published at Philadelphia. He was also research professor of Assyrian and of Semitic philosophy at the University of Pennsylvania for twenty-five years, 1886-1911 and meantime made archaeological explorations in Asiatic Turkey. He headed the University's various expeditions to Nippur, an ancient city of Babylonia between 1888 and 1914, and became an acknowledged authority on cuneiform paleography. The Babylonian section of the Imperial Ottoman Museum at Constantinople was reorganized by him between 1893 and 1909. Foreign governments conferred many orders upon him and he received several medals as well as honorary membership of foreign learned societies. His publications relate chiefly to his Assyrian researches and include valuable works on the Nippur excavations and on old Babylon. He was editor-in-chief of the University of Pennsylvania's *Bul-*

letins of the Babylon expeditions. d. 1925.

HILLSDALE COLLEGE, a coeducational institution situated at Hillsdale, Mich., founded in 1855 by the Free Baptists. Its curriculum is modern and embraces commerce, home economics, music, elocution and fine arts. The classics and sciences receive special attention. In 1933 there were 425 students and 35 teachers under the direction of J. W. Mauck. The institution was originally known as the Michigan Central College, opened at Spring Harbor, Mich. in 1844, and afterwards removed to Hillsdale.

HILO, a seaport, and the tn. second in importance of the Hawaiian Is., picturesquely situated on the E. coast of the island of Hawaii. It exports sugar, molasses, arrowroot, and rice.

HILTON, JOHN (1804-17), Eng. surgeon; surgeon to Guy's Hospital, London; pres. of Royal Coll. of Surgeons, 1867.

HILVERSUM (52° 13′ N., 5° 11′ E.), town, N. Holland.

HIMALAYA (*c.* 31° to 34° 50′ N., 70° 30′ to 96° E.), the highest system of mountains in the world, stretching, in an irregular curve, almost 1500 miles along the N. boundary of India; with a varying breadth of 100 to 160 miles, they divide India from Tibet, and lie roughly between the Indus and the Brahmaputra. The H. consist of several ranges of peaks, separated by deep gorges through which rivers flow. Rising steeply from the plain of the Ganges stands a range (some 4000-5000 ft.), between which and the higher ranges lie the beautiful and fertile valleys of Nepal and Bhutan. The greater system, starting from the Pamir Plateau in the extreme North West, is divided into

THE CREST OF SINOLCHUM, IN THE
HIMALAYAS

two main parallel chains, one lying N. of the other. The N. chain, forming a watershed between India and Tibet, has been little explored; its only point under 16,000 ft. is called Drass Pass (c. 11,300 ft.), which leads to Kashmir; and the Niti Pass (c. 16,700 ft.) connects India with E. Turkestan. The S. chain, consisting of lofty snowclad peaks, includes many of the highest mountains in the world—many rising over 20,000 ft.; the highest, Mt. Everest (28,000 ft.), is the loftiest peak known in the world; other peaks are K2 or Godwin-Austen (c. 18,260 ft.); Kinchinjunga (c. 28,150ft.); Dhawalagiri (c. 26,280 ft.); Nanda-Devi (c. 25,700 ft.); Trisul (c. 23,400 ft.). From this chain flow the Ganges, Indus, Brahmaputra, and many other rivers; on its slopes also stand many sanatoria—Simla, Darjiling, Almora, etc.—which are taken advantage of during the hot seasons.

There are few lakes; but in E. are Yamdok-cho and Chomto-dong; in W. lie the holy Tibetan lakes of Manasarowar and Rakas Tal (whence flows the Sutlej River), and also Lake Kashmir. There are numerous glaciers, and the snow-line is higher on the Indian side than on the Tibetan; metal ores exist and gold is worked in Tibet. On the Indian side, most of the inhabitants are Hindus, the Tibetans being mostly of Turanian stock. See EVEREST, MOUNT.

HIMERA (37° 58′ N., 13° 40′ E.), ancient town, Sicily, modern Thermae Himeraeae; ruined by Hannibal, 409 B.C.

HIMERIUS (315-86), Gk. philosopher; studied at Athens, wrote many speeches; his writings suffer from the over-elaboration fashionable in his day.

HINCKLEY (52° 33′ N., 1° 23′ W.), town, Leicestershire, England.

HINCMAR (c. 805-82), abp. of Reims, came to court of Louis the Pious, 844; abp., 845; had heresy of Gottschalk condemned; attacked Lothair II. of Lorraine for divorcing his queen; had various conflicts with other ecclesiastics and with Pop John VIII. over his metropolitan rights; wrote life of St. Remigius.

HINDENBURG, PAUL VON (1847-1934), Ger. soldier and president; b. Posen, E. Prussia; ed. in Junker atmosphere; served as lieutenant in the Austrian campaign, 1866; and decorated for valor in his first battle. In Franco-German War present at St. Privat, Sedan, and siege of Paris. Subsequently transferred to general staff, 1878; specialized on topography of E. Prussia, and acquired an unrivalled knowledge of its strategical features; strongly opposed the scheme for draining the region, conceiving that its swamps and lakes formed defensive zone. After commanding the two E. Prussian army corps at Königsberg and Allenstein, retired, 1911. On Aug. 22, 1914, when Russian invasion of E. Prussia reached its high-water mark, he was appointed to the command of an army for the reconquest of the country, with Ludendorff as chief of staff. In a week he had effected a complete change in the situation. At the battle of Tannenberg or Osterode (Aug. 26-31), by a bold and hazardous strategy, he won a complete and decisive victory. At once he became a popular idol, and on Sept. 25 was given the rank of field-marshal, and placed in chief command of the Austro-German forces on entire Eastern front. In Jan. 1915 he struck in the direction of Warsaw, and twice subsequently attempted to take the city, but failed. It was occupied in May, 1915, and the Russians were driven back to the Pripet marshes, but no military decision was reached. His spectacular advances gave frenzied delight to the Ger. people; honors were showered upon him, and it was accounted a pious act to drive nails of homage into his wooden effigy in Berlin. The square-headed, heavy-jawed Prussian became a subject of legend and an object of worship. In Aug. 1916 he was appointed chief of the general staff in succession to Falkenhayn, whose plans at Verdun and in the Trentino had failed. He brought with him his faithful lieutenant, Ludendorff. Nothing, however, was accomplished in the West, and the Somme battles forced the Germans to retreat to the much-vaunted 'Hindenburg Line,' which was to be the *ne plus ultra* of Allied advance. On Oct. 3 he embodied the views of G.H.Q. in a statement advising that the war should be brought to a close. After the Armistice he retained his chief command until June, 1919. In the following July he wrote to Marshal Foch offering himself as a sacrifice for the ex-Kaiser. In Nov. he gave evidence as to the responsibility for the war before the Reichstag Committee. More than once he intervened as the defender of Ludendorff, who had incurred marked unpopularity. His work, *Out of My Life*, appeared in April, 1920, his argument being that at the end of 1916 Ger. military fortunes were almost at their lowest ebb, and he and Ludendorff were called in too late to repair the mistakes that had been made; he considers that Germany lost the war, not by the enemy's skill and bravery, but by the outbreak of revolution at home, due to the failure of the political rulers. In 1923 he made speeches in which he favored the restoration of the monarchy. See WORLD WAR. Elected 2nd. President of German Republic to succeed Friedrich Ebert (1925). Although regarded as a Monarchist, he did much to bring about the common welfare of the German People, turning the extreme Nationalists against him but winning the support of the Liberal groups which favored a Republic rather than a Monarchy. It was thought in 1933 that he would resign in favor of Adolf Hitler (q. v.) leader of the powerful Nazi Party. While he did not resign, ill health and advancing age forced him gradually to relinquish his actual power to the younger and more radical Hitler to whom Hindenberg was finally forced to yield after some friction.

HINDU KUSH (35° 50′ N., 70° 30′ E.), range of mountains in Central Asia, stretching from Pamirs to Koh-i-Baba Mts. at Bamian Pass, c. 500 miles long; forms S. boundary of Afghanistan, and for some distance separates Badakhshan from Kafiristan and divides Kabul and Oxus basins. Contains sources of many important rivers; mts. crossed by many passes, most important being Khawak, leading from Badakhshan to Charikar and Kabul; Dorah, conducting to Chitral valley from Oxus; Barroghil, leading from Chi-

—By Burton Holmes, from Ewing Galloway, N. Y.

ABOVE THIS GATEWAY, IN FRENCH INDO-CHINA, ARE THE FOUR FACES OF BRAHMA, THE SUPREME HINDU DEITY.

tral and Kashmir to Upper Oxus and Yarkand; Lowarai, between valleys of Panjkora and Chitral.

HINDUISM, the name used for the religion of more than two hundred millions of the peoples of India. Hindus do not form one ecclesiastical organization, nor do they all hold one creed. Yet this congeries of peoples is more or less loosely united by certain principles which are common to them all: (1) a rigid and elaborate *caste* system—so different from anything in Western religion; (2) a pessimistic view of life which makes it something on the whole evil, and is involved with the specially Oriental doctrine of reincarnation. The origin of H. dates back to before 1000 B.C., when the Aryan tribes invading from the N. were conquering the Dravidians of India. There was some intermingling of conquerors and conquered, but not enough to prevent a rigid caste system; the conquered people were secluded not only from social but from religious privileges. The primitive Vedic religion of the Aryan conquerors had many gods, but no elaborate worship. By about 800 B. C. the class of priests was developing into the Brahman caste. Four castes were evolved—the *Brahmans*, *Kshatriyas* (warriors), *Vaisyas* (traders), and *Sudras* (serfs). Not only does caste involve something of what we mean by "class distinctions," but a Brahman might not eat food prepared by any one but a Brahman. Certain trades became hereditary in certain castes, and those born into them had to remain at them. At the same time ritual became much more elaborate, and Brahmanism as a religion tended to be crushed under a weight of ritual.

HINDUR, NALAGARH (31° 6′ N., 76° 40′ E.), state, Punjab, India. Area, 2505 sq. miles.

HINDUSTAN, OR HINDOSTAN, means the "country of the Hindus." The Persians used to call the R. Sindhu "Hindhu," and that part of the district was therefore called H. The region denoted was gradually extended, until the whole tract of country between the Himalaya Mts. and the Vindhya Mts., W. of Bengal, was so designated. In many instances even H. was used as a synonym for India, but in this sense it is not now used, and in a more restricted sense is less often employed.

HINDUSTANI. See INDIA.

HINES, WALKER DOWNER (1870), lawyer; *b.* at Russelville, Ky. Bachelor of Science of Ogden College, 1888, and in 1893, Bachelor of Laws of University of Virginia. Has been assistant attorney, assistant chief attorney, and first vice-president from 1893-1904 of Louisville and Nashville Railroads. 1904-1906 member of law firm in Louis-Ky. 1906-1918 general counsel of Atchison, Topeka and Sante Fe Railway, 1916-1918 chairman of board of directors. Chairman of the executive committee, 1908-1916. Director general of railroads, 1919-1920. Law practice in New York since October, 1927.

HINGANGHAT (20° 33′ N., 78° 53′ E.), town, Central Provinces, India.

HINGHAM, a town of Massachusetts, in Plymouth co. It is on the New York, New Haven and Hartford Railroad, and on Massachusetts Bay. It has steamship connection with New York and is a favorite summer resort. It has great historical interest and contains the oldest "meeting house" in New England, which was first occupied in 1682. It is the seat of Derby Academy. It has a high school and a public library. The fishing interests are important.

HINTERLAND, Ger. name for tract beyond district occupied by a colony, but claimed by the colony as territory which they will require for expansion.

HIOGO, HYOKO (34° 48′ N., 135° 14′ E.), town, Japan; has colossal statue of Buddha and temples; ship-building; textile manufactures.

HIONG-NU, people who had a vast empire N. of China in the Early Christian era; possibly Turks.

HIP, part of the human body called the haunch in cattle, being connection of legs and body; architect term for meeting-place of sloping sides of roof, the finial on which is called the Hip-knob.

HIP-JOINT DISEASE. See JOINT. TUBERCULOSIS.

HIPPARCHUS (190-120 B.C.), Gk. astronomer; invented trigonometry; discovered precession of equinoxes; measured sun's distance from earth.

HIPPEASTRUM, a genus of plants, natural order *Amaryllidaceoe.* It comprises fifty species of showy tropical bulbous plants w i t h funnel-shaped flowers.

HIPPIAS OF ELIS (V. cent. B.C.), Gk. sophist, a rival of Protagoras; figures in Plato's *Hippias major* and *minor.*

HIPPOCRAS, old medicinal cordial composed of wine mixed with sugar and cinnamon, ginger, or other spices, and strained.

HIPPOCRATES (V. cent. B.C.), Gk. philosopher and physician; a descendant of Æsculapius; *b.* at Cos, 460 B.C.; called 'Father of Medicine,' and first to treat it scientifically; a firm believer in recuperative force of nature, which he endeavored to stimulate and direct;wrote *Prognostics, Epidemics, Aphorisms.*

HIPPOCRENE (Gk. *hippou krene,* spring of the horse), fountain on Helicon supposed to have been formed by stroke of Pegasus's hoof; sacred to the Muses and source of inspiration to poets.

HIPPODAMUS OF MILETUS (fl. V. cent. B.C.), Gk. architect employed by Pericles at Athens.

HIPPODROME (Gk. *hippos,* horse; *dromos,* racecourse), Gk. racecourse, oblong, with semicircular end. The name is given to a famous place of entertainment in New York City.

HIPPOLYTA (classical myth.), queen of Amazons; slain by Hercules; another version makes her marry Theseus, who conquered her forces in Attica.

HIPPOLYTUS (*b.* II. cent.), presbyter of Rom. Church under bp. Zephyrinus; quarrelled with Calixtus I.; martyred in persecution, *c.* 235; wrote numerous works, but all attributed to him are probably not his; some exist in translations only.

HIPPOLYTUS (classical myth.), *s.* of Theseus, king of Athens, by Antiope or Hippolyta, the Amazon queen. His stepmother, Phaedra, conceived a passion for him, but, her advances being rejected, she accused him to her husband of having violated her chastity. Theseus

laid a curse upon him, and he met with a violent end; but was restored to life by Æsculapius.

HIPPOLYTUS, CANONS OF, a work preserved only in an Arabic trans. of a Coptic trans. of the original Gk., written in the name of H., and dealing with Church order, ordination, sacraments, prayer, almsgiving, etc.; date and authorship are uncertain, but it probably appeared in Egypt in the IV. cent. Its exact connection with the *Egyptian Church Order, Apostolic Constitutions,* and *Testament of the Lord,* with which it undoubtedly has some relation, is a complicated literary problem. Probably the canons and the Egyptian Order are derived from the same source.

HIPPONAX (VI. cent. B.C.), Gk. satirical poet; inventor of parody and the choliambus metre.

HIPPOPOTAMUS (Gk. for river-horse), the sole member of a family of artiodactyle ungulate mammals. To-day it is found only in Africa, but fossils of a larger breed of hippopotami have been found in England, the rest of Europe, and in India, etc. The common species, *H. amphibius,* inhabits rivers in all parts of Africa, but the smaller, *H. liberiensis,* is restricted to the W. of that continent. In size of H. is only a little inferior to the elephant; its legs are very stunted, so that its belly touches the ground when it walks on mud or other yielding surfaces; there is often as much as 2 in. of skin on the back and flanks, but no hair covers its dark brown hide; its small eyes are set high in the huge, ungainly head with its great snout and enormous rounded muzzle; the tail is quite short, and on each foot there are four even and hoofed toes. The animal is aquatic, nocturnal, and voracious. It is a good swimmer and diver, and as its respiration is slow, it can stay a long while under water. By day it is sleepy and languid, but by night it often comes out of the water to graze on the banks, or if it lives in a cultivated region, it will make substantial inroads into crops and cause terrible destruction. It is this bad habit which accounts for its disappearance from the fertile plains of the lower Nile. It is gregarious by nature and usually playful and good-tempered, but persistent pursuit often provokes a dangerous passion. When angered it emits a loud and piercing noise, which has been likened to the grating sound of a creaking door. Hunters chase it in a variety of ways, sometimes it is ensnared in pits, sometimes it is shot, harpooned, or pierced with spears from a canoe. The teeth are valuable as ivory, the tongue, the fat, and the jelly from the feet are favorite articles of diet, whilst the hides find many markets.

HIRAM COLLEGE, a co-educational establishment situated in Hiram, Ohio, originally known as the Eclectic Institute, founded by the Christian Church in 1850. It was incorporated as a college in 1870. It has women's dormitories, laboratories, a museum and a gymnasium. In 1932 there were 376 students and 33 teachers under the direction of K. I. Brown.

In 1934, officials of Hiram college announced plans for a new experiment in collegiate education. Briefly, the plan enabled the student to devote more time to one subject at a time rather than dividing a shorter period among many subjects.

HIROHITO (1901-), Emperor of Japan, succeeded to throne 1926, son of the Emperor Yoshohito laid stress when ascending the throne on peace and harmony at home and abroad.

HIROSHIGE, adopted name of three Japanese artists of XIX. cent. whose prints are much valued. See ARTHUR MORRISON's *The Painters of Japan.*

HIROSHIMA (34° 21′ N.; 132° 33′ E.), port, Nippon, Japan.

HIRSAU (48° 43′ N.; 8° 43′ E.), village, Württemberg, Germany; formerly site of celebrated Benedictine monastery, of which beautiful ruins remain.

HIRSCH, MAURICE DE, BARON (1831-96), Jewish capitalist and philanthropist; devoted much time and money to schemes for bettering condition of Jews; endowed the *Alliance Israelite Universelle,* 1889; gave $2,500,000 for establishment of schools in Galicia and Bukowina; founded Jewish Colonization Association, to benefit persecuted Jews.

HIRSCHBERG, a town 1120 ft. above the sea-level, 48 m. S.E. of Görlitz, and connected by rail with Glatz, Schmiedeberg and Grünthal, in Silesia, Prussia. Situated at the meeting of the Bober and Zacken rivers, it is especially noted for its beautiful surroundings, but its commerce is both varied and considerable.

HISGEN, THOMAS LEWIS (1852-), an American manufacturer and politician, *b.* in Petersburg, Ind. In 1908 he was candidate of the Independent party for president of the United States.

HISPELLUM, Ital. colony founded by Augustus; called Flavia Constans by Constantine; now *Spello*; important ruins.

HISSAR (38° N. 69° E.), district, Central Asia, between Oxus on S. and Hissar Mts. on N. Chief towns, Hissar and Kabadian. Soil fertile; rice and flax main products; towns celebrated for damascened swords and silks.

HISSAR (29° 9′ N., 75° 44′ E.), capital, H. district, Punjab, India; horse and cattle fairs. H. district has area *c.* 5000 miles.

HISTIÆUS (*d.* 494 B.C.), tyrant of Miletus, who at first Medised, but afterwards led the fruitless Ionian revolt against Darius; was captured and crucified.

HISTOLOGY, the study of microscopic physiology, dealing with cells and tissues of living things. See CELL, CYTOLOGY.

HISTORICAL SOCIETY, AMERICAN. An association of students and historical writers founded at Saratoga, New York, in September, 1884, with 50 members, now 2,500. The society aims to promote and encourage historical investigation, and its many publications cover a wide field of historical study. The American Society of Church History merged with it in 1896 as the Church History section, but in 1904 separated and became an independent body again. Among the principal committees are those on Historical Manuscripts and Public Archives. Annual meetings are held, and annual reports are issued through the Smithsonian Institute. Among the society's important publications are reprints of *Original Narratives of American History* (20 vols.); *The Study of History in Schools,* etc. The official organ of the society is The American Historical Review, a quarterly.

HISTORY is both the biography and unwritten events of the life of the human race. The beginnings of history are to be seen in the rude weapons, bones, and barrows left by what used to be called 'prehistoric' man. It is impossible to decide how far back into this early period the myths and sagas go, and how far these are inventions, how far glorifications of actual events. Niebuhr's *Romische Geschichte* 1812-32, first turned attention to their possibly historical nature, and much history has since been read into the story of Romulus and myths in general. The reverse of the process which turned heroes into supernatural beings is also seen; the Wade, who is the hero of some parts of the Eng. countryside, and is treated by Scott and others as a mediaeval personage, is possibly Woden. The point is that history, even in the old-fashioned sense, may begin with Eolithic man.

Before the first Egyptian dynasty, dated by Mariette from 5004 B.C., there is a tradition of nearly 20,000 years of rule of gods, demi-gods, and shades. With the Memphite dynasties (*c.* 4000 B.C.) Egyptian monumental history begins, and papyri, our first-written records, are found in the tombs. Inscriptions were for long the only history; among them are the cuneiform writings of Assyria, perhaps contemporary with first Egyptian papyri; they recorded important events, names of rulers, etc.; similar but fuller accounts (*Annales*) of events of the years were afterwards kept by the Romans. The Greeks never cleared their early history from its encumbrance of myth. though sceptics arose like Hecataeus of Miletus (6th cent. B.C.), and in Greece itself in age of Pericles; but Thucydides, Xenophon, and afterwards Polybius definitely set before themselves the ideal of historical veracity.

History through Gr. example has, from Roman times to the present day, been taken to be an account of events truthfully but elegantly narrated; sometimes accuracy has impinged on elegance, sometimes everything is sacrificed to the love of literary effect; sometimes scrupulous intention of accuracy is to be found in masterpieces of style, as in Thucydides, Tacitus, Brantôme, Gibbon, Macaulay, and, as many people now think, Froude. The acceptance of Christianity had as enormous an effect on historical perspective and on the growth of the spirit of historical citicism as it had on history, and a similar remark may be made about the Reformation. Discussion of questions, still unsettled, as to usages of early church trained men's minds to consider historical evidence, and from that time critical attention has been given to the past. The Fr. house of St. Maur started, in 17th cent., the work of editing texts which is now being unintermittently carried out by Record Commissions and private initiative in every modern country. The importance of the research element in modern history writing has led to system of specialists on minute points. The bibliography of history is a wide subject in itself.

HISTORY, ANCIENT. See ANCIENT HISTORY.

HIT (33° 39′ N., 42° 50′ E.), town, Turkey-in-Asia; produces naphtha, bitumen.

HITA, GINÉS PEREZ DE (*c.* 1540-*c.* 1604), Span. author; wrote well-known romance, *Guerras civiles de Granada.*

HITCHCOCK, CHARLES HENRY (1836-1919), geologist; *b.* Amherst, Mass. After his graduation from Amherst College in 1856, he became assistant State geologist of Vermont, 1857-61; State geologist of Maine, 1861-2; and of New Hampshire, 1868-78. From 1868 to 1908 he served as professor of geology at Dartmouth College. He compiled many geological maps and was a founder of the Geological Society of America.

HITCHCOCK, ETHAN ALLEN (1798-1870), major-general; *b.* Vergennes, Vt.; *d.* Sparta, Ga.; *g.s.* of Ethan Allen. He entered the artillery in 1817 as a third lieutenant upon graduating from West Point and commanded the corps of cadets from 1829 to 1833. He saw service in Florida against the Indians and in the war in Mexico, when he reached the ranks of colonel and brigadier-general. After retiring from the army he was gazetted major general of volunteers. He was interested in alchemy, Swedenborg and Dante, and published works on these subjects.

HITCHCOCK, ETHAN ALLEN (1835-1909), U. S. ambassador; *b.* Mobile, Ala.; *d.* Washington, D. C. After engaging in business in St. Louis, Mo., and in China, and serving later as president of a number of manufacturing, mining and railway companies, he was appointed by President McKinley as envoy to Russia, 1897. The Russian legation being raised to an embassy the following year, he became the first American Ambassador to the Czar's court, but soon returned to the United States to join the Cabinet as Secretary of the Interior, a post he held through the McKinley and Roosevelt administrations till 1907.

HITCHCOCK, FRANK HARRIS (1867), lawyer; *b.* Amherst, O. He graduated from Harvard in 1891 and proceeded to study law in Washington, D.C. where he was admitted to the bar three years later. Entering the government service, he became chief of the foreign markets division of the Department of Agriculture, chief clerk of the Department of Commerce and Labor, first assistant Postmaster General, and 1909-13, Postmaster General. During his direction of the Post Office the parcel post and postal savings banks were established. In 1908 he was chairman of the National Republican Committee and managed the Taft presidential campaign of that year; also the campaign for the nomination of Charles E. Hughes for President in 1916. In 1913 he resumed the practice of law in N.Y. City. Established first air mail service.

**HITCHCOCK, GILBERT MON-
ELL** (1859), statesman and publisher; *b.* Omaha, Neb. He received his
education in his native city and in
Baden-Baden, Germany, later studying law and obtaining the LL.B. degree of the University of Michigan.
He practiced in Omaha from 1881 to
1885, when he entered journalism by
establishing the Omaha Evening
World. Acquiring the Omaha Morning Herald in 1889, he combined the
two journals as the World-Herald
and became notable as its publisher.
He served three terms in the lower
house of Congress between 1903 and
1911 as a Democrat, and in the latter year was elected to the Senate,
where he remained until 1923, having
been defeated for re-election. After
the World War he was President
Wilson's chief spokesman during the
heated debates on the League of Nations (*q. v.*) in the Senate in a vain
effort to obtain the assent of the Republican majority of that chamber
to American participation in the
League's functions.

HITCHCOCK, RAYMOND, (1870-
1929) American actor and comedian.
b. Auburn, N. Y. He made his first
stage appearance in 1890 and had his
first leading part at the Tremont
Theatre in Boston, Mass. in 1903.
Visited England in 1916 and again
in 1919 with successful shows (Mr.
Manhattan & Hullo America); appeared also in "The Old Soak," "The
Caliph," "Ritz Revue" and "The
Beau's Stratagem," (1928).

**HITCHCOCK, ROSWELL
DWIGHT** (1817-1887), theologian;
b. East Machias, Me.; *d.* Somerset,
Mass. He graduated from the Amherst Thoelogical Seminary in 1848,
and later studied in Halle and Berlin. After serving as pastor of an
Exeter (N. H.) Congregational
Church, 1845-52, he became professor of revealed religion at Bowdoin
College and 1855, professor of
church history at the Union Theological Seminary, of which institution he was appointed president in
1880. He was an editor of the
American Theological Review and
wrote an analysis of the Bible.

HITLER, ADOLPH, (1889-   ),

Chancellor of the German Reich
(1933-   ), and leader of largest
political party in Germany, the Na-
zis. Born in Braunau, Austria, of
lower middle class parents, he lost
his citizenship when he enlisted in
the German army during the W.
War, and for a number of years was
refused citizenship by Germany thus
literally becoming a man without a
country. It was not until the beginning of 1932, upon taking the oath
of office as an attache of the legation of the State of Brunswick at
Berlin that he automatically became
a German citizen.

Although his name is synonomous
with the name of the party of which
he is absolute leader, Hitler did not
found the Nazi Party. In 1919, out of
curiosity, he attended a Nazi meet-
ng in Munich. Always dramatic and
with an eye to theatrical effect, Hitler leaped to his feet during the
meeting and made a speech. His
bombastic oratory soon placed him
at the head of the group and from
leader of a local unit of a national
party, he sprang to international
prominence almost overnight as the
one dominating force in German politics. Under his direction the number of men who wear the brown shirt
and swastika armband grew from
20,000 to more than 10,000,000 with
new recruits flocking daily under his
banner.

The son of a minor customs official on the Austro-German frontier,
Hitler was sent to the Realschule at
Linz by his father who wished him
to follow in his footsteps but so
whole-heartedly was he opposed to
entering the services of the Austrian
government that he purposely failed
in his examinations, declaring he was
a German Nationalist at heart. From
Linz he went to Vienna where he
worked as a carpenter for five years,
leaving there in 1912 for Munich in
order to escape military service with
the Austrian army. Two years later,
at the outbreak of the W. War, he
joined the German army and served
as a dispatch runner. At the end
of the war, he returned to Munich
where he soon became the leader of
the National Socialist German Labor

(Nazi) Party. In 1923, assisted by Gen. Erich von Ludendorf, he organized, in Munich, the revolt known as the Hitler "putsch" which was quelled in 48 hours. Hitler was arrested and sentenced to five years in prison but was released a year later, immediately resuming his Nazi activities. His dynamic energy and oratorical fervor soon rallied millions to his cause and although his magnetism drew young and old alike under his spell, it was to the young people, those who knew nothing of the horrors of war whom he lashed into a frenzy to be of service to the Fatherland. His main strength was in the rural districts among the lower classes who were hypnotized by his easy flow of words. It was the peasant, chiefly, who looked upon him as the man who could free Germany from internal depression and the yoke of foreign powers. His extreme anti-Semitic activities resulted only in an almost universal boycott of German goods by Jews the world over. So radical and frenzied did anti-Jewish feeling become in Germany under his lash that men such as Albert Einstein, Ludwig Lewissohn and many others, men of science and letters with no interest whatsoever in politics, were forced to flee their native land because of unjust persecution, leaving their property behind to be confiscated under one flimsy excuse or another. Stores owned and operated by Jews were boycotted. In the summer of 1933 Nazi guards stood in front of Jewish stores shouting that the owner was Jewish and not to patronize him.

Seeking complete mastery for himself and the Nazi party in 1932, Hitler ran for president of the German Republic but was defeated, much to his frank surprise, by Von Hindenburg by a majority of 2,000,-000 votes. As leader of the largest party in the Reichstag, he was invited by Von Hindenburg to form a majority government but so many conditions and provisos were attached to the offer that Hitler found it impossible to get sufficient support from his party in the Reichstag and was forced to decline. Von Schleicher was then given the Chancellorship but his government was short lived and two days after its collapse, Hitler became Chancellor. On the death of Von Hindenburg, he assumed the newly-created "Reichsfuhrerschaft." (See Germany).

HITTITES. The origin of the race is uncertain; described as living at Hebron; mentioned among the founders of Jerusalem; spoken of as a northern people, and as also inhabiting the s. They probably came from Cappadocia and poured into Palestine, where to a large extent they lost their racial individuality by inter-marriage with Semitic people and by adopting the Babylonian religian and customs. The Egyptian and Assyrian monuments and the cuneiform inscription of Van in Armenia have yielded much information; excavations at several centers in Asia Minor, the Tell-el-Amarna letters, and the archives of the Hatti kings have also proved invaluable aids to the study of the race.

HIVITES, people of Palestine mentioned in the Bible; expelled by the Jews (*Exodus* 3₈).

HLOTHHERE, king of Kent (673-85); slain in battle by his nephew Eadric.

HOACTZIN, OR HOATZIN (*Opisthocomus hoazin*), an interesting S. American bird, smaller than a pheasant, olive colored, varied with white, with yellow crest. The young have a remarkable habit of climbing by means of claws on each wing. Anatomically peculiar, it is probably a survival of a primitive type.

HOADLY, BENJAMIN (1676-1761), Eng. bp., author of controversial works on relation of Church and State; himself latitudinarian, he hotly disputed with High Churchmen; successively bp. of Bangor, Hereford, Salisbury, and Winchester; in 1717 preached before king sermon on kingdom of Christ, the power of the Church, which gave rise to *Bangorian Controversy.*

HOANG HO, HWANG HO, YELLOW RIVER (37° 30′ N., 118° 29′ E.), one of the principal rivers of

China; rises in the mountains of Tibet, and flowing N. E. traverses N. W. part of China and part of Mongolia; re-enters China, flowing S., E., and N.E.; enters Gulf of Pechi-li; length, 2500 miles; liable to floods.

Concord, Mass.; *d.* Worcester, Mass. He studied law at Harvard, after graduating from that university in 1846 and practiced in Worcester, Mass. Drawn into politics, he early became identified with the Free Soil

CHINESE RIVER DWELLINGS ON THE YELLOW RIVER

HOAR, EBENEZER ROCKWOOD (1816-1895), jurist and U. S. Attorney General; *b.* Concord, Mass.; *d.* there; *b.* of Geo. Frisbie Hoar (*q.v.*). He graduated from Harvard in 1838 and later practiced law. In 1849 he became judge of the Massachusetts Court of Common Pleas and judge of the State Supreme Court ten years later. He joined the national administration in 1869 as Attorney General. In 1873-75 he served on the Joint High Commission that framed the Treaty of Washington.

HOAR, GEORGE FRISBIE (1826-1904), U. S. Senator and lawyer; *b.*

party as a Republican. Between 1852 and 1857 he served in the Massachusetts legislature as assemblyman and senator, and in 1860 was city solicitor. In 1869 began his long service of 35 years in the national legislature. He served in the House of Representatives as a member for Massachusetts during four successive Congresses and in 1877 was elected to the Senate, retaining membership in that body till his death. He was a leading figure at a number of National Republican Conventions and served on the Electoral Commission which decided the Hayes-Tilden presidential contest in 1876. As a strong anti-imperialist, he stoutly opposed McKinley's policy in the Philippines. He challenged the right of the United States to retain the islands and demanded that they be returned to the Filipinos and protected from foreign interference. His scholarship was wide and embraced the sciences, classics, history and archaeology. In 1903 appeared his Autobiography of Seventy Years.

HOBART (42° 56′ S., 147° 21′ E.), capital, Tasmania; fine harbor; has two cathedrals, Parliament Houses, Government House; iron foundries, breweries.

HOBART, GARRET AUGUSTUS (1844-99), American lawyer and vice-president; b. Long Branch, N. J. He graduated at Rutgers College in 1863, and three years later was admitted to the bar. He settled at Paterson, N. J., where he built up a large practice. He held a number of local offices and served in the State Assembly (1873-78) and the State Senate 1879-85. He soon became nationally known, and in 1896 was elected vice-president of the United States on the ticket with President McKinley. His judgment was mature, his views conservative, and he was a figure of pronounced importance in Republican councils.

HOBART, GEORGE VERE (1867), author, playwright; b. at Cape Breton, Nova Scotia. Educated in Nova Scotia, 1895, managing editor of Sunday Scimitar, Cumberland Maryland, Special humorous writer on Baltimore American; sporting editor, Baltimore News. For fourteen years wrote the 'Dinkelspiel' papers on Baltimore News of which he was originator. Author of: The John Henry Books (series of comic stories in fifteen voumes), six books of comedy, Li'L Verses for Li'l Fellers (poems for children). Wrote and re-wrote comic operas, several farces and musical comedies. Co-author of drama Wildfire and Our Mrs. McChesney written for Ethel Barrymore. Author of Idle Moments in Florida, 1921. Most successful play was Experience. d. 1926.

HOBART COLLEGE, an institution of higher learning situated at Geneva, N.Y., conducted under the auspices of the Episcopal church. It had its beginnings in a theological school founded in 1813 by Trinity Church, New York City, and located at Fairfield, N. Y. In 1821 the school was removed to Geneva, where it was chartered as Geneva College. It became Hobart College in 1860 in honor of Bishop Hobart of New York, who was one of its founders and, as rector of

Trinity, obtained increased grants from that church for its support. It has a co-ordinate college for women, known as William Smith College, opened in 1908. The students in 1932 numbered 319 and the teaching staff 44 under the presidency of M. Bartlett.

HOBBEMA, MEYNDERT (c. 1638-1709), famous Dutch landscape painter; lived and died in poverty and obscurity; made unsurpassed studies of sober and peaceful landscapes, perfect in their kind; widely different manner from that of his contemporary Ruysdael, but their works often confused through dealers forging signatures.

HOBBES, THOMAS (1588-1679), Eng. philosopher; b. Malmesbury; ed. at Magdalen Hall, Oxford, and in 1608 became tutor to the s. of William Cavendish, 2nd Earl of Devonshire, remaining with this family, except for two short intervals, for the rest of his life. He travelled abroad with his pupil, who became an intimate personal friend. H. became imbued with the scientific rather than the philosophic spirit of his day. He then devoted himself to the study of the classics. Cavendish d. in 1628, and H. became tutor to the s. of Sir Gervase Clifton, 1629, then to the Earl of Devonshire, s. of his former pupil, 1631. About this time he began to devote himself to philosophy. The years 1640-51 he spent abroad. The idea of his great book, Leviathan, was forming in his mind, and he devoted most of his attention to it. His ideas were certainly affected by the civil strife of the time. The Leviathan was a great monster made up of a mass of human beings. While he anticipated later thinkers in believing that government was for the benefit of the people as a whole, he believed that the civil power residing in the people was absolute, and that no internal organisations which might conflict with it should be allowed to exist. In 1666 some believed that his 'atheistic' teaching had provoked the wrath of Heaven in the shape of the great plague, and H. was alarmed lest he might be tried for heresy. However, the king protected him, but H. was obliged to get his books printed out of England. His reputation abroad was very great. He worked on at translating Homer and other things till near the end, dying aged ninety-one. He has left the mark of his work on many subjects; in mathematics only was he thoroughly unsuccessful. He laid the foundation on which political philosophers of the XIX. cent. were to build.

HOBBY.—(1) hob or hobgoblin; (2) a slow and steady horse; (3) an occupation followed as a pastime. Classical examples of riding a h. are to be found in Sterne's *Tristram Shandy.*

HOBOKEN, a city of New Jersey, in Hudson co. It is on the Lackawanna, the West Shore, and the Lehigh Valley railroads, and on the Hudson River, opposite New York City, with which it is connected by ferries and by tubes. It has an extensive system of docks and is the terminal for several important European steamship lines. Its manufactures are of considerable importance and embraces a great diversity. It is the seat of Stevens Institute of Technology and other institutions. There are also several private preparatory schools, national banks, daily and weekly newspapers.

HOBOKEN (51° 11′ N., 4° 21′ E.) town, Belgium.

HOBSON, RICHMOND PEARSON (1870), American naval officer and author; *b.* Greensboro, Ala. He graduated at the United States Naval Academy in 1889 and later pursued studies in naval engineering and construction in Paris. He served in the navy on several cruises, but most of the time was assigned to land duty as superintendent of fleet construction. In the Spanish-American war he leaped into prominence as a national hero because of his daring in sinking the collier Merrimac across the entrance of Santiago Harbor, Cuba, with the design of blocking the exit of Cervera's fleet. While this end was not gained, the heroism of the exploit stirred the popular imagination and elicited the admiration even of the enemy. He resigned from the navy in 1904; was elected to Congress in 1907 and re-elected for the three following terms. He has lectured widely and written extensively on naval subjects. He has been an active advocate of national prohibition. His publications include *Why America Should Hold Naval Supremacy,* 1903; *Diplomacy and the Fleet,* 1908, *In Line of Duty,* 1909; *Fortification of the Panama Canal,* 1911; *Our Country's Destiny,* 1913, *America and the World War,* 1917; *The Great Reform,* 1918; *Alcohol and the Human Race,* 1919. In 1921 he organized the Amer. Alcohol Education Assoc. Pres. World Narcotic Def. Asso., 1927.

HOBSON'S CHOICE, phrase derived from Thomas Hobson (*c.* 1544-1630), the Cambridge carrier, commemorated by Milton. He insisted on horses being taken from his stable only in their regular turn—hence meaning, 'this or none.'

HOCHE, LAZARE (1768-97), Fr. soldier; commanded army of Moselle against Austrians, whom he defeated at Weissenburg; ended Vendée insurrection

and defeated Royalists at Quiberon and Penthiévre, 1795; obtained command of Sambre and Meuse force, 1796, and routed Austrians at Neuwied; War Minister, 1797; *d.* at Wetzlar.

HOCHST (50° 7′ N., 8° 30′ E.); town, Hesse-Nassau, Germany; machinery, dyes.

HOCKEY, a game which has its origin in Scotland, where it is known as shinty. The game as it is known in the United States, however, is known as ice hocking and is played almost entirely on the ice. It was introduced into the United States from Canada in 1894. It has become very popular. It is played with a vulcanized rubber disc known as the puck, which is advanced by lifting or pushing with hockey sticks about 4 feet long, terminating in a curved end. The object of the game is to drive the puck into the opponent's goal which counts as one goal. The goals are pockets of netting extending back from posts and are 6 feet wide and 4 feet high. The players number 7, which consist of 4 forwards and three for defense. Nearly all American colleges in the northern latitudes maintain hockey teams and play for records and championship during the winter.

HOCKING, JOSEPH (1855), English novelist; land surveyor, 1878; he entered ministry of United Methodist Free Church, 1884; Author of: *Zillah,* 1892; *All Men are Liars,* 1895; *And Shall Trelawney Die?,* 1897; *The Day of Judgment,* 1915; *The Path of Glory,* 1917; *Price of a Throne,* 1918; *Everlasting Arms,* 1920; *The Mystery Man,* 1930.

HOCKING, SILAS KITTO (1850), Eng. novelist; minister of the United Methodist Free Church from 1870 to 1896; devoted himself to literature; has written some sixty novels, among which are *Her Benny,* 1879; *God's Outcast,* 1898; *The Beautiful Alien,* 1916; *His Own Accuser,* 1917; *Watchers in the Dawn,* 1920.

HOCUS, OR HOCUS POCUS, a supposed corruption of *Hoc est corpus* used by priests in the Mass; was used (*temp.* James I.) as a cant-term for a juggler's trick. Its later meaning refers to a hoax with criminal intent.

HODEDA (14° 36′ N., 43° 4′ E.), fortified town, Arabia; exports coffee, grain.

HODGE, CHARLES (1797-1878), Amer. Presbyterian divine; studied in America and at Paris, Halle, and Berlin; prof. at Princeton Theological Seminary.

HODGES, GEORGE (1856-1919),

Episcopal theologian; *b.* Rome, N. Y. He graduated in divinity from the Berkeley Divinity School, Conn., in 1881, when he became assistant rector and rector of the Calvary Church, Pittsburgh, Pa. In 1894 he resigned the rectorship on his appointment as dean of the Episcopal Theological School, Cambridge, Mass. He was prominent as a Low Broad churchman and the author of a number of religious works.

HODGSON, BRIAN HOUGHTON (1800-94), Eng. administrator; Orientalist and naturalist; spent many years in the East Indian service, and was a noted authority on Buddhism and natural history; pub. *Literature and Religion of Buddhists*, 1841.

HODMEZO-VASARHELY (46° 27' N., 20° 20' E.), town, Hungary.

HODOGRAPH, curve obtained by joining ends of lines drawn from any point parallel and proportional to the velocity of a moving particle.

HODSON, WILLIAM STEPHEN RAIKES (1821-58), Brit. soldier; served against Sikhs; accused of misuse of regimental money, 1855; at outbreak of Indian Mutiny raised regiment of irregular horse, known as H.'s Horse; greatly distinguished himself during war, and at fall of Delhi took the old emperor prisoner and slew his sons; killed during attack on Lucknow.

HOE, ancient gardening tool, useful for making holes for planting; in XVII. cent. many h's commenced to be united in a Horse Hoe (grubber) for breaking up ground in fields.

HOE, RICHARD MARSH (1812-1866), inventor; *b.* New York; *d.* Florence, Italy. In association with his *b.* Peter S. Hoe, he developed printing machinery which revolutionized the methods of newspaper publication, beginning in 1846 with a rotary printing device known as 'Hoe's lightning press'. This was displaced by the web-perfecting press, which enabled printing to be done on both sides of the sheet and also provided cutting and folding mechanism. He was the *s.* of Robert Hoe, the inventor of the original Hoe printing press, an Englishman who came to the United States in 1813.

HOF.—(1) (50° 19' N., 11° 54' E.), town, Bavaria, Germany; manufactures textiles. (2) (60° 34' N., 11° 59' E.), town, Hedemarken, Norway.

HOFER, ANDREAS (1767-1810), Tyrolese statesman; with Austrian encouragement raised Tyrol against Napoleon, April, 1809; Napoleon recovered possession in July, but country rose as he departed; H. came from hiding; won battle of Iselberg against Lefebvre; ruled for three months; forced to fly in Oct. 1809; betrayed, he was shot by Napoleon's orders.

HOFFDING, HAROLD (1843-1931), Dan. philosopher; prof. Copenhagen Univ.; works trans. into many languages.

HOFFMAN, CHARLES F E N N O (1806-1884), editor and poet; *b.* New York; *d.* Harrisburg, Pa.; founded and edited the Knickerbocker Magazine. Later editor of the American Monthly Magazine and also connected editorially with the New York Mirror and Literary World; became chiefly noted as a poet. When 43 his mind failed, and he spent the rest of his life in an insane asylum at Harrisburg.

HOFFMAN, FRIEDRICH (1660-1742), Ger. physician; practiced and taught at Jena and afterwards at Minden; first prof. of Medicine, 1693, and also of Natural Philosophy at Halle; member of many foreign learned societies, and author of many medical works.

HOFFMAN, AUGUST HEINRICH, HOFFMAN VON FALLERSLEBEN (1798-1874), Ger. poet; *b.* Fallersleben, and called himself after his birthplace; prof. at Breslau Univ.; dismissed, 1842, on account of his *Unpolitische Lieder*; also wrote *Volkslieder*.

HOFFMAN, ERNST THEODOR WILHELM (1776-1822), Ger. novelist; *b.* Königsberg (Prussia); studied law; for some time musical director at Bamberg, Leipzig, and Dresden Theatres; composed several operas; became famous for *Phantasiestucke in Callots Manier* and *Die Serapionsbruder* (weird stories), and *Die Elexiere des Teufels* (novel).

HOFFMAN, MALVINA (1887-   ), American sculptor, *b.* in New York City; studied under Gutzon Borglum, Herbert Adams, and Auguste Rodin; her best work, the *Sacrifice*, is in the cathedral of St. John the Divine, N.Y.; other works that have attracted favorable comment are three portrait busts of Paderewski, *John Muir, Modern Crusader* (in the Metropolitan Museum of Art); *Bachannale Russe* (in the Luxembourg, Paris); and the stone group over the entrance to Bush House, London. She is considered one of the best women sculptors of her time.

HOFFMANN, JOHANN JOSEPH (1805-78), Ger. Orientalist; wrote various Jap. studies and *Catalogus librorum et manuscriptorum japonicorum*, 1845.

HOFMANN, AUGUST WILHELM VON (1818-92), Ger. chemist; first director of School of Practical Chem.,

London; became prof. of Chem. in Berlin, 1864. He and his pupils brought the coal-tar industry under notice. His researches on analin, rosanilin, and quinoline red are classics.

HOFMANN, JOHANN CHRISTIAN KONRAD VON (1810-77), Ger. theologian and historian; pub. *Theologische Ethik, Schutzschriften, Der Schriftbeweis.*

HOFMANN, JOSEF (CASIMIR) (1876-   ), a pianist, *b.* in Cracow, Poland. He began the study of the piano under his father, who was a prominent musician, and at the age of seven attracted the attention of Rubinstein, the great pianist. In 1887 he began a tour in the United States, but owing to his age was obliged to abandon it on account of the interference of the Society for the Prevention of Cruelty to Children. He returned to Europe and spent several years in study under leading masters of the piano. In the years following he made annual concert tours of Europe and the United States and spent much of his time in the United States. He was considered by many to be one of the two or three greatest living pianists. He composed many pieces for the piano and wrote much on musical topics.

HOFMANN, MELCHIOR (*c.* 1498-1544), Ger. Anabaptist preacher; at first a furrier, became follower of Luther; adopted extreme views on Eucharist; preached at Strassburg and Emden; became Anabaptist; sometimes thought anti-Trinitarian, but was really Valentinian.

HOFMANNSTHAL, HUGO VON (1874-1929), Austrian poet, *b.* in Vienna; ed. at the University of Vienna; the founder of the German neo-romantic school of poetry and drama; wrote *Der Rosenkavalier*; *Ariadne auf Naxos*; *Die Frau ohne Schatten*, and *Der Unbestechliche*, 1923.

HOFMEISTER, WILHELM FRIEDRICH BENEDICT (1824-77), Ger. botanist; prof. of Bot. at Heidelberg and an eminent morphological botanist; pointed out the analogies between *Coniferoe* and *Cryptogams.* He also worked on *Bryophytes, Pteriodophytes,* and the embryology of plants.

HOFMEYER, JAN HENDRICK (1845-1909), South African politician and journalist; was for many years ruling spirit in Cape Colony of Afrikander Bond; supported Cecil Rhodes till Jameson Raid 1895; tried to influence Kruger and to prevent outbreak of war between Boers and British; was in favor of federation of S. African colonies.

HOGARTH, WILLIAM (1697-1764), Eng. artist and engraver; *b.* London; *s.*

of a schoolmaster; apprenticed to an engraver, and later set up in that calling on his own account; m. Jane, *d.* of Sir James Thornhill; achieved his first artistic success with his series of six paintings representing *The Harlot's Progress,* 1731, shortly afterwards engraved by himself. This series was followed by eight scenes depicting *The Rake's Progress,* 1735; *Marriage a la Mode, Industry and Idleness, The Stage Coach, The March to Finchley,* portraits of Garrick, Lavinia Fenton, scriptural pieces, etc. H. achieved immediate success with his engravings, but his original paintings found little appreciation in his own day, and many remained unsold at the time of his death. In portraiture he was more successful. H. is now recognized as one of the great Eng. artists. His purpose, in his more famous series, was to paint a story dramatically in a set of scenes, and the best of these are at once remarkable for realism and masterly humour, for H. was not only great as an artist, but equally so as a satirist and humorist.

HOGG, JAMES (1770-1835), Scot. poet, known as 'the Ettrick Shepherd'; herded cattle and sheep in his youth; made disastrous ventures in farming; pub. *Scottish Pastorals,* 1801; *The Mountain Bard,* 1807, *The Queen's Wake,* 1813—his best work in poetry. Other writings include collections of tales, and a treatise on diseases of sheep.

HOGG, THOMAS JEFFERSON (1792-1863), Eng. author; was the Oxford associate and subsequent biographer of Shelley.

HOG ISLAND, a tract of land, S.W. of Philadelphia, on which in 1917 and the following years were created great shipyards which constituted the largest shipbuilding plant in the world. Hundreds of vessels were built here under the direction of the United States Shipping Board. The plants were disbanded and dismantled in 1922.

HOGMANAY, name given in parts of Scotland to New Year's Eve; also called *hogg-night.*

HOGSHEAD, standard measure for liquids; made 63 wine gallons or 52½ imperial gallons in 1423.

HOHENASPERG (48° 57′ N., 10° 5′ E.), former fortress, Württemberg, Germany.

HOHENFRIEDBERG, HOHENFRIEDEBERG (50° 54′ N., 16° 14′ E.), village, in Silesia, Prussia. During the War of Austrian Succession great battle was fought at H., June 3, 1745, between Prussians under Frederick the

Great, and Austrians and Saxons under Prince Charles of Lorraine; total defeat of Allies, whose losses were 15,224; Prussian losses about 4,700.

HOHENHEIM (48° 42' N., 9° 12' E.), small town, Württemberg, Germany; famous agricultural coll.

HOHENLIMBURG (51° 20' N., 7° 33' E.), town, Westphalia, Prussia.

HOHENLINDEN (48° 9' N., 11° 59' E.), village, Upper Bavaria; scene of defeat of Austrians, under Archduke John, by French, under Moreau, Dec. 3, 1800.

HOHENLOHE, Ger. family, which held title of Count from XII. cent., and attained princely rank in XVIII. cent. The family was frequently subdivided, and many of its branches are now extinct; but there remain those of Bartenstein, Jagstberg, Schillingsfürst, and Waldenburg, which represent the R.C. line of H.-Waldenburg, founded in 1551; and those of Ingelfingen, Langenburg, and Ohringen, which are descended from the Prot. family of H.-Neuenstein, founded at the same time. The most distinguished member of the family was Chlodwig Karl Victor, 1819-1901, prince of H.-Schillingsfürst; he at first entered service of Prussia, but left it in 1846; in 1866 he bceame chief minister of Bavaria; aimed at uniting N. and S. Germany; opposed Ultramontanes in 1869, and had to resign office in 1870; ambassador to France, 1873-80; appointed gov. of Alsace-Lorraine in 1855; Imperial Chancellor in 1894. Other notable members of family are: Friedrich, prince of H.-Ingelfingen, 1746-1818, who served against Napoleon and was defeated at Jena; Ludwig, 1765-1829, prince of H.-Waldenburg-Bartenstein, who became marshal of France; Alexander, 1794-1849, prince of H.-Waldenburg-Schillingsfürst, who became priest and is credited with performing supernatural cures; and H. Ingelfingen, 1827-92, prince of Kraft, who served in Franco-Ger. War of 1870-71.

HOHENSTAUFEN (48° 44' N., 9° 45' E.), village, Württemberg, Germany; site of ruined castle which belonged to H. family from 1080 till 1525, when it was destroyed in Peasant Rising.

HOHENSTAUFEN, Ger. family, holding imperial crown, 1138-1254; founded by Frederick von Büren, whose s. Frederick took name H. from H. Castle; emperors of family were Frederick I., 1152-90, Henry VI., 1190-97, Philip I., 1198-1208; Frederick II. 2112-50; Conrad IV., 1250-54.

HOHENSTEIN.—(1) (50° 47' N., 12° 43' E.), town, Saxony, Germany. Pop. 15,600. (2) (53° 34' N.. 20° 18' E.), town, E. Prussia.

HOHENZOLLERN, Ger. imperial family; name derived from castle in S. Germany; family first came into prominence in 1415, when one of its members became Elector of Brandenburg; in 1701 Frederick III., Elector of Brandenburg, became first King of Prussia, and in 1871 William I., seventh King of Prussia, became first Emperor of Germany; former Kaiser William II. is present head of family.

HOKKAIDO, Jap. term, denoting N. part of empire.

HOKUDSI (1760-1849), famous Jap. painter; works include great book of color prints, *Mangwa.*

HOLBACH, PAUL HEINRICH DIETRICH BARON D' (1723-89), Fr. philosopher; denounced Christianity as source of all ill; friend of *Encyclopoedists.*

HOLBEACH (52° 49' N., 0° 1' E.), town, Lincolnshire, England.

HOLBEIN, HANS, THE ELDER (*c.* 1460-1524), Ger. artist; painter of average ability; chiefly religious subjects; examples at Basel, Munich, and Augsburg, also at Hampton Court. He is chiefly famous as being the *f.* of an illustrious son.

HOLBEIN, HANS, THE YOUNGER (1497-1543), Ger. artist; *s.* of Hans H. (*q.v.*); *b.* Augsburg, in his youth assisted his *f.*, subsequently going to Basel, where he became a member of the painters' guild, 1619. Here and at Lucerne he was extensively engaged in portraiture, mural decoration, and the production of woodcuts, including the famous series, 'The Dance of Death.' In 1526 he visited London and executed many fine portraits of notabilities, but returned to Basel in 1528. He was settled in London again in 1532, became court painter to Henry VIII., and subsequently *d.* of the pestilence. H. ranks amongst the greatest of the old Ger. masters. His notable works include *The Ambassadors* (National Gallery), *Anne of Cleves* (Louvre), *Duke of Norfolk* (Windsor), *Jane Seymour* (Vienna).

HOLBERG, LUDWIG, BARON (1684-1754), Dan. author; *b.* Bergen; lived in England, 1706-8; became prof. of Metaphysics at Copenhagen, subsequently of Rhetoric and History. His earliest literary successes were his satirical poems, *Peder Paars*, *Hans Mikkelsen's Metamorphoses*, etc. Upon the opening of the Dan. theatre at Copenhagen, H. supplied its stage with a long series of brilliant comedies, which have taken a high place in Dan. literature. Other important works include his *Autobiography*, *History of Denmark*, and *History of the Jews*.

HOLBORN, central metropolitan borough, London, England; contains Chapel of Ethelreda, St. Andrew's Church, City Temple, Lincoln's Inn. Gray's Inn, Brit. Museum, and many other public buildings.

HOLCROFT, THOMAS (1745-1809), Eng. dramatist; his melodrama, *The Road to Ruin*, 1792, was highly successful, and is still played.

HOLDEN, CHARLES FREDERICK (1851-1915), naturalist; *b.* Lynn, Mass. After studying at the U. S. Naval Academy, he served as assistant curator at the American Museum of Natural History, New York City, from 1871 to 1875. Later he became professor of zoology at Throop University, Pasadena, Cal., also honorary curator of the University Museum, and president of that city's board of education. He was notable as a lecturer and writer on popular science and on animal and ocean life.

HOLDEN, EDWARD SINGLETON (1846-1914), astronomer and educator; *b.* St. Louis, Mo. He was educated at Washington University and the U. S. Military Academy, West Point. He became in order professor of mathematics at the Naval Academy in 1873; director of the Washington Observatory at Madison, Wis., in 1881; president of the University of California in 1885; director of the Lick Observatory, San Jose, Cal. in 1888; and in 1901 librarian at West Point. His publications include works on astronomy and a life of Sir William Herschel.

HOLDEN, SIR ISAAC, BART. (1807-97), Eng. inventor; after a life of struggle, invented a wool-comber, 1847, and established, near Paris, wool-combing industry, which brought him wealth.

HÖLDERLIN, JOHANN CHRISTIAN FRIEDRICH (1770-1843), Ger. poet; *b.* Lauffen; became insane, 1802; wrote excellent lyrics; *Empedokles* (tragedy, unfinished), *Hyperion* (romance in letters), etc.

HOLDHEIM, SAMUEL (1806-60), Jewish nationalist; rabbi at Berlin.

HOLGUIN (20° 50′ N., 76° 29′ W.), town, Cuba, W. Indies.

HOLIDAYS, originally 'holy' days, *i.e.* days on which no work should be done; in modern England Bank H's are the h's recognised by the State; these are not observed in Scotland, nor is Good Friday, which is customarily kept in England. Quebec still observes some of the old feast days (the h. properly so called), but the rest of the Dominion and the Brit. Colonies have their own new systems.

In U.S.A. there are no legal h's; the presidential proclamation of Thanksgiving Day (usually last Thursday in Nov.) makes it legal holiday in Columbia and the Territories, though it is generally observed. Other h's generally observed are Independence Day (July 4), Labor Day (first Monday in Sept.), and these are legal in most states, which have also various other statutory h's.

HOLINSHED OR HOLLINGSHEAD, RAPHAEL (*d. c.* 1580), Eng. chronicler; wrote *Chronicles of England, Scotland, and Ireland* (pub. 1578), from which Shakespeare's Eng. hist. plays were largely drawn.

HOLKAR, title or Mahratta ruler of Indore.

HOLL, FRANK (1845-88), Eng. artist; R.A., 1884; achieved distinction as painter of genre subjects, but later devoted himself to portraiture, his sitters including Gladstone, Chamberlain, Bright, Lords Wolseley and Roberts.

HOLLAND OR NETHERLANDS, mar. kingdom, N. Europe (50° 46′-53° 33′ N., 3° 21′-7° 10′ E.), consisting mainly of deltaic deposits of Rhine, Maas, and Scheldt; much of surface 8 ft. below sea-level and protected by embankments and sand dunes; highest point 655 ft. Is bounded by Germany on E., Belgium on S., and elsewhere by North Sea. Within historic times sea has invaded land, transforming Flevo lake into the Zuider Zee (South Sea); anc. continental coast-line lay along Frisian Islands (Texel, Vlieland, Terschelling, Ameland, Schiermonnikoog, Rottum, Borkum), now separated by the Wadden (Shallows) from the mainland. Since the 16th cent. over a million ac. have been reclaimed from sea, lake, and river, and schemes for recovery of Zuider Zee have been passed (June, 1918); time required is thirty-three years, and capital cost $750,000,000; four separate areas to be diked cover total area of 521,170 ac., with fresh-water lake in centre. Alluvium (59 per cent. of area) consists of fens, clays, and sands; clays—especially of newly-reclaimed polders, *i.e.*, low-lying basins embanked and then pumped dry—are most fertile; diluvial strata (40½ per cent.) chiefly sands and gravels, not very fertile.

Estuary of the Maasland Scheldt contains many islands—*e.g.*, N. and S. Beveland, Walcheren, etc. Canals and waterways (5,000 m.) much more important than railways (2,382 m). and metalled roads. Climate resembles that of England, but is more variable. Principal occupations are grazing and agriculture. Cattle of superior breeds give rise to trade in butter and cheese prepared in factories (Gouda and Edam); horticulture, especially production of bulbs, flowers, and fruit, has been carried on for centuries; fisheries of some importance; chief industries are brewing, distilling, manufacture of sugar, vinegar, bricks, and stoneware, margarine, machinery, cocoa, salt, diamond-cutting, shipbuilding; coal-mining in Limburg prov. is increasing. Holland is a free-trade country; exports are food products and commodities mentioned above; imports, cereals and flour, iron and steel, textiles, raw materials, and food products. The official cap. is the Hague, Amsterdam is the commercial cap., and Rotterdam and Flushing are the chief ports.

Population and Area.—Inhabitants of N. descended from anc. Frisians, of centre from Franks, of *s.* from Saxons; mixed with French Huguenots, Walloons, Scots, etc.; Jews mostly in Amsterdam. Area, 12,648 sq. miles.

Religion.—Religious census of 1909 gave 2,588,261 as belonging to Dutch Reformed Church, and 746-186 other Protestants; also 2,053,021 Roman Catholics; 10,082 Jansenists; 106,909 Jews. Protestants are strongest in Friesland, Groningen, and Drenthe; Roman Catholics in N. Brabant and Limburg. There is no State Church, but state makes allowances to all Churches.

Education.—Primary education is free and (since 1900) compulsory between ages of six and thirteen. Intermediate instruction in 'burgher night-schools' for those engaged in industrial and agricultural work, and in 'higher burgher schools' for technical education, is inexpensive; in connection with these are schools of agriculture, horticulture, and forestry. Above these are gymnasia, preparing for univiersities of Leyden, Utrecht, Groningen, and Amsterdam.

The government is a constitutional and hereditary monarchy, with a States-general of two chambers. The first chamber has 50 members, elected indirectly by the provincial states from the wealthiest citizens; it holds office for nine years, one-third of number retiring every three years. The second chamber, of 100 members, is elected directly by single-member constituencies for four years (electors to be 25 years old, members 30). Justice is administered by a high court

at the Hague (seat of government) and several other tribunals.

Colonial Possessions.—Holland owns parts of the E. Indies, and has less important possessions in the W. Indies. E. Indies possession (with areas in sq. m.) are: Java and Madura, 50,557; Sumatra, 161,612; Borneo, W. coast, 55,825; Borneo, S. and E., 156,912; Billiton, 1,863; Banka, 4,446; Riau-Lingga Archipelago, 16,301; Celebes, 72,070; Molucca Islands, 43,864; New Guinea, 151,789; Timor Archipelago, 17,698; Bali and Lombok, 4,065. Total area, 735,000 sq.m.; pop. 47,000,000. W. Indies possessions are: Dutch Guiana, 46,060; Curacao Colony, 403. Total area, 46,463 square miles. Total area of Dutch colonies 781,463 square miles.

History.—For one or two centuries B.C. the land we call Holland was occupied by the Frisians and Batavi. The country was conquered by Rome, but let slip in the 4th cent. on the coming of the Franks. It was converted to Christianity about the 8th cent., and formed part of the empire of the Karlings. The name Holland was given to the district which still forms the provinces of N. and S. Holland in the 11th cent., when the counts of Holland rose to importance. The various states which made up the Netherlands passed, some by marriage, some by conquest, to the dukes of Burgundy, and then by descent to the Emperor Charles V. He was a firm ruler, under whom trade made the country prosperous; but the accession of his *s.*, Philip II., in sympathy a Spaniard, and nothing of a Dutchman, meant terrible oppression for the country by king and Inquisition. The result was the famous revolt, partly political, partly religious, under William of Orange, a member of a princely house in the S. of France. William's great protagonist in war was the Duke of Alva.

In 1572 a successful rising took place of the N. provinces (the southern remained under Span. and then Austrian domination till they became Belgium). William of Orange became virtual ruler. The Union of Utecht was formed in 1579, and the provinces declared themselves free of Span. control, 1581. William was murdered at Philip's instigation in 1584. The war with Spain grew fiercer, but in 1609 a truce was signed for twelve years. But the next few years were largely taken up with religious struggles between the Orthodox and Arminian parties, with the result that the Arminians were banished. Thenceforward Holland grew rapidly, not only politically, for she became famous in arts and science as well. In the 17th cent. she exerted a greater influence in Europe than ever before or since. She became a rival of England in colonizing and transport activities, and there was war between the two countries under Cromwell and Charles II. The Dutch wars 1652-4, 1664-7, 1672-8, left things much as they were. The second war saw the Dutch fleet in the Medway and Thames. In 1672 the English and French made an abortive attempt to invade Holland, and John de Witt, who had really guided the affairs of the Dutch, became so unpopular that he was murdered. William of Orange now came into power, and the peace of Nimeguen, 1678 ended the war.

William of Orange became King of Britain in 1688, and Dutch troops fought with English in the campaigns against Louis XIV. After William's death ,in 1702, a republic was established once more, and a period of general decline set in. By the Peace of Rastatt, 1714, the Span. Netherlands which Frnace had tried to obtain, became Austrian. But the Dutch Republic ceased from that time to have much say in European politics. In 1747 William IV. of Orange was elected Stadtholder of all the seven provinces, and the office was declared hereditary in his family. War broke out with Britain as the result of a quarrel over naval matters in 1780, and by the Treaty of Paris, 1793 certain colonies were surrendered to Britain. Meanwhile there was a party adverse to the houes of Orange, and after internal disputes William of Orange was re-established under Prussian and British auspices.

But the Fr. Revolution again upset matters, and in 1795 the country was conquered by Republican troops. The Orange family fied, and the anti-Orange party was overjoyed at the Fr. victory. A Batavian republic was established; nominally, a Fr. alliance was formed; practically, the country was under Fr. domination. Britain acquired the Dutch colonies. There was a short respite from war after the Peace of Amiens, 1802, but soon came more conflicts, and in 1806 Napoleon made his b. Louis Bonaparte, King of Holland. A revolt broke out in 1813, and William I. was recognized as sovereign prince, and as king in 1815, the Belgian provinces being united to the Dutch. But a quarrel arose between the Dutch and Belgians (different in many ways by race, religion, and temperament), and an independent kingdom of Belgium was established in 1831; the constitution was revised in 1848. Qaurrels about religious education took place continually during the reign of William III., 1849-90, the f. of the present Queen Wilheimina. During her minority, 1890-8, Queen Emma, widow of William III., acted as regent. Another political question has been that of the suffrage; in 1896 it was extended so as to almost double the number of electors. In 1901 the queen married Prince Henry of Mecklenburg-Schwerin. During the S. African war, Dutch sympathies were strongly with the Boers. In 1909 Princess Juliana was born. Holland remained neutral during the Great War, and was the asylum of the Ger. Kaiser after Nov. 9, 1918, the government refusing to yield him up.

Dutch Language and Literature.— Dutch (officially *Nederlandsch*) is one of the Low-German languages, of the same family as Old English and Frisian. Its development belongs to three periods *Old* Dutch, derived from various Teutonic tribal dialects, which first began to take shape about the 9th cent.; *Middle* Dutch (12th to end of 14th cent.), which became the language of a considerable portion of Germany, Belgium, and N. France; and *Modern* Dutch, which dates from the 15th cent. Dutch is spoken not only in Holland, but in the Union of S. Africa, by colonials of Dutch descent who use a *patois* known as the 'Taal.'

The Middle Dutch period witnessed the introduction of numerous epics and romances, chiefly derived from foreign sources, including *Floris en Blancefloer*, *Reinaert* (Reynard the Fox), *Roman van Lancelot*. During the 14th cent., however, the flourishing trade of Holland had made that country one of the chief industrial markets of the world, and so with the rise of commercial prosperity there gradually came into being a more distinctive form of expression, out of which grew a literature which was characteristic of the people and the times. This literature began with Jacob van Maerlant, whose social satires, under the name of *Naturen Bloeme*, appeared about 1263, and was followed in 1284 by his greater work, *De Spieghel Historiael* (Mirror of History); after him came other writers, chiefly on historical or on moral subjects, including Jan van Boendale, 1280-1365, Jan de Weert, and Melis Stoke. The romantic school of poetry was still represented by the works of Jan van Heelu, Hein van Aken, and Dirk Potter; but their influence was not lasting, and the moralists of the Maerlant.

Modern Dutch is represented in its pioneer stage by the works of Coornhert, Spieghel, and Visscher, and a master stylist in Pieter Hoofdt, 1581-1647, whose work in history, poetry, and drama is of high character. The greatest poet Holland has produced was Joost van Vondel, 1587-1679, whose tragedies, chiefly on Scriptural subjects, are marked by great imagination and expression, and are said to have influenced Milton. Jakob Cats, 1577-1660 was a poet of another order, whose work was invariably witty though sometimes coarse, and secured a lasting popularity. Other writers of outstanding abilities belonging to this period include van der Goes, Oudaen, and the historian Geeraerdt Brandt. The 18th cent. saw a decline in Dutch poetry, but a writer of remarkable attainments arose in Willem Bilderdijck, 1756-1832, whose influence on the Dutch literature was very marked; and the 19th cent. witnessed the rise of many writers of poetry, history, fiction, and belles-lettres whose works are distinguished by charm and originality.

Flemish Literature.—As distinct from the Old Dutch literature, modern Flem. literature came into existence during the early part of the 19th cent. Its exponents include a number of poets and realistic and historical novelists, amongst whom may be named Karel Ledeganck, Jan van Beers, J. T. van Rijswijck, P. van Duyse, Peter van Kerckhoven, J. L. D. Sleeckx, Jan Snieders, Julius de Geyter, Emmanuel Hiel, and numerous others.

HOLLAND. (1) North, prov. of Netherlands (52° 35′ N., 4° 50′ E.), between Zuider Zee and North Sea. Flat low (large portion below sea-level and protected by dykes), and fertile; produces cattle, cheese, flower bulbs (Haarlem), potatoes, etc. Fishing, shipping, and shipbuilding are carried on. Chief towns, Amsterdam and Haarlem. Area, 1,070 sq. m.; pop. 1,110,000. (2) South, prov. of Netherlands (52° N., 4° 30′ E.), extending along North Sea northwards from the mouth of Maas. Low and fertile, and produces cattle, cheese, flowers, fruits, bricks, gin; shipping and shipbuilding are carried on. Chief towns, the Hague, Rotterdam. Leyden, Area, 1,166 sq. m.

HOLLAND, a city of Michigan, in Ottawa co. It is on the Pere Marquette Railroad, and on the Black river, at its mouth, and on Lake Michigan. It is an important industrial community and has manufactures of furniture, leather, pianos, hot air furnaces, etc. It is the seat of Hope College and the Western Theological Seminary, both institutions of the Dutch Reformed Church.

HOLLAND, an unbleached linen cloth originally manufactured in H.

HOLLAND, CHARLES (1733-69), Eng. actor, of days of Garrick; his *s.* Charles 1768-1849, was also a prominent player.

HOLLAND, ERNEST O. (1874), College president; *b.* in Bennington, Ind. Bachelor of Arts, University of Indiana, 1895. 1909-1910 at Columbia College, fellow in education, 1912 Doctor Philosophy. 1895-1900 taught in high schools of Indiana. 1900-1905 head of English department at Boys High School, Louisville, Ky. 1905-1907 associate professor of education, junior professor, 1908-1908, professor secondary education; 1908-1911 at University of Indiana. 1911-1916 superintendent school, Louisville, Ky. Since 1916, president of Washington State College. Member Phi Beta Kappa, Advisory Board Reconstruction Educational Alliance. Member, selection committee for Rhodes Scholarships, 1927-32.

HOLLAND, SIR HENRY, BART. (1788-1873), Eng. physician; practised medicine with great success in London; travelled much abroad, and knew most eminent people of his time; author of works on medicine, travel, and other subjects.

HOLLAND, HENRY FOX, 1ST BARON (1705-74), Brit. politician; held various offices of state; Leader of Lower House, 1755, 1762; Paymaster-Gen., 1757.

HOLLAND, HENRY RICH, 1ST EARL OF (1590-1649), Eng. soldier and politician; arranged marriage between Charles I. and Henrietta Maria; changed sides several times during Civil War; taken prisoner at St. Neots, 1647, and executed, 1649.

HOLLAND, HENRY RICHARD VASSALL FOX, 3RD BARON (1773-1840), Brit. politician; Lord Privy Seal in 'All the Talents' Cabinet, 1806; Chancellor of Duchy of Lancaster, 1830; wrote *Memoirs of Whig Party.*

HOLLAND, JOHN PHILIP (1841-1914), submarine inventor; *b.* Liscannor, County Clare, Ireland. He studied submarine navigation in Cork while following the occupation of a school teacher, and when thirty years old came to the United States, where he pursued his calling at Passaic, N. J. In 1875 he invented his first submarine device, which was tested in the Passaic river and remained below water for 24 hours. His next experimental ventures were financed by the Fenian Brotherhood, with the design of building underwater boats that could attack British shipping. Two boats were constructed and one was successfully tested, but factional differences finally ended Holland's financial support from his Irish compatriots. Towards the close of the nineteenth century the U. S. government began to be impressed by the progress of submarine science abroad and the impression which Holland's further experimental craft made on several naval officers. A competition was held, in which American and foreign inventors were invited to tender bids for building a modern submarine that met the government's specifications. Holland's device won, and while the first boat built for the government failed, subsequent boats abundantly justified the claims he made for his design. Great Britain later adopted submarines of the Holland type, as well as Russia, Japan, Holland and other countries. He may be said to be the father of the modern submarine that dealt such havoc in the World War, as the most effective types were based on his conceptions. As the science advanced the machines developed went far beyond Holland's inventive scope, but he blazed the trail that made them possible.

HOLLAND, JOSIAH GILBERT (1819-1881), editor and author; *b.* Belchertown, Mass.; *d.* New York. He was trained as a physician, graduating from the Berkshire Medical College, and practised at Springfield, Mass., but medicine failed him as a livelihood, and he turned to teaching and journalism in various parts of the country. In 1849 he became one of the editors of the Springfield Republican and subsequently part owner of that journal. In 1870 he established the magazine known as the Century, then under the name of Scribner's Monthly, and edited it with great success to his death. He became known also as a novelist, poet and essayist, and earned popularity through a multitude of contributions to the journals he edited, afterwards collected and published in book form. He wrote a life of Lincoln.

HOLLAND, PHILEMON (1552-1637), Eng. translator of Gk. and Lat. classics. His *s.* Henry, 1583-*c.* 1650, wrote *Baziliologia* 1618 and *Heroologia,* 1620.

HOLLAND, WILLIAM JACOB (1848), zoologist and paleontologist; *b.* Jamaica, West Indies. He was educated for the ministry, graduating from the Princeton Theological Seminary in 1874; and occupied the pastorate of a Pittsburgh Presbyterian church from 1874 to 1891. Afterwards he served as chancellor of the Western University of Pennsylvania for two years. In 1897 he was appointed director of the Carnegie Museum at Pittsburgh and became an authority on museum administration and zoology. His scientific writings include works on butterflies, moths and the fauna of past geological ages. *d.* 1932.

HOLLANDER, JACOB HENRY

(1871), economist; *b.* Baltimore, Md. In 1891 he graduated from Johns Hopkins University, where he became associate professor of finance, and in 1904 professor of political economy. Meantime, 1897, he acted as secretary of the Bimetallic Commission abroad and as U. S. Commissioner ofr tax-law revision in Porto Rico as well as treasurer for that island's government. In 1905 he investigated the public debt of Santo Domingo for the U. S. government and later readjusted it as financial adviser for the Dominican Republic. His writings chiefly relate to economic and financial subjects.

HOLLES, DENZIL, BARON HOLLES (1599-1860), Eng. politician; *b.* at Houghton, Nottinghamshire. H. had considerable share in Resortation of Charles II., by whom he was appointed ambassador to Paris; concluded *Treaty of Breda,* 1667.

HOLLEY, MARIETTA (1850-1926); author; *b.* Jefferson County, N. Y. When sixteen she began contributing poetry to country papers and afterwards prose contributions to national periodicals. Her writings, which revealed a distinctive humor and became popular at home and abroad, largely ambraced the sayings and doings of 'Josiah Allen's Wife' (her pseudonym) and vivacious descriptions of the diverting adventures of 'Samantha', a popular character who figures in most of her books.

HOLLIDAY, ROBERT CORTES (1880), author; *b.* in Indianapolis, Ind. Attended Art Students' League, New York, 1899-1902. University of Kansas, 1903-1904. 1904-1905 illustrator for magazines. 1906-1911 with Charles Scribner's Sons as bookseller. 1912 librarian with New York Public Library. 1913 reference librarian, New York School of Philanthropy. 1913-1914 assistant literary editor of New York Tribune, 1915 reporter and editor. Since 1916 with editorial departments of several book companies. Author: *Booth Tarkington,* 1918; *The Walking-Stick, Papers,* 1918; *Joyce Kilmer, A Memoir,* 1918; *Peeps at People,* 1919; *Broome Street Straws,* 1919; *Men and Books and Cities,* 1920; *Turns About Town,* 1921; *A Chat About Samuel Merwin,* 1921. Writes humorous and literary articles for magazines and newspapers. Instructor in writing for publication.

HOLLOWAY, THOMAS (1800-83), Eng. patent medicine manufacturer, who made large fortune from pills and ointment, and built Holloway College for women, Englefield Green, Surrey, 1887.

HOLLY, an evergreen shrub, *Ilex aquifolium*, with smooth grey bark and dark glossy leaves with spines on the margin. It will not grow in the shade of other trees. The flowers are *dioecious*. The female flowers have abortive *stamens* and the male ones an abortive *pistil*. The bright crimson berries severely irritate the digestive tract of man, but are eaten by birds. The wood, used for turned articles, is smooth, hard, white, even-grained, stains well, and when dyed black is used as imitation ebony.

HOLLYHOCK, ALTHEA ROSEA, a plant belonging to natural order *Malvaceoe*. Flowert are regular *polypetalous, hypogynous*, and the *stamens* ripen first.

HOLLYWOOD, a suburb of Los Angeles, Cal., which is notable for the moving picture interests which have studios there. It is also a favorite residential place for those connected with moving pictures. It is a part of Los Angeles.

HOLMES, ARTHUR (1872), college president. *b.* in Cincinnati, 1894-1895 at Bethany College, Bachelor of Arts 1899 of Hiram College. 1903 University of Pennsylvania, Master of Arts, 1908 Doctor of Philosophy. 1899 ordained Disciples of Christ. 1899-1904 pastor at Sixth Church, Philadelphia. 1904-1905 Memorial Church, Ann Arbor, Michigan. 1905-1908 religious and educational director of Pennsylvania Railroad department of Y. M. C. A. 1908-1909 director of psychology. 1909-1912 assistant professor, 1908-1912 assistant director Psycho-Clinic, University of Pennsylvania. President of Drake University since 1918. Author: *Decay of Rationalism*, 1909. *The Conservation of the Child* 1912. *Principles of Character Making*, 1913. *Backward Children* 1915.

HOLMES, MRS.' MARY JANE HOWES (1839-1907) novelist; *b.* Brookfield, Mass.; *d.* Brockport, N. Y. She married Daniel Holmes, a lawyer. Before engaging in authorship she was a school teacher, to which fact may be traced a didactic tendency perceptible in her numerous novels, one of which she produced annually. The circulation of her books, of which *Tempest and Sunshine* (1854) was perhaps the most popular, ran into the millions. They depicted domestic life, had a marked moral tone, and were free from sensationalism. She lacked fine literary qualities, but successfully appealed to the younger generation of her day and even later.

HOLMES, OLIVER WENDELL (1809-1894) poet, essayist, and physician. *b.* in Cambridge, August 29, 1809; *d.* in Boston, October 8, 1894. Educated at Phillips Academy, Andover, and Harvard, where he graduated in 1829. His famous poem *Old Ironsides* appeared in 1830 and was the means of saving the famous frigate 'Constitution' from destruction. After a year at the Harvard Law School he studied medicine three years in Paris and in 1836 received his degree of M.D. in the United States. He was professor of physiology and anatomy at Dartmouth, 1839-1840 and at Harvard 1842-1882 and practiced in Boston. The first of *The Autocrat of the Breakfast Table* appeared in the Atlantic Monthly. *The Professor at the Breakfast Table* was published in 1859 and *The Poet at the Breakfast Table* in 1872 and made the author famous at home and abroad. His novels were *Elsie Venner* 1861, *The Guardian Angel* 1868, and *A Mortal Antipathy* 1885. The volumes of verse *Urania* 1846 and *Astrea* 1850, brought him recognition as a poet. Among his most famous serious poems are *The Chambered Nautilus, The Last Leaf* and *The Iron Gate*, and in humorous verse, *The One Hoss Shay*, and *Evening, by a Tailor*. His later collection of poems were *Songs in Many Keys*, 1861. *Songs of Many Seasons* 1875, *The Iron Gate* 1880 and *Before the Curfew* 1887. Among miscellaneous works are 100 *Days in Europe* 1889, *Over the Teacups* and lives of Motley and Emerson. See Morse's *Life and Letters of Oliver Wendell Holmes*.

HOLMES, OLIVER WENDELL (1841-1935), Am. jurist, *b.* in Boston. He graduated from Harvard in 1861 and after service in the Civil War in which he was wounded, graduated from Harvard Law School in 1866. For many years he was professor of law at Harvard, and from 1899 to 1902 was chief justice of the Supreme Court of Massachusetts. In 1902 he was appointed associate justice of the United States Supreme Court. He was the *s.* of Oliver Wendell Holmes, the poet. Resigned, 1932.

HOLMIUM, a metal of the rare earths, at present classed as an element, with an atomic weight of 163.5. According to many authorities, however, it is probably a mixture of two or more substances. It forms with Erbium and Thulium a group of metals which are still under investigation and all of which may be found to be mixtures of greater or less complexity. It is found in yttria, a rare earth discovered in 1794 by Professor Gadolin, of Abo in Finland. From this earth, Mosander, in 1843 separated terbia, which, in turn, was shown by Soret, Cleve, Thalen and Lecoq de Boisbaudran to consist of erbia, holmia, thulia and dysprosia.

Holmia is yellow in color, and gives pale yellow salts.

HOLOGRAPH, any writing written wholly in the handwriting of the person from whom it imports to proceed. It is most often employed in the writing of wills, and the name of two witnesses are required.

HOLOFERNES. See JUDITH, BOOK OF.

HOLST, HERMANN EDUARD VON (1841-1904), German historical writer; *b.* Fellin, Livonia; *d.* Freiburg, Germany. He engaged in journalism after studying at Dorpat and Heidelberg and in 1866 came to New York City, where he became American correspondent of the *Kolnich Zeitung* and an editor of a German-American journal. He returned to Germany in 1872 to occupy the chair of history at the University of Strassburg and later that of Freiburg. After relinquishing the latter post he travelled in England and the United States, where, from 1892 to 1900 he served as professor of history at the University of Chicago. He wrote the Constitutional and Political History of the United States, 8 vols., and a life of John C. Calhoun.

HOLSTEIN. See SCHLESWIG-HOLSTEIN.

HOLSTON RIVER, one of the headstreams of the Tennessee, flowing southwest from Smith county, southwest Virginia, into Tennessee through a mountainous country. It joins two other of the Tennessee's headstreams, the Clinch river, at Kingston, Tenn., and the French Broad river, a few miles east of Knoxville. Many small mountain brooks flow from it. Its length is about 350 miles and it is partly navigable for light craft.

HOLT, HAMILTON (1872), editor and lecturer; *b.* Brooklyn, N. Y. He was educated at Yale and Columbia Universities. In 1897 he entered journalism as managing editor of the *Independent*, and from 1913 to 1921 edited and owned that periodical. He became associated with a number of international societies and as an advocate of world peace lectured on that subject throughout the country. He represented the League to Enforce Peace at the Versailles Peace Conference in 1919. He also became of note as an advocate of simplified spelling, municipal government reform, and of improved social and labor conditions. Pres. Rollins Coll., 1925.

HOLT, HENRY (1840), publisher and author; *b.* Baltimore, Md. After graduating from Yale and Columbia

Universities .1863-4) he entered the publishing business of G. P. Putnam and in 1873 established the publishing firm of Henry Holt & Co., New York City. He also edited the *Unpartisan* (formerly the *Unpopular*) Review and published works on man and nature, the cosmos and immortality, and on social and literary subjects. He also translated Edmond About's *Notary's Nose* from the French. *d.* 1926.

HOLT, LUTHER EMMETT (1855-1924), physician; *b.* Webster, N. Y. He graduated from the Columbia College of Physicians and Surgeons in 1880. From 1890 to 1901 he was professor of diseases of children of the New York Polyclinic, and thereafter at the College of Physicians and Surgeons. He became also physician-in-chief to the New York Foundling Hospital and the Babies' Hospital and a leading official of the Rockefeller Institute for Medical Research. His contributions to medical literature relate to the health and care of infants.

HOLT, WINIFRED, American sculptor and philanthropist. Was educated privately and studied anatomy, drawing and sculpture in Florence, Italy. Later she exhibited at New York, Florence and Berlin, her chief works being portraits, busts and bas reliefs. Becoming interested in befriending the sightless, she founded the New York Association for the Blind, promoted the establishment of a number of branches of that body, and organized similar societies in France in connection with aiding the World War blind. She lectured also in the United States and Canada on the work of blind soldiers. Much of her writings relate to the blind, and include a biography of Henry Fawcett, the blind Postmaster General of England.

HOLY ALLIANCE, THE (1815), a sort of treaty drwan up by the Emperor Alexander I. of Russia, in which he, the Austrian emperor, and king of Prussia, agreed to govern their dominions on principles of 'Justice, Christian Charity and Peace.' Though Alexander's intentions were good the H. A. came to stand for reactionary principles in Europe.

HOLY CROSS, COLLEGE OF THE, a Roman Catholic institution of higher learning situated at Worcester, Mass. It was established in 1843 and is controlled by the Society of Jesus. The system of education conforms to that followed in all Jesuit colleges and includes preparatory and collegiate departments. It is the oldest Catholic College in New England. In 1933 there were 1,094 students and 75 teachers, under the direction of the Trustees.

HOLY CROSS MOUNTAIN, a peak, 14,000 ft. in height, of the Saguache range and branch of the Rockies, Colorado, U. S. A., in Eagle co., 15 m. N.W. of Leadville. Its name is taken from two huge snow-filled ravines which have the appearance of a cross.

HOLY GHOST. See HOLY SPIRIT.

HOLY GRAIL. See GRAIL, THE HOLY.

HOLY ISLAND, LINDISFARNE (55° 42′ N., 1° 48′ W.), island, off Northumberland, England; connected with mainland at low tide by sandy tract; has ruined Benedictine monastery.

HOLY LAND. See PALESTINE.

HOLY ROMAN EMPIRE. See EMPIRE, HOLY ROMAN.

HOLY SEPULCHRE, KNIGHTS OF THE. See under HOSPITALLERS.

HOLY WATER. In Early Church running water was used for baptism, and was not specially consecrated. Water in baptism not only symbolised purity, but carried away sin. The h. w. now used in churches is consecrated in various rites. For royal or special baptisms water from the Jordan is used.

HOLY WEEK, week before Easter, observed in the churches by special religious exercises.

HOLYHEAD (53° 18′ N., 4° 39′ W.), port, Holy Isle, Anglesey, N. Wales; fine harbor; old church.

HOLYOAKE, GEORGE JACOB (1817-1906), Eng. journalist and pioneer of the Co-operative movement in England; named his views 'secularism.'

HOLYOKE, a city of Massachusetts, in Hampden co. It is on the Boston and Maine and the New York, New Haven and Hartford railroads, and on the Connecticut river. Excellent water power is furnished from the river which is dammed with a dam 1000 feet in length. Holyoke is a city of great industrial importance and is the leading high grade paper manufacturing locality in the world. Its other industries include the manufacture of silk, cotton and woolen goods, machinery, turbines, thread, knit goods, automobiles and tires, steam engines and wire. The city has many important buildings, public schools, high schools and libraries. It is connected by electric railway with neighboring towns and cities.

HOLYOKE, MOUNT, an elevation in Hampshire co., Mass., between Hadley and Amherst on the north and South Hadley and Granby on the south. It is two miles east of the Connecticut River. Its formation is green stone, and its highest elevation is 1,120 feet above sea level.

HOLYROOD, royal palace, Edinburgh; founded 1128, by David I., as an abbey; palace foundations laid, c. 1501; sacked by English, 1544 and 1650; rebuilt by Charles II., 1671-79.

HOLYSTONE, piece of stone used for scrubbing the decks of ships; so called because its use demands a kneeling attitude.

HOLYWELL, (53° 17′ N., 3° 13′ W.), town, Flintshire, Wales; above St. Winifred's well is Perpendicular chapel.

HOLYWOOD (54° 38′ N., 5° 50′ W.), port, County Down, Ireland; site of former monastery.

HOLZMINDEN (51° 50′ N., 9° 25′ E.), town, Brunswick, Germany.

HOMAGE, term used under the feudal system for formal acknowledgement made by tenant that military service was due from him for the lands into which he was entering; the tenant knelt, placed his hands between the lord's hands, and swore fealty.

HOMBURG-VOR-DER-HÖHE (50° 14′ N., 8° 36′ E.), town, Hesse-Nassau, Germany; noted watering-place; has saline and chalybeate springs; in vicinity is Saalburg.

HOME ECONOMICS. Owing to the great increase in the cost of household necessities during recent years, much attention has been given to intelligent and systematic control over the expenditure of the family income. Various systems of household bookkeeping have been devised, and although these differ in details, the underlying purpose of all of them is to draw attention to expenditure on individual items, in order that extravagance may be corrected, a better balanced expenditure devised, and a saving effected. To assist the would-be home economist, many specimen budgets have been drawn up, indicating in what manner the family income should be apportioned. These budgets must necessarily vary with conditions. The expenditure of the city worker on rent, lunches and carfare will obviously be greater than the dweller in a small town, while the item for food will be less for the farmer than for the rest of the community. As a general guide, however, these specimen budgets have value. One commonly given for a moderate income divides the expenditure as follows: Food, 25 per cent., rent 20 per cent., clothes 20 per cent., operating 15 per cent., higher life 20 per cent. The last item includes education, amusement, savings, books and charity. Under operating expenses are included rent, repairs, fire insurance, railroad and carfare, heat, light, water, furniture and supplies, laundry, labor, telephone, interest, taxes and doctor. It is obvious that the percentage expenditure will vary with different incomes. The item for food, for instance, for a $1000 income will probably reach at least 30 per cent. while for a $5000 income it may drop to 15 per cent. Similarly, a saving of 10 per cent. on a $1000 year income is high, while on a $5000 it should approximate 25 per cent. It is sometimes recommended that the head of the family should draw up a reasonable budget in detail for his own use, and then by comparing his actual expenditure, item by item, he can reduce expenditure whenever it appears excessive.

HOME, JOHN (1722-1808), Scot, dramatic poet; *b.* Leith; *ed.* for Church; officiated in E. Lothian; his famous play, *Douglas*, was produced in Edinburgh (1756), with great success, and was seen at Covent Garden in the year following; later became Secy. to Lord Bute, and subsequently tutor to Prince of Wales (George III.)

HOME OFFICE, department of Brit. government; at head of Home Sec., under whom are parliamentary and permanent under-sec., two permanent assistant under-sec's (one of whom is a barrister), numbers of clerks, inspectors, of factories, prisons, etc. Sec. of State for Home Department maintains law and order in England and Wales, controls prisons, administers Labor Acts, Licensing Acts, Vivisection Act, Cruelty to Animals Act, etc.

HOLY SPIRIT, THE, or HOLY GHOST, or PARACLETE, in orrhodox Christian theology, the Third Person in the Blessed Trinity. Foreshadowings of the Christian doctrine are foind in certain parts of the O.T. writings, as, for instance, in Gen. 1. 2, 1 Sam. xvi. 13, and Joel ii. 28 ff., quoted as a prophecy of the descent of the Holy Spirit at Pentecost in Acts ii. 17 ff. It becomes much clearer, however, in the N.T., where the Holy Spirit is spoken of in a way that makes His Divinity distinct in such passages as 2 Cor. iii, 16 ff., 2 Tim. iii. 16., Gal. v. 22, etc. From other pasasges still more may be gathered. Matthew xxviii. 19, 1 Pet. i. 1-14, speak of the Holy Spirit as distinct from the Father and the Son, while His Personality is insisted on in the important passage beginning John xiv. 16, as also in John xv. 26, 'But when the Comforter is come whom I will send unto you from the Father, even the Spirit of truth, which proceedeth from the Father. He shall testify of me.' In this text we have also a reference to the question of the Procession of hte Holy Ghost, which caused such serious misunderstandings between the Eastern and Western churches in later centuries. The Easterns condemned the churches of the West for the addition of the Filioque clause in the Nicene Creed, and they further denied that the procession of the Holy Spirit was 'from the Father and the Son.' It must be pointed out, however, that there is probably no real doctrinal difference involved, as the West has never held that this rather unfortunate addition to the Oecumenical Creed teaches a Dual Procession, but rather a procession *from* the Father *through* the Son. This doctrine Eastern theologians would endorse. Many questions relating to the Holy Spirit are bound up with the controversies as to the Holy Trinity which occupied the mind of the Church in post-Nicene times. The most important results, embodied in the Athanasian Creed, and the additions to the Nicene Creed, lay stress on the *personality* of the Holy Spirit.

HOME RULE, term invented by Isaac Butt in 1873 to indicate Irish demand for self-government. For history, see IRELAND. The form of self-government advocated by the Earl of Dunraven in 1905 was known as Devolution, which he thus propounded; 'One Parliament is my centre, its ultimate effective supremacy is my circumference, but emanating from that centre and within that circumscribing limit I desire to see the largest possible freedom of action and self-government relegated to Ireland.' At the present time there is a strong devolutionary movement in Scotland, and to a lesser extent in Wales.

HOMEL, Gomel (52° 26′ N., 30° 52′ E.), town, Mogilev, Russia.

HOMER, greatest epic poet; *b.* between 1100-900 B. C., in Greece; exact birthplace uncertain, traditionally Chios; known by his poems, the *Iliad* and the *Odyssey*, which were originally ascribed to him but are almost certainly of different authorship. From internal evidence it is calculated that about a century separates the poems. They existed before the introduction of writing, and were handed down by word of mouth by the *rhapsodists*, who some times perverted the order of lines or interpolated passages of their own composition. Many poems are ascribed to H., the *Homeric Hymns*, the *Thebaid*, etc., but they are of different authorship though roughly contemporaneous. His writings correspond with the Mycenean and Cretan civilisations; his style is graphic and picturesque, abounding in similes; the vocabulary is large and contains many *hapax legomena*. The *Odyssey* and *Iliad* were recited at many Gk. festivals and were taught in schools; served as model for Vergil and Apollonius of Rhodes. See also GREECE (LITERATURE).

HOMER, LOUISE (1872), operatic vocalist; *b*. Pittsburgh, Pa., as Louise Dilworth Beatty; married Sidney Homer under whom she studied singing. In 1898 she made her debut at Vichy as Lenora in La Favorita, after studying her art under Mme. Koenig, in Paris. She next appeared at Covent Garden, London, and at the Metropolitan Opera House, New York City, where she became a great favorite of opera lovers. She sang also in concerts, and made frequent tours in the U. S. Chosen one of 12 greatest American women, 1924.

HOMER, WINSLOW (1836-1910), an American painter, *b*. in Boston, Mass. He began his art studies in the studio of Frederic Randel, president of the National Academy of Design. During the Civil War he was sent to the front by *Harper's Weekly* to make sketches. His first painting, 'Prisoners from the Front,' was exhibited in 1864 and immediately gave him a high standing. His later subjects were chosen from among the fisher folk of the Maine coast and other parts of New England, among these being 'The Life Line' 1884, and 'The Lookout,' 1897. His finest painting is considered a marine, 'On the Maine Coast.'

HOMESTEAD, a borough of Pennsylvania, in Allegheny co. It is on the Pennsylvania, the Pittsburgh and Lake Erie, Bessemer and Lake Erie and other railroads, 7 miles southeast of Pittsburgh. It is one of the chief steel manufacturing cities in the country and is the seat of the steel works established by Andrew Carnegie, afterwards sold to the United States Steel Corporation. Its other manufactured products are engines, mill machinery, car wheels, valves, axles, fire brick, concrete products, tiles, ornamental iron work, fire escapes, cigars, violins, phonographs, plumbers' supplies, chemical products, and ice.

The manufacture of airplane parts also constitutes an important industry.

HOMESTEAD LAWS are statutes formally in force in America, whereby a settler may establish right to his dwelling. By an Act passed in 1862 any Amer. citizen of twenty-one years of age may claim 160 acres of public land; this he receives on condition of his settling there for five years, after which time he receives a title to it from government. The homestead is also protected by law from seizure by creditors. Similar laws obtain in various Brit. colonies.

HOMEYER, CARL GUSTAV (1795-1874), Ger. jurist and antiquarian.

HOMICIDE. See MURDER, INSANITY.

HOMILETICS (Gk. *homilein*, to gather together), science of preaching as branch of rhetoric.

HOMILY, a religious composition simpler than a sermon. Justin Martyr says that after the reading of Scripture the minister exhorted the people. Preaching has sometimes been subordinate, *e.g.* in the Middle Ages and in some Catholic countries now. An Anglican clergyman may read one of the Homilies in the Prayer Book instead of his own sermon, a practice now obsolete.

HOMŒOPATHY, system of therapeutics, founded by S. C. F. Hahnemann (1755-1843), a Ger. physician, the main theory of which is that a disease is cured by drugs which produce in a healthy person similar symptoms to those of the disease, the therapeutic effect of any drug being ascertained or 'proved' by administering it to healthy persons in gradually increasing doses. In regard to the dose of a drug which should be given in homoeopathic treatment opinions differ; but most homoeopathists are agreed that small doses are necessary, while the drugs should be administered in the same form as when it was 'proved.' Hahnemann also promulgated a theory that all chronic diseases were due, directly or indirectly, to psora (itch), syphilis, or sycosos (fig-warts) —a theory which has been entirely disproved with the advance of the science of medicine, but which has had the unforunate effect of assisting the opponents of homoeopathy to ridicule the main theory of the system, with which it has really no connection. Considerable success has attended the introduction of homoeopathic methods of treatment, and according to its advocates, the development of serum therapy (*e.g.* in diphtheria, tetanus, plague) bears out the truth of the fundamental theory. In addition, it has had a great share in influencing the diminution of the quantity of drugs considered necessary for the treatment of disease, while it has also stimulated the study of the action and effects of drugs.

The opposition with which homoeopathy was received by the medical profession in Britain has of late become somewhat lessened, and in addition to the London Homoeopathic Hospital, founded 1850, there are a number of similar hospitals and dispensaries in provincial towns. The barriers between homoeopathy and more orthodox medical treatment have, with the modern development of therapeutics, been largely broken down. In America, the theory is taught in many medical schools and universities. There are a great number of homoeopathic hospitals and journals, and a large proportion of medical practitioners work in accordance with its principles.

HOMOPTERA, the name given to one of the two sub-orders of Hemiptera whose members differ from those of the Heteroptera in that their wings cover the abdomen in a roof-like manner; the head is furnished with three ocelli, placed triangularly on the summit, and the front of the head is bent over, touching the coxae. This sub-order includes the Cicadidae, Fulgaridae, Membracidae, Cercopidae, Jassidae, Psyllidae, Aphidae, Aleurodidae, and Coccidae.

HOMS, HEMS, HUMS (34° 46′ N., 36° 46′ E.), walled town, Syria; formerly site of famous temple of the sun; produces silk.

HO-NAN (34° N., 113° E.), province, Central China; area 67,940 sq. miles; mountainous in W.; drained by Hoangho and affluents of Han-kiang.

HONAWAR, ONORE (14° 17′ N., 74° 27′ E.), port, Bombay, Brit. India.

HONDA, SAN BARTOLOMEO DE HONDA (5° 12′ N., 74° 50′ W.), town, Colombia, S. America.

HONDECOETER, MELCHIOR D' (c. 1636-95), Dutch painter of birds; belonged to a family of painters, being s. of Gisbert and Grandson of Gillis d'H., both painters.

HONDURAS, republic in Central America (14° 42′ N., 86° W.), bounded N. by Caribbean Sea; E. and S. Nicaragua; S., Pacific and Salvador; and W. Guatemala; coast-line c. 400 m.; cap. Tegucigalpa. Surface excepting narrow strip of swamp-land on the coast, is mountainous, traversed by continuation of Nicaraguan Cordillera, and form-

ing elevated tableland with fertile plains and valleys, and rising in mountain ridges—highest point being Montana de Salaque (c. 10,120 ft); many streams, including Segovia (c. 350 m.) and Ulua; only large lake is Yojoa. Climate is healthy in highlands, but oppressive in lowlands. Honduras is rich in minerals —platinum, silver, iron, etc.; bananas, coco-nuts, coffee, tobacco, and rubber are produced, sarsaparilla is exported; industries are cattle breeding and straw plaiting for hats; important towns include Jutigalpa, Comayagua, and Amalpa. Area, 44,275 sq. m.;

History—Honduras was discovered by Columbus 1502; became independent 1839; revolution 1910-11.

Government. The president is elected for four years; Congress, one house, has 42 deputies elected for four years. See under CENTRAL AMERICA.

HONDURAS, BRITISH, a British crown colony; w. side of Gulf of Honduras, in w. of Caribbean Sea (18° N., 88° 20′ W.), bounded N. by Yucatan province of Mexico, W. by Guatemala. It produces cedar, mahogany, rosewood, logwood, sugar, coffee, sarsaparilla, fruits, tortoise-shell, most of which are exported; imports cotton, yarn, cloth, hardware, general goods. Climate is moist and hot, and unsuited to Europeans. Colony is administered by lieut. governor, assisted by executive and legislative councils. Inhabitants include Europeans, Indians, mixed races. Early Brit. settlers had considerable trouble with Spaniards, who made various attempts to oust them, but were ultimately frustrated. Honduras became independent 1839; Britain's claims were finally confirmed in 1859. Belize, the cap., on good harbor, does large export trade. Area, 8,598 sq. m. See under CENTRAL AMERICA.

HONDURAS, GULF OR BAY OF, the broad basin of the Caribbean Sea, skirting Honduras, Guatemala, and British Honduras in Central America.

HONE, a variety of hard, slaty stone, close grained, containing tiny particles of quartz or silica and used on the decks of ships.

HONEGGER, ARTHUR (1892-   ), Swiss composer, b. at Havre; ed. at Zurich and the Paris conservatoire. His most famous composition is *Pacific 231*, 1924, an example of his startling modern style of composition. He also wrote the biblical drama, *King David*; the opera *Judith*, 1924; and *Antigone*.

HONEY, a sweet liquid collected by bees and other insects from the nectaries of flowers; composed chiefly of various sugars (glucose and possibly cane sugar), wax, mucilage, oil, water, mineral substance, coloring matter, and water. The bee carries it in its h. bag to the hive, where it is stored in combs composed of hexagonal cells. It is doubtful whether it undergoes any chemical change while in the bee's body. Its color, aroma, and properties depend on the parent flowers; heather h. is highly esteemed; some tropical varieties are poisonous.

Science has elaborated a centrifugal extractor; the comb is placed on a wheel and rotated rapidly, with the result that the honey is cast off into a receptacle. H. has a prominent place in it. The mead was obtained by boiling the drained h-comb.

HONEY-EATERS or **HONEY-SUCKERS**, (*Meliphagidoe*) a family of perching birds-with about 250 species, confined, with one exception, to Australia. New Zealand, and the islands of the S. Pacific. They have long bills and a long, extrusible tongue wherewith they extract honey from flowers. The Parson Bird and Bull Bird are New Zealand honey eaters.

HONEY-DEW, a sweet and sticky exudation found, especially in warm, dry weather, on the leaves and stems of many trees and plants. Some hold that it is invariably associated with Aphides, Cocci, as, for instance, *Cocus mannifera,* and other insects. For it is known that Aphides excrete from the abdomen a fluid indistinguishable from H., the theory being that they prick a hole in the leaf or stalk and so suck the excess of sugar from the flowing sap. Others believe that without these insects H. would still form whenever the tissues of the plant are broken. H., which is also called manna, has been known to fall in showers. As it closes the pores when it dries, and thus hinders the natural growth of a plant, gardeners use a syringe to wash it away.

HONEY-GUIDES, *Indicasoridoe*) a family of about 20 species of climbing picarian birds found in Africa and Western Asia. Their name is due to the fact that some forms guide travellers to nests of bees. Like cuckoos, they make no nests, but lay their eggs in those of other birds.

HONEY - LOCUST TREE, OR THREE-HORNED ACACIA, the popular name of the leguminous plant *Gleditschia triacanthos,* a native of the Carolinas and Virginia. The trunk and branches of the young tree are covered with prickles, the foliage of a light shining green, and the seeds are covered with a sweet pulp.

HONEY SPRINGS, a locality in Kansas, 25 miles south of Fort Blunt, near Elk Creek. Here, on July 17, 1863, a severe action was fought between the Confederate army under General Cooper and the Union army under General Blunt. The Confederates were defeated with a considerable loss.

HONEYSUCKLE, a twining shrub, *Lonicera Periclymenum (Woodbine, twisted Eglantine);* natural order *Caprifoliaceoe,* with sweet-scented, *bilabiate* flowers, night-moth *pollination,* and crimson berries.

HONFLEUR 49° 25 N., 0° 14′ E.), port, Calvados, N.W. France; tidal harbor; exports dairy produce, fruit, vegetables; has ruined castle and fine church.

HONG-KONG, isl. belonging to Britain and lying off S. E. coast of China at estuary of Canton R. (22° 15′ N., 114° 14′ E.), along with a small portion of the mainland on peninsula of Kowloon, constitutes crown colony of Hong-Kong; cap. Victoria; extreme length *c.* 11 m., and breadth 2 to 5 m.; separated from mainland by fine strait, which makes an excellent harbor. The interior is barren and rocky. Chief exports, tea, silk, and opium. Hong-Kong has a Brit. governor, is a naval station, and the great centre of Brit. commerce with Japan and China, was occupied by Britain *c.* 1840, ceded by the Treaty of Nanking 1842; univ. of Hong-Kong was opened March 11, 1912. Area, 32 sq. m. Sir Wm. Peel, gov., 1930.

HONITON (50° 48′ N., 3° 11′ W.,) town, Devonshire, England; noted for lace manufacture; produces butter; has XV.-cent. church.

HONOLULU, a city port, and cap. of Hawaii, Pacific Ocean (belonging to U.S.A.), situated on the S. coast of the island of Oahu. In 1907 an Act was passed by which the island and county of Oahu, and the small islands adjacent, became the 'city and county of H.' The chief industries are the manufacture of machinery and carriages, rice-milling, and ship-building. The city, too, has a plentiful water supply, and hence the vegetation is luxuriant. There is a natural harbor which is formed by a lagoon, within the coral reef which has 22 ft. of water at the entrance at high tides, and can hold a large number of ships. This and Pearl Harbor are the only safe ports in the archipelago. From 1820 to 1893 the city was the residence of the sovereign, and is now the seat of government and the foreign consuls. It is an entrepot for European and Indian goods, and has communication by steamship with

San Francisco, Seattle, Vancouver, Victoria, Sydney, and Chinese and Japanese Ports. See HAWAII.

HONOR, a legal description of a seigniory of two or more manors under the control of one baron and subject to a single jurisdiction. See MANOR.

HONORIUS I. (*d.* 638), pope; elected to papal chair, 625; excommunicated after death for his views concerning Monothelite heresy.

HONORIUS II. (*d.* 1130) became pope, 1124; ratified foundation of Knights Templars; opposed Roger of Sicily. Honorius II. was antipope from 1061-64; *d.* 1072.

HONORIUS III. (*d.* 1227) became pope, 1216; authorised orders of St. Dominic and St. Francis; promoted crusades; aided Henry III. of England.

HONORIUS IV. (*d.* 1287) elected pope, 1285; confirmed Carmelite and Augustinian eremite orders; assisted Anjou against Aragon.

HONORIUS, FLAVIUS (384-423), W· Rom. emperor from 395; reign marked by Gothic invasions; sack of Rome, 410; persecuted pagans.

HONTHORST, GERARD VAN (1590-1656), fashionable Dutch painter in the Ital. manner; executed several religious pictures and many portraits of royalties, including Charles I. of England.

HOOCH, PIETER DE (1629-77), Dutch painter of interiors; obtains wonderful effects of material, reflections of light in pots and pans, and subtle expression in countenances.

HOOD, loose head-covering attached to the cloak; moulding projecting over an arch.

HOOD, HON. HORACE LAMBERT ALEXANDER (1870-1916). Brit. admiral; entered the navy, 1883; saw service on the Nile during the operations in the Sudan, 1898. In 1904, while in command of *Hyacinth*, he commanded a naval brigade which captured the Mullah's stronghold at Illig, Somaliland; was naval attache at Washington, 1907-8; in command of the Royal Naval Coll. at Osborne, 1910-13; appointed naval secretary to the first lord of the admiralty (June 1914), and in Oct. of the same year, after the outbreak of the World War, he took command of the Dover patrol. In the battle of Jutland he was in command of the 3rd Battle-cruiser Squadron, which was attached to the main fleet under Sir John Jellicoe, and led it into action. While under a terrific fire, his flagship *Invincible* was sunk.

HOOD, JOHN BELL (1831-79), Amer. general in Confederate army in Civil War; suffered crushing defeat at Nashville.

HOOD, MOUNT, a mountain of the Cascade range on the western border of Wasco co., Oregon. It is connected by rail with Hood River. Its height is 11,225 feet. At its top is an observatory used by the Forest Rangers.

HOOD, ROBIN. See ROBIN HOOD.

HOOD, SAMUEL, VISCOUNT HOOD (1724-1816), famous Brit. admiral; after considerable service in N. America, and in W. Indies, where he distinguished himself against French at Martinique, 1781, St. Kitts and Dominica, 1782, he obtained command of Mediterranean fleet, 1793; and captured Toulon; took Corsica, 1794.

HOOD, THOMAS (1799-1845), Eng. humorist and poet; *b.* London; ed. as an engraver; became sub-editor of *London Magazeine*, 1821; pub. *Odes and Addresses to Great People*, 1825; *Whims and Oddities*, 1825; launched *Hood's Comic Annual*, 1830; was sometime edit. of Colburn's *New Monthly Magazine*; pub. *The Song of the Shirt* in *Punch*, 0843; at heart a serious writer, noted for his kindly nature.

HOOD, TOM (1835-74), Eng. humorist; *s.* of the well-known Thomas H.; author of T. H.'s *Comic Annual*.

HOOFT, PIETER CORNELISSEN (1581-1647), Dutch historian and poet; held several offices under Maurice of Orange; author of *Dutch History* in 27 vol's, *History of Henry the Great*, and several tragedies, including *Geeraerdt van Velzen* and *Baeto*; also wrote *Granida*, a fine pastoral, and lyrical poems; a master of style.

HOOGSTRATEN, SAMUEL DIRKSZ VAN (*c.* 1627-78), Dutch painter, who excelled in portrait and atmosphere.

HOOK, THEODORE EDWARD (1788-1841), Eng. novelist, dramatist, and wit; *s.* of a composer; began to write successful comic operas and sketches as a youth; was Accountant-General of Mauritius, 1813-17, but owing to the defalcations of an assistant was arrested and imprisoned; became edit. of *John Bull*, a Tory organ, 1820; his *Sayings and Doings*, 1824-28 were highly popular; his novels include *Jack Brag*, *Gilbert Gurney*, and others; famed for his improvisations and practical jokes.

HOOKAH, large tobacco pipe much used in Turkey, Persia, and other Eastern countries; the stem passes through two bowls, the lower containing water, which absorbs harmful ingredients of the smoke.

HOOKE, ROBERT (1635-1703), Eng. scientist; educated at Oxford; surveyor of London during rebuilding after Great Fire of 1666; invented anchor escapement of clocks and spring-balance wheel of watches; sec. of Royal Soc., 1677-82.

HOOKER, ISABEL BEECHER (182 - 1907), an American writer; *b.* in Litchfield, Conn., and the *d.* of Dr. Lyman Beecher. She was one of the first agitators for women's suffrage in this country and as such appeared frequently on the lecture platform. Among her writings, most of which are on the subject, is *Womanhood, its Sanctities and Fidelities.*

HOOKER, JOSEPH (1814-1879), an American soldier, *b.* in Hadley, Mass. He graduated from the military academy at West Point in 1837, and served with distinction during the Mexican War, but in 1853 he resigned, following the vocations of farmer and engineer at various times. When the Civil War broke out he immediately offered his services to the Federal Government and was sent to the front with the rank of brigadier-general He served so well during the various battles in which he participated that he was made a major-general in 1862, and as such commanded at the battle of Fredericksburg. In 1863 he was given command of the Army of the Potomac, but here showed a decided lack of administrative ability, so that he was again sent into the field of active fighting. At the battle of Chancellorsville he made so poor a showing, the Federal defeat there being attributed to his poor judgment by his superiors, and so strong was the public feeling against him that he resigned. He was then given command of the 11th and 12th corps, and given the opportunity to retrieve himself, at the Battle of Lookout Mountain, near Chattanooga, which he did so brilliantly that he has ever since been regarded as one of the great military leaders of the Civil War. In 1865 he was breveted a major-general of the regular U. S. Army.

HOOKER, RICHARD (1553-1660), Eng. theologian; *b.* Heavitree, Devon; ed. Oxford; took orders and received the living of Drayton-Beauchamps (Bucks); was appointed Master of the Temple, 1585; and subsequently held livings at Boscombe (Wilts) and Bishopsbourne (Kent). *The Four Books of the Lawes of Ecclesiastical Polity* was pub. 1594; the fifth book in 1597; and subsequent books were pub. after his death.

HOOKER, SIR JOSEPH DALTON (1817-1911), Eng. botanist and traveller, succ. his *f.* as director of Kew Botanical Gardens, 1865; pub. *Genera Plantarum* and a *Flora of the British Isles*; O.M., 1907; a friend of Darwin.

HOOKER, MOUNT, a mountain in the Rocky Mountain system in Canada, on the east boundary of British Columbia. It is 15,690 feet high.

HOOKER, THOMAS (1586-1647), Puritan theologian; lectured in Leicestershire; emigrated to Massachusetts, 1633; helped to found Hartford, Conn., 1636; wrote *The Soule's Humiliation.*

HOOKWORM DISEASE. Also known as *Ankylostomiasis, uncinariasis, miner's anaemia, tunnel disease,* etc. A disease prevalent in hot climates, especially in the south eastern portion of the United States, West Indies, and Central and South America. It is caused by a parasitic worm, known as *ankylostomum duodenale,* which lodges in the intestines. The worms, of which there may be any number from a few up to many thousands in the intestines, are from 1-60 to 1-25 inch in length, and almost cylindrical. The disease has probably existed from time immemorial, but the worm was first discovered by Dubini in 1838. In the years 1853 to 1854, Bilharz and Grieseinger definitely connected the symptoms of the disease with the presence of the worms in the body, but it is only during recent years that the wide prevalence of the disease in the United States has been realised and its causes and treatment fully understood. The early symptoms are caused by the passage of the larvae through the skin. This produces irritation followed by burning, inflammation, blisters and finally pustules. The pustules form scabs, which fall off, leaving sores. The sores heal in about two weeks and the patient then appears to recover almost completely. In another six to eight weeks, however, the later symptoms, due to the development of the worms in the intestines, appear. There is general weakness and languor, pallor, pains in the upper abdomen, indigestion and sometimes constipation. In severe cases death may ensue. The disease attacks children very readily, sometimes with tragic results. The child's bodily and mental development may be retarded to such a degree as to leave him permanently stunted and mentally deficient. The disease, however, responds readily to treatment, especially in the early stages. The expulsion of the parasites

HERBERT CLARK HOOVER (1874-
31st President of the U. S. A.

is followed by slow but almost certain recovery. The day previous to the treatment the patient fasts after the mid-day meal, and is given a strong purgative upon retiring, followed, if necessary, by a dose of laxative salts the next morning. After the bowels have acted, an anthelmintic is administered. The two most effective are oil of chenopodium (either with or without chloroform) and thymol. As the latter drug is a poison, care must be used in its administration. The drugs are given in two doses, one hour apart followed by a further dose of laxative. The patient should remain in bed, and no food should be taken until the evening meal.

HOOLIGAN, term applied in latter part of XIX. cent. to London street ruffians of criminal class. The earlier 'garrotters' were of a more brutal type, who half-strangled their victims from behind and rifled their pockets. The 'Mohacks' of the XVIII. cent., referred to in the *Spectator*, belonged to a better class, and though violence was often used, it was chiefly with humorous intent.

HOOPER, JOHN (c. 1495-1555), Prot. martyr; went to Switzerland during last reactionary years of Henry VIII.; reforming preacher under Edward VII; chaplain to Protector Somerset; bp. of Gloucester, 1550; objected to priestly vestments; bp. of Worcester *in commendam*, 1552; imprisoned on Mary's accession, 1553; burned at Gloucester, 1555; called 'Father of Nonconformity.'

HOOPOES (UPUPA), so called from their call; form a genus and family of picarian birds widely distributed in desert regions of Europe, Asia, and Africa. One species (*U. epops*), with long slender bill, crested head, and orange-brown plumage marked by black and white bars, is an occasional migrant to Britain.

HOOSAC TUNNEL, a famous tunnel through the Hoosac Mountains, in western Massachusetts, about 5 miles long. It was opened in 1875. Its total cost is about $18,000,000.

HOOVER, HERBERT CLARK (1874-), 31st president of the United States. *b.* West Branch, Iowa. He graduated at Stanford University, Cal., in 1895, took part in geological surveys during his college vacations and in 1896 became manager of mines in New Mexico and California. He went to West Australia in 1897 as chief of the mining staff of an Australian corporation. Two years later he was chief engineer of the Chinese

Imperial Bureau of Mines. He participated in American operations during the Boxer Rebellion of 1900. From that period, until 1914 he was engaged actively in important mining operations. During the World War he was chairman of the American Relief Committee in London and Belgium, 1915-16; and in 1917 was made Food Administrator of the United States by President Wilson. In that office he gained a national reputation, and, following the close of the war, made a remarkable record in feeding the inhabitants of destitute regions in Poland, Austria and other impoverished sections of Europe. His name was prominently mentioned as a candidate for the presidential nomination at the Republican National Convention in 1920. He became Secretary of Commerce in the cabinet of President Harding in March of 1921. The administration of his department has been notable for economy and efficiency. He was an active factor in the American relief afforded the starving millions of Russia in 1922 and took an important part in the guarding of the commercial interests of United States business men in 1923. In 1927, as a personal representative of Coolidge, he went to the rescue of the sufferers of the Mississippi flood, aided by the army and navy and the Red Cross. In 1928 he was elected President of the United States.

The first months of his administration were marked by the reopening of negotiations with Great Britain and other powers for the limitation of Naval Armaments and the appointment of a National Law Enforcement Commission headed by Geo. W. Wickersham to investigate and report on crime in the U. S. Congress also established a Federal Farm Board at his request. He was defeated for re-election by Governor Franklin Delano Roosevelt of New York, Democrat, by an overwhelming majority.

HOP is a twining plant, *Humulus lupulus*, natural order *Cannabineœ*, which twines in the direction of the hands of a watch (right-handed spiral). It is a perennial plant with opposite lobate leaves, and grows wild in hedges and upon river-banks. The hop is *dioecious*. The male flowers are small and terminal and borne in the axils of leaves, the floral envelope has five segments and there are five *stamens*: the female flowers are cone-like in arrangement. Each has a tubular floral envelope and is invested by a *bracteole*. The cone is made up of a series of *bracts* with two female flowers at the base of the upper surface of each. The *bracts* are membranous and covered with *glands* which secrete an oil which keeps off insects. Flowers are pollinated by the wind (*anemophilous*). The fruit is composite and is called a *Strobilus*.

HOPE, ANTHONY. See HAWKINS. ANTHONY HOPE.

HOPI, MOKI, tribe of N. Amer. Indians inhabiting S.W. of U. S. A.

HÖPKEN, ANDERS JOHAN, COUNT VON (1712-89), Swed. statesman; leader of the Hats; noted for classical style of speeches.

HOPKINS, ESEK (1718-1802), an American naval officer, *b.* in Scituate, R.I.; appointed by Congress, 1775; First Commander-in-Chief of American navy with title of Admiral. He was dismissed for allowing the 'Glasgow' to escape.

HOPKINS, JOHNS (1795-1873), an American capitalist and philanthropist,*b.* in Arundel County, Md. His father was a Quaker farmer, and until he was 17 the son remained at home, helping with the farm work. He then went to Baltimore and from a boy in a grocery store, worked his way up to success as the head of a large wholesale grocery firm, retiring in 1847 with a large fortune. He gave over $4,000,000 toward the establishment of a free hospital, and in his will left $3,000,000 for the establishment of the Johns Hopkins University.

HOPKINS, MARK (1802-1887), an American College president, *b.* in Stockbridge, Mass. He graduated from Williams College, in 1824, studied medicine and began practice in New York City, in 1828, but returned to Williams College two years later as professor of philosophy and rhetoric. In 1836 he became president, and as such showed such ability that within a few years he had raised the institution to the status of one of the best colleges in the country. He wrote *An Outline Study of Man*, 1873; *The Scriptural Idea of Man*, 1883; and *Teachings and Counsels*, 1884.

HOPKINS, SAMUEL (1721-1803), Amer. theologian; ordained 1743; made attack on slavery, arousing much opposition; wrote *Life of Jonathan Edwards* and various theological works.

HOPKINS, STEPHEN (1707-1785), an American statesman. *b.* in Providence, R.I. He was appointed chief justice of the Superior Court of Rhode Island in 1751, and in 1756 was elected governor of the province. He was a member of the Continental Congress and a signer of the Declaration of Independence.

HOPKINSON, FRANCIS (1737-91), Amer. politician and writer; delegate at Continental Congress, 1776,1777; signed Declaration of Independence; wrote *The Political Catechism, a Prophecy.*

HOPKINSVILLE, a city of Kentucky, in Christian co., of which it is the county seat. It is on the Louisville and Nashville, the Tennessee Central, and the Illinois Central railroads, 73 miles N.W. of Nashville, Tenn. Its industries include the manufacture of tobacco, lime, brick, wagons and carriages. It is the seat of several educational institutions including McLean College and Bethel Female and Southern Kentucky College. It is the seat also of the Western Kentucky Insane Asylum. It has a public library, a national bank and a high school.

HOPPER (WILLIAM) DE WOLF (1853), an American comedian, *b.* in New York City. He was educated in J. H. Morse's School, and in 1879 made his first appearance in *Our Boys*. Later he joined Daniel Frohman's Madison Square Company, where he appeared as Pittacus Green in *Hazel Kirke*. After a course in voice culture and music he joined the McCaull Opera Co., then starred at the head of his own company. He is most popularly known for his appearances in the Gilbert and Sullivan operas. With Student Prince Co., 1927-28 and concert and lecture tour, 1930-31. In 1921, he appeared in *Erminie* with Francis Wilson.

HOPPNER, JOHN (1758-1810), Eng. artist; distinguished for brilliant coloring; painted 'a Sleeping Nymph' and other classic subjects, but excelled in portraiture; a follower of Reynolds, and a rival of Lawrence.

HOPTON, RALPH, BARON HOPTON (1598-1652), Eng. Royalist in Civil War; gained Cornwall for king; won battle of Stratton, 1643.

HOQUIAM, a city of Washington, in Gray's Harbor co. It is on the Chicago, Milwaukee and St. Paul, the North ern Pacific, and the Oregon Washington and Navigation Co. railroads, and on Gray's Harbor. It has considerable commercial importance as it has an excellent harbor. It is also the center of an important lumbering region. Its industries include salmon canneries, saw mills, etc. There is a Carnegie library.

HORACE, QUINTUS HORATIUS FLACCUS (65-8 B.C.), Rom. poet; *b.* at Venusia, in Apulia; his father, of the freedman class, contrived to have him educated at the same schools as the sons of senators and magnates at Rome and at Athens. At Athens N. joined the forces of Brutus, and served in Philippi as tribune. His depreciation of his valour is an imitation of Archilochus and Alcaeus, and does not imply real cowardice. His homestead appears to have been twice confiscated, but his patron Maecenas stood by him in his time of trouble and bestowed on him the beloved Sabine farm. In 37 B.C., H. with Maecenas, Vergil, and others, made the famous journey to Brundisium (*Sat.* I. 5.) When Vergil died (19 B.C.) Horace became chief court poet and voiced the ideals of Augustus.

His *Satires* are not vindictive in tone; they employ ridicule and not invective. The *Epistles* in tone are not unlike the moral essays of Pope. The *Epodes* are less delicate in sentiment, less restrained in passion. The *Ars Poetica* and the 2nd book of the *Epistles* are poetic treatises of literary art and criticism. The *Odes*, his lyrical poems, are H's. greatest work; they are not original in sentiment or passionate in feeling, but they are polished, chaste, and perfect in expression.

HORÆ (classical myth.), the 'Seasons'; three beautiful maidens, Eunomia, Dike, and Eirene, dau's of Zeus and Themis, who presided over spring, summer and autumn, and, in a lesser degree, the hours.

HORAPOLLON (fl. IV. cent. A.D.), Greek of Egypt to whom Gk. treatises on Egyptian hieroglyphics are ascribed.

HORATII, THE THREE, three Rom. bro's, who in legendary Rom. history met in battle three bro's called the Curiatii, of the Alban nation, to decide a national dispute. Two of the Horatii were slain, the third feigned flight, then turning, slew his foes one by one.

HORATIUS COCLES, hero of Rom. legend; said to have held the Tiber bridge single-handed against the Etruscans under Lars Porsena.

HOREB (28° 33′ N., 33° 56′ E.), mountain, Palestine; alternatively called Sinai (*q.v.*).

HOREHOUND (MARRUBIUM), genus of plants of order *Labiatœ*; White H. (*M. vulgare*) is used medicinally as tonic, laxative, and as sedative for coughs.

HORIZON, circle of which the centre is the person beholding, the circumference at the eyesight limit; the dip of the farther part of an object and the h. is one of proofs of spherical shape of earth.

HORMAYR, JOSEPH, BARON VON (1782-1848), Ger. historian and politician; conducted affairs during Tirolese rebellion, 1809; Austrian imperial historiographer, 1816; afterwards entered Bavarian service. Wrote *Geschichte der Tirol.*

HORMISDAS, pope, 514-523, healed schism between Eastern and Western Churches.

HORMIZD, five Sassanid kings of Persia, of whom best known is Hormizd IV.; he became king, 578 A.D.; reformed army; warred against Romans and Turks; was deposed, 588, and slain, 590.

HORMONES, the secretions given out into the blood by glands of internal secretion, such as thyroids, parathyroids, suprarenals, and pituitarys; these substances produce chemical changes in the body which affect such important functions as growth, sex development, etc. The hormone secreted by the pancreatic glands is known as secretin, and acts as a stimulant in digestion; the extract of the suprarenal glands is called adrenalin, and its injection into the blood stream produces a rise in blood pressure (by constricting the arteries), increases the heart force, and extends to all of the sympathetic nerves; it has proved invaluable in stoppage of haemorrhage, and in heart diseases; so stimulating is its effect upon the heart that apparently dead patients have been revived by it. A third hormone extract is thyroxin, the derivative of the thyroid gland, of great use in treating myxodoema, a thyroid deficiency, and cretinism caused by atrophy of the thyroid gland; it may also be useful in goiter treatment. The pituitary hormone acts as an inhibition to the flow of urine, and is used to check the excessive flow in diabetes insipidus.

HORMUZ, OR ORMUZ (27° 3′ N., 56° 26′ E.), ancient and famous city on Persian Gulf; exact date of foundation unknown; occupied various sites during course of history. In XIII. cent. one of chief centres of trade with India; *c.* 1300, inhabitants forced to abandon city owing to Tartar raids, and settled on island of Jerun not far distant. Here fine fortified city was built; in XVI. cent. taken by Portuguese, but still of great commercial importance; Portuguese forced to surrender to Eng. a cent. later, and Persians transferred trade to Gombroon on mainland. Minaret, portion of mosque, and other traces of city still to be found on island.

HORN, ARVID BERNHARD, COUNT (1664-1742), Swed. politician; ambassador to Poland, 1704; secured Stanislaus I.'s election to Polish throne; premier, 1710; virtual ruler of Sweden, 1720-38; established new constitution.

HORN, PHILIP DE MONTMORENCY, COUNT (1518-68), Dutch statesman who, with William of Orange and Egmont, led the revolt of the Netherlands against Spain; executed at Alva's command.

HORNADAY, WILLIAM TEMPLE (1854-   ) an American zoologist, b. in Plainfield, Ind. He graduated from the Iowa State Agricultural College. During 1875-9 he visited Cuba, Florida, the West Indies, South America, India, Ceylon, the Malay Peninsula and Borneo as a collecting zoologist. Prominent in the movement for the protection of game and birds. He has written *Two Years in the Jungle*, 1885; *Camp Fires in the Canadian Rockies*, 1906; *Conservation in Theory and Practice*, 1914; *Awake, America*, 1918; *The Lying Lure of Bolshevism*, 1919; *Old Fashioned Verses*, 1919, and *Thirty Years War for Wild Life*, 1931.

HORNBEAM is a genus of trees, natural order *Cupuliferoe*, cohort *Fagales*; flowers resemble those of hazel, but the male *catkins* have no *bracteoles*.

HORNBILLS (BUCEROTIDOE), so called on account of their large, hollow, horny beaks; a family of picarian birds confined to Africa from the Sudan southwards, South-Eastern Asia, and the neighboring islands. While sitting on her eggs the female is built into the tree-hollow by a mud wall, the male feeding her until the young are hatched; arboreal and terrestrial, feeding on seeds, insects, and even reptiles.

HORNBLENDE. See AMPHIBOLE.

HORN-BOOK, article once used in elementary education, consisting of a sheet of paper bearing the alphabet, Lord's Prayer, etc., placed between a flat piece of wood, with handle, and a thin sheet of horn.

HORNE, RICHARD HENGIST (1803-84), Eng. poet and critic; pub. *Orion*, 1843, an epic poem; *Death of Marlowe, Cosmo de Medici* (tragedies); and *A New Spirit of the Age* (criticism).

HORNE, RT. HON. SIR ROBERT STEVENSON (1871-   ), Brit. statesman of Scot. birth, had brilliant career at Glasgow Univ., and was called to bar, 1896; was Conservative candidate for Stirlingshire (Jan. and Dec. 1910). During World War he did valuable work as assistant inspector-general of transportation, 1917; director of Admiralty Labor department, 1918; entered Parliament as Coalition Unionist member for Hillhead div. of Glasgow, 1918; minister of labor, 1919-20. In March 1920 he succeeded Sir Auckland Geddes at the Board of Trade, and retained this office until the conservative victory of October, 1922; privy councillor, 1919.

HORNE, THOMAS HARTWELL (1780-1862), Eng. theologian and scholar; pub. *Critical Study of the Holy Scriptures, Introduction to the Study of Bibliography*; long connected with Brit. Museum.

HORNED OWL. See OWL FAMILY.

HORNED TOAD, the popular name given to the species of *Ceratophrys*, a genus of amphibians, belonging to the order Anura and the family Cystignathidae. The name is derived from the triangular, upright, horny appendage above each eye. The head and mouth are huge, and the general appearance is toad-like. *C. cornuta* of N. Brazil is beautifully colored, as also is *C. ornata*, a species found in Uruguay, Paraguay, and N. Argentina.

HORNELL, a city of New York, in Steuben co. It is on the Pittsburgh, Shawmut and Northern, and the Erie railroads, and on Canisto river, 60 miles S. of Rochester. It is an important industrial community and has manufactures of silk products, doors, blinds, furniture, carriages, brick and tile, gloves, and machinery. It is the seat of a free academy and of two hospitals. It has a public library, national banks, etc.

HORNEMANN, FREDERICK (fl. 1800), Ger. explorer; carried out explorations in Africa for London African Association between 1797 and 1799.

HORNET (VESPA CRABRO), reddish-brown wasp; eats fruits, insects, etc.; American variety is Whitefaced H. (*V. msculata*).

HORNFELS (plural, hornfelses), a rock found in diabases, basalts, and other igneous rocks, composed of felspar, hornblende, and pyroxene; of tough, durable composition, also hard and brittle; color, dark brown and black; generally contains numerous small bright crystals of black mica.

HORNPIPE, lively dance, popular among sailors; so called because originally accompanied on a reed pipe having horn fittings at either end.

HORNSEY (51° 35′ N., 0° 6′ W.), borough, suburb of London, Middlesex, England.

HOROSCOPE, signs of the heavens at person's birth; in 'casting' the h. astrologers made diagram of 12 houses, or zodiac signs. See ASTROLOGY.

HORROCKS, JEREMIAH (1619-41); Eng. astronomer; first to show how moon follows Kepler's laws, and to account for its irregularities; revised Kepler's Rudolphine tables; predicted and first observed transit of *Venus*; first to make tidal observations.

HORSE FAMILY (*Equidae*), the most highly specialised family of odd-toed, hoofed (*Ungulate*) mammals, including horses, asses, and zebras as well as many extinct forms. The compact, clean-cut bodies long heads and tails, and maned necks of the horse and its relatives are familiar, but there are skeletal characters of more importance in separating it from its nearest allies, the Tapirs and Rhinoceroses, and these mainly reside in the teeth and limbs. The skull is very long, the eye-socket is a closed ring, and the teeth number, at highest, 44, although the early disappearance of the first cheek-tooth on each leaves 42 as the usual number. The surfaces of the back teeth, obviously grinders, are thrown into complicated crescentic folds of hard enamel, with softer cement between; and the incisors are prominent and chisel-shaped, with a central pit lined by enamel—the 'mark' whose decrease in size indicates the age of its possessor. The limbs are furnished with one hoofed digit (the third), which is functional, but it is sometimes accompanied by the second and fourth, reduced to mere splint bones, or at any rate always functionles.

Horses in a general sense are found throughout the world, but the various wild species are confined in range and are found only in the Old World, especially in Asia and Eastern Africa. Semi-wild forms occur in Australia and America, but these are the descendants of domesticated horses which have escaped from captivity, in the latter country since the Spanish conquest. In nature horses are gregarious, living, in herds the movements of which are dominated by an experienced stallion or male, the female being known as mare, and the young as foal; but they are ever on the watch and habitually move against the wind so that they may receive early notice of the scent of an enemy. They are entirely vegetarian, feeding mainly on grass, but also on young shoots of trees and herbage.

To consider less generally the members of the horse family, all the living species of which belong to the noe genus *Equus*.

Heading the list on account of its familiarity and of its usefulness to man is the domestic Horse (*E. caballus*), representatives of which roamed the plains of Europe and Asia in freedom till about the end of the XVI. cent., although the horse as a domestic animal probably dates from prehistoric times. It is characterised by a hardened lump—the 'chestnut' —on the inner side of the legs above the hock, and by the fact that the hairs of the tail grow in a tassel from its base. During the ages of servitude to man many varieties of horses have been selected and bred for special purposes. Thus perhaps most useful are the heavy carthorses, distinguished by their weight of body and stoutness of limb, the best known being the Shire, Clydesdale, and Suffolk Punch. While bred for very special purposes necessitating cleanness and lightness of limb and body are the English Racers and American Trotters, differing in descent from the cart-horses, which are comparatively pure natives of Europe, by the interbreeding with such graceful African horses as the Arab.

Closely related to the domestic horse are the active Tarpans or Wild Horses of of the steppes, probably a decaying remnant of the original wild horses of Europe; and the small, shaggy, erect-maned Prejevalski's Horse of Central Asia.

The horse, as we know it, has been traced back to Pliocene times, but the remains of earlier forms have been discovered which seem to point to the ancestral line along which the modern horse developed. The differentiation appears to have followed these directions; an increase in size, a reduction in the number of functional digits, and an increasing complexity in the structure of the teeth. Thus the Eocene *Phenacodus*, at the source of the horse group, was an animal about the size of a bull-dog and had five functional toes on each foot; *Paloeotherium* and *Anchitherium*, the former from the later Eocene, the latter about the size of a sheep, had three digits, and link the tapir group to the horses, while in the Pliocene *Hippotherium*, as big as a donkey, the middle digit was already outstandingly developed.

HORSE-CHESTNUT OR ÆSCULUS HIPPOCASTANUM, a well-known species of Hippocastanaceae, commonly grown in Britain as an ornamental plant. It has large leaves divided into five or seven long, distinct leaflets, and the white flowers are arranged in tall spikes: the fruit is a prickly capsule.

HORSE-MACKEREL, the popular name of *Caranx*, a genus of teleostean fishes belonging to the sub-order Acanthopterygii and the family Carangidae. *C. trachurus*, is common on our coasts, where the young are often found in large colonies, sheltering under medusae. They have a compressed oblong body covered with small scales.

HORSENS (55° 52′ N.; 9° 50′ E.); town, Jutland, Denmark.

HORSE RACING. See RACING.

HORSE-RADISH, COCHLEARIA ARMORACIA, natural order *Cruciferœ.* The root, long, cylindrical, and fleshy, with an enlarged upper end, is used as a condiment.

HORSE-SHOEING, the custom of protecting horses' hoofs is probably coeval with domestication of horse; machine-made shoes have been largely used since Goodenough's patent invention, 1860.

HORSETAIL, vascular cryptogam with green stem and branches and brown, scale-like leaves. One generation reproduces by spores, the next by male and female cells.

HORTENSE (1783-1837). See BEAU-HARNAIS.

HORTENSIUS, QUINTUS, dictator to end of plebeian secession at Rome, 286 B.C.; passed *lex Hortensia,* giving independent legislative power to *plebs.*

HORTENSIUS, QUINTUS (141-50 B.C.), Rom. orator; became consul in 69 B.C.; attained fame as advocate.

HORTHY, DE NAGYBANYA NIKO-LAUS (1868-   ), Hungarian admiral and regent, *b.* at Kendered; ed. at the Naval Academy at Fiume; distinguished himself as an admiral in the World War, and was appointed commander of the Austro-Hungarian fleet. After the collapse of the Monarchy, Horthy formed a counter-revolutionary party, which succeeded in quashing the rise of Bolshevism in Hungary. On March 1, 1920, he was elected regent of Hungary by the national assembly, but since the Hapsburg dynasty had been deposed he remained in the strange position of being regent to a non-existent king. However since he performed his duties in accordance with the constitution, the legitimist question was seldom raised.

HORTICULTURE. See GARDEN.

HORUS, Egyptian sun-god, represented by the hawk; divided Egyptian reverence with Osiris.

HOSANNA, salutation of the crowd when Christ made His triumphal entry into Jerusalem (*Mark* 11₉,₁₀), being part of an ancient Heb. ceremonial.

HOSE, skintight foot and leg coverings, formerly reaching to the waist; the XVI.-cent. breeches were called *trunk-hose.*

HOSEA, Old Testament minor prophet. H. was a contemporary of Isaiah, and prophesied during reigns of last six kings of Israel, from Jeroboam II. to Hoshea. The book may be divided into two parts: the first (chaps. 1-3) relates the unfaithfulness of the prophet's wife, which is used as a symbol of idolatry of nation; and the second (chaps. 4-14) is a series of accusations against Children of Israel for their wickedness, which is unsparingly denounced. H. makes use of illustrations taken from domestic and rural occupations, such as baking, reaping, and sowing. Book is frequently quoted in New Testament, quotations occurring in the Gospels of *Matthew* and *Luke,* the *Apocalypse,* and the *Epistle to the Romans.*

HOSE-PIPE, india-rubber implement for conveyance of water. The fire h.-p. is covered with carefully woven linen cloth, made circular, without seam, and done by handloom for important purposes.

HOSHANGABAB (22° 43′ N., 77° 39′ E.), town (and district), Central Provinces, India.

HOSHEA (slain 721), last king of Israel; refused to pay tribute to Shalmeneser IV., king of Assyria, who attacked Israel.

HOSHIARPUR (31° 33′ N., 75° 48′ E.), town, Punjab, India; manufactures lacquer, cottons. H. district has area of 2244 sq. miles.

HOSIERY, stockings (See HOSE) and garments similarly manufactured by knitting. Unlike weaving, knitting is supposed to have been a late mediaeval, probably Scot., invention. The stocking-frame was invented in 1589 by Lee, and completed by the addition of Jedediah Strutt's invention for rib-stitch in 1758. The warp loom was first introduced in 1775. Matthew Townsend introduced the latch needle in 1858. Circular and flat frames by which seamless h. is obtained have been invented by Fr., Ger., Belg., Eng., and Amer. manufacturers.

HOSIUS (*d.* 359), dp. of Cordova; authoritative member of Council of Nicaea, 325.

HOSIUS, STANISLAUS (1504-79), Polish cardinal, who suppressed Reformation in Poland.

HOSKINS, JOHN (*d.* 1664), Eng. miniature painter, whose works are much sought after by collectors.

HOSMER, HARRIET G. (1830-1908), an American sculptor, *b.* in Watertown, Mass. Without much training she first confined herself to modelling in clay.

then studied anatomy at a medical college in St. Louis, Mo. In 1852 she went to Rome, where she came under the influence of John Gibson, an English sculptor. Shortly after she exhibited 'Puck' in the United States, which immediately won her a high class reputation. Her 'Will-o'-the-Wisp' added to her name in the following year. Among her public works is a statue of Benton, the Missouri statesman, standing in Lafayette Park, in St. Louis.

HOSMER, JAMES KENDALL (1834), an American university president and writer, *b.* in Northfield, Mass. He graduated from Harvard University, in 1855, studied theology and was ordained a Unitarian pastor, in 1860. During the Civil War he served in the Union Army as a private. After the war he taught English and history at Antioch College, the University of Missouri, and Washington University, and during 1892-1904 was librarian of the Minneapolis Public Library. Among his books are *The Color Guard*, 1864; *A Short History of German Literature*, 1878; *A Short History of Anglo-Saxon Freedom*, 1890; *How Thankful Was Bewitched*, 1894; *A History of the Louisiana Purchase*, 1902. *d.* 1927.

HOSPICE, house of shelter for pilgrims and travellers, usually founded and maintained by some religious order.

HOSPITAL CORPS, UNITED STATES. The Medical Services of both the Army and Navy have such corps, for which recruits are enlisted and trained to qualify for tending the incapacitated and the wounded. The duties of the hospital corps are non-military, and the personnel are only subject to drills necessary for their physical efficiency. The army hospital corps consists of sergeants, corporals, cooks and privates, whose functions are to perform all needful hospital service in camp, garrison or field. The naval hospital corps undertakes like duties in naval hospitals, naval stations, navy yards and marine barracks and in subsidiary branches of the naval service, such as the coast survey. The personnel embraces pharmacists, stewards and apprentices. Enlistments for the army hospital corps are made through army medical officers, and those for the navy corps (except apprentices, who can be enlisted like other recruits) through the Surgeon-General.

HOSPITALLERS (*Ordo fratrum hospitalariorum Hierosolymitanorum* and *Ordo militioe Santci Johannis Baptistoe hospitalis Hierosolymitani*), religious military order. Its pre-Christian foundation is merely traditional. The constant

stream of pilgrims to Holy Land, from the beginning of Christian era, increased after the erection of Church of Holy Sepulchre by Constantine. Pope Gregory the Great, at close of VI. cent., founded a hospital at Jerusalem. Persians captured Jerusalem, 614, but Charlemagne established a protectorate over Holy Places, 797-99, and refounded Pope Gregory's hospital, which was served by Benedictine monks from Mount of Olives. Turks captured Jerusalem, 1070-87, and destroyed all Christian edifices. Christian merchants of Amalfi obtained permission from Turks and established a hospital, *c.* 1050, again probably served by Benedictines; still under invocation of St. Mary.

Gerard, *d.* 1120, was the true founder and first Grand Master of the later hospital, of which he became Institutor by papal bull, 1113. The Crusaders and every Western country bestowed lands on the hospital, and in 1113 the pope confirmed these grants. Gerard was succeeded by Raymond du Puy, *d.* 1158-60. Mention of a Constable in 1126 seems to point to military character already. From 1137 the Knights Hospitallers took prominent part in crusades. Augustinian rule was given to the Order before 1153, as it was confirmed by Pope Eugenius III.; threefold vow of poverty, chastity, obedience; duty to be servants of the poor(*fratres pauperibus servientes*). Successive regulations were codified by Grand Master Pierre d'Aubusson, 1489. On suppression of Templars, 1313, their lands were granted to Hospitallers.

They were forced to fly from Jerusalem, 1187; held out against Saracens at Acre till 1291; held Rhodes, 1310-1522, and became known as *Knights of Rhodes*; Turks at last took Rhodes, 1522, and knights retired of Malta, granted them by Charles V., 1530. Grand Master Philippe de Villiers de l'Isle d'Adam strenuously continued war against Turks from the Order's new home, and his successor, La Vallette, defended Malta in famous siege, 1565. In XVIII. cent. Order became merely rich aristocratic picturesque institution. Possessions in England were lost at Reformation; possessions in France confiscated, 1792. Napoleon captured Malta, 1798. Malta is still seat of the Order.

HOSPITAL SHIPS belong to one of three classes, (1) naval or military; (2) Merchant marine; (3) Civil. Military hospital ships usually exist only during a state of war, and are used for transporting wounded soldiers from the country where military operations are in progress to hospitals overseas. For instance, during the European war, hospital ships were used to transport wounded American and British soldiers from the French and other fronts to England and America. Naval hospital ships may be permanently attached to a navy, to care for sick, injured or wounded sailors, or for ship-wrecked persons. In the U. S. Navy, a hospital ship is commanded by a naval medical officer not below the rank of surgeon. Under him, are merchant officers and crew for navigation, and doctors, nurses and orderlies to care for the sick and injured. The merchant officers have full control over the navigation of the ship and the maintenance of discipline among the crew. According to an agreement of the second Geneva Convention, of 1868, merchantmen or hospital ships having wounded on board, or boats rescuing wounded or shipwrecked, are immune from attack or capture. A hospital ship must carry no arms or ammunition, except such as are necessary for protection of the wounded or for maintenance of order on board. U. S. Navy hospital ships are painted white with a broad green horizontal stripe. If the ship belongs to an organization, such as the Red Cross, the stripe is red instead of green. They fly the Red Cross flag as well as the national ensign. An example of a merchant marine hospital ship is the U. S. coastguard cutter Androscoggin, which was converted into a hospital for caring for the men of the north Atlantic fishing fleet. Two well-known civil hospital ships are the Bellevue Hospital ship for tuberculous children from New York City, and the Boston Floating Hospital.

HOSPITALS. The monastic orders that arose with the spread of Christianity were among the first to care for the sick by systematized institutions, though hospitals of a sort had been founded long before in pagan times. The elaborate hospital system of modern days had its origin in those remote monastic retreats. The Crusades produced the Hospitallers, who were knights devoted to serving the sick, and also the orders of Sisters of Mercy, Sisters of Charity and kindred bodies. The more notable hospitals of the distant past were at Alexandria, Ephesus, Constantinople and Caesarea, where St. Basil founded a great establishment with special provision for lepers. Among the earliest hospitals also was the Hotel Dieu in Paris, the first hospital in France and the oldest in existence to-day, dating from the sixth century. Three centuries later the Archbishop of Canterbury founded one in England. Famous London hospital of St. Bartholomew's had its beginnings in 1123, and that of St. Thomas in 1215. Other renowned English institutions did not appear till the eighteenth century—

Westminister in 1719, Guy's in 1725 and the Royal Infirmary of Edinburgh in 1730. The growth of universities developed the study of medicine, and many hospitals became identified as departments with schools of learning. The great hospitals in Italy, France, England and Scotland thus became noted medical schools.

American hospitals were naturally founded upon European methods, especially English, and began with the Pennsylvania Hospital, Philadelphia, established in 1730, of which Benjamin Franklin was clerk. The next American hospital of note was the New York Hospital, chartered in 1771. These led the way to the erection of hospitals in every American community, urban and rural, built and conducted on lines so far in advance of the European models that Old World hospitals now look frequently to American methods and practice to guide them in improving their efficiency.

Hospitals are either charitable institutions wholly, or semi-charitable, receiving both free and pay patients ,or receive pay patients only. They may be supported wholly or in part by federal, state or municipal funds, or maintained by religious or other organizations, or by private endowment. Among those under municipal control and reserved solely for the city poor are the Johns Hopkins Hospital, Baltimore, the Philadelphia Hospital, Bellevue and allied institutions in New York City, Massachusetts. General and Boston City Hospitals in Boston, and Cook County Hospital in Chicago. There are also many notable institutions founded by private gifts and sectarian societies throughout the country. In large part the country's hospitals that general cases, but there are many both charitable and private, devoted to the treatment of special disorders, such as ailments of the eye, ear, nose and throat, cancer and tuberculosis, and contagious skin diseases, while there are also hospitals for children and women, the incurable and the insane. Other hospitals are those maintained by the army at Hot Springs, Arkansas (where there is also a naval hospital), and at Denver Colo.; Presidio, San Francisco; Manila, Philippines; Honolulu, Hawaii; Takoma Park, State of Washington; and at El Paso, Texas. Kindred institutions are the dispensaries and clinics, where patients who do not require hospital attention are treated, and sanatoria, public and private, for invalids and convalescents.

HOSPODAR (Russian *Gospodar*), a Slavonic term meaning 'lord,' 'master', is the title which is specially applied to the head of a family or the master of a

house. It was a title of the rulers of
Wallachia and Moldavia from the 15th
century to 1866, when Rumania became
independent. The title was also used
by the grand-dukes of Lithuania and
the kings of Poland down to John
Sobieski.

HOST (Lat. *hostia,* sacrifice); the
element of bread in the Eucharist;
circular unleavened wafers marked with
emblems of the Crucifixion are used in
the R. C. Church; these emblems were
forbidden at the Reformation.

HOSTAGE, a person given up to an
enemy as a security for the performance
of certain articles of a treaty or other
conditions. On the surrender of a town,
victors and vanquished gave such personal security for fulfilment of terms, the
h's being later exchanged.

HOT AIR ENGINES are heat motors
in which the working substance (usually
air) does not experience a change in
physical state throughout the cycle.
There are two general classes of Hot Air
Engines:
(A) Those in which the air used does
not come into contact with the flame of
the heat source, but is heated by conduction from this source and also by a
regenerator which serves to conserve
some of the heat left in the air after
expansion. This would otherwise be
rejected to the refrigerator and lost. The
air, in these engines, is not discharged
at the end of the cycle, but used again;
consequently the cycle is a closed one.
(B) Those which use as a working
substance the products of combustion
of the heat source mixed with some air.
In these engines the cycle is not a closed
one, and the working substance is
exhausted at the end of the stroke.
The engine consists of a means for
heating air, or other similar gas, and a
cylinder in which the heated gas is allowed to expand, thereby acting on a
piston and doing useful work.
The theoretical heat efficiency of such
an engine is high, much higher than when
the working substance suffers a change in
physical state during the cycle (such as
the steam engine and boiler) because no
heat is lost through a change of state.
The practical efficiency of the engine
as compared with the theoretical is,
however, low for numerous reasons too
complicated to discuss here. For this
reason and because its weight per horse
power is large, this engine is used in
practice only where a very simple and
safe machine is required, *e.g.* for fog
signals in light houses—pumping small
quantities of water in dwellings, etc.
The expansion of air by heat was first
utilized by Hero of Alexandria—Egypt

in 130 B.C. in his device for mysteriously
(?) opening doors. Practical development of the Hot Air Engine was begun
in 1807 by Sir Geo. Cayley. Many other
engineers worked on the idea, notable
among them being Ericsson and Starling.

**HOTCHKISS, BENJAMIN BERK-
LEY** (1826-1885), an American inventor,
b. in Watertown, Conn. He made many
inventions in fire-arms, the most notable
of which are the Hotchkiss magazine
rifle and the Hotchkiss machine gun.

HOTCHKISS (MACHINE) GUN. A
machine gun working on much the same
principles as the Colt (Browning) gun.
The mechanism of the gun is actuated by
a helical spring. This is compressed by a
piston operated by the expanding gases
produced by the burning (explosion) of
the charge of powder. The cylinder in
which the piston operates connects with
the gun barrel at a point near the muzzle. The volume of this cylinder, and
consequently the force actuating the
piston is adjustable, thereby permitting
the regulation of the speed at which the
whole mechanism works. This arm is
unique, in that there is no separate spring
to actuate the firing pin, the main spring
performing the service in such a way that
the breech must be tightly closed before
it can act on the firing pin striker, thus
preventing the prefiring of a cartridge.
Another important feature is the arrangement whereby the breech cannot be
opened until the projectile has left the
barrel and the burnt gases have had time
to escape from the muzzle. The ammunition is fed by metal strips or clips holding 30 cartridges each. The gun is
usually sighted to 2,000 yards and can
fire 500-600 rounds per minute. It
weighs 53 lbs. without a mount.

HÔTEL-DE-VILLE, Fr. term corresponding to Eng. town hall; it usually
contains barracks, prison, court-house,
offices of local bodies, and residence of
chief magistrate. Famous H. of Paris,
burnt during riots of Commune, 1871,
has been rebuilt.

HÔTEL-DIEU (God-house) Fr. name
for important hospitals; some, like those
of Angers and Beaune, are of architectural interest.

HOTHO, HEINRICH GUSTAV
(1802-73), Ger. writer; author of an
important work on Flemish and Ger.
painters.

HOTMAN, FRANÇOIS (1524-90),
Fr. author; embraced Reformed religion;
undertook Huguenot missions to Ger.
princes; prof. of Law in various univ's;
Councillor to Henry of Navarre, 1580;
wrote *Franco-Gallia,* etc.

HOT SPRINGS NATIONAL PARK, a city of Arkansas, in Garland co., of which it is the county seat. It is on the Missouri Pacific and the Rock Island railroads and the Ouachita River. It derives its name from the radio-active thermal springs, 46 in number, which flow from the base of Hot Springs mountain at a temperature of 135 F. to 147 F. The waters are noted for their curative and rejuvenating properties. The springs are frequented by those who desire to keep physically fit. and the thermal baths are an adjunct to rejuvenation. Outstanding institutions include U.S. Army and Navy General Hospital, various other hospitals, modern schools, five banks, palatial bathing establishments and modern hotel facilities. The resort is open the year round.

HOTTENTOTS, South African aborigines (calling themselves *Khoikhoi*, Men of Men); sometimes but erroneously supposed to include Bushmen (*q.v.*) Their quaint language, with its 'click' sounds, led the early Dutch settlers to dub them H's (*i.e.* 'jabberers'). They were decimated and driven southwards by Bantu (or Kafirs) and pure H's now number only from 50,000 to 100,000; mostly in Cape of Good Hope, but several thousand survive in Ger. S.W. Africa. They are of middle statute, have yellowish-brown skins, woolly hair, and are characterised by steatopygia. Their tribes were pastoral and peaceful under patriarchal rule; they used poisoned arrows. Their folklore is described in Bleek's *Reynard in South Africa.*

HÖTZENDORFF, CONRAD VON, Austrian general; (1852-1925), War chief of Austrian general staff; constant friction with Falkenhayn, Hötzendorff believing road to success was *via* Asiago, Falkenhayn *via* Verdun. Relations improved when Hindenburg succeeded Falkenhayn. Formula of German Kaiser as to united action accepted by Austria-Hungary, Turkey, and Bulgaria, but Hötzendorff insisted on second clause guaranteeing same consideration for integrity and protection of Dual Monarchy as for German Empire.

HOUDINI, HARRY (Eric Weiss), American magician, born in Appleton, Wis., 1874, died Detroit, Mich., 1926. Developed marked ability to free himself from bonds. Became known as the Handcuff King. He exposed many spiritualistic frauds.

HOUDON, JEAN ANTOINE (1740-1828), Fr. sculptor; won *Prix de Rome*, 1761; studied in Italy for ten years; achieved great success with statue of St. Bruno; later works included statues of Washington, Cicero, and Voltaire; and busts of Napoleon, Moliere, Rousseau, Nev. and D'Alembert.

HOUGH, EMERSON (1857-1923), an American author, *b.* in Newton, Ia. He graduated from the University of Iowa, in 1880. In 1895 he made an exploring trip in the midst of winter through Yellowstone Park, the result of which was an Act of Congress, protecting the Park buffalo. Among his books are *The Singing Mouse Stories*, 1895; *The Story of the Cowboy*, 1897; *The Mississippi Bubble,* 1902; *The Young Alaskans*, 1910; *The Lady and the Pirate*, 1913; *The Young Alaskans in the Far North*, 1918; *The Sagebrusher*, 1919 and *The Covered Wagon*, 1922; *North of 36*, 1923.

HOUGHTON, ALANSON BIGELOW (1863), manufacturer; *b.* in Cambridge, Mass.; 1886 Bachelor of Arts, Harvard College. Post graduate at Berlin and Paris, 1899 entered manufacturing of glass at Corning, 1903-1910 second vice president, 1910-1918 president, chairman of board since, Corning Glass Works. Director of Metropolitan Life Insurance Company. Ex-president of Board of Education, Corning. Elected to Congress for term of 1919-1923, resigned to become Minister Plenipotentiary and Ambassador Extraordinary to Germany in 1922. 1925 he was appointed ambassador to Great Britain, succeeding Kellog. Resigned, 1929.

HOUGHTON, GEORGE CLARKE (1852-1923), an American Protestant Episcopal clergyman, *b.* in New York City. He graduated from St. Stephens College in 1867 and afterwards studied at the General Theological Seminary. He was appointed curate of Trinity parish in 1870, continuing there until 1879, when he was appointed rector of Trinity Church in Hoboken. In 1887 he became rector of the Church of the Transfiguration, better known as 'The Little Church Around the Corner', which was founded by his uncle, George H. Houghton, in 1848. This church is famous throughout the country for its liberality in matters of belief and practice. It gained its name through the willingness of Dr. Houghton to perform burial services for actors, after they had been refused by the pastor of another church, who suggested 'The Little Church Around the Corner'. Dr. Houghton remained rector of this church until his death. He wrote much on theological subjects and was one of the best known clergymen in the country.

HOUGHTON, RICHARD MONCKTON MILNES, 1ST BARON (1809-85), Eng. poet and critic; received a peerage, 1863; pub. *Poetry for the People*, 1840;

Palm Leaves, 1848; and other vol's. of verse; also a life of Keats; a generous patron of poets and authors.

HOUGHTON-LE-SPRING (54° 51′ N., 1° 29′ W.), town, Durham, England.

HOULTON, a city of Maine, in Aroostook co., of which it is the county seat. It is on the Bangor and Aroostook and the Canadian Pacific railroad. It is the center of an important farming region and its industries include foundry and machine shops, lumber mills, woolen mills, a starch factory, etc. It is the seat of the Rickert Classical Institute. It has a high school, public library, hospitals and a park.

HOUND. See Dog Family.

HOUND'S-TONGUE (CYNOGLOSSUM),genus of plants of order Boraginaceae (*q.v.*). Common hound's-tongue (*C. officinale*), has small red flowers and downy leaves.

HOUNSLOW (51° 28′ N., 0° 22′ W.), town, Middlesex, England; formerly site of priory. H. Heath was a highwayman's haunt.

HOURI, name given in the Koran to the seventy-two beautiful women who are assigned to every 'Faithful' as spouses on entering the Muhammadan paradise.

HOURS, CANONICAL, special times in the day for devotion in Catholic Church, viz. Matins, Lauds, Prime, Terce, Sect, None, Vespers (Evensong), and Compline.

HOUSE, EDWARD MANDELL (1856), American peace envoy; *b*. Houston, Texas, of English parentage. He graduated from Cornell in 1881 and thereafter devoted his attention to Democratic politics, state and national, without seeking office. In 1914 he became prominent as a confidential envoy and adviser of President Wilson, who sent him to Europe in that year on a diplomatic mission before the outbreak of the World War. In the war period he visited Europe again as the President's representative to consult with the belligerent governments. On the United States entering the conflict in 1917 he attended in London the meetings of the Supreme War Council of the Allies as chairman of the American mission, and in that capacity communicated America's views regarding the conduct of the war to the allied premiers and foreign ministers. When peace neared in 1918 he was designated by the President to act for the United States in the negotiations for the armistice

with the Central Powers. Next to President Wilson he was the most prominent American who figured on the war councils of Europe and throughout the war period was the subject of considerable attention in the American and foreign press. He edited with Charles Seymour, *What Happened at Paris*, 1921, the story of the Peace Conference of 1918-19; *Intimate Papers of Col. House* (4 Vols.), pub., 1927-28.

HOUSE BREAKING. See Theft.

HOUSE-FLY (MUSCIDÆ). With the house-fly (*Musca domestica*) are ranked the blue-bottles (*Calliphora*), green-bottles (Lucilia), and the dreaded African tsetse-fly (*Glossina*). The eggs of Muscid flies are generally laid upon dung, decaying matter, or carrion, and upon this the larvae feed. In this way they are of some value as scavengers; but otherwise they cause much trouble. The house-fly may carry germs of disease upon its feet or proboscis, and transfer these to human food; the larvae of blue-bottles and green-bottles frequently bore into the skin of sheep, causing great irritation and sometimes death; the 'screw-worm' larva of one species of *Lucilia* bores in the nasal cavities of man and higher animals; and tsetse-flies are the carriers of the organisms which cause the fatal native disease of sleeping sickness and the troublesome animal disease, nagana, in Africa.

HOUSE OF COMMONS. See Parliament.

HOUSE OF LORDS. See Parliament.

HOUSE OF REPRESENTATIVES. See Congress.

HOUSING. The assuring of proper housing conditions for populations in large cities has only in comparatively recent times become a matter of marked concern to municipal, state and national governments. It has come to be realized that not only altruism but self interest prescribe the establishment of such conditions, since the health and happiness of the people are matters of vital interest to state and nation.

The movement for better living conditions in the United States began in New York City in 1842, when attention was called to the housing situation in a special report on the sanitation of the city. Since that time, almost all the large cities of the country have adopted plans for the betterment of dwellings. Chief among these are; protection against fire and means of escape in case of fire; light and ventilation; sanitary protection, the latter including water supply, toilet accommodations and the prevention of overcrowding.

In many cities tenements must be fire-proof, and fire escapes are required in buildings over three stories in height. Light and ventilation are secured by provisions for minimum open spaces and limitation of the proportion of a lot that can be occupied by a building. In New York, water must be furnished on every floor and one toilet accommodation must exist for every two families.

Model tenements, combining artistic attractiveness with abundance of light, air and sanitary conveniences, have been built by private enterprise in over 124 cities of the United States, while nearly 700 cities have taken an active interest in the improvement of housing conditions.

In Great Britain, the movement for better housing has been largely under the direction of municipal and state governments, which have not only regulated construction but actually built thousands of model dwellings, thus differing from the United States where the actual building has been done by private concerns. The limitation on the height of houses is stricter in Great Britain than in this country. In London, Glasgow, Manchester, Liverpool and Edinburgh, vast slum areas have had their dilapidated buildings razed and model municipal tenements built in their places. The regulations in Berlin and Paris are more elaborate, though in general they aim at the same end and follow the same fundamental ideas as in the United States.

HOUSMAN, ALFRED EDWARD (1859), Eng. poet and scholar; prof. of Latin, Cambridge; author of *A Shropshire Lad*, 1896; *Manlius* (5 Vol.), 1932.

HOUSMAN, LAURENCE (1867), Eng. writer and artist; first achieved celebrity as book-illustrator; author of *An Englishwoman's Love Letters*, 1900; *A Modern Antaeus, Sabrina Warham* and *What O'clock Tales*, 1932.

HOUSSAYE, ARSÉNE (1815-96), Fr. novelist and poet; his novels include *Les Filles d' Eve, La Couronne de Bluets*, etc.; poetry, *Cent et un sonnets*, also dramas, critical and hist. works. His *s. Henri*, 1848, is a historian and academician.

HOUSTON, a city of Texas, in Harris co., of which it is the county seat. It is on the Gulf, Colorado and Sante Fe, the Southern Pacific, the International and Great Northern, the Missouri, Kansas and Texas, and other railroads, and on Buffalo Bayou, 50 miles northwest of the Gulf of Mexico with which it is connected by a ship canal accommodating large steamships. It is the second city of the State in population and first in industrial importance. It is well built on both sides of the Bayou, which is spanned by several bridges. Among the public buildings are a city hall and market house, the Houston Lyceum, the cotton exchange, a Masonic Temple, Union Station, and a post office. The city is the seat of several educational institutions including the William M. Rice Polytechnic Institute. There is an excellent street system, five public high schools and a public library. Houston is the most important city of the State in manufactures. Its industries include plants for the making of oil, furniture, iron castings, cigars, brick, pottery, jewelry, paints, chemicals, soap, etc. There are also railroad and machine shops, sugar and pump mills and cotton compresses. There are several banks and other financial institutions. The city is lighted by gas and electricity, has an abundant water supply, electric street railways and all the other essentials of a modern city. The exchanges at the United States Clearing House amount to nearly one billion dollars annually. Houston was settled in 1836 and in 1837 was the capital of the Republic of Texas.

HOUSTON, DAVID FRANKLIN. (1866), an American public official, *b.* in Monroe, N. C. He graduated from South Carolina College, in 1887, taught school for some years and during 1900-2 was professor of political science at the University of Texas. During 1902-5 he was president of that institution, and during 1908-16 he was chancellor of Washington Univ., in St. Louis, Mo. In 1913 he was appointed by Pres. Wilson Secy. of the Department of Agriculture, which position he held until 1920, after which he was Secy. of the Treas. until the end of the administration. Author of *A Critical Study of Nullification in South Carolina.* Chairman, Fed. Res. and Farm Loan Bds., 1920-21.

HOUSTON HEIGHTS, a post town of Harris co., Texas, U.S.A., 4m. N.W. of Houston. Now incorporated with city of Houston.

HOUSTON, SAM (1793-1863), an American statesman, soldier, adventurer and one of the most picturesque figures in American history. He was *b.* near Lexington, Va., but at the age of thirteen went to Tennessee with his parents. Several years later he struck into the western wilderness and for some years lived among the Indians, being adopted by one of the chiefs. In 1813 he returned to civilization, enlisted as a private in the army and chanced to come under the observation of General Jackson, whose influence caused him to be appointed Indian agent among the Cherokees. A year later he resigned, because of a clash with higher authorities, who objected to his zeal in preventing the importation of slaves through Florida, then a Spanish province. In 1823 he was elected to Congress from Tennessee, was re-elected in 1825, and in 1827 he was elected Governor of the State. He resigned two years later and abruptly left civilization to return to his Indian friends. In 1832 he appeared in Texas and during the war between the United States and Mexico was elected commander-in-chief of the Texan Army, brilliantly distinguishing himself as such. In 1836 he was elected President of the Republic of Texas, and again in 1841, and when, in 1845, Texas entered the Union as a state, he represented it in the U. S. Senate, until 1859, when he was elected Governor. In 1861 he was deposed on account of his strong anti-slavery sentiment, whereupon he retired into private life.

HOUWALD, CHRISTOPH ERNST, FREIHERR VON (1778-1845), Ger. dramatist and author; pub. *Romantische Akkorder, Jakob Thau, der Hofnarr,* etc.; also some plays.

HOVA, OR MERINA, the dominant tribes of Madagascar, occupying the plateau of Imerina; small and slightly built, yellow complexion, hair black and long; converts to Christianity.

HOVE (50° 50' N., 0° 21' W.), town, Sussex, England.

HOVEY, RICHARD (1864-1900), an American poet, b. in Normall, Ill. He graduated from Dartmouth, in 1885, after which he was, first an actor, then a journalist, and finally a lecturer on English literature at Barnard College ,in New York City. His best poems are published in two collections; *Along the Trail,* 1898 and *To the End of the Trail,* 1908. He also wrote *Songs from Vagabondia,* 1893, in collaboration with Bliss Carman.

HOWARD, old Eng. family, said to have been settled in Norfolk as far back as X. cent. In XV. cent. Sir Robert H. married the *d.* of Mowbray, Duke of Norfolk, and his *s.,* Sir John H., was in 1483 cr. Duke of Norfolk and Earl Marshal of England, an office hereditary in the family ever since. The first duke was killed at *Bosworth* and attainted; but his *s.* Thomas won battle of *Flodden,* and regained the dukedom in 1514;

third duke was uncle of Anne Boleyn and Catherine Howard, queens of Henry VIII.; his *gs.* and successor m. heiress of Arundel earldom, thus bringing that title to the H. family; this duke was afterwards attainted and beheaded for plotting in favor of Mary, Queen of Scots, 1572. The family regained dukedom from Charles II. after the Restoration. Present is 15th duke, and is premier duke of England. The Earls of Effingham, Suffolk, ahd Carlisle are of same stock.

HOWARD, BRONSON (1842-1908), Amer. playwright; among his plays are *Young Mrs. Winthrop* and *Old Love Letters.*

HOWARD, CATHERINE (1521-42), fifth queen of Henry VIII.; *d.* of Lord Edmund Howard; m. Henry, 1540; charged with unfaithfulness, and beheaded in Tower.

HOWARD, JOHN (1726-1790), famous Eng. philanthropist; *b.* in London. On being app. high sheriff of Bedford, he inspected the prison, and finding many abuses both there and in other Eng. gaols which he subsequently visited, gave himself up to securing reforms in management of prisons and prisoners. He afterwards visited the prisons of many European countries, which he described, with those of England, in his *State of Prisons* (pub. 1777). He also carried out researches on the plague.

HOWARD, KATHLEEN, an Anglo-American opera singer, *b.* in Canada. She studied singing under Oscar Saenger in New York and under Jean de Reszke, in Paris. For a time she was a choir singer in New York, then, in 1907, made her debut in Metz, Germany, with such success that she continued singing there for two years. For three seasons she was the leading contralto of the Court Opera at Darmstadt. In 1913 she appeared at Covent Garden, in London, later in the season coming to N.Y. where she was the leading contralto of the Century Opera Co. Since 1916 she has been a member of the Metropolitan Opera Co. N.Y. editor, Harper's Bazaar, 1928.

HOWARD, LELAND OSSIAN (1857), an American entomologist, *b.* in Rockford, Ill. He graduated from Cornell University, in 1877, then became assistant entomologist in the Bureau of Entomology in the U. S. Department of Agriculture, of which he has been chief since 1894. Since 1904 he has been consulting entomologist of the U. S. Public Health Service. He is the author of *Mosquitos— How They Live,* 1901; *The House Fly—Disease Carrier,*

1911; and of many government bulletins and pamphlets.

HOWARD OF EFFINGHAM, WILLIAM, 1ST BARON (c. 1510-73), Eng. admiral; gov. of Calais, 1552; Lord High Admiral, 1553; raised to peerage, 1554; highly esteemed for his public services under Henry VIII. and Elizabeth.

HOWARD OF EFFINGHAM, CHARLES, 2ND BARON (1536-1624), Eng. admiral; Lord High Admiral, 1585-1619; commanded Eng. fleet against Armada, 1588; joint-commander in expedition against Cadiz, 1596; cr. Earl of Northampton, 1596; ambassador to Spain, 1605. His first wife, Katharine Carey, according to legend, failed to deliver Essex's ring to Queen Elizabeth.

HOWARD, OLIVER OTIS (1830-1909), an American soldier, b. in Leeds, Me. He graduated from the West Point military academy, in 1854, was professor of mathematics there during 1857-61 after which he went to the front as a colonel of Volunteers. He participated in the battles of Antietam and Fredericksburg and led the 11th and 12th corps at Chancellorville and Gettysburg. Later he had command of the Army of the Tennessee, and during Sherman's 'march to the sea' he had command of the right wing of Sherman's force. After the war he was for a while president of Howard University, an educational institution for negroes in Washington, D. C., which was named in his honor. In 1886 he was promoted to the rank of major-general in the regular army. He wrote *Donald's School Days*, 1879 and *Fighting for Humanity*, 1898.

HOWARD, SIDNEY COE (1891-), American playwright and author, b. at Oakland, Cal.; ed. at the University of California and Harvard; wrote *Swords* 1921; *Casanova*, 1923; *They Knew What They Wanted* (Pulitzer prize play, 1925); *Lucky Sam McCarver*, 1925; *The Silver Cord*, 1926; *Alien Corn*, 1931, filmed; and short stories, *One Flight Up*, 1924.

HOWARD, SIR ROBERT (1626-98), Eng. dramatist; s. of Earl of Berkshire; fought on king's side in Civil War; wrote *The Committee*, 1663, a comedy, and collaborated with his bro.-in-law, Dryden, in *The Indian Queen*.

HOWARD COLLEGE, an educational institution founded in Birmingham, Ala., in 1841, under the auspices of the Baptist Church. In 1932 it had a teaching staff of 41 and a student body of 1,012. Its library contains 26,000 volumes.

HOWARD UNIVERSITY, a co-educational institution for negroes in Washington, D. C., founded in 1867 under the auspices of the Federal Government,

through the Freedman's Bureau, at the time Gen. O. O. Howard was director of that institution and therefore named from him. While it also has a department of manual training, it prepares its students largely for professional careers, having departments of law, medicine, dentistry, theology (undenominational) and music. A large portion of the negroes in the professions have graduated from it. The Federal Government contributes about $100,000 yearly towards its upkeep. In 1932 its faculty numbered 271 and its students 2,464.

HOWE, EDGAR WATSON (1853-), an American journalist and writer, b. near Treaty, Ind. For many years he edited the Atchison Daily Globe. He also wrote several books, the best known of which is *The Story of a Country Town*. Known as Sage of Potato Hill.

HOWE, ELIAS, JR., (1819-1867), an American inventor, b. in Spencer, Mass. His father was a farmer and local miller and the son remained at home as his assistant, until 1836, when he began to learn the trade of machinist. In 1845 he completed a working model of a sewing machine, which he patented. For the following nine years he was engaged in a continuous law suit to protect his patent from the infringements of manufacturers, but finally won and thereafter enjoyed a steady income from the royalties paid him by the manufacturers of sewing machines. During the Civil War he fought in the Union Army as a private, after which he established a manufacturing plant in Bridgeport, Conn.

HOWE, HENRY MARION (1848-1922), an American metallurgist, b. in Boston, Mass. He graduated from Harvard University, in 1869; professor of metallurgy at Columbia University; author of *Copper Smelting*, 1885; *Metallurgy of Steel*, 1891; *Iron, Steel and other Alloys*, 1903; and *The Metallography of Steel and Cast Iron*, 1916.

HOWE, JULIA WARD (1819-1910), an American writer, b. in New York City. She married Dr. Samuel Gridley Howe, and together they established and edited the Boston Daily Commonwealth, which they made largely an abolitionist organ. In 1861 she wrote *The Battle Hymn of the Republic*, which made her famous. After the war she became interested in the women's suffrage movement and wrote and lectured for it. She wrote *Sex and Education*, 1874; *Modern Society*, 1881; *Reminiscences*, 1819-1899, and *Sketches of Representative Women of New England*, 1905.

HOWE, MARK ANTHONY DE WOLFE (1864-), Amer. editor and

writer, *b.* in Bristol, **R. I.** He graduated from Harvard University, in 1887, was for some years associate editor of The Youth's Companion and assistant editor of the Atlantic Monthly during 1893-5. During 1913-19 he was editor of the Harvard Alumni Bulletin. Among his books are *Shadows*, 1897; *Boston, the Place of the People*, 1903; *Harmonies*, a book of Verse, 1909; *The Atlantic Monthly and its Makers*, 1919; and *George von Lengerke Meyer— His Life and Public Services*, 1919.

HOWE, RICHARD, EARL HOWE (1726-99), Brit. admiral; saw considerable service during war of Amer. Revolution; as commander of Channel fleet, relieved Gibraltar in 1782; First Lord of Admiralty 1683; on June 1, 1794, defeated French off Cape Ushant, day of this victory being long known as *Glorious First of June*.

HOWE, SAMUEL GRIDLEY (1801-1876), an American physician, *b.* in Boston, Mass. He graduated from Brown University, in 1821 and studied medicine. Moved emotionally by the writings of Byron, he went to Greece, in 1824, and participated in the Greek Revolution, eventually becoming chief surgeon of the Greek Navy. Later he also joined the revolutionists in Poland and spent some weeks in a Prussian prison. His fame, however, rested on the great work which he later accomplished in the education of the blind, after his return to the United States, in 1830. He became superintendent of the Perkins Institute for the Blind, in Massachusetts, and did much to develop the raised letter method of reading.

HOWE, WILLIAM, 5TH VISCOUNT HOWE (1729-1814), Brit. general; distinguished himself at *Abraham's Heights*, Quebec; commander-in-chief in Amer. War of Independence.

HOWEL DDA ('the God') (*d.* 950), king of Wales, 943; maintained peace and codified the laws.

HOWELL, CLARK (1863), an American editor, *b.* in Barnwall co., S. C., He graduated from the University of Georgia, in 1883 and in the following year joined the staff of the Atlanta Constitution. In 1889 he became editor, and in 1897 succeeded his father as editor-in-chief. Since then he has also been a director of the Associated Press. In 1886 he was elected to the Georgia House of Representatives, being Speaker during 1890-1. During 1900-6 he was a member of the State Senate.

HOWELL, JAMES (*d.* 1666), Brit. author; travelled extensively and famed for his Royalist sympathies; wrote *Dodona's Grove*, an allegory, and numerous other works but chiefly noted for his *Familiar Letters*, 1645-55, written in the Fleet prison.

HOWELLS, WILLIAM DEAN (1837-1920) Novelist, essayist, and poet. *B.* in Martins Ferry, Ohio, March 1, 1837; *d.* in New York, April 11, 1920. The *s.* of a country printer and newspaper editor he had no regular education, but was brought up among books and in a literary atmosphere. From 1840 to 1849 he lived at Hamilton, Ohio, which he has described in *A Boys' Town*. After some experience writing for newspapers he was appointed U. S. consul to Venice, Italy, 1861-1865. On his return to the United States he formed connections with the N. Y. Tribune, Times and The Nation, and edited the Atlantic Monthly, 1871-1881. He wrote *The Editors Study* for Harper's Monthly, 1886-1891 and was editor of The Cosmopolitan for a short time, returning to Harpers to write *The Easy Chair* for the Monthly until his death. He was a founder and the president of the American Academy of Arts and Letters. In the first rank of American novelists he was also noted as poet and essayist. Few authors in his class have been more prolific. Among his principal works are *Poems*, 1873-1886, and 1895. Novels: *Their Wedding Journey*, 1871; *A Chance Acquaintance*, 1872; *A Foregone Conclusion*, 1875; *Lady of the Aristook*, 1878; *A Modern Instance*, 1882; *A Womans Reason*, 1883; *The Rise of Silas Lapham*, 1885; *April Hopes*, 1888; *Annie Kilburn*, 1889; *The Kentons*, 1902; *New Leaf Mills*, 1913; *The Leatherwood God*, 1919. Travels: *Venetian Life*, 1866; *Italian Journeys*, *Tuscan Cities*, *Some English Towns*, *Spanish Travels* also *Years of My Youth* and *Years of My Middle Life*, 1920 and one act plays *The Mouse Trap*, *The Elevator*, etc.

HOWITT, MARY (1799-1888), an author, wife of William H., wrote much in collaboration with her husband. She wrote numerous children's books, which were very popular in their day; and she rendered a distinct service to literature by translating the novels of Frederika Bremer and many of the tales of Hans Andersen. In 1886 she published her *Reminiscences of my Later Life* (in *Good Words*). Her work was healthy, but, apart from the translations, ephemeral. There is a biography by her daughter, Margaret H., 1889.

HOWITT, WILLIAM (1791-1879), an author, began to write at an early age, and when he was thirteen, one of his poems appeared in the *Monthly Magazine*.

In 1821 he married Mary Botham, and husband and wife wrote many books in collaboration. He had no special call to authorship, and became a very miscellaneous writer. *The Book of the Season*, 1831; *A Popular History of Priestcraft*, 1833; *Pantilla, or Traditions of the Most Ancient Times*, 1835; and the *Rural Life of England*, 1838, give some idea of his scope. In 1852 he visited Tasmania and Australia, and on his return wrote several books on these places, but none of them have any particular value. His most successful work was a *Popular History of England*, 1856-62.

HOWITZER, light ordnance used in field and siege operations; of 5-in. and 6-in. calibre, throwing shells of from 50 to 120 lb.

HOWRAH (22° 31′ N., 88° 20′ E.), town, Bengal, India; jute, cotton. District has area 509 sq. miles.

HOWTH (53° 23′ N., 6° 3′ W.), town, County Dublin, Ireland.

HOY (58° 50′ N., 3° 18′ W.), mountainous island, Orkney, Scotland; has celebrated Dwarfie Stone, in which are excavated rooms.

HOYLAKE (53° 24′ N., 3° 11′ W.), town, Cheshire, England.

HOYLAND NETHER (53° 30′ N., 1° 26′ W.), town, Yorkshire, England.

HOYLE, EDMOND (1672-1769), Eng. pioneer authority on whist; wrote on games, and taught whist in London; his *Short Treatise on Whist* was pub. 1742.

HRDLICKA, ALES (1869-   ), a Bohemian-American anthropologist *b.* in Humpolec, Bohemia. He studied in his native country and in New York, later carrying on investigations among the insane and other defective classes in the New York State service. Since 1898 he has been almost continuously in the field for the U. S. National Museum as anthropologist, participating in expeditions to Mexico, the Balkans, South America, Asia, and various parts of the United States.

HSUAN-TSANG (fl. 664), Chin. writer of travels; became a Buddhist monk in early life, won great reputation for learning and sanctity, and finally visited India in order to penetrate Buddhist arcana; he traversed vast deserts alone, and left invaluable accounts of the districts through which he passed. The Ind. pilgrimage was considered specially meritorious by the Chin. Buddhists, whose writings are an important source for history of India.

HSUAN T'UNG (1906-   ), Emperor of China; selected, 1908, abdicated, 1912, but retained title. In 1924, was forced by Kuominchun to abandon his palace and retire to the Japanese Concession at Tientsin.

HUANCAVELICA (12° 55′ E., 75° 2′ W.), town, Peru, S. America.

HUARTE DE SAN JUAN (1530-92), Span. physician renounced for his writings showing the connection between psychology and physiology.

HUBBARD, ELBERT (1859-1915), an American writer, *b.* in Bloomington, Ill. Leaving his father's farm at the age of 14, he worked in a printing shop and later in a soap factory, eventually becoming part owner of the latter. Selling out his interest, he established a handicrafts colony in East Aurora, N. Y., from which he issued *The Philistine*, a monthly publication which had many admirers. He wrote a great deal of 'success' literature, which found a wide reading among those who made material success their sole ideal. Among his writings are *Little Journeys* (biographical sketches); *The Message to Garcia*, 1898, and *Hollyhocks and Goldenglow*, 1912.

HUBERT, ST. (656-728), bp. of Liége; feast-day, Nov. 3; patron saint of hunters. Legend says that he was converted by appearance of Christ on the Cross above the deer's head when shooting.

HUBLI (15° 18′ N., 75° 11′ E.), town, Bombay, India.

HUC, EVARISTE RÉGIS (1813-60), Fr. missionary; after an unsuccessful mission to Tibet, wrote *Voyage dans la Tartarie, le Thibet et la Chine*, 1851-52, and other valuable books on those regions.

HU-CHOW-FU (30° 49′ N., 120° 5′ E.), town, Cheh-kiang, China.

HUCKABACK, thick linen material much used for face towels.

HUCKLEBERRY, also called **WHORTLEBERRY, BILBERRY, BLUEBERRY WHINBERRY** (*Vaccinium myrtillus*), a small shrub with drooping wax-like, flesh-colored flowers, followed by dark blue berries of an agreeable flavor. The red W., or cowberry (*V. vitis, idoea*), occurs on mountainous heaths and bears red berries. The marsh W., or cranberry (*Oxycoccus palustris*), is a prostrate plant with dark red berries and occurs on peat bogs.

HUCKNALL TORKARD (53° 2′ N., 1° 12′ W.), town, Nottinghamshire, England.

HUDDERSFIELD (53° 39′ N., 1° 47′ W.), town, Yorkshire, England; situated in extensive coal-field; centre of 'fancy' woolen industry; manufactures iron goods, machinery; fine public buildings and park.

HUDSON, a town of Middlesex co., Mass., U. S. A., on Assabet R. 15 m. N.E. of Worcester. It has manufs. of leather, rubber shoes webbing, gossamers, paper boxes lasts, etc.

HUDSON, a city of New York, in Columbia co., of which it is the county seat. It is on the New York Central and the Boston and Albany railroads, and on the Hudson River. It is the trade center of an extensive farming and manufacturing region and is connected by steamship lines with all the Hudson River points. Its industries include the making of iron wire, woolen goods, bricks, machines, cement, textiles, etc. It is the seat of the State Home of Refuge for Women.

HUDSON BAY (c. 60 N., 87° W.), great inland sea, N. E. of North America; receives drainage of great part of Canada by Churchill, Nelson, Albany, and other rivers. Area, c. 500,000 sq. miles; connected with Atlantic by Hudson Strait. A railway is being built to connect H. B. with the centre and west of Canada. Hudson Strait is open to navigation for two or three months in the year. See map CANADA.

HUDSON FALLS, a village of New York, in Washington co.

HUDSON, HENRY (d. 1611), famous Brit. explorer. In 1607 he attempted to discover a N.E. passage to Pacific; in 1609 explored H. River; afterwards sailed to Arctic Ocean, hoping to find a N.W. passage; discovered H. Strait and Bay. On last voyage crew mutinied, and H. and others were cast adrift and never heard of again.

HUDSON RIVER, beautiful and important river in New York state, U. S. (41° 50′ N., 73° 58′ W.), called after Henry Hudson, who first explored it, 1609; rises in Adirondack Mts.; total length, c. 350 m. (tidal, c. 150). Principal tributaries are Sacondaga, Mohawk, and Wallkill. About 60 m. from New York (at mouth) the river passes through picturesque highlands into great expanse —Haverstraw and Tappan (c. 12 m. by 4½) Bays—after which a steep wall (called the Palisades), rising 300-500 ft. from brink of river (here 1 or 2 m. broad and called *North River*), extends to upper part of New York.

HUDSON'S BAY COMPANY, joint-stock company, founded 1670 by Prince Rupert and seventeen others, under charter from Charles II., for the importation of furs and skins into Gt. Britain from N. America. In 1869 its exclusive rights were ceded to the Brit. Government for $1,500,000, but the trade is still continued under certain reservations.

HUÉ (16° 24′ N., 107° 32′ E.), fortified town, Fr. Indo-China; capital of Annam; has royal palace.

HUE AND CRY, old process, in Eng. law, of pursuing felons with horn-blowing and shouting; if taken, they were summarily dealt with; later meaning, police proclamation regarding offenders, etc.

HUEHUETENANGO (15° 30′ N., 91° 41′ W.), town, Guatemala, Cent. America. Pop. 1905, c. 12,000. H. department has area of 5,700 sq. miles.

HUELVA (37° 32′ N., 6° 50′ W.), frontier province, S.W. Spain; area, 3,913 sq. miles; has valuable copper mines. Its capital is Huelva.

HUERCAL OVERA (37° 26′ N., 2° 1′ W.), town, S.E. Spain.

HUERTA, ADOLFO DE LA (1877), Mexican president; educated business man of studious habits; during revolution, 1913, acted as General Obregon's representative at Carranza's head-quarters. Appointed governor of Sonora, 1919; and succeeded Carranza as president after revolution on 1920. See MEXICO.

HUERTA, VICTORIANO (1854-1916), Mexican president and soldier; of Indian parentage; befriended by Juarez, and educated in Military Coll., Mexico City, where he had a successful career; became general, 1901; repressed the Chihuahua rebellion, 1912 and was trusted by Porfirio Diaz; was appointed military commandant of Federal District, 1913; after resignation of Porfirio Diaz, May, 1911, entered service of President Madero; combined with General Felix Diaz to make Madero a prisoner and force him to resign, upon which he became interim president. He incurred odium in U.S. for his share in murder of Madero, and this led to protracted conflict with America, Feb. 1913. After his confirmation in the office of president, Carranza and Villa headed rebellion against him. Repudiated the National Debt, thereby precipitating anarchy, only remedied by Amer. intervention. Resigned in summer of 1914.

and took up residence in U. S.; arrested, July, 1915 for violating Amer. neutrality, but died before being brought to trial.

HUESCA (42° 11′ N., 0° 10′ W.), province, Spain; area, 5,848 sq. miles; watered by Aragon and other affluents of Ebro, N. occupied by Pyrenees; produces wine, grain, fruit. Pop. 250,000. Its capital. Huesca, has a cathedral.

HUGGINS, SIR WILLIAM (1824-1910), Eng. astronomer; pioneer in stellar spectroscopy and photography; made many striking discoveries relative to origin, constitution, and condition of the heavenly bodies; list of papers in his *Atlas of Representative Stellar Spectra.*

HUGH THE GREAT (*d.* 956), Duke of the Franks and Count of Paris; founder of the fortunes of his house, and *f.* of H. Capet.

HUGH CAPET (*c.* 938-96), king of France; founder of Capetian dynasty; *s.* of Hugh, Count of Paris and Duke of France; elected and crowned, 987; warred against Charles of Lorraine, his capture of whom in 991 closed the war.

HUGH DE PUISET (*c.* 1125-95), bp. of Durham and Earl of Northumberland; exercised powerful influence upon the political affairs of the reign of Richard I.

HUGH OF ST. CHER (*c.* 1200-63), Fr. Dominican priest and cardinal; besides playing prominent part as a churchman, wrote theological works of interest.

HUGH OF ST. VICTOR (*c.* 1079-1141), canon of Hamersleben, Saxony; had great reputation as mystic in XII. cent.

HUGH, ST., OF LINCOLN, OR OF AVALON (*c.* 1140-1200), prior of first Eng. Carthusian house at Witham (Somerset); bp. of Lincoln, 1186; strong defender of rights of Church, and pious man; not to be confused with Hugh of Wells, bp. of Lincoln, or St. Hugh of Lincoln, Christian boy traditionally crucified by Jews.

HUGHES, CHARLES EVANS (1862); American jurist and executive; *b.* Glens Falls, N. Y. He studied at Madison (now Colgate) University, 1876-78; and graduated at Brown University, 1881. Graduating from Columbia Law School in 1884, he entered at once on the practice of law in New York City. He first came into national notice when in 1905 he acted as special counsel for legislative committees investigating gas and insurance management, his remarkable work

resulting in the adoption of immensely valuable reforms. In 1906 he was elected Republican governor of New York State and was re-elected two years later. His career in that office – as one of notable achievement. In 1910 he was appointed by President Taft an associate justice of the U. S. Supreme Court, and served on that bench for six years. He was nominated for President on the Republican ticket in 1916, but was defeated by Woodrow Wilson and returned to the practice of law. By presidential appointment he investigated the alleged irregularities in the building of army and navy planes during the war. In March, 1921, he became Secretary of State in President Harding's cabinet. He presided at the Conference on the Limitation of Armaments held in Washington, 1921-22, and created a sensation at the first session by his proposal for the 'scrapping' of capital ships and the establishment of the 'naval holiday.' Other important problems handled by him have been those relating to the German treaty, the question of mandates, the oil controversy and American participation in the World Court, 1923. Chief Justice U.S. Supreme Court, 1930.

HUGHES, JOHN (1797-1864), R.C. divine; went to America from Ireland, 1817; bp. of New York; keen Catholic controversialist.

HUGHES, RUPERT (1872), an American author, *b.* in Lancaster, Mo. He graduated from the Western Reserve University, in 1892. For some years he was assistant editor of Godey's Magazine, Current Literature and The Criterion, in London, then, in 1902, came to New York, where he was for three years on the staff of the Encyclopedia Britannica. Before and during the war with Germany he served in the Volunteer Corps, retiring with the rank of major. His biography of Geo. Washington, (1926-30), caused much comment. Has written and directed many motion pictures. Among his books are *The Whirlwind*, 1902; *Love Affairs of Great Musicians*, 1903; *Empty Pockets*, 1915; *The Unpardonable Sin*, 1919; *The Cup of Fury*, 1919; *What's the World Coming to?* 1920; *Monna*, 1912; and *Souls for Sale*, 1922. He wrote a number of plays, among these being *The Cat Bird*, and *Tess of the Storm Country.*

HUGHES, SIR SAMUEL (1853-1921) Canadian soldier and public official educated at Toronto Univ., and the Royal Military School; lecturer in English language, literature, and history in the Toronto Collegiate Institute, 1875-85;

joined the militia and took part in the Fenian raid, 1870; promoted lieutenant-colonel, 1897; served in South African War; member of the Dominion Parliament since 1892; minister of militia and defence, 1911-16. On outbreak of the World War he had charge of the organizing of Canadian troops, whom he later accompanied to France; appointed major-general, 1914, and knighted, 1915.

HUGHES, THOMAS (XVI. cent.), Eng. dramatist; wrote *The Misfortunes of Arthur*, played before Queen Elizabeth at Greenwich, 1588.

HUGHES, THOMAS (1822-96), Eng. judge and author; ed. Rugby and Oxford; became a County Court judge; was greatly influenced by the religious views of F. D. Maurice and Kingsley; pub. *The Manliness of Christ*, 1879. He is best known, however, by his famous story, *Tom Brown's Schooldays*, 1857; and its sequel, *Tom Brown at Oxford*, 1861.

HUGHES, RT. HON. WILLIAM MORRIS (1864), Australian statesman; *b.* in Wales; went to Australia, 1884, and entered politics as member of the Legislative Assembly of New South Wales, 1893; a position he resigned on becoming member of the Federal Parliament; devoted himself to the interest of Labor, and advocated a very advanced policy; was attorney-general in various labor administrations, 1908-15; prime minister, 1915; defeated twice on the subject of conscription, he broke with the extreme section of his party, and formed a coalition with the Liberals; again defeated in 1922; represented the Commonwealth at the Imperial War Cabinet, 1918; Australian del. to Peace Conference. Min. Ext. Affairs, 1921-23.

HUGLI, HOOGHLY (22° 57′ N., 88° 19′ E.), town, Bengal, India, on H. River; has fine mosque and various educational establishments. Pop. 29,383. H. district has area of *c.* 1,200 sq. miles.

HUGLI, HOOGHLY (21° 40′ N., 87° 50′ E.), most westerly mouth of Ganges, entering Indian Ocean, and that up which trade passes to Calcutta.

HUGO, GUSTAV VON (1764-1844), Ger. jurist; chiefly known for his *Lehrbuch eines Zivilistischen Kursus* 1792-1821.

HUGO, VICTOR MARIE (1802-85), Fr. author; *b.* at Besancon; travelled with his *f.*, General Count Hugo, 1774-1828, through Spain and Italy during Napoleonic campaigns; returned to Paris for education. From outset H.'s private and public life were troubled.

Nearly all his children died in his lifetime, and he lived his last years with his grandchildren. H. entered Parliament after Revolution of 1848; became ardent Republican, and after *coup d'etat* of Dec. 2, 1851, retired to Channel Islands until 1870; returned to Paris, and took deep interest in politics, working with all his might for abolition of capital punishment, etc. His funeral was a magnificent one, and he was laid to rest in the Pantheon as perhaps the greatest figure in Fr. Lit.

H. was the great leader of Romantic School of Fr. lit. (see under France). His poems, dramas, and romances, on every subject and in numberless forms, aroused an enthusiasm almost unparalleled in lit.; through him the current set definitely in favor of the new Romantic movement; his dramas, *Hernani*, 1830; *Le Roi s'amuse*, 1832; *Lucrece Borgia*, 1933, etc., and novels, *Le Dernier Jour d'un condamne*, 1829, *Notre-Dame de Paris*, 1831; *Les Miserables*, 1862; *Les Travailleurs de la Mer*, 1866; *L' Homme qui Rit*, 1869; were epoch-making and were only surpassed in greatness by his lyrics. H.'s rhetorical effects are somewhat alien to the austerer age which has followed; but he will always remain one of the literary giants of the XIX. cent.

HUGUENOTS, name given to Fr. Protestants who in XVI. and XVII. cent's banded themselves together to secure personal liberty and religious freedom. Long struggle began in 1562, with massacre of number of H's at Vassy by R.C. followers of the Guises, and towards close of same year the H's were defeated at *Dreux*; two months later the murder of Duke of Guise by a Calvinist fanatic put an end to hostilities, and peace of Amboise was arranged, 1563. In 1567 war again broke out, and H's were defeated at *St. Denis*; by Treaty of Longjumeau, 1568 peace was restored for a short time; but the following year saw a resumption of hostilities; the H's again suffering defeat at *Jarnac*, while Condé was murdered, 1569. Henry of Navarre and Coligny then became leaders of Prot. party, and in 1570 hostilities again came to an end by Treaty of St. Germains.

Two years later occurred the terrible massacre of St. Bartholomew's Eve, Aug. 24, 1572; the example of Paris was followed in other towns, and in two months from 20,000 to 30,000 H's were slain in France. The remainder again took up arms and were successful in obtaining in 1575 numerous concessions, some of which were subsequently revoked. In 1589 Henry of Navarre came to Fr. throne, and in 1598 he granted religious freedom by Edict of Nantes; but after his death civil war recommenced and H's were again defeated. For many years, in spite of confirmation of Edict of Nantes, they were subjected to persecution; and in 1685 the Edict was revoked, great numbers of H's fled from the country, and their church was annihilated; revived in XVIII. cent., and after various vicissitudes finally obtained equality with rest of population after the Revolution.

HUITZILOPOCHTLI, ancient Mexican war-god, to whom wholesale human sacrifice was made.

HULDA, Teutonic goddess of the spindle and marriage.

HULL (45° 23' N., 75° 46' W.), town, Quebec, Canada; paper- and sawmills.

HULL, KINGSTON-ON-HULL (53° 45' N., 0° 20' W.), river-port and borough, Yorkshire, England, with Holy Trinity Church, St. Mary's Lowgate, 1333, town hall, library, theatre, nautical school, and extensive docks. Shipbuilding, machinery, chains, ropes, canvas, chemicals, tanning, sugar-refining, etc. H. made free borough of Kingston-on-Hull by Edward I., 1299; besieged by Royalists, 1643; extensive trade with Continent, and headquarters for deepsea fisheries.

HULL (from A. S. *helan,* to cover), capsule or chrysalis; whole lower part of a ship.

HULL, ISAAC (1773-1843), an American naval officer, *b.* in Derby, Conn. He went to sea as a cabin boy at the age of 14 and became a skipper before he was 21. In 1798 he joined the Navy, and at the opening of the War of 1812 he was commander of the frigate "Constitution'. On August 19, 1812, he encountered the British ship 'Guerriére', a vessel slightly inferior to his own, and captured it. Being the first victory of the war for the United States, popular joy was unbounded and Hull was the popular hero of the time. Later he was promoted to the rank of commodore and commanded a squadron in the Mediterranean.

HULL, WILLIAM (1735-1825), an American soldier, *b.* at Derby, Conn.; he studied law and was called to the bar in 1775. He fought with distinction in the War of Independence, and received the personal thanks of Washington for his services. He was made governor of Michigan Territory by Jefferson in 1805 and held the office till 1812, when he was appointed commander of the north-western army during the war with Great Britain. He was sent with 1500 men to defend Detroit. a task which presented great difficulties and in which he failed. He was court-martialled for cowardice and sentenced to be shot, but the sentence of death was not carried out.

HULSE, JOHN (1708:90), Eng. divine who bequeathed funds to Cambridge Univ. for four lectures (Hulsean Lectures) to be delivered before the univ. annually on the evidences of the Christian religion.

HUMACAO (18° 16' N., 65° 44' W.), town, Porto Rico, W. Indies.

HUMANE SOCIETY, AMERICAN, Organized in Cleveland, Ohio, in 1877, consolidating a number of other socieities engaged in humane work. The chief aim of the society is to prevent cruelty to children and animals. One of its first activities was to secure State laws to regulate cattle trains, and protect cattle from suffering in transit. They offered $5,000 for a model cattle car, and in 1900 prizes for monographs on vivisection open to colleges and medical students. The society now includes over 300 affiliated societies. Membership 10,000. The official organ is The National Humane Review. Headquarters, Albany, New York. Gen. Mgr., 1932, N. G. Welker.

HUMANISM, literally that which attaches primary importance to man, but used more specifically of Renaissance movement of XV. cent., and beginning of modern thought.

HUMANITARIAN.—(1) humane; (2) denying divinity of Christ, while accepting God the Father; (3) erecting morality into a religion.

HUMAYUN, NASR ED-DIN, MUHAMMAD (*c.* 1510-56), emperor of Delhi; second of the Mogul line, and preserved realm acquired by his *f.,* Baber (*q.v.*), though first spent many years in fighting.

HUMBER (53° 40' N., 0° 12' W.). estuary of Trent and Yorkshire Ouse, E. coast of England, between York and Lincoln.

HUMBERT I., RANIERI CARLO GIOVANNI MARIA FERDINANDO EUGENIO (1844-1900), king of Italy, *s.* of Victor Emmanuel II.; succ. 1788; supported Triple Alliance and also maintained friendly relations with Britain; advocated colonisation on Red Sea littoral; assassinated by anarchist Bresci.

HUMBOLDT, FRIEDRICH HEINRICH ALEXANDER, BARON VON (1769-1859), Ger. naturalist and explorer; explored course of the Orinoco, the Andes, the Amazon, and Mexico. He introduced *quano* into Europe and in 1817 delineated *isothermal* lines. Besides accounts of the natural history of the regions he explored he wrote works on plant distribution, laws of temperature, magnetism, volcanoes, terrestrial magnetism, and the igneous nature of rocks. He devoted much attention to climate and the conditions which control it. As a favorite of Frederick William III, of Prussia, he could not undertake further expeditions. with the exception of a journey to Siberia, in his sixtieth year, during which he determined the height of the plateau and discovered diamonds in the gold washings of the Ural. In his seventy-sixth year he wrote the *Kosmos*, in which are embodied the results of his personal observations and his generalisations from those and his wide scientific knowledge.

HUMBOLDT, KARL WILHELM VON (1767-1835), Ger. statesman and author of valuable philological works; *b.* of above; as Prussian member of Public Instruction established Univ. of Berlin, 1809.

HUME, DAVID (1711-1776), Scot. historian and philosopher; *b.* Edinburgh; *s.* of a small landowner in Berwickshire; studied at Edinburgh Univ., and became interested in speculation; in 1739 pub. first two vol's of *Treatise of Human Nature*, but to his bitter disappointment the work was a failure; tried, unsuccessfully, to get chair of Moral Philosophy at Edinburgh, 1744; made librarian at Advocate's Library, Edinburgh, 1751. His *Philosophical Essays* were pub. in 1748, and *Political Discourses*, 1751. In 1753 H. set to work to write the history of England. His qualifications and aims in writing were distinctly above those of his day, though by no means equal to those of ours. His *Natural History of Religion* appeared in 1757. He was much honored during the visit he paid to Paris in 1763; app. Under-Sec. of State to the Home Department, 1766; in London, 1767-69; returned to Edinburgh; had a furious quarrel with Rousseau; latterly in much better financial circumstances than before; *d.* a much respected man.

H's. hist. work was important, but his *History of England* has long been superseded and does not survive to the extent *e.g.*, of Gibbon's *Decline and Fall*. In economics he was an opponent of the Mercantilists. He perceived the connection between economics and sociology, and the importance of hist. treatment. He believed firmly in free trade.

HUMERUS. See SKELETON.

HUMIDITY. See ATMOSPHERE, WEATHER.

HUMILIATI, Ital. religious order; origin uncertain, perhaps at Rome, 1178; rule granted by Innocent III., 1201, to order of priests (the third, a lay order originally, then also one of women); suppressed, 1571.

HUMMEL, JOHANN NEPOMUK (1778-1837), composer and pianist; *b.* Pressburg, Hungary; brilliant extempore player; best compositions pianoforte and chamber music.

HUMMING-BIRD, name given to members of the *Torchilidoe* on account of humming sound produced by their extremely rapid wing-pulsations. The *Torchilidoe*, which include the smallest known birds, are confined to the New World, the majority occurring in equatorial and subtropical belts, although the family's range extends from Alaska to Tierra del Fuego. The males' exquisitely lustrous and gorgeous plumage defies description, and its distribution in tufts, gorgets, crests, and the like, enhances its native brilliance. H-b's seldom rest, but flit tirelessly from blossom to blossom, feeding on honey-loving insects, by means of long, tubular, forked tongues, and doubtless assisting in fertilisation of the flowers visited. The nest is a highly finished structure, closely resembling its surroundings, being clothed with mosses and lichens. The males are exceedingly pugnacious, fighting fiercely among themselves, and also attacking, with remarkable valor, any creature passing near the sitting hen.

HUMOR (Lat. *humor*, damp) had already become an Eng. word of the same equivalence as its Lat. progenitor in 1382, but had then already been applied to what the Schoolmen named the cardinal fluids of the body—blood, choler, melancholy, and phlegm. The predominant h. became the means of classification of temperaments; thus the word is used by Shakespeare and the XVII.-cent. writers of 'comedies of h's.' In late XVII. cent. h. appears as a term for a sense of broad fun. To-day, wit is an intellectual cleverness which raises a smile; it may be unkind, unsympathetic. H. is more elemental, it is of the heart, not the intellect; it is born of incongruous incidents, and its product is laughter. Oscar Wilde was a wit; J. M. Barrie is a humorist.

In drama wit is the province of comedy; h., of farce. Notable humorists are Aristophanes, Chaucer, Dunbar, Rabelais, Molière, Cervantes, Shakespeare (great wit also), Swift, Sterne, Addison,

Fielding, Smollett, Goldsmith, Dickens, O. Wendell Holmes, Mark Twain, Max Adeler, Charles Lever, Jerome K. Jerome, W. W. Jacobs, Stephen Leacock.

HUMPHREYS, ALEXANDER CROMBIE (1851), a Scotch-American educator, b. in Edinburgh, Scotland. He came to this country as a boy and during 1872-81 worked for a commercial firm, at the same time studying at the Stevens Institute of Technology, in Jersey City, N. J. For many years he was the head of a gas producing firm. Since 1902 he has been president of the Stevens Institute of Technology. He is the author of *Lecture Notes on Some of the Business Features of Engineering Practice*, 1905. d. 1927.

HU-NAN (27° 30′ N., 111° 30′ E.), province, Central China; area, c. 83,380 sq. miles; surface hilly; lies in Yangtse-Kiang basin; coal, tea, rice.

HUNDRED (A.-S. *hund*, hundred; red signifies computation), Eng. numeral. The h. as a division of the shire may have been originally the land inhabited by 100 families; tradition ascribed the institution of the h. to Alfred the Great; but it is probably much older; division corresponding to the h. are called *wards* in N., *wapentakes* in Yorks and Midlands, *rape* in Sussex, *lathe* in Kent.

HUNDRED DAYS. See FRANCE. (History, 1815).

HUNDRED YEARS WAR, struggle between England and France, 1337-1453, originating in English claim to crown of France; from 1337 to 1364 fortune favored English; then ensued a period of French success; after 1380 French again suffered disaster, but they rallied under Joan of Arc in 1429, and the English were expelled in 1453. See ENGLAND AND FRANCE (HISTORY).

HUNEKER, JAMES GIBBONS (1860-1921), an American musical critic, b, in Philadelphia. Pa. He acquired a musical education under Georges Mathias, in Paris ,and on returning to this country became a teacher of the piano at the National Conservatory. Ten years later he joined the staff of the New York Sun as musical and dramatic critic, his writings gaining him a wide recognition. Among his books are *The Melomaniacs,* 1902; *Iconoclasts,* 1905; *Egoists,* 1909; *The Pathos of Distance,* 1913, and *The Steeplejack,* 1921.

HUNGARY, OR MAGYARIA, inland republic of Central Europe (45° 50′-48° 30′ N., 16°-23° 10′ E.), bounded B. by Czecho-Slovakia by Jugo-Slavia, W. by Austria, Surface is mainly plains of middle Danube and its trib. the Tisza (Theiss); the smaller, called the 'Little Hungarian Alföld,' or Pressburg Basin, covers an area of c. 6,000 sq. m., and lies W. of Bakony or Mávra, which separ tes it from the Great Hungarian Alföld, the largest plain in Europe, extending over c. 37,000 sq. m., and with an average height of 300 to 350 ft.; the Lower Hungarian Highlands extend between the Danube and Lake Balaton, and attain an altitude of c. 2,200 ft. in Mesek Hills. The Danube enters republic below Pozsony (Pressburg), turns S. in traversing Bakony Forest, and crosses into Jugo-Slavia, near Baja; it forms several large islands—e. g., Czallok Szent-Endre, Csepel; navigable for vessels drawing 6 ft.; Tisza rises in Carpathians, enters Hungary c. 22° E., and crosses S. border below Szegedin; navigable for steamers to Tokaj, but not generally ascended beyong Tisza Füred; country subject to river floods; many marshes. Largest lakes are Balaton (265 sq. m.) and Fertö; small lakes numerous. The Aggtelek or Baradla Cave in Gömör co., and Fonacza Cave in Bihar, with fossil remains, are among many interesting caverns.

Climate is continental; maximum rainfall of early summer is followed by remarkably dry period. The greater part of the Alföld consists of wide open, treeless steppes called pusztas, where graze vast herds of horses, cattle, buffaloes, sheep, and swine; but many acres have recently been converted to the plough, the soil being excellently adapted for the growing of wheat. Agriculture is important, and wheat, rye, barley, oats, and maize of excellent quality are grown; the land is divided among peasant proprietors, who engage largely in bee-keeping and silk culture; the forests yield oak, beach, and pine, fruits, especially apples, apricots, table grapes, peaches, plums, and pears, are largely produced; tobacco, sugar beet, and hops are grown; chief minerals are gold, silver, lead, copper, quicksilver, iron, coal, antimony, and sulphur; salt is a state monopoly. Industries include brewing and distilling, sugar and flour milling, and tobacco. Railway mileage, c. 5,388 miles; navigable rivers, 687 miles.

Population and Area.—The non-Aryan Magyars came from the Ural Mts. c. 890; they form almost the entire population. Area, c. 35,911 square miles. (See article Population).

Education and Religion.—In 1910 over 60 per cent. of Magyars could read and write. A national system of education on non-sectarian lines is under consideration; there are universities at Budapest (cap.), Pozsony, and Debreczen. All religions are tolerated.

Constitution since 1918.—After the *debacle* of Nov., 1918 (see WORLD WAR,), a republic was proclaimed under Karolyi, but ignoring President Wilson's 'self-determination' principle, Rumania, Czecho-Slovakia, and Jugo-Slavia seized parts of Hungarian territory. On Karolyi's resignation, March, 1919, the Hungarians, influenced by Bela Kun (or Cohen), who had been Lenin's secretary, set up a Soviet government. Bolshevism was fanned by Jewish refugees and repatriated prisoners from Russia. Rumanian forces occupied Budapest, and a Socialist government (Aug. 1-7) gave way to the Archduke Joseph as provisional president. On a protest by the delegates of the League of Nations he resigned, Admiral Horthy being elected provisional chief of state in March, 1920. —See map CZECHO-SLOVAKIA, AUSTRIA-HUNGARY.

History.—See AUSTRIA-HUNGARY.

Literature of Hungary was for a long time confined to Latin, under the influence of the Catholic clergy; at the close of the 18th cent., however, the natural language was revived, and Hungarian literature is now in a healthy state; the Magyars have no lack of dramatic art and excel in belles-lettres; owing to their strong political character, legal and constitutional questions have long been a popular subject with writers, statesmen, and scholars; there are many writers on jurisprudence, one work, *The Theory of Law and Civil Society*, by Prof. Pulsxky, being written in English.

The Magyars have been no less successful in literature of an historical nature, especially in monographs; these histories, written in early times in Latin, have of late made very good progress, bnt the tendency is to lean towards monographs, with a resulting dearth of more general histories; there is the same want in literary histories; the monographs, however, are of an excellent standard. A favorite subject of study is that of aesthetics, and 20th cent. writers have also made excellent progress in the departments of science proper.

HUNGER, an indefinite sensation usually referred to the stomach, but also combined with a non-localised feeling of weakness or faintness. Normal H. is not of necessity strictly periodic, but training may result in its recurrence becoming regular.

HUNGERFORD, MARGARET WOLFE (*c.* 1855-97), an Irish novelist, *b.* in Ireland. Mrs. H. made a name for herself by her breezy Irish love-stories, of which the best known are: *Molly Bawn*, 1878; *Mrs. Geoffrey*, 1881; *April's*

Lady, 1891; and *A Conquering Heroine*, 1892.

HUNS, Mongolian race who invaded Europe in IV. cent. A.D. They waged war with the Goths then inhabiting Central Europe, and drove them S. into Spain, Italy, and Balkan Peninsula, thus indirectly causing destruction of Rom. Empire. Under Attila (*q.v.*), they founded a large empire, which after his death was disintegrated. All trace of them in Europe has now been lost, although at one time they reached as far W. as Gaul. Probably akin to the White H's who invaded Persia in V. cent.

HUNT, GAILLARD (1862), an American writer, *b.* in New Orleans, La. He graduated from the Emerson Institute, in Washington, D. C., then entered the government service. From 1900 to '909, he was chief of the Bureau of Citizenship, in the Department of State, then chief of the Division of Manuscripts in the Congressional Library, till 1917. Since 1921 he has been editor for the Department of State. Among his writings are *The Seal of the United States*, 1892; *The Department of State, Its History and Functions*, 1914; and *Life in America One Hundred Years Ago*, 1914. *d.* 1924.

HUNT, HENRY JACKSON (1819-89), an American soldier, *b.* at Detroit, Mich. He served throughout the Mexican War under Scott, and distinguished himself at Contreras, Churubusco, and Chapultepec. He fought at Bull Run, 1861, and became chief of artillery in the Washington defences, and later held a similar post in the army of the Potomac. At the close of the war he assisted in the reorganisation of the United States army, and was made president of the permanent Artillery Board. In 1883, after holding various commands, he retired, and became the governor of the Soldier's Home, Washington, D.C.

HUNT, JAMES HENRY LEIGH (1784-1859), Eng. poet and essayist; *b.* Southgate; ed. Christ's Hospital; became clerk in War Office; subsequently editor of *The Examiner*, 1808; a Radical newspaper, founded by his bro.; was fined and imprisoned, 1813, for two years for publishing an uncomplimentary truth about the Prince Regent; publ. his best-known poem, *The Story of Rimini*, 1816. Amongst other journalistic ventures may be mentioned the starting of *The Indicator*, 1818; *The Companion*, 1828; *The Tatler*, 1830 and *Leigh Hunt's London Journal*, 1834. Amongst his original works may be named *Lord Byron and his Contemporaries*, 1828; *Collected Poems* 1832; *A Legend of Florence* (drama), *Sir Ralph Esher* (novel), *Imagination and Fancy, Wit and Humour, The Town*,

Men, *Women*, and *Books*, etc. His *Autobiography* was pub. 1850. H. was intimately associated with Keats, Byron, and other poets of the day.

HUNT, RICHARD MORRIS (1828-1895), an American architect, *b.* at Brattleboro, Vt. He graduated from the Ecole des Beaux Arts, in Paris, then traveled extensively with one of his former teachers. In 1855 he returned to this country. His reputation was established on a series of important works of which he was architect; the Capitol extension, in Washington, D. C., the Lenox Library building, in New York, the Yorktown Monument, in Virginia, the Presbyterian Hospital, in New York, the pedestal of the Statue of Liberty, in New York Harbor and a number of similar public buildings. He was a founder and president of the American Institute of Architects. His influence on American architecture has been very extensive.

HUNT, WILLIAM HOLMAN (1827-1910). Eng. artist; *b.* London; turned from commerce to art; formed friendship with Millais, and became one of founders of Pre-Raphaelite Brotherhood. His earlier pictures dealt chiefly with hist. subjects, but he later devoted himself to painting Biblical and allegorical pictures, and became recognised as the greatest of modern religious artists. His *The Light of the World* is at Keble Coll., Oxford, *The Hireling Shepherd* and *The Shadow of Death* at Manchester, *The Triumph of the Innocents* at Liverpool.

HUNTER, JOHN (1728-93), Scot. surgeon, anatomist, and physiologist; *b.* (Feb. 13) at Long Calderwood, East Kilbride, Lanarkshire, the youngest of ten children. H. had but little schooling; in 1748 he became assistant in his bro. William's dissecting-room in London; later took charge of his bro.'s practical class, and attended Cheselden's lectures at Chelsea Hospital; a surgeon's pupil at St. Bartholomew's, 1751; surgeon's pupil, 1754 and house-surgeon, 1756, at St. George's Hospital; staff-surgeon ih the army, 1760, serving in the Belle Isle and Portugal expeditions; retired, 1763 on half-pay, and commenced to practise as a surgeon in London, teaching, in addition, anat. and operative surgery. H. was elected F.R.S., 1767, obtained post of surgeon to St. George's Hospital, 1768, and began to take pupils, one of the first being Edward Jenner (*q.v.*). His reputation as a surgeon was now greatly increasing; app. surgeon-extraordinary to the king, 1776; built a museum and lecture-rooms for himself 1783-85; app. deputy-surgeon-general to the army, 1786; surgeon-general and

inspector-general of hospitals, 1790; awarded the Royal Society's Copley medal, 1787, and on Pott's death, 1788, became acknowledged head of surgical profession in England; *d.* suddenly on Oct. 16, 1793. In 1859 his remains were transferred to Westminster Abbey.

HUNTER, ROBERT MERCER TALIAFERRO (1809-1887), an American statesman, *b.* in Essex co., Va. He practised law and at the age of 24 was elected to the State Legislature. He was elected to Congress in 1837 and strongly opposed Clay's protective policy. He was several times returned to Congress and served as Speaker of the House. He was elected U. S. Senator in 1847 and was re-elected until the outbreak of the Civil War, when he withdrew and became Confederate Secretary of State. At the close of the Civil War he served as Treasurer of Virginia.

HUNTER, WILLIAM (1718-83), Scot. physician and anatomist; elder *b.* of John Hunter (*q.v.*); ed. at Glasgow Univ., went to London, and commenced to lecture on operative surgery, 1746; afterwards including a course on anat., in addition to practising as a surgeon. He gave up surgery for obstetrics, being app. surgeon-accoucheur at Middlesex Hospital, 1784, and at Brit. Lying-in Hospital, 1749.

HUNTING is a sport of the highest antiquity; depictions of wild beasts with hunters in pursuit are found on Assyrian abd Egyptian sculptures. Hounds were in common use, while even lions were trained to follow game. The Greeks hunted big game on horseback or by trapping, and were particularly fond of harehunting. See XENOPHON's CYNEGETICUS.

In mediaeval times the stag was extensively hunted by ˙˙ings and nobles, and stringent forest-laws were passed by William I. and other rulers. It is still practised in Devonshire; powerful hounds are employed to track down quarry. Fox-hunting (*q.v.*) is found in most English-speaking lands. Otter-hunting is practised on foot with otter hounds; hunters are armed with spear. Beagles are employed in hare-hunting, which is quite different from coursing; owing to the timidity of the quarry, this is a sport which necessitates quietness.

Big-game hunting is a sport which, owing to its expense, can be followed by comparatively few.

HUNTINGDON.—(52° 20′ N., 0° 11′ W.), county town, Huntingdonshire, England, on Ouse; has XIII.-cent. grammar school and interesting churches; birthplace of Oliver Cromwell.

HUNTINGDON, a borough of Pennsylvania, in Huntingdon co., of which it is the county seat. It is on the Juniata River. Its industries include the manufacture of boilers, sewer pipes, knit goods, etc. It is the seat of Juniata College.

HUNTINGDON, SELINA HASTINGS, COUNTESS OF (1707-91), Eng. religious worker; supporter of Methodism; founded chapels where Eng. Church liturgy was used, but her movement severed itself from Church of England, 1799; her *Connexion* still exists.

HUNTINGDONSHIRE (52° 29′ N.; 0° 15′ W.), midland co., England, bounded N. and W. by Northampton, S.W. by Bedford, E. by Cambridge. Surface mostly level, with slight risings in S.E. In N.E. is fen-district called Bedford Level. Chief towns, Huntingdon (capital), St. Ives, and Godmanchester. Principal rivers are Nene and Ouse. Chiefly agricultural county;much pasture-land; wheat chief grain grown; market-gardening and fruit-growing, brewing, tanning, iron-founding, and manufactures of paper and parchment. Among places of interest are abbeys of Ramsey and Sawtry; priories at St. Ives and St. Neots; churches at Hartford, Old Fletton, Ramsey, and Alwalton; remains of palace at Buckden; ancient castles of Kimbolton and Huntingdon, and Hinchingbrook House, seat of Cromwell family.

HUNTINGTON, a suburb of the city of Shelton, Conn. It is an agricultural and residential community, situated on the hills to the west of Shelton.

HUNTINGTON, a city of Indiana, in Huntington co., of which it is the county seat. It is on the Wabash, Chicago and Erie, and other railroads and on both sides of the Little Wabash River. It is the scene of an extensive coal mining and lime burning region and its abundant water power is utilized in its industries, which include brass, burial vaults, furnaces, pumps, paints, pianos, radiators, rubber goods, soap, etc. It is the seat of Huntington College, a business university, and two conservatories of music.

HUNTINGTON, a town of New York, in Suffolk co., on Long Island, 32 miles N.E. of Brooklyn. It contains the village of Northport. It is a popular summer resort and residential section.

HUNTINGTON, a city of West Virginia, in Cabell co. It is on the Chesapeake and Ohio and the Baltimore and Ohio Railroads, and on the Ohio and Guyandotte rivers. It is connected by boat lines with all the important river points. Its industries include the manufacture of railway cars, brick, machinery, ice, etc. Here are the railroad shops of the Chesapeake and Ohio railroads. The city is the seat of Marshall College, State Normal School. It was named for the late Collis P. Huntington. Its growth was rapid.

HUNTINGTON, ARCHER MILTON (1870), an Amer. editor and writer, *b.* New York City, adopted *s.* of Collis P. Huntington. He was privately educated in this country and in Spain. He has edited *Lady Aulnoy's Travels Into Spain,* 1899; *The Poems of the Cid,* 1897 and he has written *A Note Book in Northern Spain,* 1898.

HUNTINGTON, COLLIS POTTER (1821-1900), an American capitalist, *b.* in Harwinton, Conn. Leaving his father's farm at sixteen, he traveled throughout the country selling clocks, then settled down in Oneonta, N. Y., as a merchant. In 1849 he went out to California by way of the Isthmus of Panama, with a stock of hardware, and prospered in San Francisco. In 1860 he and Leland Stanford and Charles Crocker formed a company which promoted the scheme for building the first trans-continental railroad, the Central Pacific R. R., which was completed in 1869. At the time of his death Mr. Huntington had seen this beginning develop into an organization of 26 subsidiary corporations, owning or controlling 9,000 miles of track and several steamship companies—the Southern Pacific R. R. Co., of which he was president.

HUNTINGTON, DANIEL (1816-1906), an American painter, *b.* in New York City. He studied art under Prof. Morse, president of the National Academy of Design, in 1835, later going to Florence and Rome, and returning to New York to establish a studio in 1845. He was president of the National Academy of Design during 1877-91. Among his portraits, in which he specialized, was one of Abraham Lincoln. One of his best paintings, 'Mercy's Dream,' is now hung in the Corcoran Gallery, Washington, D. C.

HUNTINGTON, ELLSWORTH (1876), an American geographer, *b.* in Galesburg, Ill. He graduated from Beloit College, in Wisconsin, in 1897, afrer which he spent four years in Harput, Turkey, as instructor in Euphrates College. At the end of this period he made an exploration of the shores of the Euphrates River which brought him distinction in the form of a medal from the Royal Geographical Society of London. Since then he has explored extensively in Russian and Chinese Turkestan and India. He is the author of *Explorations in Turkestan*, 1905; *The Pulse of Asia*, 1907; *Palestine and Its Transformation*, 1911; *Civilization and Climate*,1915;*World Power and Evolution*, 1919; *The Red Man's Continent*, 1919; *The Principles of Human Geography*, *The Human Habit Of Living*, 1931.

HUNTSVILLE, a town of Alabama, in Madison co., of which it is the county seat. It is on the Nashville, Chattanooga and St. Louis, and the Southern railroads. Its favorable situation makes it a much frequented summer and winter resort. Its industries include the manufacture of cotton, cottonseed oil, flour, and sawmill products. It is the seat of Goodrich Training School. State Agricultural and Mechanical Institute for Negroes. and an Infirmary.

HUNYADI, JANOS (*c.* 1387-1456)' Hungarian soldier and politician; instrumental in obtaining Wladislaus of Poland's election as king of Hungary; subsequently conducted war against Turks, whom he defeated at *Hermanstadt* and near Iron Gates of Danube, 1442; he was defeated at *Varna* in 1444, when the king was slain; during heir's minority H. acted as regent; in 1448 he was defeated by Turks at *Kossovo*, and in 1456, with support of Giovanni da Capistrano, he accomplished relief of Belgrade; *d.* in following month.

HUNYADI, LASCLO (1433-57), Hungarian statesman; executed through plot of his enemies; eldest *s.* of the great Janos.

HUNZA (36° 22′ N., 74° 50′ E.), and **NAGAR** (36° 6′ N., 74° 50′ E.), towns and small states, Kashmir, Brit. India.

HUON OF BORDEAUX, a hero of Charlemagne cycle of Fr. romances, H., Duke of Guienne, being one of Charlemagne's paladins.

HU-PEH (*c.* 31° N., 113° E.), province, Central China; area, *c.* 71,410 sq. miles.

HURD, SIR ARCHIBALD (1869), Eng. journalist and writer on naval matters, pub., among other works. *Naval Efficiency, The Command of the Sea, The British Fleet in the Great War*. Since 1899 has been on editorial staff of *Daily Telegraph*, and has contributed numerous articles to the *Fortnightly Reviews, Nineteenth Century*, etc.

HURD, RICHARD (1720-1808), Eng. ecclesiastic and author; bp. successively of Lichfield and Worcester; declined primacy; pub. *Letters on Chivalry and Romance, Dissertations on Poetry, An Introduction to the Prophecies*, etc.

HURLEY, EDWARD NASH (1864), an American public official, *b.* in Galesburg, Ill. With only a common school education he was for some years a railroad worker, being a locomotive engineer up to 1888, after which he was for a while a traveling salesman. He originated and developed the pneumatic tool industry in this country. In 1913 he was American trade representative to the Latin-American republics, later becoming chairman of the Federal Trade Commission. In 1917, during the war against Germany, he was appointed chairman of the U. S. Shipping Board and president of the Emergency Fleet Corporation, which position he held till 1919. He wrote *The Awakening of Business,* 1916, and *The New Merchant Marine,* 1920. *d.* 1933.

HURON, a city of South Dakota, in Beadle co., of which it is the county seat. It is on the Chicago and Northwestern and the Great Northern railroads. It is the center of an extensive agricultural and stock raising region and is the division headquarters of the Northwestern Railroad. Its industries include flour mills, machine shops, grain elevators, etc. It is the seat of Huron College and has a high school and other public buildings.

HURON, LAKE, one of the great lakes of North America, in the basin of the St. Lawrence River. It is second in size only to Lake Superior. In position it lies between Lake Superior and Lake Michigan on the N. W. and W. and between Lake Erie and Ontario on the S. and S.E. It is surrounded on the W. and S.W. by the State of Michigan and on all the other sides by the province of Ontario. It is divided in two parts by a long peninsula and a chain of islands. On the N. and E. the parts are called North Channel and Georgian Bay. Its total length is about 280 miles and its greatest breadth about 190 miles.

HURONS, members of tribe of N. Amer. Indians, who inhabited shores of Lake H., but were early exterminated.

HURRICANE, violent storm, with rain, thunder, and lightning, common in West Indies and other places during autumn months.

HURST, FANNIE (1889), an American author, *b.* in St. Louis, Mo. She graduated from Washington University in 1909, then spent several years among the working people, being at one time a saleswoman in a department store and again making a steerage passage across the Atlantic. Her novels, which have been extremely popular, deal with life among the Jewish working people. She has written *Just Around the Corner*, 1914; *Every Soul Has Its Song*, 1915; *Gaslight Sonatas*, 1916; *Humoresque*, 1918; *Star Dust*, 1919, and *The Vertical City*, 1921. She has also written two plays: *The Land of the Free*, 1917, *Back Pay*, 1921, and *Back Street*, 1931.

HURST, JOHN FLETCHER (1834-1903), an American Methodist bishop, *b.* near Salem, Md. He graduated from Dickinson College (Carlisle, Pa.), in 1854 studied theology in Germany, held pastorates in New Jersey and New York and became a bishop in 1880. During 1891-1902 he was chancellor of the American University, in Washington, D.C. He is the author of *A History of Rationalism*, 1965; *Our Theological Century* 1876 and *A History of Methodism*, 1904.

HUSBAND, originally the owner of the house (A.-S. *hus*), with feminine 'housewife' (A.-S. *huswif*); general idea of a caretaker developed from this meaning.

HUSBAND AND WIFE. See MAR-RIAGE.

HUSBAND, WILLIAM WALTER (1871), Commissioner general of immigration. *B.* at East Highgate, Vt. Educated in Vermont. 1900-1902 reporter for St. Johnsbury Caledonia, 1902-1903 managing editor for Montpelier Daily Journal; 1903-1907 clerk of United States Senate Committee on Immigration; 1907-1911 executive secretary on United States Immigration Committee; 1911-1913 chief of contract labor division, United States Bureau o) Immigration; 1913 represented United States Department of Labor in Europe; 1916-1917 editor Immigration Journal; 1917-1919 with American Red Cross in Europe; 1918-1919 on Interallied Repatriation Commission. Since 1921 commissioner general of immigration. Author of: *Emigration Conditions in Europe* (Reports of United States Immigration Commission, Government Printing Office.) 1911.

HUSBANDRY, PATRONS OF, also known as the Grange, an American organization of farmers. In 1866 the U. S. Department of Agriculture sent one of its agents, O. H. Kelley, to investigate the condition of the farmers in the South. Finding them in an extremely impoverished situation, he attempted to afford them constructive assistance by organizing them. Thus, in 1867, were organized the first 'granges' of the American Patrons of Husbandry. At first the progress made was slow, but in 1872 the organization took on a sudden spurt and began spreading all over the country, especially in the Middle West. In 1873 there were 10,000 local granges, and in 1875 the total membership stood at 1,500,000. The object of the order was to secure better economic conditions for the farmers through joint action, and in the endeavor to accomplish this it gradually drifted into politics. In 1892 the organization backed the Populist Party, by a large majority, and when that political party disintegrated, the Grange suffered heavily, its membership dwindling to negligible quantities. During the past few years, since the close of the war against Germany, it has been recovering somewhat. In Washington State the local granges are engaged in a very successful co-operative enterprise, known as the Grange Warehouses, Inc.

HUSKISSON, WILLIAM (1770-1830), Brit. financier and politician; Sec. of Treasury, 1804; pres., Board of Trade, 1823; Colonial Sec., 1827. Advocated free trade, and secured reduction of import duties.

HUSS, JOHN (*c.* 1373-1415), Bohemian religious leader, of peasant family; studied at Prague Univ., where he lectured, becoming rector of Behtlehem chapel, 1402. H. studied Wycliffe's writings, and gradually adopted unorthodox views; proceedings taken against him, 1408; forbidden to preach or perform priestly duties; elected rector of Univ., 1409, but this led to further proceedings against him; excommunicated, 1410, and writings burnt; after further troubles obliged to leave Prague in 1412, and wrote *De Ecclesia*. In 1414 he went to the general council at Constance to defend his views, being granted a safe conduct from King Sigismund; after lengthy trial condemned July 6, 1415, and, refusing to recant, burnt. Continuing the work of Wycliffe, H. helped to prepare the way for the Reformation.

HUSSAR, name originally given in 1458 to Hungarian light cavalry soldiers; name means 'twenty,' since one man in twenty was chosen for service.

HUSSEIN IBN ALI (1851), first King of the Hedjaz, belongs to family of the Katada in which sherifate of Mecca has been vested for eight centuries; recognized by Mohammedans as senior descendant of Mohammed. From 1890 to 1908 lived as an honored prisoner at Constantinople, where he gave his four sons, Ali, Abdullah, Feisal, and their half-brother Zeid, a modern education. After Turk.

revolution, 1908, was appointed Grand Sherif and Emir of Mecca by Committee of Union and Progress, and gained great influence over surrounding Arab tribes. Refused to proclaim Holy War on behalf of Germany, and was invited by nationalist societies in Syria and Mesopotamia to lead Arab revolt. For the history of this revolt and his subsequent intervention in the war on the side of the Allies, see ARABIA. On Oct. 29, 1916, was proclaimed King of Hedjaz with concurrence of the ulema sheikhs, title being subsequently recognized by all the Allies. While Feisal and Zeid led his northern army victorious into Syria and Ali and Abdullah blockaded Medina, he set himself vigorously to organize his new kingdom. Was represented at Peace Conference by Feisal. See HEDJAZ.

HUSSITES, religious party in Bohemia, named from John Huss (*q.v.*), soon after whose death they arose. The special conditions of Bohemia aided them; the avarice and corruption of its priests was infamous, and the Slav peasantry disliked Ger. domination. The H's split into two groups—the *Utraquists* (or *Calixtines*), those whose main claim was communion in both kinds, and the *Taborites*, who were extreme. Continual fighting took place between these two and also with Ger. troops. As it seemed impossible to crush them, a treaty was signed by the H's, Rom. delegates, and King Sigismund, the main clause of which allowed communion in both kinds. This concession continued till 1620. The H's were mostly absorbed in Protestantism at the Reformation.

HUSTING, early Eng. court, of which traces are found in the old Danelagh; it survived as the county court of London city, and gave its name to election platforms.

HUTCHESON, FRANCIS (1694-1746), Brit. theologian and metaphysician; *b.* N. of Ireland; ed. Glasgow Univ., 1910-16; became minister of a dissenting congregation in Dublin, and established a school; though a dissenter, he was on good terms with the bp's of the Irish Church; in 1729 became prof. of Moral Philosophy at Glasgow; many Eng. and Irish dissenters came to study under him. His writings deal with metaphysics, logic, and ethics, of which the last are best known. H. held man has a number of senses—consciousness, sense of beauty, a public sense, a moral sense, sense of the ridiculous, etc., of which the 'moral sense' is fundamental. His philosophy follows Locke in many points (not in all), and is in opposition to Hobbes.

HUTCHINSON, a city of Kansas, in Reno co., of which it is the county seat. It is on the Atchison, Topeka and Santa Fe, the Chicago, Rock Island and Pacific, and the Missouri, Pacific and other railroads, and on the Arkansas River. The city is the largest salt producing city in the world. It is also an important meat packing and shipping center. Its other industries include the manufacture of flour, wall board, fibre products, etc. It is the seat of the State Reformatory, and has a public library and a high school.

HUTCHINSON, ANNE (1600-43); religious fanatic; *b.* in England; *m.* and emigrated to America, 1634; caused a schism in Boston congregation and was excommunicated.

HUTCHINSON, SIR JONATHAN (1828-1913), Eng. surgeon; prof. of Surgery and Pathology at Royal Coll. of Surgeons, 1877-82; pres. Royal Coll. of Surgeons, 1889; founder of the London Postgraduate School of Med.; made important researches in different branches of med., particularly regarding leprosy, and on which he became the greatest living authority; author of numerous works on medical subjects.

HUTCHINSON, THOMAS (1711-80); Brit. gov. of Massachusetts; constrained to order Brit. troops from Boston, 1770; Loyalist gov. of Massachusetts, 1717-74, though not in sympathy with government actions; superseded by Gage.

HUTCHINSON, WOODS (1862), physician, *b.* at Yorkshire, England, 1880, Bachelor of Arts, 1883, Master of Arts, Penn College; 1884 Doctor of Medicine, University of Michigan; 1884, began practice of medicine; 1891-1896 professor of anatomy, State University of Iowa; 1896-1900 at University of of Buffalo, professor of comparative pathology; 1903-1905 state health officer of Oregon; 1907-1909 clinic professor of medicine at New York Polyclinic; 1899-1900 at London Medical Graduates' College, lecturer on comparative pathology; 1899-1900 lecturer on biology, extension department, University of England. Author of: *The Gospel According to Darwin*, 1898; *Studies in Human and Comparative Pathology*, 1901; *Play as an Education*, *Acromegaly and Gigantism*, *Health and Common Sense*, 1908; *Preventable Diseases*, 1909; *Conquest of Consumption*, 1910; *Exercise and Health*, 1911; *Exercise and Health*, 1918 and many other books. *d.* 1930.

HUTCHINS, HARRY BURNS (1847,) an American University President, *b.* in Lisbon, N. H. He graduated from the University of Michigan, in 1871, was Jay professor of law there during 1884-7; professor of law at Cornell University during 1887-94; and was president of the University of Michigan from 1910 to 1920, since then being president emeritus.

HUTTEN, ULRICH VON (1488-1523), Ger. humanist and reformer; first trained as monk, but left in disgust; from 1504-15 wandered about Germany and Italy; author (in part) of famous *Epistoloe Obscurorum Virorum*; attacked Papacy and quarrelled with Erasmus, but was received by Zwingli; a passionately sincere reformer, but a man of dissolute life, headstrong, and lacking in self-control; wrote much in Latin and German.

HUTTON, CHARLES (1737-1823), Eng. mathematician, taught at Newcastle till 1773; then prof. of Mathematics at Woolwich. Pub. *Mathematical Tables*, 1785, *Mathematical and Philosophical Dictionary*, 1795-96; *Course of Mathematics*, 1798 and 1811.

HUTTON, JAMES (1726-97), Scot. geologist; ed. Edinburgh High School and Univ.; abandoned study of law for that of medicine; took M.D. (London) 1749; began study of geology as hobby and put forward theory that geology is not cosmogony; studied also atmospheric changes and several branches of physics.

HUTTON, RICHARD HOLT (1826-97), Eng. miscellaneous prose writer and edit.; joint-edit. of the *National Review*, 1855-65, and of the *Spectator*, 1861 onwards.

HUXLEY, THOMAS HENRY (1825-95), one of the greatest of Eng. zoologists and biologists; *b.* at Ealing in 1825; app. assistant-surgeon on H.M.S. *Rattlesnake*. During the four years' cruise in Australian seas, he studied the delicate surface fauna of the ocean. The result was the forsaking of medical for biological science. From 1854 till he retired in 1885, H. was palaeontologist and lecturer on Natural History at the Royal School of Mines.

Keen as he was on scientific research, H.'s mind was essentially practical, and he labored strenuously in popular lectures and 'Lay Sermons' to make abstruse science—the Evolution Theory of Darwin in particular—clear to the people. He was a member of the Fisheries Commission and of the London School Board; he was a constant critic of political and social progress, and a bitter opponent of all narrowness of thought. More than any of his predecessors, he made the study of zoo. in the univ's a practical training instead of an accumulation of hearsay information.

From examining the anatomy and relationships of Medusae, he wandered to Vertebrate Anat., where he discussed the structure and origin of the skull, the characters of fossil Ganoid Fishes, and the systematic arrangement of Birds. Besides his printed lectures and essays, he wrote many masterly general works, e.g. *Man's Place in Nature*, 1863; *Lessons in Elementary Physiology*, 1866; *Aant. of the Invertebrates*, 1870 and *The Crayfish*, 1881.

HUY (Flem. *Hoey*), town, on Meuse Belgium (50° 32' N., 5° 15' E.), distilleries; paper-mills. Captured by Germans after resistance by civil guard (Aug. 12, 1914).

HUYGENS, CHRISTIAN (1629-95), Dutch mathematician; studied civil law at Leyden, Breda, and Paris; investigated oscillations of pendulum and was first to show Saturn's ring surrounds planet; measured its inclination to ecliptic; was founder of undulatory theory of light; in *Traite de la lumiere*, 1690 gave explanation of reflection and refraction. Discovered polarisation of light.

HUYGENS, SIR CONSTANTIJN (1596-1687), Dutch poet and statesman; best works are *Batara Tempe*, *Dagwerck* (a didactic poem), and *Oogentroosi* (a consolatory poem).

HUYSMANS, JORIS KARL (1848-1907), Fr. novelist, whose realism is mixture of Zola with Maupassant, without the latter's polish; later works are psychological studies of religious experiences.

HUYSUM, JAN VAN (1682-1749), Dutch painter of wonderful vases of fruit, flowers, butterflies, etc.; considered master of this kind of painting.

HYACINTH, a genus of monocotyledonous plants; natural order, *Liliaceoe*. The hyacinth, *Hyacinthus orientalis*, is a perennial herb with a bulb. Foliage-leaves are long, narrow, parallel-veined, with sheathing bases. A bare stem terminates in a raceme of pendulous brightly colored flowers in the axils of bracts; three petaloid sepals and three petals form a single tube with six free segments.

HYACINTH, JACINTH, red stone used by ancients as ornament; variety of Zircon.

HYACINTHUS (classical myth.), beautiful youth slain accidentally by Apollo; from his blood grew Gk. hyacinth (clearly not our flower of that name), inscribed with exclamation of woe, 'Ail' Great Spartan midsummer festival, the *Hyacinthia.*

HYADES, in Gk. myth., seven maidens who watched over Dionysus; changed by Zeus into stars and placed in constellation Taurus.

HYBLA MINOR (mod. Paterno) (37° 32' N., 14° 53' E.), ancient city, Sicily, on S. slope of Mt. Etna.

HYBRIDS.—One of the chief causes of the separation of species of animals and plants has been the fact that members of a species are fertile, amongst themselves, but are not fertile with members of another species. This rule is not universal, however, for occasionally species are found which interbreed with other species, the progeny of such a union being known as hybrids, and the phenomenon as hydridism. But it must be remembered that where hybridism occurs the species concerned are *closely* related, for while a Hare and a Rabbit may interbreed occasionally, it is absurd to think of either breeding with a Porcupine, although distantly related in the same natural order of Mammals. Another general fact is that hybrids are seldom fertile amongst themselves, although there is no apparent reason why this should be so. Mules—the offspring of horses and asses—are infertile with each other, but sometimes produce young when mated again with the pure parental forms. In the animal world hybrids seem to occur in nature not infrequently amongst deer, game-birds, ducks, and fishes, *e.g.* Roach mating with Bream or Rudd, and Carp with Tench or Bream. And artificial hybrids among these and many others, such as the species of such lowly creatures as Sea Urchins, are not uncommon. In the vegetable world the artificial crossing or hybridising of species of plants has led to many new forms. It is unfortunate, 'or clearness' sake, that the word 'hybrid' is used for the progeny not only of two species, but also of two varieties of one species, when the word 'mongrel' would have indicated the latter class more distinctly. Varietal mongrels or hybrids are so much under man's control and have given rise to so many useful breeds, that they are of the utmost importance.

HYDE (53° 27' N., 2° 5' W.), town, Cheshire, England; cotton manufactures; coal mines.

HYDE, DOUGLAS (1863), Irish literary historian, poet, and folklorist, known as 'An Craoibhin Aoibhinn' (Delightful Little Branch), has played a large part in the revival of Gaelic language and literature; founder of Gaelic League, and its president up to the rise of Sinn Fein and the intrusion of politics, 1915. Works include a *Literary History of Ireland,* 1899; *Love Songs of Connacht,* 1906, and short plays for Irish-speaking actors. Chm. Folklore Inst., Ireland, 1930.

HYDE, WILLIAM DEWITT (1857-1917), an American college president, *b.* in Winchendon, Mass. He graduated from Harvard, in 1879, studied theology at Andover Theological Seminary, held a pastorate in Paterson, N. J. and became president of Bowdoin College in 1885. In this capacity he showed marked administrative ability, developing the institution into one of the best in the country. He wrote *Practical Ethics,* 1892; *Practical Idealism,* 1897, and *The Gospel of Good Will,* 1915.

HYDER ALI, HAIDAR ALI (c. 1722-82), famous soldier; native of India, who became Maharajah of Mysore; conquered Calicut and other native states; formed alliance with French, and took Arcot in 1769; defeated in several engagements by Sir Eyre Coote, 1781.

HYDE PARK, a town of Massachusetts, in Suffolk co., 8 miles S. of Boston. It is on the Neponset River and the N. Y., N. H., and Hartford Railroads. It is chiefly a residential place but has important manufactures.

HYDE PARK, a famous park in London, which contains about 400 acres. On the W. is Kensington Gardens. The park has for many years been a fashionable promenade. It contains Rotten Row, a road set apart for equestrians, and the Serpentine, a large body of water. The Albert Memorial, in memory of the Prince Consort, is in Hyde Park.

HYDERABAD, HAIDARABAD (17° 50' N., 78° 40' E.), principal native state in India, lying between provinces of Madras and Bombay in the Deccan; area, c. 82,700 sq. miles; capital, Hyderabad. Country fertile, but badly cultivated. Tableland traversed by the Godavari in N., and Kistna in S.; climate healthy; chief products are rice, wheat, maize, cotton, etc. Nizam and State are Muhammadan; otherwise mostly Hindu,

HYDERABAD, HAIDARABAD '(17° 21' N., 78° 30' E.), city; capital of above state; surrounded by walls; principal buildings are the Mecca mosque and Brit. Residency; fourth largest city and one of chief seats of Muhammadanism in India; important commercial centre; extensive water-works.

HYDERABAD, HAIDARABAD (15° 23' N., 68° 24' E.), city; capital, Hyderabad, Scind, Bombay, Brit. India; near E. bank of Indus; strongly fortified; manufactures silks, gold-work.

HYDRA, in Gk. legend, nine-headed monster inhabiting **Lerna in Argolis** slain by Heracles.

HYDRA, ancient *Hydrea* (37° 20′ N., 23° 30′ E.), small island on S.E. coast of Argolis, Greece; took prominent part in the Gk. war of independence; contains seaport of H.; active trade.

HYDRANGEA, a deciduous shrub, *Hydrangea hortensia,* with oval, strongly veined opposite leaves. The *inflorescence* is a *corymb* of pink or blue flowers; the petals are absent and sepals are petaloid.

HYDRATES are compounds, including salts, containing water of crystallization, where water molecules do not undergo rearrangement.

HYDRAULIC ENGINES are machines designed to convert into mechanical energy, the kinetic energy of moving water or the potential energy of water under pressure. Under this heading are classified Water Pressure Engines, Water Wheels, Water Turbines, Water Motors, Hydraulic Rams, etc.

Water Pressure Engines usually consist of long cylinders in which the water acts on a piston; this in turn acts on the load. Typical examples of this engine may be seen in hydraulic elevators, hydraulic presses, etc.

Water Wheels are of three types: 1— the overshot wheel, with the water entering the buckets of the wheel on top; 2—the breast wheel, in which the water enters the buckets at about the same level as the wheel axis; 3—the undershot wheel, in which the velocity of a stream of water drives the wheel by impinging on its blades. Water wheels are commonly used to drive small grist mills, saw mills, cider presses, etc.

Water Turbines are classified as Impulse Turbines, when all the energy of the water is changed to kinetic energy before it acts on the turbine runner, and as Reaction Turbines when only part of the energy is converted into kinetic energy before entering the turbine buckets. This class of hydraulic engine is widely used to drive electric generators, where the head of water or discharge is high.

Water Motors, built somewhat on the lines of a reciprocating steam engine, take water at a pressure and utilize its potential energy. The velocity of the water is kept as low as possible. The efficiency of this device being only about 50%, they are seldom used.

Hydraulic Rams utilize the kinetic energy of a stream of water in a pipe to force a smaller quantity of water to a height greater than that of the head on the ram. The efficiency of this device is rather low, but its convenience, simplicity and the absence of moving parts (except valves), renders it quite popular in rural districts for supplying water for domestic purposes for a comparatively low water fall.

A Hydraulic Engine, utilizing pulsations in a closed pipe system has been proposed. The pulsations are imparted to the incompressible water by a pump-like apparatus; the motor also resembles a valveless pump. In this system there is no flow of water, the pulsations transmitting the energy. Its future however is doubtful since other power transmitting systems are more efficient and convenient.

HYDRAZINE, DIAMIDOGEN (H_2N. NH_2), is a colorless liquid, B.P. 113°·5 C., formed by complex organic decomposition. It is heavier than and soluble in water, and at 0° C. forms colorless crystals. It reacts vigorously with the *halogens* and is a strong reducing agent.

HYDROCARBONS. A large group of compounds composed of hydrogen and carbon combined in varying proportions. The three principal groups of hydrocarbons are known as (1) saturated (2) unsaturated, (3) hydrocarbons containing a ring structure. Saturated hydrocarbons are those in which all four valencies of the carbon atom are satisfied. They have the general formula $C_n H_{2n} + 2$. The paraffins belong to this group, including marsh gas, CH_4, which is the simplest hydrocarbon known, and most of the constituents of petroleum oil. Unsaturated hydrocarbons, having the general formula C_nH_{2n}, or $C_nH_{2n_2}$, contain unsatisfied carbon bonds and will therefore unite directly with other elements, such as chlorine, without any disturbance of the hydrogen atoms in the molecule. One of the best known of the unsaturated hydrocarbons is acetylene, C_2H_2. Others are ethylene, C_2H_4, propylene, C_3H_6, butylene, C_4H_8. The hydrocarbons of ring structure imclude a number of compounds of great commercial importance, among them being benzene, C_6H_6, toluene, C_7H_8, naphthalene, $C_{10}H_8$, anthracene, $C_{14}H_{10}$. Combination of one type with another frequently occurs in nature, so that the number of natural hydrocarbons is enormous. Decaying vegetable and animal matter, under favorable conditions, gives rise to hydrocarbons, natural gas and coal gas consist largely of them, and petroleum and shale oils are made up almost entirely of a mixture of hydrocarbons of varying complexity.

HYDROCARBONS, BENZINE. See BENZINE HYDROCARBONS.

HYDROCELE, collection of fluid, usually serous, in vicinity of the testis or spermatic cord, commonly due to chronic inflammation, perhaps syphilitic, of testis, manifested as a fluctuating swelling of the scrotum with a dragging feeling; treated by slight operation of tapping, injecting various substances, or excising part of tunica vaginalis and draining.

HYDROCEPHALUS, condition of brain in which the ventricles or cavities are distended with fluid, due either to malformation or to chronic inflammation it is either congenital or develops in the first few months of life, and the upper part of the head is increased in size out of proportion to the rest of the body; the brain may be pressed on by the fluid, so that the intelligence is impaired, and hydrocephalics do not usually live long. Treatment is unsatisfactory, and best is merely maintenance of the health of the individual with nourishing foods and tonics.

HYDROCHLORIC ACID (HCl), colorless gas, liquefying under cold and pressure, liquid boiling at —83·6 C.; when dry, inactive with metals; readily soluble in water, saturated solution at 15° C. having S.G. 1·21; solution called Muriatic Acid, Spirits of Salt; manufactured by strong sulphuric acid on common salt (see also ALKALI); commercial a. is yellow and used for making bleaching powder and in soldering; forms chlorides.

HYDROCYANIC ACID, PRUSSIC ACID.

HYDRO-DYNAMICS. See HYDRO-MECHANICS.

HYDROGEN (H=1) is a tasteless, odorless, and colorless gas. It is the lightest known substance and therefore constitutes the standard of *Atomic Weight* and *Valence.* At—253° C. it is a colorless liquid. *Hydrogen* burns in air and oxygen with a non-luminous blue flame. It is prepared— (1) by the action of metals on water, different metals abstracting the oxygen at cold, moderate, and high temperatures; (2) by the action of a suitable acid on a suitable metal. All acids contain *hydrogen.* Hydrogen, either as a gas at a high temperature, or in the nascent condition at ordinary temperature, is a reducing agent, for it abstracts *oxygen* from compounds. A mxiture of *hydrogen and oxygen* when ignited unite with explosive violence to form water. The position of *hydrogen* in the *periodic* system is not definite. As a univalent element it must be placed at the head of either the alkali metals or the halogens, but it resembles neither closely.

HYDROGEN PEROXIDE (H_2O_2); unstable viscid iiquid obtained by combination of hydrated peroxide of barium and sulphuric acid (dilute); strong oxidising agent employed largely in bleaching and dyeing.

HYDROGRAPHY. See MAP.

HYDROMECHANICS is the study of the dynamical properties of fluids and their application as motive power for machinery. *Hydrostatics* is the study of fluids in equilibrium or at rest. *Hydrodynamics* is concerned with fluids in motion. For these purposes, a fluid is defined as any substance which can yield continuously to any force which tends to divide it along any plane. If through any body we draw an imaginary plane surface, the stress (tension, pressure, or shearing force) acting across this plane can be resolved into two components—one perpendicular to, the other along the plane. In a solid, both components may be present; in a fluid at rest, the perpendicular component alone can be present. Fluids, therefore, include both liquids and gases.

The basis for the first division of the subject— *Hydrostatics*—is given by the principle just enunciated, that in a fluid at rest the stress in any plane drawn through the fluid must always be normal to that plane. This stress generally takes the form of a pressure, which is measured *at* any point by the thrust or pressure exerted over unit area including the point. It may be expressed in atmospheres, pounds weight, or tons weight per square inch or square foot, or (if the C.G.S. system be adopted) in dynes per square centimetre. The principal theorems of hydrostatics may be summarized as follows, it being understood, of course, that they apply to fluids *at rest* or *in equilibrium*: (1) The pressure at any point of a fluid is the same in all directions. (2) Pressure is transmissible from one point to another in the same mass of fluid—*i.e.*, any additional pressure applied to an incompressible fluid will be transmitted equally to every point of the fluid. (3) In liquids acted on by gravity, the pressure is uniform over all points in the same horizontal plane, and therefore the free surface of a liquid at rest under gravity is a horizontal plane. (4) The pressure at any point in a homogeneous liq id acted on by gravity is proportional to the depth of the point below the free surface; hence liquids 'find their level,' as the saying is, and where two liquids do not mix, their surface of separation is a horizontal plane. (5) The pressure on any plane area immersed in a fluid is equal to the weight of a column of the liquid whose cross-sectional area is equal to the immersed area and whose height is equal to the depth below the free surface of the centre of gravity of the immersed area. (6) Any body which is wholly or partially immersed in a fluid acted on by gravity experiences an upward thrust equal in amount to the weight of fluid displaced by the body, and this thrust acts vertically upwards through the centre of gravity of the displaced fluid (*Archimedes' principle*). (7) In order that a body floating freely in a fluid may be in equilibrium, the condition involved in (6) above must be satisfied, and, further, the centres of gravity of the displaced fluid and of the floating body must lie in the same vertical line.

These theorems (for the proofs of which the reader is referred to any treatise on the subject) have a very extensive application in the sciences, arts, and industries, and we have only space to mention a few in illustration. The transmissibility of fluid pressure is applied to the conveyance of power from one point to another. At a central station, hydraulic presses or accumulators apply pressure to a body of water; pipes in communication with the presses convey the pressure to cranes, motors, lifts, and other hydraulic machines The principle that water finds its own level is familiar to all. The variation of pressure with depth is the principle of Hare's Hydrometer, and of similar methods of determining the density of liquids. It is also illustrated by the diminishing pressure of the atmosphere as we ascend from sea-level, but in this case the rate of diminution is complicated by the fact that air is compressible. In the case of the water in an ocean, the proportionate increase of pressure with depth is more nearly correct, owing to the low compressibility of water. The expression given in (5) above for the total thrust on an immersed surface is constantly in use for calculating the stresses on dock gates, reservoir walls, dams. and other immersed surfaces.

Archimedes' principle, taken together with the conditions of equilibrium given in (7), introduces the whole question as to the equilibrium of ships, submarines, diving-bells, caissons, balloons, and all other bodies which are supported vertically by the upward thrust of the fluid in which they are wholly or partially immersed. In this connection, the question of *stability* of equilibrium of a floating body arises, and thus introduces matters of the utmost importance in naval architecture. The principle of Archimedes also forms the basis of a method for ascertaining the *specific gravity* of a body. For if the upward thrust of a body when totally immersed in water is equal to the weight of an equal volume of water, the weight of the body when weighed in water will be diminished by this amount. Hence the ratio of the weight of the body to the difference between the weights in water and air gives the specific gravity. Obviously, also, the ratio of the diminutions in weight of the same body when weighed n a given liquid and in water is equal to the specific gravity of the liquid. In the case of a body specifically lighter than water, it floats in water with that proportion of its whole volume immersed which equals the specific gravity of the body. This is the basis for the construction of *hydrometers*, which are used to give direct readings of the specific gravity of liquids.

In *Hydrodynamics*, we start with the assumption that liquids are perfect—*i.e.*, that the relative motions of their parts are not impeded by viscous friction. There is no liquid in nature which satisfies this condition, but in many liquids the effects of viscosity are so slight that they may be neglected. Later on in the treatment of the subject, the equations of motion are modified so as to allow for viscosity, but their complicated character has rendered their solution difficult except in a few simpler cases. It is not possible to give here any explanation of the hydrodynamical equations, but one or two of the leading ideas connected with them may be mentioned. The motions of a fluid may be treated in two ways. We may fix attention on a given volume of space and take into account the amounts of fluid which enter or leave that space. Or we may choose a certain small volume of the liquid and study the changes which, during its motion, it may undergo in shape, position, speed, pressure, etc. In either case we are led to the equations which describe the motion of the fluid. The whole mass may then be mapped out by lines which at each point have the same direction as the velocity of the fluid at that point. These are termed *lines of flow*, or *stream-lines*. Following the gravitational analogy, according to which water, in flowing down a hillside, always takes the steepest possible course, we can draw a series of surfaces in the fluid such that they are always at right angles to the stream-lines.

Such surfaces are termed *surfaces of equivelocity potential*, and the fluid will always move from places of higher to places of lower velocity potential. The term *irrotational* is applied to those species of fluid motion in which a velocity potential exists, in order to distinguish them from cases of rotational or vortex motion where such potential does not exist. Another way of looking at irrotational motion is to imagine that each stream-line begins at some point where fluid is continuously produced and ends at some point where it is continuously annihilated—that is, to start from a *source* and end at a *sink*. In rotational or vortex motion, a cylindrical portion of the fluid of very small diameter is in rotation about its axis. Such motion is accompanied by a tension between the ends of the vortex and a pressure on its cylindrical surface or boundary. It can be proved that, in a perfect fluid, vortex motion cannot be created, and if in existence it cannot be destroyed. In a viscous fluid, however, vortices can be produced; but if left to itself without a supply of energy from without, the vortex is destroyed in time by the viscous forces in the fluid.

HYDROMETER is an instrument for determining the *density* of liquids and solids. It is an application of the principle that when a body floats in fluid under the action of gravity the weight of the body is equal to that of the fluid displaced. Boyle was the first to employ h's. A h. consists of a glass bulb with a long stem sealed and graduated. The bulb is weighted with mercury or small shot, a sufficient vuantity being used to immerse the whole of the bulb in the heaviest liquid in which it is to be used. The height and diameter of the stem must be such that the h. will float in the lightest liquid in which it is to be used. The point to which the h. sinks in the lightest liquid, and that to which it rises in the heaviest liquid, are then marked on the stem with the densities of these liquids, and the distance between graduated. The *density* of any liquid not greater or less than those marked on the stem can be obtained by placing the h. in a tall cylindrical vessel full of the liquid and reading the mark to which it sinks. Care must be taken that no air-bubbles adhere to its surface and that it does not touch the sides of the vessel.—Nicholson's Hydrometer, made of metal, has a pan above and below the bulb and only one mark on the stem. From these pans the weights in air and water of a solid are obtained, and the formula weight in air divided by weight in water is the required density.

HYDROPATHY, the treatment of disease by pure water, is a method which has been employed since ancient times, Hippocrates, Galen, and other classical medical writers praising it highly. In the XVIII. cent. water began to be used externally and internally for fevers, and Priessnitz, 1799-1851, a farmer at Gräfenberg, Silesia, treated sprains, wounds, and many other conditions, with great success, by applying water to every part of the body; and during the first half of the XIX cent. treatment by water became very popular, hydropathic establishments springing up in numbers in England, France, Germany, and America. Water is best drunk about an hour before meals; only very little, and that hot, during meals; while early in the morning and late at night, water is benefit in flushing out the stomach and bowels. In the form of steam, water has a valuable effect in irritation or inflammation of the respiratory passages and lungs. The methods of applying water externally to the body include hot or cold packing, for cooling or inducing sweating; hot-air baths (Turkish) to stimulate the nervous and vascular systems and for the treatment of gout and rheumatism; spray, shower, plunge, douche, needle baths, having a stimulating and tonic effect on the system; sitz, head, and foot baths. for local congestions and inflammations; and hot and cold fomentations or poultices for numerous local conditions, wounds, sprains, etc.

HYDROPHOBIA, an infectious disease occurring among certain animals, particularly dogs and other animals of the canine species, and communicable by them to man, infection being most usually carried by a bite of a rabid animal. The first symptom of the disease in a dog is a change in its habits; it is gloomy and restless; the restlessness increases, the animal snaps at everything and tears up and swallows all kinds of unusual things; the eyes are dull, the mouth continually open, and it has a characteristic high-toned bark; it becomes much excited in the presence of another dog and tries to attack it; gradually convulsions, paralysis, and coma come on and death ensues.

In man the incubation period is from about a fortnight to seven or eight months, bnt six weeks is the average period. The first symptoms are mental depression and restlessness, sleeplessness and nervous excitability; the symptoms become worse and the person suffers much from thirst, but on making the effort to drink is seized with a spasm of the muscles of swallowing and breathing; these and other paroxysms increase in severity, then weakness and paralysis develop, convulsions and coma ensue, and result in death.

The former treatment was to excite the part infected or to apply to it a caustic or the actual cautery, but the researches of Pasteur have revolutionised the treatment. It depends on the fact that a virus can be extracted from the tissues of a rabid animal and then either attenuated or intensified. The spinal cords of rabbits which have been inoculated are dried for different periods, the diminution of virulence being proportional of the length of time they are kept, and emulsions made from them are injected into the individual affected, the strength of the virulence of the emulsion being gradually increased up to the standard strength. An individual so treated does not exhibit any symptom of hydrophobia.

HYDROPLANE is, strictly speaking, a craft which, under power, skims along the surface of water. The bottom is so constructed with planes that when movement starts the craft rises to and then skims along the surface. The term is also often applied to what is more correctly described as the *hydro-aeroplane* This is an aeroplane fitted with a base in the form of a pontoon or boat with a hydroplaning bottom. When under power, the base is lifted to the surface by the combined aeroplane and hydroplane action. It may then be controlled as a hydroplane.

HYDROSTATICS. See HYDROMECHANICS.

HYDROXIDES, compounds containing hydrogen and oxygen not in form of water, thus differing from hydrates (*q.v.*); mostly basic in action; common h. is Sodinm H. (NaOH).

HYDROXYLAMINE, HYDROXY-AMMONIA (NH₂. OH), is a liquid which with acids forms salts; prepared by acting on nitric acid with nascent hydrogen.

HYDROZOA, the name given to a class of Coelenterata belonging to the sub-.hylum Cnidaria; it is coincident with Hydromedusae or Craspedota, with the addition of the Acalephae. This class includes polyps, colonies of polyps which produce medusae by budding, and medusae which rise directly from the egg. The polyps, which are small in size, are generally attached permanently to foreign bodies ,but sometimes as in Siphonophora, the whole colony may be free-swimming. The first polyp assumes an upstanding position termed the hydranth, which lengthens and buds until it forms a colony or hydrosome. The generative cells, which are always ripening and discharging, may arise in a variety of places, but always migrate to the ectoderm of the gonophore. H. feed chiefly on animal substances, and with few exceptions are

marine organisms, The class is divided into the orders Hydridae, Hydrocorallinae, Tubulariae, Campanulariae, Trachomedusae, Narcomedusae, and Siphonophora.

HYENAS (HYÆNIDÆ), a family of carnivores comprising seventeen species and races, confined to the tropical and sub-tropical areas of the Old World. Remains of the Cave-Hyena have been found in Britain.

HYÉRES (43° 7′ N., 6° 5′ E.), town, dep. Var, France, near Mediterranean, on Riviera; noted winter health-resort; trade in fruits and salt; birthplace of Massillon.

HYGEIIA, Gk. goddess of health, *d.* of Æsculapius, god of med.; bore snake in her hand.

HYGIENE, the science of the preservation of health, including all principles concerning the well-being of man physically and mentally, and in regard to his environment. See DIGESTION, FOOD, BACTERIOLOGY, VENTILATION, PUBLIC HEALTH.

HYGROMETER (Gk. *hygros,* damp), apparatus for gauging humidity of atmosphere; commonest form is 'wet and dry bulb h.,' consisting of two thermometers, one with moistened bulb. The difference between the two marks the humidity, and may amount to several degrees on a dry day, or nothing if air is saturated. Daniel's h., 1820 was bent tube containing ether, each end terminating in a bulb, one of which was covered with cloth. Evaporation took place when ether was poured upon cloth, and this resulted in cooling of cloth-covered bulb and condensation of ether inside the tube, producing moisture upon surface of other bulb. The temperature at which this condensation takes place is called the 'dew-point.'

The first h. was invented in 1676 by Coniers.

HYKSOS, SHEPHERD KINGS, an Asiatic race who conquered Egypt in XV. cent. B.C., and kept possession of country for several cent's., after which a rebellion occurred, and they are expelled; they have been identified with the Jews by some writers, including Josephus.

HYLAS (classical myth.), *s.* of Theiodamas, and beloved by Herakles; removed from earth by water-nymphs.

HYMANS, PAUL (1854), a Belgian statesman. He was *b.* in Brussels, and was educated at the University of Brussels. From 1900 he was a member of the House of Representatives from Brussels. For several years he was professor at the University of Brussels. He was English Ambassador in 1915 and in 1917 was Minister of Foreign Affairs for Belgium; first president, League of Nations, 1920. Belgian delegate to Disarmament Conference, 1932. He wrote several works on historical subjects.

HYMEN, Gk. god of marriage, *s.* of Apollo and Urania; represented with veil and torch.

HYMENOPTERA (Gk. *hymen*, marriage; *pteron*, a wing), an order with between 30,000 and 40,000 members, which include Saw-Flies, Gall-Flies, Ichneumon Flies, Bees, Wasps, Ants, etc., and includes the most highly developed of insects. The name signifies that the upper and under wings on each side are 'wedded' or linked together in flight by a row of hooks in the latter, which catch in a hard rim of the former. H. are generally active, neat insects, with four usually transparent wings, strong mandibles, often with a 'waist,' the females furnished with a saw, sting, or boring or piercing ovipositor; and the larva undergoing a complete and abrupt metamorphosis in assuming the adult form.

HYMETTUS, modern Trello Vouni (37° 56′ N., 23° 49′ E.), mountain, Attica, Greece; famous for its honey; height 3,370 ft.

HYMN (Gr. *hymnos*) denotes a poem written in memory of heroes, or addressed to the gods. The historic antecedents of Christian hymns are to be sought in anc. Israel, the words hymn and psalm being practically interchangeable. It is recorded of Christ and His disciples that they sang an hymn after the institution of the Lord's Supper. Hymnody developed in Eastern Christian Churches before those of the West. In the West the introduction of hymns was due to St. Hilary of Poitiers and St. Ambrose of Milan, the latter of whom was the real founder of hymnody in the West. St. Benedict of Nursia (*d. c.* 541), by fitting of hymns to his Order of Worship, secured their widespread hold. The hymn 'The royal banners forward go' is attributed to Venantius Fortunatus (7th cent.); 'Come, Holy Ghost, our souls inspire,' to Charles the Bald (9th cent.). From the 11th to the 16th century the hymns produced were chiefly monastic in origin and character, that of St. Bernard of Cluny (12th cent.) being one of the best—'The times are very evil.'

HYNDMAN, HENRY MAYERS (1842-1921), founder of British Socialism, *b.* in London, son of a wealthy man; ed. at Trinity College and traveled extensively. Became imbued with socialist ideas of Karl Marx and in 1881 published the first socialist book since the failure of Owenism. Many prominent English socialists of the present generation were either his colleagues or pupils in the Social Democratic Federation. Upon the outbreak of the World War, he became a strong nationalist and broke with his party, which expelled him, whereupon he formed the National Socialist Party with a few of his followers.

HYOID BONE, a U-shaped bone lying immediately above the thyroid cartilage of the larynx, and near the root of the tongue to the muscles of which it gives attachment.

HYPATIA (370-415), *d.* of Theon; lecturer, Platonic school at Alexandria, founded by Plotinus; mathematician and philosopher; murdered by fanatics.

HYPERBOLA, a conic section obtained by cutting a cone with a plane perpendicular to base of cone.

HYPERBOLE (Gk. *huperballein*, to throw beyond), term of rhetoric for exaggeration.

HYPERBOREANS, in Gk. legend, people who lived in unknown regions of north (*i.e.* of the north wind, Boreas).

HYPEREIDES (*c.* 390-322 B.C.), Attic orator; pupil of Isocrates; opposed Philip and Alexander of Macedon; advocated Lamian War; was captured and killed by Antipater.

HYPERION, a Titan in Gk. mythology; *s.* of Uranus and Gaea and *f.* of Helios; title-character of unfinished masterpiece of Keats.

HYPERSTHENE, mineral found in Skye and Labrador; orthorhombic, with bronze lustre, or brown or green coloration; belong to pyroxene group; S.G. *c.* 3.5.

HYPERTROPHY, overgrowth of an organ or other part of the body, either through increase in the size of the components of the tissues or through increase in their number, or by a combination of both. H. is due to increased exercise of a part in its functions or to increase of its blood supply; some forms of h. *e.g.* goitre, elephantiasis, are due to disease.

HYPNOTISM, a term including everything relating to the induction of a state resembling sleep; called hypnosis. Such terms as *mesmerism* and *animal magnetism* are sometimes used to describe certain aspects of it. This state differs from sleep in an increased and extreme suggestibility of the individual, in a loss of sensitiveness of the sense organs, in a tendency to anaesthesia, and in an increased rapidity of the pulse and the respirations. Usually an individual awakened from hypnosis does not remember what has happened during the state, but the memory of this may be brought back by post-hypnotic suggestion. Somnambulism, or sleep-walking, is a state resembling hypnosis, which seems to be induced generally under the influence of mental excitement, and is hereditary in some persons.

Hypnosis is induced usually by the subject fixing his eyes on some small object in such a position that there is slight muscular strain in gazing at it, and passively allowing the hypnotizer to suggest to him the ideas of weariness of the limbs, heaviness of the eyes, and sleep. Some hypnotizers pass the hands monotonously and slowly close to or over the face. Soon the eyes close, the subject becomes drowsy, but instead of allowing him to pass into a natural sleep the hypnotizer, by speaking, etc., keeps in contact with him and thus maintains control. In this state the subject knows what is going on around him, but is only able to do what the hypnotizer allows or commands him, and he may pass into a deeper state of hypnosis, resembling coma, in which he is more profoundly influenced than in the lighter stages. Under suggestion the subject may use limbs with much greater strength than ordinarily, while anaesthesia of a part of the body so deep that a surgical operation may be performed, may also be brought about by suggestion.

Several theories regarding hypnosis have been propounded, but the explanation which seems to give most promise of solution of the problem, upon which research is still being made, is that hypnosis is the temporary blocking of the nervous links between the different systems of neutral dispositions (the conditions of the rise of ideas to consciousness) of the brain, so that each idea works out its effects free from the interference or inhibition of antagonistic ideas, and thus is more effective than normally.

In the United States and the Continent of Europe hypnotism has been employed to a considerable extent in the treatment of physical and mental disease. See AUTO-SUGGESTION.

HYPOCAUST . Gk. *hupo*, beneath; *kauein*, to burn), Rom. chamber containing heating apparatus.

HYPOCHLOROUS ACID (HClO), strong bleaching agent formed by combinations of nitric acid (dilute) and bleaching powder.

HYPOCHONDRIASIS, nervous condition characterised by mental depression and delusions regarding the state of the health; the general health and appetite are usually quite good, but no persuasion as to the real condition is of any avail; in its most advanced form h. is a form of insanity. The condition yields to psychoanalysis and moderate exercise, and such interests as serve to turn the sufferer's mind to other matters.

HYPOSTASIS, personality (*persona*), an independent and incommunicable existence; used to mean person of the Trinity in early Christian controversies.

HYPOSTYLE (Gk. *hupo*, under; *stulos*, a column,) architectural term for Egyptian and classical buildings in which rows of columns support flat ceiling.

HYPOTENUSE (subtending), t h e longest side of a rightangled triangle, which lies opposite the right angle. The middle point of the H. is the centre of the triangle's circumscribed circle, and hence equidistant from the angles. The square described on the H. equals the sum of the squares on the other two sides.

HYPOTHEC (Gk. *hupotheke*, thing pledged), right given by Scot. law over effects of a debtor (Engl. lien.) ;

HYPOTHESIS, supposition accepted by scientific thought as a guide to further inquiry; requires verification before being held to be a demonstrated theory.

HYPOTRACHELIUM (Gk. *hupo*, under; *trachelos*, neck), name given by Rom. architect Vitruvius to moulding between the annulet of the capital and the shaft in Gk. buildings.

HYRCANIA, modern Astarabad (36° 40' N., 54° 30' E.), ancient district, Persia. S. of Caspian Sea.

HYRCANUS, JOHN I. (d. 105 B. C.), Jewish chief priest (135); youngest of Simon Maccabeus; forced to acknowledge suzerainty of Antiochus, but conquered Samaria and restored Jewish prosperity. His unfortunate grandson, John Hyrcanus II. (executed 30 B. C.), Jewish chief priest (78-40), was the obedient vassal of the Romans.

HYSSOP (*Hyssopus officinalis*), small perennial herb of natural order *Labitoe*, with thin quandrangular stems, elliptical leaves growing in pairs, and spikes of small violet flowers; grows in S. Europe and as far as Central Asia; an infusion of the leaves was formerly used to relieve bruises, swellings, catarrh, etc. Hedge H. (*Gratiola officinalis*) is a herb of natural order *Scrophulariadeoe*, with cylindrical stems and solitary reddish flowers, native of S. Europe; once used as a drug with purgative, diuretic and emetic action; formerly a remedy for dropsy and gout.

HYSTASPES.—(1) legendary Persian ruler of time of Zoroaster; (2) father of Darius I.

HYSTERIA, a form of disturbance of the nervous system, characterised by exaggeration of reflex and mental excitability with diminished will-power and control over the emotions. The causes are hereditary predisposition to nervous disease, nerve exhaustion, various conditions of the genital system, and the condition often appears at such a time as puberty, pregnancy, or the climacteric. Women are affected very much more than men, most frequently girls betwen fifteen and twenty-five. The symptoms are varied, and may stimulate many different conditions, common symptoms being (1) *sensory disturbances*, hyperaesthesia or anaesthesia; (2) *motor disturbances*, epilepsy, spasms, (*e.g.* vaginismus, (spasms of vagina), globus hystericus (spasms of throat), paralytis; (3) *visceral disturbances*, palpitation, vomiting; (4) *mental disturbances*, melancholia, apathy, craving for sympathy, etc. Moral influence has been found to be of greater value than drugs. Treatment—Psychoanalysis, complete rest and in some cases, tonics.

HYSTERON-PROTERON, Gk. name given to that figure of speech which reverses the natural order (generally for emphasis.)

HYTHE (51° 5′ N., 1° 5′ E.), market town and watering-place, Kent, England, near Eng. Channel; one of the Cinque Ports.

I

I (Phœnician and Heb. *yodh*; Gk. *iota*), ninth letter in Eng. alphabet, adopted from Lat. use of Gk. *iota*; the form was a zigzag, straightened by the Gk's; dot added to distinguish it among m's and n's in Middle Ages.

I.O.U. ('I owe you'), private document of simple nature witnessing indebtedness; of no legal value.

IAMBIC, term in prosody for verse composed of *iambi*, feet of two syllables with first short, second long. (e. g.)

IAMBLICHUS, (fl. 300 A.D.), Syrian philosopher; a pupil of Porphyry. Fragments of his works survive, but *On the Egyptian Mysteries*, often ascribed to him, is not really his. I. was a Neo-Platonist of great learning, and constructed an elaborate theological scheme. The Emperor Julian thought him as great as Plato. I. believed in an Absolute, and many other deities, arranged in groups.

IAMBLICHUS, (fl. II. cent. A.D.), Syrian Gk.; author of love-romance, *Babuloniaka*, of which only fragments are extant.

IAPETUS, (classical myth), Titan *s.* of Uranus and Gæa, and *f.* of Prometheus, Atlas, etc.; *grandfather* of Deucalion, and possibly to be identified with Hebrew Japhet.

IAPYDES, race of Illyria subjugated by Romans, II. to I. cent. B.C.

IAZYGES, Sarmatian tribe now extinct, which gave Rome trouble on the Danube, I.-IV. cent. A.D.

IBADAN, (8° 22′ N., 4° 3′ E.), town, in Yoruba, S. Nigeria, Brit. W. Africa.

IBAGUÉ, SAN BONIFACIO DE IBAGUÉ (4° 30′ N., 75° 15′ W.), town, Colombia, S. America; commercial centre of an agricultural district, producing cacao, tobacco, sugar-cane.

IBÁÑEZ, VICENTE BLASCO. See BLASCO IBÁÑEZ.

IBARRA (0° 23′ N., 77° 53′ W.); city Ecuador, S. America; at foot of volcano of Imbabura; cotton and woolen industries.

IBERIANS.—All is obscure concerning the origin of this ancient people; sometimes the term 'Iberian' was applied anciently to all who dwelt in Spain, but it was also given to the tribes dwelling particularly round the Ebro. Found in Spain, Southern France, Corsica, Sardinia, Sicily, and in Celtic Britain.

IBERIS, CANDYTUFT, g e n u s of plants, order Cruciferæ; annual C. is popular garden flower.

IBERVILLE, PIERRE LE MOYNE, SIEUR D' (1661-1706), a French-Canadian naval and military commander, b. at Montreal. He took part in the destruction of Schenectady, 1690. In 1699 he founded Fort Biloxi (afterwards Mobile) at the mouth of the Mississippi in Biloxi Bay, and planted a French colony there.

IBEX (*Capra*), animal of Goat family; varieties: Alpine I. (*c. ibex*), Arab. I. (*c. walic*), Himalaya I. (*c. siberica*), Abyssinian I. (*c. walie*); have long, ridged horns; gregarious, but males and females form different flocks after breeding-time.

IBIS (*Ibis Æthiopica*), a bird allied to storks and spoonbills; head and neck dark and naked; plumage white, apart from glossy black dorsal feathers; beak long and curved; held sacred by ancient Egyptians, and often found in mummified condition.

IBLIS (Arab. from Gk. *diabolos*), fallen angel whose history is related in the *Koran.*

IBN' ABD RABBIHI (860-940), Arab. poet; author of valuable anthology.

IBN'ARABI (1165-1240), Muhammadan theological writer and mystic; chief work, the valuable *Alfutûhât almakkarja* (The Messan Revelations).

IBN BATUTA, ABU ABDULLAH MUHAMMAD (1304-78), Arab. traveller and writer; *b.* at Tangier; spent many years travelling in Asia, Africa, and Europe, visiting Egypt, Palestine, Persia, Mesopotamia, Arabia, A s i a Minor, Russia, India, China, and Spain;

he made pilgrimage to Mecca four times, and during visit to India was appointed kazi at Delhi; wrote an interesting account of his travels.

IBN GABIROL, AVICEBRON (XI. cent.), Jewish thinker; wrote poetic, liturgical, and philosophical works; his philosophy was influenced by Neoplatonism and sometimes thought heretical by Jews; his Arabic work trans. into Latin influenced the Schoolmen.

IBN KHALDUN (1332-1406), Arab historian; served various rulers, at Fez Tlemcen, and Tunis; app. cadi at Cairo, 1384, 1399; author of *Universal History*, a work dealing chiefly with Arabs and Berbers.

IBRAHIM PASHA (1789-1848) adopted *s.* of Muhammad Ali, viceroy of Egypt; supported Turkey in Gk. War of Independence, and was defeated by Allies at Navarino, 1827; twice invaded Syria; defeated Turks at Nezib, 1839; viceroy of Egypt, 1858.

IBSEN, HENRIK (1828-1906), Norweg. dramatist and poet; *b.* Skien; served seven years in a chemist's shop at Grimstad; wrote blank-verse plays, which were produced, and took part in stage-management, 1850 onwards, at Bergen. *The Warriors in Helgeland*, a romantic dramatic poem, was printed in 1858, but refused by managers. His first great protest against social conventions was *Love's Comedy*; its hero makes eloquent poetic diatribes (furnishing Shaw with some attractive characters), and epitomizes the moral in the last line—'A health to Amor, late of earth, in tea.' *Brand*, a beautiful lyric against moral deadness, appeared in 1866; its theme was repeated in the greater *Peer Gynt*, with its marvellous songs. From this time Ibsen's position in literature was assured. He now abandoned verse and substituted analysis and irony for lyrical attacks on middle-class vices. *The Pillars of Society*, 1877, started an exposure of the *bourgeoisie*, a constant theme of novelists and playwrights since. *A Doll's House*, 1879, *Hedda Gabler*, 1890, and other plays have largely destroyed the 19th cent. ideal of womanliness. In *An Enemy of the People*, 1882, he shows up the cowardice of public opinion. In *The Wild Duck*, 1884, Ibsen ironically ridicules the attempts of reformers. In numerous other plays he analyzed modern life and created characters which have become literary personalities. *The Master-Builder*, 1892, perhaps his chief work, has hardly yet become absorbed into common thought. Ibsen's plays have revolutionized dramatic art by their realism and their consummate mastery of stage technique.

IBYCUS (fl. VI. cent. B.C.), poet of Gk. colony of Rhegium; fragments remain; cranes discovered his murderers.

ICA, ECCA or **YCA** (14° S., 75° 52' W.), maritime department, Peru, S. America, between Lima and Arequipa; capital, Ica; wine, fruits.

ICE is solid water, and is precipitated as snow, frost, or hail. It consists of colorless crystals of hexagonal form, with a well-marked habit of twinning. Ice at 0° C. is less dense than water, and floats on it. Ice contracts on melting.

Iceberg is a mass of ice floating in water, retaining its equilibrium by submersion of *c.* 87 per cent. of its bulk; frequently 300 ft. high; of great danger to vessels (*e.g. Titanic*); if in quantities, icebergs affect surrounding temp. considerably. *Ice-floes* are floating fields of ice driven together by pressure of bergs.

Ice-breaker, a steamer specially constructed for forcing a passage through ice-bound waters; it may be used to clear a passage for other vessels or simply for itself. The bow is shaped to mount and crush the ice downwards, and is very strong.

ICE, ARTIFICIAL, the production of ice through various chemical or mechanical means. As an industry the artificial production of ice only became important in about 1880, but fifty years before that machines had been perfected which could produce it, though not cheaply enough to make them a commercial success. Prof. A. C. Twining, of New Haven, Conn., was one of the most prominent inventors in this line of effort, in the early fifties. Such machines require steam power to work them, and their action consists in evaporating pure ammonia in a vacuum, and again condensing the vapor to a liquid, so as to be used afresh. By such machines 20° F. below zero has been easily obtained. By the modern method pure ammonia is brought to the boiling point by the pressure of a steam pump. After it is transformed into a gas it passes into cooling pipes, where it condenses, thus producing cold artificially. These pipes pass about the tanks containing the water to be frozen. Over 5,000 patents have been issued on ice machinery. There are several thousand ice plants in the U. S. most of them in the S., where natural ice is not easily procurable, and in large cities in the N., such as N. Y., where the demand is large. The development of the electric refrigeration machine for domestic and industrial use has enjoyed widespread popularity, obviating the necessity of purchasing ice, artificial or natural, in cakes.

ICE CRYSTALS. See Ice.

ICEBERG (Ger. *Berg*. mountain), a hill of ice rising often as much as 270 ft. above the sea. It is a floating mass which has broken away from some glacier or ice-sheet in the Polar regions, and which sails away from its frozen home into warmer and navigable waters. When the I. first breaks away, the fracture is green or blue, but when it comes within view of whalers and other vessels, its cliff-like faces and graceful pinnacles glisten in the sunshine with a dazzling white. During its first flight, an I. strews the sea with pebbles and rocks and other detritus—the remnant of its glacier days. As it enters warmer zones, it melts, disintegrates, tilts, and often overturns. From the specific gravity of ice, it is calculated that only one-ninth of ice mountains appears above the ocean surface and, as their speed is often considerable, it is clear that they are a grave source of peril to passing ships: it was collision with an I. which caused the wreck of the *Titanic*, 1912.

ICELAND MOSS, a lichen, *Cetraria islandica*, found in Iceland and N. Europe; edible.

ICELAND, an isl. in the N. Sea (63° 23'-66° 33'N., 13° 22'-24° 35' W.), *c.* 500 m. N.W. of Shetland Islands and 250 m. S.E. of Greenland; N., E. and W. shores much indented by fiords; surface consists of ice-covered plateaus 1,500 to 2,000 ft., culminating in Oräfa Jökull, 6,425 ft., near S.E., coast; numerous small lakes, many being crater basins or moraine lakes. Glacier fields cover 5,000 sq. m.; in interior are large areas covered by recent lavas. Over twenty of the many volcanoes have been active in modern times; the best known are Hecla, 5,108 ft., Katla, and Askja; more than seventy earthquakes occurred in last cent.; hot springs and geysers are common. Scenery is very fine. Chief industry is breeding of cattle and sheep; principal exports: salt fish, especially cod, butter, oil, mutton, and wool; go mainly to U.K. In 1906 a telegraph cable from Shetlands by Faroes to Seydisfjord and Reykjavik (cap.) was laid; there are no railways. Only *c.* 7,000 sq. m. of area are habitable. See Map of Europe.

Iceland was discovered and colonized by Norsemen between 870 and 950, though Irish (Culdee) monks appear to have visited the isl. and partly settled there, from 795 onwards. The earliest immigrants arrived in four main streams the first and fourth from Norway, the second from the Norse kingdom of Dub-lin, the third from the Orkneys and Western (*i.e.* Hebridean) islands. Christianity became established *c.* 1,000. At first the Icelanders constituted themselves into a sort of aristocratic republic of franklins, whose central authority was the Althing, or national assembly, which met every summer, and was at once framer, interpreter, and executor of the laws. But internal conflicts led, 1262-71, to island falling under the supremecy of Norway. From *c.* 1280, though *de jure* only from 1388, Iceland was a dependency of the Danish crown. The restoration of national self-government was finally secured in 1918, when Iceland became a free and independent state under Christian X., King of Denmark. Area, 39,709 sq. miles. Pop. 92,000.

Language and Literature.—The language spoken and written in Iceland at the present day is almost precisely the same as that spoken and written at the date of its colonization in the 9th cent.—*i.e.*, the anc. Norræna (Northern) or Dan. tongue, which presents close affinities to A.S. The language employed in the runic monuments was also closely akin to anc. Icelandic.

Iceland possesses a rich literature which counts two periods of especial fruitfulness—(1) from about the middle of the 11th to the end of the 13th cent., and (2) from the beginning of the 19th cent. to the present time. The literature of the older period may be grouped in three divisions—the anc. mythical and heroic songs, the scaldic poetry, and the sagas. The most valuable of the mythic or mythological songs are the *Völuspa*, or 'Wise Woman's Prophecy'; *Hamarsheimt*, or 'Fetching Home the Hammer'; *Hymiskvida*, or the 'Song of Hymir'; *Vafthrudnismál*, or the 'Sayings of Vafthrudnir'; *Grimnismál*, or 'Sayings of Grimnir'; *Havamál*, or 'Sayings of the High One'; and the fragmentary *Rigsmál* —in which the doings of the gods Odin, Thor, etc., are sung. The most famous writers of scaldic poems were Egil Skallagrimsson, 904-90, whose lament for his son contain remarkably fine poetry; Eyvind, *c.* 910-95; Kormak, *c.* 937-67; Halfred the Troublesome, *c.* 968-1014; and Sighvat Thordarson, the friend of St. Olaf and Magnus, kings of Norway. But prose saga is the peculiar and crowning product of Icelandic genius. Of a mythical-heroic cast are the *Gylfaginning*, *Völsungasaga*, *Ragnar Lodbrok*, *Hrolf Kraka*, and *Orvar Odd*; while the following have a historical foundation: *Ynglinga*, *Orkneyinga*, *Færeyinga*, *Laxdæla*, *Eyrbyggja*, *Gretti*, *Egil*, *Vija-Glum*, *Kormak*, *Gisli*, *Njal* and *Gunnlaug*. The chief sources for this anc. Icelandic literature are two collections known as the

Elder Edda and the *Younger Edda*. The latter was put together by Snorri Sturluson, 1178-1241, and embraces the mythical-heroic sagas. The *Elder Edda*, which preserves the anc. mythical songs, was attributed (though upon the slenderest grounds) to Sæmund, who flourished about 1100. Ari, a contemporary of Sæmund, wrote chronicles (*Konungabok*) and a wonderful Domesday Book of Iceland (*Landnamabok*). Snorri Sturluson also compiled the chronicle known as *Heimskringla*, or 'Story of the Kings so Norway,' and as a chronicler had a worthy successor in his nephew, Sturla Thordarson, 1214-84. The relatively barren stretch between the earlier and the later literary periods can furnish the names of only three poets—Stefan Olafsson, 1620-88, Hallgrimur Petursson, 1614-74, and Eggert Olafsson, 1726-68; the eccles, historian, Finnur Jonsson, 1704-89, who wrote in Latin; and the general translator (*e.g.*, of *Paradise Lost*), Jon Thorlaksson, 1744-1819. The pioneers of the later reawakening were the last named, who also wrote original poems, Sigurdur Petursson, 1759-1827, Benedikt Gröndal, 1762-1825, and Magnus Stephensen, 1762-1833. The real awakening took place between 1830 and 1880, the most potent organ being the magazine *Fjölnir*, 1835, etc., to which poems, new both in form and in subject were contributed by Bjarni Thorarensen, 1786-1841, and Jonas Halgrimsson, 1807-45. They had a very useful ally in the philologist, Konrad Gislason, 1808-91. Sigurdur Breidfjord, 1798-1846, Steingrimur Thorsteinsson and Matthias Jochumsson have been succeeded by a younger school with more modern and realistic tendencies, represented by Pall Olafsson, Hjalmar Jonsson, 1796-1875, the younger Benedikt Gröndal, Thorsteinn Erlingsson, and Hannes Hafstein. The two most distinguished novelists of the 19th cent. were Jon Thoroddsen, 1819-68, and Gestur Palsson, 1852-91. Outside the bounds of pure literature the most distinguished names are those of Jon Sigurdsson, 1811-79, historian and political writer; the folklorist Jon Arnason, 1819-88; and Thorvaldur Thoroddsen, who has explored Iceland, and written about her geography.

ICELAND SPAR, a clear colorless variety of calcite ($CaCO_3$) found in Iceland. It forms large rhombohedra having a specific gravity of 2·7 and a hardness=3. The value of I. S. lies in its having a strong double refraction, which makes it pre-eminently suited for polariscopes, Nicot's prisms, and other optical purposes. The supply from Iceland, where crystals of very large size are found, is nearly exhausted, and no substitute has been found to compare with it.

ICE-PLANT (*Mesembryanthemum crystallinum*), creeping plant bearing white flowers; leaves have glistening appearance, whence name.

ICE-YACHTING, sport carried on principally in Scandinavia, Gulf of Finland, and N. America; a sailing-vessel is used, with runner-plank instead of keel. A speed of over 80 miles an hour can be attained with a favourable wind.

I-CHANG (30° 48′ N., 111° 32′ E.), town, treaty port, Hu-peh, China, on Yang-tze-kiang.

ICHNEUMON, a small mammal allied to weasel, living in Egypt and N. Africa generally; feeds on snakes and on crocodile eggs.

ICHNEUMON FLIES (*Ichneumonidæ*), a family of Hymenopterous insects, with long, thin bodies, and long ovipositors. They pierce and lay their eggs in the larvæ of other insects, on which the young feed. Many agricultural pests are thus kept in check.

ICHNOGRAPHY, architectural name for ground-plan or horizontal section of a building.

ICHTHYOLOGY.—Günther, in his *Study of Fishes*, 1880, defines I. as 'the branch of zoology which treats of the internal and external structure of fishes, their mode of life, and their distribution in space and time,' and perhaps to these should now be added a study of the economic aspect of the group. See FISHES AND FISHERIES.

ICHTHYOSAURS.—Fish-like reptiles of fish-lizards which existed in immense numbers in the Mesozoic era, and of which fossil remains are found in Europe, North America, the East Indies, Australia, and South Africa. At Lyme Regis in England, and at Württemberg, in Germany, the fossils are very numerous. It is assumed that these creatures were modified from ancestors who were land animals, as they have the characteristics of reptiles. They resembled, in some respects, the modern whale. Their bodies were round and tapering, their heads large, with long snouts, and along the jaws were rows of pointed teeth, as many as four hundred having been found in one mouth. There was practically no neck. In place of limbs were broad paddles, and the creature had a vertical, fish-like tail, and a triangular fin on the back. The skin was smooth and the eyes were surrounded with wedge-shaped, sclerotic plates. The remains which have been found vary greatly in size, the smallest being about three feet in length

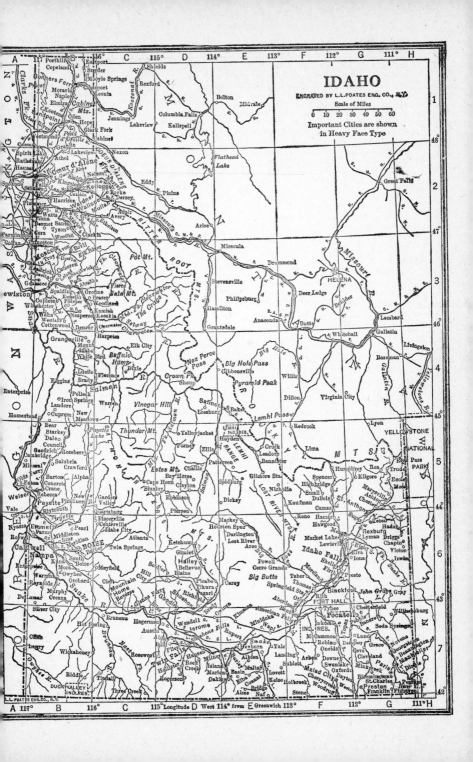

IDAHO

ENGRAVED BY L.L.POATES ENG. CO., N.Y.

Scale of Miles

0 10 20 30 40 50 60

Important Cities are shown
in Heavy Face Type

and the largest nearly forty feet. Thirty-five species have been identified, and some, if not all, were viviparous, as is shown by the fact that the young have been found in the abdominal cavity of some of the specimens. There is evidence to show that the ichthyosaurs were predacious, and fed on fish. They are some what of a biological curiosity, as nothing is known regarding their origin or descent. Apparently none of them survived beyond the cretaceous period of the Mesozoic era.

ICKES, HAROLD L. (1874—). b. Frankstown Township, Blair County, Pa., March 15, 1874. Received his A. B. from the University of Chicago in 1897 and his J. D. *cum laude* in 1907. After graduation he became a reporter on Chicago papers until 1901.

Ickes entered national politics as a delegate at large to the Progressive National Convention in 1916; but was a delegate to the Republican National Convention in 1920. In 1924 he managed a vigorous campaign for Hiram Johnson, and the campaign of Hugh S. Magill. He organized the successful Progressive Republican League to support Roosevelt in Chicago and the west.

Ickes was president of the Peoples' Protective League in 1922; a member of the board of the Chicago Government Planning Association; and became Chairman of the Peoples' Traction League in 1929. In 1933 President Roosevelt appointed him Secretary of the Interior. He also had almost complete administrative control of all public relief measures.

ICONOCLASTS. A breaker or destroyer of images. In the primitive Church there was a general feeling against the use of art in Christian worship. This was owing partly to the idolatry which accompanied heathen worship. That they, like the Jews, had no images in their churches amazed their heathen neighbors. From the IV. cent. paintings and sculptures were employed in Christian worship. Only then the symbol of the cross came into use, and there was strong prejudice

against a crucifix. The famous *iconoclastic* controversy arose in the Eastern Empire in the VIII. cent. The attack on images was begun by Leo III., *d.* 740; it was continued by Constantine V., but the Empress Irene restored them; another iconoclastic reaction took place, but came to an end with the Emperor Theophilus, *d.* 826. The later Church did not take up the position of the extreme I's that were themselves possessed of sacramental power, neither did it reject them altogether. In the Eastern Church *icons* like flat pictures are used, whereas the Catholic Church in the West has always believed in images, crucifixes, etc., as means of instruction.

ICONOGRAPHY (Gk. *eikon,* image; *graphein,* to describe), writing about engravings; history of Christian relics or pictures.

ICONOSTASIS (Gk. *eikon,* image; *stasis,* standing), division in Gk. churches between outer choir and inner sanctuary; adorned with *ikons, i.e.,* pictures of saints, etc.

ICTINUD, Gk. architect of temple of Apollo, of which sculptures are in Brit. Museum, of Parthenon, 433 B. C.

IDA (d. 559), king of Bernicia; established Anglian rule over Bernicia, 547.

IDA (Turkish *Kaz-Dagh*), a mountain range in Asia Minor, which extends through Phrygia and Mysia, and commands the ancient plain of Troy. Mount Gargarus, 5748 ft. high, its loftiest peak, was the seat of the temple erected to Cybele, the *Idœa Mater.*

IDAHO, a W. state of U. S. (45° 30′ N., 114° 8′ W.), bounded N. by Brit. Columbia and Montana, E. by Montana and Wyoming, S. by Utah and Nevada, W. by Oregon and Washington. Principal city is Boise City. Except small area in S. the surface is rugged and mountainous; the S. E. region lies in the Great Basin of U. S., while the rest, some 70,000 sq. m., lies in the drainage basin of the Columbia R.; in the N. and E., part of the Rocky Mountain system is embraced, the principal range being the Salmon R. range, separating Idaho from Montana; other ranges are the Saw Tooth and Baise, on the Columbian Plateau; a prominent physical feature are the Snake R. Plains; the more important lakes are Pend d'Oreille, Cœur d'Alene, and Naniksu, in the Pan-Handle in the N.; and the John Day and Bear lakes in the S. E. There is abundant vegetation in the N. and center; forests extend on the W. slopes of the Bitter Root and Cœur d'Alene Mts. The climate is healthy. Mineral deposits which are owned by the state, include gold, copper, lead, silver, and coal, while in the S. E. soda, gypsum, and sulphur are found; there are many state forests; grain farming is mostly confined to river valleys, but extensive irrigation works have been carried out, the most important crop being wheat; other crops are oats, barley, potatoes, hay, etc.; the principal industries are lumber and timber working, flour and grist milling; stock raising is carried on. Admitted into Union, 1890. Legislature consists of senate, 37 members, and house of representatives, 65 members; state represented in Congress by two senators and two representatives. A large percentage of the people are Mormons. Area, 83,888 sq. m., including 534 sq. m. of water. Pop. 445,032. See Map of U. S.

IDAHO FALLS, a city of Idaho, in Bonneville Co., of which it is the co. seat. It is surrounded by an extensive agricultural region which is well irri-

gated. It is on several important railroads. Its industries include a sugar factory. There is a Carnegie library and other public buildings.

IDAHO, UNIVERSITY OF.—An educational institution for both sexes at Moscow, Idaho, founded in 1889, and opened in 1892. The tuition is free except in law and music. It is governed by the State Board of Education and the curricula comprises a classical course, general science, forestry, home economics, education, civil, mechanical and electrical engineering, agriculture, and law. The Agricultural Extension Division, headquarters, State House, Boise, supplies lectures, demonstration trains, movable school houses, etc. Annual income, about $1,500,000. President, 1933, M. G. Neale. Students, 2,000, Faculty, 157.

IDALIUM (Gk. Sugal), an ancient tn. of Cyprus, was situated almost in the centre of the island, on the site now occupied by the village Dalin or Idalion. It was sacred to the worship of Aphrodite, who was hence named Idalia. The town was destroyed by earthquake before the time of Pliny.

IDAR, EDAR (23° 50' N., 73° E.), native states, Gujarat, Bombay, India.

IDAS (Gk. myth), *s.* of Aphareus and *bro.* of Lynceus; successfully rivalled Apollo for Marpessa's hand; slew Castor and then wounded Pollux, who had slain Lynceus, but was struck by thunderbolt of Zeus; strongest of mortals.

IDDESLEIGH, STAFFORD, HENRY NORTHCOTE, 1ST EARL OF (1818-87), Eng. politician; held various offices of state, and as Chancellor of Exchequer in Disraeli's Ministry introduced sinking fund for reduction of National Debt, 1874; Foreign Minister, 1886.

IDE, HENRY CLAY (1844-1921), American jurist and diplomat; *b.* in Barnet, Vermont, September 18, 1844; *d.* June 13, 1921; graduated from Dartmouth, 1866; State Attorney, 1876-1878; Senator, Vermont, 1882-1885; United Commissioner to Samoa, 1891; Chief Justice of Samoa, 1893-1897; member of Taft Commission, 1900; secretary of finance and justice Philippines, 1901; Vice-Governor, 1904; Governor-General, 1906; Ambassador to Spain, 1909-1913; Author *Land of the Registration Act,* 1903; *The Internal Regsitration Law of the Philippines,* 1904.

IDEA, term which has been used in a great variety of meanings: (1) In Plato, Ideas (or Forms) are universal natures,

not 'in the mind but the objects of knowledge; (2) in later Platonism, they are conceptions in the mind of God; (3) in Locke, they are objects of knowledge, but tend to be regarded as representations of things in the mind; in Berkeley and Hume they are definitely subjective; (4) and (5) for the Kantian and Hegelian uses, see KANT and HEGEL; (6) in modern psychology idea generally means a process of conceiving and imaging at once, ot an object conceived and imagined at once.

IDEALISM, in a general sense, means the tendency to regard everything from an ideal or imaginative standpoint; its use in philosophy is to denote that theory of the universe according to which everything (either really or as perceived) consists of *ideas.* I. has different forms: in the absolute I. of Hegel the universe consists of ideas entirely, but ideas of the universal mind not ours; in other forms of absolute I. objects have no ultimate reality except in the minds of those who perceive them—this is more properly termed *subjective* I. In Kant's I. all human experience consists of ideas, though this does not preclude the existence of objects outside our minds. I. can fairly be said to have begun with Plato. The Platonic theory of ideas is that beyond our world of sense there is an ideal world. They stand as types from which objects in our world derive whatever reality they possess. Aristotle somewhat modifies this, and makes the individual dependent on the universal will. He showed that matter cannot really be opposed to mind, nor the particular to the universal. It was not Aristotle's I. but his formal grouping into categories which the mediæval Schoolmen followed. Of modern idealists the first was really Bp. Berkeley. In some respects he carried on the work of Locke. Berkeley held that things have no real existence apart from a mind which can perceive them, though it need not be our mind but the mind of God. Though many would refuse to follow him here, he at least was the first to show that, whatever a thing be in itself we can only know it by our own senses —a most important step in advance of that unthinking view which would make a thing just what it appears.

IDEALOGY. See PSYCHOLOGY.

IDELGRAPH, palæographical term for picture-writing, such as hieroglyphics.

IDENTIFICATION, science of the anthropometric system of identification of criminals by finger-prints was adopted, 1901, with remarkable results, and has become the recognized way of keeping record of prisoners.

IDENTITY. See Psychology.

IDES, 15th day of Rom. month.

IDIOCY. See Insanity.

IDIOM (Gk. *idios*, peculiar to an individual or thing), form of a particular language or language of a particular locality.

IDIOSYNCRASY, peculiar physical or mental condition characteristic of an individual, often taking the form, for example, of an undue feeling of discomfort in the presence of certain animals, odors, etc., or of undue susceptibility to certain drugs, or of eccentricity of habits.

IDLE (53° 50′ N., 1° 45′ W.), town, W. Riding, Yorkshire, England; woolen goods.

IDOLATRY.—Worship of idols or 'graven images' was not, as some have supposed, first stage in religious evolution, but posterior to animism. The idol worshipper fails to distinguish between his god and the idol, in whom he thinks his god dwells. 'Idolatry' in New Testament is used loosely for pagan rites.

IDOEMENEUS, in Gk. legend, king of Crete who when sailing to Trojan War promised to Poseidon in return for protection the first thing he met on landing; this was his *s.*, whom he sacrificed; Crete being smitten with plague, his subjects banished him.

IDRISI, EDRISI (*c.* A.D. 1099-1154), Arab. geographer; *b.* at Ceuta, of famous Muhammadan family; studied at Cordova; travelled through Asia Minor, Egypt, Morocco, Spain, and Portugal. Pub. geographical work, 1154; constructed a globe of silver, divided it on the Ptolemaic system, and wrote explanatory book, pub. in 1592, and several times reissued and translated.

IDUMÆA, Gk. for Edom, territory of Moab; first inhabited by Horites, then by Edomites; for some time under suzerainty of kingdom of Judah, but later independent, then conquered by Assyria; Edomites were settled in S. Palestine, II. cent. B.C.

IDUN, IDUNA, Scandanavian goddess of spring and summer; seized by Loki (winter).

IDYLL, IDYL, name given by Gk's to short creative work, at first of general but afterwards of pastoral nature; *cf.* I's of Theocritus, Bion, Moschus.

IESI, OR JESI, a tn. of Italy in the prov. of Ancona, situated on the l. b. of the Esino, 17 m. S.W. of Ancona. It is noted as the birthplace of the Emperor

Frederick II., and possesses a fine cathedral.

IF, an islet of Bouches-du-Rhône dept., off the S. coast of France, opposite Marseilles in the Gulf of Lyons. It was once covered with yews ('ifs'). Its fortress Château d'If, built by Francis I., 1529, is famous. It was used as a state prison later, Mirabeau and Philippe Egalité being imprisoned there. In Dumas' *Count of Monte Cristo* the hero is confined there.

IGLAU (49° 23′ N., 15° 35′ E.), town, Czecho-Slovakia; textiles, tobacco.

IGLESIAS (39° 19′ N., 8° 32′ E.), town, Sardinia; bp's see; lead and zinc mines.

IGNATIEFF, COUNT NICHOLAS PAVLOVICH, (1832-1908), Russ. diplomatist, who made treaties advantageous to his country with China, Khiva, and Bokhara.

IGNATIUS (*d. c.* 117 A.D.), one of Apostolic Fathers (*q.v.*). Though so famous, very little known of him. His epistles are preserved in three recensions, and controversy has raged over the complicated literary problem they present. I. contains seven epistles preserved in Greek, also Latin, Armenian, Syriac, and Coptic versions; II. contains these seven and six others, Gk., and Lat. version; III. (discovered by Cureton, 1845), three of first seven, preserved in Syriac. The controversy over the claims of I. and II. to be the original was mostly theological. Scholars mostly now recognize II. as original and III. as shortened from it. Ignatious defends Episcopacy and protests against Docetism and Judaising tendencies in Church.

IGNATIUS, ST. (*c.* 790-878), Patriarch of Constantinople, was the son of Michael I., Emperor of the East. He was compelled to enter a monastery, whence he rose to the patriarchate through the favor of the Empress Theodora. He was an opponent of the iconoclasts. The influence of his brother Bardas, whom he had ex-communicated led to his being forced to abdicate in 866, but he was restored in the following year.

IGNATIUS, LOYOLA. See Loyola.

IGNATIUS'S BEANS, seeds of *Strychnos Ignatii*, containing strychnine; found in Philippines; so named by Jesuits.

IGNEOUS ROCKS. See Rocks: Geology.

IGNIS FATUUS (Lat., foolish fire), a luminous appearance occasionally seen in marshy places and church-yards. It is usually visible shortly after sunset in autumn, and has been recorded in many countries. The light, which resembles a flame, is seldom pure white, and may be red, green, blue, or yellow. Accounts differ greatly, some observers speak of it as being fixed, and others as moving. Experiments have proved that it is not due to true combustion. Theories explaining its occurrence have been in turn discredited. These include the burning of marsh gas, phosphuretted hydrogen, and phosphorescent vapor. Many local names are given to the phenomenon, *e.g.* Will-o'-the-Wisp, Jack-a-lantern, etc. and its manifestations have given rise to a wealth of story and legend.

IGNITION.—This term is applied to combustions in which the fuel (material to be burned), unites with oxygen at such a rapid rate, that the reaction is accompanied by flame.

All combustible material, considered chemically, unites with oxygen at any temperature, although in most instances the reaction at ordinary temperatures is so slow that it cannot be detected without accurate scientific apparatus. Like all chemical reactions this union may be increased by the application of heat. In general their speed is doubled by a rise in temperature of 10° C. (18° F.). Eventually a point is reached at which the union proceeds so rapidly that the material bursts into flame, *i.e.*, the reaction itself generates sufficient heat to heat particles of unburned material to incandescence.

For all combustible substances there is a characteristic temperature called the 'ignition point.' If a very small portion be heated to this point, the entire mass quickly ignites, owing to the heat which is generated by the local reaction. When the speed of such ignition exceeds moderate limits, a so-called 'explosion' occurs. Waves of explosion may travel as fast as 5 miles per second.

The application of this phenomenon is very extensive. The striking of a match consists in locally heating its surface by friction to the ignition point. Similarly the match applied to paper heats a small section. The ignition point or 'flame point' of gasoline and kerosene is regulated by law, and oils which catch fire below this temperature cannot be sold. Such laws have minimized the dangers of explosion and fire in the domestic use of mineral oils. All gasoline engines are supplied with 'ignition systems,' which are a means of locally heating the explosive mixture of gasoline and air, by an electric spark, this constituting the most convenient and easily controlled method of ignition.

IGNORAMUS (Lat. pres. tense 1st person plural of verb 'to know not'), word formerly written by jury on dorse of bill of indictment which they did not find 'true'; term for stupid person.

IGNORANCE OF THE LAW does not in law excuse a man from the consequences of his acts.

IGNORANTINES, name of a religious order instituted at Rheims, 1680, now with 14,000 members from all parts of the world.

IGUALADA (41° 35' N., 1° 34' E.); town, Barcelona, Spain, on Noya; textiles.

IGUANA, see LIZARDS.

IGUANODON (*Iguana*, and Gk. meaning tooth), a genus of ornithopod dinosaurs, found fossil in Jurassic and Lower Cretaceous rocks of Europe. The I. was described by Mantell in 1825, from specimens found in Kent, England. It was from 15 to 25 ft. long; the head large and narrow, and the massive body terminated in and long and very strong tail. The fore-limbs were small and adapted for grasping the leaves and branches of plants on which it fed. All the bones were hollow. The structure of the skeleton is altogehter very remarkable. It lived in great numbers in the swampy regions of England and Belgium, and other parts of Europe during the Jurassic period. Several species of the I. are known, mostly from the Wealden and Purbeck beds.

IGUVIUM, modern **GUBBIO.**—Ancient town, Umbria, Central Italy; *c.* 23 miles N.N.E. of Perusia, with Rom. remains. Famous *Eugubine Tables,* 7 in number, with religious writings in Lat. and Umbrian, were discovered, 1444, and kept in town-house. I. was famed for majolica work up to XV. cent.; an important town in pre-Rom. period; received Rom. citizenship after Social War; destroyed by Goths, 552.

IKI-SHIMA (33° 55' N., 129° 45' E.); small island of Japan, N.W. of Kiushiu; area, 5,858 sq. miles.

ILAGAN (17° 5' N., 121° 50' E.); town, Luzon, Philippine Islands; tobacco region.

ILCHESTER, ancient *Ischalis* (51° N., 2° 41' W.), decayed town, Somersetshire, England, on Yeo.

ILDEFONSO, SAINT (607-667); a Spanish prelate and theologian, *b.* at Toledo; was a pupil of St. Isidore, became abbot of Agali, and attended the ninth council of Toledo in 653. In 658 he succeeded his uncle Eugenius as Archbishop of Toledo. He added fourteen lives to St. Isidore's *De Viris illustribus*, and wrote several theological works.

ILE-DE-FRANCE, ancient province, France; enclosed between rivers Seine, Marne, Oise, Aisne, and Ourcq; correspond to departments Seine, Seine-et-Oise, Seine-et-Marne, Aisne, Oise, and a small part of Nievre and Loiret; capital, Paris.

ILETSK, ITELSKOI-GORODOK (51° 29′ N., 53° 29′ E.), town, Orenburg, Russia, near junction of Ilek and Ural; salt-works.

ILEX, a cosmopolitan genus of plants in the order Aquifoliaceæ, which consists of between one and two hundred species. *I. aquifolium*, the common holly, is found chiefly in Central Europe; it is valued as an ornamental tree and for its fine-grained, heavy, compact timber; the berries are poisonous and have violent emetic effects. *I. Paraguayensis*, the maté plant, is val ed for its leaves, which are dried and used like common tea, under the name of Paraguay tea. The I. so frequently mentioned by classical authors is *Quercus Ilex*, the hohm-or holly-oak, a species of Fagaceæ found round the Mediterranean.

ILFORD (51° 34′ N., 0° 5′ E.), town, Essex, England; photographic material works.

ILFRACOMBE (51° 12′ N., 4° 7′ W.), watering-place and seaport, Devonshire, England, on Bristol Channel.

ILHAVO (40° 34′ N., 8° 38′ W.), seaport town, Aveiro, Portugal; manufactures glass, porcelain.

ILI (45° N., 75° 30′ E.), river, Central Asia; rises in Tian-Shan mts., and flowing W., then N.W., enters Lake Balkash; length, 900 miles; navigable in lower course.

ILIAD, see HOMER.

ILIGAN BAY, on the N. coast of Mindanao, Philippine Is. The R. Iligan flows into it at the S.E. corner and here lies the town of Iligan with a large trade in rice, spices, and hemp.

ILION, a city of New York, in Herkimer co. It is on the New York Central and West Shore railroads, and on the Mohawk River and on the Erie and New York State Barge canals. It is an important industrial center and has plants for the making of fire-arms, typewriters, cash registers, office equipment, etc. There are a hospital and library.

ILIUM, TROY (*q.v.*).

ILKESTON (52° 58′ N., 1° 20′ W.), market town, Derbyshire, England; hosiery, lace; coal and iron mines.

ILKLEY (53° 55′ N., 1° 50′ W.), town, health-resort, W. Riding, Yorkshire, England.

ILL (48° 30′ N., 7° 30′ E.), river, Alsace, Germany; joins Rhine 9 miles below Strasburg; length, 125 miles.

ILLAWARA (34° 30′ S., 150° 30′ E.); maritime district, New South Wales Australia; fertile; coal and iron mines.

ILLE-ET-VILAINE (48° 10′ N., 1° 40′ W.), maritime department, N.W. France, formed from part of ancient Brittany; mostly level, with occasional marshes and numerous lakes; watered chiefly by the Ille and Vilaine; fine horses and cattle are reared; cereals, flax, hemp, apples, and pears grown; produces cider, butter, and cheese; iron mines, slate quarries; oyster fisheries; capital, Rennes.

ILLEGITIMACY is the condition of being born out of lawful wedlock. An illegitimate child cannot inherit by right of succession—for in law he has no father—but otherwise is under no legal disabilities. Engl. law recognizes that the offspring is legitimate no matter how soon the birth takes place after marriage, but declares the offspring illegitimate when born of parents incompetent to marry, *i.e.* persons who are within the prohibited degrees of consanguinity or affinity. In most countries of Continental Europe special provision is made for the care of illegitimate children, and in the years following the World War nearly all these countries, and England, passed measures providing for their care and maintenance.

ILLER (48° 20′ N., 10° E.), river, Bavaria, Germany; joins Danube near Ulm; length, *c.* 100 miles.

ILLIMANI MOUNTAIN, one of the loftiest mountains of the Bolivian Andes, in the Eastern Cordillera Range, S. America.

ILLINGTON, MARGARET (1881); actress; *b.* at Bloomington, Illinois; educated at Illinois Weslayan University, and studied at Chicago Musical College; made professional debut at Criterion Theatre, New York, 1900, in 'The Pride of Jennico'; 1902-1903, played in stock company at Lyceum Theatre, New York; leading role, 1903, 'The Japanese Nightingale;' 1904, 'The Two Orphans;' 1905, 'Mrs. Leffingwell's Boots'; 1906, at London, England, 'The Lion and the Mouse',

'His House in Order'; 1906, at Empire Theatre, New York, 'The Thief'; 1907, 1911-1912, star in 'Kindling'; 1913-1914, 'Within the Law'; 1915-16, 'The Lie'; 1916-1917, 'Our Little Wife'; 1917-1918, co-star with John Drew in 'The Gay Lord Quex.'

ILLINOIS, N. central state of U.S. (40° N., 89° 30' W.), bounded N. by Wisconsin, E. by Lake Michigan and Indiana, S.E. and S. by the Ohio R. (which separates it from Kentucky), S.W. and W. by Mississippi R. (which separates it from Missouri and Iowa). Cap. is Springfield. Situated in the prairie-plain region, partly in the valley of the Mississippi and touching the Great Lake dist. in the N.E., the surface slopes gently to the S. and S.W.; the average height above sea-level is 600 ft., highest elevation being Charles Mound, c. 1,200 ft., on the boundary between Illinois and Wisconsin; bluffs are encountered along the principal rivers, the best known being Starved Rock. There are several elevations, the largest stretching across the S. from 6 to 10 m. broad, and reaching c. 1,050 ft. above sea-level. See Map of U.S.

There are almost 300 streams, mostly tributaries of the Mississippi, but some, tributaries of the Wabash and Ohio rivers; the most important river is the Illinois, at times broadening into vast lakes—notably the lovely Peoria Lake; several shallow lakes lie to the N.E. The soil, especially in the river valleys, is exceedingly fertile. The climate is varied the mean annual temp. being some 11° F. higher in the S. than in the N., which again varies; but summers and winters are both severe.

The chief mineral product is coal, Illinois being the third largest producer in U.S., and the coalfields extending over a vast area of c. 42,900 sq. m.; there are also many petroleum wells; zinc is worked, as also are lead, limestone, salt, and fluor-spar. Illinois is the richest of the U.S. in agriculture; the chief cereal crops being corn, wheat, oats, and hay; tobacco is grown, and an active live-stock industry carried on. Chief industries are slaughtering and meat packing, iron and steel foundries. Commerce is conducted by rivers, lakes, canals, and electric and other railways.

Chicago—the largest city—is second largest in America; other important cities are Peoria, East St. Louis, Quincy, Springfield, Rockford, and Joliet. There are many universities. The name of the state is derived from Illinois confederacy of Indians—the original inhabitants; explored, 1673, by a Frenchman, Joliet; passed into the hands of English, 1763, and admitted to Union as state in 1818.

Legislature consists of senate, 51 members, and house of representatives, 153 members. Area, 56,665 sq. m. (622 sq. m. of water).

ILLINOIS AND MICHIGAN CANAL. See CANAL.

ILLINOIS COLLEGE.—A co-educational institution, the oldest in the state, established in 1829 at Jacksonville, Illinois, under the auspices of a group of seven eastern college men known as the 'Yale Band.' A conservatory of music is a feature of the college, and there is a preparatory department, Whipple Academy. Endowed funds, $455,000. President, 1933 Harold C. Jaquith, Ph.D. Total student body, 397. Faculty, 24.

ILLINOIS INDIANS.—A confederacy of Algonquin tribes, once inhabiting S. Wisconsin, N. Illinois and sections of Iowa and Missouri. Almost constant wars with the Sioux and Fox tribes, and traders' rum, reduced them in 1750 to about 2,000. In 1800 only 150 remained, the Kankakeas and Peorias, who sold their lands to Illinois and moved, first to Missouri, and now are settled in the N.E. corner of Oklahoma, and number between 200 and 300. It was their custom to practice polygamy and to wrap their dead in skins and attach them to trees. Their huts consisted of wooden frames covered with mats or rushes.

ILLINOIS RIVER.—The most important affluent of the upper Mississippi, formed by the junction of the Kankakee, Des Plaines, and Du Page rivers in Grundy Count, 45 miles S.W. of Chicago. It is 500 miles long and its whole course is within the state of Illinois, being navigable to La Salle. It joins the Mississippi about 24 miles above the mouth of the Missouri. Ottawa and Peoria are the principal cities on the river.

ILLINOIS STATE NORMAL UNIVERSITY, THE.—Founded in 1857, and located at Normal, a suburb of Bloomington. The oldest State Normal institution in the Mississippi Valley. Its purpose it to provide teachers for the state; and students are required to sign a pledge on entrance that they intend to become teachers. The tuition is free; the Board of Education of Illinois is the governing body. The University provides a four-years' course to prepare High School teachers, principals, and superintendents. There is a Normal School for teachers of elementary and rural schools; a University High School, and an elementary training school. The last two furnish training for student-teachers. There are also special courses in manual training, art, vocal music,

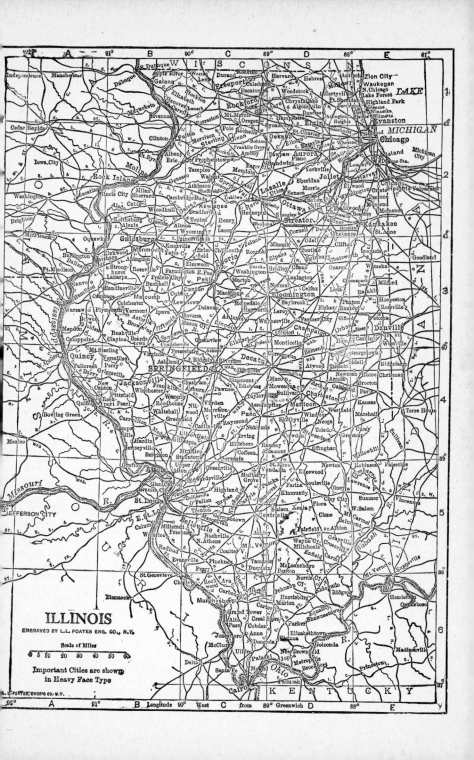

ILLINOIS

ENGRAVED BY L.L. POATES ENG. CO., N.Y.

Scale of Miles

5 10 20 30 40 50 60

Important Cities are shown
in Heavy Face Type

household economics, commerce, and agriculture. The income was about $551,000 from the State treasury, and interest from funds given by the Federal Government in 1818. Students in all departments, including summer sessions, 2,605; teachers, including the Training School, 189.

ILLINOIS, UNIVERSITY OF.—An institution for higher education, established in 1867, at Urbana, Illinois. The departments of medicine, law, and dentistry are located in Chicago. Since 1876 a Summer Session has been held. It confers on graduates the degrees B.A., and B.S. The University issues a number of publications, including 'The Law Bulletin', Medical Bulletin', University of Illinois Studies in Psychology', Studies in Language and Literature', Studies in Education'. The library contains 916,452 volumes. Income from invested funds, etc., $6,535,781; of this the State appropriates $700,000. President, Harry W. Chase. Students, 14,594; teachers, 1,223, 1932-33.

ILLINOIS WESLEYAN UNIVERSITY.—A Methodist Episcopal coeducational institution, founded at Bloomington, Illinois, in 1850. It maintains a preparatory and law school, and confers the degrees B.A., B.S., and LL.B. The library contains 35,000 volumes. Value of property, about $973,-730. Endowment, $1,000,000. Students, 702; faculty, 60, 1933.

ILLUMINATI (Lat. 'enlightened'), term assumed originally by sects of Christian mystics, who claimed that their minds were illuminated by supernatural light; title assumed by Rosicrucians and modern associations of political idealists.

ILLITERACY.—Inability to read or write. The methods of collecting data on illiteracy differ widely in various countries, so that comparisons can only be approximated. In some countries inability to sign a marriage certificate, or of army recruits to read, are proofs of illiteracy, while only a few nations prepare a census. Tests made of recruits in the United States during the war period showed that there was more illiteracy in this country than had been hitherto suspected. While the 1930 census shows a gain of 1.7 per cent in literacy, it is a melancholy thought that the United States contains 4,283,753 persons over 10 years of age who can neither read nor write. In 1930, out of 111,330,656 persons over 10, the illiterates numbered 4,283,753 or 4.3 per cent. In 1920, it was 6.0 per cent. There were, in 1920, 1,242,572 illiterate native whites, and 1,763,740 of white foreign born. Negroes, 1,842,161, or 22.9 per cent.

Since the World War no attempt has been made to take a census of illiteracy in Europe, and the following figures apply to 1910, and a little later: Illiteracy in Austria, among persons over 11, was 13.7 per cent; Belgium, over 10, 12.7. per cent; England-Wales, marriages, 14.8; France, over 10, 14.1; German Empire, army recruits, 0.06, marriages, 4.1; Italy, 37.0 over 10, army recruits, 31.1, marriages, 38.7; Netherlands, army recruits, 0.8, marriages, 2.2; Russia, 69.0, army 61.7; Spain, over 10, 58.7; Ireland, 9.2, over 9, marriages, 8.1; Sweden, army, 0.2; Switzerland, army, 03.

ILLUMINATION, ART OF, the ornamentation of manuscript. The Celtic and Teutonic races of Europe had their own art before coming into contact with Rome, Celtic civilization being at its height in the VI. cent. B.C., and the ornamentation which they afterwards applied to MSS. was largely copied from the characteristic forms of their metalwork. Byzantine art, however, which retained the classical tradition, exercised a considerable influence on Italy, where the Eastern Empire retained possessions until XI. cent., and through Italy on Europe. The earliest examples extant of Byzantine illumination, VI. cent., are of extreme splendor, some of silver writing on purple vellum, others with gaily painted designs on gilded vellum, and gracefully drawn figures in miniature as illustrations. Initials have been called attention to by the apparently independent instinct of all schools of illuminators, but all may have been influenced in some way not now to be traced by the Byzantine tradition. The great moment of the commencement of a book was not, however, celebrated so impressively in the Byzantine as in the Western schools. The great age of Byzantine illumination was the XI. cent. The characteristic Celtic interlacing of geometric designs, dragons, etc., in medallion and leaf-shapes, appear in the elaborate borders of Celtic MSS. and in the tail of the intricate initials, and the human figure is sometimes equally elaborately conventionalised with the animal. Celtic school had more influence than the Rom. on England until the Conquest. In France, Merovingian illumination of a simple kind was replaced in 800 by the Carolingian school which culminated in the X. cent.; it was marked by splendor of pigment and some success in the drawing of the miniatures. Illumination of XII.-XV. cent's has some features of ornaments of architecture of those cent's, and the miniature initial was a characteristic feature. Eng. work was noted in XIII. and XIV. cent's but the greatest of all were the Ital. and Flemish schools of the early Renaissance.

mastery of perspective and figure-drawing appearing for the first time.

ILLUMINATION, the amount of light falling upon an object. If an object is illuminated it must be opaque, *i.e.*must not absorb all the light. The eye is a very poor judge of intensity of I., but it judges equality of I. fairly accurately, and all I. experiments take account of this. I. depends on the candle-power of the source and its distance.

ILLUSION, a term loosely applied both to delusions and hallucinations, or, in other words, to pervertions of the senses and perverted ideas. Psychologists differ as to the more appropriate application of the term. Esquirol, the celebrated French alienist, 1772-1842, in classifying mental diseases, distinguished the two states by referring hallucinations to an exicted state of the brain affecting the *remembrance* of the sensations of sight and causing the subject to see what is commonly termed visions or apparitions, and defining I. as the false interpretation of a sensation actually perceived. Dr. Ferrier, while including both under the generic name of Is., differentiates between an I. of the senses and a delusion of the mind. He defines Is. generally as sensations without a corresponding external object, giving the names *spectral illusion*, phantom, or phantasm, where the eye is or seems to be the seat of sensation, and the term *vivid idea* or *conception* when the I. is due to an act of ideation. The whole distinction is sharply drawn by regarding an I. as a mockery, false show, or deceptive appearance, and an hallucination, delusion, or 'illusive transformation' (Ferrier) as a chimerical thought. Popularly, any transformed appearance of a real object, any appearance without a corresponding physical or external object, and any distorted, exaggerated, or misconceived notion or idea constitute Is. The distinction is important according to Dr. Tuke in regard to insanity, because, while the sane may easily transform a real object into something else than it is, the perception of an object externally projected without the slighest corresponding reality indicates some serious disturbance of the nervous system. Both Is. and delusions, however, are consistent with sanity. A scientist closely concentrating his mind and senses on some experimental work may well have visual and auditory Is. conjured up by a subtle interaction of some external object upon strained or expectant senses, without thereby being mentally diseased. Is. may occur quite early in life, and are more common to males than females. According to Dr. Ferrier, some who have experienced Is.

have been remarkable for active memories, great ability, and extreme sensitiveness, while others were by no means so endowed; and, again, some are in perfect health, while others are suffering at the time from either trifling indispositions curable by dieting or from serious inflammatory and febrile diseases. In the criminal law, the term delusional insanity appears to embrace Is. and hallucinations indifferently, provided the reason is involved.

ILLUSTRATION. — The history of illustration commences with the Egyptian *Book of the Dead*. There remain no Gk. or Roman writings which can be dated with certainty before the Christian era, but it is known that illustration was practised by the Romans. It is found in the 3rd cent. *Iliad* of the Ambrosian Library at Milan, developed in the miniatures of Christian art (see ILLUMINATION, ART OF), and became an important feature of printed books. The earliest impressions of the printing press, where text and illustration were both engraved on wood together, are known as xylographic books. Bohner's illustrated *Fabulæ* were printed at Bamberg in 1461, Burgh's illustrated *Parvus et Magnus Catho* in England *c.* 1481. One of the earliest and greatest illustrators was Albrecht Dürer, 1471 1528. England hardly entered the field of art in any line in the 15th and 16th centuries, but took the lead in illustration in the 18th and 19th centuries. Not only in his set illustrations as for Butler's *Hudibras*, 1726, but in *Marriage a la Mode*, *The Rake's Progress*, etc., Hogarth gave interest to 'subjects of a modern kind and moral nature,' and thus stimulated illustration. Wood engraving gave place to metal for illustration in the 16th cent., but the former method was revived at the close of the 18th cent. by Thomas Berwick, whose *Quadrupeds*, 1790, and *British Birds*, 1797-1804, were mode s of illustration; the use of lithography in 1796 marked the beginning of cheap illustration.

At the same time the early 19th cent. used steel for *editions de luxe*, such as Whitaker's *History of Richmondshire*, illustrated by Turner. The most wonderful perhaps of all illustrations, Blake's *Illustrations to the Book of Job*, belong to this period. Cruikshank, Leech, and Hablot K. Browne were followed by Tenniel, Mulready, and others, and they by the Pre-Raphælites, whose works, engraved by the Dalziels in *Good Words*, etc., made 'the Sixties' a great period in illustration. *Punch* has held a unique position among periodicals for excellence of illustration since its commencement, and the *Graphic*, founded 1869, has had work of best black-and-white artists. Modern illustration has been revolutionized by photogravure and, since 1875, by process; while color-illustration (see PRINTING) has reached a high degree of excellence. William Morris, who founded the Kelmscott Press in 1891, represents a second Pre-Raphælite movement, but the general trend of illustration is against mediævalism. A list of prominent illustrators of late times must include Abbey, Mrs. Allingham, Barnard, Beardsley, Tom Browne, Caldecott, Caton Woodville, Crane, Fildes, Frost, Furniss, Garth, Jones, Charles Dana Gibson, H. C. Christy, M. L. Blumenthal, Neysa McMein, W. A. Rogers, Grace Greenaway, Gregory, Hall, Herkomer, Holt, Phil May, Millet, Nicholson, Parsons, Partridge, Pennell, Herbert Railton, Raven Hill, Reinhardt, Renouard, Ricketts, Sambourne, Savage, Shannon, Sullivan, Hugh Thomson, Townsend, Strang, Sturge Moore, Woods.

ILLUSTRES (Lat. 'illustrious ones'), title of chief dignitaries of later Rom. empire.

ILLYRIA, wide extent of country along W. shore of Adriatic, between Fiume and Durazzo; stretches inland to Danube and Servian Morava; embraces modern provinces of Dalmatia, Bosnia, Herzegovina, and Montenegro; also S. half of Croatia-Slavonia, W. part of Servia, the sanjak of Novibazar, and extreme N. of Albania; inhabitants never clearly identified; coast colonised by Greeks, VI. and VII. cent's B.C., but some 300 years later Latin civilization spread rapidly. After long history of continued warfare, I. (excepting some mountain tribes) ultimately became entirely Serbo-Croatian, in population, language, and culture. See Map of Europe.

ILMEN (58° 15′ N., 31° 30′ E.), freshwater lake, near Novgorod, European Russia; area, c. 360 sq. miles.

ILMENAU (50° 41′ N., 10° 54′ E.), town, summer resort, grand-duchy Saxe-Weimar, Germany; porcelain and glass.

ILMENITE, a mineral similar to hæmetite in appearance; opaque and slightly magnetic; generally found in gneisses and schists together with magnetite.

ILOILO (10° 50′ N., 122° 42′ E.), seaport, Panay, Philippine Islands; exports sugar, tobacco, rice.

ILORIN, ILLORIN (8° 27′ N., 4° 30′ E.), town and province, N. Nigeria, W. Africa; important trading centre; wood-

carving and leather industries.

ILSENBURG (51° 52′ N., 10° 40′ E.), small town, health-resort in the Harz, Saxony Germany; iron works.

IMAGE, term used in psychology for the impress made by an object on the eye, or for a mental impress; in theol. and art for any likeness of a person or thing; I's have played a considerable part in some religions (see ICONOCLASTS); in the Anglican Church adoration of I's is forbidden in art. XXII.

IMAGE WORSHIP.—In most great religions images have been important, not the least so in Christianity. There are different conceptions of an image: (1) it is that and nothing more; (2) it is the abode of the person or deity whom it represents, or retains a mysterious connection with him. Thus by getting possession of a man's image one could injure the man himself. This idea is called *sympathe ic magic.* Images are forbidden to Mohammadans. Eating, moving, and other acts have been ascribed to images of Christ, the Virgin, and Saints, as to those of heathern gods of antiquity (See ICONOCLASTS.).

IMAGINATION, used genera ly for calling up to the mind ideas other than those conveyed by senses, and, in psychology, for calling up ideas formerly received through the senses.

IMAM, the title of the caliph or leader of the Mohammadans; various sects have disputed as to nature and extent of his powers.

IMAUS, the ancient name for a part of the Himalaya Mts.

IMBECILE, weak, especially mentally weak; used of a state of mental weakness less advanced than idiocy. See INSANITY.

IMBERT, ARTHUR DE SAINT-AMAND (1834-1900), a French historian and biographer, b. in Paris. He was connected with the government in an official capacity, and late in life began the study of the lives of the women of the old French court of the First Empire, and the Restoration. This study resulted in a number of volumes and biographies of these women, which are considered the first authority on this subject. His studies ot the women of the court of Napoleon are especially valuable.

IMBREX (from Lat. *imber*, rain), Lat. term for roof-tile curved to carry off rain.

IMBROS (40° 10′ N., 25° 40′ E.), Turkish island, in Ægean Sea; fertile; seat of Gk. bp.

IMERITIA, IMERETIA (42° N., 43° E.), district, forming part of Kutais, Transcaucasia, Russia.

IMITATION, copying the movements of a model, or the results of such movements. It may be (1) impulsive, e.g. 'contagious' coughing and yawning, or (a higher type, presupposing more attention) the rythmical movements of a spectator of dancing; (2) inventional, arising from admiration of the agent copied, or of the dexterity copied, or from desire for a remoter end to which acquirement of the dexterity is a necessary means. The tendency to imitate is in most respects similar to instinctive tendencies, and is the young child's or animal's earliest mode of acquiring the habits of the race.

IMITATION OF CHRIST, famous devotional book dating from XV. cent.; authorship much disputed; some have ascribed it to John Gerson of Paris, and others to a John Gersen who probably never lived; but these do not now find many defenders. It must be either anonymous or (much more probably) by St. Thomas A. Kempis, 1380-1471; he lived near Utrecht, and the I. certainly emanates from Holland.

IMMACULATE CONCEPTION, see MARY.

IMMANENCE, meaning 'indwelling' as opposed to 'transcendence'; so the I. of God is the view of Him as a spiritual force in the universe, not a power controlling it from without.

IMMANUEL, BEN SOLOMON (c. 1265-c. 1330), Jewish satirical poet of Italy in Dante's time.

IMMERMANN, KARL LEBERECHT (1796-1840), Ger. Romantic dramatist and novelist; b. Magdeburg; best works: Merlin (dramatic poem), Die Epigonen and Münchhausen (novels).

IMMIGRANTS, EDUCATION OF. See AMERICANIZATION.

IMMIGRATION.—All the new countries have their immigration problems, due mostly to a lack of the most desired immigrants in sufficient numbers. In the case of the United States, the problem became one peculiar to itself; it received too many immigrants, even of the type formerly most welcomed. In that respect the United States stood alone among the countries that have grown by immigration. Its policy regarding incomers, always selective, consequently became drastically restrictive. Of the old countries Great Britain alone confronted an immigration problem, due to the influx, chiefly into London, of hordes of poor Russian and Polish Jews, the most desirable of whom used the British metropolis as a half-way house en route to the United States, leaving a large residue of their unfit brethren (including criminals) behind them to aggravate London's population and economic evils. Australia and the other British dominions cannot get the immigration they want, but, like her mother country and the United States, guard against the entry of undesirables. The Latin-American republics are equally anxious to develop their resources by desirable immigration, and it is warmly encouraged.

The check on immigration to the United States had its stimulus largely in the protests of American labor against the competition of incoming European workers whose cheapness lowered the standard of living established by the higher pay the unions succeeded in obtaining from capital.

Another cause was a racial hostility to the incoming swarms of S. Europeans, Slavs and Orientals, whose settlement was views as imperilling the supremacy of Americans of Anglo-Saxon and Teutonic stock. A third cause, though less manifest on the surface, was religious, expressed in an objection to any large infusion of new population from the Catholic countries of Europe.

Immigrants flocked to America from the beginning to better themselves. Economic forces, rather than the religious or political freedom offered, peopled the United States. A mistaken stress has been laid upon Old-World tyranny as a causation for the westward movement of population. That is only true of a comparative few of the earliest settlers. the modern immigrant wandered from his homeland, as his forefathers did, in search of a more assured means of livelihood and prosperity. There are no records of the migration before 1820, when 8,385 immigrants entered. By decades immigration grew from 151,824, in 1820-1830, to 8,795,386, in 1901-1910. In the middle of the nineteenth century the influx came chiefly from Ireland and Germany. Conditions in Russia brought later a Hebrew wave. Then with the twentieth century as it advanced came the flood from Italy and Austria-Hungary, the immigration from which countries reached, in 1899-1921, well over 3,000,000 respectively.

The World War of 1914-1918 checked immigration to a level that made the annual influx a negligible factor in the country's economic life. In 1914;

1,218,480 aliens entered. The next year, with the war in full blast, the number declined to 326,700, and in 1916, to 298,826. War immigration reached its lowest point in 1918, when only 110,618 entered American ports.

Restrictive legislation did not come until 1917. The measure passed in that year was in part due to the War and the need of excluding (or deporting) an undesirable type of alien produced by the conflict. The head tax, imposed on all entering aliens was increased to $8.00. Unwanted immigrants were reclassified, and safeguards against illiteracy increased. Later, other measures were adopted by Congress aimed at protecting the country from the entry of anarchists and propagandists against the established order. It was, however, the Immigration Restriction Act of 1921, which definitely put into force the long-considered experiment of checking an increase of population from foreign sources. This measure limited the number of aliens to be admitted to 3 per cent of the number of foreign-born persons of such nationality resident in the United States. This temporary measure was made permanent by the Immigration Act of 1924. This further restricted immigration by making the percentage permissible two per cent of the nationals as they were distributed by the census of 1890. It repealed 'The gentleman's agreement'' with Japan, and practically cut off immigration from that country. In 1930 foreign born pop. of U. S. was 14,204,149.

IMMORTALITY.—Belief in I. has been widespread, but not universal. It developed in Judaism comparatively late, but it has always formed a part, perhaps the chief part, of the Christian hope, and exists in many other religions. In early Christianity it was allied with the expectation of the speedy end of the world. Many arguments have been used to uphold it, and although no one of them can prove it, the sum-total possesses great cumulative force. Besides the feeling that another world is required to redress this, it can be said matter is eternal, so must spirit be too; the materialistic argument against it can be met by the assertion we do know that we are something more than our bodies. The pantheistic view that we shall be absorbed into divine life fails to satisfy those who believe there will be intensification rather than annulling of our personality.

IMMUNITY, resistance to a certain disease or to a certain organism, either natural or artificially produced by different means.

IMOLA, ancient *Forum Cornelii* (44° 2' N., 11° 43' E.), town, Bologna, Italy.

IMP, formerly scion, then child; from phrase 'I. of Satan' came modern use.

IMPACT. See ENERGY; PHYSICS.

IMPEACHMENT. — The accusation and trial of a person for treason, high crimes or misdemeanors. In England, the House of Commons is the prosecutor, and the House of Lords the trial court. In the United States, impeachment is by the Lower House of Congress, or by the Senate of a State Legislature. In some states the trial is held in the common courts of justice, and in others, judges of the highest appelate court sit with the senators and take part in the proceedings. Impeachment in England dates from the 15th century, and one of the most famous cases was that of Lord Bacon, in 1621, who was convicted, removed from office, and heavily fined. Since the early years of the 19th century, impeachment has become practically obsolete in Great Britain. In some of our states, under their constitution, a two-thirds vote is necessary for impeachment, and the only punishment is removal from office. In England, any punishment, even capital, is legal, but the House of Commons has the power to pardon. With us, impeachment is excepted from pardoning power. In some jurisdictions only state officers are subject to impeachment, county and municipal officers being excepted. Judicial opinions differ on the question of impeachment as to whether an official can be impeached after leaving office. In certain cases, impeached offenders can be punished by the courts for the same crime.

IMPERIAL CHAMBER (Ger. *Reichskammergericht*), from 1495 till its dissolution Court of Holy Rom. Empire; consisted of 16, then 18, judges and officials app. by empire; took place of old Imperial Court whose members were emperor's nominees. Its work was unsystematic and often taken over by the Aulic Council.

IMPERIAL CITIES in former times were cities in Germany which were directly under the emperor and owed allegiance to no intermediate lord; name became common in VIII. cent. (Ger. *Reichstadt*); cities attained their status by imperial grant or by buying their freedom from the intermediate lord; examples are Basel, Cologne, Mainz, Strassburg, Worms.

IMPERIALISM, in modern usage, signifies either extended rule over various and often distant parts of the world or the desire to federate or unite more closely these distant dependencies with the mother country.

During the IX. cent. most European countries were engaged in more or less determined efforts to extend their colonial possessions—France, in N. Africa, and E. Asia; Germany, in Africa and the Pacific, and Italy, on the Red Sea littoral. Along with this proceeded a remarkable development of naval strength. The policy of Great Britain was profoundly affected by these events.

Imperial Federation.—The desire arose for a closer federation between the mother country and the colonies, to be promoted by such schemes as improved telegraphic and postal communication within the empire, periodical conferences in Britain at which ministers of state confer with ministers from the colonies on subjects of imperial interest, preferential tariffs, etc. In 1884 an Imperial Federation League was founded. First conference of representatives of self-governing colonies took place in 1887, when Australia undertook certain obligations in regard to naval defence. In 1893 the league was dissolved and the Imperial Federation (Defence) Committee was constituted to carry out a definite scheme based on partitipation by the colonies in the work and cost of imperial defence. In same year second colonial conference was held, direct fruit of which was offer of an ironclad by Cape Colony and the provision of coal by Natl. In 1902 advantage was taken of the presence of colonial premiers at the coronation of Edward VII. to hold a third conference, the result of which was further grants towards the defence of the empire. German naval activity in 1909 resulted in an offer by Australia and New Zealand to contribute each a battleship to the imperial navy. At a subsequent imperial conference Canada and Australia undertook to build navies of their own.

IMPEY, SIR ELIJAH (1732-1809), chief-justice of Bengal; supported Warren Hastings; impeached in 1783 for action in trial of Maharajah Nand Kumar, but acquitted.

IMPHAL, MANIPUR (24° 48′ N., 94° E.), town, capital Manipur, Assam, India.

IMPLEMENTS AND MACHINERY, AGRICULTURAL, may be classified, according to the sequence of agricultural operations, as follows: Implements used (1) in preparing the soil for crops; (2) in sowing seeds or manures; (3) in cultivating growing crops; (4) in harvesting or securing crops; (5) in preparing crops for market; (6) in preparing crops for home consumption; (7) dairy implements and utensils; (8) implements required for estate work.

Implements used in Preparing Soil for Crops.—These include ploughs, cultivators, harrows, rollers, and land pressers, all of which have to a great extent preserved their original form, although they have been adapted to steam and oil, and probably may be to electric motor power. The plough turns the furrow completely over, and exposes a fresh surface to atmospheric action, and is therefore the most thorough of all cultivating implements. Cultivators, grubbers, or scarifiers tear and pulverize the soil by means of curved teeth, and, when worked by steam, in many cases supersede the plough. Harrows are used to render the surface fine for the reception of the seed, and to cover it; but the heavier forms do service similar to that of cultivators. Rollers are used to break clods, but still more to consolidate the seedbed after sowing, and to smooth the surface. They are plain, or toothed, or formed of segments or rings, and vary in weight from the light wooden to the heavier iron toothed and ringed rollers. Pressers are composed of two or three heavy iron wheels, placed at such a distance from each other, on a frame, as to follow two or three ploughs, and press the furrows as they are turned over. The adaptation of these implements to steam power has given rise to many forms. Thus, balance plough carries from eight to sixteen ploughs, half of which are in work, while the other half are suspended on the opposite side of the frame. At the end of the furrow the idle ploughs are lowered into work, and the working ploughs are hoisted out of work by the same movement. The powerful 7-tine cultivator is steered round the ends by the driver, and in both cases the steersman is seated on the implement. The most important of all implements, a satisfactory digger, has yet to be invented.

Implements used in Sowing Seeds or Manures.—These include various forms of drills, broad-cast sowers, seed-barrows, and manure distributors. They are all designed to supersede hand sowing, but they are neither more rapid nor cheaper than that method, although they sow the seed in rows and require less. Drills deposit the seed below the surface by means of hollow coulters; while broadcast machines and seed-barrows scatter it on the surface, or in ordinary pressed furrows, where the plants come up in rows. Drills include dry-drills, corn-drills, turnip-drills, clover-drills, bean-barrows, and potato-planters.

Implements used in Cultivating Growing Crops.—Besides hand-hoes, which are largely employed, this class includes various forms of horse-hoes. They vary from one-row scufflers for potato sultivation or root crops grown on the ridge system to multiple hoes for taking three or more drills.

Implements used in Harvesting or Securing Crops include harvesters or self-binders, reaping machines, mowing machines, loaders, stackers, swathe-turners, horse-rakes, hay-tedders, and sweeps. The self-binder delivers its sheaves, neatly tied with string, at the rate of thirty a minute, and will cut and tie up an acre of corn in an hour. There are also several kinds of mechanical potato-diggers and root-toppers in use.

Implements used in Preparing Crops for Market.—The threshing machine stands at the head of the list in this class. A good modern threshing machine separates and delivers simultaneously the straw, the cavings, the chaff, and seeds of weeds. In many modern threshing machines a chaff-cutter is attached, which delivers the cut straw into bags; or an apparatus is added which ties the straw in bundles. In others, the wheat is delivered at the proper weight into sacks ready for delivery. The finishing threshing machine combines the operation usually performed by the winnowing machine, the hummeller, and the screen. The inequalities of sample, or rather of bulk, in a large rick cause many farmers to prefer a single-blast machine, and the bulk of the corn is then turned over on a floor and rendered equal in character. It is afterwards winnowed or screened, and weighed up for market.

Implements used in Preparing Crops for Home Consumption.—These include grist-mills, kibblers, bruisers, chaff-cutters, boilers, root-splicers, pulpers and shredders, and oil-cake breakers. They are best arranged in connection with a fixed steam or oil engine, to drive a shafting with pulleys placed at intervals; each pulley carries a belt, which is passed over a corresponding pulley on each instrument.

IMPLUVIUM (Lat. from *impluere*, to rain into), receptacle in atrium of Rom. house for rain falling through *compluvium* of roof.

IMPOSITION (Lat. *imponere*, to place upon), arrangement of type after composition in printing.

IMPOST, architectural term for part of door-post on which arch rests; often forms capital of a pilaster, or is moulded; also name applied to taxes.

IMPOTENCE, inability of male to perform function of reproduction; may arise from excessive nervous strain, disease, or excess.

IMPRESSIONISM IN PAINTING.— The term 'impressionism' is said to have originated with Edouard Manet (regarded as founder of the school), who, in the preface to a catalogue of his works at the Exposition Universelle, 1867, claimed that the painter's function was to render his own 'impression' of things seen; Claude Monet's picture *The Impressionist* also served to fix the term as a general designation of certain new aims and ideals in art. These group themselves roughly under three heads: (1) the reproduction of the actual (of which Manet's work is representative); (2) the quest of the beauty and mystery of light (led by Claude Monet), hence term 'luminarists'; (3) the effort to seize some instantaneous and vivid aspect of life, and to reproduce that impression, untrammelled by detail (Degas or Renoir represents this last). Under the influence of the great Romanticist Delacroix, the two ideals of *actuality* and *light* had already been severally expressed in landscape by Courbet and Corot, Delacroix in his turn having been influenced by Turner and Constable. Impressionism has, however, no nationality; its exponents are found in every land; besides the long roll of Fr. impressionists, from Monet to the latest Fr. 'salonist,' we have the Swed. Zorn, the Norewg. Thaulow, the Dutch Maris, the Scot. Guthrie, etc.; while Whistler and Sargent stand for America. Impressionism and the later Eng. post-impressionism met with much antagonism at first; Manet's earliest impressionist pictures were exhibited in the Salon des Refusés, 1863, and at his death his fine portrait of *Claude Monet in his Studio*. Witness also the bitter Ruskin-Whistler controversy. In considering impressionism we have to take into account the extraordinary influence of modern Jap. art on the truth-seekers and light-seekers of the West.

IMPRESSMENT, the seizing and compelling men to enter navy; practice was resorted to in this country from the XIV. cent. till reign of George III., laws being passed to regulate the system; it has now died out, although these laws have not been repealed. Right to exercise power of I. is claimed by all sovereign authorities, and it has been resorted to by all European states. The impressment of sailors from American ships by English vessels of war was one of the chief causes for the War of 1812.

IMPRISONMENT, punishment by incarceration (with or without hard labor) for offences which are not serious enough for penal servitude. I. in first division amounts to little more than confinement— prisoners may wear ordinary clothes, receive friends, etc.; in second division, special rules somewhat similar to above are in force; while criminal offenders are placed in third division (hard labor). The maximum term is generally two years.

IMPROVISATORE, poet or musician who has gift of composing without study and recites as he composes; apparently common in Middle Ages, but only appears as a freak in modern times.

INCANTATION (Lat. *cantare*, to sing), spell fashioned on the belief universal in primitive men that words placed in a certain order have magical power.

INCARNATION (from Lat. *incarnari*, to be made flesh; from *in* + *caro*, flesh), in Christian theology, the act by which the Second Person of the Blessed Trinity assumed human form and human nature. In many other religions, and especially in those of India, are there accounts of the taking of human flesh by the gods in order to secure a fuller revelation to the world, but these differ essentially from the orthodox Christian belief in the I. of Jesus Christ, which lays stress on the fact that the Logos, eternally divine, then became also essentially human, so that Christ was 'perfect God and perfect Man; one not by conversion of the Godhead into flesh, but by taking of the manhood unto God.'

INCAS, see under Peru.

IN CŒNA DOMINI (Lat. 'at the Lord's Supper'), papal bull, thus commencing, issued yearly against heretics, 1363-1770.

INCE-IN-MAKERFIELD (53° 31' N., 2° 37' W.), town, Lancashire, England; collieries, ironworks.

INCENSE, a term given to various substances which when burnt give off a sweet smell—generally used in religious worship. It was used in many ancient Oriental worships, particularly in Egypt, as appears from various monuments. It was common, too, in ancient India, where its use still survives—even among Mohammadans, who elsewhere do not use it much—and in Persia and Babylonia; it is also used in Buddhist countries. The ancient Greeks burnt I. to their gods, and it was employed in Rome on festal occasions. Among the Jews the burning of I. accompanied animal sacrifices, and in the Temple its object was partly fumigatory to overcome the stench of the blood of the slaughtered beasts. In the Christian Church its use is not definitely proved before the V. cent., as the Early Fathers do not refer to it, but it was certainly used in the catacombs at Rome, though this may have been for sanitary reasons. Its use was regular in the Middle Ages, and is enjoined at certain portions of sung Mass in the Rom. Missal. It is likewise common in the Gk. and Eastern Churches, where there are liturgical formulæ for the censing of the bread and wine. In England, according to the uses of Sarum and Bangor, the altar was to be censed during Mass, but at the Reformation its use was generally abandoned. It was revived together with so many other ancient customs in the XIX. cent.

INCEST (Lat. *incestus*, unchaste), sexual intercourse between persons who could not marry on account of affinity.

INCH, 12th part of an Eng. ft.; divided formerly into 3 barleycorns and supposed to measure 3 barleycorns placed end to end.

INCHBALD, MRS. ELIZABETH (1753-1821), Eng. actress, dramatist, and novelist; beautiful and skilful player, but never overcame impediment in speech; the writings show too much cultivation of 'sentiment.'

INCHCOLM and **INCHKEITH**, islands in Forth Scotland.

INCIDENCE, ANGLE OF, is a term used for the angle made by the direction of a disturbance impinging on the surface of a medium with the normal to the surface.

INCLINED PLANE, a rigid plane inclined at an angle to the horizon. It is a mechanical instrument used to facilitate the lifting of heavy bodies. In the case of an incline of 1 in 6, a power of 1 lb. will support a weight of 6 lbs., thus giving a mechanical advantage of 6.

INCLINOMETER, instrument for measuring the *dip* (inclination of earth's magnetic field to horizontal). Two kinds of I's are in use—the *dipping needle* and the *earth inductor*. The former is a suitably mounted, light, magnetised needle, free to move about a horizontal axis; the latter, a coil of wire spun about a diameter, adjusted until no current is induced. The inclination of the needle, or of the diameter of the coil, to the horizontal measures the dip.

INCOME TAX.—The imposition of a tax levy on incomes is an old device for obtaining government revenue. It appeared in the Middle Ages, in Italy, and later in France. England raised money on taxing incomes centuries before she inaugurated the modern method by establishing an income tax as a fiscal expedient in 1799 to meet the huge outlays caused by the Napoleonic wars, an impost that lasted till hostilities ceased. In 1842 she revived the tax, and it has since been in operation, an integral part of the country's fiscal system, despite Gladstone's attempt to repeal it in 1874.

By the time the United States adopted, 1913, the income tax as a stable source of revenue, the system had long been firmly established in almost every other country of importance. Not that it was wholly new to Americans. The colonies drew revenue from incomes, and quite a number of the States resorted to the same method of filling their treasuries long before the national government did. State taxation of incomes, as pursued early in the XIX. cent., was a failure. When the Civil War came only 6 States, Massachusetts, South Carolina, Pennsylvania, Virginia, North Carolina, and Alabama, were making such a levy. In a number of other states the tax had been abandoned. During that war a number of Southern States adopted the tax in addition to those named. The Federal Government also levied an impost on incomes to meet war emergencies, the tax lasting from 1861 to 1872. In 1894 an attempt to revive the Federal Income Tax failed through the unconstitutionality of the proposed measure. State income tax meantime languished, the only levies in force by the close of the XIX. cent. being those of Massachusetts, Virginia, North Carolina, and Louisiana. The tax of the last named state soon after disappeared. With almost no exceptions, the state administration of the income tax laws was poor, the yield small, and the taxes generally unpopular.

In the XX. cent., the need of revenue compelled a number of the States to pay more and more attention to the income tax. Wisconsin led the way, in 1911, by devising a new tax system for personal and corporation incomes, and by the close of 1920 there were ten other states, Mississippi, Oklahoma, Massachusetts, Missouri, Delaware, Virginia, New York, North Dakota, and New Mexico, making similar levies by improved methods. Connecticut, Montana, and West Virginia tax the net incomes of corporations, without corresponding taxation on incomes of individuals. South Carolina stood out in 1919, by abolishing her State income tax altogether. Ohio tried to establish an income tax in that year, but the measure was repudiated by the Legislature.

The Federal Income Tax of 1913 imposed a graduated tax of one per cent on incomes from $3,000 upward, with an additional tax of one per cent. on in-comes of $20,000 upward. In 1916 (the middle of the World War period), the normal rate was doubled from one to two per cent. and the additional rate increased by scale, so that the extra tax fell heavy on very large incomes. In 1917, American entry into the war produced the War Revenue Act, which increased the income tax assessments by making the extra levy apply to all incomes above $5,000, instead of $20,000, and reduced the amounts that could be exempted. In 1919, the taxable incomes were widened to include those exceeding $1,000, the normal rate was raised to four per cent, which became eight per cent on incomes exceeding $8,000, while the surtax was applied to incomes above $8,000, beginning at one per cent, and graduating upward to 65 per cent on incomes of $1,000,000. Further amendments, and reductions were made by Congress in 1923 and 1924, but an effort to repeal the surtax on large incomes was defeated in 1924, although it was urged by President Coolidge and Secretary Mellon. Taxes on smaller incomes were greatly reduced.

Under the Revenue Act of 1928, income exemptions were $1,500 for single individuals; $3,500 for heads of families; $3,000 for corporations with a net income below $25,000. Under personal income there was a further allowance of $400 made for each child under 18 and for every dependent person.

Corporation income taxes, June 30, 1932, were $629,566,115, a decrease of $369,826,583 from the previous year. Individual income taxes were $427,190,681 for the same year, $406,457,216 lower than the preceding year. The income tax collection was $1,056,756,697. This was $803,283,799 lower than the year before.

INCREMENT, UNEARNED, denotes increase in value of land resulting, not from any expenditure of labor or money on the part of the owner, but from independent causes.

INCUBATION AND INCUBATORS. —Incubation, originally the sitting of a hen on her eggs, now means the exposure of a living organism to a uniform temperature, under suitable conditions of moisture and ventilation; incubators are enclosed spaces with devices for securing this. For each organism there is a maximum, minimum, and optimum temperature. Incubation should be conducted at the optimum temperature and never reach the maximum or minimum. Incubators are employed to hatch, a practice known to the early Chinese and Egyptians. The latter employed *Mamals*, large closed brick ovens in which thousands of eggs were hatched. These were heated by low fires, which, after the twelfth day were allowed to go out. Modern egg incubators are heated by hot air or hot water. The essential is that the incubator shall maintain a constant temperature, notwithstanding changes in temperature of the outer air, fluctuations in gas pressure, and the occasional opening of the incubator. After the tenth day the chick, having developed a fœtal respiratory organ, produces more heat, and the incubator should automatically adjust itself to this. The providing of increased air for respiration increases evaporation, and the eggs should be provided with additional moisture.

Hot-air incubators are double-walled metal cylinders, the space between the walls being packed with non-conducting material. In the centre of the floor there is a box with pipes which, after traversing the incubator, open to the exterior at the top. Inside the box there is a lamp which heats the air. The hot air then circulates through the pipes in the incubator. Fresh air is supplied to the incubator by a tube on either side of the heating box. A jar of water supplies sufficient moisture. The temperature is regulated by a valve over the main pipe from the heating chamber. Increase in temperature opens the valve, decrease closes it. The valve is worked by the expansion of a column of mercury actuating a system of levers.

Bacteriological incubators may be hot or cool; the former are kept at 37° C., the latter at 20° C. Cool incubators are used for gelatin cultures of pathogenic bacteria or to grow non-pathogenic bacteria and moulds. The temperature is maintained in summer by the passage of cold water round the walls and in winter by warm water. The hot incubators for pathogenic bacteria are square double-walled metal boxes covered with wood. Warm water is poured into the space between the metal walls and heated underneath by oil, gas, or electricity. The flame is regulated by a system of levers which can decrease or increase it when the temperature of the water makes a valve open or shut. The temperature of such an incubator remains constant for months. The air surrounding the incubator should be kept as still as possible and should be some degrees below the temperature of the incubator. A very carefully regulated and ventilated form of this incubator is used to rear prematurely born infants. When the child has grown sufficiently the temperature is gradually decreased.

INCUBUS (Lat. *incubare*, to lie upon), demon supposed to visit women and engender witches, etc.; the feminine form was the *succuba*.

INCUMBENT (Lat. *incumbere*, to lean upon; the reason for this name is not known), holder of a benefice in Anglican Church.

INCUNABULA (Lat. cradle; plural of *incunabulum*), title (nationalized in various countries) given to printed books of XV. cent.; of these there are about 30,000. Bibliographies are Beughem, *I. typographiæ*, 1688; Panzer, *Annales typographici*, 1793 and 1803; Hain, *Repertorium*, bibliographicum, 1826-38; Proctor, *Index to the Early Printed Books in the Brit. Museum*, 1898; Copinger, *Supplement to Hain's Repertorium*, 1898-1902. Many facsimiles were printed in the late XIX. cent.

INDABA, intertribal conference of Kaffirs.

INDEMNITY, a contract, express or implied, to keep a person immune from liability under a contract into which he has entered, or intends to enter. Contracts of fire, marine, and accident insurance (but not life assurance), are instances of such contracts.

INDENTURE, name for legal deed between two or more parties. Formerly the duplicates of the agreement were written on one parchment, which was then cut into two by indented line, so that the deed and counterpart could be fitted into one another and thus give evidence of being the same agreement.

INDEPENDENCE, a city of Kansas, in Montgomery co., of which it is the county seat. It is on the Atchison, Topeka and Santa Fe, and the Missouri and Pacific railroads, and on Verdigris River. It is surrounded by extensive gas and oil field area, and its industries, include cotton mills, planing mills, flour, mills, cement works, machine shops, glass works, brick plant, revolving door plant, etc. Its public buildings include hospitals, a public library, court house and Memorial Convention Hall. It has high schools and a park system.

INDEPENDENCE, a city of Missouri, in Jackson co., of which it is the county seat. It is on the Chicago and Alton, the Kansas City Southern, and the Missouri and Pacific railroads. It is four miles S. of the Missouri River, and 10 miles E. of Kansas City. It has several important industrial establishments. The public buildings include a high school and a public library. There are two large parks. Independence has considerable historic interest. It was occupied in 1831 by the Mormons, who remained there until 1838. It was a noted gathering place for emigrants who journeyed across the plains. Pop., 1920, 11,686.

INDEPENDENCE, DECLARATION OF. See DECLARATION OF INDEPENDENCE.

INDEPENDENCE HALL, a building in Philadelphia, where, on July 4, 1776, the Declaration of Independence was adopted by Congress and read to the people. The Continental Congress met there. It is now used as an historical museum.

INDEPENDENT CATHOLIC CHURCH IN THE UNITED STATES, THE POLISH.—A religious body formed of the Polish Catholics of Chicago, who separated from the orthodox church, by the Rev. Anthony Kozlowski. He is said to have been consecrated a bishop while attending a conference of Old Catholics in Europe. The Independent Catholics own much property in Chicago, and have built an orphanage, hospital, and academic and industrial schools, and a home for the aged.

INDEPENDENTS, name given to churches where the individual church is supreme; often called 'Congregationalist.'

INDEX, list of words about which book contains information, arranged in alphabetical order. In learned books there used to be, and still often is, an *I. personum, I. locorum,* and *I. rerum.*

INDEX LIBRORUM PROHIBITORUM, or simply 'The Index,' list of books which R.C. Church officially prohibits her members from having or reading. First list was issued by Pope Paul IV., in 1557; reissued from time to time, and recast by Leo XIII., 1897, when books defending heresy were prohibited, but not necessarily books by heretics not so doing; likewise immoral books must not be read. Special permission can be given to scholars and others to read prohibited works.

INDIA, the central peninsula of S. Asia (8° 4'-37° N., 61°-101° E.), includes terr. over which Brit. king as Emperor of India exercises dominion or suzerainty. (For Fr. and Port. possessions, see separate articles.) Four distinct regions are recognized: (1) the mountains north, (2) the Indo-Gangetic valley, (3) the Deccan, (4) Burma (see separate article). Area, 1,805,252 sq. m.   Pop., 1931, 351,399,880. See Map of Asia.

(1) The Himalayas, consisting of successive folded ranges, sweep for 1,500 m. from Kashmir to Assam; mean elevation, 18,000 ft.; breadth, 200 m.; peaks, Everest, 29,002 ft., Kanchanjanga, 27,815 ft., and Dhaulagiri, 26,826 ft. Beneath them is rank vegetation of Tarai trough; the more recent Sivaliks, from Hardwar to

Beas R., enclose duns (valleys) of which Dehra Dun is largest. In N.W. also is mountain frontier consisting of offshoots of Hindu-Kush through which Kabul R. and Khaibar Pass come; S. of highland of Waziristan is recent range of Sulaiman Mts. (Takht-i-Sulaiman, 11,800 ft.), crossed by Bolan Pass; farther S. Hala Mts. reach Karachi.

(2) Alluvial plains, stretching from Arabian Sea to Bay of Bengal, owe their fertility or sterility to the rivers Indus, Jumna, Ganges, and Brahmaputra. The Aravali range forms divide between Indus and Ganges systems.   The Indus collects the waters of the Jhelum, Chedus and Ganges systems.   The Indus collects the waters of the Jhelum, Chenab, Ravi, Beas, and Sutlej, which give the Punjab ('five rivers') its name; thence the Indus flows in ever-changing channels to Sind.   The Ganges bursts through the Sivalik Hills at Hardwar, receives the Jumna ar Allahabad, and unites with the Brahmaputra to form the vast delat of 160 m. along the Bay of Bengal; the deltaic coastal belt forms the Sundarbans.

(3) The Deccan plateau (average height 1,500-2,000 ft.) is highest in W. Ghats, which extend S. to Nilgiri Hills and Cardamom Mts. separated by Polghat. In N.E. are coal basins of Gondwana system.   Drainage is to E. by Godavari, 800 m., Kistna, 800 m., and Kavari, to W. by Tapti and Narbada; the E. rivers form extensive deltas.

The largest native states are Rajputana, Kashmir, Haidarabad, Baluchistan, Central India Agency, Behar, and Orissa.

Climate.—The climate varies from the cold of the perpetual snows of the Himalayas to the intense, moist heat of the plains and the dry heat of the plateau, while other differences are caused by the continental conditions of the N. and the insular conditions of the S.   The S.W. (summer) and N.E. (winter) monsoons are much modified by local configuration. The three seasons are: hot (March to May), wet (June to Oct., later in S. Madras), and cool.   The rainfall varies from 8 in. in Sind and Cutch to 12 in. in Rajputana; 21½ in the Punjab plains; 31 in the N. Deccan; 40-60 in Central India, W. Bengal, and Orissa; 65 in Lower Bengal; 95 in Assam and Cachar; 114 in the E. Ghats; 139 in the W. Ghats; and 152-73 in Lower Burma; while among the Assam hills it is said to reach 500 in.   Owing to density of population and great evaporation, any failure of the regular rains is disastrous and leads to serious famine.   The subsoil of the great Indo-Gangetic plain of the north is Recent Alluvium, that of the Himalayas possibly at points Cambrian, with Crystalline, Upper and Lower Tertiary rocks, Volcanic and Cretaceous strata. Large districts of E. and S. peninsula have Crystalline rocks; fringing Crystalline rocks of the Deccan is a strip of Recent Alluvium along the Bay of Bengal.

Occupations. — Agriculture predominates, and has been extended by irrigation to the Punjab, Sind, etc.; the government irrigation works water *c.* 45 million ac. and the annual yield of promised crops is estimated at $100,000,000. The most important Ind. crops are rice, pulse, wheat, and other grains; cotton, jute, and other fibres; tea, tobacco, sugar. Agricultural departments supply information to cultivators, and distribute seeds. Special attention is paid to afforestation; the state has reserved *c.* 107,353 sq. m. of forests, and controls in addition *c.* 249,154 sq. m.; Burma yields much teak. Mining is important; coal, petroleum (chiefly in Burma and Assam), manganese, gold (Mysore), monazite, wolfram, salt, and saltpetre are mined.

Industries.—The native village handicrafts suffer from the competition of factory products. Cotton is manufactured on a large scale, especially in Bombay; jute in Bengal; woolen and silk goods, paper, and timber.

Commerce.—The sea-borne trade of India is second only to that of the U.K. in the Brit. Empire. Chief exports: jute manufactures; grain, pulse, and flour; raw cotton and cotton manufactures; tea; raw jute; oil seeds and oils; leather, hides, and skins, etc. Imports: manufactured goods, sugar; chemicals, etc. Trade is mainly with U.K., Japan (which rapidly increased her share during the World War), and U.S. There is a land trade with Nepal and the Shan States.

Communications.—Most of the railways are state owned. Of the total mileage (42,813 in 1931) about half is on standard gauge (5 ft. 6 in.); nearly all the remainder is on meter gauge. Good metal roads run in all directions. The largest ports are Calcutta, Bombay, Karachi, Rangoon, and Madras.

The towns with over 200,000 inhabitants are the former cap., Calcutta (1,485,582 with the suburbs), Bombay, Madras, Hyderabad, Rangoon, Lucknow, Delhi (made the cap. in 1911), Lahore, Ahmedabad, and Benares.

History.—The earliest peoples found in India are the Dravidians, who were driven S. and into the less eligible hill districts by an Aryan invasion. This took place possibly in the second millenium B.C., possibly earlier, and is commemorated in the contemporaneaous poem the *Rig-Veda.* By the VI. cent.

B.C., sixteen Aryan states had been established S. of the Himalayas, and Brahmanism, apparently not known to the Dravidians, was flourishing. In the VI. cent. Buddhism and Jainism were taught. The Hindu epic the *Mahabharata* gives a legendary history of this period. Magadha (Behar) became the chief state. The invasion of Alexander the Great in 327 B.C., a famous event in European history, left a permanent mark on India, and inscriptions and art show. Alexander reached the Hydaspes (Jhelum) and retired, leaving garrisons to secure his conquests. He died, 333, before revisiting India, which, shortly afterwards, became part of the Seleucid Empire. The Indian monarch Chanddragupta, 321-297, recovered a good deal of territory from the Greeks and founded the dynasty of the Mauryas, which lasted until 184 B.C.; and despite various efforts of the Seleucidæ, India broke away from Macedonian rule, the process being completed by Kadphises (*fl.* A.D. 1st cent.), founder of the great Kushan dynasty, which had its seat at Peshawar. History has not yet been disentangled from legend for these early centuries, but the invasions of the White Huns in the V. and VI. cent's B.C. stand forth. In the early days of militant Mohammedanism India successfully repelled several Arab inroads, but in 1001-24 the great Turk. leader, Mahmud, established the Ghazni dynasty in India, 1024-1186. There followed the Mongol invasion of Jenghiz Khan in 1219, and the inroad of Tartar hordes under Timour (Tamerlane of Eastern legend) in 1397, who captured Delhi in 1398. Timour established his rule in Hindustan, but the Persian sultan, Baber, who established his rule in India, 1519-26, was the true founder of the great Mogul Empire, famous until the close of the XVII. cent. Renowned rulers were Akbar, 1556-1605; his son, Ishangir, who ruled until 1627; Shah Jehan, who built the Taj Mahal as well as the fort, palace, and Jama Masjid at Delhi; and Aurungzebe, *d.* 1707, the most brilliant of the line. The last King of Delhi was deposed by the Brit. in 1858 for taking part in the Mutiny of 1857.

Trade with India was carried on by European states from beginnings of history, its mart being Alexandria. The Cape route was discovered by Vasco da Gama, 1497-98, who, in 1502, established a Port. station at Cochin. The Dutch founded their E. India Co. in 1602, the French in 1664. The Eng. E. India Co. received its first charter from Queen Elizabeth in 1600. In the next cent. and a half it continued to be merely a trading company, with stations at Surat, Bombay. Madras, and Calcutta, and ousted in turn Port. and Dutch rivals. A new era commenced in 1748, when Dupleix, the brilliant Fr. governor, interferred in disputes between rival princes for the throne. Britain followed suit, and won first great success at Arcot, in 1751 (see CLIVE). Clive was sent in 1757 to take vengeance on Surajah Dowlah. the Nabob of Bengal, for the outrage of the 'Black Hole of Calcutta,' and by his victory at Plassy laid the foundation of Brit. rule in India. The success of Sir Eyre Coote at Wandewash, in 1760, led to the extinction of Fr. rule in India. Warren Hastings, gov.-gen. under the India Act of 1773, played an important part in building the Brit. Empire. He subdued the Mahratta princes, and collected the army with which Sir Eyre Coote crushed Haidar Ali, Sultan of Mysore, at Porto Novo, 1781. Marquis Wellesley, gov.-gen. 1798-1805, induced the Nizam of the Deccan and other native princes to accept Brit. protection, stormed Seringapatam, cap. of Haidar Ali's successor, Tippoo, and subdued the Maharattas, his brother Arthur, future Duke of Wellington, winning the hard-fought battle of Assaye, 1803. Lord Hastings, gov.-gen. 1813, reduced Nepal to submission without depriving it of independence.

Britain was now practically supreme over peninsula S. of a line from the mouth of the Indus to that of the Ganges, and over the basin of the Ganges itself. Between 1848 and 1856 the Marquis of Dalhousie annexed more territory than any other gov.-gen. before or since. By the defeat of the Sikhs at Gujarat and elsewhere the Punjab was brought under Brit. rule. S. Burma, including the port of Rangoon, was annexed, and, most important of Dalhousie's achievements, Oudh, 'the garden of India.' His high-handed proceedings in Oudh had much to do with the Indian Mutiny. The Mutiny broke out in 1857 at Meerut; the chief centers of the war were Delhi, Cawnpore, and Lucknow. Cawnpore was the scene of the 'Bloody Well'; Lucknow is celebrated for the relief brought to the Brit. garrison by General Havelock. With the capture of Delhi, the headquarters of the rebel troops, the back of the rebellion was broken. The Derby-Disraeli ministry then transferred the government from the E. India Co. to the crown, 1858. The company was dissolved in 1874. The last flames of the Mutiny, kept alight by Nana Sahib, were quenched by Lord Canning, 1859-62; but the unrest in many parts, especially Bengal, has been a serious danger ever since. There were terrible famines in 1861, 1866, 1868-9, 1874, 1876-7, 1897-7, and 1899. Sir John (afterwards Lord) Lawrence, who

became viceroy in 1864, had to meet Hindu discontent and famine in Orissa. After some losses of Brit. forces, he made an agreement with the Bhutanese, 1865. The Earl of Mayo became viceroy in 1869, and was faced with serious deficiency of the revenue, and wide dislike of the new income tax (abolished 1873). After his assassination by a convict in 1872, Lord Ellenborough succeeded, and was followed by Lord Northbrook in 1872, and by Lord Lytton, 1876-80.

In 1876 Queen Victoria was proclaimed Empress of India in London, and the next year at Delhi. Invasions of N.W. tribes culminated, 1878-80, in the Afghan War, by which Britain obtained possession of the mountain passes. Lord Ripon, viceroy, 1880-4, by various democratic measures, including his scheme of local self-government, which developed municipal institutions, and by the attempt to extend the jurisdiction of the criminal courts in the districts over European British subjects, independently of the race or nationality of the judge, won much unpopularity. This attempt ended in the compromise of 1884. He enjoyed, however, unusual native good will. Lord Dufferin, 1884-8, introduced various reforms, annexed Upper Burma, 1886, and passed an Income Tax Bill, 1886. Lord Lansdowne, 1888-94, and Lord Elgin, 1894-99, restored the finances, the former introducing gold standard.

In Lord Elgin's time there were a number of risings along the N.W. frontier. In 1895 the Brit. agent in Chitral was beseiged, and had to be rescued by an expeditionary force. Two years later the Wazirs, Swalis, and Mohmands attacked the Brit. positions in Malakand, and the Afridis closed the Khaibar Pass. Peace was only established after a prolonged campaign (the Tirah campaign). During the 1896-7 famine bubonic plague made its appearance, and the measures taken to prevent the spread of the disease caused rioting in Bombay and elsewhere. Lord Curzon, 1889-1905, reorganized the N.W. Provinces, naming them the United Provinces. In 1904 the pro-Russian attitude of the Dalai Lama of Tibet necessitated an expedition to Lhasa. The Dalai Lama abdicated, and a treaty was concluded with his successor. In 1905 Bengal was divided into the provinces of E. Bengal and Assam. The great Punjab earthquake took place the same year. Lord Curzon continued the development of India on Western lines, but eased the burden of taxation. He resigned after a serious dispute with Lord Kitchener, commander-in-chief, as to the respective authorities of the latter and the military member of the governor's council in time of war. The matter was decided in 1906 to the satisfaction of Lord Kitchener and the new viceroy, Lord Minto, 1905-10.

Plague had been raging in the Punjab since 1897, and in 1907 there was an alarming increase of sedition there and in Bengal. Severe measures of repression were taken against both Mohammedans and Hindus. Lord Morley now brought forward measures for giving natives a certain amount of representation, and native satisfaction was expressed for the India Council's Act, 1909. Lord Hardinge succeeded as viceroy in 1910. George V. visited India in 1911-12, was proclaimed emperor at Delhi Durbar and declared Delhi cap. in place of Calcutta. An attempt was made on the viceroy's life during the state entry into Delhi. The development of communications, the growing use of the Eng. language, and Eng. education, which has evolved a certain common outlook amongst the increasing products of the universities, have brought about a great increase in material prosperity, but have also profoundly affected Indian thought. World movements acting on the dawning sense of nationality in India have effected an intellectual revolution. They have produced certain malignant forces, such as the outbreak of anarchism, but also certain healthy forces such as the desire for progress and larger powers of self-government. The years 1914 and 1915 were comparatively peaceful. In the latter year, however, the Lahore Conspiracy Case revealed a plot for upsetting the government, probably instigated by Germany. In the spring of 1916 Lord Hardinge was succeeded by Lord Chelmsford. During the year the foundation stone of the Hindu university at Benares was laid. In 1917 the political truce which had been observed since the war commenced was broken. In Madras in particular, Mrs. Annie Besant entered upon a campaign of active criticism against the government, with the result that her liberties and those of her two most active supporters were restricted. The excitement thus caused was allayed by the official announcement that the goal of the imperial government in India was the attainment of full self-government within the empire, and that while Parliament would be the judge of the time and place of the steps to this end, substantial measures would be taken without delay. Mr. Montagu, secretary of state for India, visited the country during the year, and in Nov., 1918, Parliament duly endorsed his proposals.

The outstanding historical incident since that time has been the series of disturbances in the Bombay Presidency, in Delhi, and in the Punjab in April, 1919. The most serious outbreaks occurred at Amritsar, where rioting and the murder of a number of Europeans took place. On the afternoon of April 13, Brigadier-general Dyer, with a small force, opened fire upon a dense crowd in a confined space, with the result that 379 persons were killed and probably three times as many wounded. A commission, with Lord Hunter at the head, was appointed in October, 1919, to investigate, and its report was published as a parl. paper on May 27, 1920. The majority report held that the outbreaks were acts of rebellion, as distinguished from mere riot and political opposition, partly due to resentment against the Rowlatt bills and to the Satya-Graha or civil disobedience movement started by Mr. Ghandi. They also held that the authorities were justified in declaring martial law, but that the action of General Dyer in starting firing without giving the assembled people time to disperse, and the continuance of the firing after the crowd had begun to disperse, was due to a mistaken conception of duty. The government of India endorsed this view, and also held that the administration of martial law in the Punjab was marred in certain instances by the misuse of power and injudicious and irresponsible acts largely due to the inexperience of the officers, combined with an absence of executive instructions for dealing with a situation so abnormal. Subsequently, upon the appeal of General Dyer, the War Council inquired into his case, generally concurring in the findings of the Hunter Commission. After an animated debate the House of Commons adopted the same view by a majority of 100, July 8, 1920.

The most important vernaculars (of which there are 147) of India are the Aryan (spoken by over 200,000,000 natives) and the Dravidian (spoken by 56,000,000), probably the indigenous speech. The former are the speeches of nearly all the tribes of N. India, the latter belong to the S. and the hill tribes of the center. The chief races are the Turko-Iranian of the N. (including the Afghans, Baluchi, and Brahui of Baluchistan and the N.W. Frontier Prov.), the Indo-Aryan of the Punjab, Rajputana, and Kashmir (represented by the Rajputs, Khatris, and Jats), the Scytho-Dravidian of the W. (represented by the Mahrattas and possibly by the Kunbis and Coorgs), the Aryo-Dravidian of Behar, the United Provinces, and parts of Rajputana (including Hindi), the Mongolo-Dravidian of Bengal and Orissa, the Mongoloid of the N. frontier, and the Dravidian of the Indo-Gangetic plain and the Central Provinces. The caste system of India is an extreme example of the differences in social rank always produced by foreign conquests; the tribes who conquered the original Dravidians must, however, have largely adopted their speech. According to the census there are in India 239,195,140 Hindus, 4,335,771 Sikhs, 1,252,105 Jains, 12,-786,806 Buddhists, 109,752 Parsis, 8,280,347 Animists, 77,677,545 Mohammedans, 24,141 Jews. Christians, in 1921, numbered 3,858,000. In 1930-31 there were 227,189 recognized schools having an enrollment of 12,056,837 students. Of these, 32,910 were for girls, with an enrollment of 1,389,241 with an additional 817,284 girls enrolled in boys' schools. Unrecognized schools totalled 34,879 with an enrollment of 632,249. The sixteen universities had 8,189 men students, 224 arts and science colleges for men had an enrollment of 65,291 and 20 similar schools for women had 1,546 students. There were 588 professional and training schools with a total of 42,097 men students and 230 such institutions for women with 7,068 students. There remains an enormous proportion of illiteracy. Many schools have been founded and maintained by Missionaries connected with the Christian Church. Newspapers are pub. in twenty-two dialects.

Government of India.—In 1858, an Act was passed transferring the government of India from the E. India Co. to the crown. This Act made no important change in the administration of India, but the gov-gen. became known as the viceroy. He is the sole representative of the crown in India, and is assisted by a council composed of high officials, each of whom is responsible for a special part of the administration. The distribution of functions between the government of India and the provincial administrations or states fluctuates; broadly speaking, it may be said that the tendency of the day is to confine the government of India to control, and the local governments to administration. The government of India retains in its own hands all matters relating to foreign relations, defence, general taxation, currency, debt, tariffs, post, telegraphs, and railways. The ordinary internal administration—the assessment and collection of revenue, education, medical and sanitary arrangements, and irrigation, buildings, and roads—falls within the purview of the local government. In all these matters the government of India exercises a general and constant control. It prescribes lines of general policy, and tests their application from the annual administration reports of the local authorities. It directly administers certain imperial departments, such as railways, post office, telegraphs, the survey of India, and geology. There is a wide field of appeal to the government from officials or private individuals who feel aggrieved by

the action of local governments. The supervision of the principal native states rests directly with the gov.-gen. in council, but local governments have also certain responsibilities.

To bring the administration into close touch with public opinion, the executive council was expanded in 1861, by additional members into a great legislative council, and the representative system was introduced in 1892. Further reforms were introduced in 1909, and the 1919 Act established an Indian legislature consisting of the viceroy and two chambers, the council of state, consisting of 60 members, of whom not more than 20 are officials, and the legislative assembly, containing 140 members, of whom 26 are official members. These chambers may sit jointly for the adjustment of differences. The term of office of the council of state is five years, and that of the legislative assembly three years, but dissolution may take place earlier, or the term may be extended by the viceroy, who has also the power, with the assent of the Brit. Parliament, of enacting certain measures against the wish of the council or assembly.

Provincial Governments.—British India is divided into eight large provinces and six lesser charges, each of which is termed a local government. The eight major provinces are the presidencies of Madras, Bombay, and Bengal; the lieut.-governorships of the United Provinces, the Punjab, Burma, and Behar; and the chief commissionerships of the Central Provinces. The minor provinces are Assam, the N.W. Frontier Province, Baluchistan, Coorg, Ajmere Merwara, and the Andaman Islands. The three presidencies occupy a superior position. The civil administration of each is vested in a governor-in-council appointed by the crown and assisted by a council of three members (two members of the civil service) and, under the Indian Councils Act of 1909, of a fourth who is usually an Indian. Lieut.-governors are appointed by the gov.-gen., and must have served for at least ten years in India. Chief commissioners are in theory delegates of the gov.-gen., but in practice have powers little short of lieut.-governors. The Act of 1909 more than doubled the number of members of the *provincial councils*. Election by specially constituted electorates was introduced, and power was given to members to debate and move resolutions on the provincial financial statements and on questions of general public interest, also to ask supplementary questions. The rules for discussion of the annual financial statement are similar to those applicable to the supreme council.

Local Administration.—The administrative system is based on repeated subdivision of territory, each administrative area being in the responsible charge of a member of the civil service who is subordinate to the officer next in rank above him. The most important of these units is the district, and India is divided into 250 districts, with an average area of 4,430 sq. m., and an average pop. of 931,000. The head of a district is styled the collector and district magistrate or the deputy commissioner. He is the representative of the government, and embodies the power of the state. He is concerned in the first place with the land and land revenue, and has magisterial powers. He also guides and controls the working of municipal government.

Local control over certain branches of the administration is secured by the constitution of local boards and municipalities, the former exercising authority over a dist. or taluka, and the latter over a city or town. These bodies are composed of members either nominated by government or elected by the people, who are empowered to expend funds derived from levies on the land revenue, tolls and ferries, on education, sanitation, the construction of roads and tanks, and general improvements. The tendency of recent years has been to increase the elective and reduce the nominated element.

India and World War.—The declaration of war was followed in India by unprecedented demonstrations of loyalty on all sides, and the numerous offers of help or personal service made by the chiefs and people aroused in Britain a feeling of intense gratitude. India was not included in the actual theater of war, except when Madras was subjected to a slight bombardment by the Ger. cruiser *Emden*, but up to Dec., 1914, shipping in the Bay of Bengal and in the Arabian Sea was on several occasions interfered with, and a number of vessels were sunk by enemy ships. Legislation was adopted prohibiting the activity of hostile trading firms, but a general exemption was issued in favor of companies which had no hostile foreigners as officers or merely had capital of amount less than one-third in enemy hands.

An exemption was also made on political grounds in favor of Asiatic subjects of Turkey. An Enemy Trading Ordinance was promulgated in June, 1916, similar in character to the Brit. Trading with the Enemy Act, but was very sparingly exercised. Interment was practiced in the case of less than 500 persons. The control and marketing of Ind. wheat was taken over by the government, and was successful in reducing Ind. prices to a safe level and placing at the disposal of the population of the U. K. the Ind. surplus.

In March, 1922, Mohandas Gandhi (*see* GANDHI), was arrested and sentenced to six years imprisonment for attempting to create ill-feeling in India, with the ultimate object of overthrowing the government. In pleading guilty, Gandhi requested "the highest penalty that can be inflicted upon me for what in law is a deliberate crime and what appears to me to be the highest duty of a citizen." In January, 1924, following an operation for appendicitis, he was released from prison, and returned to his people to find that he was no longer their leader.

For several years Gandhi remained in comparative seclusion, though constantly attempting to regain his lost prestige. Finally he was again the Mahatma ("Great Soul") to his people, and, in May 1930, his non-violent campaign led to his imprisonment in the Poona jail. While there, Gandhi, through mysterious communication with the outside world, not only retained but strengthened his hold on his followers. In January, 1931, he was released.

In February, 1931, Gandhi conversed with Viceroy Irwin and a "truce" pact was drawn up. A group of Indian Communists in Karachi accused Gandhi of betraying India by his pact with the Viceroy, but he calmed them by his threat: "The day that my inner voice tells me my country no longer needs me I will starve myself to death."

At the same time Gandhi's power was threatened at the 45th Congress of the Indian Nationalist Party by the younger element in the party which demanded violent resistance and blamed him for the hanging of three Indians at the hand of British Justice. However, all opposition was withdrawn when Gandhi again delivered his starvation ultimatum. The Irwin-Gandhi truce was promptly ratified and Gandhi was appointed to head the delegation to a Second Indian Round Table Conference in London.

Prior to Gandhi's release riots became general, particularly in Bombay, Calcutta and Rangoon. The Peshawur country was attacked by Afridi tribesmen from the Himalayan foothills and were subdued only through air raids by British planes.

During August, the Simon commission completed its investigation and presented its report reaffirming self-government as the goal of British policy; suggesting an elastic all-India Federation with as much local autonomy as possible; and, advising the separation of Burma from India—a sort of "United States of India" under the British Crown. The Maharaja of Bikanir stated, immediately following the report, that the rulers of the native states would support a dominion constitution if these states could be assured of equality with British India.

In November of 1930, the Indian Round Table Conference at London convened to determine the destiny of 350,000,000 people of conflicting racial strains and religious beliefs, 222 languages, and 2,300 castes and sub-castes. Also, there were more than 500 autonomous states to be considered.

There were 86 delegates at the conference—57 from British provinces, 16 from the autonomous Indian States, and 13 members of the British Parliament.

At the close of the Conference, Premier MacDonald summed up the outstanding points:

"1. Amnesty for India's 50,000 political prisoners, if civil order is restored in India.

"2. An invitation to the Indian extremists to participate in the negotiations still to come, before the new Indian Government is established.

"3. Establishment of full responsible self-government in India, with the Imperial British Government reserving control of finance, foreign affairs and defense.

"4. Extension of the voting franchise in India, and the lifting of restrictions based on religion and caste.

"5. Establishment of a Legislature of the two Houses modeled along the lines of the Congress of the United States.

"6. Encouragement of Indians to settle their own commercial problems.

"7. Uninterrupted continuance of negotiations to settle the details of the new government.' '

However, it is not considered that the outcome of the conference was very encouraging. The India of today demands more than mere promises.

Late in January, 1931, Viceroy Irwin completely reversed his theories concerning treatment of the Nationalist leaders. He ordered the release of all principals, including Mahatma Gandhi, who immediately continued his "non-violent" campaign.

Viceroy Irwin and Gandhi finally agreed, late in February, to discuss the situation. Irwin promised (1) immediate modification of the laws constituting the British salt monopoly in India, and (2) release from jail of many of Gandhi's followers. Gandhi (1) pledged the Indian National Congress to call off "civil disobedience" and the boycott on British goods; (2) waived his demands for investigations of "police atrocities," for remission of fines collected in connection with "civil disobedience," and for release of native soldiers and policemen jailed for mutiny and disobedience; and (3) agreed to stop all "aggressive picketing" by Nationalists.

Six thousand delegates had gathered in Karachi for the 45th Congress of the Indian Nationalist Party. It was rumored that Gandhi was drawing near his Waterloo. The party's younger element led by Subhas Chandra Bose, Mayor of Calcutta, and Pandit Jawarhabal Nehru, retiring President of the Congress, demanded violent resistance to the British. This group was further incited by the hanging at Lahore of Bhagat Singh, Sukh Dev, and Raj Guru. Gandhi was blamed by his opponents for the execution of these men at the hands of British Justice.

A stirring oration by Nebru opened the Congress. With burning words he was swaying the crowd when Gandhi suddenly appeared. As if by magic, opposition seemed to leave the minds of people; the speaker stopped and later announced his withdrawal of all opposition to the Mahatma. Mayor Bose likewise withdrew his opposition before the next meeting of the delegates, and Gandhi had again stated his "starvation ultimatum." The Irwin-Gandhi truce was soon ratified by unanimous vote, and Gandhi was appointed to head the Congress delegation at the Second Indian Round Table Conference to be held in London.

Lord Willingdon—formerly Governor of Bombay, Governor of Madras, and Governor-General of Canada succeeded Viceroy Irwin, April, 1931.

During 1932-33 much friction was again manifested when Gandhi, still campaigning for justice for his 40;-000,000 Untouchables, began another fast. He broke it after 6 days when the Hindus and Untouchables worked out a compromise, satisfactory to him and approved by the British government.

After the Third Round Table Conference in March, 1933, a plan was announced whereby the British govment and the divergent Hindu states, castes and sects hoped to find harmony. This was the new Indian Federal Constitution which, however, could not become effective until the various Princes accepted its provisions and a sound, non-political reserve bank had been established.

INDIA, FRENCH.—The Fr. possessions in India comprise Pondicherry, Chandernagore, Karikal, Mahe, and Yanaon; administered by the governor of Pondicherry.

INDIA, PORTUGUESE. — The Port. possessions in India comprise Diu, Damao, and Goa. Area, 1,638 sq. miles.

INDIA RUBBER. See RUBBER.

INDIAN CORN. See CORN, INDIAN.

INDIAN INK. See INK.

INDIAN MUTINY, Rebellion of nat. of Bengal, 1857. The immediate

THE TAJ MAHAL, INDIA

cause of outbreak is supposed to have been the introduction into the army of cartridges, greased with cows' and pigs' fat, the handling of which was abhorrent both to Hindus and Muhammedans; but discontent with British rule had long been gaining ground. After several slight outbreaks early in the year the mutiny began in earnest, with the revolt of the native regiments at Meerut, in May, 1857, when the Sepoys murdered the Eng. officers and massacred European residents; the mutineers then marched towards Delhi, which they captured and retained for four months.

In July occurred the terrible massacre of English at Cawnpore by the Nana, whom Havelock defeated on the following day; on Sept. 14, Delhi was at last stormed and taken by English; and Lucknow, which at first was defended by Sir Henry Lawrence, was partially relieved by Havelock in Sept., 1857, and in Nov. by Sir Colin Campbell (afterwards Lord Clyde), who finally captured it in July, 1858.

Others who distinguished themselves during the mutiny were Lord Canning, Gov.-Gen., who conducted affairs in Calcutta; Sir John Lawrence, who enlisted support of Sikhs and contributed greatly to Brit. success by sending large contingent to Delhi; General Outram, who served under Havelock; General Nicholson, killed in storming of Delhi; and Sir Hugh Rose, who conducted campaign in Central India, and by his capture of Jhansi and other positions practically ended the war. On re-establishment of Brit. authority, a royal proclamation announced that the governing power of the East India Company was abolished, and that henceforth the sovereign of England would be supreme ruler of India.

INDIAN OCEAN (c. 4° N., 75° E.), bounded W. by Africa, N. by Asia, E. by Australia and Malay Archikpelago; divided in N. by Ind. Peninsula into Bay of Bangal (E.) and Arabian Sea (W.); mean depth, c. 2,300 fathoms; area, c. 17,320,300 sq. miles; receives many important rivers from Asiatic continent; chief islands are Madagascar, Mauritius, Réunion, and Comoro Islands.

INDIAN RESERVATIONS, territory set aside for the exclusive use of Indians by the United States Government. This practice was begun even in colonial days, by Massachusetts, Connecticut, and Rhode Island, the terms of the treaties usually being that in exchange for the greater part of their hunting lands the Indians would be left unmolested in more restricted territory, and receive annual allowances in the form of clothing, provisions and other means of livelihood, to take the place of their loss of hunting grounds. After the Revolution, this policy was pursued by the Federal Government, notably in the allocation of Indian Territory to the five 'civilized tribes,' the Cherokees, Seminoles, Creeks, Choctaws, and Chickasaws. Many evils followed in the wake of this policy; the Indians were demoralized by Government support, and there was constant aggression on the part of white settlers to obtain land in the reservations with the most fertile soil, the Government often being obliged to send out troops to drive out squatters. The Dawes Act, passed by Congress, in 1887, marked a change in this policy, by providing for individual ownership of land by the Indians, together with a program of popular education and assistance in agricultural enterprise. This course has been slowly pursued with success, and at the present time the area of Indian reservations has been considerably reduced. In 1930 the Indian population of the U. S. was 170,350 males and 162,047 females. It has been estimated that in 1492 there were 846,000 Indians. Oklahoma has the largest Indian pop., 92,725 with Arizona second with 43,726.

INDIAN TERRITORY, an area of about 30,000 sq. miles, which had been set apart as an Indian reservation, in 1834, with Kansas on the N., Missouri and Arkansas on the E., and Texas on the S. and W. After the Civil War, when the West was being settled, strong pressure was brought to bear on the Government to open this section up to settlement, and finally, in 1889, it was decided to purchase that part known as Oklahoma from the indians and declare it open for settlement. The rest of the territory remained closed, but in 1894, Congress authorized a survey, the country being until then almost unknown. It was inhabited by what were known as 'the five civilized tribes,' the Cherokees, Chickasaws, Choctaws, Creeks and Seminoles. Federal appropriations for the Indian Service for 1932 amounted to $25,612,046 and $3,415,046 from tribal funds, making a total of $29,027,092. The appropriations for 1933 were $4,860,271 less than the amount appropriated for 1932.

Oklahoma has far more Indians than any other state with Arizona ranking second. The discovery of oil on Indian property in Oklahoma in 1929 has made many of them independently wealthy.

INDIANA, N. central state of U.S. 39° 46' N., 86° 20' W.), lying between Lake Michigan and the Ohio R.—which constitutes S. boundary line — and

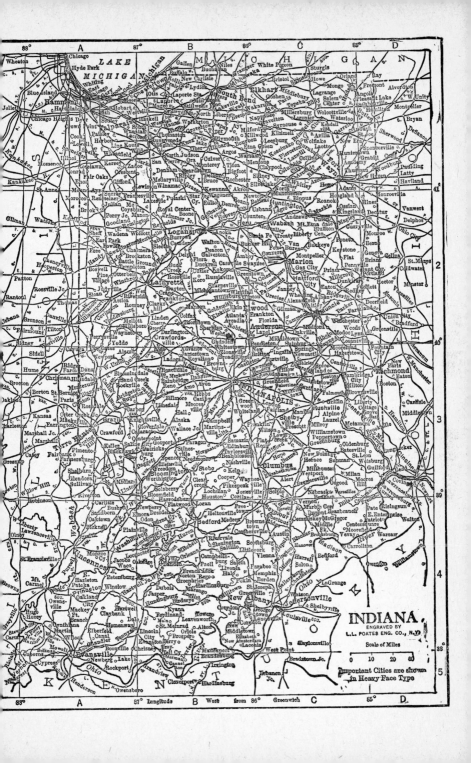

INDIANA

ENGRAVED BY
L.L. POATES ENG. CO., N.Y.

Scale of Miles

Important Cities are shown
in Heavy Face Type

bounded N. by lake and state of Michigan, E. by Ohio, S. and S.E. by Kentucky, and W. by Illinois. The cap. is Indianapolis. The surface is mostly undulating prairie, with a gentle S. slope, and having a range of sand-hills in the N.; S. of this the country is flat and marshy with shallow lakes; and along the Ohio R., in S., a chain of hills ('Knobs') rises steeply.

The most important river is the Wabash, a trib. of the Ohio, and measuring over 500 m., of which c. 350 are navigable; it is the boundary between Indiana and Illinois; other rivers are the Kankakee (trib. of the Illinois), and the St. Joseph and Elkhart into Lake Michigan, the Maumee into Lake Erie, and White Water into the Ohio. English Lake (part of the Kankakee) is the only large lake. See Map of U. S.

The climate is equable; the soil—excepting sandy region S. of Lake Michigan—is exceedingly fertile, especially the Wabash valley. The state coalfields have an area of about 6,500 sq. m.; petroleum, natural gas, sandstone, limestone, and cement are worked. The land is largely agricultural—the chief crops being corn, wheat, oats, hay, and potatoes; tobacco is also grown, as well as fruits and vegetables of all varieties. Manufactures and industries are important, and include clay working, flour, and grist milling, slaughtering and meat packing, iron and steel foundries, as well as woolen works and manufacturing of agricultural implements. Indianapolis is an important center for live stock. Natural facilities for transport are provided by the Ohio and Wabash rivers and Lake Michigan; there are extensive railways. Admitted to the Union as state in 1816. Legislature consists of senate (50 members) and house of representatives (100 members); two senators and 13 representatives go to Congress. Area, 36,354 sq. m. (including 309 sq. m. of water).

INDIANA, a borough of Pennsylvania, in Indiana co. It is an important industrial community, and has glass works, tanneries, lumber, and flour mills. It has also important coal mining interests. It is the seat of a State Normal School.

INDIANA, UNIVERSITY OF.— Founded in 1820, it was opened in 1824 as the Indiana Seminary, and adopted the name of college in 1827, and university in 1838. Since 1867 it has been co-educational. The tuition is free, a board of trustees making reports biennially. The courses include, languages, science, and history; the degrees, Ph.D., and A.M., being conferred for graduate work. Law and medical schools are attached, and a biological station is maintained at Winona Lake. President, 1933, W. L. Bryan. Students, 4,550, faculty, 322.

INDIANAPOLIS, a city of Indiana, the capital of the State, and the county seat of Marion co. It is the largest and most important city of Indiana, and in the geographical center of manufactures in the U. S. It is on 16 railroads, and on the White River. The city has an area of 51 sq. miles. It is situated on both sides of the river, but chiefly on the E. bank. The two parts of the city are connected by several bridges. Indianapolis, on account of its situation, is preeminently an industrial city. It has exceptional shipping facilities and is near ample fuel supplies. There are approximately 850 manufacturing establishments, and nearly 4,300 retail concerns. In addition to these, there are over 300 wholesale and jobbing houses which carry on extensive business with all parts of the Central West. One of the most important industries is slaughtering and meat packing. Over 3,000,000 head of livestock are received annually by the stock yards. Other industries of importance are automobiles and accessories, foundry, machine shop and metal trades, wearing apparel, food products, pharmaceuticals and furniture. The city is well laid out and has nearly 800 miles of improved streets. There are over 500 miles of sewers and nearly 500 miles of water mains. The city is maintained on a high standard of government. It is the seat of many important State institutions, including the State Institute for the Blind, a school for the deaf, Indiana Girls' School, Indiana Women's Prison, and Central Hospital for the Insane. It is also the seat of the School of Medicine of Indiana University, and of the Indiana University Extension Center. It has one of the finest libraries in the U. S., which contains nearly 225,000 volumes. There is also an excellent State Library and Museum in the State House. The school system has a high order of merit. There are about 90 public school buildings, over 30 of which are equipped with manual training and domestic science courses. In addition to these there are about 20 Catholic parochial schools, two academies for young women, and three Catholic institutions for boys. Other educational institutions are Butler College, Indiana Central University, College of Music and Fine Arts, and many private schools for boys and girls. The city has several excellent hospitals and many handsome office buildings, theatres and apartment houses. Indianapolis was settled in 1819, and was given its present name in 1821. It became the capital of the State in 1825. From the introduction of natural gas as fuel, in 1889, its growth was remarkably rapid.

INDIANS, AMERICAN, OR RED, were called Indians by British as being inhabitants of what the early discoverers of America believed to be the W. Indies, but are known to most nations as Red-skins (*e.g.*, Fr. *Peaux-rouges*). They are confined to the Amer. continent, and now generally believed to be a Mongolian people separated from Asia by the comparatively recent subsidence of the 'Pacific continent.' In the convenient approximation to racial division of the classification Black, Brown (or Red), Yellow, and White, they constitute the Brown group (see RACES OF MANKIND). The Palæolithic remains show early habitation. The numerous tribes may be divided into these main stocks: (1) N. America: Algonquin, Athabascan, Eskimo, Iroquois, Muskhogean, Pawnee, Pueblo, Salish, Shoshone, Siouan; (2) Central America: Cuna, Lencan, Maya-Quichè, Mixtec, Nahuan, Opata-Pima; (3) S. America: Antisuyu, Araucan, Arawak, Aymara, Bororo, Botocudo, Carib, Chibcha, Chiquito, Choco, Chuncho, Fuegian, Jivaro, Mataco, Pano, Payagua, Puelche, Quichua, Tehuelche, Ticuna, Toba, Tupi-Guarani, Warrau, Zaparo. The largest remaining tribes are the Sioux, Cherokees, Choctaws, and Creeks. Over 60 different languages, all polysynthetic, have been recorded in N. America.

At present there are about six million Indians in N. America, Mexico and Central America, about 4½ million in S. America, in both cases including half-breeds, of which there are about 1½ million in S. America, where, however, the estimate of the Ind. population is only a rough one, owing to the amount of almost unexplored forest region. The half-breeds of N. America belong chiefly to the 'Five Civilized Tribes,' of whom *c.* 60,000 (*i.e.*, two-thirds) are pure Indians. Excluding Alaska, there are about 300,000 pure Indians in the U.S., mostly resident in Ind. reservations (tracts of land set apart for their habitation), the chief being in Arizona, S. Dakota, Montana, and Oklahoma. Alaska has *c.* 30,000 Indians. The very few Indians who have abandoned their tribes in the U.S. pay taxes but have no political rights. The Indians of Arizona and New Mexico, who are U.S. citizens by treaty, exercise no political rights, and have so far shown no political interest. The total Indians of Canada are *c.* 111,000. The various estimates of the numbers of Indians vary, but seldom fall below the figures given above. The various stocks are characterized by copper-colored skin, lank black hair, high cheek bones, long, deep-set eyes, and powerful, often aquiline noses. They vary in stature and development, the finest specimens being found among the Patagonians of S. America and the Iroquois, Pawnees, and Sioux of the U.S. and Canada.

Before they were ousted by Europeans they were skilled hunters, trained observers, of extraordinarily acute senses, capable of enduring without a murmur great hardships and torture, which they freely employed on others, and they have never shown any liking for European comforts or any sympathy with European ideals. Most of them were still in the Stone Age when Columbus landed. Iron seems never to have been known to the makers of the old civilizations of Peru and Mexico. The Indians are of the utmost importance for the study of primitive institutions and religions, and this importance has been recognized in late years by a growing number of students. The matriarchate was common, if not universal, and at the close of the XVIII. cent. European commissioners still found that the tribe was to be treated with through its head women; polygamy is rare, monogamy the rule; the chieftainship was very rarely hereditary, the strongest man of the tribe being chosen by varying systems of election. The 'medicine-men'—*i. e.*, magicians—have great power. Their tales of the Creation are interesting as giving prominence to the Deluge. Their well-known belief in a future happy hunting-ground seems widely spread, but is not universal. The ghosts of the dead take animal forms or appear as skeletons or unsubstantial bodies, and may inflict harm on the living. Many tribes believe in reincarnation as human beings. In their creed is a strong element of animism, but over all deities and spirits is 'Atiuch' or the 'Father' or 'Manito,' to whom alone direct prayer is offered. He is sometimes conceived as the sun. Corn is worshipped, credited with miraculous powers, and named the 'Mother.'

Reverence for certain animals, the white eagle, beaver, buffalo, etc., is seen in the curiously picturesque names of chieftains and braves—White Bear, Many Horses, Buffalo Ribs—and in names of women, such as White Antelope.

In the XVII. and XVIII. cents. the British and French were continual rivals for the favor of the Indians, and the dispatches of Eng. colonial governors to the home government often express admiration of Fr. methods of dealing with the natives. There were 'friendly' or Brit. Indians and Fr. Indians. The early colonists lived in constant dread of the

'Indian peril,' and the state of New York was particularly exposed until Fr. alliance with the Algonquins led to the Iroquois becoming firm friends of the British. These two peoples played an important part in the history of N. America. The Iroquois inhabited the district round St. Lawrence R. and the Great Lakes, part of New York state, and lands in Virginia, the Carolinas, and Georgia. Their tribes included the federation formed by Hiawatha, important in Brit. colonial history as the Five Nations, which became Six Nations by the accession of the Tuscaroras. The Cherokees of this stock were the chief tribe with which the Carolinas and Virginia had to deal in the XVIII. cent. They were transferred bodily to the other side of the Mississippi in 1838. The Iroquois, however, by their bitter enmity to the French in Canada, did much towards the establishment of Brit. N. America. The Athabascan tribes were of great importance in western N. America; the Apaches and Navajos are said to be able to run down the deer while hunting, and the grim, mysterious, and skilled Apache has given his name to the Parisian thug, while Navajo blankets are widely known. The Siouan tribes formerly spread over the N. and center of the present U.S. To this stock belonged the now extinct tribe of Catawbas, prominent in the history of S. Carolina, and it includes the Assiniboines and famous Dakotas, or confederate Sioux, who were allies of the British in the XVIII. cent.

The Sioux, roused by a religious prophet, gave much trouble in the late XIX. cent. General Custer was slain by a force under Sitting Bull while invading Sioux territory, in 1876, but they were put down by Sheridan, and in 1889, sold 11,000,000 ac., parcel of the Dakota reservation, to the U.S. A rising in Badlands, S. Dakota, followed immediately after, 1890, other tribes joined and the Indians laid waste surrounding territory. Before the close of the year General Miles's forces captured and slew Sitting Bull, his son, Crow Foot, etc. A small heroic band under Big Foot sought to revenge Sitting Bull's death, but were exterminated at Wounded Knee Creek, 1890; further forces surrendered to Crook and Miles, 1891. Risings of the Chippewa, 1892, and Navajo, 1893, followed. Unrest ceased with the union of Ind. Terr. and Okla., 1907. See IND. RESERVATIONS and IND. TERRITORY.

INDICATOR, an instrument for recording diagrammatically on a card the behavior of steam in the cylinder of an engine. The piston is connected with a lever, the end of which carries a pencil (usually a brass point) for making the diagram. The actual movement of the piston is magnified in the diagram. The indicator card (of metal) is wrapped round a drum, which is made to oscillate on its axis, being connected with the crosshead of the engine by a cord passing round a groove at its base. Various springs serve to adjust the indicator cylinder to varying conditions. The expansion and compression curves thus obtained are in the form of rectangular hyperbolas.

INDICTMENT, the charges preferred in writing for offenses in law punishable upon summary conviction, or after trial by jury, constitute an I, and the counts of an I, are its several parts, charging distinct offenses. Indictable offenses must be tried before a jury and the accusation must be set down in writing.

INDIES, LAWS OF THE, name applied either to Span. colonial law code in general, or to the special codes of certain colonies.

INDIGESTION, see DIGESTION.

INDIGO is a dye-stuff which exists in the leaf of plants of genus *Indigofera,* natural order *Leguminosæ,* as a glucoside *indican,* $C_{14}H_{17}O_6N_3H_2O$. An enzyme in the leaf acting on a water extract of the colorless glucoside in presence of atmospheric oxygen gives indigotine, the coloring matter of indigo. About one-half per cent indigo is obtained from leaves and after evaporation sold as 3-in. cubes. A 20 per cent paste made by melting the carboxylic acid of phenylglycocoll with caustic alkalies has supplanted the natural Indian product.

INDIGO BIRD (*Cyanospiza cyanea*), a small bird of the finch family, native of the U. S. A. It is about 5½ in. long, the adult male of a beautiful blue color, whilst the female and young are of a bluish grey. It has a sweet song, something like a canary, and frequents open spaces.

INDIUM. — In. Atomic Weight, 114.8. A metal belonging to the aluminum group, and first discovered in 1863, by Reich and Richter in zinc blende. It is a white metal, softer than lead and easily malleable. It is not affected by air or by moisture. It has a specific gravity of 7.1 and a melting point of 155° C. It can be obtained from the oxide by reduction in a current of hydrogen, or by fusion with sodium, or it can be prepared electrolytically from solutions of the chloride, nitrate or sulphate. It dissolves slowly in hydrochloric and dilute sulphuric acid, but rapidly in nitric acid. When heated on charcoal in the blowpipe, it gives a blue coloration to the flame and forms an incrustation of oxide. It combines with selenium and tellurium, forming black metallic masses.

INDIVIDUALISM, view that governmental interference with conduct of individual citizens should be jealously restrained; opposed to collectivism and socialism.

INDO-ARYAN LANGUAGES, important group of seven languages—Hindi, Marāthi, Bangāli, Panjābi, Gujrāti, Sindhi, Uriya—belonging to Indo-European family. All descended from Sanskrit (*q.v.*), to which they bear same relation as European Romance languages to Latin, and from which principal portion of vocabulary and whole inflectional system are derived. Usual theory is that they arose from Prakrits, or local dialectical forms of Aryan speech (Sanskritic and non-Sanskritic), which received great stimulus from adoption as medium of Buddhist teaching.

Three classes of materials entered into formation of Indo-Aryan languages: (1) *Tatsama*, words unaltered from pure classical Sanskrit; (2) *Tadbhava*, words Sanskrit and Prākrit, much changed in process of derivation; (3) *Desaja*, words obtained by contact with aboriginal and other races conquered by Indian Aryans.

In first few cent's. A.D., change took place from synthetic to analytical. Alphabets employed are all varieties of Devanāgari (Sanskrit). Most important of seven languages is Hindi, which, written in pure Devanāgari, spoken by *c.* 100,000,000, understood throughout N. India, bids fair to become national language. There are two varieties of Hindi, western and eastern, Hindustani (*q.v.*), being dialect of former.

Distribution.—Hindi, United Prov., Central Prov., C. India, Panjab, etc.; Bengāli, 50 millions, Bengal;, Panjābi, 17 millions, Panjab; Marāthi, 19 millions, Bombay, Haidarabad, C. Prov.; Gujrāti, 10 millions, Bombay, Baroda; Uriya, 10 millions, Orissa; Sindhi, 3 millions, Sind.

INDO-CHINA, Fr., general term for Fr. colonial possessions in S.E. peninsula of Asia (8° 30'-23° 25' N., 100°-109° 20' E.); consists of five states—the colony of Cochin-China, protectorates of Annam, Cambodia, Tongking, and Laos—and Kwang-Chau. Was leased from China for 99 years, 1898, in addition to territory around Battambang ceded by Siam, 1907. Area, *c.* 277,504 sq. m.; pop., 21,599,582, of whom 23,700 are Europeans. The region is under a gov.-gen., and each state has a resident superior or lieutenant-governor for executive purposes, except Cochin-China, which being a direct Fr. colony has a governor at its head. In 1887 further

unity was imparted to Indo-China, when Annam, Tongking, and Cambodia, were united into a customs union; but financial and political unity was not established until 1898. The principal exports are rice, products of fisheries, maize, cotton yarn, pepper, coal, hides, rubber, and sugar. There are about 1,000 m. of railway open, and goods can go direct from Haipong to Yün-nan, 538 m. The beginning of French influence in S.E. Asia may be traced to missionary efforts, begun in XVII. cent. in Siam, whence they spread to Tongking and Annam. The revolution in France retarded progression, and it was not till 1861-2 that French became masters of principal part of Cochin-China. In 1882, the third republic resolved upon a highly aggressive policy, and from that year the French steadily pressed their conquests until they possessed all the country E. of the Mekong. See Map of S. Asia.

INDO - EUROPEAN LANGUAGES are a group of languages with certain characteristics in common, and otherwise called Aryan, or Indo-Germanic. The following are the Indo-European languages: A., the so-called *Centum* group—(1) Greek, (2) Italic, (3) Celtic, (4) Germanic or Teutonic (including Swedish, Danish, Norwegian, Icelandic, English Frisian, Dutch, Flemish, German); B., the so-called *Satem* group—(1) Aryan (including Sanskrit, Zend, and Old Persian), (2) Armenian, (3) Balto-Slavonia group (including Old Bulgarian, Russian, Servian, Polish), (4) Albanian.

The resemblances between these languages of Europe and Asia force on our attention the problem of their hist. connection, their relation to the original language, and the original land of the parent race. Round these problems there have been long and divers controversies. Some claim the East as the orignal home of the languages; others claim the West; the claims for the East being older. The obviously great antiquity of the language of the Hindus was the basis on which the theories of an Eastern origin were built. Linguistic evidence seemed to point to Central Asia as the original home of the parent race. But claims began to be put forward for Europe, and various tracts were suggested as the original home, *e.g.*, South Russia, West Germany, the region of the Baltic, and Scandinavia.

The inhabitants of Europe may be divided into two distinct classes—the dolichocephalic and the brachycephalic, and the pivot of the problem is ultimately which of these two classes is the Aryan. Modern opinion seems to favor the dolichocephalic race; or, to be more exact, European civilization and culture are regarded as derived from the Aryan race, the tall, fair, dolichocephalic peoples most purely represented today by the English, Germans, and Scandinavians. This theory is technically called Aryanism.

INDONESIAN, Indo-inhabitants to be found in Malaysia, etc.

INDORE (22° 42′ N.; 75° 54′ E.); native state, Central India; consists of various isolated tracts; capital, Indore; commercial centre.

INDORSEMENT, ENDORSEMENT, writing on back (Lat. *dorsum*) of document as descriptive, or, in case of money, as quit claim, the possessor becoming owner.

INDO-SCYTHIANS, Asiatic races of N. India.

INDRA, Hindu deity represented as covered with eyes and riding on an elephant.

INDRE (46° 50′ N.; 1° 30′ E.), department, Central France, formed principally from ancient province Berry; surface flat; watered by the Indre; produces cereals, fruit, wine; capital, Châteauroux.

INDRE-ET-LOIRE (47° 16′ N.; 0° 45′ E.), department, Central France, formed principally from ancient province Touraine; produces grain, fruits, wine; capital, Tours.

INDUCTION, in logic, the process of reasoning from particular instances to a general law; the opposite of *Deduction* (*q.v.*).

INDUCTION. — Electrification or magnetization may be produced in a body merely by its proximity to a charged or magnetized object. Electric currents may be set up in a closed circuit by changing the intensity or direction of a magnetic field in the vicinity. Such phenomena are called induction.

To illustrate.—If a charged body, *A*, be brought close to an object, *B*, which is not charged, a charge is *induced* on *B*. Those parts, *B*, which are closest to *A* acquire a charge opposite in kind (sign) to that originally present on *A*, while the more remote parts of *B* hold a charge similar to the original. When the bodies are separated the induced charge disappears. Similarly, if a bar of magnetizable material be held close to one pole of a magnet, the bar becomes magnetized, the ends acquiring opposite polarities. The end nearer the magnet is of polarity opposite that of the adjacent pole (of the magnet). If the material of the bar is such that it does not easily retain magnetism, its magnetic properties disappear when it is moved away from the magnet.

If a magnet be plunged into the center of a coil of wire, the ends of which are connected, a current will flow in one direction on the coil while the magnet is being inserted into the coil, and in the other direction while the magnet is being withdrawn. If an electro-magnet is used, currents may be *induced* in the wire by allowing the magnet to remain stationary in or near the wire while the strength of the magnet is varied. When the strength is being increased, currents will flow in the coil in one direction, and in the other direction while the intensity of the magnetic field is being decreased. While the magnetic field remains constant no currents are *induced* in the coil.

INDUCTION COILS utilize the principle of electro-magnetic induction to convert a low potential uni-directional current into a high potential oscillating current. They consist of a core of soft iron wires, on which are wound two coils of wire, one primary and one secondary, and a means of rapidly making and breaking the primary coil circuit. The primary is usually wound next the core and consists of comparatively few turns of heavy wire; the size and the number of turns depend on the voltage to be applied to, and the voltage to be produced by, the coil.

The secondary coil is composed of a very large number of turns of extremely fine wire, usually wound in sections. These, while separated by good insulation, are wired together so as to form one continuous winding. The interrupter which makes and breaks the primary circuit usually consists of a light iron armature, so placed as to be attracted by the core when it becomes magnetized. This armature carries a platinum or silver contact which rests normally against a similar fixed contact, but is drawn away from it when the armature is attracted by the core. The contacts are in series with the primary circuit, and complete it until the current magnetized the core which attracts the armature thus breaking the circuit. This demagnetizes the core, thereby releasing the armature and again completing the circuit through the contacts. As long as the battery is connected this action continues with great rapidity.

Every time the circuit is made a magnetic field is generated which cuts the secondary coil inducing in it a current in one direction. When the circuit is broken the field is destroyed which induces a current in the secondary in the reverse direction. These coils are extensively used in the operation of X-ray tubes, ignition systems, and wireless telegraphy transmitters.

INDUCTION MOTORS.—This name designates that type of alternating current motors in which currents are induced in the windings on the rotor of the motor. These in turn generate the magnetic fields necessary to produce rotation. These motors consist of, 1st., a rotor made up of disks of laminated iron; in slots on their periphery are placed the rotor or secondary winding of copper wire; 2nd., a stator also composed of iron laminations with slots in their inner surface in which are placed the stator or primary windings. The winding on the latter is similar to that of an alternating current generator. The winding on the rotor may (A) be similar to that of the stator, with the ends connected to an external resistance through slip rings; the motor is then called a Wound Rotor Machine; (B) consist of copper bars in the slots referred to above, their ends connected by two rings of copper; in this case the motor is of the Squirrel Cage type. In polyphase motors, when the field is energized, the pulsating fields, generated by each phase combine to form a rotating field. This cuts the rotor windings, generating current in them, the reaction of which causes the rotor to follow the rotating field. The rotor must always lag a certain amount (called the slip), in order that the current may be generated in its windings. Single phase motors will not start themselves, but when started, the rotor windings generate a pulsating field which combines with that of the stator, resulting in a rotating field which produces the action noted above. There are two common methods of starting single phase motors: (1) 'shading coils' of high impedence, so wound on the stator as to produce an out-of-phase magnetic field, which combines with the main field to produce a rotating one; (2) the motor is started as a repulsion motor and after attaining a certain speed the brushes are lifted and the windings short-circuited by an automatic device.

INDULGENCE, in R.C. theology the remission of the temporal punishment which often remains due to sin after its guilt has been forgiven.' Pope Urban II. granted a plenary I. for the first crusade, 1095; and since then I's, plenary or partial, have been frequent. The abuse of I's was one of the signs of decay of the mediæval Church. According to the official R.C. view the Saints have done more than was necessary in expiation of their own sins, and the benefit of this can be transferred to others.

INDULINES are amidated azonium salts which dye blue, bluish-red, and black. Rosindulines and Napthindulines are basic. The salts give red fluorescent solutions.

INDULT (from Lat. *indulgere*, to permit), papal license for non-performance of religious duty.

INDUNA, Kaffir magnate.

INDUS (24° N., 67° 30' E.); river, India; rises in S.W. Tibet near sources of Sutlej; general course N.W. through Ladak, Kashmir, etc.; turns S.W. in N.W. Frontier Province, flows through Punjab and Sind, and enters Arabian Sea by numerous mouths; chief tributaries, Zanskar, Shayok, Kabul, and Punjnud (five united rivers); delta begins at Hyderabad (chief town); total length, 1,800 miles; navigation begins near Attock; drainage basin, 375,000 sq. miles; fish and crocodiles abound; subject to great floods.

INDUSTRIA (c. 45° 10' N.; 8° E.); ancient town, Liguria, Italy.

INDUSTRIAL CHEMISTRY. See CHEMISTRY, INDUSTRIAL.

INDUSTRIAL EDUCATION. See VOCATIONAL EDUCATION.

INDUSTRIAL SCHOOL, voluntary school for giving manual and commercial training to the poor.

INDUSTRIAL WORKERS OF THE WORLD, a labor organization based on 'industrial union' principles and on the theory of syndicalism. It was organized in Chicago, in 1905, by a group of radicals, discontented with the compromising spirit of the crafts unions. It differs from the latter in that organization is by industry, rather than by craft; it insists on a transfer system, enabling itinerant workers to join locals whenever they arrive in new locatities; low iniation fees and monthly dues; salary of officers not to exceed average wage of workers; no contracts or agreements are signed with employers; and no big union treasuries are sanctioned. It advocates the general strike as a weapon of offense and defense, and it stands unequivocally for the abolition of the capitalist system, for which is to be substituted what is called syndicalism; industries to be governed democratically by the workers themselves, each industry to be more or less autonomous. In 1917 the organization had a membership of about 100,000 recruited principally among the lumber workers of the N.W., the metal mine workers in the Rocky Mountain region and among the agricultural workers. It has conducted many important strikes, notably in Lawrence, Mass., among the textile workers, in 1911, and among the silk workers, in Paterson, N. J., in 1912, and in 1917, among the lumber workers in Washington, Idaho, and Montana. The Thirteenth Convention of the organization was held in Chicago, in May, 1921, and while there was no lessening of the spirit of militancy, by 1930 the membership had dwindled to a handful.

INDUSTRIAL MANAGEMENT, a science which has developed with the growth of large-scale industry. Formerly the manufacturer set up his manufacturing plant under his personal management and sold his goods on the open market, the result being largely a matter of chance. With increased output, personal supervision became less possible on the part of the individual owner, and scientific system became as imperative as in the administration of a state or municipality. There thus developed the 'efficiency engineer,' whose business it is to serve the large business enterprise in a consultative capacity, making periodical surveys of the business organization as an accountant examines the books. The science is divided into four main phases: (1) finance; (2) production; (3) selling; and (4) personnel, the latter being the human and most uncertain element. The first and second elements belong more properly to banking and applied science, and it is therefore that the marketing of goods and the personnel of the organization concern the efficiency engineer more deeply. The first, selling, has developed into a specialty involving a profound knowledge of the distributive processes of the economic system, as well as the psychology of the purchasing public, including that important aspect of it, advertising. In this latter field large, alaborately organized firms specialize separately, taking full charge of this phase of their business for many large corporations. Here the study of organs for publicity is conducted with the same intensive effort that the geologist studies rock formations. The other chief aspect of selling is salesmanship, which is usually carried on by each manufacturing corporation directly, but under the supervision of experts commanding large salaries. Art, or the personal equation, enters into this phase of the administration, rather than science, since it is the personality of the salesman which counts. The head of the sales force, therefore, requires a profound knowledge of human character, not only in picking out the best salesmen, but in choosing the proper raw material from which qualified salesmen may be trained. It is in the fourth phase of Industrial Management, personnel, that

the efficiency engineer has the widest scope for the exercise of his profession. This phase may again be divided into two aspects; the psychology of the workers, from the office boy up to the factory foreman; and the arrangement of their labor to the highest point of economy. In the employment bureau of the large corporation which has adopted the up-to-date methods of industrial management, applicants for positions are subjected to long series of psychological tests, from which it is possible, first, to judge whether the applicant is fitted for the work, and, secondly, for what kind of work in the establishment he is most fitted. Studies are also made of the many thousands of movements made on the part of the workers, with the object of eliminating unnecessary effort. This latter phase has at times been carried to such extreme as to defeat its own object, the workers themselves reacting against the system. Another contributing element is the initiation of welfare work among the employees of large establishments, for the psychological effect it has on the efficiency of their labor.

INDUSTRIES, NATIONALIZATION OF. See Bolshevism.

INDY, PAUL MARIE THÉODORE VINCENT D' (1851), Fr. composer, one of the leading musicians of the day, although, owing to choice of subjects, his music does not suit the popular taste so well as that of some of his contemporaries. Some of his works are *Le Chant de la Cloche, 1884; Ferval, 1897; Médee, 1898; Sauge Fleurei, 1907;* and a study of *Cesar Franck, 1907. d. 1932.*

INE, king of West Saxons fron 688 to 726; issued important code of laws.

INEBOLI (41° 57′ N., 33° 47′ E.), seaport, Asia Minor, on Black Sea; wool and mohair.

INFALLIBILITY, a theological term used of Pope, Church, or Bible, though for the last *Inspiration* is more commonly found. The doctrine of Papal I. is of gradual growth; defined by the Vatican Council of 1870. By this the Pope is infallible when he speaks on faith or morals *ex cathedra*, that is formally and finally as teacher of all Christians. Those who strongly defended this view were called *Ultramontane*: the rejection of it by a small minority led to the formation of the *Old Catholics*.

INFAMY, technical term among Rom. for publicity given to disgraceful conduct; in England legal state of a person once convicted of a crime.

INFANT, in law, means a person, male or female, under twenty-one years of age. In some legal systems, *e.g.* in those of Ohio, Kansas, and other of the United States, females cease to be Is. at eighteen. Infancy is an important status in the law, more especially in regard to contractual capacity, and responsibility for crime.

INFANTE, title of younger sons of kings of Spain and Portugal, eldest *s.* being called prince.

INFANTICIDE, a common crime in ancient Greece and Rome, and until comparatively recent times (in the matter of female infants) in China and India. It is a capital offense, and when the exposure or abandonment of a new-born child has resulted in death, and a verdict of wilful murder has been returned, the capital sentence is pronounced. But public opinion has long refused to sanction the hanging of a mother who in despair and distraction of mind has abandoned her illegitimate child, and the death sentence is always revised and imprisonment substituted.

INFANTILE PARALYSIS.— Otherwise known as Poliomyelitis. A disease which chiefly attacks young children, although there are occasional cases among adults. It affects the spinal cord and its membranes and sometimes the brain. It is infectious, especially in the early stages. Dr. Frederick Eberson, Assistant Clinical Professor of Medicine at the University of California, announced that he had isolated the germ of infantile paralysis. It is a minute organism, reproducable through several generations of its life cycle. The disease gains access through the nasal passages. It occurs mainly in temperate zones, and appears as widespread epidemics usually during the summer and early fall, although winter epidemics have occurred. The early symptoms are vague. There is some gastro-intestinal disturbance, or mild respiratory trouble, with headaches, backaches, restlessness and irritability. In two or three days, local paralysis occurs, usually affecting the legs. There is acute inflammation of the spinal cord, causing swelling and pressure on the nerve structures. In very light cases, paralysis may be so slight as to be unnoticeable. In fact, it is believed that many cases go unrecognized, mild poliomyelitis being mistaken for intestinal disorder, and in such cases there is much danger of the disease being spread among other children who may develop the more serious symptoms. The disease reaches its acute stage, as a rule, within the first eight days, but recovery is usually slow. Comparatively little is known regarding the methods of treatment.

In 1933 Kramer announced immunized vaccine success., immunizing monkeys. The treatment of the resulting paralysis meets with varying degrees of success. In some cases, the lower limbs cease to develop and become practically lifeless, showing little or no improvement after years of treatment. In other cases a slow but steady improvement is noticed, and recovery may be practically complete. The treatment most favored is scientific exercising along lines which develop, in the patient, a conscious will to perform movements. Electrical treatment and massage are sometimes used, but are considered of little value by many authorities.

INFANT MORTALITY, term technically used to denote the number of infants who die within one year from birth and the proportion that these deaths bear to the death rate of the entire population. Stastistics in the United States are much less accurate on this subject than in many countries abroad. The different States vary in the strictness of their laws regarding these matters and the vigor with which they are enforced. In some states where excellent laws obtain, they are only in part obeyed. Reliance has to be placed therefore on records from a sufficient number of large cities, where, as a rule, the figures are fairly complete, and an average of which gives sufficient ground for generalization. It is known that about 2,500,000 babies are born in the United States every year. A much larger proportion of these die within the first year than in any other period of existence. They also die more frequently where the population is most dense. Some of the causes for the high infant mortality are premature birth, heredity, intemperance, too early marriage of parents, neglect, ignorance. lack of hygienic surroundings, and the many infantile diseases that break the babe's fragile hold on life. Of these causes, perhaps unsanitary conditions are the most fatal. Contrasting towns of the same State, Fall River and Lynn, Mass., the rate of infant mortality was 239.7 per thousand in the former, and only 140.7 per thousand in the latter. The first is overcrowded with tenement houses; the second has better buildings, larger open spaces, and the parents are engaged in healthier occupations.

In 1932, out of a population of 27,-703,149 in leading American cities, the total deaths were 312,047. Of these, the deaths under one year of age totaled 113,661. The death rate for infants is much greater among the colored people than among the white. In 1920, for instance, 82 white babies and 132 negro babies out of 1,000 of each color born, died in their first year of life. In New York City, the number per thousand dying before the expiration of the first year was 83 white and 157 colored.

A marked improvement in infant mortality is shown in the figures for 1921, where the total deaths in the same cities, though the population itself must have increased considerably in that period, were 327,550, while deaths under one year numbered 48,067. Part of this improvement is due to the housing laws which require a larger amount of air space in tenements; part to the conquests made by science in the treatment of infantile diseases, such as diphtheria, baby pneumonia, and scarlet fever; part to the efforts of health officers of various cities who have established educational centers for mothers on the subject of care of children, and part to the widespread discussion and suggestions in newspapers and magazines. It is too early as yet to assume what effect prohibition will have upon the figures of infant mortality, although it is known that hitherto intemperance on the part of either or both parents has had a most deleterious effect on the vitality of the new born and their chances for life.

INFANTRY. In its largest sense the word includes fighting men on foot of all kinds; in a narrower sense, regularly organized and disciplined foot soldiers. The earliest infantry were the tribal gatherings, and later the militia called to arms in war time for the defense of a state or city. The earliest regular infantry formed the m a i n strength of armies raised by the old empires of the Euphrates and Tigris region and the valley of the Nile. A monument of the former region, the stele of Enneatum in the Louvre, 5,000 years old, shows men armed with helmet, shield, and spear formed up in close order. The Greeks relied on civic militias, trained to athletic exercises as part of the ordinary education of the younger men, and sufficiently drilled to move in broad column with levelled spears in front. Philip of Macedon developed this formation into the phalanx, armed with long pikes, so that the weapons of three ranks projected from the front of the attacking column. But the mass had little manœuvring power, and was not adapted to meet a flank attack. The flanks of the phalanx were covered by more mobile, light-armed detachments. The Romans of the republican period, however, developed a new infantry organization and tactics which in a comparatively short time enabled them to defeat both the Gr. and the Carthaginian armies, which derived their infantry methods from Gr. mercenaries. The Roman legion was essentially an infantry force with a small cavalry detachment. The rigidity of the phalanx was avoided. The maniples, or companies, were drawn up, not in an unbroken line, but with intervals between them, and behind these intervals were placed the companies of the second line. The men were not closely locked together, but given room to use their weapons freely. The short, heavy spear of the legionary as not a pike but a javelin. It was hurled at close quarters, and then the short-bladed sword was drawn, and, covered by his shield, the soldier closed with his adversary before he could recover from the impact of the spear. The legionary was a swordsman, and once the volley of spears and the rush of swords broke anywhere into a hostile line the company could hew its way to right or left, while company after company broke in to reinforce the attack on the crumbling line or mass of the enemy. These tactics made the Romans masters of all the Mediterranean world. The legionary was also trained to entrenchment work, and carried a heavy load of baggage, so that transport was reduced to a minimum.

During the decline of the empire there was a growing dependence on mercenary troops enlisted from 'Barbarian' nations, and the cavalry arm was increased to cope with the mounted raiders of the new peoples that were pressing on the frontiers. With the coming of invaders from eartern Europe and from Asia, largely mounted warriors, cavalry became more important than infantry, and through the earlier Middle Ages the heavily armed man-at-arms was the main strength of armies. Infantry began again to become important in the XIV. cent., when the Swiss Confederates showed that an array of pikes and halberds could defy the mounted men; the militia of the Flem. cities gave the same proof of the power of steady infantry; and the Eng. archers proved that the arrow flight could destroy charging knights and men-at-arms before they could come to close quarters. The introduction of musketry added to the value of the foot soldier, and the first regular regiments of infantry, the Span. *tercios* of the XVI. cent., well-disciplined bodies of musketeers combined with pikemen, were for nearly a hundred years all but invincible in pitched battles. In the XVII. cent. the invention of the bayonet made the protection of the pikemen no longer necessary for the musketeer, and infantry began to assume its modern form, while at the same time the cavalry began to form a less and less numerous element of regular armies, and became at last an auxiliary arm. The XVIII. cent. saw the introduction of light infantry or skirmishers, fighting in dispersed order to cover the advance of the closed bodies of infantry, and as fire effect increased through the improvement of the musket, the line became a reliable fighting formation. In the XIX. cent. the introduction first of the rifle, then of the breech-loader and magazine rifle, increased both the range and efficiency of infantry fire, and made the cavalry charge against steady infantry hopeless, and the foot soldier, assisted by artillery fire, became the battle winner. With the increase of infantry fire effect, close-ordered movements on the battlefield gave way to various forms of dispersed order, and the use of cover and entrenchments. Infantry is now the main strength of all armies, and even the cavalry soldier is armed with the rifle and trained to fight on foot.

INFECTION. SEE DISEASE, GERM THEORY OF.

INFERNAL MACHINES, a name given to mechanical contrivances with a dangerous explosive and used for a nefarious purpose. Such machines are generally made to look quite harmless and frequently have some clockwork arrangement by which the explosive is fired after a certain lapse of time.

INFINITE, that which is without end. It is impossible to conceive a point in past time without something before, or in future time without something after; so also in space; hence idea of infinity. But infinity cannot be imagined. Some assert space and time are finite.

INFINITY, perhaps the most difficult conception mathematicians have to make. Infinity is defined as being that quantity which is greater than every assignable quantity, and is denoted by the sign ∞. It is most easily conceived as a limit, e.g. as the quantities $\frac{1}{2}$, $\frac{1}{3}$, $\frac{1}{4}$, $\frac{1}{n}$ . . . – . . . get smaller and smaller, so n gets larger, and larger and the limit to which n tends, as the infinitesimal $\frac{1}{n}$ tends to zero, is ∞. In higher geometry parallel lines are those which meet at infinity, and the asymptotes of an hyperbola are the tangents to the curve at points on it infinitely distant. All points at infinity are on the line at infinity, whose equation in areals is $x+y+z=0$, and all circles pass through two imaginary points known as the circular points at infinity.

INFIRMARY, see HOSPITAL.

INFLAMMATION may be defined as the reaction of the tissues to an irritant; and the term irritant includes physical and chemical agents, heat and cold, a crush or a blow, as well as those toxic agents known as micro-organisms. Celsus (b. about 50 B.C.) is said to have enumerated *rubor*, *tumor*, *calor*, and *dolor* ('redness,' 'swelling,' 'heat,' and 'pain') as the four marks of inflammation; and although these four cardinal signs are not necessarily all present in every inflammation, they to some extent furnish an index to the severity of the process. Interference with function also occurs. The result of irritation of the tissues is dilatation of the vessels and escape of white blood corpuscles or leucocytes into the tissues. Metchnikoff has demonstrated the destruction of bacteria by these white blood-cells. In the course of this struggle many of them die, and pus consists of myriads of these dead corpuscles. The most favorable termination of acute inflammation is resolution, which leaves practically no material trace of the process. In many cases, however, acute inflammation subsides into a chronic state. If at all extensive, acute inflammation is attended by rise of temp. and by general malaise, especially when pus is formed and retained in a confined space. Rigors may follow the formation of pus, or the spread of the inflammation and the septic organisms by the lymphatics to new centers of infection.

Treatment.—As far as possible the affected part should be put at complete rest; the local application of heat, a sharp purge, and a milk diet are usually indicated. If suppuration occurs, free incision is called for.

INFLORESCENCE, in plants, is the manner in which their flowers are arranged. The simplest form of all is a solitary terminal flower, e.g. daffodil, but more often there is a more or less complex system of branching (q.v.) in which the branches do not develop into foliage-shoots but bear flowers. The stalk upon which the flowers are borne is known as the *peduncle* or *rachis*; if the flowers spring directly from the peduncle they are said to be *sessile*, but if they depend from a secondary stalk they are said to possess *pedicels*. An I. found at the apex of a shoot is *terminal*, if found in the axils of leaves it is *axillary*. noted for eloquence.

INFLUENZA, an acute infectious disease caused by a specific bacillus, *Bacillus influenzæ*, characterized by fever and by symptoms affecting the respiratory, digestive, or nervous systems. It occurs in epidemics, appearing most frequently in the winter months, and has spread, at one time or another, to practically all parts of the world, adults between the ages of twenty and forty being attacked most often, children and aged persons less frequently. Infection is from the secretions of the mucous membrane of the nasal passages and the trachea and bronchial tubes. The incubation period of the disease is from two to six days. The onset is sudden, with pains in the back and loins, and headache, often accompanied by giddiness and nausea or vomiting. The temp. rises quickly, varying from 100° to 104°, and a feeling of weakness and discomfort is marked. After a few days the disease may assume one of four varieties: *respiratory*, with bronchitis or broncho-pneumonia developing; *gastro-intestinal*, with pain in the abdomen, vomiting, and diarrhœa; *nervous*, with great depression, insomnia, severe headache and other pain, irregular heart, and perhaps delirium; *febrile*, with pronounced prostration and high temp., especially in children. The death-rate in proportion to the number of cases is not high. In the epidemic of 1890 it was 1.6 per 1,000. But in the extraordinary epidemics of so-called 'Spanish influenza,' which swept across the whole world in 1918 and 1919, this mortality was greatly exceeded. Most of the fatal cases were complicated by pneumonia. There were severe epidemics of influenza in the United States in 1921 and 1922.

The treatment is rest in bed, warmth, and nourishing foods, complications being treated as they arise. For the pains at the commencement of an attack, salicylate of soda is valuable, phenacetin if headache is pronounced, while quinine, phenol, and a host of other drugs have been employed. Vaccines, both prophylactic and curative, have been tried, but the evidence of their value is not conclusive.

INFORMER, legal term for person who brings a suit against another as a law-breaker; a *common I.* is one who shares the profits of convictions. The system was brought to an art in the later Rom. Empire, and was common in Ireland during the XVIII. and XIX. cent's.

INFUSORIA, the highest class of Protozoa, with many members which are among the most familiar of the group. Their name is due to the fact that, where any infusion of vegetable matter is exposed to the air, Infusoria abound therein in a short time. As the other classes of Protozoa are distinguished by the presence or absence of characteristic locomotor organs, so the infusorians are known by the coating of fine, short, vibratile hairs or cilia, which, present often in hundreds or even thousands, enable them to swim through the water or glide over solid substances. The free-swimming forms are generally round or oval in shape, while the gliding forms are flattened, with a permanent creeping surface; but the essential structures are the same—a protoplasmic body formed of external ectoplasm and internal endoplasm, containing usually two nuclei (*macronucleus* and *micronucleus*), food vacuoles and numerous contractile vacuoles, and furnished frequently with a mouth and œsophagus which guide the food to the endoplasm.

As is often the case in Protozoa, the bodies of many Infusoria are preserved from desiccation in continuous dry weather by the formation of a protective covering—*encystment*—but this process is also related to reproduction and to lack of food. When encystment precedes reproduction the contents of the cyst break up into very many minute individuals; but a more usual mode of reproduction is that of simple division, where an individual splits into two—crosswise if free, lengthwise if fixed.

Most Infusoria live in the sea or in fresh water, where they swim independently or are attached to rocks, seaweeds, zoophytes, etc., by means of a long contractile stalk or by adhesive organs, or simply by modified cilia. They live on small organisms, such as bacteria, diatoms, and minute Protozoa, which are wafted towards the mouth (where it is present) by the continuous action of the neighboring cilia. Some Infusoria are parasitic, and live in the bodies of other animals, upon the juices of which they feed. The parasitic forms, however, do little apparent harm, with the exception of one form (*Ichthyophtheirus*), which occasionally causes fatal epidemics amongst fresh-water fishes.

The class Infusoria falls into two distinct groups:—

Sub-class I., *Ciliata*, in which cilia occur throughout life—some without mouths (*Astomata*), such as *Opalina*, parasitic in the food canal of frogs; or the group of *Gymnostomata*, with simple porelike mouths; or the large permanently open-mouthed *Hymenostomata*, of which the common slipper animalcule or *Paramœcium* is a member. Or there are forms distinguished by a spiral band of well-developed cilia which leads to the mouth (*Spirigera*), including the sedentary *Stentor*, which has a body covered with an even, fine coating of cilia, and which builds a gelatinous tube within which it can withdraw for refuge; the closely related sluggish *Balantidium* is parasitic in the human food canal.

INGALLS, DAVID SINTON (1899-
), b. Cleveland, Ohio; ed. prep. sch.
Cleveland, O. B. A. Yale, 1920 LL.B
Harvard, 1923. Admitted to Ohio bar
1923. Practiced in Cleveland. Member
Ohio House of Rep., 1927-29. Asst. Sec.
of navy for Aeronautics, 1929-32. Rep.
Cand. for Gov. of Ohio, 1932, defeated.
Appointed Dir. Dept. Pub. Welfare,
City of Cleveland, 1933.

INGALLS, JOHN JAMES (1833-
1900). American lawyer; b. in Middle-
ton, Mass., December 29, 1933; d. at
Las Vegas, New Mexico, August 16,
1900. Graduating from Williams College
in 1855 and admitted to the bar in 1857,
he practiced law at Atchison, Kansas
and was a delegate to the first Constitutional Convention. Secretary of the
Territorial Council, 1860; to the State
Senate, 1861; state senator, 1862. In
the Civil War he was judge-advocate to
the Kansas militia, 1863-1865, and for
three years edited the 'Atchison Cham-
pion.' The Republicans elected him
U.S. senator, 1873, 1879, and 1889.
Charges of bribery were brought against
his election in 1879, but he was exoner-
ated. President pro-tem. of the senate
in 1887. He was defeated for senator in
1891 by the Farmers Alliance. He was
noted for eloquence.

INGE, WILLIAM RALPH (1860),
Dean of St. Paul's. London, since 1911;
formerly Lady Margaret prof. of divinity, Cambridge, 1907-11; Gifford lecturer at St. Andrews, 1917-18. Has written numerous works, incl'.ding *Society in
Rome under the Cæsars, 1886*; *Studies of
English Mystics, 1906*; *The Church and
the Age, 1912*; *The Philosophy of Plotinus,
1918.*

INGEBORG (c. 1176 to c. 1238),
queen of France, whose repudiation by
Philip Augustus led to his excommuni-
cation, 1196, and the placing of France
under an interdict.

**INGELHEIM, NIEDERE, AND IN-
GELHEIM OBER** (c. 49° 58' N., 8° 6'
E.), two small contiguous towns, Hesse,
Germany, on Selz; wine.

INGELOW, JEAN (1820-97), Eng.
poet and novelist, who became known
by publication of poems in 1863; her
best-known novels: *Off the Skelligs* and
Fated to be Free.

**INGEMANN, BERNHARD SEVER-
IN** (1789-1862), most popular Dan. poet
and novelist of his day; his writings are
somewhat mawkish, but graceful and
finished.

INGENOHL, FRIEDRICH VON
(1857), Ger. sailor. He became admiral
of High Seas Fleet, 1908. In January,
1913, he was promoted to the command-
ership-in-chief of Ger. navy, and retained
this position until after the battle of
Dogger Bank, Jan. 24, 1915, when he
was superseded.

INGERSOLL (43° 3' N., 80° 58' W.);
town, Ontario, Canada, on Thames;
agricultural implements; furniture.

INGERSOLL, ERNEST (1852), American naturalist; b. in Monroe, Michigan, March 13, 1852. He was educated
at Oberling College, the Lawrence
Scientific School, and the Museum of
Comparative Zoology, Harvard. Appointed an expert by the U.S. Fish Commission he became noted for his writings
and lectures on scientific subjects. An
officer of the National Association of
Audubon Societies. He edited the
'Farmer's Practical Library.' Author,
*Nests and Eggs of North American Birds,
1880-1881*; *Oyster Industry of the United
1881*; *Knocking 'Round the Rockies,
1883*; *The Crest of the Continent, 1884*;
Wild Neighbors, 1897; *Book of the Ocean,
1898*; and *Wild Life in Orchard and
Field, 1902*; *Wit of the Wild, 1906*; *Animal Competitors, 1911*, and *Dragons and
Dragon Lore, 1928.*

INGERSOLL ROBERT GREEN
(1822-1899), and American lecturer; b.
in Dresden, N. Y. At the age of twelve
he accompanied his family to Illinois,
where he studied law and began to practice, in Peoria. He became interested in
politics and joined the Democratic
Party, but after the Civil War, during
which he served in the Federal Army as
a colonel of volunteers, he became a
Republican, because of his anti-slavery
sentiments. In 1868 he was Attorney-
general of Illinois, and in 1876 he made
a speech at the Republican National
Convention, held in Cincinnati, which
gave him a national reputation. After
this period he began to make extensive
lecture tours throughout the country,
people flocking in multitudes to listen to
his arraignment of religion and its institutions. His logic was based largely on
the writings of Thomas Paine, but it was
his oratory rather than his processes of
reasoning which carried conviction to
his hearers. He was a master of irony
and invective and probably had more
influence than any other man in this
country in diminishing the congregations
of the churches. He wrote *The Gods and
Other Lectures, 1786*; *Some Mistakes of
Moses, 1879*; and *Prose Poems and
Selections, 1884.*

INGERSOLL, R O Y A L RODNEY (1847), Rear-Admiral, United States Navy; *b.* in Michigan, 1868; graduate of United States Naval Academy; served as naval officer all over the world; commissioned captain, 1903; rear-admiral 1908; commander of United States Ship missioned captain, 1903; rear-admiral, commander of United States Ship Supply during Spanish American War, 1908; commander of Maryland, Chief of staff Atlantic Fleet, on voyage from Hampton Roads to the Pacific, member general board of the Navy, 1905; retired, 1909; president special board on naval ordnance, 1917-1919. Author, *Text-Book of Ordnance and Gunnery, 1887*; *Exterior Ballistics, 1891*; *Elastic Strength of Guns, 1891. d. 1931.*

INGHAM, CHARLES CROMWELL (1796-1863), prominent Amer. portrait painter.

INGHIRAMA, FRANCESCO (1772-1846), Ital. antiquary; made valuable Estruscan researches. His *bro.*, Giovanni I. (1779-1851), wrote astronomical books.

INGHIRAMI, TOMMASCO (1470-1516), distinguished Ital. humanist.

INGLEBY, CLEMENT MANSFIELD (1832-86), Eng. scholar; author of books on Shakespeare.

INGLEFIELD, SIR EDWARD AUGUSTUS, KT. (1820-94), distinguished Eng. Arctic navigator; made admiral, 1879.

I N G L I S, SIR JOHN EARDLEY WILMOT (1814-62), Brit. general. During the Indian Mutiny he commanded the Residency at Lucknow from death of Lawrence to relief by Havelock, 1857.

INGOLSTADT (48° 47′ N., 11° 25′ E.), fortified town, Bavaria, Germany, on Danube; seat of a univ., founded 1472, transferred in 1800 to Landshut, and in 1826 to Munich; manufacturers cannon and gun-powder.

INGRAHAM, JOSEPH HOLT (1809-1860), American novelist; *b.* at Portland, Maine, in 1809; he went to sea as a boy; took part in revolutions in S. America; graduated from Bowdoin College, in 1832; subsequently teaching school in Natcheze Mississippi. He wrote a popular success, *The Southwest by a Yankee, in 1836*; and a series of sensational romances, followed including, *Lafitte, Captain Kyd*, etc. In 1855 he was ordained a priest of the Protestant Episcopal church and wrote the biblical romances, *Prince of the House of David, 1855*; *The Pillar of Fire, 1857*; and *The Throne of David, 1860*.

INGRAM, JAMES (1774-1850), Eng. scholar, edit. *Saxon Chronicle, 1832*.

INGRAM, J O H N KELLS (1823-1907), Irish literary man, political philosopher, and philologist.

INGRES, JEAN AUGUSTE DOMINIQUE (1780-1867), Fr. painter; belonged to the classical school, withstood the Romantic inrush and lived to enjoy short classical revival of the Second Empire; *b.* at Montauban; became pupil of David, 1796, and speedily his rival; executed portraits of Napoleon and other pictures, including famous *Girl after Bathing*; numerous historial subjects followed, including the *Chapelle Sistine*; elected to the Institute, 1825, and for a while most prominent painter of France. Among best works are *Ambassadors of Agamemnon, Stratonice*, and *La Source*.

INHAMBANE (23° 50′ S., 35° 20′ E.); seaport (and district), Portug. E. Africa; exports rubber, wax, oil-nuts.

INHERITANCE.—According to law, if a person dies intestate his *real* property passes according to certain rules. The person who last held it is the *purchaser*, unless he can be proved to have inherited. It descends first to lineal descendants, male coming before female, and the issue of a dead heir before the next living *bro.* or *sister*. If there are no descendants then it passes to ancestors. Relatives of the half-blood inherit much as relatives of the whole, with certain differences.

INHERITANCE TAX, an assessment levied on legatees of property. It is a tax of considerable antiquity, dating back to Roman times, and is in force today in most countries, where it has demonstrated its value as a producer of revenue to the state with a minimum of hardship to the persons taxed. In England it is counted upon heavily for budget purposes. In the United States it was in force during the Civil War, but was afterward abolished, though it has again been instituted by the Federal Government, as well as by the great majority of the States of the Union. The Federal tax takes no cognizance of any estate less than $50,000 in value. For amounts in excess of that figure the tax is 1 per cent on the first $50,000, and increases gradually until it reaches 25 per cent on estates exceeding $10,000,000. In most of the States there is an exemption ranging from $2,000 to $20,000 to near relatives and graduated taxes on the excess over the exemption of from 1 to 25 per cent, the latter figure only being imposed on exceptionally large bequests. In Alabama and Florida, there are no State inheritance taxes. In Texas and Maryland, bequests to parents, husband, or wife, and lineal descendants are exempt from tax. There has been considerable controversy over the wisdom and expediency of inheritance taxes, but the great weight of opinion is in favor of their being levied. The tax is easily ascertainable, simple of collection, and involves little hardship on the legatee, as it is paid at a time when the latter is in the receipt of a considerable sum of money or other property, usually unearned, and often unexpected. Moreover the exemptions relieve the recipients of small amounts almost or altogether from tax, while on larger estates the burden weighs most heavily where it can be borne.

⌐ **INHIBITION** (from Lat. *inhibere*, to prevent). In psychology, the suppression of one nervous process by another. Yields to psychoanalysis.

IN HOC SIGNO VINCES, a Latin expression meaning 'In this sign thou shalt conquer'. According to the legend this appeared on a flaming cross in the sky to the Roman emperor Constantine I., before the battle in which he defeated Maxentius.

INISFAIL (Gaelic for island of the *fail*, or stone), Ireland; the country which possessed the *fail*, or stone, on which Jacob slept. This stone was afterwards taken to Scone in Scotland, and thence to Westminister Abbey, where it forms part of Coronation Chair.

INITIATIVE, a term that has acquired a political significance in its application to a movement by which legislation is passed through the driving force of a popular mandate expressed in votes at a special election, or by which proposed legislation is either approved or rejected by the same means. In other words, the people take the *iniative* in requiring a tardy legislature to pass some measure which the latter may disfavor, or itself wants to pass judgment upon a measure before a legislature enacts it into law. The movement had its origin in Switzerland and aimed at obtaining for the electorate a more direct share in legislation. In that country a single voter at a popular assembly of the smaller cantons could require a proposal to be submitted to the vote; in the larger cantons there must be a number of petitioners, varying according to the size of the communities. The initiative was finally adopted as a method of proposing constitutional amendments. In the United States, South Dakota, 1898, first adopted the initiave (with its accompanying referendum if necessary). Oregon came next, 1902, with a constitutional amendment providing that on a petition of 8

per cent of the voters a proposed measure could be submitted to popular vote, and must become law if favored by a majority. A number of other states passed similar laws that opened a channel to popular approval or otherwise proposed measures. In practice the operation of the initiative and referendum is the determination of legislation by the voters at large, as the legislature's duty, after the people have spoken in merely formal action putting the popular mandate into effect where it is affirmative. See ELECTORAL REFORM.

INJECTION, the act of throwing a substance into one or other of the cavities of the body; or the substance so injected. The substance is generally employed as an aqueous solution and is intended to have a curative effect by direct action on the organ into which it is injected or to which it is readily conveyed by the natural processes of the body. Hypodermic Is. are made by piercing the skin and introducing the active substance into the subcutaneous tissues by means of a small syringe. Intravenous I. is the introduction of a solution directly into a vein. Intramuscular I. is the introduction of a solution into the substance of a muscle. Vaginal, urethral, and rectal Is. are introduced into the vagina, urethra, and rectum respectively.

INJUNCTION.—A legal remedy for the enforcement of covenants, particularly negative covenants. Thus, where a tenant covenants not to carry on a particular trade the court will grant an I. to restrain him from doing so, or an I. may be obtained from the courts to restrain the publication and sale of books and newspapers pending the trial for breach of contract, or to prevent a public singer from singing in certain places when the contract has been made to sing elsewhere.

INK contains dissolved or suspended coloring matter; it should not mould nor form a thick deposit; it should be non-erasable, non-poisonous, and non-corrosive. Since the XI. cent. ink has been made from an iron salt and tannin. Tannin inks are made by fermenting *galls* with yeast and mixing the tannic acid so obtained with ferrous sulphate. Gum arabic is added to suspend the precipitate. Oxidation by air develops the intensity of the color. Colored inks are obtained by adding different pigments. *Printing ink* contains lampblack, linseed oil, and some yellow soap. *China* or *Indian Ink* is soot from wood or lamp-black mixed with glue from ox skin, and made into cakes. *Copying inks* are made from logwood. ammonia alum, and metallic salt. They are corrosive. The color develops by oxidation. *Aniline inks* are non-corrosive, and have no sediment, but are fugitive. *Marking ink*, indelible ink for marking linen, etc., is a solution of silver nitrate or other salts. *Secret* or *invisible inks* (*sympathetic inks*) are chlorides of nickel, cobalt, etc., which become visible only on the application of heat or a chemical agent.

INKERMANN, village in the Crimea, 33 miles from Sebastopol; noted for defeat of the Russians by the English and French, on Nov. 5, 1854.

INLAND WATERWAYS. See INTERNAL IMPROVEMENTS.

INLAYING, method of decoration by inserting one material into another, differing in nature or color; different kinds are bidri, damascene, buhl work, marquetry, pietra dura, mosaic.

INMAN, HENRY (1801-46), Ameri. artist, who executed many portraits of celebrities.

INN (48° 34′ N., 13° 28′ E.), river, Central Europe; ancient *Enus*; rises in Swiss canton of Grisons; joins Danube at Passau; length, 320 miles; navigable to Hall.

INN.—An 'inn' has been defined as 'a house, the owner of which holds out that he will receive all travellers and sojourners who are willing to pay a price adequate to the sort of accommodation provided.' Generally a hotel is an inn. The ale-house, or tavern, is merely a refreshment-house, and a fully licensed public-house is not necessarily an inn. Neither is a boarding-house, for the proprietor of the latter makes what arrangements he, or she, pleases with the boarders. But the innkeeper is bound by law to receive and afford proper entertainment to every one who offers himself as a guest, if there be sufficient room and no good reason for refusal. In the event of neglect or non-fulfilment of duty on the part of the innkeeper proceedings should be taken against the person who is, in fact, the innkeeper.

INNERLEITHEN (55° 37′ N., 3° 5′ W.), town, health-resort, Peeblesshire, Scotland, seat of Woolen industry; saline springs (Scot. *Roman's Well*).

INNESS, GEORGE (1825-1894) American painter; *b.* in Newburg, N. Y., May 1, 1825; *d.* at Bridge of Allen, Scotland, August 3, 1894. He displayed high artistic talent from boyhood, and when he opened a studio of his own a liberal patron sent him to Europe, where he spent several years at work in France and Italy. In 1850 he settled at Eagleswood, near Perth Amboy, New Jersey. He ranks with the best American landscape painters, and his pictures are highly prized by collectors. Five of his paintings are in the Metropolitan, New York. Among notable works are: *Close of a Stormy Day, An Autumn Morning, Autumn Gold, Passing Storm,* and *Moonrise.*

INNESS, GEORGE, JR. (1854) American painter; *b.* in Paris, January 5, 1854; *s.* of George Innes, with whom he studied in Rome, 1870-1874, and then under Bonnat in Paris, in 1875. He exhibited at the National Academy of Design, in 1877, and became a member of the Academy in 1879; awarded a gold medal by the Paris Salon, 1899, and has since been a frequent exhibitor; decorated by French Government. He is best known as a landscape and animal painter. Representative works are, *A Mild Day, 1887,* and *Morning on the River, 1902.* Since 1913 he has had an artistic connection with the *Century Magazine.* Author of *Life, Art and Letters of George Inness, 1917. d. 1926.*

INNOCENT, INNOCENTIUS.—The name of numerous popes, of whom the most important are:—

Innocent I., reigned 402-17; confirmed actions of Synod of Carthage, 416; commemorated in Rom. Church, July 28.

Innocent II., reigned 1130-43; supported St. Bernard against Abelard and Arnold of Brescia.

Innocent III., reigned 1198-1216; one of the greatest of the popes; exercised enormous power; as pope and as an Ital. prince he opposed imperial power; enforced his decisions on marriage question on Philip of France and Peter of Aragon, more significant still were his relations with King John and his putting England under interdict; promoted Fourth Crusade, 1204, and crushed the Albigenses; *d.* soon after presiding at the Lateran Council of 1216. I. was a statesman rather than a theologian, and under him the papacy reached the height of its power.

Innocent IV., reigned 1243-54; engaged in long conflict with Emperor Frederick II., carrying on the lofty ideal of power of Innocent III.; had more personal ambition and less loftiness of aim than his predecessor; promoted study of canon law.

Innocent VI., reigned 1352-62, at Avignon; a firm ruler, he carried through various reforms, but has sometimes been charged with nepotism.

Innocent VII., reigned 1401-06; tried to summon general council in 1404, which never assembled.

Innocent VIII., reigned 1484-92; unsuccessfully preached a crusade; without real ability, and guilty of nepotism; influenced by Cardinal della Rovere (Julius II.).

Innocent X., reigned 1644-55; condemned the Jansenists, 1653; largely swayed by his *sister-in-law*, Donna Olimpia Maidalchini.

Innocent XI., reigned 1676-89; carried out reforms in papal court, and tried to secure greater simplicity and spirituality in Church life; came into conflict with the Jesuits; took some part in politics, opposing Louis XIV. over *Declaration of Gallican Liberties*, which I. resisted; an unsuccessful attempt was made to canonise him.

Innocent XII., reigned 1691-1700; a reforming pope, tried to abolish nepotism by declaring popes should not give offices to relatives.

Innocent XIII., reigned 1721-24; supported Old Pretender and opposed the Jesuits.

INNOCENTS' DAY, CHILDERMAS, Church holiday to commemorate massacre of innocents by Herod; Dec. 28., in Rom. Church; considered unlucky.

INNS OF COURT.—In England, corporate bodies, of which all barristers and students of law must be members. (The phrase is also applied to the buildings belonging to these societies.) Four of these courts exist in London: The *Inner Temple*, the *Middle Temple*, *Lincoln's Inn*, and *Gray's Inn*—all the smaller inns have long been abolished. Each of these societies is governed by a body of benchers. The privileges of the inn are to admit men to become students of law, and to confer the right, by calling them to the Bar, to practise in the Law Courts. Each student, before admission, must pass an entrance examination or produce a certificate from a university, and before being called to the Bar must keep twelve terms (three years) and pass other examinations. In Ireland, King's Inn, Dublin, is the only Inn of Court. In Scotland, there are no Inns of Court, and an advocate, corresponding to the Eng. barrister, is trained in the Faculty of Advocates.

INNSBRUCK (47° 17' N., 11° 24' E.), town, Austria, capital of Tyrol; beautifully situated at head of Brenner Pass; seat univ., founded 1677. Among principal edifices are Franciscan Church (with magnificent monument to Maximilian I.), imperial castle, and Ferdinandeum museum; textile and glass-paint industries.

INNUENDO (from Lat. *innuere*, to nod towards), method of defamation by insinuation which may constitute libel.

INOCULATION, the communication of disease accidentally or intentionally to a healthy subject by the introduction of certain products of disease into the body through the skin or the mucous membrane. The chief diseases so transmitted in man are anthrax, hydrophobia, small-pox, and syphilis. Before Jenner introduced vaccination (*q.v.*), I. of small-pox was practised. The disease as thus transmitted was far less dangerous than the ordinary small-pox, and, further, rendered the inoculated subject much less liable to a future attack. Its disadvantages are obvious, in that it tended to keep the disease alive, and further to increase its spread, but it was invaluable to those who had been inoculated, and was of great service prior to Jenner's discovery. In 1840 the practice of I. with small-pox was forbidden by law. Pasteur's treatment for hydrophobia and all serum injections are based on a similar principle to that explained above.

INORGANIC CHEMISTRY. See Chemistry.

INOUYE, KAORU, MARQUESS (1835-1929), Jap. Meiji statesman, who won some success for European innovations.

INOWRAZLAW, HOHENSALZA (52° 47' N., 18° 15' E.), town, Posen, Poland; iron-works; salt-works in vicinity.

INQUEST (Lat. *inquisitio*, search), legal inquiry made by Coroner and jury; held in cases of death from unusual causes.

INQUISITION, THE.—In the IV. cent. the Christian Church, which till then had been persecuted, became itself persecuting. Laws were passed in the Christianised Empire against heretics. In the Dark Ages there was not much persecution, but about the X. cent. rigorous measures were adopted, and in various countries heretics were burnt. It came to be established that heretics, after being condemned by the Church courts, should be handed over to the 'secular arm' for punishment. The Emperors Frederick I. and Frederick II. and Pope Innocent III. urged increased severity. Gregory IX. really created the mediæval inquisition which he entrusted to the Dominicans. The judicial procedure of the I. was quite different from that to which we are accustomed. The accused was assumed to be guilty; he did not know who had accused him, and all proceedings were in secret. Hardly a case is known of complete acquittal, but if the prisoner confessed, he had to suffer various pains and penalties, such as scourging, penance, imprisonment. Torture was frequently used to extort confession, and every effort made to induce the heretic to accuse others also. Those who were obdurate were liable to be burnt. The heretic's goods were confiscated, the spoils going sometimes to the secular monarch, sometimes to the Church, and occasionally confiscation was so great as to involve impoverishment in a district where the I. had been acted. The I. extended its activities to the suppression of heretical lit. and to magic.

The I. never had a real existence in England, although from the XV. cent. onwards heretics were burned at the stake, particularly in the Marian persecution. In France the Albigenses were suppressed in the XIII. cent. with great cruelty, and the Waldenses in the XIV. In Italy persecution was often for political reasons, and in Germany heretical mystics suffered most.

It is the *Spanish I.*, however, of which the influence was greatest. Owing to the independent policy of Span. kings, the I. never did much in the Middle Ages. It was reorganized by Ferdinand and Isabella, in 1480. Despite its independence of the Holy See it was recognized by the popes. (It is noteworthy that while no country in Europe was more orthodox than Spain, none was so jealous of papal interference.) No class in Spain was exempt from its vigilance, but some came off worse than others—*e.g.* the descendants of converted Moors or Jews were always regarded with suspicion. The Span. I., after having been twice temporarily abolished, finally disappeared, in 1834. Its work had been more thorough and far-reaching in Spain in modern, than elsewhere in mediæval times.

INSANITY, a term applied to certain varieties of mental disease in which the disorder of mind is so severe as to produce disorder of conduct in the affected subject. The term is really more a legal than a medical one, as a certain degree of irresponsibility must exist before the subject may be legally confined against his will. Milder forms of mental disease exist in which the conduct of the patient remains rational. The great aim of modern mental healing (PSYCHIATRY) is to have all cases of mental disease, whether certifiable or not, treated by specialist physicians in special hospitals, unless the patients can bear the expense of having such treatment in their own homes.

Insanity may be due to actual structural disease of the brain, or may be of the nature of an intellectual anomaly which renders impossible the adaptation of the subject to his normal surroundings. In both cases the practical point is that the sufferer from insanity must be forcibly confined in order to protect the community from him, or in order to protect him from the evil consequences to himself of his own conduct.

It has been calculated that among civilized peoples the ratio of insane to sane is about 1 to 300, but the proportion varies in different countries.

The most important cause of most varieties of insanity is a hereditary tendency to mental disease, about 60 to 70 per cent of the insane having a hereditary taint; the predisposition develops into an actual manifestation of disease on an exciting cause arising. The marriage of near relatives does not necessarily produce insanity in the offspring—*i.e.*, not unless there is already a family tendency to the disease. Many bodily diseases are potent exciting causes—*e.g.*, epilepsy, syphilis, alcoholism, influenza, pellagra. Privation, emotional shock, and severe continued strain of all kinds are most important in producing many kinds of mental breakdown. The onset of insanity may also be intimately connected with the following important periods of human life—viz., puberty, adolescence, the climacteric, and the decline of old age. Pregnancy, child-bearing, and lactation must also be mentioned.

The classification of the various types of insanity has gradually been undergoing modification since it was first laid down according to mental symptoms by Philippe Pinel, 1745-1826, but the following description depends on the classification adopted by the leading schools of psychiatry all the world over.

Insanity arising in infancy or early childhood is known either as *Idiocy* in the lower mental types or as *Imbecility* in the higher. This kind of insanity may or may not be accompanied by gross disease of the brain, such as hydrocephalus, and is very often associated with epileptic fits. Cretinism is a condition of undeveloped intellect due to absence or atrophy of thyroid gland.

Among the insanities due to actual structural disease of the brain are general paralysis of the insane and senile dementia.

General Paralysis of the Insane is a common and always fatal disease, the causation of which is intimately connected with syphilis. Progressive feeble-mindedness is the chief symptom, but this is usually accompanied by a peculiarly happy mental state in which delusions of wealth, grandeur, and omnipotence are prominent; the delusions are very extravagant and changeable. Bodily emaciation and paralysis gradually get worse along with the dementia, the speech from being slurring in the early stages becomes inarticulate, all bodily control is lost, and death usually supervenes in from one to three years. No treatment has ever cured the disease.

Senile Dementia is the insanity of old age. Loss of memory is usually the first symptom, and is followed by various degrees of weakness of mind, up to apparent absence of any mind at all. These patients are sometimes very violent and difficult to manage. Senile dementia never improves. The length of time the patient lives depends on his bodily health.

Epilepsy is very often associated with insanity of the most violent and serious kind. The main characteristics of the insane epileptic are irritability and impulsiveness. He is the most difficult of all patients to manage, and is very frequently homicidal and sometimes suicidal as well. He seldom improves, and may live for many years.

Insanity may be caused by definite bodily diseases or intoxications.

Alcoholic Insanity may take the form of *Delirium Tremens.* In this case the subject has been soaking himself in spirits to the exclusion of food. The delirium, which is characterized by mental confusion and vivid visual hallucinations of an unpleasant nature, ensues when the alcoholic stops drinking suddenly, as he must under the circumstances. The patient always recovers if properly treated, but convalescence is slow, as the stomach is always very much upset. No alcohol should be administered in treating the patient. *Chronic Alcoholism* may result in permanent impairment of intellect. *Dipsomania* is the inability to resist periodic outbursts of extremely excessive and usually solitary drinking; this type of case is much the worst from the sociological point of view, and is also commoner than is usually supposed. The subject struggles against the craving, which, however, usually gets the upper hand, as in all drug habits. The dipsomaniac is the patient who is to be found in the ordinary inebriate home.

Popular and medical opinion regard alcohol as the principal direct cause of insanity; this is a most inaccurate statement, as it is extremely rare for alcohol to produce chronic mental disease. The unstable person cannot tolerate large quantities. Alcohol, on the other hand, is a most potent factor in producing serious bodily disease, and in laying the foundation of a family tendency to nervous and mental illnesses.

Acute and Subacute Delirious Insanity comprises a very important group of conditions which are the result of nervous exhaustion plus the invasion of the brain by poisonous infections the nature of which has been determined in a few cases only. The patient is deteriorated in bodily condition, the alimentary system is usually out of gear, and there may be actual fever. The mental condition is one of confusion; the patient is not properly conscious of his surroundings, may be very restless and violent, and often has visual and other hallucinations. The result is either death or recovery, and depends almost entirely on the early provision of expert medical and nursing attention. The injudicious use of certain sedative drugs (especially chloral) has damaged the chances of many cases. Forced feeding may be necessary. Hospital treatment is essential. *Acute Puerperal Insanity* belongs to this group, and requires the same careful treatment.

The remainder of the diseases to be described may be called the mental diseases *par excellence*, as their onset is not connected with any particular change in the brain or general bodily illness. The altered personality of the subject is the first thing which draws attention to the illness.

Melancholia consists of mental depression (misery) so severe that the patient loses all sense of proportion of his trouble and ceases to behave rationally. A suicidal tendency is the most important symptom, and for this reason the patients need the most careful observation; unfortunately, however, suicide often takes place before the mental disease has been recognized. In many cases depressive delusions are present; the nature of these may vary from beliefs in financial ruin to those of eternal damnation, according to the type of person affected. The bodily health suffers, and as a rule, the patient becomes much emaciated, as a result of self-imposed starvation.

Mania consists of extreme and irrational happiness. The patients are very talkative and may be very noisy and violent. The bodily health is not very much upset. True mania is uncommon, and the term is often wrongly applied to all sorts of other conditions. Recovery occurs frequently, but in smaller percentage of cases than melancholia.

Folie Circulaire or *Alternating Insanity* is a combination of mania and melancholia in successive phases. The periods of insanity may range in duration from a few days to many months. The outlook is bad, as the disease is a constitutional mental habit.

Dementia Præcox, Primary Dementia and *Adolescent Insanity* are some of the names which have been applied to a large and very important group of cases. The disease begins very insidiously, usually at the age of from twenty-five to thirty-five, and is characteristized by mental reserve, stolidity, and gradual estrangement from the outside world. Vivid hallucinations of hearing are the rule, and the patient often develops strange mannerisms and fixed attitudes. The mental life of the patient ultimately ceases to have any connection with his surroundings, and becomes a fantastic tissue of day-dreams, delusions, and hallucinations. The patients commonly live a long time, and form a large proportion of the permanent population of our menta hospitals. There is a strong family tendency to the desease.

Systematized Delusional Insanity (Paranoia) is a rare intellectual anomaly of which good examples are to be found in every large institution for the insane. The disease usually manifests itself after the age of thirty-five, and consists of a sense of personal superiority which at first leads the subject to believe that he is being persecuted by other persons, and so is being prevented from fulfilling the exalted destiny which is in store for him. He commonly makes himself a nuisance to his employers or to the public at large. Later on the grandiosity of the patient knows no bounds, and he will argue that the reason why he is shut up is because a royal princess wants to marry him, because he is the real cause of current political troubles, or because he is the incarnation of the Deity, and the government know how great his power might be. He is not usually a difficult patient to manage, as with all his apparently disadvantageous surroundings he can never get rid of his self-satisfaction at being so much better than other people. This is a mental disease which gradually progresses and does not affect length of life. Abortive types of this kind of insanity are common enough in everyday life.

War and Insanity.—During the World War the commonest types of insanity met with among soldiers as a result of fighting service were the delirium of exhaustion and melancholia. The recovery rate was very high.

It must be clearly understood that the term 'shell-shock' refers entirely to hysterical and neurasthenic breakdowns, which, though they should be classed as mental illnesses, are seldom so severe as to lead to insanity otherwise than in the form of transitory mental confusion.

Treatment.—Although it appears that that the anc. Egyptians and Greeks treated the insane as suffering from disease, this was succeeded by the mediæval idea that they were possessed of devils, and the treatment applied was scourging, torture, plunging afflicted persons into pools of water until they were nearly drowned, and chaining them up in dungeons. In somewhat later times the harmless insane wandered about the country or were taken care of at holy shrines, and those considered dangerous were put in chains in prisons along with criminals. Asylums where the insane were detained were built (or in some cases former monasteries, etc., were

used) in the 17th and 18th centuries, but the treatment was much as before. More humane treatment was first advocated by Pinel and Esquirol in France, at the end of the 18th cent. It was not, however, until near the middle of the 19th cent. that physical restraint began to be abolished from asylums, and a scientific treatment, with light work and exercise in the open air, began to be introduced.

Short attacks of delirious insanity and alcoholism and such comparatively transient states as acute puerperal insanity may be treated quite well at home under a good nurse and the supervision of a physician, but a good modern mental hospital has the advantages of a healthy and systematized régime and dietary under skilled nursing and medical supervision, and proper accommodation for violent and invalid cases. In fact, instead of the old asylums of detention with strait waistcoats and other appliances, they are nowadays mental hospitals, conducted on scientific principles. Indeed, certain mild forms of insanity can well be treated in special wards of general hospitals.

The treatment consists in plenty of nourishing food—over-feeding rather than under-feeding. Cod-liver oil, malt extract, and the like are valuable in cases where nutrition is poor, and in many such cases wines and malt liquors are of distinct benefit. Quinine, iron, and dilute mineral acids are valuable tonics, but nerve stimulants—*e.g.*, strychnine—require more care in administration, as they may lead to mental excitement. Moderate exercise in fresh air is most important, simple open-air work, such as gardening, social amusements, dancing, etc., in moderation, help to divert patients' minds from morbid thoughts into more healthy channels.. *Hypnotism* is employed with benefit in the treatment of some types of insanity, particularly in cases of morbid obsession.

INSCRIPTIONS. See Palaeography Cuneiform Inscriptions; Archaeology.

INSECTIVORA (Insect Eaters), are Mammalia of the class Rodentia, usually small in size and nocturnal in habit. They may possess a smooth velvety fur, as in the mole (*Talpa*), or have a covering of spiny erectible quills, as in the hedgehog (*Erinaceus*). They run partly or wholly upon the sole of the foot, and the first digits of both feet (corresponding to the human thumb and great toe respectively) are not apposable. In addition to moles and hedgehogs, the order also includes shrews, tree-shrews, potamogale (an elongate animal and a powerful swimmer, inhabiting the river banks of the W. African tropics), and galopithecus (a bat-like creature inhabiting S.W. Asia, which possesses a membranous skin-fold, the *patagium*, by means of which it is able to glide parachute-fashion from tree to tree). In nearly all, the snout is peculiarly delicate and sensitive and projects beyond the apex of the upper jaw. The teeth are characteristic, the mandible bearing more than two incisors, whilst the molars possess tuberculate roots. The milk dentition is extremely transitory, and is absorbed in the majority of cases before birth. The brain is small, the cerebrum leaving the cerebellum exposed, and being, with the exception of a lateral groove, quite smooth. The characters of the molars, and the small, smooth brain, are strongly indicative of the primitive character of the group, and this is confirmed by the absence of scrotal sac and the abdominal position of the testes. With the exception of the West African elephant-shrews, the urinogenital and anal apertures are partially or wholly enclosed in a common skinfold suggesting a cloaca.

The order, which is not represented in Australasia, first makes its appearance in the Lower Eocene. The fossil forms are more or less synthetic in type, and suggest nearer affinities with the marsupials, the wholly extinct creodonts, and the lemurs than do their modern representatives. The I. are grouped in twelve families, of which the *Soricidæ* (shrews), *Talpidæ* (moles), and *Erinaceidæ* (hedgehogs) have Brit. representatives. The wide and often extremely limited geographical distribution of many of the families lends further support to the primitive character of the order.

INSECTIVOROUS PLANTS, besides feeding in the usual way, capture and devour insects. Varieties: (1) with leaves provided with pit-like traps filled with a viscid fluid—*e.g.*, *Drosophyllum lusitanicum* of Portugal and Morocco; (2) with no pits on leaves, but secreting a viscid fluid—*e.g.*, sundew; (3) with viscid fluid, along with a movement to capture insect—*e.g.*, Venus's fly-trap. In each case the viscid fluid possesses digestive or dissolving qualities. In this way the plant obtains a supply of nitrogenous matter in circumstances where the usual means of supply may be deficient.

INSECTS belong to the invertebrate group of Arthropoda. There are over a quarter of a million species known today, and the likelihood is that the study of entomology in the future will reveal many thousands more. Thus I. are by far the largest class of animals, and can further claim a very remote

ancestry, as the Lower Silurian rocks in the earliest ages known to geologists show distinct traces of them. 'A typical I.' stands considerably higher in the biological scale than Peripatus or Myriopods. Its body is enveloped in a horny substance called chitin, and is structurally composed of three segments, which are frequently so narrowly united that the I. seems cut up into three parts—a phenomenon which has given the class its name (*insect*, Lat. for 'cut into'). These three divisions are the head, thorax, and abdomen. The adult I. has wings, with the exception of the caterpillar, etc., a centralised body with only three pairs of locomotor limbs, whence it is called a Hexapod ('six legs'), and carries on its respiration by means of airtubes or tracheæ, whence it ranks with other Tracheata.

The classification of insects is based upon variation in structure, especially upon the various types of wings and mouth arrangements: (1) 'Aptera' (wingless, sugar-lice and springtails. There is no metamorphosis; (2) 'Neuroptera' (nerve-winged), May-flies, caddis-flies, scorpion-flies, and dragon-flies, white ants, and book-lice. These have four glassy and membraneous wings, a complete metamorphosis, and a mouth of the biting type; (3) 'Lepidoptera' (scale-winged), butterflies and moths. These have four wings with delicate, colored scales and a complete metamorphosis. The mouth is furnished with a proboscis, and the larvæ are characteristic; (4) 'Orthoptera' (straight-winged): earwig, cockroack, locust, grasshopper, and cricket. These are 'ametabola,' have 'cerci' appended to the abdomen, and have the front pair of wings leathery and smaller than the back wings; (5) 'Hymenoptera' (membrane-winged): wasps, bees, and ants. Their mouths are both biting and suctorial. They have four transparent, membranous wings, and undergo a remarkable transformation; (6) 'Diptera' or 'Flies' (two-winged): house-fly, horse-fly, and bluebottle-fly, gnat, daddy-longlegs, and mosquito. Their metamorphosis is very complete, their mouths are mostly suctorial, their two wings are transparent and membranous and their larvæ are both legless and headless (maggots); (7) 'Hemiptera' (half-winged): aphis (green-fly), cochineal insect, water-boatman, lice, bugs, and cicada. These undergo slight metamorphosis and have suctorial mouths, and four wings, which is either membranous or horny with a membranous apex; (8) 'Coleoptera' (sheath-winged): water-beetle, stag-beetle, and tiger-beetle, etc., glow-worm, and cock-chafer. Members of this class experience a complete transformation and have biting mouths, but their salient characteristic is the horny sheath ('elytra') of which their front or upper wings are composed, so that the delicate membrane of the hind or lower pair is quite hidden from view.

Life and General Characteristics.—I. have most diverse haunts and frequent underground cased, hot springs, and even the sea; nevertheless, the majority are aerial and dwellers on land. In tropical and temperate climates they abound, but they are represented even in the polar regions. Many, as, for instance, the pond-skater, whirligig beetle, water-scorpion, and gnat, are aquatic for the earlier days of their lives. Generally speaking, adult I. are short-lived and die within a twelvemonth; the adult Ephemerid, as its name implies, does not live beyond twenty-four hours, but the queen bee flourishes for some years, and a queen ant will rarely last for thirteen. The food of insects is very various. Some steal the pollen and nectar from the flowers; others feed on weaker species of their own kind; others act as internal or external parasites of higher animals; others again grow fat on putrescent matter, and yet another section suck juices from living organisms. Parents will often gather a store to feed their young, even though they themselves die before the larvæ are hatched. A number of I. are able to express sorrow, anger, or fear, or to convey information or make love by means of sound. This may be produced by the rubbing together of the rough surfaces of the outer cuticle, or by the buzzing vibrations of leaf-like appendages near the stigmata of the air-tubes, or by the quick flutter of their wings. Thus grasshoppers scrape their legs against their wing ribs and male crickets chirp by rubbing their wing-cases together. Many Hymenoptera produce their noise by the second means, whilst the whirring sound of bees and flies is due to wing motion. The death's head moth emits a noise by blowing air out of its mouth. Sometimes the noise is purely automatic. If left unchecked I. would multiply with an alarming rapidity. Fortunately, however, inclement weather, and the predilection which birds, ant-eaters, frogs, and fishes, show for them as food, counteracts their amazing fecundity. As with higher animals, so certain I. are naturally protected by having an outward appearance which exactly counterfeits their actual surroundings. This is the case with moss and leaf I. and with humming-bird moths. Other I. are saved from molestation by disgusting fluid discharges, an unpleasant smell, a hard skin, or an offensive weapon like a sting. The social species, ants, bees, termites, and wasps, offer a most instructive and fascinating field for

study by reason of their intelligence, architectural skill, and developed communistic life.

Economic Value.—Unconsciously I. play a great part in the cross-fertilisation of flowers as they carry pollen from one bloom to another. The 'myrmecophilous' (ant-loving) plants are actually guarded by ants from other and hostile intruders. Man owes a debt of gratitude to the hive-bee for its honey and wax, to the silk moth for its silk, and to the cochineal I. for a dye. But there are many species which seem purely harmful and destructive. Cattle, sheep, and horses are annoyed by the bot-fly; crops, orchards, and vines are a prey to a whole army of greedy parasitic I., and the havoc caused by a locust swarm is often untold. House flies are strongly suspected as the agents which carry pathological or disease-bearing germs in a number of infectious outbreaks; the mosquito is probably largely responsible for the horrible disease called *Elephantiasis arabum.*

INSECTS, COTTON. See COTTON INSECTS.

INSOMNIA, inability to sleep. which is usually accompanied by emaciation, dryness of the skin, and nervous disturbances, may be due to anæmia or hyperæmia of the brain, secondary to diseases of the heart, lungs, and other organs; while the abnormal state of the blood in gout, rheumatism, etc., or through excessive use of tobacco or alcohol, will also produce insomnia. It may be due also to overwork, or nervous derangements, neurasthenia, etc., from various causes. The treatment depends on the cause, which, if possible, should be removed by suitable remedies. A glass of warm milk or cocoa, taken before retiring, will, in almost all cases of simple, uncomplicated insomnia, pave the way to sound sleep.

INSPECTOR GENERAL, the head of a department in the U. S. Army. The duty of the Inspector General and his staff is to make periodical inspections of the army and all its institutions, including even the homes for disabled veterans, and to keep the Secretary of War constantly informed regarding such matters as equipment, stores, armament, disposition of garrisons, personnel, etc. It is also his duty to suggest improvements, such as the adoption of new types of artillery, small arms, etc., and to suggest remedies where he is obliged to report certain defects. In 1923, the Inspector General of the United States was Major-General Eli A. Helmick, of Indiana.

INSPIRATION (Lat. 'inbreathing').—
The idea that a human being can be an
organ or vehicle for the manifestation of
the divine, or can receive divine communications, appears in all religions.
Often the inspired person is in a state
of great emotional excitement. The Old
Testament prophet was at first a seer,
then moral, spiritual, and to some extent
predictive. I. is most frequently used in
connection with sacred writings; all great
religions have their sacred books; in
Muhammadanism the conception of I.
of the Koran is more rigid than that of
the Bible has ever been among the
Ians. In the Christian Church the literal
and verbal inerrancy of Scripture has
been largely believed in, but it is now
generally abandoned. Another view is
that the Bible is infallible in matters of
faith and morals, though not always
necessarily in others. Most Christian
theologians would now accept the Bible
as spiritually more inspired than any
other book, and as containing all things
necessary to salvation, but would admit
moral and spiritual progress.

INSTERBURG (54° 37′ N., 21° 50′
E.), town, E. Prussia, Germany; iron
foundries, tanneries.

INSTINCT, a word used in a vague
and popular and also in a more exact
scientific sense, in which it is defined as
meaning those mental faculties which are
for a specific end, but which do not
necessarily imply conscious knowledge
on the part of the creature who exercises
them. Some would try to separate the
biological and psychological aspects of
instinct among animals, but it is in the
connection of the two that the problem
really consists. The term 'habit' is
applied to dispositions and secondary
automatic actions acquired after birth.
Intelligence presupposes individual experience with conscious purpose; the activities of instinct are performed without
previous experience and without conscious purpose other than the satisfaction of response to the immediate and
appropriate stimulus. The instincts of
animals popularly so-called are only
partly instincts proper, and partly what
they have acquired. Many instinctive
actions, again, as due to imitation. The
problem of instinct is closely connected
with heredity. There is undoubtedly
such a thing as racial preparation, and
the capacity for certain actions is inherited. As animals rise in the scale
their instincts become more and more
associated with intelligence, until in the
highest animals instinct tends to lapse
and intelligence to predominate.

INSTITUTE (Lat. *instituere*, to establish, appoint), name given to laws and
commentaries thereon (see JUSTINIAN);
to places in which training is given, or
to associations for scientific purposes.
The *Institut de France* (established 1795)
comprises the five Academies.

INSTITUTE OF FRANCE. See
ACADEMY.

INSTITUTIONAL CHURCH, one
which makes social activities besides
worship important in Church life (some
think to the exclusion of religion).

**INSTITUTE FOR MEDICAL RE-
SEARCH, ROCKEFELLER.** See ROCK-
EFELLER FOUNDATION.

INSTRUMENT OF GOVERNMENT,
a paper constitution drawn up in Dec.,
1653, by officers of the army, making
Cromwell Protector under control of
Council of State and a reformed Lower
House; Cromwell ruled under it till
1657, when it was superseded by the
Humble Petition and Advice.

INSTRUMENTATION is virtually
synonymous with ORCHESTRATION, and
signifies the distribution of parts of a
musical composition among the various
instruments of the orchestra. The history and development of I. run parallel,
as it were, to the history and development of the orchestra. Up to the XVIII.
cent. the orchestra served almost exclusively as an accompaniment to vocal
music (opera, choral, etc.). Within these
limitations, however, marked progress
was made in the art of I. by Scarlatti,
Bach, and Händel. With Gluck the orchestra and orchestration attained more
importance in opera, while Haydn laid
foundation of symphonic music. In
Mozart's day the orchestra was still
small (about forty instruments), and
brass and percussion parts were insig-
nificant, almost artificial. Beethoven
gave a greater share to brasses and
drums, and improved the rôle of almost
every instrument. XIX. cent. inventions led to an enormous advance in tone,
compass, and flexibility of winds in particular. New instruments were introduced and the orchestra was considerably
enlarged. The art and science of I.
naturally became more complex as the
orchestra's capabilities increased. Wagner first fully realised the dramatic power
of orchestral music, and by applying new
laws and original ideas to the improved
instruments of his day, attained effects
never previously attempted or possible.
Tchaikovsky and the Russ. school gave
even greater prominence to brass and
percussion instruments, and imparted
new coloring to orchestral music. The
modern masters, Strauss and Debussy,
strive after emotional effects which add

still further to the difficulties and complexities of I.

INSULIN. See DIABETES.

INSURANCE.

At the end of the calender year, 1932, there was $100,-154,372,632 worth of life insurance alone in force in the U. S. while the U. S. Department of Commerce, for the previous year, estimated the total worth of life insurance in force in the world at that time at $136,000,-000,000. Marine insurance is probably the oldest form, records having been traced back to the start of the 15th cent. when merchants insured their goods and vessels against the perils and hazards of sea voyages. Since it was the custom at that time for the merchant to accompany his goods, he was also insured as was the capt. of the boat. The average length of these policies was one year and since there were no organized companies then to assume liability, individuals appeared who were willing to take the risks and the term *underwriter* came into being. As far as is known, premiums on this early type of life insurance were approx. 5%, regardless of age or health. Life insurance as a paying business received its first impetus from Robert Chandler who, in 1574 was given a patent by Queen Elizabeth to open a Chamber of Insurance in London. The first general life insurance company in America was founded in Philadelphia in 1812 but it was not until the early forties that life insurance in America began to flourish as a paying business.

An insurance contract between two parties, expressed by a policy and sustained by the periodical payment of given sums known as premiums, obligates one party (the insurer or underwriter) to protect the other (the insured) against losses to which the insured's health, business, or property may be subject. Personal insurance covers sickness, accident, old age, maternity, risks of traveling, and unemployment. Property insurance takes a multitude of forms. Great underwriting bodies, like Lloyds of London and American marine insurance corporations protect shipowners against loss of their craft and cargoes at sea. Equal protection is available against losses from destruction of property by fire, bad weather, or other causes on land. The farmer insures his livestock to offset losses from disease, and his crops from the unforseeable risks of climate, such as unpropitious frosts. The breaking of plate-glass windows can be insured as can the risks of loss of or damage to automobiles. There is also burglary insurance, protection from damage by steam boiler explosions, and from elevator and vehicular accidents. Employes, such as railroad, construction and manufacturing companies, protect their resources against claims for damages arising from accidents to their workmen, while employees are guarded against loss of income, due to accident by being provided with industrial insurance. Industrial, or working-class insur., mentioned above, differs from ordinary life insurance in that the premiums are payable weekly in small sums, some as low as five cents, instead of in larger sums at longer periods, and covers the lives of workers from the ages of one year to 65 years with no sex distinction. Another invaluable form of insurance is that which safeguards firms from losses due to bad debts, known as credit insurance. Yet another business protection is provided by surety or bond companies, who insure employers against thefts committed by dishonest subordinates.

Governments have been drawn into the insurance system in competition with private companies. England insures her post office employees and other workers against unemployment. New Zealand conducts a successful life insurance department, though without offering any marked advantages above those of private companies. Old Germany devised a compulsory insurance system for workmen. In the World War the United States successfully established an insurance bureau for men who were injured, incapacitated or died, as a result of military service.

There is little government regulation of insurance co.'s in Eng., but in the United States such supervision is quite extensive, each State regulating the business within its own borders as it sees fit. The control of insurance has been reserved to the individual States by a Supreme Court ruling which held that the conduct of insurance was not interstate commerce, and therefor not subject to federal regulation.

INTAGLIO, representation of an object made by cutting away the object from the ground, not, as in relief, cutting away the ground from the object.

INTELLIGENCE IN ANIMALS. —I. has been defined as the 'conscious adaptation of means to ends.' It is closely connected as regards animals with instinct. Romanes asserted and Mivart denied that animals possess I. and reason. But a distinction is drawn by psychologists between perceptual and conceptual thought, the former involving the perception of some relation between two things, the other abstract analysis. Much human and, at any rate, most animal thought is 'perceptual,' but it is still an open question whether animals are capable of 'conceptual' thoughtas human beings undoubtedly are.

INTELLIGENCE TESTS.—For many years psychologists have sought to devise tests whereby human intelligence could be measured and compared with some definite standard. Intelligence has been defined as the ability to solve problems presented to sense, and care must be taken not to confuse intelligence with knowledge. While the intelligence of a child increases with its age, and while in many cases this growth of intelligence may continue into years of adulthood and may be, and probably is, fostered by education, yet it is perfectly possible for a poorly educated person to possess more innate intelligence than one highly educated. In 1905, Binet and Simon, French psychologists, published the first series of tests for measuring intelligence. In 1908 they published a second series, and in later years the tests have been modified and improved by other scientists. The tests were designed for determining the degree of intelligence possessed by children of different ages. By experimentation, a normal standard for each age was determined, and a child was fied as to his normality or abnormality according to his ability to pass the tests for his age, or for ages less or greater than his own. There were fifty-six tests in the 1908 series, and they were designed to cover the ages between three and twelve years. Recently, however, intelligence tests have been much used to classify adults. During the war, one-and-a-half million men in the U.S. Army were subjected to these tests and classified. Two typed of tests were employed, one based on the Binet-Simon method, the other on a so-called 'point scale,' designed by R. M. Yerkes, J W. Bridges, and R. S. Hardwick. The ability to pass these tests does not depend, in any way, upon the degree of learning. Simple tasks are given the examinee, and simple problems are given him to solve. For instance, he is required to make, or complete, simple patterns, to complete sentences, or to point out errors in simple statements. Intelligence tests are being used more and more in place or ordinary entrance examinations to colleges and universities. Questions in these tests necessarily tax the intelligence more than in those designed for children or uneducated adults. An example may be given in the following question recently used in a college examination· 'If you found a Roman coin dated 55 B.C., in whose reign would you conclude that it was made?' The correct answer, of course, is that the Romans had no knowledge of the date of Christ's birth before he was born and therefore could not have dated their coins 55 B.C. A coin with such a date, therefore, must clearly be fraudulent, and the date would be no indication as to when it was made. It will be seen that no knowledge of Roman history is required for such an answer. The question tests the ability of the examinee to think clearly and quickly. Adults who show the mentality of a child are called morons.

INTENDANTS, officials of Fr. kings, before Revolution. *Intendants des finances* were under controller-general of finances. *Intendants des provinces* from about 1570 had considerable authority in provinces; they came in collision with provincials gov's and with parliaments over administration; very powerful in XVIII. cent.

INTENSIVE AGRICULTURE. See AGRICULTURE.

INTENT, element of purpose which, with attempt at offense, constitutes legal crime; the I. is an important question in criminal, but is not considered in civil matters. Many legal documents have saving clause, by which the verbal expression is to be interpreted 'according to the true I. and meaning of these presents.'

INTERCALARY DAYS, days inserted in the calendar to restore correspondence of solar and civil year; this is secured by leap-year system.

INTERCHURCH WORLD MOVEMENT, an organization founded by a number of broad minded clergymen and laymen of the Protestant denominations for the purpose of creating a vital institution of the Church. The effort came with the momentum engendered among the churches by war service, during which the various denominations had cooperated so effectively that it was felt that this spirit might be brought to survive into the peace period. A large number of wealthy Americans became so enthusiastic over the idea that the organization took on huge proportions, a large building being required to house the various offices. Among the many projects planned by the officers was that of investigating industrial conditions, with the object of suggesting measures leading to the amelioriation of the poverty of the working classes. One of these investigations, known as the 'Pittsburgh Survey,' which was conducted during 1919-20, resulted in a report so radical in spirit that the majority of the wealthy patrons of the organization were incensed, the report more than indicating that the employees of the steel corporations were sorely oppressed by their employers. With the withdrawal of this financial support the organization disintegrated, its affairs being wound up in 1922.

INTERCOLUMNIATION, spacing of columns in classical architecture, differing in different orders.

INTERDICT, forbidding of divine worship and administration of sacraments by ecclesiastical authority as punishment for sin; pronounced by Pope against persons or countries.

INTEREST, an allowance made for the use of borrowed money or capital. The ratio which the I. bears to the loan or principal per annum is the rate per cent. I. is payable periodically, usually half-yearly in commercial transactions, but frequently monthly in the case of loans by registered moneylenders or by persons who ought to be so registered. I. is either simple or compound, the former being payable on the principal alone, the latter on the amount of the principal and interest as and when it fall due. The exaction of I. was prohibited in England as early as 1197, and the prohibition rested, as elsewhere, upon religious grounds.

It is an economic commonplace that the rate of I. is the same in all trades in the same country and at the same time—a law which rests for its validity on the elimination from profits, of compensation for risk, of dishonorable reputation and everything but pure I. on capital. But the risk in some occupations being greater, and some trades requiring more superintendence t h a n

others, there must always be differences in the rate of I. or profits in different trades at the same time; and in those trades or businesses in which the rate is higher than the bank rates—their criterion of the average rate—some economists contradistinguish such higher rate by the name *false I.* It is an accepted position in economics that as wealth and population increase the rate of I. declines, because, among other causes, wealthy and populous communities afford less and less scope for any given quantity of labor and capital, a tendency which is the root principle of the Ricardian theory of rent; and again the increasing export of capital tends to produce a uniform rate for all countries.

INTERGRAPH. See CALCULATING MACHINES.

INTERIM (Lat. meanwhile), name given to temporary settlements of controversial points during the Refromation, by order of the emperor, to remain in force until a general council should meet—noted I's are those of Ratisbon (or Regensburg), 1541. Augsburg and Leipzig, 1548.

INTERLAKEN (46° 42' N., 7° 52' E.), town, Swiss canton of Berne, on Aar, between lakes Thum and Brienz; tourist centre.

INTERLUDE (Lat. *inter*, between; *ludus*, play), a short piece or musical phrase performed between the acts of a play or between the verses of a hymn. In drama, a short performance given between the parts of a play or in the intervals of a banquet or court pageant.

INTERNAL IMPROVEMENTS. — The question of improving roads, waterways, and harbors, of the United States was discussed by Congress in the early days of the Republic, but there were so many other more pressing matters to decide in organizing the new government that many years passed before anything important was done. In 1806, the Federal government built a wagon road from the Potomac to the Ohio river, which was carried to Wheeling in 1820, and then to Columbus, Indianapolis, and St. Louis. The first canals mentioned in early history were built in Pennsylvania, in 1790-1810. In Maryland, in 1784. The Erie Canal (*q.v*) was built in 1823, by New York State, to the Genessee River, and was connected with Lake Erie in 1825. The first mile of railroad was built by the Baltimore & Ohio, in 1828, followed by the Charleston & Hamburg, 1829, and the Mohawk and Hudson, 1830. The first efforts of the Federal government to improve the waterways of the country are not recorded, but in 1922 there were

26,410 miles of navigable streams in the United States. The River and Harbor Bill of March, 1921, appropriated $15,000,000 under the direction of the Secretary of War, for 1923-1924, for projects, etc. and later in the year the President and Director of the Budget asked for $27,885,260, for present works, their maintenance, etc. The Chief Engineer of the U.S.A. in his report to the Secretary of War, in 1922, recommended $43,000,000 appropriation for the year, exclusive of the Muscle Shoals, Alabama, project. By the Federal Aid Act of 1916 to 1921, 28,135 miles of highways were under Federal Aid at a cost of half a billion dollars, of which the government supplied 40 per cent. The Federal Act of November 9, 1921, appropriated $75,000,000 for roads to states contributing dollar for dollar exclusively from state treasuries.

INTERNAL REVENUE. — F u n d s raised for government purposes in the United States by the imposition of taxes upon domestic products or activities, as distinguished from customs duties on goods imported from abroad. The system dates back to the very foundation of our government, have been inaugurated by the first Secretary of the Treasury, Alexander Hamilton. The Government had assumed debts incurred by the States in the Revolutionary struggle, which they themselves were unable to meet. To discharge these obligations, for which the customs were inadequate, Hamilton proposed a tax on distilled spirits. Against the most bitter opposition he secured Congressional approbation of a measure, 1791, imposing a tax on this product of from 11 to 30 cents a gallon, according to its alchoholic content. So vigorously was this tax fought by the liquor interests that the opposition finally resulted in the so-called Whiskey Rebellion. This was summarily repressed, and the right of the Federal Government to impose such a tax was firmly established. Once the principle was accepted, it had unlimited applications. Snuff and sugar were taxed; government stamps were required to be affixed to deeds, legal documents and negotiable instruments. The laws were repealed in 1802, when the Federalists were ousted from power, but reimposed with many additions during the war of 1812, to meet the pressing necessities of the Government. Following the conflict, they were again repealed, and from that time to the outbreak of the Civil War, government revenue was derived from the customs. In 1862 the office of the Commissioner of Internal Revenue was created with an organization of inspectors and collectors forming a system

which has remained in force up to the present time. During the Civil War, not only liquors and tobacco, but almost eveyr conceivable object had to bear its share of taxes for the financing of the conflict. Most of these were distinctly war taxes and were repealed by 1870. Whiskey, beer, tobacco and stamp taxes were still retained. To these has now been added the income tax, the greatest revenue producer of all.

The Internal Revenue System is pliable and elastic. Taxes can be raised or lowered, imposed or repealed, as the exigencies of the government require or permit. The cost of administration is only about two and one-quarter per cent of the amount collected. The Internal Revenue receipts for 1933 were $1,604,-052,691, as contrasted with customs receipts for the same period of $250,-747,991.

INTERNATIONAL, THE, an international association of working men, founded 1864, in London; came to an end at Philadelphia, in 1876; most important members were Karl Marx and Bakunin, leaders respectively of moderate and extreme factions. See SOCIALISM.

INTERNATIONAL CONFERENCES, AMERICAN. See INTERNATIONAL AMERICAN CONFERENCES.

INTERNATIONAL LANGUAGE. See UNIVERSAL LANGUAGE.

INTERNATIONAL LAW (also called *jus inter gentes*, or erroneously *jus gentium*), the usages observed in relations between civilized states. International law may be divided into the Natural and the Conventional elements. The former, generally known as the *Law of Nature*, is based on those principles which are supposed to be universally accepted as rules of conduct for both states and individuals in their dealings with each other; it is thus a moral rather than a legal obligation. The Conventional element is the result of obligations imposed upon states by treaties and agreements between themselves, and of precedents and cases whereby the customary practice has been established. In many European states the writings of lawyers on the subject are also regarded as law. The chief question which has to be decided is that of the lawfulness or unlawfulness of war; and to prevent war the states may refer their disputes to international arbitration. Up to the World War this practice was becoming increasingly common, and several nations had made it obligatory *inter se* by treaty.

The state as the unit of international law has certain rights which other states must recognize. These include: (1) the right to do whatever is necessary for its own conservation; (2) the right to acquire new dominions; (3) to buy or sell property; (4) to choose its own form of government or to change it; (5) to increase its army and navy and to develop its commerce. And among the obligations morally binding on states are: (1) to allow no plots against sovereign of a foreign state to be organized within its bounds; (2) to put down sedition; (3) to protect its subjects in foreign countries; (4) to see that justice is impartially administered. In arbitration treaties issues affecting the 'vital interests' of the contracting parties are usually excluded from the application of that method of settlement, interference with a nation's rights or independence being regarded as a legitimate *casus belli*. In international law the sea beyond the three-mile limit is regarded as free to all, every nation having rights of navigation and fishing on the high seas. Only ships of war and merchant vessels are recognized in international law; the former are armed vessels used in public service; they are considered to be part of the national territory of the state to which they belong, and when entering the ports of foreign states are not subject to the local jurisdiction of these states. Merchant vessels, on the other hand, are subject to the laws of any foreign state whose ports they may enter. Pirate vessels are not recognized and may be seized; and by most states ships engaged in slave trade are treated as pirates. In 1899 the International Peace Conference met at the Hague, and arranged for the constitution of a permanent arbitration court, to which disputes between states might be referred. In August, 1913, the Palace of Peace, instituted by the 'Carnegie Foundation' at the Hague, was inaugurated, and a year later Europe was engaged in the most widespread and sanguinary war of the ages.

International law differs from ordinary law in two respects: (1) it is not made by any legislative authority; (2) it cannot be enforced by any superior power. In all international disputes the final tribunal is war or arbitarion. The utter breakdown of international law during the World War revealed its weakness in the most glaring manner, and led to the constitution of a League of Nations, which should promote international co-operation and achieve international peace and security by the acceptance of obligations not to resort to war, and by the firm establishment of the understandings of international law as the actual rule of conduct among governments. See under LEAGUE OF NATIONS.

INTERIOR, DEPT. OF. See CABINET.

INTERMITTENT FEVER. See MALARIA.

INTERPELLATION, term in legislative procedure for interruption, with the consent of the Assembly, of ministerial business, by question attacking ministerial policy; sometimes weapon of obstruction.

INTERREGNUM, period between death of king and election of successor; in Middle Ages this often meant lapse of government.

INTERREX (Lat. *inter.*, between; *rex*, king), official app. by Rom. senate on death of a king to govern until appointment of new king (period called an *interregnum*), sometimes ten *interreges* were elected with duty of choosing a king. Under the republic an inter-consular 'I.' was sometimes appointed.

INTERSTATE COMMERCE, connotes the free and untrammelled conduct of trade between persons throughout United States, irrespective of State lines. The term has its chief significance in its opposite relation to Intrastate Commerce, which expresses trade transactions carried on within the boundaries of a State. Interstate commerce is under Federal control; intrastate commerce is regulated by each State. The phrase has come to mean largely the transportation of commodities over the great systems of railroads that pierce the country unimpeded by State boundaries. In other words, the railroads, as a national means of transit, came to dominate interstate commerce. Interstate railroad traffic and interstate commerce accordingly pass current as interchangeable terms, though the jurisdiction of the Interstate Commerce Commission (the Federal body that controls the railroads) also embraces the supervision of water-borne traffic when connected with a railroad, the regulation of interstate pip (oil) lines, as well as of telegraphs, telephones, and cables. A trade in commodities and transport thereof, originating and completed within a State is intrastate commerce, subject to State, not Federal, regulation; but a transaction that calls for transshipment of the goods from one State to another becomes interstate commerce, since delivery necessitates the use of transit facilities that operate in more than one State.

The control of interstate commerce in its intimate connection with railroad traffic became imperative following the great expansion of railroads after the Civil War. Interstate commerce, as such, could take care of itself; but the railroads, plunging past State lines and scorning State control, ran wild in their liberty, like overgrown, refactory children. Competition was stifled by pools, rate discriminations became a scandal, favored shippers were enriched by the ruin of business rivals, and the development of towns and localities were at the mercy of lines which dictated whether a community should or should not have transportation. Most of the traffic lay wholly outside State control.

The Interstate Commerce Commission was created by Congress, in 1887, to remedy the evils arising from the unregulated and unscrupulous operation of railroads between the States. It set out to obtain just transportation charges, check discrimination favoring one shipper at the expense of his competitor, and prevent the pooling of freights. Following this measure came the Sherman Anti-trust Law, 1890, which further regulated the transit of interstate commerce by defining as illegal all combinations that throttled competition and were thus in restraint of trade or commerce between the States. Under this law the mergers of the Northern Pacific and Great Northern, 1903, and of the Union Pacific and Southern Pacific, railroad systems were dissolved by the U.S. Supreme Court. The original law establishing the Commission was amplified by other measures, strengthening that body's powers, such as giving it authority to fix railroad rates and preventing the granting of illegal rebates. The rates established by the Commission are unappealable unless contested on constitutional grounds. See RAILROADS.

INTERSTATE COMMERCE COMMISSION, a body of seven members, formed to administer the Interstate Commerce laws, the first of which was passed by Congress in February, 1887, as a result of the agitation against the practice of the railroads in favoring certain shippers. Since then the jurisdiction and the powers of the Commission have been frequently broadened by amendments. Generally speaking, its function is to regulate the control of the railroads of the country in the public interest, especially in the matter of passenger and freight rates, which may not be changed without its consent. Carriers are compelled to report to it annually and whenever demanded for special reasons. It has the power to examine the books of all carriers. It has the power to compel testimony, in which regard it enjoys the same status as a Federal court. It also has the power to enforce whatever labor laws may be passed for the protection of employees, etc. In 1933, the chairman of the Commission was Patrick J. Farrell.

INTERVAL, in music, is the difference in pitch between two sounds; the ratio between the frequencies (vebrations) of two notes. Intervals are reckoned from the lower note upwards, both notes being included. They are classed according to the number of degrees of the stave—*i.e.*, alphabetical letters—included, not according to number of tones or semi-tones contained. Intervals are subdivided into different classes, according to number of semi-tones contained: fourths, fifths, and octaves are called perfect; seconds, thirds, sixths, and sevenths are called major and minor. A diminished interval is one that contains a semi-tone less than a perfect or a minor interval, while an augmented interval contains a semitone more than a perfect or a major interval.

INTERVALE, term used geographically in America for low-lying land between hills.

INTESTACY.—In the case of persons dying without making a will (*i.e.* interstate).

INTESTINE, the lower part of the alimentary canal, divided in man into small and large intestines, communicating by the ileo-cæcal valve. See DIGESTION.

Intestinal Obstruction may be *acute,* caused by strangulation by bands or adhesions, by volvulus or rotation of the intestine on its own axis so as to produce strangulation, by acute intussusception or the telescoping of one portion of the intestine into the part below, by the termination of chronic obstruction, by kinking or through peritonitis; or the obstruction may be *chronic*, due to impaction of fæces or foreign bodies, to stricture, tumors, and other affections of the intestinal wall, or to compression of the intestine from tumors or adhesions without. The symptoms of the former are sudden severe pain, later becoming continuous, in the region of the umbilicus, shock and collapse. There is persistent vomiting, which soon becomes very offensive, the bowels do not move, the abdomen becomes distended, and peritonitis comes on if the obstruction is not relieved by immediate operation. In regard to chronic obstruction, there are colicky pains, with constipation alternating with diarrhœa, and finally acute obstruction takes place. The treatment before the case becomes acute is a fluid diet, enemata, and small doses of cascara or calomel. Operative treatment is generally carried out at an early stage.

INTOXICATION, poisoning by drugs or other poisonous substances; used chiefly as denoting the condition produced by excessive consumption of alcohol.

INTRANSIGEANTS (irreconcilables); political party uncomprisingly hostile to an existing government, the term being used chiefly in Spain, 1873, France, and Italy.

INTUITION, a philosophical term for that which is directly perceived or apprehended, whether in logic or ethics, as opposed to that arrived at by a reasoning process.

INVALIDES, HOTEL DES. See PARIS.

INVENTORY, BENEFIT OF (Lat. *beneficium inventarii*), term in Rom. and Common law for right of heir to enter into estate without being liable for encumbrances beyond its value as inventoried.

INVERARAY (54° 14′ N.; 5° 4′ W.), seaport, county town, Argyllshire, Scotland, on Loch Fyne; herring fishery. I. Castle, built 1744-61, is seat of Duke of Argyll.

INVERCARGILL (46° 26′ S.; 168° 23′ E.), town, Otago, South Island, New Zealand, on New River estuary; breweries, foundries; exports, preserved meat, wool, and timber.

INVERNESS (57° 28′ N.; 4° 13′ W.), royal burgh, seaport, and county town, Inverness-shire, Scotland, on Ness; tweed centre; 'Capital of Highlands'; near end of Caledonian Canal; has coasting trade; woolen industries, breweries, distilleries. I. was ancient Pictish capital; has remains of castle built by Cromwell and destroyed by Jacobites, in 1746; scene of 'Northern Meeting'; has Episcopal cathedral; famed for purity of Eng. accent.

INVERNESS-SHIRE (57° N.; 4° 40′ W.), Highland county, Scotland, extending from Moray Firth on E. to Atlantic and Outer Hebrides on W.; area, *c.* 4,200 sq. miles; county town, Inverness. Surface is mostly wooded country, rough hill-grazing, heath, peat, and stony waste little cultivated; deer-forests and grouse-moors; excellent fishing; many wild glens. I. is largest and most mountainous county in Scotland; flat strip near Inverness gradually rises into mountainland, culminating in Ben Nevis, 4,406 ft., in S.W., highest point in Brit. Isles. There are many rivers, the largest being Spey, Ness, Beauly, and Lochy. Among the numerous lochs are Ness, Morar (deepest in Brit. Isles), Shiel, Archaig, Lochy, Ericht, and Laggan. Caledonian Canal traverses I. A geological 'fault' runs across Scotland through I.; slight earth-

quake shocks frequent; interesting signs of glaciation.

INVESTITURE. — In feudal times some token of I. was commonly given when a man was installed in lands or office. Many of the bp's and abbots held land under the Crown from the days of Charlemagne and were invested with ring and crozier on appointment to their sees. This soon was plainly objectionable, for simony and other abuses became common. The Lateran Synod of 1559 forbade clerical I. by a layman, and papal prohibitions followed in 1078, 1080, 1087, 1089. The final prohibition came from the Lateran Council of 1123. In England the struggle over I. was between Abp. Anselm and Henry I.

INVOLUTION, in math's the raising of a quantity to a given power, *e.g* .42= 16. *Evolution,* the extracting of roots (*e.g.* $\sqrt{16+4}$) is included with I. under *Theory of indices.* See ALGEBRA.

IO.—(1) legendary dau. of Inachus, king of Argos; beloved by Zeus, who, to save her from Hera, changed her into white heifer; Hera sent to Argus to guard her, but Hermes slew him; eventually was restored to human form. (2) (Astron.) an asteroid, and also a satellite of Jupiter.

IODINE (I. At. Wt. 126·8), non-metallic element with bluish-black metallic luster; S.G. 4·95, M.P. 115° C.; B.P. 200° C. Formerly it was manufactured from *kelp,* a species of seaweed, but it is now worked up from the salts of which large natural deposits exist. In presence of potassium iodide, I. dissolves in water, forming a brown solution. It forms a brown solution in alcohol and in ether, and a violet solution in carbon disulphide and in chloroform. With starch I. gives an intense blue coloration. I. is present in the thyroid gland, and from the earliest times bodies containing I. have been much prized medicinally. There are two series of salts, *Iodides* and *Iodates,* and two acids, *Hydriodic Acid* (HI) and *Iodic Acid* (HIO_3). Of the *Halogens,* I. has the least affinity for other elements.

IODOFORM, CHI_3, yellow cry stalline substance with strong smell; antiseptic and disinfectant; much used in surgery.

IOLA, a city of Kansas, in Allen co.; of which it is the county seat. It is on the Kansas and Texas, the Missouri Pacific, and the Atchison, Topeka and Santa Fe railroads, and on the Neosho River. In the neighborhood are extensive natural gas wells which are utilized for industrial purposes. The industries include cement works, foundry, and machine shops, brick plants, creamery, ice plant, etc. There are several public buildings.

ION, OF CHIOS (*d.* 421 B.C.), Gk. poet and historian; won prize for tragedy at Athens.

IONA, ICOLMKILL (56° 19′ N., 6° 29′ W.), island, at S.W. corner of Mull, Inner Hebrides, Scotland; about 3½ miles long and 1½ miles wide; area, *c.* 2,000 acres; scarcely half cultivated; coast rocky and surface mostly rough. I's chief interest lies in association with St. Columba (*q.v.*) and introduction of Christianity into Scotland; great center of learning and religion, VI. cent. onwards; frequently ravaged by Norsemen; abounds in hist. antiquities; ruins of ancient nunnery, monastery, and chapels; also restored ruins of cathedral, with choir, sacristy, transepts, and a 70-ft. tower, as well as Columba's tomb and numerous crosses and carved stones.

IONIA, a city of Michigan, in Ionia co., of which it is the county seat. It is on the Pere Marquette and the Grand Trunk railroads, and on the Grand River, 35 miles E. of Grand Rapids. It has many important industries, including the manufacture of tile, auto bodies, florists' supplies, furniture, tools, dies, clothing, etc. Ample water power is furnished by the river. It is the seat of the State Reformatory and the State Hospital for Criminal Insane. It has also large railroad repair shops. Its public buildings include six schools and a library.

IONIAN ISLANDS (38° 30′ N., 20° 30′ E.), group of islands on W. coast of Greece, consisting of seven islands:Corfu, Cephalonia, Paxos, S a n t a   M a u r a (Leuka), Ithaca, Cerigo (Kythēra), Zrante (Zakynthos); surface mountainous; highest peak, Monte Nero, 5,310 ft., in Cephalonia; subject to frequent earthquakes; rich in marble, sulphur, salt, coal, wine, olives, currants, fruit. Formed into a province called Thema of Cephelenia, IX. cent.; gradually taken by Venetians from XIII. cent. onwards; Passed to France, 1797; made an independent state, 1800; retaken by French, 1807; came under the protection of Brit., 1815; ceded to Greece, 1863. Area, *c.* 1,100 sq. miles.

IONIAN SCHOOL OF PHILOSO-PHY, name given to group of philosophers about 600–400 B.C., who interpreted the universe scientifically rather than, like others, metaphysically. They may fairly be said to have started European philosophy. Thales declared

water to be the underlying principle of all things. Anaximenes thought it was air, and Hippo moisture. Anaxagoras thought the Universe the work of mind, conceived as thin substance.

IONIANS, inhabitants of Attica (held by some to have been the cradle of the race), Euboea, W. coast of Asia Minor, Cycladic Islands, and of colonies in Thrace, Propontis, Pontus, and Egypt. Origin of name is unknown, but Homer and Herodotus use it. A mythical ancentry is attributed to Ion.

IONIC ARCHITECTURE. See ARCH-ITECTURE.

IONISATION, the dissociation of a molecule into electrically charged ions (*q.v.*). The phenomenon, according to the ionic hypothesis, can occur either in a gas or in the solutions of compounds. Before an electric current can pass through a gas or a solution, it is held that some ionisation must occur. In the case of a gas which is a poor conductor, ionisation may be brought about by passing X-rays through it, whereupon it become a good conductor. Similarly, a gas subjected to strong electrostatic discharge becomes ionised. An elaboration of the theory maintains that the ions of the gas travel with immense velocity and collide with neutral molecules. These molecules, by the force of the collision, are themselves broken up into ions, which in turn collide with other molecules. In this way, an enormous increase in the number of ions is brought about. The solutions of all salts are supposed to be more or less ionised, and when the two poles of a battery are dipped into a solution, the positively c h a r g e d ions (metallic) travel to the negative pole, while the negatively charged ions (acidic) travel to the positive pole. As soon as the charged ions come in contact with oppositely charged electrodes, they lose their charge and thereby become ordinary atoms, or groups of atoms as the case may be, with ordinary chemical activity. The ionic hypothesis has been much attacked by some chemists of high standing, but while there are still many points connected with it which require explanation, it undoubtedly contains much truth and it serves a useful purpose until such time as the phenomena it seeks to explain can be further elucidated. (See also DISSOCIATION.)

IONS, the term originally used by Faraday to describe the components of a chemical compound set free when an electric current is passed through its solution. The word is derived from the Gk., and means 'traveller,' and those parts of the decomposing compound which travel to the anode are called

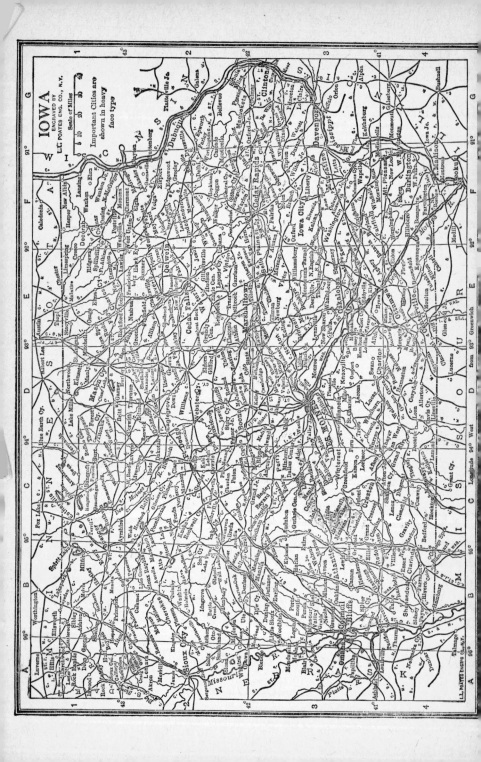

IOWA

ENGRAVED BY
L.L. POATES ENG. CO., N.Y.

Important Cities are
shown in heavy
face type

Scale of Miles

anions, while those which go to the kathode are termed *kations*. It is assumed that when a salt is dissolved in water, there occurs a certain amount of dissociation, (*q.v.*) ions, consisting of atoms or groups of atoms, being produced. These ions carry either a positive or a negative charge of electricity, and each molecule, on dissociation, forms two ions having equal and opposite charges. It should be carefully noted that ions are not held to be identical with chemical atoms. Thus, a solution of sodium chloride may contain positively charged sodium ions and negatively charges chlorine ions, but seeing that metallic sodium reacts violently with water it is clear that there cannot exist, in the solution, any free sodium atoms. The ionic hypothesis is that the ions of sodium and chlorine are highly charged, electrically, and that the presence of these charges keep the ordinary chemical activities in abeyance. Dr. R. A. Millikan, an American physicist, was awarded the Nobel prize in Nov. 1923 for isolating the ion. See also IONISATION.

IOVILÆ, name given locally to Osco-Umbrian monuments (of V. and preceding cent's. B.C.) in Italy.

IOWA, N. central state of U.S. (42° N., 93° 30' W.); bounded N. by Minnesota; E. by Mississippi R., which separates it from Wisconsin and Illinois; S. by Missouri; W. by Missouri and Big Sioux rivers (separating it from Nebraska and S. Dakota). Surface is mostly rolling tableland or prairie (average elevation being scarcely 1,000 ft. above sealevel), broken by vertical cliffs at river banks in N.E., and bluffs near rivers in S.W. Iowa is divided into two drainage systems: the larger, on the E., drained by tributaries of the Mississippi—Des Moines, Skunk, and Iowa; and on the W. by tributaries of the Missouri. There are several small lakes in the N. The climate is healthy. Valuable deposits of coal, which is of good quality, extend over 19,000 sq. m.; other minerals are lead, gypsum, limestone, clay, etc. The land is almost entirely devoted to farming—about half to the growing of cereals, chiefly corn, wheat, barley, oats, rye, potatoes, hay, etc.; naturally, industries are mainly agricultural and livestock rearing; other industries are meat packing and preparing food stuffs; dairy farming and poultry keeping are also of importance. There are no important manufactures. The chief towns are Des Moines (cap.), Dubuque, Sioux, Davenport, Council Bluffs, and Cedar Rapids. Iowa was organized as territory, 1838, and admitted as state of U.S., 1846. The state has a lieut.-governor, a senate and house of representatives, and sends 2 senators and 11 representatives to Congress. Area, 57,147 sq. m. (561 sq. m. water). See Map of U. S.

IOWA CITY, a city of Iowa, in Johnson co., of which it is the county seat. It is on the C., R. I. & P. and Rock Island Short Line railroads, the Cedar Rapids and Iowa City Interurban, and on the Iowa River. It is the trade center for a large agricultural area and its industries are of importance. Only air naval station between Chicago and Omaha. Also has important aviation field. Power is furnished by the river. It is the seat of the State University of Iowa, and other educational institutions. There are hospitals, a Masonic Temple, and other public buildings.

IOWA RIVER, a stream that rises in Hancock county, near the Minnesota state line, and flowing in a S.E. direction empties into the Mississippi N. of Burlington. It is 300 miles long, and is navigable to Iowa City, 80 miles from its mouth.

IOWA STATE COLLEGE OF AGRICULTURAL AND MECHANICAL ARTS.—A co-educational and technical institution at Ames, Iowa, founded in 1868. There are five divisions of instruction — agriculture, e n g i n ee r-ing, household economy, industrial science, and veterinary medicine. The campus and farms cover 1,300 acres. The land is valued at $5,150,000, and the buildings cost $3,350,000. The library contains over 133,064 volumes. Professors, 792; total students registered, 7,296.

IOWA STATE UNIVERSITY.—A co-educational institution at Iowa City, established in 1847. It provides courses in liberal arts, applied science, medicine, dentistry, law, and graduate. There are also schools of pharmacy, correspondence, and for trained nurses. A University armory, psychopathic hospital and nurses home were completed in 1921, and a chemistry building, and Iowa Memorial building for service men in 1922. Over 1,500 students attend the summer session. The library contains 411,448 volumes. Total income about $5,000,000. President, W. A. Jessup, Ph.D. Students, 7,470; teachers, 600, 1931-32.

IOWA WESLEYAN UNIVERSITY.—institution for both sexes, at Mount Pleasant, Iowa, established in 1844, under the auspices of the Methodist Episcopal church. Admission is non-sectarian. The library contains over 25,000 volumes. Productive funds,

$420,310. Students, 306; teachers, 22, 1931-32. President, J. E. Coons.

IPEK (42° 34′ N., 20° 27′ E.); town, Albania; until 1690 seat of the Serbian patriarchs.

IPHICRATES (*d. c.* 353 B.C.); Athenian general, distinguished in Corinthian War, 395-87, Egypt, 378-74, and against Sparta, 372-71; inventor of new armor.

IPHIGENIA (classical myth.), Gk. legendary character, fixed to some extent by Euripides and other poets; *dau.* of Agamemnon and Clytæmnestra; sacrificed to Artemis (Euripides' *I. in Aulis*); according to one of the floating stories, she was miraculously caught away by Artemis; with her *bro.* Orestes became chief character of another play of Euripides', *I. in Tauris.*

IPSWICH (1) (52° 4′ N., 1° 10′ E.), seaport, Suffolk, England, on Orwell estuary. Noteworthy public buildings are the town hall, corn exchange, museum, and church of St. Mary le Tower. I. has a grammar school refounded by Queen Elizabeth, in 1565; manufactures agricultural implements; artificial manures; and has breweries and tanneries; sacked by the Danes in 991 and 1000.

IPSWICH, a town in Massachusetts, in Essex co. It is on the Boston and Main railroad, and on the Ipswich River. The industries include planing mills, grist mills, and plants for the making of hosiery, boats, and canoes. There is a library, a home for aged women, a house of correction, and a high school. Ipswich is one of the oldest towns in Massachusetts, and was settled under the name of Agawam, in 1633, by John Winthrop.

IQUIQUE (20° 10′ S.; 70° 7′ W.); seaport, Chile, S. America; exports nitrate of soda and iodine.

IQUITOS (3° 40′ S.; 72° 57′ W.), town, river port, Peru, S. America, on Upper Amazon; center of trade; exports rubber.

IQUITOS, tribe of uncivilised S. Amer. Indians.

IRAK (34° 30′ S.; 50° E.); fertile province, Persia; carpet-weaving industry; capital, Sultanabad.

IRAK-AJEMI (34° N.; 52° E.); province, Central Persia; produces grain and fruits; contains Teheran, the capital, and Isaphan. Area, 138,190 sq. miles.

IRAK, OR IRAQ, KINGDOM OF, a kingdom which comprises in its area practically the land known as Mesopotamia, and including the former Turkish vilayets of Bazra, Bagdad, and Mosul. It is bounded on the N. by Kurdistan, on the E. by Persia, on the S. by the Persian Gulf and Kuwait, and on the W. by the Arabian and Syrian deserts. It has a total area of 116,500 sq. miles and a population of about 3,000,000. The capital is Bagdad, and the chief port Bazra. In 1921 Mesopotamia, which was occupied by the British during the World War, became the Kingdom of Irak, a mandate of Great Britain. Prince Feisal, son of Hussein Ibn Ali, King of Hedjaz, was crowned the constitutional sovereign. In 1922 a treaty of alliance was signed between Great Britain and Irak, in which Feisal agreed to be guided by Great Britain in national and financial matters for 30 years, in return for armed protection when necessary. In 1932 Great Britain gave up her mandate and Irak became an independent kingdom and member of the League of Nations. In 1933 Feisal died and was succeeded by his son, Ghazi. The chief value of the territory lies in its rich oil deposits, particularly in Mosul. The "Mosul question" was hotly disputed by Turkey, and the border between Turkey and Irak had to be settled by the League of Nations. The petroleum fields are being developed by the Anglo-Persian Oil Co. and the Turkish Petroleum Co.

IRAN. See PERSIA.

IRANIAN LANGUAGES the languages which make up the Indo-Iranian group of Indo-European languages. The most important of the modern Iranian languages is literary Persian, written and spoken by well-educated Persians.

IRAWADI or **IRRAWADDY,** the principal river of Burma, India, rises in the northeast of Assam, near Tibet, and flows generally south into the Bay of Bengal, over a course approximately 1,250 miles long. Near the Bay it flows through a dozen mouths, forming a delta 18,000 miles square. The river is navigable for 900 miles and serves as the chief means of communication between the interior of Burma and southwestern China and Tibet. Along its banks are situated the principal cities of Burma, as well as extensive rice fields.

IRBIT, the capital of Perm, a district in the U.S.S.R., at the junction of the Irbit and Nitza rivers. It is famous for its annual fair in February.